Childhood & Adolescence

Third Edition

Childhood & Adolescence

A Psychology of the Growing Person

L. Joseph Stone
Joseph Church

Random House, New York

Third Edition

9876543

Copyright © 1973 by L. Joseph Stone and
Joseph Church
Copyright © 1957, 1968 by Random
House, Inc.

Library of Congress Cataloging in Publication
Data

Stone, Lawrence Joseph, 1912—
    Childhood and adolescence.

    Bibliography: p.
    1. Child study.   2. Adolescent psychology.
I. Church, Joseph, joint author.   II. Title.
BF721.S82   1973   155.4   72-2876

ISBN 0–394–31723–8
Manufactured in the United States of America.
Composed by Cherry Hill Composition,
Pennsauken, N.J. Printed and bound by
Von Hoffman Press, St. Louis, Mo.

Cover Photo by Sebastian Milito

Photo Research by Olivia Buehl

Design by James McGuire

preface

A book is the product of many people in addition to its authors. In the first edition of this book, published in 1957, we gave thanks to the mentors and colleagues who had contributed to our thinking, and fifteen years later we find ourselves still indebted to Heinz Werner, Gardner and Lois Murphy, Otto Klineberg, L. K. Frank, K. M. Dallenbach, R. B. MacLeod, Max Wertheimer, Bruno Klopfer, Margaret Mead, Benjamin Spock, Mary Essex, Eveline Omwake, Barbara Biber, and Eugene Lerner, all of whom helped shape what we hope is a humanistically scientific approach to the study of human psychological development. Our erstwhile editor, Charles D. Lieber, first proposed this book and has continued to give us sage counsel over the years. Our present editor, Richard Kennedy, and our manuscript editor, Susan Rothstein, have been consistently cooperative with a pair of sometimes fractious authors. Olivia Buehl has played her role of picture editor with devotion and sensitivity.

We think it does no injustice to our teachers and associates to say that we have learned most from the children we have known in various settings around the world. Each of us owes his own children special gratitude for the bits of their lives that we have observed and enjoyed and which they have allowed us to smuggle into these pages.

Our students have given us continuous feedback, and we have tried to benefit from their comments. Numerous readers have written us over the years, and we are grateful for their suggestions. The present edition owes special thanks to Dr. Roy Gendron, Psychologist, Poughkeepsie Public Schools, and Prof. Emma McConnell, Director of Teacher Education, Vassar College, for their critical reading of Chapters 10 and 11.

In the pages that follow, we pay tribute to some of the many thinkers and researchers whose fertile output makes it necessary to keep revising this book. The high quality of the research available to us makes us proud to be part of the enterprise of developmental psychology.

L.J.S.
J.C.

contents

Contents

Contents

x

Contents

the
birth
of the
baby

A moment after he has emerged from his mother's body, the newborn baby is dangling by his feet from the doctor's upraised hand, a trickle of fluid draining from his nose and mouth. A smart slap on the bottom, and he gives a thin, reedy wail. The birth cry marks the baby's first breath and serves as a boundary between his former waterborne, parasitic existence and his status as an air-breathing, separate organism. He is still attached to his mother by his umbilical cord, but this has ceased functioning as a life line and will shortly be clamped off and severed—a painless operation. In another fifteen or twenty minutes, the placenta in which the umbilical cord terminates, having separated from the lining of the mother's womb, will be delivered, with its attached membranes, as the afterbirth. The **neonate** immediately has drops of silver nitrate solution (or penicillin ointment) put into his eyes as insurance against infection, he is labeled with his family's name and given a brief physical examination, and a new human being is on the long road to maturity.

One of the odd by-products of our urban-suburban civilization is that many Americans never see a newborn baby until confronted with their own. Many new parents, whose expectations are based on the idealized "newborn" babies shown in advertisements (usually babies two or three months old), are taken aback at their first sight of their tiny, wet, sticky, possibly red and wizened baby. It is because so many people are unfamiliar with neonates that we must begin with a description of the baby's physical appearance. Later on, we shall talk a good deal about the biological and psychological individuality that exists from birth—and indeed from conception—but let us first describe newbornness in general, the still somewhat fetal character that neonates have in common. Note that we speak of the baby as a neonate not only as he is within the first few minutes after birth but also during the first few weeks of postnatal life.

Physical Appearance of the Neonate

The newborn baby seems incredibly small: average weight 7 pounds (3+ kg.) (although we have a newspaper clipping announcing the birth of a baby weighing 17 pounds [7.7 kg.]), average length 20 inches (51 cm.); since he* keeps his legs drawn up, he is likely to look even smaller. His proportions are very different from those of later life: his head makes up a quarter of his overall length (try to picture an adult with these proportions) and seems to rest directly on his puny shoulders, his neck being all but invisible; his almost useless legs are about a third of his total length. When he is held vertical under the arms, his head lolls and his bowed legs hang helplessly. His feet, which seem disproportionately long, are bent inward at the ankles, so that the soles are almost parallel. His facial proportions, too, will undergo many changes; his cranial vault is well developed, but his features are small and unarticulated, and he seems virtually chinless. His nose may have been flattened and his head squeezed out of shape **(molded)** in his passage through the birth canal. This molding disappears within a

* Except where sex differences are an issue, we shall refer throughout to the child as "he." This is to avoid the awkwardness of "he or she" and the feelingless neutrality of "it."

4

week or two. The neonate may still be wearing his fetal hair, dark and coarse, not only on his crown but sometimes elsewhere: low across his brows or far down his back, for instance. This hair, if present, will eventually be replaced by a regular crop, either gradually or after an intervening period of baldness. The baby at birth is still wet with the **amniotic fluid** in which he was immersed before birth and his skin is coated with a cheeselike protective substance, the **vernix caseosa**, which, when it dries, gives his skin a chalky cast. Depending on his maturity, his coloring may range from pale livid to rosy pink, perhaps tinged with the so-called **normal physiological jaundice of the newborn** (see below). Both eye and skin pigments are slow to develop, so that virtually all babies are born with smoky blue eyes and even Negro neonates may have light skins for the first few days. The neonate's skull has six soft spots, or **fontanels**, openings covered with a tough, resilient membrane; the most conspicuous of these is at the very top of the head and may not close over until age one and a half.

The genitals of the newborn are at first surprisingly large and prominent. Neonates —both boys and girls—in many cases have enlarged breasts which may secrete a milklike substance called "witch's milk," and girls may have a brief "menstrual" flow shortly after birth. These phenomena are caused by hormones absorbed from the mother's bloodstream, and subside rapidly.

The neonate is likely to look scrawny because he has not yet fully developed his layers of body fat, except for the fat pads that fill out his cheeks. The fat pads play an important part in sucking and, incidentally, keep the baby's toothless mouth from having the withered look of an old person's. Premature babies (defined not by

The moment of birth. Note the baby's size relative to the adult hands, the enlarged genitals and breasts, and the absence of maternal blood.

Wayne Miller, Magnum

5

A crying neonate. The baby seems to be giving a Moro response. Note the engorged breasts and the lack of tears.

age since conception but by a birth weight of less than 5 pounds [2¼ kg.; the European cutoff point, however, is 2½ kg.]) have underdeveloped fat pads and look remarkably senile. At the other extreme, very mature neonates may well be plumped out with body fat and so resemble the pink pudginess shown in advertisements.

We should not be misled by the unprepossessing, almost larval look of the average neonate. All his body structures are present, some ready for full functioning, others only in rudimentary form. He is a real human being, down to the last eyelash and the miniature nails on fingers and toes. All the nerve cells are present at birth, but in immature form—the brain more than doubles in size, from 350 cc. to 750 cc., between birth and age one, and doubles again by age six. In the neonate's jaws are buds for two sets of teeth. The newborn girl's ovaries contain what is thought by some to be a lifetime supply of rudimentary ova, although mature sperm cells do not form in the testes of the boy until middle childhood.

The "feel" of a neonate is something to be experienced. A skilled adult can hold him in one hand, fingertips bracing the back of his skull, the heel of the palm holding his shoulders, the forearm supporting his almost nonexistent buttocks. But not all newborn babies feel alike to hold. Some remain compactly and comfortably curled, like kittens, others sprawl like bundles of loosely joined sticks, some are tense and stiff, still others squirm and writhe or flail. Even at this age, we see the beginnings of marked individual differences in behavior.

Contrasts between full-term (A. and B.) and premature (C. and D.) neonates. Note the limp sprawl of the baby in C. and the difficulty in raising the head to clear nose and mouth in D.

A.

B.

C.

D.

Basic Life
Processes
in the Neonate

If the neonate is to grow and flourish, his first order of business is to stay alive. Although our concern in this book is not primarily with the physiological processes that maintain life, these are so central in the existence of the newborn baby that we must see how they settle down to dependable operation before we go on to examine the rudiments of behavior in the neonate.

The complete transition from fetal to postnatal ways of living takes between two weeks and a month. It is the end of this transition that marks the end of the neonatal period and the beginning of infancy. The transition begins, however, with the birth cry; and when we consider the drastic change of environment involved in being born, from the dark, waterborne passivity of the womb to autonomous life in the light and air, the neonate does a remarkable job of adapting. His various body mechanisms may work unevenly and inharmoniously, but they do work, and the baby is a lot more durable than he seems to anxious parents.

Prior to birth, as we have said, the baby lived in total darkness, suspended in a fluid bath (the amniotic fluid) at a constant temperature, and cushioned against mechanical buffetings. He received oxygen, water, nutrients, and other substances (some perhaps beneficial and others demonstrably harmful) directly into his bloodstream through the umbilical cord that joined him by his navel to the placenta and so to his mother's bloodstream (see p. 27), and discharged body wastes and other bloodborne materials into the blood flowing to the placenta. Although most pre-

natal metabolic wastes are disposed of in this way, once the fetus's kidneys are working he excretes small amounts of urine directly into the amniotic fluid. In addition, he swallows mucus and amniotic fluid containing shed skin and hair, and solid wastes are formed in the bowel as **meconium**, a greenish-black, tarry substance which also contains bile from the liver. (Meconium is not ordinarily excreted before birth.) Once he is born, the baby's body must shift to new patterns of circulation and must do for itself the jobs of respiration, digestion, and temperature control.

Respiration

Breathing is a new activity for the neonate. The baby's first breath may be stimulated simply by his being exposed to air, it may be set off by a sneeze or a yawn, or it may be stimulated by the traditional (in our society) slap on the bottom, producing the birth cry which sets in chain the whole complicated reflex pattern of lifelong inhalation and exhalation. Almost any sort of stimulation can be used to start the baby breathing, as by massage; by dipping him into warm water, or cold water, or an alternation of both; by mouth-to-mouth breathing; or by various more drastic measures that are sometimes called for. The neonate's lungs are at first congested with mucus and perhaps amniotic fluid, and he may have to spend a few days with his head lower than his feet to facilitate drainage. The muscle groups active in breathing are poorly coordinated for some weeks after birth, and the neonate's respiration tends to be noisy, shallow, and irregular. Because the soft palate has not yet been integrated into respiration, the neonate's breath may rattle in his throat in an alarming but innocuous way.

Circulation

The shift from fetal to postnatal circulation begins with the first breath. The abdominal muscles surrounding the umbilical vessels contract, and circulation through the cord slows down immediately and ceases within a few minutes, making it possible to clamp off and sever the cord. The navel opening heals over within five days, and the dried, atrophied stump of umbilical cord drops off in a week or two. Increased pressure in the left atrium of the heart closes a flap over the **foramen ovale**, the opening between the left and right ventricles, and the foramen grows permanently closed within ten days. The shutting off of the umbilical arteries forces blood to the lungs, which now take over the job of aeration previously done by the pools of maternal blood surrounding the capillaries from the infant's side of the circulatory system of the placenta. The oxygen level of the blood reaches 90 percent of normal within three hours after birth. The acid-alkaline balance (pH) of the blood is normal in a week or so, and blood pressure is normal within ten days.

A day or so after birth, a number of babies develop what has been called normal physiological jaundice of the newborn (or, more technically, **icterus neonatorum**). The jaundice is caused by the presence in the blood of a substance called bilirubin, produced when red blood cells break down and perhaps involving liver function. The authorities differ on the cause of the breaking down of the red corpuscles, some holding that the baby is born with a surplus which has to be eliminated, others suspecting that it is due to incompatibilities of ABO blood types between mother and child, which sometimes, it now appears, lead to disorders comparable to those produced by Rh incompatibility, discussed on page 34. In any case, moderate icterus of brief duration seems to be self-limiting and with no serious consequences for the baby; nevertheless, it has to be watched closely to differentiate it from much rarer severe jaundice and kernicterus, which can lead to brain damage. There is growing evidence of specific genetic factors in some of these conditions, related to enzyme deficiencies and inadequate metabolism of various substances. At last count, some twelve hereditary enzyme defects had been identified (Knox, 1969), including phenylketonuria as well as albinism and G-6-P D (Doxiades et al., 1964), which involves susceptibility to the fumes of common moth balls and may also make the child more vulnerable to lead poisoning. The technique of **amniocentesis**, by which amniotic fluid containing fetal tissues can be withdrawn with a needle through the mother's belly wall between gestation ages seventeen and twenty-two weeks, is making it possible to diagnose some of the more serious defects prenatally. One of these is Tay-Sachs disease, which involves brain degeneration and early death (O'Brien et al., 1971); another is Fabry's disease, produced by faulty galactose metabolism (Brady et al., 1971).

Digestion

The baby, unlike the fetus, must take in sustenance through his mouth, digest it in his alimentary tract, and eliminate wastes by urination and defecation. (We leave out of account sweating, the shedding of dead skin and hair, and the cropping of dead or superfluous tissue as in nail or hair trimming. We also ignore the fetus's ingestion and digestion of amniotic fluid containing body wastes and its secretion of small amounts of urine.)

From birth the normal baby's digestive tract is equipped with enzymes to handle all the basic foods except some starches, and in a short time the neonate takes in from his surroundings the beneficent bacteria needed for digestion. (Since vitamin K, which is important for blood clotting, is produced by the intestinal bacteria, any lesion in the first few days holds the threat of serious hemorrhage.) It is assumed in many American hospitals that babies cannot eat for a day or two after they are born. Certainly the mother's milk does not "come in" until eighteen or twenty-four hours after birth, but her breasts may meanwhile secrete a milklike substance called **colostrum**, thought by some to have nutritional value. Observations of babies born into various "primitive" societies, however, where they are breast-fed by wet nurses right after birth, would suggest that neonates are indeed capable of managing food almost at once. Whenever he begins, the newborn is likely to be an unskilled eater. At first, he takes fluids in 1- or 2-ounce doses, of which a good part may be promptly regurgitated, and more often than not the baby, at least in the American hospital regime, loses weight for the first few days of life. The excretion of meconium and the elimination of mucus and other wastes further this weight loss. A fair number of babies, from the age of two or three weeks, suffer badly from colic, marked by severe gastric pain. The cause of colic is unknown. It usually clears up spontaneously by age three months.

Temperature regulation

Mechanisms to keep body temperature steady develop slowly, so the neonate is at the mercy of environmental fluctuations and can easily become chilled or overheated. His sweat glands begin operating only when he is about a month old. The absence of sweating makes it easier for the newborn to conserve heat and body fluids. Parents, in adjusting the household temperature to the baby's needs, tend to err on the side of keeping him too warm and may in the process interfere with the normal development of temperature-regulating mechanisms.

Immunity and susceptibility

Among the substances absorbed by the fetus from his mother's blood through the placenta are antibodies which give him several months of immunity to various infections. Indeed, the so-called "teething" sicknesses from age six months onward probably represent simply the coincidental wearing off of earlier immunities acquired from the mother. Medical lore, supported by a good deal of observation, has it that mother's milk also supplies the baby with antibodies. As far as we know, the only experimental verification for this belief comes from studies of the increased resistance to staphylococcus infection in mice fed human milk (Gyorgy et al., 1962). In spite of his borrowed antibodies, the newborn baby is highly susceptible to infections of the gastrointestinal tract, respiratory system, and skin. (A goodly number of babies also develop early such allergic reactions as hay fever and eczema.) It takes the baby some years to build up his own system of resistances, and the parents meanwhile have to protect him against infection. Some parents, of course, are overprotective, to the point where they may seriously restrict the baby's experiences. Moreover, overprotection retards the necessary formation of the baby's own immunities, and may have the paradoxical result of making him more vulnerable rather than less. Babies in the United States and many other countries get a series of immunizing inoculations and vaccinations during their first couple of years, further bolstering resistance, although a number of pediatricians have begun to suspect that this practice has been overdone.

Behavioral
Capacities
of the Neonate

The past decade and a half has seen a revolution in the study and understanding of neonatal psychology. When we consider that people have been having and rearing babies for as long as there have been people, it is amazing how little was securely known about the newborn's capabilities. Recently, however, there has been an outpouring of research by investigators too numerous to list. For a more detailed account, see the recent compilation by Stone et al. (1972). This research has completely changed our thinking about the neonate and given us a new respect for his abilities. The revolution was brought about by several factors: a sharpened awareness that one cannot understand development

without knowing its origins; improved observations, ingenious procedures, and sophisticated instrumentation; the shrewd use of "indicator" responses, those physiological reactions to sensory stimulation, such as changes in heart rate, brain waves, or skin conductance, which signal that the baby has taken in sensory stimulation; recognition that the baby's **state**—whether he is alert or asleep or somewhere in between, whether he is calm or distressed, hungry or sated—is an important consideration in evaluating his behavior; and using the baby's limited ways of acting upon the world to let him tell us how he perceives and connects events. Experimenters have learned to use subdued stimuli and gentle handling—the neonate's real capacities get obscured when overzealous observers subject him to excessive stimulation. We have rediscovered that human development has a number of nonhuman analogs, so that work with animal species permits experimental manipulations impossible with human subjects. Most investigators currently agree that human neonates **habituate** rather quickly, that they stop responding to a stimulus as the novelty wears off; thus, our measurements have to take account of whether a response comes early in a series or late. As we shall see shortly, the fact of habituation has been turned to good use in the study of perceptual discrimination.

A newborn spends much of his time sleeping, perhaps twenty hours a day. Studies of states (summarized by Korner, 1971) recognize two kinds of neonatal sleep. **Regular sleep** is marked by slow, even breathing and a minimum of grimacing and body movements. **Irregular sleep** is characterized by quick, uneven breathing, frequent body movements and changes

A.   University of Colorado Medical Center

B.

A neonate being wired up for the recording of physiological indicator responses. Polygraphic tracings in A.
show rapid eye movements (REM) in the two curves
marked EOG, or electroculogram. The squiggle at the
right of the EMG (electromyogram) tracing indicates
body movement. The RESP (respiration) record shows
some irregularities. The tracings in B. show the smooth-
ness of regular, quiet sleep.

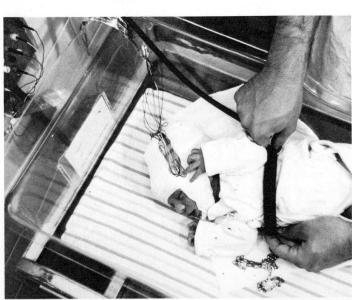

of facial expression, and **rapid eye movements** (REM, associated with dreaming in
adults), visible through the lids. Between
sleep and waking is **drowsiness**, in which
the baby's eyes open and close and he
moves little. In **alert inactivity**, the baby's
eyes are bright and shiny, and he is largely
inactive. This state is most likely to occur
right after a feeding (or the elimination
that often follows a feeding). The inactive
but alert neonate may stare fixedly at a face
or a spot of light that happens to fall
within his field of view, and will try to
track a slowly moving object (although
Bower et al. [1971] hold that babies initially follow movement patterns rather than
the object itself). **Waking activity** is
marked by diffuse body movements, unsee-
ing eyes, and uneven breathing. The state
of **crying** is accompanied by agitated movements.

When a neonate is crying and an adult
picks him up, he ordinarily quiets immediately—if only temporarily—which shows
his responsiveness to the sensations that go
with being held, cuddled, and rocked.
Ambrose (1969) has isolated movement, as
perceived via the semicircular canals of the
inner ear, as a key influence in soothing the
baby: he has constructed a "vestibulator,"
a stabilimeter (a spring-mounted bassinet
ordinarily used to measure the baby's
movements) with a motor that imparts an
up-down motion of about 2¾ inches
(about 7 cm.) sixty to seventy times per
minute, which effectively quiets crying
newborns. That movement is not the
whole story, of course, is indicated by the
soothing effects of swaddling (see p. 16).
According to Korner and Thoman (1970),
vestibular stimulation is important in
bringing the baby to visual alertness and
scanning, and works even better when

combined with holding the baby upright against an adult body. Rocking soothes rat infants, too (Thoman and Korner, 1971). Asleep or awake, the neonate is subject to fits and starts and tremors reflecting the spread of stimulation in his still-immature nervous system. Korner (1969), however, reports that startles and rhythmic mouthing occur most often during regular sleep, that reflex smiles and erections of the penis are found most often during irregular sleep, and that all such manifestations decline in drowsiness. She also observes sex differences, with smiles and sucking movements more frequent in girl neonates than in boys, and startles more frequent in boys; such sex differences are likely to be obliterated, though, by individual differences in the "preferred" channel of discharge.

Neonatal REM, and the associated brain wave patterns indicative of dreaming, were first reported by Roffwarg et al. (1966). We still do not understand the significance of REM sleep in newborns—it is as though the physiological mechanisms of dreaming are present from the beginning, anticipating the arrival of something to dream about. In any event, REM sleep is more common in the neonatal period than at later ages. Emde and Koenig (1969) observe REM in a variety of states; smiling is associated with sleeping and drowsy REM, and frowning goes with REM in all states: sleeping, drowsy, sucking, crying, and fussing.

John Fay

Prone sleeping posture in a neonate.

Posture and movement

Most babies quite early have a preference for lying on either their backs or their bellies, as shown by agitated movements or

13

▲

The neonate unites thumb and mouth.

crying when placed in the less favored position and by relaxation in the favored one—the mother's becoming sensitive to such cues is an important part of learning to communicate with her baby. On back or belly, the baby keeps his arms and legs flexed, his fingers curled more or less tightly into fists, and his head turned to one favored side. Babies who regularly lie on their backs are likely to develop a bald spot and some flattening of the skull at the place where it meets the mattress. This flattening is harmless and disappears, although not always completely, as the baby begins to vary his sleeping position, somewhere around age six months. When in distress, the newborn squirms, twists his head from side to side, and flails his limbs —not randomly but, as high-speed movies show, in a highly stereotyped pattern.

Lying alone on a table or in a bassinet, the neonate is virtually helpless, but he becomes a different creature when in contact with a responding human adult. That is, his state changes, and with it his capabilities, according to his behavioral context. This shows up most strikingly when the baby is hungry and he engages in complex **rooting** behavior: like newborn mammals of other species, he "searches" the adult body with his mouth as though for a nipple; he clutches firmly at whatever handholds he finds—clothing, hair, folds of skin —and propels himself, if not restrained, with trunk, arms, and legs, so actively that the adult may wonder if, like the Duchess's baby in *Alice in Wonderland*, he isn't changing into a small pig. In settings where there are limited opportunities to learn traditional child-care practices by observing them, most first-time mothers who are breast-feeding their babies have to be shown how to get themselves and the neonate into position for nursing, and how to put the breast into the baby's mouth. But as long as the mother plays her part properly, the neonate adapts reciprocally. Films made by Helen Blauvelt show that when the neonate is picked up to be carried against an adult shoulder, he presses his cheek against the adult's. The usual adult response is to press back, which only pushes the baby's head over to the other side. If, instead, the adult tilts her (or his) away from the baby's, the baby's head slides down to the base of the adult's neck, and when the adult straightens up her head, the two are perfectly interlocked. Blauvelt and McKenna (1961) have described a number of patterns of mother-child adaptations and compared them to those observed in sheep and goats; in these nonhuman species, such reciprocal adaptations, so uniform that they seem like ritual, play an important part in establishing immediately the mother-child bond essential to the young animal's survival and sanity (if the bond is not formed, the young animal is likely to show disturbed behavior). In the same vein, Spitz (1966) has spoken of the "intricate ballet" of early adaptations in the mother-infant dyad.

The newborn has only a limited command of his hands, which he tends to keep fisted when not in use. As we know, people learn to use their hands in an enormous variety of ways—to feed themselves, to draw and write, to pick their noses, to pick pockets, to make love, to mold clay, to handle tools—but it is possible to specify quite briefly the neonate's repertory. He may, in waving his arms, score his face with his fingernails, for which reason his shirt sleeves may have to be folded or sewn closed over his hands; but it will be at least a month before he can scratch at an insect bite or a patch of eczema. He does grasp when his hand is properly stimulated, but he does not yet reach out to grasp things that he merely sees (B. L. White, 1963), although Bower et al. (1970a) find evidence of beginning reaching from a few days of age. He clings when rooting, and when nursing he soon begins to clasp the breast or bottle, but he does not yet cling monkey fashion to the adult who holds him upright against the adult's body. He may be able to suck his thumb at birth—it appears that some fetuses suck their thumbs prenatally —but many newborn babies cannot find

Behavioral capacities of the neonate

their mouths with their hands, try as they may, while others, when hungry, hook a whole hand into the mouth.

Emotions

The newborn baby's emotional expression is often intense, but it lacks variety. Distress, whether from hunger, pain, heat, cold, or whatever, comes out as tearless crying, thrashing, and turning red all over. (Although the tear glands play no part in neonates' crying, they act continuously to bathe the eyeballs and will step up their activity to wash away irritants.) Crowell and associates (1965) have demonstrated that newborns show a galvanic skin response, which is one autonomic index of emotionality in older subjects. As we have already said, newborn babies evince a "**pleasure smile**" (Wolff, 1959; Chastaing, 1957; Ambrose, 1961), which must be distinguished from both the **social smile**, which appears during the second month in response to the human face or voice, and the "**gas smile**," the twisted precursor of a burp (although Wolff [1963] reports smiling to a high-pitched human voice as early as age three weeks). For the most part, however, the neonate is blankly unemotional.

More than half a century ago, the famous behaviorist John B. Watson (1919, pp. 199–201) postulated three basic emotions present at birth and linked to reliable, untrained stimuli: fear, produced by loss of support; rage, produced by restraint; and love, evoked by fondling. He held that these emotions, by associative conditioning, later became attached to new stimuli (for conditioning theory, see pp. 183–191). Subsequent observations have failed to support Watson's hypothesis. Although

loss of support (or a loud noise or a flash of bright light) will provoke a Moro response (described on p. 23), careful observation by the Shermans (Sherman, 1927), Bridges (1932), and others indicates that one cannot differentiate among unpleasant emotions in the newborn. Further, one can produce vigorous crying and kicking in the neonate by partially immobilizing him, but snug swaddling arrests crying and struggling and soothes the baby (Wolff, 1959; Lipton et al., 1965). Although, as we have said, rocking has a calming effect on rat neonates, swaddling does not (Thoman and Korner, 1971). An interesting cultural difference is to be seen in the reactions of American women who have given birth in Soviet hospitals. While the Russian mothers accept swaddling as routine, American mothers typically report initial feelings of horror at seeing their babies wrapped up like mummies, and then dawning amazement as they realize that the baby seems to find it more pleasant than not. Finally, there is no indication that the neonate feels affection toward anybody or anything, although such affection develops rapidly in the first few months. We might mention here the early beginnings of an important form of social behavior, imitation of other people's actions; the earliest recorded imitation appears at ten or twenty days of age, when the baby imitates the adult's sticking out his tongue (Zazzo, 1957). Gardner and Gardner (1970) report imitative tongue protrusion in a six-week-old, and some evidence of imitating mouth opening.

Sensory capacities and perception

The neonate's sense organs are in good working order, but he still has a long way to go in making use of the information they bring him. We must bear in mind, too, that there are decided individual differences in sensitivities to various kinds of stimulation, and in strengths of reaction thereto. There is some slim evidence to suggest that some newborns, within a few minutes after birth, turn to look in the direction of a sound (Wertheimer, 1961). Turkewitz et al. (1966) report a somewhat unreliable reflexlike eye-turning to sound. Some primitive coordination of visual and auditory space is suggested by an experiment by Aronson and Rosenbloom (1971). When the baby (ages four to eight weeks) sees his mother (or another person), in one location, but hears her voice coming from someplace else (via a speaker), he shows signs of pronounced distress.

Within a day or two, the neonate can track a moving object with his eyes, although not too reliably. A few babies right after birth can turn their heads to follow a moving object, and most can do so within a few weeks. Schiff (1965) demonstrated that infant monkeys reacted with great agitation to a rapidly approaching large object (actually an expanding shadow projected on a screen in front of the subject, creating the impression of impending collision). More recently, Ball and Tronick (1971) have found this same **looming effect** in human babies as young as two weeks, as have Bower et al. (1970b); the babies react by throwing back their heads, raising their arms, and in many cases crying. However, if the projected shadow was made to appear on a course that would miss the baby, he simply followed its progress without emotion.

Fantz (1963) has shown that the newborn baby discriminates patterns; thus, the neonate spends more time looking at black-and-white forms than at unfigured

Eve Arnold, Magnum

A snugly swaddled Russian newborn. Observe that the baby, contrary to American intuitions, shows no distress at being tightly confined.

Dr. Robert Fantz

colored areas, and shapes arranged to make a crude approximation of a human face are looked at significantly longer than the same shapes in a random arrangement. Salapatek and Kessen (1966) dispute Fantz's interpretation, since in their more detailed studies of the scanning movements with which the baby inspects simple forms like triangles, the neonate typically fastens on an isolated feature such as an edge or an angle and does not scan the figure as a whole. The issue is moot on at least two counts. First, we know that what one sees is not merely the point at which the eye is aimed. Second, there may well be differences in scanning patterns depending on whether one is looking at a none too interesting figure like a triangle or a much more interesting facelike one. Observations by Carpenter and her associates (1970; Friedman et al., 1970a, 1970b) provide strong support for pattern discrimination by newborns. Jirari (1970), too, finds form preferences in the neonate. Observations by Haith (1969) and others tell us that, for the first few months, babies scan horizontally more than vertically. If the baby's eyes encounter a vertical edge, as where a black area meets a white one, his gaze clings to the edge; horizontal edges, however, go undetected. Haith also finds, using infrared light, that when the visible light goes out, the newborn baby (even if he was asleep) opens his eyes and scans the darkness. The neonate's eyes have a fixed focus at about 7½ inches (19 cm.), which may mean that more distant objects are seen as blurred (Haynes et al., 1965). This finding bears comparison with a related one by Bruner that we shall be describing in a moment. We have said that the newborn's rapid habituation to repeated stimuli can be used to study perceptual discrimination; for reasons that will become clear, studies of habituation will be discussed under the topic of learning.

The baby's tactual sense is obviously important in his being soothed; it helps guide his rooting behavior, in which olfactory cues also probably play a part. Behavioral biologists tell us about **pheromones**, airborne chemical "messages" secreted by one or another of an organism's (plant or animal) organs. The most widely known of the pheromones are the sex attractants of such insects as the cockroach or the gypsy moth; sex attractants hold promise as methods of pest control, since synthetic versions can be used to lure insects into a trap. Leon and Moltz (1971) have found that the rat mother, when her pups are sixteen days old and just beginning to move about on their own, starts to produce a pheromone which very effectively draws the young back to her. To get back to the human baby, he reacts with distress to unpleasant odors like ammonia and asafetida (Engen et al., 1963; Lipsitt et al., 1963). He likewise reacts aversively to unpleasant tastes, such as that of quinine (Pratt, 1954). Dubignon and Campbell (1969) have found that the neonate shows a clear preference for milk over a 5 percent dextrose solution. Although the neonate seems indifferent to whether he is held head up or head down, the vestibular apparatus of his inner ear is working. We have already seen that vestibular stimulation calms the crying neonate. In addition, the newborn shows the same kinds of eye movements (**nystagmus**) as adults after he has been spun on a turntable. One gets the same results if the baby is kept stationary inside a rotating drum with vertical stripes on its inner surface, or, as in a study by Tauber and Koffler (1966), by switching lights on and off to give an impression of rotation. The neonate's sensitivity to pain, as measured by his reactions to pin pricks or mild electric shocks, increases rapidly in the first few days (Lipsitt and Levy, 1959). Circumcision on day three, routinely carried out without anesthetic in American hospitals, now is being called into question. While we cannot agree with those of a psychoanalytic persuasion who feel that the neonate experiences circumcision as castration, there is clear evidence of pain and stress (Emde et al., 1971). The baby's reaction to internal pain, as of colic or hunger cramps, is even more pronounced. It is not clear whether the newborn tries to push away anything that obstructs his breathing. If he does, it is weakly and ineffectually. Observation shows that he cannot rid himself of a cleaning tissue spread over his face, and pediatric lore has it that pillows are a lethal menace to babies.

There is some reason to believe that stimuli which are noxious to the newborn are noxious because of their strong intensity, rather than their specific qualities as perceived by an adult. Well into infancy, the child reacts aversively to strong light and loud noises, and later to strongly flavored foods. On the other hand, we must point out that infants are often impervious to stimuli that are very prominent for older children and adults. The young baby may not react at all, for instance, to thunder, fire sirens, or the racket of trash cans being emptied. The smells that adults find disgusting, such as the odors of body wastes, affect the neonate not at all. At the same time, the baby may be upset by stimulation that seems innocuous to adults, such as the crackling of stiff paper.

The use of indicator responses such as change in heartbeat or respiration has made it possible to study systematically the newborn's hearing. Bartoshuk (1964) has shown that heartbeat varies directly with loudness (obviously, both heartbeat and loudness have to be within a reasonable range). Both Eisenberg (1969) and Connolly (1970) have shown extremely early discrimination of pitch and loudness, and Eisenberg has shown special responsiveness, in terms of both alerting and quieting, to the human voice by the age of a few weeks. As we shall see in a moment, the baby can discriminate even articificial syllables within the first month. Psychophysical studies of the kind we have been describing are providing the means for early diagnosis of impaired vision and hearing.

Learning

Until just a few years ago, nobody knew for sure whether newborn babies could learn. Studies of neonatal learning were mostly limited to the method of classical conditioning (see pp. 183–185). Attempts to associate such stimuli as a flash of light or the sound of a buzzer with such responses as sucking or autonomic reactions to electric shock yielded equivocal results. (As did related attempts to condition movements of the fetus.) Then, after a long hiatus, Siqueland and Lipsitt (1966) and Papousek (1967)—these dates refer to publications, not to when the studies were actually carried out—by combining the methods of classical and instrumental conditioning (see pp. 183–189), showed that head-turning could be conditioned to particular sounds, provided the neonate received immediate reinforcement in the form of milk or dextrose squirted into his

mouth. More recently it has proved possible to dispense with both the classical conditional signal that an act would be rewarded and the concrete reinforcer of milk or dextrose, using instead cognitive reinforcers such as an interesting event. The currently popular conditioned response is non-nutritive sucking on a nipple equipped with switches that control a display apparatus. Bruner (Center for Cognitive Studies, 1968–1969; these findings are similar to ones reported by Siqueland, below), for instance, has shown that babies learn to suck faster or slower, whichever is called for, to bring a picture into sharper focus, as though perceptual clarity were a strong motive from birth on. Siqueland (1969) gives the baby what he calls "conjugate reinforcement": that is, the strength of the reinforcer is directly related to the strength of the response, so that, for instance, the baby can suck harder to raise the illumination of a picture or the volume of a record player. Note again how these learned responses are tied to perceptual experience. Indeed, workers such as Siqueland disclaim interest in learning as such, but use learning as an index of perception, attention, and motivation. From this standpoint, what is called reinforcement can be viewed as feedback, which gives the baby information about the effectiveness of his own behavior. We cannot stress enough that responsive human beings are an especially fertile source of feedback for the baby. The early social interchange which seems so important to the baby's total development, and which the baby himself soon learns to initiate and control, has been dubbed "the game" by J. S. Watson (1970), and has led Stone et al. (1972) to speak of the baby's early "social addiction."

Habituation, whether measured by straying attention, lack of change in heartbeat, or the resumption of sucking unrelated to the stimulus conditions, is taken to mean that the baby has learned what the stimulus is about and has lost interest. There are individual differences in rate of habituation (Eisenberg et al., 1966), as in just about everything else. Some workers have suggested, cautiously, that fast habituaters are brighter than slow habituaters. If this hunch is verified, it would be a downward extension of older findings that bright school-age children "satiate" faster than less bright ones on boring, highly repetitive tasks like filling page after page with short pencil strokes (Lewin, 1954). The really intriguing finding about habituation is that a new stimulus, to which the baby will again respond, need differ in only minute detail from the old, habituated one, indicating that babies as young as one month of age are capable of very fine perceptual discriminations, as between the syllables *buh* and *puh* (Eimas et al., 1971).

These findings on neonatal learning should not really surprise us. The chief block seems to have been psychologists' preoccupation with classical conditioning as the model for all learning. Now that perceptual learning has become a respectable topic, advances should proceed rapidly. Certain things could have been found out through simple observations in real-life settings, of course. It is obvious that the baby, before the end of the neonatal period, learns to recognize his nursing bottle, as shown by the way he opens his mouth and strains toward the bottle. We have known for some time that goslings and ducklings and lambs and kids learn to know their mothers within a few hours after hatching or birth. More recently,

Siqueland's apparatus which permits the baby to control a visual display by varying his sucking.

Jason Lauré, courtesy Dr. Lewis P. Lipsitt

A.

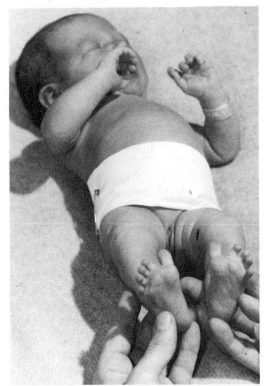

B.

▲

Neonatal reflexes. A. Grasp reflex of the toes. B. The Babinski response. C. and D. The Moro response to loss of support.

Stanley et al. (1970) have shown that puppies under a week old, rewarded with a milk-bearing nipple for the correct choice, learn to discriminate between wire-mesh and terry-cloth surfaces. (They show a preference for the terry cloth from the beginning, but milk associated with the mesh overcomes this preference.)

Reflexes

There is a wide array of reactions which can be rather dependably elicited in the newborn and which are often called **reflexes**. Some of these have little behavioral significance but may be very useful to the physician for diagnostic purposes, like the familiar knee-jerk (patellar) reflex. One of these, the **plantar** (sole of the foot) **response**, is interesting because it changes with development. If one strokes the sole of the neonate's foot, his toes fan up and outward in the **Babinski response**. Later in infancy and thence throughout life except in conditions of brain damage or stupor, the toes do the opposite, they curl downward. The **Babkin response** (Babkin, 1956) is produced by pressing on the neonate's palms while he is lying on his back. The baby reacts by opening wide his mouth, turning his head to the midline (remember that neonates typically keep their head turned to one side), and sometimes by raising his head. Other reflexes have practical adaptive value but are primarily vegetative, that is, automatic and ordinarily involuntary. Such are the pupils' contraction to an increase in light

C.

D. Dr. Heinz Prechtl and David Beintema, *The Neurological
Examination of the Full-term Newborn Infant*

and salivation when something is placed in the mouth. Then there are "reflexes" involving complex motor behavior, such as the rooting response. These should probably not be called reflexes (if these are thought of as fixed response units), since they can be varied adaptively instead of following a rigid pattern, since they cannot be elicited unless the baby is in the proper motivational state, and since later on they will be superseded by new and more mature forms of action.

Of considerable importance to the neonate's survival is the **sucking response**, present at or shortly after birth. Although the sucking response can also be elicited in isolation, it is usually one component in the more inclusive **rooting response**, described earlier. Tactile stimulation of the lips or cheek causes the baby to turn his head toward the source of stimulation (a nipple is the usual stimulus, but an experimenter's finger will work as well), try to take it into his mouth, and begin to suck (Prechtl, 1958). If the stimulus is indeed a milk-producing nipple, sucking, swallow-

ing, and breathing occur in fairly well coordinated alternation. The sucking response may not appear unless the baby is hungry, but this is not a hard condition to meet. According to Kron et al. (1968), neonates show striking and consistently maintained individual differences in rate and force of sucking. Kron and his fellow workers also report a distinct change in and stabilization of sucking behavior in the first few days. The head-turning portion of the sucking response implies that if one wants the young baby to face in a given direction, as when one wants to take his picture, it does no good to push against his cheek—he turns his head toward the push rather than away from it. One should, it follows, touch the cheek on the side toward which one wants him to turn. If restraining a baby's head causes him distress, as Watson proposed, conceivably it is because he is being stimulated to turn his head in two directions at once.

We have already mentioned the **Moro response**, which can be set off by any sudden, intense stimulation, such as a loud noise. The neonate reacts by stretching wide his arms and legs, often crying at the same time, and then hugging himself together again. The tension subsides visibly within a few seconds. There is then usually a refractory phase, as with many other responses, during which the response cannot be elicited. Repeated stimulation leads to habituation.

Apart from the scant "voluntary" use of the hands which we mentioned earlier, the neonate shows a **grasping reflex** when his palm or fingers are stimulated. He reacts by taking a firm grip on the rod or finger used to stimulate him—so firm in some babies that they can hang by their hands for as long as a minute (Pratt, 1954). Voluntary grasping supplants reflex grasping between three and four months of age, but even then, once the baby has something in his hand, the still-persistent grasp reflex makes it impossible for him to let go. One can also elicit a vestigial grasp reflex of the toes by stimulating the sole of the foot just at the base of the toes (note that the Babinski response is triggered by stroking the middle of the sole, where the arch will be).

If the baby is supported horizontal on his belly, he may perform swimming movements (**swimming reflex**). We are skeptical about claims that newborn babies "instinctively" know how to swim, and we suggest that any psychologist who cares to test the hypothesis should try it on his own newborn baby. If the neonate is held vertical with his feet lightly touching a firm surface, he may move his feet up and down as though walking (**stepping reflex**). These two responses disappear shortly after birth, to reappear later in more mature form. If the neonate is lying prone and the bottoms of his feet come in con-

This newborn's grasp reflex is strong enough to support his own weight, although the adult on the right is taking no chances.

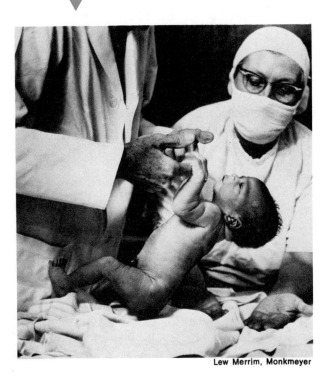

Lew Merrim, Monkmeyer

tact with a surface, he pushes against it, in some cases with sufficient force to move his body; this **push-back response** probably accounts for reports of newborn babies "crawling." At a slightly later age, the baby pushes back with his feet when supine.

Within the first hour after birth, given the right stimulus conditions, the baby shows such important vegetative reflexes as vomiting, sneezing, hiccoughing, yawning, and blinking. Boy babies, as we have already said, have erections of the penis. These tend to precede urination, and they also occur regularly during sleep (Wolff, 1959; Korner, 1969), especially irregular sleep when REM is most pronounced. This pattern of erections during sleep is very similar to that found in adult males of all ages (Fisher et al., 1965). Attempts to identify analogous cycles of clitoral erections in females are still inconclusive (ibid.).

Limitations of the neonate

Our description might lead the reader to conclude that any handling of the newborn would produce great outbursts of reflex activity. Such is not the case. In fact, during routine care such as dressing and undressing, bathing, and medical examinations, most babies for the first several months are remarkably passive, placid, and malleable. Most of the newborn's response capabilities are likely to go unnoticed by parents. At the same time, parents may anthropomorphically (or "adultomorphically") credit the baby with qualities of mind, morality, and purpose that the scientific observer is unable to confirm.

For all his rudimentary humanity, the neonate still lacks a great many capacities. The only vocal sounds he makes are crying and the noises that go with digestion and indigestion. He cannot yet (with some rare exceptions) raise his head, roll over (except by accident), or move his thumb and fingers separately. His hands do not reach out to things at a distance, although, as we have said, Bower et al. (1970a) find signs of beginning reaching. He cannot control elimination. He begins almost at once to pay attention to human faces, but he cannot yet tell one face from another. He does not know that he has feet. He has nothing to remember and remembers nothing, although studies of early learning tell us that experience begins to take hold almost at once. His life is governed largely by the rhythms of his digestive tract and other physiological processes, the rise and ebb of wakefulness, the triggers that set off reflex discharges, and the kind mercies of those who take care of him.

*Individual differences
and individuality*

Right from birth, as we have said, the baby manifests an individual uniqueness that is the product both of his special genetic make-up and of conditions in the uterine environment. Newborn babies are decidedly different from one another—in the tonus of their bodies, the forcefulness or sluggishness with which they react, the speed at which they move their limbs, the zeal and vigor with which they attack the nipple, the patterning of bursts of sucking, their sensitivity to light or sound or touch, their irritability, their alertness, their sleeping rhythms. They differ in size and shape, in the absolute and relative size of body organs, in blood chemistry, and in hormonal balance. Within a short time, the very proteins of the body become so individualized that they reject tissues transplanted from other persons. These, of course, are differences along single dimensions on which people can be scaled between polar opposites like fast and slow. Needless to say, any number of people can share the same scale position on any single dimension. However, combinations of scale positions on many dimensions produce a cluster of characteristics which make each person unique, unlike anybody else in the whole world. Birns (1965) has shown individual differences in responses to four kinds of stimuli: a soft tone, a loud tone, a cold disk applied to the skin, and a pacifier. Kron et al. (1968), as we have said, have found differences in strength and rate of sucking. Eisenberg et al. (1966) have found differences in rate of habituation. Korner and Thoman (1970) relate differences in visual alertness to patterns of maternal care. And so on.

Let us stress an obvious but often neglected fact. People change as they grow, but they still retain their individuality. We know very little as yet about the meaning for later development of anatomical, physiological, and psychological differences observable at birth. Predictions made from early behavior to later functioning work out at better than chance expectations, but there are too many exceptions, including some very dramatic reversals, for us to have much confidence in the prognostic value of neonatal characteristics (Escalona and Heider, 1959; Kagan and Moss, 1962; Thomas et al., 1963). Nevertheless, it seems probable that the differences between any two individuals would mean that they would respond to and take in

and integrate even highly similar life experiences in different ways. We shall set forth as we go along some of the evidence for the radical role of the psychological environment in determining the course of development, but while experience may transform the individual it in no way diminishes his individuality. Even such an event as oxygen deficiency at birth, which is significantly associated with later intellectual impairment, has a differential effect on different individuals; as Graham and her collaborators (Graham et al., 1962) have pointed out, too many individuals escape the expected consequences of traumatic birth for us to make predictions in the particular case.

Prenatal Development

Now the baby is safely born, and the reader has some acquaintance with his lineaments, but before we follow the neonate toward adulthood, we must turn back and see where he has come from. For the baby at birth is already nine months old, and is considered a year old in the reckoning of some Oriental cultures. In addition, he has a genetic history linking him with a multitude of ancestors back to the dawn of life. (Our practice of drawing a family tree as spreading out from a single pair of founders is more than somewhat misleading; not only can a single couple have a throng of descendants, but a child has many progenitors, doubling in number each generation back—two parents, four grandparents, eight great-grandparents, and so on.) We shall first sketch the child's development from conception to birth, and then go still further back for a brief look at some principles of genetic inheritance.

The total gestation period is estimated at 266 days on the average. However, since it is usually impossible to date conception exactly, pregnancy is reckoned from the beginning of the last menstruation, and the normal term is set at forty weeks.

The successive metamorphoses by which a single cell becomes a human being are a remarkable history, and the reader is urged to consult a book on human embryology or gestation for a detailed account. Here we can offer only a few highlights important to our understanding of later development. The single cell which will become a child is itself formed from the fusion of two germ cells, an **ovum** from the mother and a **sperm** cell from the father. The cell thus formed is called a **zygote.** Through a series of cell divisions the zygote is transformed over a two-week period into a **blastocyst,** a hollow sphere with an inner cell mass at one side. It is from this cell mass that the baby himself will develop. Most of the blastocyst is devoted to the baby's housing and life support systems. The key structures that develop are the **placenta**, by which the baby is attached to the mother, and the double-walled balloonlike sac filled with amniotic fluid in which the baby floats. The inner membrane of this sac is called the **amnion**, and the outer membrane the **chorion.**

It is important to understand the structure and function of the placenta. When fully developed, the human placenta is a disk-shaped fleshy slab, 6 to 8 inches (15 to 20 cm.) across, slightly more than an inch (25 mm.) thick, and weighing about a pound (slightly under one-half kilogram). On the maternal side it is a spongy-surfaced mass of blood vessels implanted in the lining of the uterus, or womb; these vessels are bathed in maternal blood and can exchange various substances with it. More details in a moment. The placenta is smooth on the side to which the baby is connected by the umbilical cord, a rubbery tube containing a vein that carries fresh blood from the placenta to the baby and two arteries carrying waste-laden blood to the placenta. Within the placenta, the umbilical vein and arteries branch out into the countless tendrils that are bathed in maternal blood. The baby's heart, which begins beating three to four weeks after conception, pumps blood through his body and the cord and placenta. Wastes, such as carbon dioxide, are absorbed through the walls of the placental vessels into the mother's blood, and the fresh blood draws from the mother's blood nutrients—oxygen, water, sugars, fats, amino acids, minerals, and so forth—and other substances such as hormones, antibodies, viruses, and blood fractions, which we shall discuss later, and carries them back to the baby. Notice that the baby's and the mother's blood normally never mix, all transactions taking place via the placental screen. The mother's blood supplies all the nutritive raw materials for the baby's growth, but the blastocyst, even as it burrows into the uterine lining, begins synthesizing complex amino acids and carbohydrates. The placenta serves not only as a filter through which selected materials pass back and forth between the mother's and the baby's blood, but also as an endocrine gland, secreting hormones which become an integral part of the mother's physiology and presumably help regulate the baby's own growth. Some authorities believe that the slowing down of placental hormone secretions helps start the birth process. The chorion and amnion grow out from the edges of the placenta to enclose the baby.

Prenatal development

The child himself emerges from the inner cell mass of the blastocyst, formed in the first two weeks. Between that time and a conception age of eight weeks, all the baby's anatomy is taking rudimentary shape. During this six-week period the developing organism is known as an **embryo**. It is during the embryonic stage that the baby is most vulnerable to environmental insults of the kind we shall talk about later. Some idea of the appearance of the embryo can be gained from the accompanying photographs.

It is about two weeks into the embryonic period, or about four weeks after conception, when the mother is aware of pregnancy. Most obviously, menstruation is by that time two weeks overdue. In addition, the woman may feel a heaviness and fullness of the breasts and see an enlargement and darkening of the nipples and surrounding areolas. She may have to urinate more often than usual. She may have morning sickness, the nausea that afflicts some two-thirds of women in the early weeks or months of pregnancy. There are various possible emotional attitudes toward being pregnant, from elation to panic. Particular attitudes mixed in with somatic symptoms and perhaps psychosomatic reactions can produce great individual differences in the experience of pregnancy. Most women, though, if their pregnancy is voluntary, find it a mixture of discomfort and rewards, hopes and anxieties, pain and delight. Many women report that later pregnancy is a time of unparalleled physical well-being.

Toward the end of the embryonic period, the baby-to-be is about 1¼ inches (3 cm.) long. He has limbs and digits and humanlike facial features. The endocrine system has taken shape and the male embryo's testes produce androgens. There is still no visible difference between the sexes, however. An embryo removed from the womb will show some isolated reflex movements when stimulated, indicating at least rudimentary nerve transmission.

From about eight weeks on, the developing creature is known as a fetus. The fetal period is given over to the elaboration and growth of structures laid down in the embryonic stage. By about the twelfth week, an expert can distinguish the sexes in surgically removed fetuses, although the testes do not descend from the male's abdominal cavity into the scrotum until age twenty-eight weeks or later. A fetus as young as ten weeks, when it is less than 3 inches (7½ cm.) long and weighs less than an ounce (29 g.), makes breathing movements if removed from the mother's body. It makes sucking movements of the lips in response to stimulation, and the feet show the Babinski response. Before age sixteen weeks, reflex swallowing begins and the fetus ingests small amounts of amniotic fluid. Between twenty and twenty-eight weeks of age, the fetus comes to be densely covered with downy lanugo hair, which is shed, although not always completely, shortly before birth. One can hear the fetus's heartbeat, with the help of a stethoscope, before age twenty weeks, and about the same time the mother experiences the "quickening," fetal movements that she can feel. The quickening is felt first as a mild fluttering, but later in pregnancy as good solid kicks. Twenty weeks is the midpoint of pregnancy, and the mother's con-

Stages in prenatal development. A. A two-cell organism thirty hours after fertilization. B. A living three-and-a-half-day-old human morula. C. A twenty-four-day-old embryo. D. An embryo at four-and-a-half weeks. E. A fourteen-week fetus. Note amniotic sac, umbilical cord, and placenta. F. Fetus at sixteen weeks. G. Fetus at about twenty-two weeks; despite its apparent maturity, the fetus at this age cannot survive outside the womb.

The birth of the baby

A.　Dr. Landrum B. Shettles

B.　Dr. Landrum B. Shettles

C.　Dr. Landrum B. Shettles

D.　Dr. Landrum B. Shettles

E.　Dr. Landrum B. Shettles

F.　Edith L. Potter, *Fundamentals of Human Reproduction*

G.　Edith L. Potter, *Fundamentals of Human Reproduction*

dition will usually be obvious to other people. Any morning sickness will probably be past, and she will be entering the most comfortable period of pregnancy. A fetus born at this time will inevitably die quickly, although babies weighing as little as 12 ounces (340 g.), indicating an age of just over 20 weeks, have been known to survive.

Toward age twenty-four weeks, the eyelids, previously fused shut, separate, and the fetus opens and closes his eyes. The sebaceous glands start operating and produce the vernix caseosa. A twenty-eight-week-old fetus, some 15 inches (38 cm.) long and 2½ pounds (1+ kg.), stands a fair chance of surviving birth, but keeping him alive may require large doses of oxygen and a small consequent risk of blindness associated with retrolental fibroplasia (see p. 000). There are other hazards and vulnerabilities that go with prematurity (Braine et al., 1966). One danger that has only lately come to be recognized is that the isolation imposed on the premature baby to protect him from infection also involves social deprivation. Siqueland (1970) reports good effects from providing human stimulation (cuddling, rocking, talking, crooning) for premature babies. Freedman (1969) has simply arranged that the baby's isolation chamber be made to rock in a 12 degree arc twelve times a minute; this rocking motion soothes premature babies and leads to increased smiling in those babies that smile. In the last few weeks of gestation, the baby is filling out so quickly that a difference of only a few days in age at birth may make a decided difference in his appearance.

During the final weeks of pregnancy, the mother will probably feel healthy, but she is likely to suffer some discomforts of a mechanical sort. Her inner organs are becoming crowded by the expanding fetus. She must make postural adjustments to a new distribution of weight—note the sway-backed stance of many women in late pregnancy. In the last few weeks, many women experience their bodies as awkward and cumbersome and look forward to childbirth as a welcome liberation.

Prenatal Environmental Influences

The normal process of prenatal development is so usual that we tend to take it for granted. The zygote, we must remind ourselves, does not contain a miniature model of the creature it is to become, so that it has only to grow bigger, but instead a wealth of information, coded in molecular form, which regulates successive steps in the evolution of the organism. Note that the genetic code does not stop operating at birth. The entire business of growing up and growing old constitutes, together with prenatal development, a single, continuing process. We shall talk more in a little while about genetics, but here we must mention two aspects of the way genetic constitution is expressed in development. We must remember, first, that every cell of an organism contains exactly the same genetic information as every other cell of that organism, but this information is used differently by different cells at different periods of development. The same information, in other words, is used to manufacture different sorts of tissue—skin, bone, blood, muscle—and different kids of organs —eyes, teeth, liver, brain, whatever. Second, the units in the genetic code, like the words in sentences, change meaning according to their context. Both these statements can be reduced to one by saying that genetic mechanisms operate in various ways according to their environmental contexts. We must stress that there are many different levels of relevant environments, some inside the organism and some outside it. The gene does it work in the context of its position on the chromosome. The chromosome operates in the context of other chromosomes. The cell nucleus operates in the context of the surrounding cell matter. The single cell acts according to its position in the cell cluster. Events in the cell cluster as a whole (even as a zygote in the Fallopian tube) are governed by environing conditions of temperature, electrical potential, chemical balance, orientation with respect to the uterine wall, gravity, and atmospheric pressure. We cannot neglect the nutrients which are used to construct the organism. Eventually, of course, personal, social, and affective influences work on the organism's very biology.

It is fortunate that the intrauterine environment is usually quite stable, varying only within very narrow limits, since experimental manipulation of the prenatal environment of animal embryos shows that even minor alterations can produce serious deformities. (The study of developmental anomalies is called **teratology**—the science of monsters—or, if one prefers a truly impressive label, **dysmorphogenesis**.) In addition to the general conditions mentioned above, the following agents are some that have been found to alter embryonic development in one species or another: poisons, drugs, viruses, x-rays and other forms of ionizing radiation, abnormal blood conditions of the mother (such as hormone imbalance, anemia, or the presence of anomalous proteins), excess or deficiency of certain vitamins, oxygen lack, protein deficiency, and iodine deficiency (Mintz, 1958; Montagu, 1962).

Among the deformities produced by environmental factors are anencephaly (lack of a brain), harelip, phocomelia (the "seal flippers" syndrome caused by, among other things, the drug thalidomide), cleft palate, syndactyly (failure of the digits to separate), extra members or missing members, reversal or ambiguity of sex, and a host of other conditions, some minor and some so severe as to lead to spontaneous abortion. Certain birth deformities in livestock, which ranchers used to attribute to poor heredity, have recently been traced to the eating of toxic weeds by pregnant animals (Ripley, 1971). While only a relatively few pregnancies eventuate in such developmental disasters, recent teratological research is of great interest for the light it throws on general principles of growth. Moreover, such research promises to bring many of the newly understood factors under control, and to eliminate vague fears of "hereditary taints." What we do not yet know very much about is ways of manipulating the prenatal environment to produce superior forms of somatic development; for the time being it seems safest to say that the normal environment is the ideal one. However, there is now evidence from the study of rats that injection of pituitary growth hormone into the pregnant mother has favorable effects on the development of the brain in the offspring (Zamenhof et al., 1966). Notice, too, the inescapable reciprocity of the influences; not only does the mother affect the development of the baby, but the zygote, embryo, and fetus are a part of the mother's environment and modify her physiology from the moment of conception.

Whether teratogenic agents have an

Prenatal environmental influences

effect, and what the effect is likely to be, varies with certain conditions: the **time** of development at which the agent is introduced, the **part of the organism** that is affected, how large a **dose** is present, and both **strain** and **individual differences** among organisms. Note, too, that teratogens can act on the embryo in two different ways: directly, as in the case of rubella (German measles) virus or x-rays, or indirectly, by altering the mother's physiological state in ways that will have an effect on the developing baby. Now let us look more closely at the governing variables of prenatal environment influences. Because things generally go so smoothly, we can often see the operation of important principles best when development goes awry. This should not, however, make our account seem a panorama of disasters.

Timing

It is a principle of embryonic development that organs and organ systems emerge in a fixed sequence, with just so much time allowed for each—though the times, of course, overlap. That is, in the total time-table of growth, each organ system has its own **critical period.** During its critical period, the organ system is both highly responsive to growth-stimulating influences and highly vulnerable to disruptive ones. Put another way, it is the part of the organism that is growing most rapidly that is most sensitive to deleterious agents. If the organ system does not develop normally during its critical period, it does not have a second chance—the focus of growth shifts to successive systems.

The importance of timing is illustrated by the differential effects of grossly exces-

sive amounts of vitamin A given to pregnant white rats at different stages of gestation: between eight and ten days, the most likely consequence is anencephaly; between eleven and seventeen days, cleft palate; between eighteen and twenty days, cataract (Mintz, 1958). Some teratogens, such as thalidomide, seem to act only at one stage of development, and are innocuous at other times. Others (like the vitamin excess mentioned) act at any time but have different effects depending on the stage of development. Thus, maternal rubella (German measles) during the embryonic period may cause brain damage, blindness, deafness, or peripheral deformities in the offspring, depending on the time of infection. It is estimated that 30,000 defects and 20,000 fetal deaths resulted from the epidemic of 1963–1965 in the United States. (Because rubella is a mild, inconsequential disease except for its effects in the early months of pregnancy, many physicians recommend that girls be given every opportunity to contract it in childhood. A vaccine is available, but doubts have been raised about whether the immunity it gives is long-lasting.) It further follows from what we have said that the same anomaly can be produced by more than one teratogen.

Let us emphasize that the effects we are speaking of, which alter the basic design of the organism (its **morphology**), occur only during the germinal and embryonic periods when the baby's anatomy is first taking shape. During the fetal period, various agents can produce permanent damage, but they no longer modify the basic structural design. The fetus reacts to maternal illnesses, to poisons, to maternal fatigue (which finds chemical expression in the bloodstream), to nicotine, and to alcohol.

Narcotics-addicted mothers are likely to give birth to narcotics-addicted neonates (see references in Bowes et al., 1970).

A topic that has received much attention recently (e.g., Cravioto, 1968; Scrimshaw, 1969) is the relationship between maternal nutrition and physical development. Recent research has led to the discarding of two cherished hypotheses, one of which supplanted still another myth about fifteen years ago, which said that every baby cost its mother a tooth. The first fractured hypothesis is that the unborn baby has first call on the nutritional resources of the mother, that her needs get attended to only after his have been met. It now appears that the mother's body nourishes itself first and gives the child the leftovers. For this reason, obstetricians no longer encourage pregnant women to gain as little weight as possible. The second abandoned hypothesis is the doctrine of "brain sparing," which says that the brain is the last part of the body to be affected by nutritional deficiencies. In fact, there appear to be critical periods for brain development, and malnutrition, especially protein shortage, during these times can impair brain tissue formation. Brain development continues very rapid for the first three years after birth, but we can also infer from the neonate's abilities that a great deal has gone on before birth. According to Dayton (1969), the development of body tissue, including brain, goes on in three stages. The first is hyperplasia, the proliferation of cells, which takes place in the brains of human babies during fetal and early postnatal life. Malnutrition during this period leads to a reduced number of brain cells, with no recovery possible. This means, of course, that babies born to malnourished mothers, and who are themselves malnourished early in life, may from then on have permanent psychological impairments. Malnutrition seems to be a factor for babies who are not premature but are unusually tiny at birth and are called "small-for-dates."

Locus of effects, size of dose, and organism differences

Some portions of the organism are structurally more central to total functioning than others; if these central systems are deformed, then other, secondary, often widespread deformities follow in their wake. If, on the other hand, it is one of the peripheral systems that is affected, then the damage may be quite circumscribed. We may, of course, be misled by the most striking feature of an anomalous condition and fail to see that it is only a part of a syndrome. For instance, the stunted limbs for which phocomelia is named are only one of the effects produced by thalidomide. Other features of the "thalidomide syndrome" are a temporary strawberry mark extending from the forehead down the nose and across the upper lip, and, with varying incidence, a saddle-shaped or flattened nose, a missing external ear and a downward displacement of the auditory canal (hearing, however, is normal), and malformations of the alimentary tract and of the heart and circulatory system (Taussig, 1962).

Some teratogens have no effect unless they surpass a certain minimum dose. On the other hand, the threshold may be a dual one. Either too little or too much vitamin A can pose a threat. A debate is in progress on whether there is a threshold effect for ionizing radiation. Sternglass

(1963) and others hold that there is no threshold, that any exposure to radiation can be dangerous both for unborn babies and adults; the effect of raising the dose is simply to raise the probability that a gene, chromosome, or other vulnerable structure will be struck.

The same teratogen may have different effects or no effects depending on the species involved. Even closely related strains may show different reactions to the same agent, and individual members of the same strain—including litter mates—may respond differently.

Although we have been talking about environmentally induced abnormalities of physical development, the very same principles of environmental regulation apply to normal development. As we said earlier, the hereditary make-up of the organism is not a single fixed entity that simply unfolds on schedule. It contains many possible modes of expression, varying with all its contexts. For instance, worker bees and queen bees are both genetic females, but only the queens, fed during childhood on an exclusive diet of royal jelly, become fertile adult females. The workers, brought up on pollen and nectar, become sexless adults.

Old and new conceptions of prenatal influences

The prenatal environmental influences we are talking about are, of course, quite different in kind from those which have always figured in old wives' tales: the pregnant woman who sees a tree struck by lightning gives birth to a child who will have a blaze of white in his hair; the woman who listens to good music through-out pregnancy will produce a musically talented child; by thinking pleasant thoughts, one guarantees a child of cheerful disposition. Unlike these magical influences, the ones we are discussing require direct physical action on the tissues of the embryo, as by x-rays, by the transmission of biochemical agents from the mother's blood to the child's, or by privation of materials needed for normal growth. At the same time, there is firm evidence from animal experimentation (Montagu, 1962, ch. 8), and suggestive evidence from the study of human beings (ibid.), that the mother's emotional state can have a bearing on her unborn child's development. Emotional arousal involves physiological changes, and the endocrine and neurohumoral products of arousal can be passed from the mother's blood to the child's. The exact relationships are still unclear, but is is evident—at the rat and mouse level—that severe or prolonged stress to the mother (commonly used stressors are electric shock, immersion in ice water, and crowded living conditions) can affect the infant's body size, adrenal size and activity, anxiety level, learning ability, and longevity.

Rh incompatibility

One important form of prenatal influence, illustrating reciprocal action between genetic and environmental factors, is that of blood incompatibility between a mother whose blood is Rh negative (that is, does not contain Rh factor) and a baby whose blood is Rh positive. Rh factor is a genetically determined blood component found in all rhesus monkeys (whence "Rh") and 85 percent of white people (as against nearly 100 percent of other racial groups). When

Rh factor is introduced into Rh negative blood, as sometimes used to happen in transfusions before the Rh factor had been recognized, antibodies that combat the Rh factor are produced. When an Rh negative woman mates with an Rh positive man (the only potentially dangerous combination), she may conceive an Rh positive child (if the father carries two Rh positive genes, the child is certain to be Rh positive; if he carries one Rh positive and one Rh negative gene, then the chances are half-and-half). If the unborn child is Rh positive, and even a small rupture of the placental capillary structure allows some of his blood to mingle with his mother's, this may lead, as in the case of transfusion, to the production of Rh antibodies in the mother. However, the antibodies are usually produced too slowly to affect a first Rh positive fetus. If, however, the mother carries subsequent Rh positive children and receives additional Rh positive blood, her now-sensitized blood steps up production of antibodies which may enter the fetal bloodstream and cause destruction of its Rh positive red blood cells. The damage caused by Rh antibodies to the baby's Rh positive blood can sometimes lead to miscarriage or, at or shortly after birth, to death or brain defects. Fortunately, total transfusion techniques for the newborn have been developed which can prevent damage from Rh incompatibility. Indeed, techniques have been worked out for transfusing the fetus's blood before birth. For reasons unknown, Rh reactions appear somewhat less frequently than purely statistical considerations would lead one to expect. In addition, there is hope that Rh antibody production can be blocked by treating the mother with gamma globulin (Freda et al., 1966).

It should be apparent that an Rh negative mother's production of antibodies is but a special case of the so-called immune response by which the body fights off an invasion by alien tissue. The intriguing if rather frightening possibility has been raised, but by no means proved, that the baby's placental tissues may sometimes serve as an antigen which provokes an immune response by the mother (Billington, 1970; Currie, 1970; Curzen, 1970; Kirby, 1970).

In spite of the diversity of possible unwanted environmental influences, most embryos develop in essentially normal conditions and are born sound of body. The interest of prenatal influences for this book's purposes is to illustrate very concretely the lifelong interplay of genetic and environmental forces. The important lesson, first formulated in these terms by Hebb (1953), is that all aspects of development are determined 100 percent by heredity and 100 percent by environment, since neither can operate without the other—a sometimes neglected consideration. From this standpoint, it is meaningless to try to quantify the "relative contributions" of each. Rather, following Anastasi (1958), the question is one of how the interaction takes place. We shall return to this issue later (pp. 331–341).

Biological Inheritance

A complete account of modern genetics, the science of how biological characteristics are transmitted from one generation to the next, would be far beyond the scope of this work, and once again we urge the reader to consult an appropriate book in the field. Thus, we shall talk about genes and chromosomes, but leave to specialists the treatment of the underlying DNA and RNA. We shall begin with a brief presentation of some standard genetic notions and then go on to discuss some of the more recent findings in this field, and some principles that the reader may find helpful in thinking about how hereditary traits find expression.

Eugenics, euthenics, and euphenics

Genetics has several useful applications. Perhaps the most important of these is in **eugenics**, the improvement of a species—human, animal, or plant—by selective breeding, matching parents to produce certain desired traits in their offspring and preventing unions likely to yield unfavorable traits. Eugenic procedures are standard practice in animal husbandry and agriculture, although many of the selective breeding techniques used by farmers were devised centuries before Gregor Mendel fathered the science of genetics. Even with help of modern knowledge, selective breeding may go badly awry; the corn blight that recently threatened crops in the United States traveled rapidly because resistance to it had been bred out of the most popular strains.

At the human level, we find crude eugenic measures in the practice, at various times and places, of infanticide, by which unwanted or unfit members were eliminated from the species; in Hitler's lunatic campaign of racial purification (with some uncomfortable contemporary parallels); and in the scattered and rarely invoked

laws ordaining sterilization of criminals, mental defectives, psychotics, epileptics, or other people whom a given society might deem substandard. Instead of restrictive eugenic measures, most geneticists would recommend matings across as many geographical and social barriers as possible with a view to increasing human heterogeneity. Some combinations would work out badly and others well, but the odds in favor of superior combinations would be increased over what they are now, and selective factors should work to limit the propagation of the unsuccessful combinations. This is not quite the same thing as the notion of **heterosis**, or hybrid vigor, which says that the progeny of mixed matings are always, on average, superior to those of inbred lines. We do not find the evidence altogether convincing.

Genetic counseling of prospective parents used to be a restricted undertaking. The counselor had to reconstruct his clients' pedigrees as best he could and try to project from his knowledge the probabilities that certain traits would occur in a given proportion of the children. Since 1964, it has been possible to examine the chromosomes of living people and to detect certain abnormalities that might restrain people from reproducing. As we have said, amniocentesis permits prenatal diagnosis of some genetic defects, so that genetic counseling can be extended past conception.

Eugenics is often contrasted with **euthenics**, ways of improving the species by manipulating the environment. Advocates of eugenics and euthenics have often been at odds with each other, although it should be obvious that measures of both sorts can go hand in hand. Both sorts of measures encounter tremendous psychological resistance, eugenic ones because people rebel at any hint of programed matings, and euthenic ones because the beneficiaries of the status quo want to keep things just as they are.

Finally, somewhere on the horizon, there is **euphenics,** direct manipulation of the genetic material itself. The isolation of single genes has become possible, one can now fertilize a human egg in the test tube and grow it to the blastocyst stage, and animal eggs have been taken into the embryonic stage in the laboratory. The techniques are well along, but the social implications and issues are only at the beginning.

Sources of genetic knowledge

Even with new techniques for studying human chromosomes, most of our knowledge of genetic mechanisms, like our knowledge of prenatal development, comes largely from studies of nonhuman species. Unlike fruit flies and mice, human beings cannot be bred under controlled laboratory conditions. This means that we have no way of regulating matings, for which we should be grateful, and also that we have no way of keeping environments standard, which we would have to do to be confident that the variations we observed were genetic in origin. A favored technique in human genetics, comparing identical twins raised together with twins raised in separate environments (and with nonidentical twins, siblings, and unrelated persons), has several limitations. First, identical twins reared apart are by no means numerous. Second, we have only the crudest beginnings of a systematic way to specify and contrast significant aspects of the environ-

ment. Third, we generally cannot know in advance that a pair of twins will be separated, which means that such cases are only discovered some time after the fact, and we have to reconstruct their early histories from often questionable evidence. There is the further practical difficulty in human genetics that people live too long, and have to wait too long to reproduce, to make good subjects for even nonlaboratory research. The human geneticist is often less an experimental scientist than an archivist, tracing traits back through historical and family documents and hospital records.

Hereditary mechanisms

The trait-carrying elements of heredity are thought to be **genes,** giant molecules in the **chromosomes,** which are rodlike bodies in the cell nucleus, visible under the microscope during periods of cell division. All organisms produced by a sexual mating have two sets of chromosomes, arranged in pairs, one set—half of each pair—inherited from each parent. Human beings normally have 23 pairs, or 46 chromosomes. Ordinarily, when a cell divides, the chromosomes split lengthwise in two, so that there are 92, which are then divided equally between the two resulting cells. Germ cells, spermatozoa and ova, however, have a peculiarity. At one stage of development (**meiosis,** or **reduction division**), instead of the individual chromosomes splitting, the chromosome pairs simply separate, with one set going to one new cell and the other to the other. That is, the mature human germ cell contains only 23 chromosomes rather than 46. When a sperm and ovum combine, each contributes

Biological inheritance

its 23 chromosomes so that the zygote has the usual 46. Since some people still entertain the notion that it is either the father or the mother who is exclusively responsible for the child's heredity, it is important to note that the child gets half his chromosomes from each parent. Which parent the child "takes after," whether in appearance or behavior, is a complicated matter that cannot be resolved by references to "your side of the family." Even where certain trait resemblances are clear, the child may take after the other parent in other respects. In meiosis, the chromosomes do not divide themselves neatly according to their (grand) maternal and (grand) paternal origins. In other words, the set of 23 chromosomes that one parent passes on to his or her offspring may include some chromosomes inherited from that parent's father and some from the mother. Furthermore, although the numerous genes that make up a single chromosome generally stay together as a unit, there is evidence that corresponding genes sometimes trade places with each other between members of a chromosome pair, so that the chromosomes themselves may change in character. Hence, a given parent has not two kinds but a great variety of germ cells, each sperm or ovum representing a different sorting and shuffling of potentialities. These facts help explain how members of the same family resemble each other, since each child has 46 chromosomes drawn from a pool of only 92, and how at the same time they can be quite dissimilar, since their chromosomal inheritance can be any one of a vast number of possible combinations of genes.

We still do not understand the subtle differences in composition among the genes that control different structures or that determine the different forms that a given structure can take: noses can be straight or hooked or retroussé, hair can be blond or brown or red or black, or straight or wavy or kinky, and so forth for all the varieties of human constitution. The fact is, nevertheless, that many physical characteristics do have a stable pattern of inheritance. With an exception to be noted in a moment, there are two genes for every trait. Certain traits occur given the presence of a single gene without regard to the contribution of the second, counterpart gene. Such traits are called **dominant**. Among dominant human traits are brown or hazel eyes, blood types A, B, and AB, high blood pressure, Rh positive factor, and allergy. Other characteristics occur only when two like genes are present; these are called **recessive** traits: blue eyes, adherent ear lobes, normal vision, and so forth. When a dominant gene is paired with a recessive gene, only the dominant trait is expressed. In such cases, we must distinguish between **phenotype**, the phenomenal or observable characteristic, and **genotype**, the underlying genetic make-up which does not necessarily correspond to the phenotype. Thus, a phenotypically brown-eyed person who genotypically has a pairing of brown-eye and blue-eye genes (either of which can be passed on to his offspring) will look just like an individual who has two genes for brown eye color. It follows that two phenotypically brown-eyed parents each of whom carries a recessive blue-eye gene can have blue-eyed children. The same genotype-phenotype terminology can be applied to environmentally caused modifications; thus, as we noted earlier, the queen and worker bee are genotypically the same but phenotypically very different. A number of traits are partially dominant, so that a single gene produces an intermediate effect, for example, medium skin pigmentation or wavy hair. Some genes may be dominant in one biological context but not in another. For instance, baldness is dominant in men but recessive in women (although there are more bald women—that is, women with two genes for baldness—than the reader may realize).

The example of baldness should remind us that not all our genetic make-up has found full expression at birth—remember such genetically influenced characteristics as growth rate, adult stature, age of onset of puberty, and the different ways in which men's beards grow. The serious degenerative condition of the nervous system called Huntington's chorea, which is hereditary, is usually not manifested until adulthood; by the time it is recognized, the sufferer may already have children of his own. Other genetic traits may appear only in special circumstances. Sickle cell trait, an abnormal form of hemoglobin which can lead to dangerous clotting, and is found in West African and American Negroes (and to a lesser extent in several Mediterranean peoples), is normally a recessive trait. The person who carries two sickle cell genes suffers a severe and sometimes fatal anemia. The carrier of a single gene, however, may also develop anemia when his oxygen supply is reduced, as by great exertion, high altitude, respiratory infections, or alcohol. Recently, several black soldiers died following strenuous exercise at a camp in the mountains, presumably because of their sickle cell make-up. Sickle cell is thought to have survived in Africa because it confers resistance to malaria. Its incidence in the United States, where its antimalarial virtues are slight, seems to be dwindling to some minimum (Porter, 1968, p. 324).

Genetic sex determination

The two members of any pair of normal chromosomes are very much like each other, with one important exception. In males, one chromosome, designated X, is paired with an undersized one called Y. It is the Y-chromosome that determines maleness at the human (and mammalian) level. (In some nonmammalian species, it is the other way around. Reproduction in certain species may be wholly or partly by **parthenogenesis**, or virgin birth. Some parthenogenetic fishes are exclusively female; among the bees, the queens and workers are genetic females with fathers, whereas the male drones are born parthenogenetically.) The human sperm, then, are of two kinds: half carry an X-chromosome and half carry a Y. All ova are X. When a sperm carrying an X-chromosome and its constituent genes joins with an ovum, the result is XX, and a female has been conceived. When a Y-carrying sperm fertilizes an ovum, producing XY, a male zygote is formed. The Y-chromosome acts by differentiating the primordial gonads as testes rather than ovaries, and the testicular hormones govern the further elaboration of the male's primary and secondary sex characteristics.

Although XX and XY are the two normal patterns, others can occur through errors in chromosome replication: XXY, XXX, XXXX, XXXXY, or a single X without the second gene (XO). This last case produces an underdeveloped female. Any combination containing a Y produces some version of maleness. One type that has been in the news is XYY, associated with unusual tallness, acne, and in some cases abnormalities of the genitalia. The XYY genotype has been linked to criminal behavior (Telfer et al., 1967). Before one leaps to any conclusions about the hereditary nature of criminality, however, one should consider three points. First, despite some lurid cases, we do not know what proportion of XYY males engage in antisocial behavior; we do know, on the other hand, that some XYY's lead perfectly ordinary lives. Second, some persons with perfectly normal sex genotypes are also chronic criminals, which means that other factors must be operating. Third, even if XYY types are more likely than others to become felons, we have to take account of possible social and psychological mediation, since their somewhat anomalous physical appearance may lead to estrangement and hostility. In connection with these deviations from normal sex determination we should mention the fact of "mosaics," people whose cells are of two different kinds, such as XX/XO or XX/XY. Nobody understands mosaicism, but it has been suggested that two ova might be fertilized and then join in a double zygote. Finally, in at least some females, it appears that one of the two X-chromosomes may be partially inactivated, so that development is governed largely by a single X (Lyon, 1966).

The Y-chromosome carries fewer genes than the X, so that some genes on the X have no matching counterparts on the Y. Certain of these genes are responsible for what have been named **sex-linked recessive traits.** These are produced by genes on the X-chromosome which are recessive when paired with an offsetting normal gene in the XX female but which find full expression in the male, whose Y-chromosome lacks the matching gene with its counteractive effect. Perhaps the best known of the sex-linked recessives are red-green color blindness (other forms are only partially sex-linked) and hemophilia, or bleeder's disease, a condition in which the blood does not clot, so that even a minor wound can cause a fatal hemorrhage. Fabry's disease, which we mentioned in connection with the "inborn errors of metabolism," is a sex-linked recessive. These conditions can appear in women only in the rare instances when both X-chromosomes bear the gene for the trait. Thus, while sex-linked recessive traits are not confined to males, they are much more common in males than in females. For instance, red-green color blindness is found in some 8 percent of men but only .4 percent of women. It should be remembered that the male always inherits his sex-linked recessive from his mother, who supplies his X-chromosome.

We said earlier that half the sperm cells are X and half Y, but this assertion has to be qualified. In many species, including man, more males are conceived than females. The **sex ratio**, the number of males per 100 females, varies in human populations from 103 to 107 at birth. At later ages, because of higher mortality among males, the sex ratio shifts in the opposite direction in most societies. Either more Y sperm than X are produced, or Y sperm have some sort of advantage in fertilization.

Mutations and evolution

As we have seen, cell division involves duplication of the nucleus, so that each "daughter" cell has a full complement of chromosomes and genes. Ordinarily a gene reproduces itself with total fidelity, so that a person's genes are exact copies of the ones that his parents contributed to the zygote. Occasionally, however, there occurs a **mutation**, a change in the structure of the gene, which leads to a minor or major change in physical constitution.

The occurrence of mutations is thought to provide the raw materials on which natural selection operates to produce evolution. Mutations constantly appear, almost as though to be tried out, with the maladaptive mutants failing to reproduce and the fitter ones (in terms of the given environment) multiplying. We must emphasize that biological fitness is defined strictly in terms of being able to reproduce one's kind, and not in terms of personal survival. This emphasis is necessary because many people who try to apply Darwinian notions to social matters tend to define fitness in terms of such traits as superior fighting ability. While fitness obviously includes the ability to evade would-be predators and catch prey, it also depends on sexual attractiveness and fertility, having the right foodstuffs available and the right enzymes to digest them, the parental responsiveness that insures survival of the young, physiological mechanisms suited to the surrounding conditions of moisture and temperature, and so forth. It should also be made clear that fitness is inevitably relative to particular environments. Thus, stable, nonmutant mechanisms that serve a species well may prove ill-suited if the ecological context changes too drastically. Natural and man-made alterations produced by flood, drought, fire, housing and highway construction, and pollution of all kinds can dislocate or destroy whole ecosystems. People are only now coming to terms with the inescapable fact that the balance of nature is an intricately interconnected system, and that trifling with it is likely to lead to unforeseen and possibly disastrous effects.

As viable mutations accumulate over generations, new species emerge. It used to be thought that mutations occurred spontaneously or perhaps even in response to a mystical evolutionary driving force, or **élan vital**, toward improvement of the species. Nowadays, most mutations are believed to be the product of natural radiation from terrestrial and cosmic sources. At least some part of the current uproar over the release of nuclear energy stems from apprehension that we may be conducting a mammoth but unplanned experiment in evolution. There are other sources of mutations, of course. Some chemicals are mutagens, as we have learned from the controversy about food additives, pesticides, and defoliants. A virus can sometimes replace and function as a gene, which may be one of the mechanisms in cancer.

New ways of thinking in genetics

The simple gene-chromosome model we have sketched works reasonably well as far as we have gone. Supplementary concepts are needed, however, to account for the full range of phenomena. A lot of attention has been given to traits governed by a single gene: eye color, blood type, free versus adherent ear lobes, whatever can be discretely categorized. Of much greater interest to psychologists, though, are the so-called **distributive** traits, which are matters of more or less, like height. Such traits conform to the principle of **gene interaction**, that is, they are regulated by more than one gene and so are called **polygenic** (Medawar, 1959). Those psychological traits which may have important genetic determinants are all distributive and hence polygenic—intelligence, temperament, schizophrenia, proneness to violence—which makes obsolete much of the debate about their origins. For it seems to be the case that polygenic traits are highly sensitive to environmental influence. It used to be thought that height was strongly determined by the genes, and we have had to accommodate to the fact that stature increases dramatically as the standard of living rises (obviously we have to stop somewhere, or we will go the way of the dinosaurs). There is the further difficulty, though, that traits like intelligence are probably not distributed continuously. As long as we lump together all the various abilities sampled on an intelligence test into a unitary IQ, we can point to some sort of a normal distribution. Unfortunately, the distribution curve may be a very poor picture of what exists in the real world. Thus, before we make any firm assertions about the genetic bases of behavior, we have to improve our understanding of the trait itself. We must also, at some point, be able to say what the concrete organic correlates of behavioral variation consist of. It is not genes that behave, but organisms.

We might mention in passing the principle of **pleiotropy**, which says that one gene may control a variety of traits, perhaps in interaction with subordinate genes. We should also mention the fact of **expressivity,** that the same gene may lead to different forms of the same trait in different individuals. For instance, allergy, to the extent that it is hereditary, may be expressed as hay fever in one person and eczema in another; the presence of the gene may mean that this person is sensitive to ragweed pollen and that one to Brazil nuts.

We now return to a phenomenon touched upon in connection with sex determination. An error during cell division can lead to the formation of an extra chromosome, the loss of part of one chromosome to another, or the loss of a chromosome altogether. Most of such departures from **diploidy** (the fact that chromosomes come in pairs) are lethal, but there are four kinds of chromosome which people can have three of and still survive, and one kind, the X, that people can have only one of and still live. Abnormal complements of chromosomes have been associated with Down's syndrome (mongolism), skeletal anomalies, leukemia, and the sex patterns already mentioned. A recent study of 4,500 babies born in New Haven (Lubs and Ruddle, 1970) indicates that some .5 percent of babies have chromosomal anomalies. There was a steady increase in incidence with the age of the mother, from .2 percent in the fifteen-to-nineteen-year-old group to 1.6 percent in the forty-to-forty-four group. (Fourteen of the twenty-two babies involved were phenotypically normal.) The interesting point about these conditions is that, like mutations, they are genetic without necessarily being inherited. There is, however, heated disagreement about how these anomalies arise. Everyone agrees that they are more common in the offspring of older mothers, and, since females carry their lifetime supply of ova around with them from an early age, older mothers have older ova. The endogenous school (German, 1970) believes that aging processes in the egg increase the likelihood of an abnormal segregation of chromosomes during cell division; or that there may be a delay in the release or fertilization of older eggs, with the same result (Edwards and Fowler, 1970). The exogenous school believes that the anomalies are produced by agents such as viruses or ionizing radiation, and that older women simply have had more exposure to these agents, increasing the probability that one or more ova will be affected. In areas having a high level of natural radiation, all sorts of anomalies are more common than in low-radiation regions. Whenever a new virus is introduced into a community, the number of birth defects rises temporarily until the women of the community have developed antibodies. Robinson and Puck (1965) tentatively ascribe a five-month increase in chromosomal anomalies to an earlier outbreak of rubella, and Stoller (1968) reports that a wave of infectious hepatitis was followed nine months later by a rise in mongolism and hydrocephaly. It is not sexism that keeps attention focused on the mother; there undoubtedly are sperm containing anomalies, but far fewer in proportion to the vast sperm total, lowering the probability that they will be involved in reproduction, and those that occur are soon discharged. Note, too, that there are several forms of mongolism. The most common kind, associated with an extra chromosome 21, lasts only one generation. A rarer kind may lie latent in the parental cells .and become manifest in only an occasional daughter.

In all this discussion we have sidestepped a logical problem that arises in talking about genetics. This is the difficulty of saying what we mean by "trait." Sometimes the word designates a distinct anatomical feature, such as wings or an eye or a finger, which can take different forms; it may refer

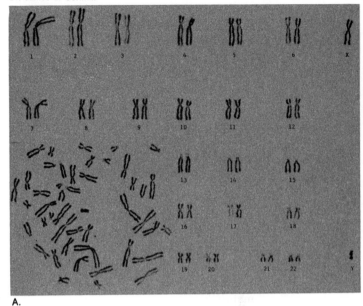

A.

Human chromosomes. The inserts show how the chromosomes look when arrested during the process of cell division. The larger displays are karyotypes, with the chromosomes arranged according to type. A. Normal male chromosomes. B. Chromosomes from a male victim of Down's syndrome; note the three number 21 chromosomes.

B.

to the particular form that a feature can take, such as the curliness of hair; it may mean the presence or absence of some component, such as eye pigment or an enzyme or a sixth toe; it may denote a pattern of related traits, as in mongolism, which involves many physical anomalies; or it may refer to some anatomically unlocalized characteristic of the way the total organism functions, such as intelligence. Part of the difficulty disappears when we keep in mind the distinction between single-gene and polygenic traits. Some remains, though, because we do not know how or where the organism's total morphology is encoded in the zygote nucleus, or the successive morphologies through which the organism passes en route to maturity.

Biology and psychology—
the place of genetics

If our later chapters seem to slight genetic factors, it is not because we think them insignificant but because we have used up most of what we want to say about them. Our main point is that a person's genetic endowment by no means determines his total development as a person, although a culture may dictate that certain physical traits imply particular psychological traits, setting the stage for a self-fulfilling prophecy. This does not mean that we can shape people at will, without regard to their organic constitution; it means that each unique organism will make something different of its experience and develop into itself. We know, of course, that some experiences are more likely to be important than others, and we know that some constitutional traits are more likely to play a

role than others. Where the individual's constitution enters significantly into his personal relationships, as in sex differences, extremes of beauty or ugliness, responsiveness and unresponsiveness, deformity or impaired mobility, sensory handicaps, or organic impediments to learning, understanding, or thinking, we shall take due account of it. A genetic consideration that will recur simply because people have inflated it to monstrous dimensions is race. Let us state flatly that all psychological studies of racial differences have been hopelessly confounded by factors of culture, economics, and social status, and will continue to be as long as race is an important element in popular thinking. Let us state further that racial attitudes and research in the United States are a sorry joke because race is treated as dichotomous (as in "black" and "white"), whereas in fact it it distributive, with racial mixture the rule rather than the exception. We must also bear in mind the fact of prenatal influences, so that constitutional conditions, **even when congenital** (present at birth), are not necessarily genetic. We do know something about the psychological correlates of certain genetic pathologies (yet even mongoloids have a wide spread of intelligence), but we know next to nothing about the psychological implications of normal physical variations.

Hence, the authors' stress on experience in the following chapters is not to be taken as antibiologism. Quite to the contrary. We would like to see the standard concepts of the biological sciences expanded so that they can deal with behavior and psychological development. So far, we have only the rudiments of an organismic-ecological biology of the total functioning person relating to his surroundings. A complete biology, of course, goes well beyond genetics and will give an integrated account of what are now treated as isolated physiological subsystems—digestive, respiratory, reproductive, and so on. We need a holistic biology that can assimilate the new discoveries from the frontiers of biochemistry and at the same time give us means for the biological phrasing of such higher-order activities as manipulation, play, empathy, language, learning, knowledge, and imagination. Until that happy day, the authors will concentrate on the psychological analysis of behavior.

The Birth Process

Having introduced the reader to the newborn baby and then turned back successively to the baby's prenatal incarnations and to his ancestry, we must now bring the child once more into the world. Toward the end of pregnancy, the fetus turns head down and comes to rest with his head in the lower part of the uterus, now well down in the mother's pelvic basin. The baby is then in position for the usually headfirst passage into the light and air. As he turns head down, the mother's high-prowed profile sags; pressure against her upper abdomen is eased and she breathes more freely. It is from this relief from pressure that the baby's change of position is called the **lightening**. The lightening may come as early as four weeks before birth, or it may wait until the onset of **labor**, the process by which the baby is expelled from the mother's body. The specific trigger (or triggers) for the start of labor is unknown, though some of the hormonal components are understood. Once begun, labor consists of spontaneous rhythmic contractions of the involuntary longitudinal uterine muscles, aided by the voluntary abdominal musculature, and the relaxation of the circular muscles of the cervix. The muscular contractions gradually squeeze the baby out of the uterus and through the vagina into the open.

The mother may be made aware of the onset of labor by any of three signs. One sign is labor pains, produced by the recurrent uterine contractions, initially of mild intensity and spaced fifteen or twenty minutes apart, and then of steadily increasing duration, frequency, and sharpness. Labor pains may begin in the back, but migrate forward as they continue. (False labor pains, which cannot always be distinguished from genuine ones, have sent many a woman on a futile trip to the hospital.) Another first sign may be a "showing," the appearance from the vagina of a small clot of mucus brightly spotted with blood—this is a plug that had formed in the cervix and now is released as the cervix begins to relax and dilate. Yet another sign may be a gush of clear fluid from the vagina; this follows what is called the "bursting of the bag of waters," the rupturing of the amniotic sac that has enclosed the fetus, releasing the amniotic fluid.

Obstetricians recognize **three stages of labor**. The first and longest part is the period when the cervix is being dilated to permit passage of the baby's head. (The pelvic girdle has already enlarged during pregnancy, facilitating birth.) The mother is usually encouraged to remain active during the first stage, since there is nothing she can do to help the process, which at first involves only the involuntary musculature, and since activity may reduce her discomfort. The first stage lasts an average of fourteen hours for first babies, but with great individual variation, and considerably less for subsequent deliveries, as policemen and taxi drivers well know.

The second stage of labor includes the baby's passage through the vagina and his delivery into the outside world. This stage may last from under twenty minutes to an hour and a half. The mother can actively speed the birth process during the second stage by "bearing down," tightening her (voluntary) abdominal muscles in concert with the uterine contractions. This participation by the mother seems also to help reduce pain. The baby's head turns so that the back of his skull appears first. The vaginal and surrounding tissues have softened during pregnancy and can be stretched considerably; if it appears that the tissues are in danger of tearing, the doctor makes a small lateral nick (episiotomy) to enlarge the opening. Such a cut heals neatly, as a tear might not. Once the occiput has been forced out, the rest of the baby's head comes quickly free, face down and draining. The doctor (or midwife) supports the head with one hand and draws gently on the baby. The rest of him, with the shoulders oriented vertically, in line with the long axis of the vulva, slips out rapidly and easily. The doctor holds the baby aloft by the ankles and, if breathing has not begun spontaneously, slaps him on the buttocks to get him started. As soon as the blood vessels of the umbilical cord stop pulsating, the cord is clamped and cut. Drops are put into the baby's eyes to prevent gonococcal infection—penicillin is widely used, but the new penicillin-resistant strains of gonorrhea may require a change. An identifying band is fastened around the baby's wrist or ankle and, in most hospitals, his footprint is taken on an identification card bearing the mother's thumbprint. These measures, of course, are a precaution against giving mothers the wrong babies. Then, if the baby's muscle tone, color, and breathing indicate that he is functioning normally, he is put aside while the doctor and nurse attend to the mother. This first evaluation of the baby has been systematized in the Apgar Score (Apgar, 1965), the sum of ratings on five three-point scales: breathing effort, muscle tone, heart rate, reflex irritability, and color (from grayish to rosy). The scores are good gross predictors of the baby's chances for healthy survival and a useful means of identifying neonates who need special care. Still more elaborate and finer-grained techniques of neonatal assessment are being tried experimentally by Rosenblith (1961) and Brazelton (1970), based on the work of Graham and her associates (Graham, 1956). Prechtl (1968) is working on physiologically oriented assessment techniques, including prenatal maternal factors.

The third and final stage of labor consists of the delivery of the **afterbirth**, the placenta with its attached amniotic and chorionic membranes and remainder of the cord. The third stage takes less than twenty minutes and is virtually painless. The doctor carefully examines the afterbirth to make sure that all of it has been expelled and that there are no abnormalities. The mother is given hormone injections which hasten shrinkage of the uterus, pressing shut any broken blood vessels, and, if she is planning to nurse her baby, which stimulate milk production. Note that these hormone injections are the human equivalent of behavior found in other mammals—even herbivorous mothers, such as sheep and goats, become carnivorous and eat the hormone-rich placenta. The licking of newborn animals in which their mothers engage, and which is so essential both to the infant's survival and to the formation of a bond between mother and young, is probably stimulated by hormones in the amniotic fluid that coats the infant. To return to the human mother, the doctor or nurse will, if necessary, knead her abdomen to restore tone to the uterine muscles. The mother loses a pint of blood or less in giving birth—about what she would donate to a blood bank. For the next ten to fourteen days, the uterine lining disintegrates and is shed in a process (the **lochia**) resembling menstruation.

We have described the usual birth sequence, in which the baby emerges head-first, in what is called a **vertex presentation**. An occasional baby does not turn head downward in the womb, and is born buttocks first, with somewhat more difficulty, in what is called a **breech presentation**. Some babies, because of the mother's physical condition or because the baby is disproportionately large, or to forestall the consequences of Rh incompatibility, are delivered surgically, by Caesarian section. If the uterine contractions weaken or stop during labor, the baby may have to be delivered by forceps, tongs that fit around the baby's head and enable the doctor to draw him from the mother's body. The use of forceps during the first stage of labor or early in the second is referred to as high-forceps delivery and is a dangerous procedure, since inaccurate placement of the forceps and the greater force needed to pull out the baby may disfigure him or cause brain damage. For a time, high-forceps deliveries were popular because they shortened both the mother's and the doctor's labors, but recognition of the dangers involved has now led most physicians to consider the use of high forceps an emergency procedure. Low forceps, as one might expect, refers to the use of forceps at the stage of actual delivery, and involves less risk, since the forceps can be placed quite accurately. The use of forceps is virtually routine in some hospitals and is almost completely shunned in others.

"Natural" childbirth

Attitudes toward the birth process have varied widely from era to era and from place to place. For many years it was thought proper that women should suffer in giving birth as punishment for Original Sin. The first use of anesthetics in delivery was condemned from the pulpit as flying in the face of the Divine Will. Eventually, as we know, the entire process of birth was turned over to the physician and his instruments, the mother being anesthetized unconscious, partly in an attempt to avoid all pain. More recently mothers and doctors have come to a more balanced view.

If the mother chooses to have no anesthetics during the labor or to take them only sparingly at the final, most painful point of delivery, the process is called "natural" childbirth. The mother may also have had a course of exercises during pregnancy, designed to limber her body, and lessons in how to cooperate in the birth process. There can be distinct satisfactions for the mother in "being there" when her baby is born and in participating in the act of birth. We suspect, too, that minimal use of anesthetics reduces the chance of birth complications for the baby. There is a good deal of evidence that most anesthetics adversely affect the baby's activity, alertness, and general functioning for hours and days after birth (Stechler, 1964; Bowes et al., 1970). How natural a childbirth a mother has must be decided in terms of her individual temperament. And if natural childbirth is to include the father's presence in the delivery room, his temperament must be considered, too.

The advantages of natural childbirth have sometimes been obscured by its more fanatical advocates, who proclaim dogmatically that childbirth is inherently painless and is made painful only through fears instilled by a cultural mythology. It seems safer to say that taking part in the act of birth reduces the mother's pain, to point out that the pain of childbirth limits itself by numbing the mother's tissues, and that memory of the pain of childbirth evaporates quickly. As we shall emphasize repeatedly, sound development can take place only in a social milieu, and it makes no sense to speak of "natural" as opposed to "artificial" human practices, on the analogy of the animal "in the wild." The Noble Savage is an imaginary creature; people all over the world, even in the most "primitive" preliterate societies, are as various and "artificial" in their childbirth practices as in the conduct of all the other affairs of life. And those who would wholly emulate the happy primitive should first consider the figures on health, longevity, and infant and maternal mortality in technical and non-technical civilizations. We must remember, of course, that the folklore of childbirth, including the notion that the bed of pain is punishment for Original Sin, is still rampant and may produce exaggerated and groundless fears in many women. These fears may be further reinforced by the surgical atmosphere of hospitals.

A. Gregory Bateson and Margaret Mead, *First Days in the Life of a New Guinea Baby*/N.Y.U. Film

The management of childbirth. A. A twenty-minute-old Iatmul, New Guinea, baby. The mother is on the right with an older sibling. The woman on the left is the wet nurse who will suckle the baby until his mother's milk appears. It will take several days for the baby's skin pigment to develop. He will soon be coated with mud to protect him against insects. B. A standard United States hospital nursery. This one is in Honolulu, which explains the racial pattern. C. Rooming-in.

Childbirth in the hospital

Our description of the birth process assumes that the baby is born in a hospital, as is nowadays true of almost all American infants. The trend to having babies in the hospital with a physician in attendance has contributed, along with improved community and individual hygiene and better diets, to a sharp drop in infant and maternal death rates over the past half century. For instance, in 1900, 162.4 of every 1,000 American babies under a year old died. This figure had dropped to 99.9 per 1,000 in 1915 and to 23.3 per 1,000 in 1966. But note that while the infant mortality rate among white babies dropped from 98.6 per 1,000 live births in 1915 to 20.6 in 1966, the rate for nonwhite babies

B. Farrell Grehan, Photo Researchers   C. Suzanne Szasz

dropped only from 181.2 to 38.8 in the same period, reflecting the systematic exclusion of Negroes, Indians, and other nonwhites from the material benefits of citizenship. We may take what consolation we can from the contrast in South Africa: 25.9 for whites, 127.6 for nonwhites. In the period 1915–1935, the maternal mortality rate per 10,000 live births fluctuated between 58.2 and 79.9; in 1966 it was 2.9. (But nonwhite maternal deaths are three and a half times as frequent as white.) The United States 1966 infant mortality rate of 23.7 per 1,000 live births (not counting neonatal deaths) may be compared to rates of 12.6 in Sweden, 14.7 in the Netherlands, 13.7 in Iceland, and 15.7 in Finland (U.S. Department of Commerce, 1968).

However, the services of a doctor and the facilities of a hospital are essential only in those unusual instances when something goes wrong. That a normal birth does not require any particular setting or assistance is shown by the many successful births that occur in taxicabs, with driver, policeman, or fireman acting as midwife, or even at home when the mother is alone. As other countries become more American-

ized, there is a movement toward hospital births. But in the British Isles and on the Continent, the professional nurse-midwife still officiates at a large proportion of births, calling in the physician or arranging hospitalization in the event of complications. In this country, physicians have come to prefer their familiar, dependable, centralized resources provided by a hospital, and mothers the sense of specialized techniques always in reserve.

As is so often the case, the very real advantages of a hospital setting are bought at the cost of certain psychological disadvantages. First and foremost, hospital personnel are oriented to the treatment of serious pathology and sometimes forget that mothers and their babies are normal, healthy people. In their well-founded zeal for medical sterility, hospitals have brought about a certain emotional sterility as well. Fathers and other children are regarded as hotbeds of contagion and are rigorously kept away from the baby until he has left the hospital. The mother cannot be wholly excluded, but she too is suspect and is kept apart from the baby as much as possible, all the babies being to-

The birth process

49

A premature baby being handled inside his Isolette.

Elizabeth Wilcox

gether in a nursery except at feeding times. A few years ago, just as many hospitals became aware of the psychological need for relaxing their hygienic regulations, antibiotic-resistant strains of staphylococcus became a serious—for neonates, deadly—menace, and new and still more stringent sanitary measures had to be instituted. The hierarchical organization of the hospital, with authority concentrated in the physician and transmitted through nurses and attendants, favors the establishment of rigid procedures and routines which may be at odds with the psychological needs of individual mothers and their babies and may further intimidate patients already awed by an atmosphere of medical omniscience and omnipotence. Since doctors and nurses are in short supply, they cannot easily vary their procedures and may be forced into time-saving routines. The obstetrician may be tempted to dose the mother heavily with anesthetics or to use medications and forceps to hasten delivery. The mother may be discouraged, overtly or more subtly, from breast-feeding her baby, since successful breast-feeding requires that the baby be brought to the mother for all his feedings around the clock and that a first-time mother be instructed in the techniques of breast-feeding. Cumulatively, the ways of hospitals may convey to parents an uneasy feeling that their baby belongs not to them but to the hospital. Let us note, however, that the hospital nowadays has less time—usually three or four or five days—to work its effect than in the era of the two-week hospital stay when mothers were kept immobilized for a ten-day lying-in period and then allowed to sit on the edge of the bed and "dangle" briefly. In Hawaii, it is customary for the mother to leave the hospital on the day after birth, reflecting the native tradition.

ROOMING-IN.   One arrangement that combines the benefits of hospital delivery with a close mother-child relationship is found in programs of **rooming-in**. Here the baby lives in his mother's hospital room, and she begins early to take care of him. The father, subject to reasonable sanitary precautions, can visit mother and child. As it turns out, mothers, fathers, and babies thrive under rooming-in. For one thing, a generally healthy mother need no longer be kept in enforced idleness, wondering if the baby she hears crying in the nursery is hers. The mother gets some practice in caring for her baby before she suddenly has to take him home and be wholly responsible for him with no expert to turn to. Mother and child can get an early start on the business of coming to know each other and to adapt to each other's rhythms. Most important, the parents can feel that the baby is really theirs.

Interestingly enough, rooming-in simplifies hospital administration and cuts costs. When we stop to think about it, keeping babies in a centrally located nursery is efficient only if they receive all their care there, assembly-line fashion. If babies have to be distributed to their mothers for feeding and then collected again after meals, the coming and going is highly inefficient, especially if some of the babies happen not to be hungry on the hospital's schedule and in the not too rare event that the wrong baby gets deposited with the wrong mother, with consequent fireworks (since the babies are all clearly labeled, mismatchings are quickly set straight but can nevertheless occasion some emotionality). Another welcome by-product is that the chances of nursery epidemics are reduced when neonates are kept apart from each other in their mothers' rooms.

Like natural childbirth, rooming-in does not have to be an all-or-none matter. Just as maternal and paternal (and the obstetrician's) temperament have to govern just how "natural" a childbirth will be, so can degrees of rooming-in be provided to suit varying individual tastes. Mothers with other children may look upon the lying-in period as a rare opportunity for luxurious living uncluttered by workaday responsibilities. Similarly, the lying-in period has been shortened, in keeping with the principle of "early ambulation" followed in modern surgery, but many such mothers would like to indulge themselves with a few extra days of bed rest and, quite legitimately, resist being hurried onto their feet and out of the hospital.

The birth process

51

2

the infant: one

Development during infancy—from the age of a few weeks until the baby is walking securely and beginning to talk—is a dramatic thing to watch. Striking and radical changes take place within this relatively brief period. During these first fifteen months or so outside the womb, the baby changes from a helpless—if sometimes noisy—neonate unable to change position, to a high-powered, willful pedestrian investigating and exploiting everything within reach in the most active way possible, tasting, chewing, fondling, probing, tugging, pushing, pounding, and tearing. As a child's activity increases, his sleeping time decreases. Some newborn babies spend all their time sleeping except at mealtimes or when in distress; by the end of infancy, the child may sleep as little as ten hours at night, with one or two naps during the day—there are great individual differences (as we shall keep emphasizing) in this respect as in all the others. In the first year, the baby adds almost 8 inches (20+ cm.) to his length and gains about 15 pounds (7 kg.), trebling his birth weight. He acquires a dozen temporary teeth and a full head of hair. Early in infancy his face loses its neonatal look and becomes the smooth chubby face of a baby.

Socially, the infant progresses from blank, unblinking staring at faces to smiling at people, to demanding company, to laughing, to active participation in social games. After midyear, he will know that some people are strangers and may hide his face or shriek with dismay when they come near. The term "infancy" comes from the Latin *infans*, which means "not speaking" —and no matter how much he vocalizes, or how much his vocalizations change during this period, his babblings stop short of true speech. By the time he is a year old, how-

ever, he can understand a great many words and phrases, listens attentively to those he does not understand, and may (there are great individual differences) use a few words of his own. The limited emotional repertory with which he began life differentiates into half a dozen recognizable kinds of feeling states: pain-distress, aversion, anger, fear, affection, elation, and perhaps others.

From being a neonate whose existence is dominated by his own volatile inner processes with only a rudimentary awareness of the world around him, the baby moves on in infancy to a quite elaborate knowledge of his surroundings, of people and objects and their attributes, of space and spatial relations, of causal sequences, of his own body and its workings, and of countless possibilities for action. But the world becomes a place in which to learn and live and act only by virtue of the emotional attachments and meanings that are formed in this crucial period for the development of basic attitudes of optimism or pessimism, of trust or mistrust.

In this chapter, we shall begin the detailed description of infancy with an account of developmental landmarks, the conspicuous transformations of behavior (along with what they tell us about the baby's perceiving, feeling, and thinking) that appear in a fairly stable sequence in the first year or so. We could arrange these landmarks under such headings as posture and locomotion, emotions and their differentiation, social relations, perception and cognition, tastes and preferences, and learning. To do so, however, would give us a logical but artificial set of parallel strands. Instead, we prefer to examine the baby's total development chronologically, describing diverse sorts of behavior that first occur at about the same time. This is in hopes of conveying some sense of the baby's integrated functioning. Even so, we shall not be describing the whole baby, but only certain abstractions from the totality. We hope that these will be relevant and meaningful abstractions that reflect the organization of behavior and development in real babies, but meanwhile it must be the reader's task to keep in mind the baby as a flesh-and-blood creature living at home with his doting but no doubt harried parents and, in various families, brothers and sisters and uncles and aunts and grandparents.

Landmarks in the Infant's Behavioral Development

A word of warning is in order. The ages we give for the appearance of items of behavior are approximate. The so-called developmental scales (the major ones are the Bayley [1969], Cattell [1940], Gesell [1925], and Griffiths [1954]) from which many of the items are drawn have some serious defects as guidelines to the normal course of infant development. They take little account of the wide but perfectly normal range of ages at which a given kind of behavior may emerge. They assume that behavioral development during infancy is for the most part **autogenous**, that is, a product simply of growth and maturation, whereas we have come to know a great deal about the effects of social and cultural influences on development, even in early infancy and even on growth and mat-

uration. In fact, it seems that infancy itself has changed in the last twenty-five years, so that today's babies—at least the measured and observed ones in American research centers—are decidedly different creatures from yesterday's and develop much faster. This apparent acceleration plays a part in the controversy surrounding reports of precocious development in some African babies (see p. 100).

The changes that we think we have seen can be related in part to improved medical care, sanitation, and diet, so that babies are healthier and stronger than they used to be. Equally important, parental attitudes and practices have changed, thanks in large measure (in the United States) to Dr. Benjamin Spock, whose widely read book on child care has been a powerful influence in the last twenty years, so that parents are better able to relax and enjoy babies. There is greater faith in the competence of babies, and they are given increased freedom to explore and manipulate. Affluence, of course, plays a part in all this, and babies are given more playthings and exposed to ever-greater varieties of stimulation.

In general, infants seem to be more advanced in their functioning than in times past, and though the authors are not always happy about the fosterings of precocity that can be observed, it seems to be true that the older scales of baby development underestimate the abilities of infants brought up under favorable conditions. Another difficulty with baby scales is that they tend to overstress the easily measurable physical side of development, with minimal attention to cognition, which makes their occasional use as infant intelligence tests doubly illogical. The use of such tests may reveal gross impairments, and they have considerable utility in comparisons of groups, but they do a poor job of predicting later intelligence in the individual case. Both the scales and the authors are guilty of the error of ethnocentrism, of assuming that development in a broadly Western setting is representative of development everywhere. We know in fact that development follows quite different patterns and proceeds at different rates in other social settings. We shall make mention of some of these differences later, but not enough is known to permit a coherent account of differences around the world, or even in all segments of United States society. Even in the area of physical growth, we are only now beginning to get a worldwide picture (Meredith, 1969a, 1969b). Ironically enough, such data are likely to obsolesce as fast as they can be gathered and published, since physical growth is highly susceptible to changing standards of living. Our description is by necessity mostly of Western development, with no implication intended that this is the one right way to grow up.

Our knowledge of infancy, like our knowledge of the neonatal period, has been revolutionized in the last decade and a half (Stone et al., 1972). Our former ignorance is in some degree inexplicable. Babies have been around for a long time, and some of them have even resided in psychologists' households, but somehow very few people got around to noticing what they were like. In part, it may be that the endless mechanics of dealing with these immature, demanding creatures obscured some of the more interesting aspects of their development. In part, it was the inaccessibility of large numbers of subjects for research. The child goes underground into the bosom of his family from the time he leaves the hospital at a few days of age until he resurfaces several years later in the nursery

school. Even when psychologists took the trouble to seek out babies, they were likely, as we have said, to focus only on the most obvious, easily measured physical aspects of development. Now, with the growing realization that the baby is psychologically active from birth on, there is a new willingness on the part of psychologists to go to where the babies are—their homes, well-baby clinics, and pediatricians' offices. If the day care movement ever takes firm hold, research subjects will be available in unprecedented abundance. There has come to pass also a new and more receptive attitude on the part of pediatricians, public health workers, and psychiatrists; they are more interested in research than before, and in research on normal and healthy babies as well as on sick or disturbed ones. It should be remembered that a pediatrician's practice today is devoted more to preventing illness and educating parents than to treating sick children. Parents, too, deserve credit for the willingness and even enthusiasm with which they cooperate in research.

One to three months

In the first chapter, we described the behavioral capabilities of the neonate as he exists for about a month after birth, and the reader may wish to go back and review the repertory the baby brings with him into the world or develops in the first weeks (pp. 11–26). During his second month, the baby is awake more than he was as a neonate and shows more sustained response to an increasing variety of sights and sounds. By age one month, many babies, when prone, can raise their heads slightly to look at something (some especially mature babies do so at birth) or, held in the feeding position, strain for the nipple, although a number of perfectly healthy babies cannot raise their heads until age two months or later. Notice that raising the head and opening the mouth as the nipple comes into view implies that the baby now recognizes the bottle visually, at a distance, instead of having to wait until the nipple actually touches the region of his mouth. Indeed, there is accumulating evidence that the baby distinguishes between faces from a few weeks of age. At the age of a month, however, when he is in the feeding position, he may react to almost anything held before his eyes—a gray or white cube, a sphere, a cylinder, a cone, or even a loosely bunched cleaning tissue—as though it were a bottle. Here we have an example of the baby's **physiognomic** perceiving, reacting to the global properties of things rather than to specific attributes (which is the starting stage of adult perception in new situations). We expect the range of equivalence to be narrowed until the baby reacts only to a close copy of an actual bottle, with the nipple aimed at his mouth, as he learns to discriminate the essential features of the bottle and to rule out irrelevant ones.

In his second month, the baby's crying will stop at the sight of his mother, or when other people caress him. Many babies, before they are two months old, stop crying at the approaching footsteps of the mother. By about age six or eight weeks, most babies respond with a smile to a moving human face seen in front view—or, for that matter (given physiognomic perception), to a crude approximation of a face (Spitz, 1946; Ambrose, 1961). Emde and Harmon (1972) find faint signs of social smiling as early as age two weeks. By six weeks, the baby shows some ability to shut out distressing or overstimulating people

by averting his gaze. By this age, the baby sheds tears when he cries; his earlier crying was real and vociferous but usually tearless. He now, in addition to his crying and the sounds that go with digestion, produces vocalizations described by Gesell (Gesell et al., 1938) as "small throaty sounds." He still cannot really change position (at least in our bassinet- and crib-bound culture), but he may arch his back and flail from side to side when in distress. He sometimes kicks his legs in the air, but he ordinarily keeps them flexed, knees wide apart, as though squatting. He eats at frequent intervals and still takes two or more night feedings. If he is howling with hunger, he now calms down as soon as he is held in the nursing position, even before the bottle comes into view. He can track a moving person or a trinket through an arc of 100 degrees or more (some babies swivel their heads around to look over their shoulders), but if he loses sight of a moving object he does not search for it. At age two months, supine babies begin to blink when something approaches their eyes at a fast clip (White, 1963). The "looming response" (p. 17) appears in younger babies only when they are propped sitting.

At about age two months, when an adult leans over and talks to him—it matters little what is said, and gibberish works as well as speech—the baby writhes about and works his mouth as though struggling to answer back. Some babies actually squeeze out a few strangled sounds. Later, this kind of response gets elaborated into babbled conversations between adult and child.

Early in the third month, the baby begins to reach out and bat at dangling objects, but he does not yet open his fingers to try to grasp things. This first reaching out to things may signal the start of the

Landmarks in the infant's behavioral development

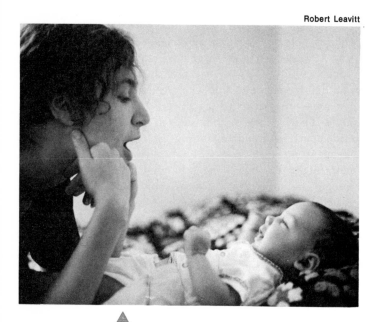

A "conversation" with a two-month-old.

gradual transition from an inert, passive orientation to an active, manipulative, exploratory one. Interestingly enough, reaching toward objects is one form of behavior very much subject to environmental, experiential influences. Burton White and his associates (White and Held, 1966) have shown that babies living in the barren, unstimulating conditions provided by some institutions do not reach out to grasp until almost five months. But when such babies were given even small amounts of extra stimulation in the form of interesting stabiles (like a mobile in structure but stationary) to look at, or a few minutes a day of additional adult handling, play, cuddling, and talking, they too reached out to grasp at just past age three months, a phenomenal advance. Accommodation of the lens of the eye is essentially complete by age three months, and the eyes converge on an object as it approaches the baby's nose.

The baby becomes more social, even to the point of enjoying mild roughhousing. Vocalizations change to gurgles and coos, which the baby utters both spontaneously and in response to people. By this age, the baby smiles in delight when the adult pretends to be angry, whereas genuine anger provokes shrieks of dismay. Some babies, in the vicinity of age three months, begin to croon or hum to music. Those babies who have suffered colic in early life are likely to be free of it by age three months, to the benefit of their and their parents' dispositions.

Three to six months

In many ways, age three months is a transition point. The change in the baby is often summarized by saying that he is "becoming human." It is hard to define the subtle ways in which "becoming human" expresses itself, but the baby has lost his neonatal look and is physically a highly individualized infant. He seems to be newly alert and responsive and gives the impression of having a beginning inner life. There even seems to be a shift in brain-wave patterns at this age. In part, the baby's new status may have to do with his differential reaction to familiar and unfamiliar people. He greets members of his household with smiles and wriggles and gurgles, whereas strangers may be met with a solemn, reserved, watchful stare. By now, he is building up stable expectations of rhythms and people. Whatever the manifestations, parents seem to have no difficulty recognizing the change when it occurs (Church, 1968, pp. 13, 180–181). As noted above, babies given the right kinds of stimulation reach out at this age and grasp things they see. Visually guided grasping seems to symbolize the beginnings of a more general shift from an inert, passive orientation to the world to a more active one.

By age three months—and sometimes earlier—many babies "sleep through" the night, from an evening feeding to five or six or seven in the morning. The age at which a baby sleeps through seems to be a matter both of the baby's physical maturity and also of parental experience, since, according to a study by Moore and Ucko (1957), second and subsequent babies sleep through at younger ages than firstborn ones. The baby's readiness to sleep through is usually shown by his taking sizable amounts at daytime feedings, by the diminishing fervor of his crying when he wakes up during the night, and by his relative indifference to the bottle when he is given a nighttime feeding. Some babies wake up during the night not so much because they are hungry as because they are ready for a period of play and sociability; such episodes are usually transitory. The baby's ability to sleep through is related to a general stabilization of physiological rhythms that goes on during infancy.

Roughly coincidental with his beginning to sleep through the night, the baby's evening bedtime behavior may show an interesting change. Previously, when sleepy and put to bed, he was likely to fuss or whimper briefly and then drift off to sleep. Now, as though recognizing that bedtime means the end of companionship and activity, many babies begin to react with cries of woe and anger. This bedtime screaming may be the first use of the voice in something resembling voluntary communication. For the baby who acts this way does not merely scream and go on screaming. Instead, he yells briefly and then stops, as though listening for a reaction. Indeed, in our experience, if a parent starts toward the baby's sleeping place, the baby will stay quiet as long as the parent keeps moving in the right direction. If the parent, heartened by silence and hopeful that the baby has gone to sleep, stops to listen, there will be a series of howls, punctuated by silences, each howl more forceful and prolonged than the one before, apparently as a way of insisting that the parent keep coming.

The baby's resistance to going to sleep means several days of torment for parents, humanely responsive to the baby's distress and the possibility that he may suffer some lasting harm without their intervention, but frazzled and fatigued by the demands of child care—piled on top of everything else—and desperate for repose. However, even the most indulgent of parents will find that they have to draw a line between social times and sleeping times, and the baby may simply have to be allowed to scream himself to sleep. According to Spock (1957)—and experience supports him —once the parents steel themselves not to respond to the baby's bedtime crying, the baby will cry for some twenty minutes (which feels like an eternity to the anxious parents) the first night, less the next two or three nights, and thereafter not at all. To the surprise and relief of guilt-ridden parents, the baby awakes the next morning refreshed and with no trace of rancor or resentment. We might mention that the process may be eased by leaving a soft light on in the baby's room, or even by allowing the baby to fall asleep in a bassinet or cradle right in the midst of family activity.

We stress this matter of bedtime and sleeping through because it reveals a new level of awareness on the baby's part, because it marks the time when parents can have some time to themselves and can themselves sleep through, thus enjoying parenthood and each other more, and also because it exemplifies a very important general phenomenon, the establishment of semiautonomous internal "**biological clocks.**" That is, the baby's cyclic daily (**circadian**) rhythms of activity and repose, of hunger, ingestion, and elimination, and of accompanying physiological changes such as regular fluctuations in body temperature seem to be set initially by recurring events in the environment, particularly by the family's schedules and routines. Sander (1969) finds that a change of primary caretakers when the baby is as young as ten days old causes considerable distress. Sander implicates the difference of rhythms between caretakers as a major source of stress. Over a period of several months, these rhythms become self-sustaining (although obviously not immutable) and relatively insensitive to random departures from the usual round.

At the risk of digression, we might point out that biological clocks are common to virtually all species, including man, bees, oysters, and flowering peas (Brown, 1959). Furthermore, the environmental programing of cycles seems to be produced not only by such obvious regularities as feeding schedules and the alternation of daylight and darkness, but also by such unlikely-seeming forces as the gravitational pull of the moon. For instance, oysters along the east coast open and close with the rise and fall of the tides. When moved to the Middle West and kept in a pan of shallow water, oysters for a time continue to open and close in concert with the tidal ebb and flow of their home waters. Gradually, however, they shift to the nonexistent tidal pattern of their new location, indicating that their cycles are not a response to the tides as such but directly to the geodetic forces that produce tides. It seems to follow that some of what we have been inclined to dismiss as superstition, such as the farmer's wanting to plant his crops by the dark of the moon, or the supposed relation between phases of the moon and women's menstrual cycles, may turn out to have some basis in fact.

Our society's great concern with time and schedules is often absurd to behold. Nevertheless, there seem to be some advantages to the stabilization of the baby's physiological rhythms, for the parent because it simplifies child care and for the baby because it appears to liberate him for play, exploration, and learning and to provide a foundation for his eventual mastery of time.

By age three or four months the baby

may enjoy the playful fright that comes when a parent says "Boo!" and then smiles and tickles him. It may give him hiccoughs, but as often as not he enjoys these, too. It is toward four months that many babies laugh (rather than merely smile or gurgle) for the first time, in the form of a hearty chuckle, perhaps in response to having the belly nuzzled or nudged by an adult. By this time, if not earlier, the baby takes active pleasure in his bath. From about three months on, when the baby is awake and on his back, he no longer keeps his head turned to the favored side but holds it in the midline, his gaze aimed straight up, although he turns head and eyes freely to see where a voice is coming from. As we said in Chapter 1, some neonates may search for the source of a sound, but the general rule seems to be that the baby will turn his head and eyes toward a familiar voice at two or three months, and to other sounds at four or five months—he hears the sounds at earlier ages, as indicated by his change of state, but he doesn't necessarily turn to the source.

The four-month-old baby can be propped in a sitting position for short periods, and can half-recline indefinitely in the baby carriers that have come into widespread use in the United States. He may begin to eat solid foods—more accurately, strained, mushy solids. At first, eating entails a fair amount of spluttering, choking, coughing, and spitting—and even gagging and vomiting—but it is usually easy to tell, each time that one tries, whether the baby is agreeably disposed toward food in this new form. (In a number of cultures this does not seem to matter and masses of mush are relentlessly crammed into the infant's mouth.) An incidental observation is that adults, spooning solids into young babies, cannot resist making empathic

Eating "solid" food. Note how the baby's eyes focus on the adult hand, and the way he opens his mouth in anticipation of the spoon.

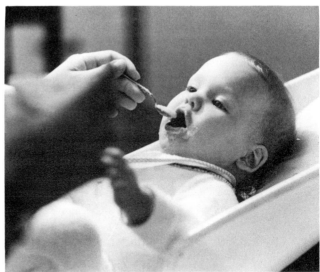

Suzanne Szasz

61

feeding movements with their own mouths, as though magically but unconsciously inducing the baby to do the same.

As we have said, the baby growing up in a normally stimulating situation reaches out to take hold of things given visually by the time he is three or four months old. If the thing to be grasped is in the midline, the baby is likely to use both hands (Bruner, 1968). The baby spreads his fingers to grasp, but his thumb is not yet opposed to his fingers (a few babies show thumb opposition almost from the beginning), and his hand bends backward at the wrist in a strained, spastic manner that parents may find alarming. When picking up things from the floor or a table top, the baby does best by corralling them with his forearm and sweeping them against his body. Although the baby can pick something up in his hand, he cannot yet intentionally let go. Either the thing he is holding gets knocked out of his hand when he moves it, or drops unnoticed from his relaxing fingers as his attention strays to something new. If he really wants to get rid of something he is holding, he rubs it against his body until it is worked loose from his grip. A development of this period, seemingly associated both with the baby's newfound skill in grasping and with his growing self-awareness, is his ability to reach up and remove a cleaning tissue spread over his face. At three months, the baby waves his arms ineffectually in the vicinity of his head, which he wags from side to side; by four months he can wipe the tissue away with his hand or arm, and before five months he simply reaches up, grasps it, and pulls it away—although there may be a delay of several seconds during which the baby seems to be considering the proper course of action. By age five

months, quite a few babies will remove the tissue and then put it back again as though playing peek-a-boo.

By age four months, if one holds the baby during preparations for a meal, he will wait, another clear sign that he anticipates things to come. It is a tense kind of waiting, marked by escaping bleats and whimpers and by straining toward the warming bottle or the room where he is customarily fed. Sometime in this period, instead of howling the moment he wakes up in the morning, the baby begins to lie in his crib softly crooning and crowing and babbling awhile before yelling to be picked up. Parents often become aware of this change almost as of something wrong. Instead of being dragged awake by the baby's screams, they come to of their own accord into a somewhat uncanny stillness hardly broken by the unprecedented sounds of good cheer from the infant.

As the baby approaches age five months, he can go four or five hours between feedings (longer, of course, during the night) and consumes generous amounts of milk and solids at each meal. He settles down to a pattern of two or three well-defined naps during the day, quite different from his earlier drifting in and out of sleep. He studies and plays with his fingers, one hand carrying the other to his eyes for visual inspection and to his mouth for tasting. Whatever he picks up goes to his mouth for sampling—and this will probably continue to be true for another year or more. If he cannot pick something up, he may pull his mouth to it. He still has to be braced in a sitting position, but he can stay this way for ever-longer periods before his head begins to loll and his body to slump. Notice how his horizons broaden as he shifts from recumbent to upright.

The provisions made for babies in different households or different cultures may make a vast difference in perceptual scope. Prone, the four- to five-month-old baby can push his chest and shoulders clear and hold his head erect, as in the classic family album photograph of the nude baby on the fur rug. During his waking periods, the baby can stay contentedly alone at least long enough to let his mother finish a few household tasks uninterrupted. It helps to keep him content to give him something to look at, such as a mobile, or to finger, such as a suspended doll or rattle, or to listen to, such as music or a family conversation. The five-month-old baby given patches of different colors to look at begins to show clear preferences, with "warm" colors (red, orange, yellow) being looked at more than "cool" ones (green, blue, violet), and intense and fully saturated colors being preferred to weak and dull hues (Spears, 1964; Staples, 1932; Valentine, 1913–1914). By this time, the baby's ankles have begun to straighten so that the soles of his feet no longer stare each other in the face.

Between five and six months of age, the baby becomes able not only to grasp but also to hold on to, manipulate, and let go of rings and rattles and rags. He uses both hands in a coordinated way to handle things, to stretch out a piece of cloth while he inspects its intricacies, and he can transfer things from one hand to the other. It seems to be the case that the baby turns any new object around so as to examine the far side, indicating, as does the baby's reaching out to grasp things, that objects never exist for him as flat projections but instead are perceived as continuing on around out of view, like proper solid things (Piaget, 1932). This applies equally to really two-dimensional patterns, like de-

L. Joseph Stone

Self-discovery. A five-month-old examines her fingers.

The baby can push his chest and shoulders clear and hold his head erect, as in the classic family album photograph.

Suzanne Szasz

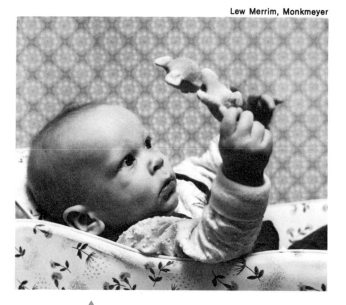

The exploration of objects. Note how the fingers of the left hand seem to be tracing the toy's contours while the right hand holds it fast.

signs on his playpen pad, which the baby tries to pick up. At a somewhat older age, having failed to pick up a design or picture, the baby may lower his eyes to the surface as though to peer at the hidden side. This phenomenon of **implicit perception**, of being aware of the presence of things or parts of things that are not directly perceived, is an important part of adult perception, but we shall talk later about differences in what is perceptually given for the baby as compared with the adult. There seem to be two different reasons that the baby may examine an object from several angles. The first, and more primitive, seems to be that the baby is looking for the best orientation to get the object into his mouth. The second, more sophisticated one, seems to be curiosity about what the far side is like, about what surprises may lie around the bend. Now, when the baby puts things into his mouth, it may be with a view to chewing on them rather than simple mouthing or tasting or sucking; his baby teeth are beginning to push through the gums, and chewing relieves the discomfort. This is the time when many breast-fed babies are weaned to bottle or cup, sometimes to protect the mother against the baby's new urge to bite.

Middle infancy

At this point, we shift our time frame to take account of the increasing diversity in rates of development after the first few months. "Middle infancy" is a period when the child can sit up comfortably but not yet creep. It is around the age of six months that the baby is likely to discover his feet (for some babies, this discovery comes as early as age four months). He does not at first experience them as part of himself, but as strange objects which occasionally swim into view above the horizon of his belly (most six-month-olds are pretty chubby) and which his hands clutch at and capture and bring to his eyes for viewing and, within a month or so, to his mouth for tasting and chewing. To get ahead of our story for a moment, the baby's pained surprise when he bites down on his foot, as though he hadn't expected it to hurt (or at least to hurt *him*), is one among many indications that knowledge of his own body is not given to the baby at birth, simply by virtue of its being an operating biological entity, but that the body, its extent and its capacities for feeling and action, is learned through a series of discoveries during a long apprenticeship. The baby's knowledge of his body can be at several levels, however, since he can make use of different parts of his body before he explicitly discovers them. Thus, he could not grasp and handle his kicking feet if his feet did not cooperate at least to the extent of stopping kicking. Somewhat later, his feet raise themselves to be caught. At a still-later age, but before they assume their main function of walking, the feet act as prehensile tools, assistant hands that fetch things out of reach of the hands or that support an object while the hands play with it.

At six months, the baby may be able to roll completely over (most babies can turn from back to belly before they can turn from belly to back), although there are wide individual variations in the age at which rolling over becomes possible. The stepping reflex—set off by supporting the baby upright with his feet lightly touching a firm surface—returns about now, having disappeared shortly after birth. Indeed,

Self-discovery. A six-month-old plays with her feet.

Vivienne

65

Rolling over from back to belly.

many babies of this age—or even younger—can lock their knees and stand on an adult lap with the adult's encircling arm for support. Most babies in our three-meals-a-day society settle down at about this time to a schedule of three meals a day plus occasional juice, snacks, and, if there is an interval between supper and bedtime, a bottle just before going to sleep. The bedtime bottle staves off hunger pangs as a threat to sleep and, just as important, provides a final period of social contact, cuddling, and soothing before the end of the day's activities.

Somewhere between five and eight months of age, and characteristically at six months, about half of all babies show a decided fear of strangers, or **stranger anxiety** (Schaffer and Emerson, 1964). We have already mentioned the reserve that the three-month-old shows toward strangers—what Bronson (1971) calls "wariness";

now he is likely to scream, clutch at the parent, and strain to put as much distance as possible between himself and the stranger. Stranger anxiety is important in practical terms, since it affects leaving the baby with new caretakers while the mother goes outside the home, and because many a visiting grandparent or aunt or uncle has suffered wounded feelings at the hands of a rejecting baby who has been rushed through the process of getting acquainted or reacquainted. The wise stranger keeps his distance, knowing that the baby's reaction to a novel stimulus has components of both fear and curiosity. With a bit of patience on the visitor's part, the baby's curiosity dominates his fear, and aversion soon changes to friendliness. Stranger anxiety is also an important consideration for the scientist doing research with infants. One cannot test a baby in a tearful panic. In addition, one must remember that stranger anxiety applies both to people and to strange things and places, and the research setting and test materials may at

Lew Merrim, Monkmeyer

first be just as threatening to the baby as the unfamiliar researcher. Rheingold (1969b) has studied the differential reactions of babies placed alone or with their mothers in an unfamiliar setting. She has also shown (Rheingold and Eckerman, 1969) that the lure of toys can pull the baby away from his mother into a strange room, especially if the baby is given time to warm up to the new situation.

Stranger anxiety is interesting also in terms of developmental principles. It indicates that the baby has acquired during the first six-month period of his life a scheme of the familiar (and ordinarily has formed powerful emotional attachments to it) so that a contrast of the strange becomes possible. The attachments that the baby forms for his family (and house and yard and crib and playthings) have their infrahuman analogies, although the processes are decidedly different. (We shall discuss these analogies in the next chapter under the name of **imprinting**.)

Whether stranger anxiety appears, and

how strongly, seems to depend on how varied the baby's caretakers have been. Those babies who have known only a few adults are likely to display marked stranger anxiety (Schaffer and Emerson, 1964). Those who have been taken care of by many adults, as in the kibbutzim of Israel, tend not to (Spiro, 1958; Caldwell, 1963). Robson et al. (1969) report that girls show stranger anxiety at an earlier age than boys. Collard (1968) has shown that kittens reared by a single human experimenter develop stranger anxiety, whereas those with a variety of caretakers do not. No one, to our knowledge, has seriously investigated whether children raised from early infancy by a nursemaid form a primary bond to the nurse rather than to the parents, but casual observations lead us to suspect that this may sometimes be the case. There is a further question whether stranger anxiety is good or bad. It is our hunch that it is good insofar as it reflects a strong emotional attachment which should facilitate cultural learning and may foretell a later

Landmarks in the infant's behavioral development

67

generalized capacity for strong affection. It seems to be good, too, in that it shows clear perceptual discrimination among people. On the negative side, stranger anxiety may mean excessively limited social contact or it may represent an attachment so strong as to interfere with the normal weanings from infantile ways. In general, development entails relinquishing old attachments and forming new ones—at later stages, of different kinds, such as friendship, erotic love, parental love, commitment to a field of endeavor, loyalties to institutions and principles, feelings for art objects and keepsakes. The sometimes painful fact of relinquishment is celebrated in Philip Roth's novel *Letting Go* (1962).

Furthermore, if we take it as a normal part of development that the child will grow away from identification with his family toward identification with humanity at large, too thorough an identification with the family can obstruct independence of thinking and the assumption of new and different systems of values. Here we are talking about the phenomenon of **ethnocentrism**, an unquestioning acceptance of one's own culture's outlook on and evaluation of things, so pervasive that it seems inconceivable (or deranged or depraved) that anyone could possibly think differently. One common outcome of ethnocentrism is that people of alien cultural backgrounds (including people from other regions or strata of our own society) may strike us as so peculiar as to seem subhuman. Such prejudice appears not only as hostility or fear of the kind found between Negroes and whites in the United States, and across comparable divisions of population in all too many other parts of the world, but also in a patronizing attitude which sees representatives of "exotic" cultures as "quaint." Fortunately, as we shall see later, in complex societies there are some inherent mechanisms that help to some degree to counteract ethnocentrism.

Although the strange is often threatening, novelty can also be an attractive quality as a departure from the humdrum habitual. On the negative side, novelty produces fear reactions, as in stranger anxiety or even when the baby sees his father partly disguised with shaving-cream lather. At the infrahuman level, we have Helen Bruce's finding (1960) that exposing freshly impregnated female mice to strange males tends to block pregnancy. However, a further analysis by Eleftheriou et al. (1962) indicates that a great variety of unfamiliar stimuli will produce the same effect, which implies that it is novelty as such that is the disruptive stimulus. On the other hand, we know that novelty can often produce fascination or amusement. Indeed, in contrast to the findings just reported, Ehrman (1966) discovered that strange male fruit flies mate more successfully than those belonging to the same strain as the females. We have already seen how the newborn baby habituates to a repeated stimulus but realerts as soon as even a minor change is introduced.

Researchers like Morgan and Ricciuti (1969) and Ainsworth et al. (in press) have done much to advance our understanding of stranger anxiety. However, there has been little attempt to distinguish degrees of strangeness. We propose four levels: the intimate, the familiar, the unfamiliar, and the totally strange, like a member of a race never before encountered. Melson and McCall (1970) found a complex relationship in habituation to novel visual and auditory stimulation, but there is some reason to think that it is the brighter babies who habituate most quickly. Kagan, Lewis, and McCall's **discrepancy hypothesis** (Kagan, 1970; Lewis, 1967; McCall and Kagan, 1967), which is closely related to Hebb and Riesen's (1943) observations on distortions of the familiar, may help explain why babies react favorably or unfavorably to a novel stimulus. The discrepancy hypothesis says that a small change from what is familiar is attractive, while a larger change is aversive. Unfortunately, it is not possible to specify precisely what constitutes a small or large discrepancy, particularly in the matter of qualitative differences, as between one person's face and another's. Rheingold and Eckerman (1969) draw a distinction between the novel, which is attractive, and the strange, which is disturbing. Again, however, we have no way to predict what will be which.

To return to our discussion of milestones, it is in the six- to nine-month age period that some babies begin to hold out their arms in anticipation of being picked up, although others do not do so until a year of age, and a few perfectly normal babies never do at all. However, near-total avoidance of human contact may indicate disturbance. By age six months, the baby is highly responsive to his parents' moods and emotions and may even, according to M. M. Lewis (1959), show distress to words conveying displeasure but spoken matter-of-factly. The baby enjoys hiding his face with a corner of a blanket, peering out from time to time as though to see if anything has changed. His vocalizations are becoming more mature and differentiated, with consonants emerging between the vowel sounds; cooing sounds give way to gurgles, and gurgling to babbling, where the child tries out a great variety of speech

sounds—apparently the same all over the world. The conversationlike exchanges of nonsense sounds between parent and baby that began at age two or three months are by now a stable pattern of play, a pattern of central importance in the infant's emotional and linguistic development.

The baby's first teeth, ordinarily the two center lowers, are likely to erupt during the seventh month. Teething may be preceded by some discomfort, and usually is marked by a compelling urge to chew on things. Once his teeth have appeared, the baby begins to chew—even milk and baby foods. Salivation increases, and since the baby has not yet learned to keep his mouth closed and swallow his spittle, he is likely to drool copiously from now until age two or later, when his set of "milk teeth" is complete. We have already said that the immunities given by antibodies absorbed prenatally from the mother's blood wear off at about this time, so that teething coincides with—but does not, as old wives' tales would have it, cause—a new vulnerability to illness. Moreover, as the baby gets older he is exposed to more people and places, and so has more opportunity to pick up infections. Sicknesses during infancy and toddlerhood may produce raging fevers, as high as 104° or 105° (41° C), which may be accompanied by convulsions, delirium, or even hallucinations. Alarming as such symptoms are, generally healthy babies with good medical care usually recover rapidly with no discernible ill effects. The breast-fed baby may have received supplementary antibodies from his mother's milk, but weaning from the breast also tends to coincide with teething, when the baby starts biting on the nipple, and breast-fed babies too become vulnerable to sickness.

During his seventh month, the baby will

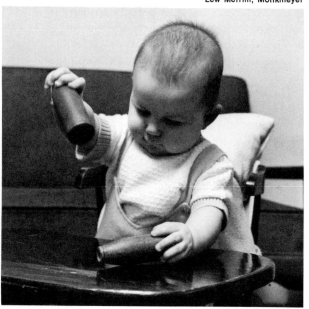

The older infant plays with two things at one time.

probably begin to be able to stay sitting up without support, but he still has to be helped into a sitting position. He also assumes the Buddha-like pose characteristic of infancy, and as he plays with something on the floor in front of him, he may droop forward until he is helplessly nose against floor. He will be content to play in his playpen, provided he is not left there too long and particularly if his mother is within sight or hearing. We should note that the early self-reliance expected of babies in European-style cultures is seen as inhuman in societies where babies and young children are carried—by mothers or older children—almost constantly during the daytime hours. Furthermore, in some societies it is considered animal-like and degrading for the child to play or creep on the ground.

In those cultures that use a feeding table or highchair, the baby amuses himself by banging objects together on the table top or tray. He may even discover the delightful game of dropping things overboard. At some point this becomes an even more delightful social game in which parents play the role of retrievers, but at first, accidental dropping aside, it seems to be a way of exploring spatial relations in which the baby watches or listens for the impact of the dropped object. Later, this ability to release things into space and the knowledge of what becomes of them is assimilated to the all-important social exchange of the game of drop-and-retrieve.

This is an early manifestation of the child's fascination with repetitive playing with new discoveries until they are fully mastered. The adult is likely to find such repetition boring and foolish and perverse, unless he can see the analogy to his own involvement with some new gadget. It is hard for the adult, who takes so much for granted, to realize how new and fresh the world is for the baby, how many things there are to discover and experiment with and assimilate. It may help if the adult can remember discovering the way raindrops trickle down a window pane, fusing and sticking and accumulating and branching, and how the better part of a rainy day during his childhood could go to tracing the movements of the raindrops, or discovering how one can fog a window pane or mirror by breathing on it, and then trace designs in the mist.

Parents who quickly get their fill of the drop-and-fetch game have tried various escapes. It does no good to fasten the plaything to the table with a length of string. In the first place, this spoils the point of the game, which is social interaction which the baby himself can control. Second, the baby cannot yet perceive the spatial relation by which the string is an instrument for hauling in the plaything. At a slightly later age, he may discover, in playing with the string, that moving the string causes the attached plaything to move and then that pulling on the string brings the toy closer. At first, however, he can utilize this knowledge only to the extent of making a single wide sweep of his arm, which may bring the plaything within reach but which can also send it flying. It is later still before the baby can shift his grip to a point on the string nearer the lure, and later again before he is able to reel it in hand over hand.

Another by-product of the baby's new skill in the use of his hands is that he may have to be given a spoon to hold while he is being fed solids, or else, once his first ravenous hunger has been appeased, he will be more interested in the spoon his mother is holding than in the food it con-

The baby may be more interested in the spoon than in the food it contains.

Raimondo Borea

71

tains. By this age, many babies have decided food preferences and will clamp their lips and jaws tight when an unfavored food is offered. Some babies approach unfamiliar foodstuffs with their nose, as though the odor is the deciding factor in whether the food should be given a try. Most babies seem insensitive to routine smells of cooking, people, body wastes, and so forth, but take delight in sniffing at flowers and other sources of novel odors.

The baby at this age enjoys a passive form of peek-a-boo in which the adult drapes a piece of cloth over the baby's head and face and then at the proper moment snatches it away and exclaims, "Boo!" Note that the suspense of being shut off from the world for more than a few seconds at a time becomes unbearable for the baby, and he may frantically claw at the cloth. There are two general principles hidden in this simple observation. The first is that when the baby is shut off from the world, he is also shut off from himself. We all need sensory stimulation from the outside world to maintain our sense of identity, as has been demonstrated by experiments in sensory deprivation (Bexton et al., 1954). Witkin et al. (1954) have shown that the younger the person, the more important visual information is for staying oriented. The second principle concerns affective arousal and comes from Dumas' (1923) theory of emotion. This principle says that all mild emotional arousal is pleasant. It is obvious that we get pleasure from being petted or fondled or from their verbal equivalents, such as words of endearment or compliments, but we also enjoy the mock-fright of a ghost story or the safe terror of a roller-coaster ride. As emotions become more intense, they differentiate more sharply into pleas-

ant and unpleasant. At a still more intense level of arousal, all emotions become disagreeable, so that what was pleasant at an intermediate level becomes painful. At the final level of arousal described by Dumas, just to complete the picture, functioning either disintegrates or is paralyzed. The baby's feelings of mock-dissolution in a game of peek-a-boo can shift very rapidly to panic—a sense that he and the world are actually on their way out of existence, and the baby needs a good deal of time and testing of the world's durability before he can feel comfortable shut off from it. At a later age, the baby himself can control the cloth in playing peek-a-boo.

Although one can elicit a few sorts of imitation beginning shortly after birth, it is from age six months on that imitation, provoked and unprovoked, flowers most abundantly (Uzgiris, 1971). Once again, there are wide individual differences. The baby imitates such gestures as those involved in breaking an egg into a bowl or in brushing away a fly. Within a short time he will imitate such functional acts as using a sponge or cleaning tissue to wipe up spilled fluids. Social games with the parents evolve out of the baby's imitating what they do and also from the parents' imitating the baby, particularly the sounds he makes in babbling. The baby quickly learns the behavior needed to cue parental participation in social games: slapping the highchair tray, sham-coughing, sniffing, puffing out the cheeks to have the air squeezed out, puckering the lips as though to whistle (many babies enjoy using a forefinger to plug up and so turn off parental whistling). From somewhere around six months, the baby joins in heartily when he hears his parents laughing, even though he has no idea what the joke is about, and at a slightly later age he tries to start new rounds of merriment by making a strained laughing sound. Notice that long before he can talk, the baby is inventing ways of communicating his wants to other people, and that his wants far transcend mere satisfaction of physical needs.

As the baby approaches seven months, he makes crawling movements when on his belly. Although these are mostly abortive, he may succeed in propelling himself for short distances—forward, sideways, or backward, more as chance dictates than from any intention of his. By this age, quite a few babies travel short distances by rolling over and over. Somewhere between ages six and eight months, the baby becomes able to hold on to an adult's fingers and half-pull himself, half let himself be pulled into a sitting position. A little later, he can sit up by himself, different babies accomplishing this in different ways. Some babies, from a prone position, walk their hands under the chest until the trunk is almost erect, simultaneously swinging their legs forward and around. Another style of sitting up is to lie on one side with knees drawn up and to half-push, half-rock the body sidewise into a vertical position, with the buttocks as the pivot and the head traveling in a 90 degree arc—the reader must bear in mind how different a baby's proportions are from a grownup's. As we have said, infants sit with their feet together close to the body, sometimes with ankles crossed. Toddlers, by contrast, will squat, kneel, or sit with legs jutting straight forward. The preschool child sits with knees slightly spread and forelegs folded back like wings, his heels by his hips.

As the baby approaches eight months, he will probably become able to crawl. (Crawling differs from creeping in that one crawls on one's belly, whereas one creeps with the torso clear of the ground.) Typically, the baby crawls by dragging himself along with his forearms and pushing with legs and feet (plus whatever other wriggling and writhing may be involved), but there are many possible individual styles. Some babies crawl feet first, some use only their arms, some travel by swiveling on their arched bellies, some, as we have said, by rolling from place to place; we shall presently describe some varieties of creeping as well. Some babies enjoy rocking on their bellies, an activity which may incidentally pump out gobbets of vomit. (In general, infants do a good bit of mechanical vomiting unrelated to gastrointestinal infections or motion sickness.) We should note here that some babies neither creep nor crawl, but stay where they are put, until they are able to walk.

At about this age, the baby begins to try to feed himself with a spoon, making a splendid mess of food, himself, and surroundings. The problem is partly one of poor muscular control, but partly also of not knowing too precisely where his mouth is. Here we must point to a distinction: even though the baby at this age has no difficulty popping a thumb into his mouth, this is a different task from inserting a spoon, where one must take account of the size and position of the object intervening between hand and mouth. Even with the simpler task of eating a piece of toast or a slice of apple, one can observe that the baby has to poke around to find his mouth. Moreover, when eating a cracker, he may try to put it in at right angles to his mouth, and be at a loss to know why it won't go in. A spoon presents the additional complication that it has to be aimed right and, besides, must be kept right side up lest

Landmarks in the infant's behavioral development

gravity rob it of its cargo. One can reproduce the baby's movements in trying to use a spoon by holding one's thumbnail up, and then making a scooping movement away from the body, up and around and back toward the mouth, with the thumbnail turned down, like an airplane at the top of a loop. The reader who finds it hard to imagine how the baby's body regions can be so imprecisely localized might remember the standard test for drunkenness of having to touch a fingertip to the nose with eyes closed, or the neurological test of having to close the eyes and bring the tips of the index fingers together, or the game of having to wriggle a particular finger while the fingers are interlaced and the arms crossed.

By age eight months, the baby will have acquired one or two additional teeth, and each remaining month of infancy will bring him another pair. Between eight and nine months, the baby's thumb becomes fully opposed, and he can grasp pincers-fashion with great accuracy. This means that he can feed himself pellets of food, such as green peas or bits of meat, as well as lick his fingers dipped into soft foods, gnaw at larger chunks grasped in his whole hand, and cram food into his mouth with his palm. As we have noted, the baby practices new skills tirelessly until they have been thoroughly incorporated into his repertory; thus with pincers grasping: with thumb and forefinger he practices picking up bits of fluff, snippets of cloth or thread, crumbs, specks of dust, grains of sand or dirt—the tinier the better, it would seem. He uses his whole hand to try to grasp shadows, sunbeams, and tobacco smoke. Indeed, later in the first year he may practice picking up wholly imaginary granules, which he carefully deposits in his other, cupped hand or sets down on a shelf or

A.   Suzanne Szas

▲

A. Crawling. B. Creeping. C. Bear-walking.

gives to a cooperative adult. By age eight or nine months, the baby will have outgrown his bathinette or dishpan or kitchen sink and will move to the family tub. This means endless opportunities for exploration and experimentation, especially if the baby has a supply of washcloths, plastic cups, floating toys, and so forth. The water must be kept shallow, however, or the baby, whose buoyancy works against his balance, will topple, and more than one baby left untended in a tub has drowned.

On dry ground, the baby can get onto hands and knees, either by pushing up from a prone or by tilting forward from a sitting position. At first, the infant can only rock back and forth on hands and knees; a short while later, he learns how to shift his weight so as to free one limb after the other in creeping. Notice that creeping seems to require a certain amount of conscious deliberation—the baby has to figure out where he is and what to do next. Once he has found the combination, of course,

B.   Wil Blanche, DPI
C.   John Fay

creeping quickly becomes smooth and automatic and often incredibly rapid. As we have said, there are numerous individual styles of creeping. Some babies leapfrog forward, moving both hands together and both legs. Bearwalking, with legs held straight, is sometimes the first form of creeping, while for some babies it is an advanced form midway between creeping and walking. One little girl we know used one leg simply for support and poled herself along with the other, like a gondolier. Some infants move sitting, either by hitching themselves along or by pulling or pushing with the hands. One baby used her feet oar-fashion, placing them forward and then sliding them outwards to the sides, which propelled her rump along the floor. At a more advanced stage of creeping, a baby may push himself along with his feet, sliding his hands on a sheet of paper or a rag. The creeping baby may take any one of a number of approaches to carrying something with him. He may simply drag it along in one hand, he may hold it off the floor and travel three-legged, or he may carry it in his mouth, dog-fashion.

The creeping baby

Once the baby can move about easily, one can demonstrate the "**visual cliff**" **effect**, the fact that he will stop short at the edge of a precipice, even when in fact there is a sheet of heavy plate glass covering the void to prevent him from falling (Walk and Gibson, 1961). Research by Campos et al. (1970), based on changes in heartbeat, indicates that babies react to the visual cliff well in advance of creeping. The visual cliff reaction is important because it shows that perception of depth is innate or develops very early. (But we can just as well infer depth perception from the baby's first reaching out to swat at a dangling toy.) The visual cliff response has been observed in newly hatched chicks and in white rats whose eyes have just opened, as well as in various other species, attesting to its wide distribution in animals for which it is a meaningful form of behavior. One should not conclude, however, that it is safe to leave an infant unguarded on a bed or table. The baby has to see the cliff to take account of it, and he is liable to

Landmarks in the infant's behavioral development

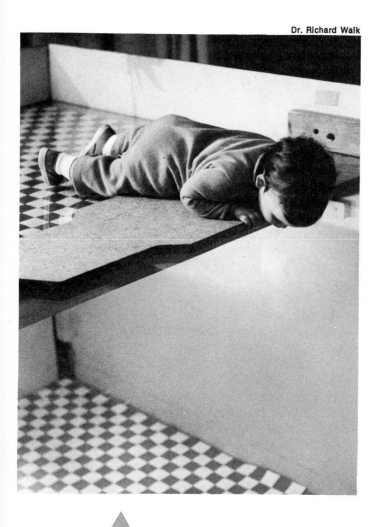

Dr. Richard Walk

A child peers cautiously at the deep side of the visual cliff.

play his well-liked game of flopping backward onto the bed when sitting with his back at the brink. Or, if he is rolling toward the brink, he may not see it until too late. In addition, some babies react to the drop-off as inviting rather than menacing and have to be restrained from flinging themselves into space (we propose the name of "Geronimo response" for this reaction). Some babies (and some puppies we have observed) want so badly to get down on the floor that they seem oblivious to the danger of falling as they try frantically to get down. The creeping baby learns very readily to go up a flight of stairs, but coming down remains beyond his powers for some time. The visual cliff effect usually restrains him from trying to go downstairs headfirst, and his body awareness has not reached the point where he can figure out the process of going down backward, feet-first. It is only at about age eleven months that one can teach the baby to creep backward downstairs or to slide feetfirst off a bed or couch. The basis of the baby's perception of the visual cliff is thought to be **motion parallax**, the fact that objects at different distances from the observer have a differential displacement on the retina. The importance of motion parallax for the baby's depth perception has received further confirmation in a study by Bower (1965). In addition, Walk and Dodge (1962) showed that a ten-and-half-month-old, blind in one eye since age five and a half months, avoided the drop-off, supporting the idea that binocular cues are not necessary for depth perception.

The baby's creeping further reveals his ability to detour around obstacles to get to something he wants. The ability to detour requires a more sophisticated perception of spatial relations than may be obvious. A chicken separated from corn by a short length of wire fence may starve to death without ever discovering that she has only to walk around the fence to get at the food. If the baby is given the task of getting a doll that is separated from him by a transparent screen, it is not usually before age one year that he can reach around the screen instead of persistently trying to penetrate it to get at the doll. Research by Kenneth Kaye (1971) indicates, however, that the solution to this task can be taught to babies as young as six months. Kaye identified three spontaneous teaching strategies used by the babies' mothers: **shoving**, attempting to move the baby's hand to the lure, which worked not at all; **shaping**, moving the lure by stages behind the barrier, which produced only unstable learning; and **showing**, giving the baby a performance to imitate, which worked very well indeed. This finding is akin to one by Phyllis Chesler (1969) that kittens learn better by watching their mothers solve a problem than by watching other adult cats. Church (1970) has found that babies can learn by imitation to pour from one cup to another and to use a stick to get a lure beyond the reach of their hand. Not long after he begins creeping, the baby wends his way snakelike through the rungs of chairs, beneath coffee tables, and in general through and around whatever passageways space offers him for exploration.

We have already mentioned some of the social games that babies begin to enjoy at this age. Others include give-and-take, passing a toy back and forth with an adult. Here parents may get another inkling of the baby's devotion to repetitive activities, the baby's interest continuing long after the adult has grown bored. Although the infant gladly hands things to an adult in a game of give-and-take, he now for the first time shows frustration and even resentment when something is taken away from him. Earlier, his reaction, if any, probably did not go beyond a mild and momentary perplexity. An important ingredient in the baby's frustration seems to be that now objects are **conserved,** that is, they continue to exist for him when they pass out of his perceptual ken, whereas at earlier ages the baby acted as though objects that went out of view went right out of existence. This new **object permanence** also makes possible the game of finding things that his parents have hidden. Although he can find a toy hidden under a box while he was watching, if there are two similar boxes he will not know which one to look under. He can learn with repeated trials, but no one, to our knowledge, has so far systematically investigated what cues the baby can learn to respond to— position (whether to the left or the right), color differences, size differences, different designs on the box, or whatever. If one hides a small object consistently in the same hand, the baby will learn after a few trials to reach for the correct hand; if one then changes hands, he will continue indefinitely to try the previously correct hand, eventually in the form of a ritualistic vestigial touching, before going on to the now-correct hand. We shall return to the matter of conservation later.

The baby takes gleeful pleasure in this-little-piggy and allied games, in just being talked to or sung to, in being swung by his armpits (one must be careful about picking the baby up by his upper arms lest one dislocate his shoulders) between an adult's legs or being jiggled high in the air, in being tumbled about on a bed, including being shoved over from a sitting position.

Late in this period the creeping baby enjoys being chased by a mock-ferocious adult, and will initiate the game by paddling away, looking over his shoulder for the adult to follow and perhaps even making cries in imitation of those the adult utters in chasing him. While it is important that the baby not be caught too quickly, it is also the case, as with peek-a-boo, that the catching not be too long delayed and the suspense too prolonged. In much the same way, the baby may now begin a favorite pastime of late infancy, that of running away or hiding from his parents when they try to get him for a bath or bedtime or whatever. Even if the infant is not yet mobile and so is unable to take refuge in a closet or behind a door, he may begin to feign total preoccupation with what he is doing whenever his parents want his attention. Along the same lines, he takes great delight in his parents' simulated inability to see him as they search in all sorts of unlikely hiding places, calling out, "Where's Baby?" Again the tension cannot be too long maintained or the delicious excitement turns into frustration and panic.

It is worth pausing to mention that not much before age three does the child have any notion that successful concealment also requires silence; when hiding, he squeals and giggles with great abandon, apparently not realizing that he is betraying his whereabouts. By age nine months, many babies resent extended confinement in a playpen. The now-mobile baby wants to be out exploring the wonders of the house or yard or park, and parents have to impose their first taboos on dangerous or damageable objects and locations.

It is characteristic of United States middle-class babyhood that the infant has monthly medical checkups in the course of which he receives a number of immunizing injections or vaccinations. As David Levy (1960) has pointed out, this practice makes for a natural experiment by which to study the acquisition of a particular fear. What we would expect is a steadily expanding gradient of anticipation of pain: at first the baby reacts only when the needle goes in; then, when the doctor or nurse approaches; then when being undressed for the examination; then when entering the examining room; then in the waiting room; and ultimately, by whatever intuition the baby senses it, when leaving home to go to the doctor—as one mother put it, "We always take a taxi to come to the doctor's. Now, whenever he sees the taxi pull up to the house (note that this one-year-old could differentiate between taxicabs and cars in general, presumably on the basis of distinctive markings) he starts to howl." It is only at about age two, when the inoculations are much more widely spaced, that many babies can make friends with doctors and nurses. The sequence we have described can indeed be observed in many babies, but other babies seem not to find injections particularly bothersome, others seem not to anticipate the injection and react only after the fact, and others seem to develop a stolid stoicism that endures medical procedures without flinching. We are at a loss to account for these widely varied individual styles. We should also point out that there are other features of medical examinations besides injections that babies find distressing—the handling, the having things done to oneself, are also disagreeable to a number of babies.

During the final quarter of his first year the baby continues the transition, by stages we shall describe in a moment, from a horizontal to a vertical organism. He becomes less passive and no longer lies quietly while being changed or cleaned or dressed. Instead, he wriggles and twists and has to be given a plaything to keep him occupied and tractable—he may even get his first angry smack on the bottom from a parent who finds it impossible to cope with a flailing baby and a soiled diaper at the same time. On the other hand, he begins to cooperate in getting dressed, holding out an arm to go through the sleeve, raising head and shoulders to allow the shirt to pass behind his back, and so forth, so that dressing the child becomes much less a matter of stuffing him into his clothes. Even so, it may be as late as age three before one no longer has to remind the child to "push" his arm or leg through or into a garment. If, as is often the case, the baby's customary plaything while being changed is his diaper pins (closed, we hope it is superfluous to add), one may see his first primitive awareness of number: if he is given or can find only one safety pin, he looks around for its mate.

His self-awareness reaches a new stage at about ten months when he recognizes himself in the mirror. (There is some evidence that culturally deprived children as old as age four years do not recognize their own reflection or photograph [Baltimore City Public Schools, 1964].) He was earlier able to recognize the person holding him, as shown by his comparing person and reflection, but his reaction to his own image develops more slowly, from simple interest to playfulness to affection to clear recognition, manifested by his reaching up to touch the hat he sees mirrored in the glass or comparing his overalls with their reflection. It is only later that one sees the child posing and posturing before the mirror, or draping himself with odd garments and admiring the effect. A charming study by Gallup (1970) shows that chimpanzees

The ten-month-old recognizes his reflection in the mirror.

Donna J. Harris, The Merrill-Palmer Institute

79

learn to recognize their own reflection; for instance, they groom themselves in front of the mirror, discovering and removing a food particle lodged in the teeth, and reacting with distress to a change in appearance brought about by the experimenter while the animal was sedated. Monkeys, by contrast, do not recognize themselves; that is, they treat the reflection as though it were another animal. Another step in self-discovery may come as early as age nine months, when the baby begins to shout or shriek as a way of letting people know that he wants something, like his dinner. When shrieking, he may for the first time discover the sound of his own voice and then make vocal sounds just so that he can listen to them.

Late in the first year, the baby becomes able to play advanced games like pat-a-cake. At first he claps his fists together, then his palms, but he is not likely to produce a clapping sound for a long time to come. If he sees people clapping on television, he may join in this mass game of pat-a-cake. The infant imitates such actions as picking up a sheet of paper and holding it above his head; blowing out a match and kissing movements of the lips; prominent inanimate sounds like the backfire of a car; and babble sounds such as *ba-ba* and *da-da*. He can throw things, but with very little control. He comes to understand a great many things that are said to him, mostly in the form of simple commands and requests but also cue words and phrases for familiar games and routine activities like bathing and eating. For instance, here is a mother's account of the behavior of her daughter at age ten months one week:

Debbie surprised us today by bringing "Red Fox" on request from her room to the dining room (a distance of 40 feet [13 m.] through several rooms—and a major feat for her to creep the distance both ways, dragging this 12-inch-high animal with her on the return trip). We had not realized she knew its "name" or that she could distinguish between it and "Bear" and "Heffalump," but she demonstrated to us then that she knew each of these equally well by bringing them, too (Church, 1968, pp. 42–43).

In his understanding of words that refer to events that are part of his regular schedule, the infant is probably helped by his biological clock, which signals when things are due to happen.

At about ten months of age the baby becomes able to solve such deceptively easy-seeming problems as how to remove a bead from a transparent widemouthed jar: at first the baby tries to grasp the bead (or whatever lure is used) directly, through the glass; at a later age—typically between ten and twelve months—he can see that the way to reach the lure is to put his hand through the opening; still later, he knows that he can up-end the container and pour the bead out. It should not be supposed that the transparent container is invisible to the baby; he may steady the jar by grasping its rim as he tries to penetrate its wall. With opaque containers, where visibility correlates perfectly with accessibility, the baby has no trouble, and enjoys putting things into and taking them out of receptacles. He explores apertures and crevices with a probing forefinger. Indeed, many a baby goes through a period where his forefinger seems to lead the way through the world. With palm and fingertips he palpates textures, quite literally getting the feel of surfaces such as fur and fabric and brick and glass and wire screening. If not restrained, the all-inquisitive infant tries to eat dirt, leaves, bottle caps, cigar and cigarette butts, dead insects—the potential list is endless. He learns to unscrew the caps from bottles and toothpaste tubes, sometimes with lamentable results. He can turn an electric light on and off by pulling a string, although at first he does not control the direction of his pull, and it takes him a while to learn to relax the string so that the switch can reset itself at the end of each yank. He can work simple cupboard latches and he tugs at knobs to open doors and drawers. He can switch on a radio or television set and twist the knob to regulate the volume. Some babies we have observed use the right hand to turn a knob clockwise and the left to turn it counterclockwise. Babies learn that there may be a delay between turning on a TV set and the appearance of picture and sound, although a baby can obviously have no understanding of the set's warming up. The baby may seek to accelerate the emergence of sound by turning the volume to its highest setting, and then be so frightened by the ensuing blast of sound that he cannot go near the set.

The infant learns that toy cars roll forward and back but not sideways. He learns to distinguish among free-rolling, friction-motor, and wind-up cars. He cannot yet work the key on a wind-up car or other mechanical toy and hands it to the adult for winding. He likes to empty pots and pans from their cabinets, to bang them together and to mouth the handles, and to disassemble complicated pieces like double boilers and percolators. At this age, he takes such things apart, but it will be some months before he has either the inclination or ability to put them back together. Late in the first year, though, he may be able to place pierced blocks on a peg. He also practices putting things in things and setting things on other things. He is sensitive only to gross differences in size and seems baffled that he cannot put a large object into a small container. He has to learn by trial and error that he cannot rest a plaything on a vertical or steeply sloping surface, but this learning does not teach him that he can roll a car down an incline, a discovery he makes at about a year and a half. It sometimes seems that babies have a hard time perceiving extended plane surfaces, since we have observed babies doing things like trying to pass a spoon from one hand to the other through a feeding-table top and creeping head on into a wall as though unaware that it existed, like the trapped wasp which seems to be trying to fly through the ceiling. It is possible that such surfaces seen close up have for the baby something of the character of a **Ganzfeld**, a homogeneous surface that fills the field of view and gives the impression of a space-filling fog (Cohen, 1957).

Late in the first year, the baby becomes aware that some things have a "correct" up-down spatial orientation and goes around almost compulsively righting overturned objects. This awareness extends even to such unfamiliar abstract forms as a wooden cone or graduated disks stacked on a central spindle to make a tower. While some babies seem indifferent to the up-down, front-to-back orientation of books and magazines, others learn to position them "correctly" before reading. Babies usually turn the pages a handful at a time. He shows his recognition of pictured objects by rocking when he sees a picture of a rocking horse; even before he can speak, he may meow at the picture of a cat or make motorlike sounds at the picture of a car. Some such behavior is clearly an imitation of adults, but a great deal of it seems spontaneous. He does not at first distinguish clearly between printed forms and

Landmarks in the infant's behavioral development

solid three-dimensional objects, as shown by his attempts to pick up the designs on his playpen pad, or letters, designs, and pictures in books.

In his progress from quadruped to biped, the baby goes through a fairly stable sequence of stages. The ages we shall give should not be taken too seriously—we hear of so many babies nowadays walking at between seven and ten months of age that we suspect that the published norms (approximately thirteen months) are obsolete, assuming they were correct earlier. Hindley et al. (1966) report differences in age of walking according to nationality, with Stockholm babies walking at an average age of 12.51 months, Paris babies at 13.81 months, and babies in Brussels, London, and Zurich at ages between these extremes. In any event, the range of normal individual differences is so wide (perhaps eight to twenty months)—and we do not even know much about such development in other societies—that it is probably meaningless to speak of an "average" age for walking. The authors were recently fascinated to watch a motorically precocious six-month-old creep to a large doll cradle, climb in, stand up, and examine his reflection in a mirror, bracing himself by gripping the mirror's frame and shifting his weight as the cradle rocked slightly under him. We shall describe progress toward walking as it is described in textbooks, however, regardless of when this occurs for any given baby, since the sequence seems to be a stable one.

By age ten months the textbook baby can support his weight when standing, although an adult must give him balance. By eleven months he can be pulled to standing and then, if his grip is transferred to a piece of furniture, he can balance himself. He may even take a few steps holding on

with both hands to an adult's fingers. By age one, he can pull himself to his feet. The first few times he does so, he does not know how to get down again and may cry in alarm until someone comes and lowers him. He soon learns, however, to let go and thud onto his seat—a distance, after all, of only 9 or 10 inches, besides which his backside is well padded with fat (if he is well nourished) and diapers (if he is European or American). He is able to "cruise," sidestepping while he supports himself on furniture or on playpen railing. Then he stands without holding on; he bounces in place, either to music or, apparently, just for the fun of it. And then, one day—parents usually sense its coming and wait tensely—he gathers himself together and, with hands held high and to the side for balance, he toddles. His first few ventures on foot may last no more than three or four steps, but the baby has clearly made a transition. He almost immediately learns to stand up without holding on to anything—seated, he may draw his feet under him and simply push up; on hands and knees, he shifts his weight backward from knees to feet and then straightens up at the hips and waist. For another month or more, the baby may still prefer to creep when he has a definite destination, but meanwhile he assiduously practices walking until the time comes when he creeps only as a joke. This joke, incidentally, tells us something about the baby's self-awareness, since he seems able to draw a distinction between the walking baby he now is and the creeping baby he just used to be.

From creeping to walking. A. Pulling oneself to standing. B. Standing holding on. The baby's knees tell us that he still gets about by creeping. C. Balinese walking rail. Compare with the more familiar imprisoning playpen. D. Cruising. E. First steps. F. A toddler toddling.

A.   Vivienne, DPI

C.   Gregory Bateson and Margaret Mead,
                        Balinese Character

D.   Suzanne Szasz

B.   Anita Sabarese, DPI

F.   George W. Martin, DPI

E.

Suzanne Szasz

The reader should bear in mind that the newly walking baby is some 29 inches (74 cm.) tall, which means in Western households that the top of his head will be just below the level of an ordinary table top; by stretching, he can just barely see what is on the table. He will not be able to grasp a doorknob, some 38 inches (97 cm.) from the floor, until almost age two. To return to Witkin's studies of reliance on visual cues for orientation in space (field dependence) as compared to internal cues (field independence), if development begins with field dependence, one would predict that the baby who can stand up in a normal environment would be unable to do so if clues to verticality were abolished, as by placing him in a spherical chamber or one whose walls were greatly out of plumb.

One can observe the baby's growing knowledge of his own body late in the first year as he explores the adult's facial features and then feels his own corresponding ones. If he plays with one adult ear, he feels both. He may even be able to comply with the request, "Show me your ear" (or nose or eye or mouth or teeth or tongue), but, as we said before, these are not clearly localized and he may have to grope a bit to find them. Also, if he suffers an insect bite or is otherwise injured, he may not be able to indicate the site of the pain he obviously feels. The baby at this time may first discover and play with his own genitals. This discovery seems to come earlier in boys than in girls, presumably because the boy's penis is visible and accessible to him in a way that the girl's vulva is not to her. The boy's discovery of his penis comes not out of some inner motivational state but out of his noticing something down there and grabbing it. A diapered society,

By late infancy, the baby can drink from a cup held with both hands. Note the trickles of spilt milk on the bib and the raised pinkie of the left hand, a common manifestation.

Suzanne Szasz

of course, tends to delay such discovery. Most normal babies by the age of a year masturbate occasionally, especially at bedtime, but babies given adequate attention and playthings do not concentrate on this source of pleasure. Genital stimulation early in infancy seems to have a soothing effect, as suggested by its use in some cultures to quiet a crying baby. By late infancy, however, genital play seems to produce actual pleasure, but with nothing like the intensity of adult sexual experience.

Around one year of age, the infant waves bye-bye, usually by closing and opening his fist. He can pile one small wooden cube, somewhat precariously, atop another. As we have said, he can fit pierced blocks on a peg, but if they are graduated in size, he cannot yet arrange them in order. Nor can he pile or fit together a set of nesting boxes. He can sometimes get a spoonful of food into his mouth, but the spoon is still likely to reach his mouth upside down. He can drink from a glass, but he has to hold it with both hands. Similarly, he can hold his own bedtime bottle, if he has one, although many babies enjoy the social contact involved in a parent's holding the bottle or holding him while he holds the bottle. He not only enjoys receiving affection but is able to return it with warm hugs and very wet, open-mouth kisses. He tries to sing and enjoys listening to songs, rhymes, and jingles, and being danced around to music in an adult's arms. He may be able to hide a plaything under or behind a couch or in a closet and then retrieve it a day or so later. This is a real-life equivalent of the delayed-reaction experiment, which tests the child's (or animal's) ability to remember the location of a concealed object, except that here it is the baby, not the experimenter, who hides the lure (Hunter, 1913). In general,

babies perform much better on tasks they set themselves than on those devised by adults. The one-year-old may be able to draw a few strokes with a crayon—often on floor or walls. An occasional bright one-year-old can figure out, apparently without prior demonstration, that he can use a stick to reach and retrieve some desired object lying beyond his grasp, and most one-year-olds can be taught, by demonstration, how to do this.

During the first few months of the second year, as the baby is making the shift from infancy to toddlerhood, he achieves a stable bipedal stance and locomotion, he perfects and integrates his already acquired manipulatory skills, and begins to say a few words or almost-words. He anticipates his interests as a toddler when he combines walking with grasping to lug, shove, and haul outsized objects. Now he enjoys his herculean efforts for their own sake; later on, they will be subordinated to higher-order activities such as block-building. When the child begins carrying things while walking, his first preference seems to be for large things hugged to his body with both arms, failing which he will carry two smaller things, one for each arm. Apparently, the urge to carry is great, for we have many times observed a baby pick up a bit of thread or lint or dust, hug it against his chest, and walk.

Perception in Infancy and Beyond

Now that we have surveyed some key features of development during infancy, it is time to examine in more detail a recurring theme of this book, self-world relations.

This topic does not end with infancy, and we shall have to violate our age-periods scheme in order to make sense. We must begin by understanding that the same physical reality can be perceived very differently by different people. Some of these perceptual differences have to do with differences in individual outlooks, while some are related to differences among groups. Social anthropologists are interested in the perceptual differences among cultural groups. Men and women debate, and sometimes quarrel about, sex differences in perceiving. The woman may see in rich detail a dress-shop window which for her male companion is only an undifferentiated blur, all but invisible; the reverse may hold true for the display window of a hardware store. And the developmental psychologist is concerned with age differences. What we perceive is only partly a product of the sensory information that impinges on our sense receptors both from outside and from deep within our bodies. We attend to only a limited portion of the sensory information available to us, and what we attend to can be organized in a multiplicity of ways. How the world appears to us is influenced by our knowledge of how things work, especially when it comes to taking account of governing forces that lie beyond perception, such as x-rays, ultrasounds, magnetism, infrared and ultraviolet light, bacteria, viruses, and the principles of growth. What we perceive is not always clearly distinguished from what we feel, think, believe, crave, and fear. In sum, the world is organized for us as a sphere of meanings and relationships, and not merely as a collection of things. We can draw a distinction between sophisticated modes of perceiving, in which the forces that actuate events are those that are derived from science, and primitive modes, in which the world is held together and animated by demons, spirit forces, and magic. Alan Moorehead (1966) gives a sensitive account of how he perceived snakes as dangerous and something to be killed, and how, through experience, he later learned to overcome (but not completely) the horror that snakes provoked in him.

As nearly as we can reconstruct the perceptual experience of the very young baby from his behavior, the world at first is only a diffuse field in which objects come and go but without a stable framework. The waking baby will alert to almost any nearby sight or sound, but if it does not hold any threat of harm or promise of gratification, he quickly loses interest, or habituates. Soon after, connections begin to develop among things, but the connection is invariably personal, through the infant. His mother's presence may portend changing, soothing, and pleasure, but he has little comprehension of the operations involved. Orange juice may signify that a bath will follow, but these are related for him as a familiar sequence of sensations, not as events in a world that includes his mother's schedule, too. Similarly, he has no idea of the geographical framework relating the kitchen where he gets his juice and the bathroom where he is bathed. The difficult thing for most adults to grasp is that, although everything is related to "my" wants and feelings, there is at first no *me*. There simply are states of hunger or wetness, or orange-flavored-fluid-followed-by-warm-immersion, all in a context of familiar person and place. But there is no *I am* hungry or *I feel* tired or *I taste* orange juice. The baby's experience is personal, because it is only his feelings of which he is aware, but he has not yet defined himself as an entity, just as he at first has no knowledge of a world that exists apart from his own feelings. This state of affairs in which the child's universe is centered upon himself, without his being aware of himself at the center, has been named **egocentrism** by Piaget (1954). We shall return repeatedly to the theme of egocentrism.

We have already noted many aspects of perceptual development during infancy. In the visual sphere, we have seen the newborn baby's preference for moderately complex forms over simple ones, and for facelike shapes over nonsense patterns. We have seen him react fearfully to what seems to be a rapidly approaching object. We have seen him learn to recognize his nursing bottle at a distance, to distinguish between familiar faces and strange ones, and even to fear strange faces. We have seen him become able to reach out and grasp a dangling plaything. He learns to inspect objects visually and manipulate them in various ways. At first, solid objects lack permanence for him, so that objects that vanish seem to go out of existence, and he fails to recognize his unfamiliarly accoutred father or mother. Then, when he begins to hunt for objects that have disappeared, we know that permanence is becoming the rule. We have seen him react to two-dimensional designs as though they were three-dimensional solids. Late in infancy, he becomes sensitive to the up-down dimension of things. As he becomes able to creep, we see him adapting to spatial arrangements, as when he avoids drop-offs or detours around an obstacle. He learns about transparent barriers and the need to go around them, too. Visually given textures invite his fingers to reach out and palpate them. The baby's first rooting be-

havior reveals a sensitivity to tactile information, and we have seen how he uses his mouth as a sense organ by which to know objects. From an early age, contact with adults and the movements they impart comfort him and give him pleasure.

In the auditory sphere, we have seen how selective the baby's hearing is at first. We have noted his early sensitivity to the human voice and the way he strains, as early as age two months, to try to answer back when talked to. From the age of a few months, he turns to see where a voice is coming from; at later ages, he searches for the sources of other kinds of sounds. He reacts to approaching footsteps, and by late infancy he recognizes the sound of his father's approaching car. He becomes responsive to music and may even show decided musical preferences. He becomes able to imitate sounds, and by the end of infancy understands a certain amount of language. We know less about the development of the sense of smell, but it is apparent that the baby's olfactory apparatus operates from birth on. Similarly, the baby develops food preferences, and he comes to recognize visually those foods he likes and dislikes.

In the realm of self-perception, we have seen the baby discover his own hands and feet and become able to use them. He learns to localize certain sensations, so that he can scratch at an itchy place or rub his eyes when sleepy. He learns where his eyes are, and his mouth, and his ears, and so forth. He becomes able to feed himself. He learns to recognize himself in the mirror. He discovers his navel and genitalia, and learns about the sensations caressing of the genitalia brings. He learns control of his body in manipulation and locomotion. He acquires a certain degree of self-control, as in waiting and in observing taboos. He becomes playful, and may even begin to play with his own identity. He becomes self-assertive and obstinate. In general, his burgeoning emotions tell us about his broadening awareness of things, of their characteristics and possibilities. Let us go on now to look at these aspects of perception more carefully.

There is some indirect evidence that the baby's active manipulation and his movements through space play a vital role in organizing his world. For instance, Held and Hein (1963) have shown that kittens whose visual experience is all gained from being moved passively through space (specifically, in a cart propelled by another, actively moving kitten) show defective spatial vision, as in the visual cliff situation. They attribute this (Hein et al., 1970) to the lack of any coherent relation between whatever spontaneous movements the kitten makes and changes that go on in the visual environment. The same authors also report the intriguing finding that if kittens experience active movement with one eye covered, the correct depth perception does not transfer to the previously covered eye. The Austrian psychologist Ivo Kohler (1964) has demonstrated that the effects of wearing distorting lenses gradually disappear as the adult subject moves about in the world, at first gropingly and then, as he becomes reoriented, normally. Once perception has stabilized, on the other hand, movement seems to play a lesser role, since adult subjects who have taken curarelike drugs, which produce a temporary but total flaccid paralysis, report that perceptual experience is even intensified under the influence of the drug (Smith et al., 1947). The importance of active movement in the initial structuring

of space may help us understand some of the cognitive limitations that go with "deprivation," which often has as one of its features that children are discouraged from moving about; in institutions where babies are kept immobilized in cribs, even walking may be long delayed (Dennis and Najarian, 1957).

We have already mentioned that very young infants scan the environment horizontally, but not vertically (Haith, 1968). It is not certain when the change to up-down scanning takes place, but during early infancy overhead space seems decidedly less meaningful for the baby than left-right and footward space. Some observations of our own suggest that babies who seek the source of a sound when it is to the side or below eye level fail to do so when the sound is overhead. Similarly, tickling various parts of the baby's body with a twisted cleaning tissue will produce a response, except when it is the top of the baby's head that is tickled. Clanton (Center for Cognitive Studies, 1968–1969) reports a shift during infancy in gazing patterns. At first, the eyes turn before the head does, which is interpreted as a reaction dominated by the stimulus. Later, the head begins to turn before the eyes do, which is interpreted as a self-determined act.

Another interesting feature of the baby's perception is the things he does not attend to. Loud and conspicuous noises that the adult finds hard to ignore, such as thunderstorms, sirens, the racket of trash cans being emptied and thrown back onto the sidewalk, the shrilling of the telephone bell, seem to go unnoticed. By contrast, though, the baby may scream in dismay at a sneeze or cough, he alerts to his mother's tiptoed approach, and, at a later age when he has learned to recognize the noise of airplanes, he detects them flying in the far distance. It is also important to realize that the baby may be focused on something besides what we assume. When we find him apparently staring out the window, at least some of the time he seems to be looking at the glass and the reflections thereon rather than through it. Similarly, the baby discovers reflections, especially his own, on the shiny surfaces of toasters, hub caps, or whatever, including very tiny ones. When the baby examines the draperies, he may be looking at the design or even at the weave of the cloth.

At all ages, we accept the world as given to our senses as real and complete—typically, the color-blind person does not discover his impairment until somebody else points it out to him. However, the adult, unlike the baby, recognizes that the world contains several kinds of reality (what philosophers call **orders**, or **levels, of reality**). Dreams and pain and other such subjective events are real enough, but they are real in a different sense from cabbages and auto accidents and oxygen and photographs and sentences. Insofar as these realities exist for the young child, they seem to be fused into a common realm where dreams occupy everyday space, thoughts influence objects, feelings take incarnate shape, material objects dissolve into nothingness or change identity without warning, and where the common denominator of causation is magic. Piaget calls this tendency to accept everything as real and real in the same way as everything else **realism.**

We must distinguish between **perceptual realism** of the kind we are talking about and "realism" in the ordinary sense of realistic, either as hard-headed practicality or fidelity to nature. Realism also comes in

such special versions as **picture realism**, as seen in the child's petting a pictured animal, trying to pick up a pictured string bean, or trying to listen to the ticking of a pictured watch (as did the Hayes's home-reared chimpanzee, Viki [Hayes, 1951]); **word realism**, whereby a statement is treated as though it were a fact; and **moral realism**, whereby moral and ethical rules are assumed to be absolute, timeless, and built into the natural order of things. We see a suspension of realism in social games where the baby adopts a playful orientation to things, as in peek-a-boo, and a reassertion of realism when the game goes on too long and the baby acts as though he had indeed come to the end of the line. The looming effect (Schiff, 1965; Ball and Tronick, 1971; see p. 17) works as well whether it is produced by a real object or simply by a rapidly expanding shadow. The chimpanzee shows as much fear of a motion picture of a snake as of a real snake. The three-year-old can lose himself in his play to the extent of trying to eat his sand cake, and we as adults can be so absorbed in a movie or a story as to cry at the death of the hero or gloat at the downfall of the villain, to the point of forgetting where we really are. As we shall see later, preschool-age children assume that the television dramas they watch are real events enacted by real characters enclosed within the set. It is a long, slow developmental process learning to sort out the many orders of reality and of reality-like fantasy.

A complicating effect of realism is that we all tend to assume that the reality we perceive is everybody's reality, as though everyone had the same knowledge, understanding, interests, values, moral standards, and vantage point in space. This assumption produces the attitude called **egocentrism,** the failure to realize that one's outlook is peculiarly one's own, with a corresponding inability to take account of other, differing perspectives on a given state of affairs. Egocentrism provides the foundation for **ethnocentrism,** taking for granted the ways of behaving, the values, and the ideas of the people among whom one grows up. Ethnocentrism is a shared blindness masquerading as knowledge; it is akin to the shared geocentrism that made people think for millennia that the earth was the center around which the universe revolved, and which resisted so bitterly the radical notion put forward by Galileo, Copernicus, and others that the earth was merely one satellite of one star among countless other stars.

Note that egocentrism, as used in the description of immature behavior, does not mean egotism; it does not mean either selfishness or preoccupation with self. It is perfectly possible to be quite generous in an egocentric way, as when someone gives a present, in all love and benevolence, that is more suited to the donor than to the recipient. We can see this in the way a young child affectionately and self-sacrificingly bestows his sodden toast upon his mother or father. Egocentric behavior occurs not because the child is full of his own importance or preoccupied with thoughts of self but precisely because he is insufficiently aware of himself and the personal nature of his experience, his biased, idiosyncratic outlook on things. Ideally, with maturity, one moves away from egocentrism and ethnocentrism toward **relativism,** the ability to take account of how things look to other people and in other cultural perspectives, but even adults give abundant evidence of egocentrism—a

mother may weep because her children didn't like some foodstuff she had prepared as a special treat. Relativism, it might be added, does not mean a relinquishing of values, but it often enables us to think critically about the values that we do hold.

In most experimental and philosophical accounts of perception, it is assumed that the person contemplates and analyzes the features of the objects around him, and then reconstitutes objects and their spatial and causal relationships from elements of sensation, by a kind of unconscious cerebration. Analytical, contemplative perceiving does occur, but the more usual procedure is to take things in and react to them at a glance. Instead of attending to the detailed properties of things, we apprehend them **physiognomically,** that is, in terms of their overall, expressive qualities, so named on the analogy of the unanalytic way we perceive the human physiognomy and the play of facial expression. Physiognomic perceiving lasts through life, so that even after we have scrutinized something analytically, and so perhaps changed its physiognomy, we continue to react to it globally, as when we identify a particular make of car. Learning to read requires a certain amount of analysis of words and letters, but once reading has been mastered, we read physiognomically. This is why we easily miss typographical errors, misread unfamiliar words as familiar ones, and seldom notice the typeface in which a book is printed. We grasp the general sense (correctly or incorrectly) of what we read, ignoring or only half-noticing the physical characteristics of the little black squiggles that are the "stimulus" for reading. In fact, if color names are printed in inks of a color different from the name, the expert reader has to make a special effort to see the color of the ink (Comalli et al., 1962; Sichel and Chandler, 1969).

The physiognomies of things contain as well what Koffka calls their **demand qualities**, which elicit particular feelings and behavior, often without prior learning. For the baby, knobs have the demand quality of graspability and pullability, crevices that of forefinger-pokeability, textures, of palpability, funny faces that of risibility, just as for the adult wet paint demands to be touched and the baby's cheek to be pinched.

Demand quality points to another neglected fact of perception, which is that we react to objects somatically and emotionally in a single sweep of behavior, and not in stages where we first perceive something, then identify it, and then have feelings about it. The general term here is perceptual **participation**, that is, we participate directly in happenings in our surroundings, as though they and we were all segments of the same organism. One of the most striking forms of participation is **empathy**, where we become so involved in some external action that we do it, too, as when we help the pole-vaulter over the bar, restrain the comedian from falling over the precipice, apply "body English" to a billiard or golf or bowling ball, yawn in concert with another, clear our throat to remove the frog in somebody else's, writhe and grunt with the wrestlers on television, or open our mouth as we feed the baby. Empathy seems to be the basis of early imitation, such as the young baby's attempted imitation of parental vocalizations and mouth movements. The way one baby cries in response to another baby's crying is another example of empathy. With age and experience, we come to perceive more objectively and to interpose judgment between perception and action (although it is

obvious, from the misunderstandings of everyday life and from students' answers on examinations, that we misperceive much of what we hear) and the somatic components of perceiving become more subdued. Nevertheless, with the proper recording instruments, such as those linked to a polygraph, or "lie detector," we can show that even in adults the very simplest stimuli, such as the click of a telegraph key, produce reverberations throughout the body (Davis et al., 1955, 1959; Lacey, 1956).

An important feature of immature perception is **synesthesia**, the fact that stimulation in one sense modality produces effects in other modalities. The almost universal adult synesthesia is the way odor contributes to flavor, as we become aware when we get a cold and foods lose their familiar "taste." A small number of adults have color-hearing, so that various sound patterns produce characteristic color sensations. It is reported that color-hearing is a common effect of the psychedelic drugs such as mescaline, LSD, and psilocybin, so that hearing music is accompanied by shifting colors of objects, prismatic effects along edges, and sometimes patterns of color flowing through the air. While the undrugged adult knows that sounds have a visible source, he does not think of the sounds themselves as visible entities. The baby, by contrast, often acts as though he expects to be able to see sounds, as when he quickly pulls an adult's hands apart as though looking for the handclap they have just made, or looks about the room as though seeking the chord that has just been struck on the piano. We even have an instance of a little girl trying to hear the ticking of a watch by holding it to her eyes (Church, 1968,

A.

George Zimbel, Monkmeyer

B.

George Zimbel, Monkmeyer

Object permanence. A. and B. The vanished object has gone out of existence. C. The baby pulls aside the blanket to get at the hidden plaything.

p. 213). For just as sensations are not clearly catalogued for the baby, his awareness of the functioning of his sense receptors is vague and poorly localized. There also seems to be an anticipatory synesthesia, whereby we sense from the visual appearance of something whether it will be rough or smooth to the touch, or wet or sticky or slimy, or hard or elastic or brittle, or warm or cool, or heavy or light. In the same vein, many sounds seem to carry faint visual or kinesthetic images of the things that produce them, as when we hear "a person walking." Even so diffuse a sense as smell may evoke an image of the object that produces the odor, as when we smell an orange (not merely the odor of orange), and this tells us its location in space.

Some of the associations and anticipatory synesthesias seem to be learned rather than organically built in, and these are called **intersensory effects** (Birch and Lef-

ford, 1963; Blank and Bridger, 1964). Whereas true synesthesias diminish with age, so that we become less likely to confuse taste and smell, sight and sound, temperature and texture, we expect an increase, at least to some maximum, in intersensory effects. We learn to judge food flavors from appearances, and it is only when we sample an alien cuisine that we are taken by surprise by flavors we had not expected. The baby apparently sees sandpaper as rough to the touch, but, to judge by his surprise when the soap bubble bursts, he did not see the latter as fragile. As far as he is concerned, there would be nothing incongruous about striking two wooden sticks together and getting a tinkling sound, or dropping a glass on a cement floor and having it land with a whoosh. He has to learn over a period of years how experience in one modality is correlated with experience in others. He has to learn, for instance, that in general, size is positively correlated with weight, but he also has to learn the exceptions, that there are big lightweight things like balloons and foam plastic rafts and eiderdown pillows,

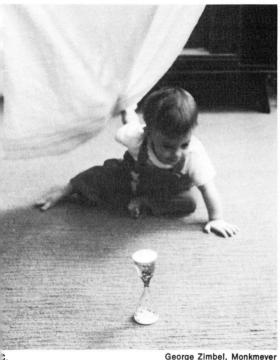

George Zimbel, Monkmeyer

and small heavy ones like chunks of gold and lead. Transfer of knowledge between modalities is a complicated matter, still incompletely mapped. For instance, a child of preschool age may be able to recognize by touch alone things that he has previously known only visually, but not the reverse: he may not recognize visually things he has previously known only by touch (Caviness and Gibson, 1962; Lobb, 1965). When, however, an object is made to look as though it is in a different location from where an adult subject's hand tells him it is, it is always the visually given location that is chosen, even when it is incorrect (Rock and Victor, 1964).

We mentioned earlier another important perceptual principle, what Piaget calls **object permanence**. The adult takes it for granted that a material object can go on existing even when not present to the senses. The young infant, by contrast, acts as though an object that has disappeared has evaporated. If one simply places a piece of cloth over a toy the infant is looking at, or lowers behind a screen a toy that the baby is following with his eyes, the infant immediately loses interest, with no sign of surprise or regret or any attempt to look for the vanished object. In other words, for babies younger than six to eight months objects lack permanence. Gratch (1972) has shown that about half of a group of six-month-olds could not continue their grip on a plaything after it was covered with an opaque cloth, and none of his subjects finished grasping an object covered during the act of reaching for it.

However, the case of permanence or impermanence is not a simple one. In the first place, it appears that certain privileged objects, such as parents, may be permanent from almost the beginning of infancy. The baby's howling at evening bedtime, at age two or three months, may imply awareness of being separated from a stable object. But there is a yet more subtle process at work. Piaget tends to conceptualize cognitive development largely as mastering concepts in mathematics and the physical sciences. An important physical concept is the law of conservation, which says that matter or energy can be transformed or dissipated but never destroyed. Thus, the child should become increasingly attuned to the stabilities and regularities of the world. But as far as the evidence of the senses goes, lots of material substantial things (without mention of dreams and sensations and smoke and mist and lights and sounds) are unstable: milk disappears from the bottle and food from the plate,

Perception in infancy and beyond

93

fat cools and congeals, ice melts, balloons shrink and shrivel, flowers bloom and wither, wastes are flushed down the toilet, water dries up or disappears down the drain. What the baby has to do is sort out the stable and the unstable, and when one considers the variety of things he encounters and the poverty of precedent he has to draw on, he does an altogether remarkable job.

Permanence used to be called **conservation**, on the analogy of the physical law. More recently, however, this term has become restricted to the conservation of quantity—number, area, and volume. The young child seems to take it for granted that when one alters the physical configuration of an array or a mass of stuff, one also changes its amount. Thus, a vertical column of three dots may not be seen as numerically equivalent to a horizontal row of three dots. Or if one changes the spacing between the dots, the child may be led to believe that the number has changed. If one pours a given volume of liquid into a container of a different shape, the child sees the change of shape as a change of quantity. These observations are not in dispute. There is, however, a flaming controversy about whether one can, by various training techniques, accelerate the child's ability to perceive quantity as constant despite various perceptual transformations. Without taking sides, we can agree with Kohnstamm (1970) that the research addressed to this question is seriously deficient on a number of counts. Even if teaching techniques could not be found to convey the idea of conservation to the child well ahead of schedule, this would still not mean that experience is of no account in its development. It seems likely that favorable experience over a period of several years might well induce conservation, even if no short-term teaching were possible. In fact, the experimenters in this field keep finding very young subjects who do conserve quite adequately.

Permanence and conservation apply to whole objects or groups of objects. But one can also talk about the conservation of the attributes of objects, which is more commonly labeled perceptual **constancy**. It is a fundamental and amazing fact that a given object looks to be the same size, shape, and color, and indeed to retain its identity as itself, under a great variety of viewing conditions. (There are also constancies in hearing, touch, and so forth, but the phenomenon is easiest to illustrate in the realm of vision.) In actuality, as an object moves toward or away from us, the image it projects on the retina changes size, but the object itself continues to appear the same size. Its color stays constant even when the illumination changes, and we see it as having the same shape even though the retinal projection undergoes all sorts of transformations. For instance, we see tables as having square corners, even though, in the customary perspectives, the corners are not projected to the retina as right angles.

There has long been a recurring controversy about whether constancy develops in the life history of the individual or is present from the start. The controversy is still unresolved, but there seem to be a few safe generalizations. First of all, we must distinguish between how objects exist for the baby as something to interact with and how they exist as objects to be contemplated. Apparently, as in the experiments mentioned above, unhandled objects are less stable than handled ones. A second distinction is between the baby's orientation to things relative to himself and to things relative to each other. For instance, in creeping or toddling through space, the baby avoids steeply pitched surfaces, seemingly in the knowledge (however ill-defined) that they will send him tumbling. (But he is as likely to try to cross a bridge made of cardboard as one made of wood.) On the other hand, as we have said, it seems to come as a surprise to him that a plaything set down on an incline will slide or roll or tumble. When it comes to grasping things and putting them in his mouth, the baby handles them appropriately with respect to size. When it comes to fitting two things together, though, or putting one thing inside another, he seems incredibly insensitive to size relations. Furthermore, size constancy seems to break down for the baby beyond a certain distance, so that the two-year-old, seeing people at the far end of the block, can point with surprise to the "little people." There is some indirect experimental support for this supposition in a study by Zeigler and Leibowitz (1957), comparing size constancy in seven-to-nine-year-olds with adults. Both groups showed approximately perfect constancy to a distance of 10 feet (3 m.); beyond that distance, constancy deteriorated, but much more so for the children than the adults. All of us, babies and adults alike, have trouble with size and distance in the up-down dimension of space. All of us are subject to the moon illusion, the fact that the moon looks much larger at the horizon than high in the sky, and most of us know the sensation of watching an airplane come in to land and seeing it jump from toy size to airplane size as it approaches. Similarly, we know that people and cars lose their reality viewed from a tall building. The baby reaches up to embrace his mother as she leans out of a third-story window, or he tries to grasp the moon. As far as we know, nobody has ever tried to study color constancy in babies, but it could be done with a discrimination-learning task.

In general, the baby's constancy is more easily tricked than the older child's or adult's, as when he fails to recognize a partly disguised parent. His judgments improve with age and experience, his coordination of objects in space becomes more accurate, and his perceptions become more objective and less affect- and action-dominated. But there is every reason to suppose that the baby begins life with a rudimentary constancy.

Two further characteristics of the world as perceived by immature human organisms deserve mention, even though we are not sure how they apply in babyhood. These are called **phenomenalism** and **dynamism**. Phenomenalism refers to the fact that babies (and many adults) seem to accept the surface appearances of things without wondering about their deeper structure. This applies particularly to learning about causal chains. The baby learns, pragmatically, a great many causal sequences: he knows how to turn a light on and off; he knows how to pour from a cup (although he may not know how to stop pouring); he knows how to turn on a radio; he knows that if he pulls the cat's tail, he is liable to get scratched, and so on. At the same time, he is not curious about their hidden mechanics. Indeed, a great many adults have no notion about what intervenes between flicking a wall switch and the shining forth of a light, of why water comes out of a faucet, of how airplanes fly, of how a car works, or even of the workings of their own bodies. One can demonstrate an interesting specimen of adult phenomenalism by asking a group of subjects to draw an island, not as it is represented on a map but as it would be seen from the side, in profile, including what is under the water as well as what is above; they are to start their drawings with a horizontal line representing the surface of the water. It turns out that almost all school-age children and a great many adults (especially females)—even well-educated adults—conceive of islands as floating, not as the peaks of mountains thrusting up from the ocean floor. A large number of subjects reveal their phenomenalism by evading the task, letting the lines showing the submerged flanks of the island peter out or run off the side of the page without coming to any resolution. We have tried this task with residents of the island of Oahu, in Hawaii, and get about the same proportion of floating and indefinite islands as with mainland dwellers.

In place of the many specific causal factors that the scientist is concerned with, the baby—or the naive adult—seems to get along with a generalized dynamism, as though the world were pregnant with some magical force that supplies the motive power for particular events. Many causal doctrines of bygone days, such as animism, animal magnetism, mesmerism, mind over matter, spiritualism, and the like, can be seen as dynamism made concrete and explicit.

Self-perception

Implicit in everything we have said so far is that perception of the world is always simultaneously perception of oneself. We perceive ourselves in several ways. Some parts of our bodies are available to visual

inspection, while other parts can be seen only with a mirror or an arrangement of mirrors, and most of what lies beneath the skin can ordinarily not be seen at all. Most of our inner anatomy has no clearcut perceptual representation for us. When we are in good equilibrium, our physiological functioning is a blend of sensations, although we can make some functions stand out, as when we attend to our breathing or our heartbeat. Various physiological imbalances have their own perceptual qualities, as in pain, aches, illness, hunger, fever, thirst, fatigue, sexual arousal, and the physiological components of emotion, such as sweating or the "butterflies in the stomach" that accompany anxiety. We experience our own behavior in terms of the spatial displacements we make and in terms of the feedback we receive from our surroundings. (We are not explicitly aware, except in difficult terrain, of the way the ground feeds back information to our feet in walking, but when that feedback is shut off, as in certain neurological conditions, walking becomes a very difficult matter.) We also experience our own behavior in terms of motivation, emotion, and esthetic and moral considerations.

In general, these self-awarenesses are blended into a total self-awareness, but we can sort out most of the constituents if we try. Somewhere in the course of development, we come to have a sense of identity, of who we are and what we believe in, what we want out of life, what our virtues and failings and competences and inadequacies are. We develop a certain amount of perspective on ourselves so that we can judge our own acts in terms both of how they look to others and of how they measure up to abstract, ideal standards; when we fail to measure up to abstract moral standards, we feel guilt, and when we fail to meet abstract standards of competence, we feel shame (Lynd, 1966). We become able, within limits, to shape our own characters and destinies, and we come to have a conscience and to be concerned for other people.

To return to the baby's self-awareness, his implicit knowledge of his own body is fairly well advanced by the end of infancy, as indicated by his ability to deal adaptively with objects. His active exploration of hands, feet, genitals, navel, and facial features seems to suggest that he has brought some parts of his body into explicit consciousness and so made them his own. He still seems peculiarly insensitive to some body states. He may, for example, carry on normally even though he has a fever or is badly chilled. When he does know that something is wrong, it may be expressed as a general malaise or a being out of sorts, as though the discomfort were not clearly represented to him. He rubs or scratches accurately at itchy patches or places where one tickles his skin with a cleaning tissue, but he may not be able to locate sharp pain such as that caused by an insect bite—he feels the pain, as we have said, but he does not seem to know where it is. By the end of infancy, he will probably respond to his own name, which is most likely the beginning of a verbal definition of self, an important ingredient in the formation of an identity. We shall have a good deal more to say about the evolution of self-awareness in later chapters.

Let us look now at the conditions, personal, social and physical, which shape development and make it possible.

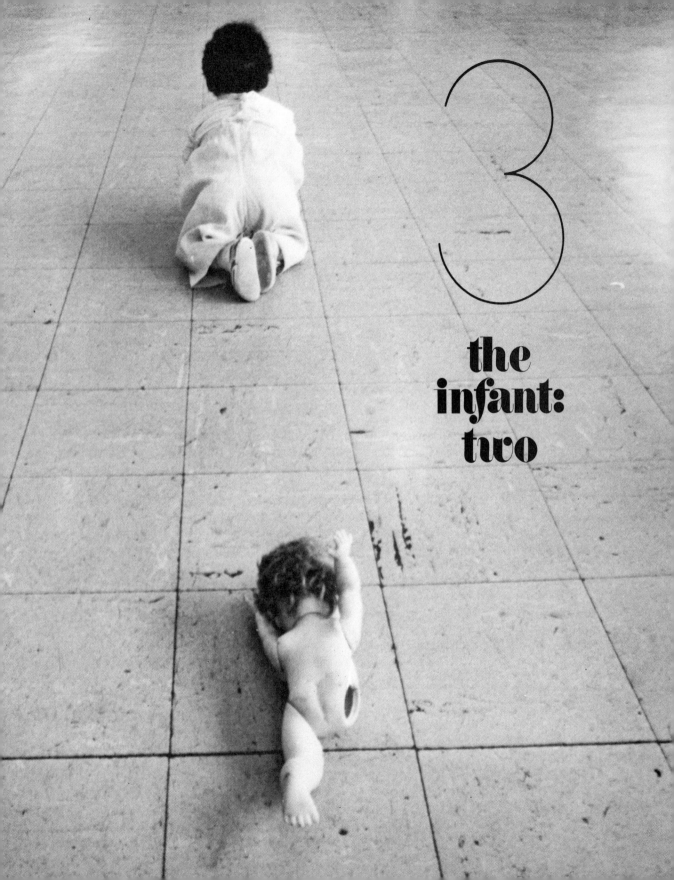

3

the infant: two

So far, we have talked about the infant's development almost as though it took place in a vacuum. In this chapter, we shall shift our focus from the baby himself to the environmental context in which he develops and in which we shall also see him after infancy. For it must be remembered that the baby is always potentially a great many different people, and which of these he becomes depends on the context in which he develops.

As in prenatal development, there are many levels of relevant context. There is the natural world of earth and vegetation and atmosphere and animal life, all linked together in cyclical exchanges of water, oxygen, nitrogen, carbon dioxide, and so forth, which make life possible. The baby, as a living organism, is part of the symbiotic whole, just as he is subject to the law of gravity and can survive only within a narrow range of atmospheric pressures. Within the natural environment there is the man-made environment of rush-mat huts and perpetual smoky fires of dung-cakes and of farms and cities and highways and vehicles and cribs and plumbing and television sets, and also institutions and ideas and knowledge and works of art, and all the more or less codified personal, economic, and political arrangements which tie societies together—often, to be sure, in antihuman ways.

The larger society does not at first act on the baby directly, but insofar as it affects his parents, it can, through them, influence his development. We shall talk more later in this chapter about culture, but we should pause here to say that even such basics as postural and motor development of the kind described in the last chapter may vary from culture to culture. Ainsworth (1967), Geber and Dean (1957),

Geber in later studies, and Kilbride et al. (1970) found evidence that Bagandan infants living in intact "bush" culture in Africa showed considerable motor precocity as compared to Europeanized, city-dwelling Bagandan babies. This precocity was sharply reversed late in the second year of life when, in keeping with local weaning practices, the child was abruptly separated from his mother, perhaps to live with his grandmother some miles away. Geber even reported precocity at birth. She stressed the influence of child-care practices on early precocity and its reversal. The neonatal findings would have to be accounted for by prenatal influences, genetic factors, or, possibly, extra-long gestation. While there has been some support for these findings from other African studies, all of these reports have been called into question by Warren (1972). Parkin and Warren (1969) did not find neonatal precocity, but their methods differed from Geber's.

Cultural conditioning apart, we must stress that parents, much as they would like to, cannot wholly regulate their baby's development. Even if we knew all the answers to how to proceed in every individual instance, and even if parents could always act according to principle and not on impulse and emotion, there would still exist the incalculables of natural disasters, epidemics, wars, economic crises, accidents, bereavements, whatever can shape a family and thus its children—including, of course, unexpected good fortune. The most conspicuous level of environment for the baby is the persons in his family and the interactions that go on among them. Parents may have to take the initiative in the earliest exchanges between baby and adult, but the baby can be a potent stimulus to parental action and can provide a good deal of feedback through his cries or his smiles of contentment or gurgles of active enjoyment. In a very short time, as J. S. Watson (1970) points out, the baby learns how to initiate and control parental reactions by his own displays of pleasure. It is out of these circular exchanges (which Watson has dubbed "The Game") that the baby's general emotional orientation to the world begins to emerge.

The Foundations of Basic Trust

Erik Erikson, whose thinking derives from Freud but who has modified the psychoanalytic scheme of psychosexual development (see pp. 175–183) along cognitive lines, has proposed that infancy is the time in which the child learns—obviously, at first in some unformulated way—whether the world is a good and satisfying place to live in or a source of pain, misery, frustration, and uncertainty. These contrasting orientations are designated as **basic trust** and **basic mistrust**. Basic trust and mistrust are initially feelings about people, but they provide the foundations for attitudes of optimism or pessimism to the world in general. The baby has physical needs, for nourishment, cleansing, sleep, warmth, and so forth. Equally important, he has psychological needs, for response, contact, cuddling, rocking, talk, play and playthings, and the various ways affection shows itself. It is the satisfaction of his needs that gives the baby a sense of the world as a good, stable, pleasant, and, ultimately, manageable place to be—in sum, basic trust. When

his needs are insufficiently met, the world takes on, to varying degrees, a dominant cast of threat and frustration—in other words, the baby develops basic mistrust. Observe that the way parents meet needs can produce either a benign or a vicious circle. The baby whose needs are reasonably well met becomes a satisfying baby who calls forth an ever-growing abundance of love and attention. The baby whose needs are not adequately met becomes irritable, demanding, and ever less lovable. An attitude of basic trust permits the development of variegated emotional responding across a full range from pleasant to unpleasant, whereas serious basic mistrust keeps emotional response in the limited range from distress to dull apathy. And out of variegated emotional functioning we would expect the growth of openness to experience and of the ability to master reality.

Note that meeting needs, especially as the baby grows older, does not always mean giving him whatever he wants the instant he wants it. A reasonable amount of delay in giving the baby a feeding or in picking him up after sleep is not going to damage him, even if he acts as though the world were coming to an end. It is when gratification is too long and too consistently delayed that panic sets in. The baby has no time perspective, the crisis seems to him to drag on interminably, he is helpless to do anything about it, and a tiny seed of distrust has been planted.

Eventually, of course, he is attended to. His panic subsides, but it leaves a residue of fear and distrust. It is not only the factual meeting of needs that counts, but the quality of the attention given to the baby. If parents are grudging, if they are hostile or impatient, their movements may

Helen Miljakovich, Nancy Palmer Agency

be rough and jerky and abrupt. If they feel anxious, their movements may be hesitant, fumbling, and erratic. Handling which lacks the definite, tenderly firm quality of a self-assured, loving parent seems to disorient and frighten a baby. The baby needs handling that expresses love and confidence. With it, he can tolerate a fair amount of normal hardship. Obviously, new parents need some practice before they can operate smoothly with their infant, and what we have said should not be interpreted to mean that there is no room for mistakes. There is bound to be some clumsiness, but within a total context of love and good will and sensitivity, initial clumsiness is of no great consequence.

Some of the things that are good for the baby hurt, like immunizing injections, and self-confident parents have to be ready to hold a squalling baby immobile while the needle goes in. Since the baby is not always a good judge of what is safe or unsafe, parents have to impose limits on his behavior. They have to help the baby sleep through the night and—gradually—to eat on a schedule approximating their own. Since an attitude of absolute trust toward a sometimes treacherous world would probably not be desirable, even if it were attainable, it may be just as well that life contains some built-in irritations and frustrations to temper a baby's basic trust, even in a benign, nurturing setting. A favorable emotional climate is not bland but temperate, with storms and seasons and rain and sunshine, mirroring family circumstances.

We should also make clear that there is no one way to love a baby. Babies are individuals and need different amounts and kinds of affection. Parents, too, are individuals and have different ways of expressing their affection. Some parents are lavish with physical demonstrations of their feelings; others are not, but still manage to convey them. Some parents are soft and tender, some are bluff and hearty, some are sober, some ironic. Furthermore, nobody can love his baby equally at all times and in all circumstances. Babies are sometimes cranky and sometimes exasperating. They can destroy the parents' sleep or a favorite treasure. What is important in terms of the baby's sense of trust is the reliability of his parents' love, the clarity with which it shows through transitory vicissitudes, through the inevitable strains and anxieties.

The evidence for the importance of early parent-child relations for basic trust as a secure foundation for later development comes from several kinds of sources. One fairly ancient tradition, drawn forcefully to our attention by such modern-day workers as Bowlby (1969), Goldfarb (1945), Ribble (1965), and Spitz (1951), and well exemplified by a study by Provence and Lipton (1962), compares babies reared in institutions with babies raised normally in their families. In general, rearing in institutions seems to have serious consequences for later emotional and intellectual development. Here we must pause to specify that we mean institutionlike institutions, not those few that seek to approximate family living conditions. Among the consequences pointed to by various observers are inconsolable distress which finally fades into blunted responsiveness, perceptual retardation, as in B. L. White's (1963) studies of visually-guided grasping, motor retardation and linguistic impairment, as in studies by Dennis and associates (e.g., Dennis and Najarian, 1957), increased susceptibility to infection, repetitive rocking and more bizarre ritualistic mannerisms, impaired learning ability, and general

 Fathers play an important role in development from infancy on.

apathy. Notice that the people who work in institutions are often not aware that anything is wrong: their charges are seen as "good" babies, quiet and undemanding and, at later ages, polite and easily managed. Salimbene gives an account of a thirteenth-century experiment by Frederick II, in which babies were deliberately subjected to institutionlike experiences, and its unforeseen results:

. . . He wanted to find out what kind of speech and what manner of speech children would have when they grew up if they spoke to no one beforehand. So he bade foster mothers and nurses to suckle the children, to bathe and wash them, but in no way to prattle with them, or to speak to them, for he wanted to learn whether they would speak the Hebrew language, which was the oldest, or Greek, or Latin, or Arabic, or perhaps the language of their parents, of whom they had been born. But he laboured in vain because the children all died. For they could not live without the petting and joyful faces and loving words of their foster mothers. And so the songs are called "swaddling songs" which a woman sings while she is rocking the cradle, to put a child to sleep, and without them a child sleeps badly and has no rest (Ross and McLaughlin, 1949).

Now it is obvious that not all institution children die, though they are more likely to than family-reared ones, and we do not even know what proportion of them find their way into mental hospitals; but it is clear that, as a rule, children raised in the barren, unstimulating setting of an orphanage are in various degrees psychologically stunted and deformed. Skeels (1966) published an extraordinary thirty-year follow-up study comparing the development of thirteen babies transferred from an orphanage to a school for defective girls, where they were individually adopted by

An orphanage in Nigeria.

Dr. Lois B. Murphy

104

the inmates, with twelve others who were left in the orphanage. All thirteen of the transferred babies had normal adult lives. Only four of those left in the orphanage became more or less normal adults, and only one finished high school and held a skilled job. It is worth noting that all twenty-five children were originally considered mentally retarded and hence unfit for adoption. In fact, eleven of those transferred were eventually adopted, whereas none of those who stayed in the orphanage were.

Yarrow et al. (1971), in a ten-year follow-up study of fifty-three adopted children, found a strong positive relationship between such maternal variables as physical contact, appropriateness of stimulation, responsiveness to the child, sensitivity to the child's individuality, and depth of emotional involvement, and favorable emotional and intellectual development in boys. The maternal variables studied had no discernible relationship to girls' development. According to Yarrow and Goodwin (1972) about half of babies show moderate to severe disturbance when transferred from a temporary foster home to a permanent adoptive home.

Some of our evidence on the importance of early experience comes from studies of infrahuman species. When we study human babies, we cannot manipulate their life histories but have to capitalize on social accidents for knowledge. With non-human animals, by contrast, we can actually manipulate their environments experimentally. Harry Harlow's (1958, 1962; Sackett, 1965) experiments in which baby rhesus monkeys were "reared" by either a roughly monkey-sized and -shaped dummy covered with soft, cuddlesome terry cloth and warmed from within by a light bulb,

B.

Mother love. A. One of Harlow's monkeys lavishes affection on his terry-cloth surrogate mother. B. A monkey stays in contact with the terry-cloth mother even as he nurses from the wire mother. C. Typical posture of monkey raised in isolation.

C.

or by a similar surrogate whose wire mesh frame was left uncovered, showed that those monkeys which had a choice of surrogates formed much stronger attachments to the terry-cloth one, which provided "contact comfort," even when it was always the bare wire frame mother which provided milk. This finding indicates that the infant's attachment to the mother is not based solely on her satisfying his hunger needs (although Igel and Calvin [1960], in a similar study with puppies, found that both contact comfort and nursing were important). Monkeys reared with terry-cloth surrogates showed much greater emotional security and curiosity than did those reared with wire mothers. The young monkey reintroduced to the terry-cloth mother after a year's separation bolts to her, embraces her, and clings passionately. Unfortunately, as we have said, the love and security gained from the terry-cloth surrogate are not a sufficient condition for normal monkey development, and Harlow's animals grew up neurotic and sexually inadequate.

A favorite research topic of recent years is **imprinting**, a term which some authors would like to generalize to all mother-child attachments, including the human (we feel that the differences are too great to apply "imprinting" to human attachments except as a metaphor). In its strict sense, imprinting refers to the bond formed between the mother and the hatchling goose or duck or chicken. Shortly after hatching, the gosling (which we may take as the prototype, although there are some species and strain differences) will follow the first moving object which comes within its field of view (the mother's calling and answering calls from the hatchlings probably also play a part [Hess, 1964]) and thereafter is attached to that particular object. Ordinarily,

the first moving object is the mother goose, but, in her absence, a football or tin can dangling from a conveyor belt, or the renowned ethologist Dr. Konrad Lorenz (who has been a pioneer in the study of imprinting) waddling, honking, and flapping his arms, will serve almost as well. We know that the gosling or baby turkey imprinted to a human being grows up to court human beings as though seeking to make them sexual partners (Lorenz, 1952; Schein and Hale, 1959). We are not aware of what effect imprinting to such inanimate objects as a tin can or a football has on the behavior of these birds as adults—it is possible that such birds end up on the experimenter's dinner table somewhat short of full maturity. The authors have wondered about the role siblings play for each other in the imprinting process, since the duck or chicken may hatch out a half-dozen young at a time, and, in theory at least, the young might be expected to imprint on one another. There is also some evidence to show that auditory experience before hatching, while the chick is still in the egg, may play a significant role in the imprinting process (Gottlieb and Kuo, 1965; Grier et al., 1967).

The case is somewhat different with higher mammals such as sheep and goats. Immediately after birth, the mother goat, presumably stimulated by her own tissue needs and the hormones present in the placenta and in the amniotic fluid coating the kid, eats the placenta and begins licking the baby. Her licking stimulates the kid into wakefulness and he staggers to his feet. Then begins a reciprocal stimulus-response sequence that has all the earmarks of a ritualized dance. The mother licks the kid from nose to tail, edging her body alongside his so that as her tongue moves down his body, he is in a position to nose along the underside of hers, ready to take hold of the nipple. However, just as he is about to nurse, the mother reaches his tail, turns around so that they are once again head to head, and the process is repeated. This goes on for two hours or more, until the mother stands still and allows the kid to nurse. Out of this stimulus-response ritual comes a stable bond between nanny and kid. If the mother and young are kept apart for as long as four hours after birth, the ritual does not take place and the attachment fails to occur. Or, if the ritual is prematurely interrupted, an odd thing happens: the kid nurses and, sated, wanders away. The next time he is hungry, however, he approaches mother goats at random, as though he did not know which was his mother, and is butted away. Even if he approaches his own mother, *she* does not recognize *him* and will not permit him to nurse. Failure to form the usual bond dooms the kid to death by starvation, or, if human beings intervene and feed him, abnormal development is likely (Blauvelt, 1955; Moore, 1960). If he is left with the flock, various neurotic symptoms appear. If he is raised in a human setting, he is permanently alienated from goat society. The effect of human rearing is especially visible in the sheep, which develops such unsheeplike traits as solitary independence (Scott, 1958).

It is believed there is a critical period (p. 32) for imprinting, so that beyond about three days after hatching, it can no longer take place. Some authors hold that the critical period for imprinting is brought to an end by the appearance of the "flight response," the tendency of the young bird to avoid unfamiliar objects after a few days of age, making impossible the proximity needed for imprinting. These experts view the flight response as the infrahuman equivalent of stranger anxiety. This position assumes that the flight response appears autogenously, as a product of maturation, as the next developmental step after an approach period. It is our view that the flight response, like all fear, is a response to strangeness, and that strangeness can only be perceived against a framework of the familiar. Thus, in our view, the young fowl which avoids normal imprinting objects does so because he has already formed a deviant attachment, as to his pen, and everything else appears strange and frightening. Indeed, Moltz and Stettner (1961) have shown that the critical period for imprinting can be considerably extended if the animal is kept in an almost structureless environment after hatching. There is also experimental evidence to show that some supposedly automatic fear reactions need not appear at all. For instance, young fowl flee panic-stricken if a hawklike form is "flown" across the barnyard, which may seem like an instinctive fear. However, Melzack and associates (1959) have shown that if young chickens are exposed to the hawk shape from the time they are hatched, this fear does not develop. Kuo (1967), likewise, has completely and permanently altered dog-cat and cat-rat relationships by manipulating early experience.

A series of studies by Denenberg and associates bears on the importance of early mother-child relationships in animal development, including the fascinating finding that male mice reared by white-rat mothers with white-rat "siblings" rarely fought with other male mice, whereas all of those reared by mouse mothers but without agemates fought when paired with another male (Denenberg et al., 1963). It further appears that the experience a female white rat has as an infant affects the emotionality

The foundations of basic trust

Mark R. Rosenzweig

Enriched rearing. A. Standard laboratory environment, with door of one cage open to show interior. B. A rat "nursery school" of the kind used in the Berkeley studies.

Mark R. Rosenzweig

of the young she later bears (Denenberg and Whimbey, 1963a).

We cannot mention all the illuminating findings from the field of animal development, but they all seem to point to the fact that manipulations of early experience, including biochemical—especially hormonal—influences, can have profound effects on physiology, temperament, sexuality, intelligence, and just about every other kind of function that has been investigated. A classic study by Forgays and Forgays (1952) shows that rats brought up in an enriched environment of other young rats, mazes, ramps, exercise wheels, swings—the best analogy is a white-rat nursery school—are brighter than rats reared in ordinary bare laboratory cages. (The methods of assessing intellectual differences among rats are as open to question as those used with humans, but we will not labor the point here.) This kind of study has been extended by C. J. Smith (1959), who found that rats raised in an enriched environment showed specialized functioning of brain tissue, while rats reared in an unstimulating cage environment did not, and by Bennett et al. (1964), who found differences in brain biochemistry associated with rearing conditions. Thompson (Thompson and Schaefer, 1961) was among the first to show that "gentling," daily handling by the human experimenter, affected the animal's emotional development—the age of the animal and the nature of the gentling seem to determine whether the animal is made more or less fearful.

S. Levine (1962) has shown that stress to the mother during pregnancy (as by electric shock or immersion in cold water), or to the young animal, increases adrenal gland size and activity and can affect body weight. He has also found (Levine, 1969) that human handling affects the relationship between animal mother and child. Schneirla and his associates (Rosenblatt et al., 1961) demonstrated estrangement in young kittens removed temporarily from the litter; Scott and Fuller (Scott, 1962; Scott and Fuller, 1965) have shown impaired social relations (to human beings as well as dogs) in dogs reared in isolation; Ader (1962) found that rats weaned early are more susceptible to gastric ulcers than rats weaned later; whereas LaBarba et al. (1970) found that early weaning increases resistance to carcinoma in mice. Kavanau (1967) showed that wild deer mice are immeasurably brighter than those reared in the laboratory—indeed, he claims that learning in wild mice is more like that of monkeys and apes than of the mice most people study. Kavanau also confirms the observation of others that mice resist being forced to do things, and apparently function best when they can control the environment.

Sometimes the significant manipulations are unintentional, as demonstrated in studies by, among others, Denenberg and Whimbey (1963b) and Hatch et al. (1963). Extra-experimental animal husbandry practices, including such seemingly innocuous things as how often one changes the shavings in the cage, can affect development. An important implication of these findings is that animals raised in typical laboratory conditions are liable to be sick or feebleminded, which has a bearing on how we interpret medical and psychological research done with such animals.

On the borderline between animal and human development are so-called feral children, supposed to have been raised by and to have identified with wild animal foster parents. Accounts of all such cases seem to be either fraudulent or erroneous (Evans, 1958; Ogburn and Bose, 1959), so the reader is warned to treat skeptically tales about "wolf boys" and "antelope girls." On the other hand, there have been a number of well-authenticated cases of "closet children" (Montagu, 1955, ch. 11), brought up with virtually no contact with the world outside the space in which they were confined, and the severe physical and psychological deficits these children showed. In at least one such case, a six-and-a-half-year-old girl who had been isolated with her mute mother and had no language, there was marked progress in language development after twenty-two months of special instruction (Mason, 1942), and at age fourteen she appeared to be a normal seventh-grader (K. Davis, 1947; Stone, 1954).

A third set of findings on the effects of early parent-child relations, with implications for the formation of basic trust, comes from studies which seek to relate specific child-care practices, such as ways of managing feeding or toilet training or discipline, to particular personality traits later in life. A review by Caldwell (1964) shows that our faith in this approach has been largely disappointed and it should probably be abandoned. This is not to say that such practices have no effect. We know from animal studies that maternal temperament has a powerful impact on the young, but we know next to nothing about the significant specifics of child care. It seems probable that it is the total quality of parental behavior, expressed, as we have said, in such things as smooth and assured or nervous and erratic or angry and impatient handling, in tones of voice, in amount of talking and play, that makes the most difference (Klatskin et al., 1956). White and his associates (Litman, 1969; LaCrosse, 1969) describe five types of mothers whose caretaking they relate to children's current

The foundations of basic trust

and later competence: the competent, the almost competent, the overwhelmed, the rigid and controlling, and the smothering mother. A major ingredient of maternal competence, as in the study by Yarrow cited earlier, seems to be the ability to attune oneself to the baby in a smooth flow of reciprocal feedback which helps the baby make sense of the world and himself. In general, it is very hard to study antecedent-consequent relations in human development simply because so many things impinge on the total process, even if we could be sure we were getting accurate information about child-rearing attitudes and practices, which some studies suggest we cannot. Retrospective studies are especially suspect (Burton, 1970; Haggard et al., 1960; Pyles et al., 1935).

Schaefer (1965) has analyzed some of the global styles of mothering in what he calls a "spherical model." In this scheme, the mother's behavior toward the child is scored on each of the three intersecting dimensions of acceptance–rejection, psychological control–psychological autonomy, and firm control–lax control. Within the "conceptual space" defined by these dimensions one can locate points representing such maternal orientations as acceptance of individuation, loving involvement, protectiveness, intrusiveness, and hostile indifference.

This is an ingenious and useful scheme, but it does not go far enough. It makes no provision for cognitive stimulation, opportunities and encouragements to explore space, objects and their qualities of taste and texture and pliability and weight and shape, and the relations among objects, the way they come apart and fit together and move and act on each other, and the sensations that arise inside the baby's own body. It omits the way parents convey values to babies, telling by their own behavior what is wicked or virtuous, beautiful or ugly, important or trivial, nasty or nice, and all the other qualities that give meaning to life. It is silent on the extent to which maternal behavior is a product of individual personality or is dictated by cultural convention. Within our own society, for instance, there are well-defined differences in child-rearing practices associated with social class (Tulkin, 1970). It does not tell us how or whether the mother sees her treatment of the child in relation to what kind of person she would like him to become. Perhaps the chief lack, though, is that it puts the full onus of responsibility on the mother. This is in line with most people's thinking, as though the mother deserves all the credit when her children turn out well and all the blame when they come to a bad end. This view leaves out of account, first, the role of the father, both directly, in his dealings with the child, and indirectly, in his sharing of the common family enterprise and in the support—or lack of it—that he gives the mother. It ignores family circumstances that may affect maternal behavior, such things as money problems, illness, competing demands from other children, or simple ignorance of how to care for babies. It says nothing about the presence or absence of in-laws who may be helpful or harassing. Finally, it leaves the baby a cipher in the family equation.

How babies get treated by their parents is in some measure a product of the baby's own qualities, actual or perceived. We have assumed too easily that caretaking patterns spring directly from parental personalities, forgetting the extent to which the baby as stimulus regulates his parents. A review by Harper (1971) shows that control by the infant is a widespread phenomenon among mammals. Bell (1968, 1971) has been one of the more forceful spokesmen for the need to take account of the feelings different babies evoke in their caretakers. Moss (1967) points to the way the baby's sex, age, and momentary state modify maternal behavior. Rothbart and Maccoby (1966) have shown that both fathers and mothers react differently to sons and daughters. Some babies call forth cuddling, and others actively resist it (Schaffer and Emerson, 1965). Babies vary in physical attractiveness, too. It is not enough to say that there are some babies only a mother could love. There are some babies who, for whatever reason, do not call forth love in their own particular mothers or fathers.

Apart from characteristics of the baby, parents themselves may have reasons of their own for not responding. They may be so immersed in other concerns that they are insensitive to whatever charms the baby may have. The baby may remind his mother too vividly of her own carnal nature, he may have come at the wrong time in her marriage, he may look like a hated adult of her childhood, or he may symbolize the end of carefree youth and of beauty. And such influences may be powerful without ever coming clearly into awareness. Fortunately, such reactions are the exception. As Rheingold (1969a) states, the baby socializes his parents as much as they socialize him: "of men and women he makes fathers and mothers."

We have been speaking of conditions which are more or less conducive to the formation of basic trust and normal emotional and intellectual development. The lack of favorable conditions used to be ascribed to "maternal deprivation." In fact, as we can see, a great many kinds of deprivation may be involved besides those that go with loving maternal care and stimulation. The baby may be deprived of sensory stimulation in general, like adult subjects who are experimentally shut off from the customary—if largely unnoticed—barrage of sights, sounds, kinesthetic and skin stimulation, and the information these bring. Most adult subjects in conditions of extreme sensory deprivation disintegrate psychologically. We would assume that babies kept isolated from the world, whether in institutions or simply neglected at home, would also suffer sensory deprivation and so would have limited opportunities to explore the material world and to acquire ways of symbolizing experience. But even babies given abundant social and emotional stimulation may be denied opportunities for exploration and mastery, and may be exposed to only the most primitive models for language development; these children suffer what we might call cognitive deprivation. We shall return to this topic throughout the book, since adequate stimulation seems crucial to fully human development. It does not follow, though, that the more stimulation the better. It has been observed in many poor families, who are likely to live in overcrowded conditions, that babies may suffer from stimulus overload, a chaotic welter of noise and activity that overwhelms the baby's capacity for taking in and digesting information.

We have been talking about things that might be missing from the lives of babies who could belong to parents of great good will, but we must also mention that some parents at some times are not parents of good will, and pediatricians and emergency ward doctors recognize the "**battered child syndrome.**" Statistics are hard to keep and compare, but it is clear that a lot of brutality gets practiced on children, including neonates and infants. The known cases of such abuse in the United States are increasing, perhaps because of recent laws requiring doctors to report cases and freeing them of legal liability in doing so. It seems reasonable to assume that most people who practice damaging violence on children are seriously disturbed or are persons under unbearable pressures and tensions, for whom the cries of a hungry or sick or lonely baby are the last nerve-shattering turn of the screw; and the chances are that such people didn't really want the baby in the first place. In some cases, however, child-beating expresses a stark and cold-blooded moralism which seeks to purge the baby of its supposed selfishness and perversity. Whatever the parental motives, the consequences are dire. Elmer (1967) and Elmer and Gregg (1967) report that half of a sample of twenty abused children were retarded, and eight of the other ten below normal. It further appears that punitively reared children fail to develop normal self-control, which fits with the common observation that violence is likely to breed violence, even if it succeeds in producing short-term submission. A study by Sherbert Frazier (Johnson, 1971) of ninety convicted murderers found that they had all been victims of severe abuse as children. It is also clear that many people who beat babies to the point of injury or death could, in more favorable conditions, cherish and care for those same babies perfectly well. These extremes should not distract us from the fact that most parents convey, and most babies learn, an orientation of basic trust.

In this context, we should mention programs of **cognitive enrichment** for infants and toddlers, designated to compensate for and counteract the kinds of deprivation we have been talking about (Gordon, 1969; Karnes et al., 1970; Schaefer, 1969;

Weikart and Lambie, 1969). There are three main approaches to infant enrichment. One approach seeks to train mothers to provide more of the appropriate kinds of stimulation (and materials) that babies need. A second sends "tutors" into the home at regular intervals to work directly with the baby. A third aims to make intellectual stimulation an integral part of programs of day care (Caldwell, 1971; Keister, 1970). All of these approaches have had some success. There is current agitation for a rapid expansion of day care facilities in this country, on the model of those in Israel, France, and the U.S.S.R. While there is much to be said for the day care movement, its more fervent supporters are liable to overlook three important considerations. First, good day care centers are very expensive to operate; a number of ambitious commercial ventures in this field have gone under rapidly. Second, it is no trifling matter to train competent workers for day care centers, especially if one wants these centers to yield positive benefits for the child, and not merely to do him no harm. Third, there appears to be diminishing enthusiasm for day care centers in some countries where they already exist (Anonymous, March 22, 1971). An incidental consideration is that one of the purposes of day care, to free mothers to work, loses much of its point if there are no jobs to be had.

Changing Trends in Child Care

People have been giving and receiving advice on how to rear children at least from Biblical times, as witness the injunction to "Spare the rod and spoil the child." Until relatively recently, though, people have simply known and taken for granted, on the basis of tradition, what should be done to and for children. Let us make clear that these givens of folk wisdom were by no means the same from one society to the next, or even in different segments of complex societies, but each group had its own tradition-sanctioned ways. Obviously, these ways had enough validity to keep the species going, but the historical record of large-scale human folly, depravity, pettiness, and cruelty gives us reason to think that improvements can be made.

In stable societies, where relatives are likely to live close together and to act collaboratively as an extended family, there are abundant opportunities to observe and absorb the accustomed practices of the society. In modern European societies, and most particularly in the United States since the end of World War I, where there is a great deal of economic and geographical mobility, and where each generation is supposed to outgrow the inadequacies of the one before, families fragment and there is limited occasion to transmit and acquire (or even to find consensus on) the culturally accepted ways of dealing with children—or of doing many other things besides. Increasingly, it is assumed that one learns personal and social functions and skills and values from schools and books and newspaper columns and magazines addressed to special groups—women or teen-agers—in sum, from the Expert. This despite the fact that American anti-intellectualism simultaneously contains a strand of contempt for the expert—the farmer once sneered at the agronomist, the office worker at the efficiency expert and, more recently, the systems analyst, the businessman at the economist or organizations theorist, and, above all, the parent and

Ken Heyman

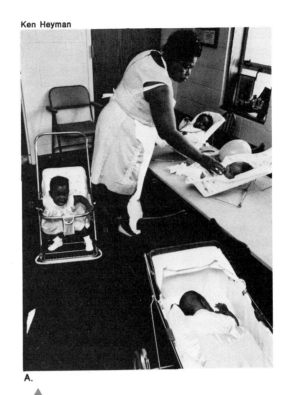

A.

Day care. A. United States. B. Hungary.

B.

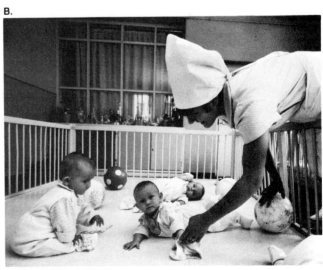

Ken Heyman

113

grandparent at the child psychologist or psychiatrist. In the folklore, it was assumed that the child-care expert was a bachelor or old maid who would disintegrate if saddled with the actual responsibilities of looking after a child. Nevertheless, advice to parents has long been a readily marketable commodity and is supplied in never-abating plenty—along with the latest gadgets—to an insatiably avid public.

The apparent conflict between disdain for the expert and a servile seeking for his counsel may perhaps be reconciled by noting two things. First, parents are truly uncertain of themselves and badly want guidance. Second, they seem to seek out and listen to those experts, or those parts of a given expert's preachments, that best suit their own opinions. That is, they are looking for confirmation for what they already do, rather than for new ways of doing things. David Levy (1954) has discussed how mothers both fail to comprehend pediatricians' recommendations and, in addition, act only on so much of what they comprehend as suits their own ideas. Even when they try, people are likely to grasp unfamiliar notions in a distorted way, and the authors, when cast in the roles of experts and teachers, have seen their own ideas come back to them in some very strange guises indeed.

Mothers were told in a 1912 treatise (Clock, 1912) that babies should not be breast-fed if the mother had hysteria or epilepsy, that worry, anxiety, and nervous excitement poisoned the mother's milk (they may indeed interfere with lactation), that constipation in the nursing mother produced constipation in the baby, that breast milk was exhausted after about seven months (apparently this expert had never heard of the societies in which chil-

dren are nursed up to age three or four years), that pacifiers produced "great harm" as well as disease, that if one started toilet training at age six weeks one might reasonably hope that the job would be completed, with "much patience and perseverance," by age eighteen months (it apparently didn't occur to anyone then, despite what actual experience might have taught them, that one might start toilet training at age seventeen months and finish the job thirty days later). Between ages one and two years the baby's diet was to consist of fruit, fluids, toast, soup, and gruel. No meat could be given before age two, after which, up to age three, the child might have some scraped beef or white meat of chicken.

If these prescriptions sound slightly unreal today, when babies are given synthetic formula at below room temperature from a disposable bottle, when baby foods are given from early infancy and by age ten months the American baby is gnawing beef from a bone or eating chicken livers and rice or chunks of cheddar cheese, probably some of our current beliefs will seem fully as antiquated in another few years. For this reason, the reader is asked always to exercise a proper skepticism. It is also worth emphasizing that in 1912 only about 80 percent of babies born alive lived to see their first birthday; that there were not at that time techniques and widespread centers for immunization against whooping cough, diphtheria, poliomyelitis, measles, and the like; there were no antibiotics; and sanitary conditions were far more primitive than they are today, all of which justified a preoccupation with physical health.

One can follow the shifting currents of expert advice on child care, along with changes in underlying values, in successive editions of the United States Government manual *Infant Care* (U.S. Department of Health, Education, and Welfare, Children's Bureau), first published in 1914. (Martha Wolfenstein [1951], who has traced these changes, has summarized them as the "emergence of fun morality," whereby it is—or was in the 1950s—not only all right to have a good time, but morally obligatory.) The early editions are in keeping with the spirit of John B. Watson, the father of behaviorist psychology in the United States. Behaviorism sought to place psychology on a secure scientific footing by eliminating from consideration all such elusive subjective states as motives, will, urges, cravings, ideas, intentions, aspirations, and the like, and by confining study to the directly observable and measurable behavior of the organism. In this view, all behavior is externally determined (or at least triggered) by unconditioned and conditioned stimuli, and stable, recurring behavior patterns are seen as habits. Thus, the main goal in this framework of child-rearing is to instill the proper habits and to avoid teaching undesirable ones. The flavor of Watson's thinking is given in the following widely quoted passage:

There is a sensible way of treating children. Treat them as though they were young adults. Dress them, bathe them with care and circumspection. Let your behavior always be objective and kindly firm. Never hug and kiss them, never let them sit in your lap. If you must, kiss them once on the forehead when they say good night. Shake hands with them in the morning. Give them a pat on the head if they have made an extraordinarily good job of a difficult task. Try it out. In a week's time you will find how easy it is to be perfectly objective with your child and at the same time kindly. You will be utterly ashamed of the mawkish, sentimental way you have been handling it (Watson, 1928).

Oddly enough, though, this streamlined mechanistic view managed to incorporate a Victorian or even medieval moralism according to which the baby was a greedy, scheming, power-mad creature in whom filthy, bestial habits could and would crop up without warning if the parent did not *nip it in the bud* but turned maudlin and indulgent. Something of the rigor of the habit-training way of thinking is given in this quotation from the 1938 edition of *Infant Care*, by which time the habits approach was already coming to be regarded by many people as obsolete:

. . . Immediately after birth he will begin to form habits, which if they are the right kind will be useful to him all his life. Regularity from birth on is of first importance.

Through training in regularity of feeding, sleeping, and elimination . . . the tiny baby will receive his first lessons in character building. He should learn that hunger will be satisfied only so often, that when he is put into his bed he must go to sleep, that crying will not result in his being picked up or played with whenever he likes. He will begin to learn that he is part of a world bigger than that of his own desires.

It is not simply that love and affection were left unemphasized; they were regarded by Watson and like-minded thinkers as downright insidious, as Watson indicates:

In conclusion won't you then remember when you are tempted to pet your child that mother love is a dangerous instrument? An instrument which may inflict a never healing wound, a wound which may make infancy unhappy, adolescence a nightmare, an instrument which may wreck your adult son or daughter's vocational future and their chances for marital happiness (Watson, 1928, p. 87).

While Watson was properly modest in his claims for the efficacy of his procedures, he saw as the outcome ". . . a child as free as possible of sensitivities to people and one who, almost from birth, is relatively independent of the family situation" (Watson, 1928, p. 186). One is tempted to infer that Watson himself had been deeply hurt in his interpersonal relations and proposed this almost psychopathic style of life as a defense against pain.

In the next chapter, we shall describe in some detail various theoretical orientations to behavior and development. Here we must mention them insofar as they played a part in the advice on child-rearing given to parents. Sigmund Freud was an influential figure who, although he came into prominence in avant-garde psychiatric and literary circles before Watson's time, became a competing force in American child psychology only in the 1920s. Freudian doctrines underwent a subtle sea change in traveling from Europe to the United States. Freud had a pessimistic, Victorian, moralistic outlook and saw man fated by his animal nature to live in lust and violence until the slow process of social evolution would remake him into a truly human being. Americans misinterpreted Freud's emphasis on animality (perhaps in the context of Darwinian thought) as an endorsement, and libertarians rallied round the Freudian banner in opposition to the supposed puritanism of Watson's behaviorism. In the American version of Freud's teachings man is made neurotic by the arbitrary, artificial restraints imposed by society on the free expression of impulses; and the secret of successful child-rearing as popularized in the 1930s and 1940s was

to avoid frustrating and inhibiting the child. Aggression was seen as the product of frustration, and not, as in Freud's own later version, as internally motivated by a death-wish or drive to destruction. (Notice how Freud's view of aggression, and the need to sublimate it in nondestructive activities, is echoed by latter-day instinct theorists like Konrad Lorenz.) What seems to have happened is that Freudian psychology thrived in the United States when grafted onto the thinking of anthropologists like Ruth Benedict and Margaret Mead, who stressed the crucial role of the social and cultural environment for the formation of character. The merger of anthropology and psychoanalysis is most clearly seen in the writings of such authors as Erik Erikson, Erich Fromm, and Karen Horney, who have been much more sociological and environmentalistic in their views (as was Freud's one-time associate Alfred Adler) than traditional Freudians. Sometimes, though, the anthropological view of human nature has been anticultural and has taken the form of Romantic Naturalism, first set forth by Jean Jacques Rousseau and happily embraced by some of the less discriminating progressive educators, which says that the ideal condition for man is that of the happy, noble savage living in a state of nature. This view is strongly implicit in some of the writings of Ashley Montagu and also in the nonanthropological works of Arnold Gesell and his collaborators. The Romantic-Naturalist child contains in himself the seeds of successful development, and to impose the outworn moralities and ideologies of a decadent society is to threaten the child's well-being at its very core. Notice that Gesell and Montagu owe less to Freud than do the anthropologically oriented psychoanalysts and the psychoanalytically oriented anthropologists, but their prescriptions for child-rearing are very similar.

One other strand that should be mentioned is John Dewey's pragmatism, which merely said that much of what we teach children is obsolete and of no earthly use to them, but which got interpreted by some people to mean that we should teach children only practical skills, as in Life Adjustment courses or in vocational education. Dewey was not particularly concerned with infancy, but his teachings were very much in the air in the 1920s and 1930s.

B. F. Skinner, about whose thinking we shall have more to say in the next chapter and who describes himself as a radical neobehaviorist, proposes in his Utopian novel *Walden Two* (1948) another ideal system of child-rearing based on several assumptions. First of all, human behavior is thought of as shaped by forces lying outside the organism, either in stimuli present at the time of behavior or else in its past history. Notions of self-control, self-determination, will, and purpose are delusions with which people needlessly torment themselves. One behaves as one does because initially random acts set off by need states are selectively reinforced (rewarded) in terms of whether they serve to reduce the need. Eventually, the organism learns which instrumental acts (called by Skinner **operants**) work in which circumstances, and behavior becomes orderly, effective, and to all appearances sensible. To find happiness, one should surrender control to a scientifically engineered society in which child-rearing according to the principles of operant conditioning will insure cooperative, industrious, conflict-free, and ideology-free individuals who will while away their leisure hours with art and music and suchlike creative endeavors.

Children are taught by being rewarded for socially useful behavior, whereas aberrant behavior receives no response of any kind and so withers away for lack of external reinforcement. (Internal reinforcement or token reinforcement works only after learning has taken place with real reinforcers.) Punishment should not be used, because it inhibits only the overt act, not the tendency to perform that act, which tendency is perpetuated by the reinforcing effect of punishment. Children are taught to work for delayed reinforcement, and thus to tolerate inevitable frustrations and delays, by gradually stretching out the interval between operant act and reward. Like many Utopia-makers, Skinner paints a coolly rational or rationalistic world without guts, without strong passions, without illness or grief or jealousy, without responsibility or the need to make decisions. One would gather that sexuality in the Walden Two colony is a bloodless coupling for purposes (in Skinner's system, societies are allowed to have purposes, even if individuals are not) of carefully programed reproduction, and such humor as is practiced is of a dry, cerebral, pedantic sort.

More than a few people find Skinner's vision appealing to the point of wanting to found Walden Twos of their own. It is a pity, therefore, to have to express the conviction that the bland bliss of Walden Two is probably unattainable. It is almost certainly unattainable by Skinner's means, since his principles of learning, while highly useful and correct for application to a narrow range of conditions, are inadequate and irrelevant for much of the important learning that goes on in life. Sylvia Bell (1971) has shown, for instance, that responding to a baby's crying does not reinforce and so increase crying, but instead reduces it. Chomsky (1959) has pointed out that if one had to learn language according to Skinner's rules, a whole lifetime might go by before one acquired the simplest rudiments. Solomon's (1963) studies on the effects of punishment yield results contrary to what Skinner would predict, and so on down the line. This is not to discourage people from seeking the Nirvana of Walden Two, but to apprise them that they may meet difficulties.

Skinner's system apart, by the late 1940s doctrinaire approaches to child-rearing were almost a thing of the past, and the needs-centered, down-to-earth, humane eclecticism of Benjamin Spock (a psychoanalytically trained but pragmatic pediatrician and psychiatrist) had swept the field. Spock's frequent injunction to "Enjoy your baby!" may smack of the fun morality we mentioned earlier, but it certainly makes a lot better sense than what has been dubbed "self-conscious parenthood," which smacks of drudgery and fear and indecision. For as various doctrines of development have threatened all sorts of dire consequences stemming from unfortunate infantile experiences, and as traditional ways have slipped out of the twentieth-century grasp, many parents have become unable to act without endless soul-searching and worrying about what later effects this or that way of acting will have. In general, parents who have a certain amount of confidence in themselves and in their babies operate every bit as well by intuition as the self-conscious parent who holds the baby with one hand, delaying a decision while the forefinger of the other hand runs through the index in Dr. Authoritative's *Manual of Expert Child Care*.

It comes as a surprise to many parents to realize that, if they know in general what to expect of a baby at different ages and what his needs and capabilities are,

the baby pretty well instructs them what to do if they will only learn to read his "language of behavior." He will not automatically be "spoiled" by the attempt to understand him; automatic indulgence and unswerving habit-training are far greater dangers.

This language takes two forms. First, there is the expressive quality of the manifestations of the baby's distress. From a very early age, the baby's cries of hunger, fatigue, anger, pain, and so forth, are fairly easy to tell apart. Sometimes there are postural cues. For instance, it is sometimes hard to tell whether the baby's cries signify hunger or colic, but the baby tends to stretch out and arch his back when hungry, and to double up in the throes of colic. The second form of the language of behavior is the feedback a parent receives from the baby when trying to meet its needs. If the parent tries to feed a colicky baby, the baby may indeed try briefly to nurse, but after a few swallows will spit out the nipple and resume crying, indicating that the adult has not yet singled out the right need and its remedy. Of course, it is not merely the turning off of crying that guides parental behavior, but also the baby's smiles and gurgles of satisfaction.

By late infancy, the baby can make dialogues with his parents more nearly explicit. By reaching out his arms and straining in the general direction of something he wants, usually to the accompaniment of shrieks or murmurs, he can convey that he wants something and where the adult should look for it. Characteristically, the adult offers the baby likely objects; wrong guesses are met by brief, angry shrieks; when the right object is offered, the baby accepts it with a grunt of satisfaction. We have already spoken of how the baby becomes able to initiate social games. At a still more advanced, but still prelinguistic, stage, the baby can communicate with tokens. If he tries to climb into his feeding table, it signifies that he is hungry; he may bring a phonograph record that he wants to hear played; he brings his coat or sweater as a way of saying that he wants to go out. Notice the analogy here with the dog who brings his dish to announce his hunger, or his leash to request a walk, or a stick to be thrown and retrieved. Even the mooing of the cows as they crowd around the pasture gate at dusk tells us that they are ready to return to the barn for milking.

When we stop to think about it, we take it for granted that we can read the language of behavior of, for instance, cats, dogs, and horses, and respond appropriately, so it should hardly be surprising that the behavior of young human beings can make sense to us—especially since they have not yet learned our many devices for covering up our true feelings. In general, in all our roles as adult human beings we respond not only to the words people speak but to the total array of information they transmit in everything they do. We read their motives, pretensions, doubts, and hidden feelings in their gestures, posture, tone of voice, dress—in short, in their language of behavior—and we can in the same way take cues from the baby.

Issues in Infant Care

While the main aim of this book is descriptive rather than prescriptive—that is, it seeks to tell the reader what children are like and how they develop, rather than how to live with them or manage them or mold them—talking about practical applications should help clarify our particular way of looking at children. It is our conviction that a concern with practical questions keeps science alive and reality-bound, and even though we cannot claim omniscience, we can at least point out where some common practices are founded on fallacy. In addition, the discussion of practical problems is the best framework in which to present some further substantive facts of behavior and development. While we shall be talking about infancy in general, the reader should keep in mind that parental practices have to change as the infant develops.

Attention, spoiling, and discipline

Perhaps as a carry-over from the "habits" era, many parents still fear that they may give the baby too much attention, thereby spoiling him and giving him the upper hand in parent-child relations. And when it comes to discipline, the ambivalence of parents is enough to shake them in two. On the one hand, lack of discipline is thought to produce tyrannical, egotistical monsters with a whim of iron and a bulldozer approach to human relations. On the other hand, in keeping with the teachings of Romantic Naturalism, discipline will mar and embitter the child and teach him to be a cringing, obsequious authoritarian —and cause him to hate his parents, who seem to fear being found out by the analyst thirty years later.

When babies cry, it is because they need something, not that they (or we) always know what. Among the things they need is human attention, initially in great abundance. "Attention," after all, is nothing but the loving closeness and stimulation that we have been talking about. It is out of attention that powerful bonds grow up between adult and child, and it is these bonds that make later communication possible—including the communication involved in discipline. It is possible that some adults are put off by so intimate a relationship, even with a baby, or are afraid of the unfamiliar potency of the emotions that go with it, and it is for such reasons that they are reluctant to give the baby a full measure of "attention."

Usually, with the one exception of evening bedtime (once the baby has given evidence that he is ready to sleep the night through), spoiling does not seem to be an issue in infancy. Later in childhood, over-indulgence—particularly of an undiscriminating, buying-favor sort, unrelated to the child's needs—can certainly have some untoward effects, but babies thrive on genuine attention and the handling, talking, singing, and all the rest, that go to make it up. As the baby becomes more secure about the solidity and reliability of his personal relations, he himself will be able to turn away from preoccupation with his parents and move into an active exploration of his nonhuman surroundings, returning from time to time to enjoy his parents' company on an ever more mature basis. It is a hangover from the habit-training view that sees the baby never stopping demanding what he is given now. If anything, the greatest danger at this age is probably the failure to satisfy the baby's cravings for attention, leading to an increased need which, like the neurotic needs of adults, becomes at the extreme insatiable. In other words, premature attempts to cultivate the baby's "powers of self-reliance" may have exactly the opposite effect.

In general, amply loved babies are not interested in getting the better of anybody. As we shall discuss later, our society teaches us two versions of human nature, and the one that many people seem to learn best is that human beings are innately selfish, competitive, and out to do in others before they get done in themselves. By the magic of the self-fulfilling prophecy, that is a kind of person our society produces in great plenty. However, there is nothing inherent in the baby that causes him to seek dominance over others. Basic trust works both ways, and parents have to have some faith in the baby. The self-fulfilling prophecy works both ways, too, and, as a rule, babies are loving, sympathetic, and generous in direct proportion to their having been treated lovingly, sympathetically, and generously—and in terms of their real needs. Hence, both Watson and Rousseau find justification—and contradiction. For there is a well-meaning but oversolicitous kind of mother who hurries to do something about every expression of discomfort before either the baby or mother has a chance to find out what, if anything, is really called for. Often she seems to be seeking the child's explicit gratitude for her maternal ministrations. In this way, the wrong need may get gratified, leaving the baby with a vague, restless dissatisfaction that may later come out as "spoiled" behavior. A similar pattern may originate in parental insecurity: the mother feels so inadequate, or is so afraid of losing the baby's love, or feels so guilty about a lack of genuine affection for him, that she gratifies his needs blindly. Spoiling may also result from capricious teasing, or inconsistent meetings of needs, leaving the child fearful that he may never get what he wants, and dissatisfied when he gets it. Teasing is usually described disapprovingly as what some other cultures do to babies, but it is only necessary to watch American parents and American visitors to see how much we enjoy getting a rise out of children of all ages, even though we are "only kidding."

Even if it is true that unstinting affection and need-gratification in infancy do produce a trusting, affectionate, essentially cooperative individual, parents tend to wonder, won't such an individual be so badly disqualified for life in our savagely competitive society that we will have done him a disservice? In answer, there is reason to think that warm-hearted people who are ready to like and trust other people need not aways end up as victims. It is not usually the person who has developed self-respect who turns into a doormat or a punching-bag for others. There remains, besides, a question of values, of whether parents want their child to grow up pretty much like everybody else, or whether they want him to approach some ideal of the human condition, even at the risk of some strain and conflict with his surroundings. Conformity begins in infancy.

The bonds of trust and affection that grow out of attention and need-gratification greatly simplify problems of discipline in infancy. During the first year, discipline is largely a matter of keeping the child apart from things that might injure him or which he is likely to destroy. Infants have no sense of property, their own or other people's. They may develop fetishistic attachments to dolls and blankets, but their main concern with objects is having access to them so that they can explore them. The baby who has lots of opportunity to poke into things does not feel more than momentarily aggrieved when some things are forbidden to him. Nor does he cease loving the parents who remove forbidden objects from his grasp or tell him "No!" as he reaches for something that cannot be kept out of his grasp. In general, parents who love their baby and have their baby's welfare at heart need not fear losing the baby's love or doing him an injury by acting like strong adults. There is no doubt that child-rearing demands some self-sacrifice on the part of parents, but self-sacrifice has to be balanced by a decent respect for their own needs as adults.

Feeding and scheduling

In other cultures, in the more ignorant and less expert-ridden areas of our own society, and even in middle-class American society sixty years ago, before the habit-formers proclaimed their doctrines of regularity, the usual practice was to feed babies when they were hungry, subject to the reservation that the mother's breast milk might not be ready at the time the baby grew hungry. In the past half century, middle-class society has been through a revolution and a counterrevolution, plus a few incidental upheavals. The habits approach, basing its dicta on some rather flimsy statistics purporting to show the average time it takes babies' stomachs to empty (not even the time it takes the average baby's stomach to empty), called for a strict schedule, from the time the baby came home from the hospital, of feeding every four hours on the dot (some physicians prescribed three-hour intervals for very small or immature babies), whether the baby had been screaming with hunger for an hour past or was so sound asleep that he had to be jiggled and prodded awake.

A.

B.

▲

Nursing. A. Bottle-feeding. B. Breast-feeding, United States. C. Breast-feeding, Indonesia.

Beyond the daily timetable to which a mother was to adhere religiously, the authorities plotted out well in advance a calendar schedule telling when all babies were to be weaned and when introduced to which new foodstuffs.

Partly because the mechanistic rigidities of the habits approach went against the parental grain (although many parents went doggedly ahead applying the methods of "science," no matter what their own feelings might be, and others who departed from the Right Way felt guilty about their lack of character), and partly in response to the naturalistic teachings of the anthropologists, **demand feeding**, based on the parents' perceptions of when the baby is actually hungry, began to supersede scheduled feeding, both in what parents did and in what pediatricians prescribed. One of the discoveries that emerged is that demand feeding, with a very little assistance from parents, moves

toward a stable scheduling according to which the baby consumes more food at more widely spaced intervals until he comes into equilibrium with the accepted patterns of his culture. That is, social patterns set the cycle of hunger and satiety that are one component in his biological clock.

One incidental issue that has now been fairly well resolved in principle is the dispute between the breast-feeders and the bottle-feeders. We suspect that the evangelistic zeal of the bottle-feeders during the behaviorist era expressed a complex of attitudes. There may have been a conviction that bottle-feeding was sanitary, whereas breast-feeding was not. Bottle-feeding may have been one more means of taking parenthood away from parents and bringing it under medical control, and in many hospitals there were—and are—covert and open pressures by doctors or nurses to use formula-feeding. A contributing value may have been that our society went through a period of machine-worship during which people dreamed of living in a world of pure reason uncluttered by the

The infant: two

122

demands of biology. Women were to be liberated from the constant demands of motherhood and from the reminder of their animal and primitive natures. The Watsonian ethic would decry breast-feeding because it fostered the sentimentality and the mother love that were so dangerous to human welfare. Women themselves felt that breast-feeding tied them down, and they took to bottle-feeding to escape the fatigue and discomforts that go with breast-feeding and because of a conviction that breast-feeding would rob them of their figures, youth, beauty, and allure.

The breast-feeders, who, in this almost entirely bottle-fed nation, are nowadays the apostolic reformers, could invoke the argument of naturalness, plus the more practical ones of the superior nutritive value of human milk by comparison with cow's milk and the convenience of breast-feeding—no formula to be mixed, bottled, and stored, and no sterilization needed. As we have said, mother's milk is also thought to carry antibodies which enhance the baby's resistance to infection (Gyorgy et al., 1962). The psychiatrically and psycho-analytically oriented pressed the argument that breast-feeding gave mother and baby a chance to be alone together in close contact, where the mother could croon and whisper to the baby, and he, in turn, could stare at and learn to know his mother's face and feel close and warm and supported. But it is possible—and advisable—to give a bottle with exactly these same provisions, if the baby is held, rather than left in the bassinet or crib with a bottle propped next to his mouth. (One objection to leaving the baby with a bottle is that, unless his head is held slightly raised, there is danger that milk will enter the Eustachian tubes and cause infection.) Finally, the irrefutable contention was advanced that, whatever breast-feeding meant for the baby, some mothers found in it a deeply pleasurable experience, taking satisfaction in the wholeness of their feminine biology.

It seems to us (and we believe we express a current consensus) that, for women living in good hygienic conditions, personal feelings are the only sensible criterion for deciding between breast and bottle. Where sanitation is unsatisfactory, or milk expensive or difficult to come by, breast-feeding is the only safe way to nourish a young baby, and the new popularity of bottle-feeding among women in economically depressed societies has sometimes been ruinous for the health of their babies.

Another aspect of feeding is **weaning**, which refers to both the transition from breast or bottle to cup and the transition from milk (or whatever milk substitutes are currently in vogue) to solids. The literature suggests that weaning too was once—and still is in some societies—a matter of bitter battles between mother and

Issues in infant care

123

child, to the point where many American mothers felt it necessary to have the baby witness a ceremonial smashing of his bottles. Many cultures have special procedures for weaning: spreading a bitter substance on the mother's nipples, or, as in several African tribes, sending the baby on a long visit to grandmother. We should say again that in many non-Western societies weaning does not take place until age two or three or even four, and may be deliberately delayed as a fairly effective contraceptive technique. In societies with low-protein diets, late weaning helps protect children from kwashiorkor, a protein deficiency disease which produces damage of the central nervous system. Before the coming of the missionaries, a baby born before the previous one was old enough to wean was killed. When the missionaries forbade infanticide, it became necessary to displace the older baby in favor of the younger, and kwashiorkor became more common.

A recent study (Zamenhof et al., 1971) indicates that rats born to protein-deprived mothers had fewer brain cells and lower brain weights than controls, and, moreover, that female rats born to protein-deprived mothers but raised on normal diets gave birth to offspring with reduced brain weight and cell counts. How this effect of malnutrition in the grandmother was passed on through the mother to the grandchildren is not understood, although it seems likely that the mothers suffered other physiological abnormalities because of the protein restriction. It should be emphasized that delayed weaning will not by itself solve problems of malnutrition. Babies need proteins of a kind not supplied by mother's milk, so that prolonged nursing does only part of the job.

Nowadays, in most of United States society, weaning seems to take place without trauma to mother or child, probably because modern pediatric practice makes the transition—both the presentation of the new and the withdrawal of the old—gradual and at first tentative, but beginning early, so that the baby comes to take it for granted that nourishment comes in a variety of flavors, textures, consistencies, temperatures, and containers. Due account is taken of the baby's readiness for change: his general emotional security, the absence of physical (especially digestive) upsets, and the increased drooling that suggests new digestive capabilities. There are also situational factors to be considered. The baby is most amenable to feeding innovations when he is wide awake and after his first, voracious hunger has been appeased. When he is tired or very hungry, the urge to suck is strong, and he will have little patience for spoons or cups. Individual differences show up, some babies taking to new foodstuffs and feeding methods with great gusto, some matter-of-factly, some cautiously, and some not at all. Some babies are ready at an early age, others not until much later, and parents can respond appropriately. As in other areas of child-rearing, a certain amount of trial and error is called for, which is no strain for the self-confident parent who can watch the baby's reactions and adapt to the information transmitted via the language of behavior.

An exception to what we have just said is to be found among some recent converts to breast-feeding who have been influenced by its more evangelical advocates. Conversations with a number of young mothers have shown that many of them experience great conflict over weaning, and postpone it to as late as two years. These mothers want to stop nursing, because they find it fatiguing, because they would like to lose weight, and because their mates would like them to be somewhat less mother figures and rather more sex objects. On the other hand, they have been led to believe that early weaning is a betrayal of the mother role and does irreparable harm to their babies' physical and mental health. Indeed, most of them have no clear idea of what constitutes early weaning. It is our opinion that the benefits of breast-feeding to mother and child have been pretty well fulfilled by the time the baby is about six months old, and gradual weaning should begin before then.

In the first decades of the century, experts on nutrition discovered some important principles of what constitutes a sound human diet. Unfortunately, though, in their application of these principles to the feeding of babies and children, the nutritionists were often as rigid, dogmatic, arbitrary, and magicalistic as their intuition-guided forerunners had been.

A key turning point in dietetics came with the publication of Clara Davis's (1939) findings on the **self-selection of diets** by recently weaned infants. The babies of their own accord ate the proper proportions of the right food components: proteins, carbohydrates, fats, vitamins, minerals. It is important to stress that Davis's subjects did not ration their intake of different substances meal by meal after the manner of a dietician's chart; it was only in the long run of weeks that their diets balanced out in the correct proportions. Along the way, babies sometimes went on "jags," sticking to one food, such as bananas, for days at a time. A second essential point is that the babies ate needed foodstuffs even when these were patently distasteful, as in the case of salt, which some children took straight, grimacing all the while. In general, the babies were oblivious to what the adult would consider palatable or unpalatable combinations of foods, or the sequence in which foods should be eaten at a given meal. Because of its fundamental implications, Davis's study needs to be repeated with a larger sample of babies of different ages and with more varied and elaborate foodstuffs—caviar and salami, for instance, not to mention sweets—than the commonplace, bland staples used in her original investigation.

It would be impractical for parents to feed their babies cafeteria-style in an attempt to apply Davis's findings literally. However, parents can learn from Davis's study not to be upset by a baby's aversion—usually temporary if it is not made an issue of—to particular foods, or to be alarmed when he goes on food jags. They can also try offering a widely variegated diet—perhaps in the form of morsels from the adults' plates—to babies from a young age, letting the baby decide which things he finds appetizing and which he wants second helpings of. (We assume a family with adequate means to afford varied and adequate fare. In cases of poverty and malnutrition there is a tendency after weaning for the child to share with the adults a diet of excessive carbohydrates and inadequate protein; and, for reasons we shall see, to prefer the familiar foods and resist innovations.) Actually, a relaxed attitude—within broad limits—about the baby's diet seems to be the rule nowadays, which may be one reason that so-called feeding problems, once common, have become a rarity in this country's middle class.

Davis's findings illustrate the principle which Cannon (1939) called the **wisdom of** the body. Briefly put, this principle says that the organism has some capacity to recognize—not consciously or logically or analytically, but at the appetitive level of what seems attractive—those foodstuffs which contain nutrients in which the body is deficient. Such selection was first observed in cases of physiological malfunction. For instance, people suffering from Addison's disease, which affects the adrenal glands and so interferes with salt metabolism, spontaneously increase salt consumption to compensate. In the same way, rats with their adrenal glands removed become highly sensitive to the presence of salt and can detect extremely minute quantities dissolved in water, as shown by their greater consumption of weak saline than of plain water (Richter, 1942–1943). Again, children who eat plaster (which is rich in calcium) from the walls are sometimes found to be suffering from calcium deficiency. People have hypothesized that pregnant women who develop "cravings" do so in response to actual dietary lacks, but the evidence is slight.

Since some people have interpreted the wisdom of the body to mean that the child can safely be left to govern his own intake, we must emphasize that it is far from perfect. Although the wisdom of the body may steer us toward nourishing food, it does not warn us away from poisons. Children do not hesitate to sample the contents of medicine bottles and soap packages and pesticide canisters or lead-laden paint or chips of putty, as the regional poison control centers that have been established in the United States can testify. The wisdom of the body does not signal to us which is the delectable mushroom and which the deadly toadstool. Foods low in nutritive value may be more attractive than nour-

Kwashiorkor, or protein deficiency disease, in a Brazilian one-year-old girl. The shriveled skin is typical. This baby is unable to vocalize.

Jean Speiser, UNICEF Photo

126

ishing ones and may even block consumption of needed nutrients by dulling the appetite. This clearly happens in the case of those children who seem to live on potato chips, soda pop, and candy. It seems to be the case that a liking for a narrow and perhaps prestigeful range of European foodstuffs, to the abandonment of the local diet of fish, coconut, fruits, and taro, accounts for the fact that many Tahitians lose their permanent teeth by late adolescence. Culturally defined food habits tend to corrupt the body's wisdom. In many societies with inadequate diets, vital nutritional supplements are there for the taking but are ignored in favor of what the culture defines as food. Many Americans would rather suffer malnutrition than eat "trash" fish such as squid, octopus, eels, or sea urchins, or the recently created fish flour, or "exotic" cuts of meat such as sweetbreads, testicles, brains, or kidneys, or the fat and marrow that are so essential in Eskimo diet. Tomatoes, a valuable source of vitamins and minerals, were long shunned as poisonous.

A curious, sometimes individual, but often cultural phenomenon is **pica**, the regular eating of non-nutritive substances (Kessler, 1966, pp. 106–108). For instance, a number of people in the southern United States regularly eat clay, now moist as it comes from the ground, now sun-dried, now oven-baked. Some like it in wafers, others prefer it in chunks. Some have a special penchant for the gray kind, others like the yellow or the red. All of us have probably known mild pica in the form of chewing the erasers off pencils or consuming small wads of paper, and some children seem to have cravings for wood or even soap. All such eating seems unrelated to or even at odds with the wisdom of the body. A dangerous variety of pica that has been getting less attention than it deserves is the eating of paint flakes or putty impregnated with lead-based paint. Many older buildings, and especially those in slums, still shed poisonous paint into the environment, where it is eaten by children whose normal inclination to pica may be amplified by ever-present hunger pangs. Although lead paint is a threat mainly in decaying buildings, it is still being widely used and will remain a danger for years to come.

Thumb-sucking and comfort devices

Sucking is an essential part of the neonate's equipment for survival. During infancy it becomes, in addition, a need which demands gratification in its own right. When the sucking need does not get gratified in the course of nursing, the baby makes up for it by sucking on other things —his thumb, a corner of his blanket, rattles, and so forth. Ena Roberts (1944), a follower of David Levy, found that finger-sucking was related to too brief feeding time in the early months, or to an abrupt change from long feeding times to short ones. Unfortunately, Roberts's findings are equivocal, since she had no way to measure food intake to be sure that both thumb-suckers and nonsuckers were getting the same amount to eat. Levy (1934, 1938) himself, in a classic series of studies, has demonstrated compensatory mouthing in puppies and pecking in chicks. Puppies fed from a free-flowing nipple, which gratified their hunger without gratifying their need to suck, sucked avidly at themselves, each other, curtain fringes, and proferred human fingers. Similarly, chicks given only a limited opportunity to peck, although adequately fed, pecked at each other's bodies until the feathers came out. A difficulty with this observation is that what looks like compensatory pecking may instead be the pecking that goes into establishing a dominance hierarchy, a pecking order, so we need a comparison with normally reared chicks before we can safely interpret Levy's findings. Another possibly relevant factor in such studies is that of space—a number of authors have pointed out that rearing animals in crowded conditions produces disturbed behavior of various kinds (Calhoun, 1962; Thiessen and Rodgers, 1961). On the other hand, chicks fed by hand and thus completely deprived of pecking experience starved to death when later left to eat in the ordinary way. It appears that pecking may have to be stimulated during a critical period early in life to become functional. In the same way, Sears and associates (Davis et al., 1948) have evidence to suggest that if the human baby is cup-fed from the very beginning, the sucking need is never established. However, we can detect no visible benefit to either baby or mother in bypassing the usual sucking activity of infancy.

If we understand that sucking, beyond its role in feeding, is an autonomous need, then thumb-sucking in infancy no longer appears a dirty, disgusting "habit" which the child threatens to carry with him into adulthood and which must be stopped immediately, if need be with the help of the splints and cuffs and mittens and bitter-tasting medicines once featured in infant-care manuals and mail-order catalogues. During infancy, thumb-sucking is not really a problem, and it usually stops spontaneously by the end of the preschool years. The relationship, if any, between thumb-sucking and malocclusion of the teeth is by no means clear, but it is likely that only the most persistent thumb-sucking—which may express other psychological needs, as for extra love and attention—is a menace to the dental arch, though even here the evidence is not very impressive.

One possible alternative to the readily available thumb if the baby needs extra sucking is a pacifier, provided it is kept reasonably clean. (In practice, it is usually a good idea to have several pacifiers ready for action.) It must be said, however, that some mothers and some babies prefer thumbs to pacifiers. But children who use pacifiers seem more willing to give them up in due time than thumb-suckers their thumbs, and very few children seem to begin thumb-sucking after relinquishing their pacifiers. In infancy, the pacifier (or the thumb) may also serve, perhaps in an illusory way, to allay hunger temporarily and so help in spacing out the baby's feedings.

A major function of thumb-sucking seems to be that of closing off contact with the outside world at bedtime so that sleep can come. The parents can muffle the baby against noise, the baby can close his eyes against light, but the only way to desensitize those most vigilant receptors, the hand and the mouth, is to incorporate them into a closed circuit of internal activity. At bedtime, along with thumb-sucking, there often goes a great variety of other self-directed activities which are called comfort rituals. Some of the frequent ones are twisting a lock of hair, holding on to an ear, fingering a blanket, or cuddling a favorite—often tattered and disreputable—doll.

Fewer parents these days than formerly are likely to regard such behavior as symptoms of psychopathology, especially now that the Peanuts' blanket-trailing Linus has become a familiar figure around the world. Bedtime masturbation is quite common beginning late in the first year and can be seen as another way of shutting out the world to find sleep. Elaborate measures to curb infantile masturbation—even daytime masturbation—are probably inappropriate. The desirable course seems to be to give the baby a reasonable amount of freedom to find out about the body that he is, without unintentionally giving masturbation more importance than the parents really wish to. Too great a concern with controlling the baby's behavior can lead to such absurdities as keeping the baby's hands under the covers to prevent thumbsucking and outside the covers to prevent masturbation.

Toilet training

As we suggested earlier, toilet training belongs in toddlerhood, but since one still hears that babies can be "trained" by age six months—or four months, or one month—it seems a good idea to say something about it here. Some babies, beginning at a very early age, have a very stable schedule of defecation. When this is the case, and if the baby defecates while awake (many have bowel movements predominantly in their sleep), parents can capitalize on the baby's schedule and, once he is old enough to sit up comfortably, put him on the pot when a bowel movement is due. Even when the baby has an irregular pattern of defecation, an alert mother can tell from his behavior and expression that a bowel movement is imminent and place him on the pot. But take note that it is the mother who is trained, not the baby. What this sort of procedure accomplishes is to save one or two soiled diapers and clean-ups a day and familiarize the baby with the toilet as a comfortable place to be. If the toilet becomes a prison, problems can arise. If the baby's spontaneous defecation schedule changes, as it is likely to do, or if the baby has no schedule to begin with, it is worse than useless to try to get him to eliminate on parental demand.

Ordinarily, bowel control comes after the child can walk, and bladder control somewhat later, with daytime bladder control preceding nighttime control. But while it is pointless and perhaps even injurious to begin toilet training before the child is able to learn, it is likewise not a good idea to postpone it too long. That is, there seems to be a critical period roughly between ages one and a half and two years or so in which toilet training happens quite easily (provided the baby's life is going well in general), and outside which it can be very strenuous. But as in feeding and weaning, the best results come from noting carefully the baby's response to tentative trials, and establishing toilet training with his interest and cooperation.

Sleeping

The chief point about sleeping is that many healthy, lively babies past the age of a few months may never want to let go of the interesting world long enough to go to sleep, so it falls to the parents, supreme in their self-confidence, to create the occasion for naps and nighttime sleep. The baby provides abundant cues, by sagging, yawning, and irritability, when he needs to sleep. Once the baby has been put to bed and is asleep, how long he sleeps can usually be left up to him. But babies can be encouraged to conform to the patterns of early-rising or late-sleeping parents. Everyday observations indicate that most babies can learn to sleep in either noisy or quiet surroundings, but once they are used to one or the other, that is what they require. Many babies have a period of fussy crying before they fall asleep; this is easily distinguished from cries of genuine distress and does not call for any parental action. When babies are truly unhappy at bedtime, they have to be soothed and comforted in a way that does not provoke further wakefulness. In very young infants, this may take the form of rocking, crooning, stroking the head, or gently patting the back. Somewhat older infants may need to have a familiar adult stand by the crib for a few minutes, acting as a secure reference point before the baby can free himself from outside stimulation and let himself go to sleep. When the baby is taken visiting and put to bed in strange surroundings, extra measures will almost certainly have to be taken to permit him to get to sleep, and extra adult tolerance needed of the irritability and vulnerability that are likely to go with delayed or omitted naps.

Early cultivation of motor skills

As we have mentioned, there has recently been a vogue for teaching skills like swimming beginning at the age of a few months. We have often been asked our opinion about such practices, and we can only say that we see no harm in them—subject to some reservations. We have seen babies less than a year old minnowing happily through the water; we have

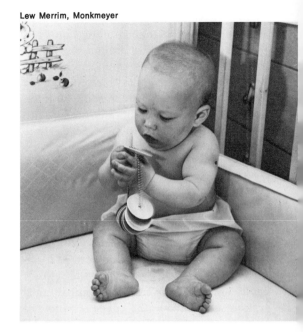

Playthings make an important contribution to the child's cognitive development.

watched babies younger than two on skis or getting the feel of a surfboard on a ripple of wave; we have seen three-year-olds pirouetting on tiptoe; and these youngsters seemed, to all outward appearances, psychologically unscarred.

One reservation that we have is that children may be cast prematurely in the role of performer, of the show-off and deliberate charmer who feeds on the audience's approval and applause. Another caution is that the child's skills may outrun his common sense. The baby who can swim may not know which water is safe to swim in and which water isn't. We recently witnessed a less-than-two-year-old happily pedaling his tricycle straight down the middle of a street, blithely riding through stop signs, to the verge of a major

The infant: two

130

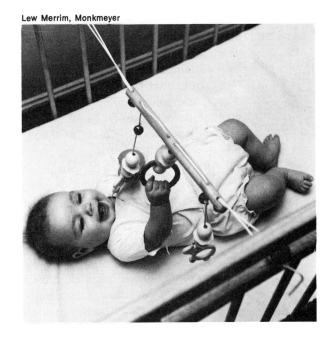

thoroughfare. A third warning is against forcing. Not only is there a threat to the baby's welfare in forcing him to persevere in an activity which he resists (at later ages, when the child can view events in better perspective, it may indeed be necessary at times to force him to do things like chores and homework), but forcing may boomerang and instill a lifelong loathing of what might have become an enjoyable activity if teaching it had been deferred to a later age. It may be worth emphasizing that babies given plenty of scope get abundant exercise on their own, and need no special encouragement to be active in the use of their bodies.

Toys for babies

Normal cognitive development takes place in a series of interchanges between the baby and the world around him. He comes to a first basic organization of reality through watching, listening, tasting, smelling, touching, manipulating, and being acted on by the things he encounters. It is now well established that, at least in the United States, from an early age there are pronounced differences in cognitive competence between children of poor parents and children of the relatively well-to-do. It is likely that a comparable distinction would be evident in most societies, but we do not know. It is probable that the greater cognitive adequacy of middle-class children can be traced to the greater number, variety, and accessibility of the objects they encounter, though this is generally coupled with the greater availability of mothers or caretakers who make objects available, respond to the child's use of them, encourage further experimentation, and talk to him about them (Rubenstein, 1967). This becomes vital when we consider the problems of cognitive enrich-

Issues in infant care

ment for children who do not get enough of the right kinds of stimulation. Rheingold and Samuels (1969) see playthings as maintaining good emotional tone and preventing what for many babies becomes chronic boredom. Compensatory enrichment should probably begin in infancy rather than at age three or four, and people who want to cultivate the cognitive capacities of infants should be aware of what kinds of materials are likely to work best.

We assume, of course, that no parent (or day care center) will ever think that playthings can take the place of human company and affection and the social games of infancy and early childhood, but as babies get older they increasingly like to explore the possibilities of raw materials and things and spatial and causal relations —particularly with the occasional involvement of the adult. The baby's interactions with both things and people provide the occasion of what Horowitz (1968) calls **contingent learning**, the way the baby's behavior feeds back to him in the reactions of things and people .

Babies enjoy and benefit from the opportunity to handle (and mouth and chew on), to take apart, and eventually to put together all sorts of things. Many of the most educational materials and objects occur as a matter of course in many homes. Among the important learning materials are very simple ones: paper to crumple and flatten and tear and suck and chew on; rags to use likewise; clothespins and teething rings to teethe on; plastic dishes to bang on table top or floor; mirrors in which to admire oneself; paper bags and empty boxes to put things in and things to put into them, including, in late infancy, grocery cartons the child can climb in and out of and hide under; and kitchen uten-

sils and pots and pans to use in myriad ways. Parents can well consider household effects to be the baby's basic playthings, and access to them becomes more feasible as the family rises above the subsistence level. Freedom to dabble with his fingers in cooked cereal and other such foodstuffs is important in the baby's coming to know the world and its properties, even at the cost of some additional mess.

Besides what the regular household provides, toymakers have come up with some ingenious and useful devices (in many cases, homemade equivalents are easy to make and just as good). Mobiles that hang above a bassinet or crib seem to fascinate very young babies, but very soon it is important to have things within reach. Let us take exception to the idea that one should attach movable displays to the baby's wrist or ankle with a length of string; the baby may indeed take some temporary pleasure in being able to set something in motion, but he may be subject to severe frustration when he finds that he cannot avoid contingent reinforcement for his movements. Babies who are reaching out to bat at and grasp dangling objects enjoy having an arrangement of curtain rings and horizontal bars to hit and tug at, especially if these are suspended on springs, and even more especially if moving them actuates bells or rattles. Rattles and soft dolls suspended by lengths of elastic also give the baby something to set swaying, to grasp, to pull and release, and to mouth or chew on. Slightly older babies (past six months) can operate the kind of music box which is wound by means of a drawstring. There is no reason similar contrivances could not be built to yield all manner of sound effects. In late infancy and early toddlerhood, blocks with holes and rods that fit through the holes get played with at successively more mature levels. Once the child can creep, the spatial arrangements of house and furniture become playthings for the baby to explore with his whole body, weaving through chair rungs, squeezing backward into narrow spaces, detouring around footstools, opening and emptying drawers, and clambering into low cupboards. So-called activity panels or gadget boards, equipped with knobs and cranks and gears, with doors that open to reveal mirrors or pictures or simply the world on the far side of the board, and miscellaneous locks and latches on the doors, are appealing to babies and young children, although most commercial versions are less imaginative than what an inspired parent could construct. For instance, one such panel we built for research purposes included a low-wattage light bulb worked by a pull-chain switch, and a battery-powered doorbell and button. A large transparent plastic bottle loosely filled with spools, blocks, clothespins, and such makes an excellent plaything for babies a year and older. These, of course, are only a small sample of what a baby given considerable freedom to explore will find for himself, including, as we have said, such taboo but rewarding playthings as tubes of toothpaste, bottles of shampoo, and rolls of toilet paper. It is essential that day care programs which aspire to emotional and intellectual enrichment be aware of the possibilities.

The Baby's Cultural Heritage

It is clear that the family a baby is born into has its own special characteristics. Any given family, though, is also part of a larger social unit whose members share characteristic beliefs about the nature of reality, from which beliefs follow common ways of thinking, feeling, judging, and acting. Some of the group's ways of acting are practical adaptations to the conditions of life: the Eskimo builds shelters of ice or hard-packed snow, the dweller in the tropics, one of thatch; the island or seacoast dweller evolves a lore of the sea, the inland dweller, a lore of the mountains or forest or prairie; and so on. But interwoven with these ecologically practical arrangements are beliefs, assumptions, values, expectations, life styles, etiquette, that may have little to do with the immediate exigencies of food, shelter, health, safety, amusement, or procreation. Indeed, in every culture, many deeply ingrained assumptions, no matter how useful they may once have been, are now counterproductive. It was once taken for granted that to have many children was good, but with surplus people overwhelming the planet the assumption looks weak. Our established beliefs about what is right for males and females stand solidly athwart the road to a new understanding between the sexes.

Collectively, the ways of a given society are called its **culture** (in large and complex societies, different groups are said to have their own **subcultures**). A culture includes institutions (government, laws, the military, the family, religion, and so forth), customs, observances, practical skills, ritual observances, moral codes, standards of cleanliness, styles of dress, and countless other manifestations. More fundamental, though, is the cognitive framework, in varying degrees consciously elaborated, which implies and justifies the surface manifestations. According to which culture he is born into, the child will learn a special, all-inclusive (but not necessarily, as we shall see in a moment, completely explicit or logically consistent) view of human nature and destiny, material reality, and—in most cultures—the workings of the supernatural. This view is communicated to the child in part explicitly, in the teachings of his elders, but even more without any explicit statement or justification, in the traditional ways of doing things, in ritual observances, in emotional reactions to events, in tones of voice, in fixed relationships to different people in the social structure, and in manner and style of movement.

We shall point out later in this chapter some of the things all cultures have in common, representing what we take to be some universals or imperatives of the human condition, but for the time being we want to stress that cultures differ, that the differences are many and deep, and are not something external to the individual person or veneers overlying a common human nature. Rather, a particular culture is one special version of human nature, an orientation to life that is assimilated, so to speak, into the individual's very bones. It is because our culturally given outlook becomes so intimately a part of ourselves that most people never discover that they share a culture. It is easy to grasp that other peoples have bizarre beliefs and outlandish practices and food and clothing, have a set of delusions which we may label a culture, but for us our beliefs and perceptions and value judgments are always the obviously factual and correct ones.

The American culture

Until recently, most anthropologists have been of European origin, and the logical thing for them to do was to travel afield and observe the behavior of "exotic," non-European people. For the purposes of this book, however, it may be more instructive to begin by pointing to some of the features of United States culture as various experts and amateurs, imported and domestic, have delineated it (for a useful historical survey, see Commager, 1947). Americans live in a highly technical, largely urban society (even the suburbs are becoming urbanized, with new suburbs of their own growing along the fringes), which already dictates some proportion of their behavior. They live in small nuclear families in sharply differentiated clumps and neighborhoods, whose design is mostly unintentional but follows economic and ethnic lines. Their mechanized society depends upon an intricate division of labor, which tends to demand highly specialized skills unlike the learning of an array of traditional crafts in simpler societies. The less well established change abodes frequently—the city poor try to stay one jump ahead of the rats and the landlord, the middle executives and technicians of the large corporations get transplanted from office to office, the upwardly mobile seek new dwellings in "better" neighborhoods, the blacks move north, and young people renounce farm and small town for the city—while the settled travel freely. At home, Americans are likely to prefer passive entertainment dispensed by electronic mass media, and they are not likely to search out information and diverse opinions on the issues of the day. Instead of exchanging news and gossip while they pound their washing on a rock or sit together plaiting mats and baskets, American women gather at the laundromat or beauty parlor or supermarket, often in considerable isolation one from another.

American men, because they work at specialized occupations, form friendships among members of the same guild. Only American school-age children are able to preserve some vestiges of tribal life, and even they, as Robert Paul Smith (1957) has pointed out, are increasingly being regimented not only into the ways of schools, but into the Little League, scouting, the use of prefabricated, highly complex play materials, summer camp, the round of after-school lessons, and regular visits to the orthodontist. More and more Americans live in a state of siege, behind multiply-locked and barred doors and windows, firearms and guard dogs at the ready. They feel under attack from professional burglars, junkie rip-off artists, wanton vandals, snipers, young people, and militants.

Americans value success, and assume that each generation will outstrip the one before it. McClelland (1961) and others have used themes from children's books to assess the emphasis placed on high achievement in a given society. Rudin (1968), in a fascinating if not completely conclusive study, found that these themes predicted death rates from causes associated with emotional disturbances twenty-five years later. Societies in which children's books extolled achievement motivation had high death rates from ulcers and hypertension, whereas those in which a need for power was dominant had high death rates from murder, suicide, and from cirrhosis of the liver, associated with heavy drinking. In this country, there is very little sympathy for the failure, the ne'er-do-well, the dropout, or the mendicant (except for the highly-paid professional fund raiser); and the person who has stopped rising through the organization or system is discarded or, more kindly, shunted into a dead-end sinecure which

he and his fellows try to pretend is not the limbo of the might-have-beens. Americans believe in progress when it is measured by growth or by technical innovation. At the same time, they are conservative in their social views, which may account for some of their ambivalence about intellectuals, who are valued when they can solve practical problems but who are mistrusted because they are likely to harbor radical, hence disturbing, ideas. In the same way, Americans value education, but not because it enriches personal experience and liberates thinking; more often it is because education enhances earning power and gives access to the right circles that it is deemed important. Americans tend to be optimistic, but, as de Tocqueville observed, their optimism tends to overflow into delusions of omnipotence and then, when they find that a problem resists solution, they may be plunged into total pessimistic impotence. Efficiency is highly esteemed, and with it an emphasis on hurry and working fast, which leaves little time for leisurely savoring of life, contemplation, and examination of goals.

Although the United States is far from the world's worst offender, a strong current of violence runs through American culture, visible in the conduct of foreign policy, the frequent brutality practiced by and toward policemen, the way bigots, North and South, treat Negroes, in motion picture and television dramas, labor struggles, and increasingly among revolutionaries. The daily newspapers are our witness. American men and, even more, women esteem youth, conceal their age, and look forward with reluctance and dread to maturity—let alone old age.

In former times, American society set great store by time sense and delay of gratification, on doing without immediate

The baby's cultural heritage

rewards for the sake of greater ones later on (this, of course, is how industrial societies, capitalist and communist, get built), but this value is being eroded both by the cult of youth, which says that one must snatch one's pleasures while they are still pleasurable, and by the credit-card and installment-plan philosophy of enjoy now, pay later, which helps keep the economy buoyant. It is considered disastrous for the economy not to expand steadily, even if the key to expansion is the manufacture of weapons. Even as times change, delay of gratification and punctuality are still middle-class virtues not prized by the lower classes.

Americans believe that marriage is good and that everybody should get married but this ethic is complicated by the fact that American men and women are thoroughly ambivalent about sexuality and about each other. It sometimes seems that American men would rather watch pornographic movies, which are purveyed in great profusion (not to mention live sex shows), than go to bed with an actual woman, and would rather bed down with a casual pick-up or a prostitute than with a woman with whom a close and open human relationship has to be formed. Fringe phenomena like mate-swapping and group sex are symptomatic of the difficulty we have reconciling sex and marriage. Divorces are relatively frequent and a growing number of children must cope with life in terms of a single parent or of shuttling between combinations of parents and stepparents.

If American culture is full of rifts and inconsistencies and incongruities, perhaps the most basic one is the two contradictory moral codes every American child learns (though such a duality is hardly an American monopoly). Whatever his religion, ev-

ery American child is taught something akin to the Christian ethic, embodying such virtues as charity, forbearance, compassion, altruism, humility, and cooperation, corresponding, as we have said, to an attitude of basic trust with some ascetic overtones added on. But he also learns the American business ethic of dog eat dog, the survival of the fittest, which blesses and demands such traits as aggressiveness, competitiveness, acquisitiveness, self-preservation, guile, and ruthlessness. It is interesting that those groups in American and European society who resisted Darwin's theory of evolution on religious grounds nonetheless embraced eagerly a **Social Darwinism** that promised to justify the law of the jungle as a governing principle in human affairs and, moreover, justified the established social hierarchy as naturally ordained. Needless to say, implicit Social Darwinism was around long before Darwin was born, and it had an explicit medieval antecedent in the divine right of kings. (As we said earlier, Social Darwinism departs from biological Darwinism in stressing individual survival rather than survival of the species.) As it works out in practice, a majority of American women and a minority of American men come to espouse the Christian ethic; a larger number of American men live primarily by the business ethic, with some concessions to Christianity when dealing with "our kind of people" and on the Sabbath. We sometimes encounter some grotesque rationalizations seeking to reconcile the business and Christian ethics: "How I Found Christ and Made a Million Dollars." Social Darwinism seems to underlie the doctrine of Manifest Destiny, which was invoked to sanctify American expansion toward and across the Pacific, and the "realism" or "pragmatism" of current American politics. A great number of American men, however, seem to live in perpetual and painful conflict, never quite sure how to act and never quite free of misgivings once they have acted. It may be that such moral conflicts find somatic expression, which would help account for the mass hypochrondria implied in our gargantuan consumption of laxatives, stomach remedies, headache remedies, dietary supplements, and magical nostrums, without mention of recurring fads and cults such as the present enthusiasm for macrobiotic and organic foods and vitamin C in massive doses to ward off colds.

What we have said is only partly accurate, of course, because we are in the middle of rapid and turbulent change. One odd by-product of the change in the material situation and in values has been the growth of a new sort of Protestant ethic. The original version, as set forth by Max Weber, saw the businessman as acting less for his own gain than as God's agent, so that he preached and, in varying degrees, practiced thrift, honesty, austerity, and chastity. Because he adhered to such virtues, he could feel that he was of the Lord's anointed, predestined to Salvation, and that he and a country dedicated to these principles could do no wrong. His contemporary descendant, while still preaching much the same fundamentalist theology, social conservatism, and blood-and-fire patriotism, has become a devoted if sometimes frantic and frustrated hedonist, with life's great goods defined by sports cars and private planes and helicopters, gadgets, swimming pools, the casinos of Las Vegas, compulsive sexuality, fine clothes and jewelry, and luxury cruises to tax-deductible conventions.

This subculture characterizes many of our leading citizens and is subscribed to by a great many—probably most—young people. At the same time, we must recognize a number of new emergents in our society. In Charles Reich's (1970) analysis, United States society has passed through two eras, each marked by a different form of consciousness. During the era of rugged individualism, which lasted until the time of the Great Depression, Consciousness I prevailed, in which self-centered, competitive striving was the rule. With the coming of the New Deal, the corporate state took form, bringing with it Consciousness II, in which individual identity was submerged in the interests of a paternalistic society in which government and business were merged in the pursuit of welfare. Now, according to Reich, society is about to be transformed by Consciousness III, observable in the Youth Movement. Consciousness III betokens the revival of noncomformist individuality, but now in a cooperative rather than competitive spirit, with great emphasis on intimacy, love, intensity of personal experience, sexual freedom, democracy, pacifism, internationalism, and esthetics perhaps helped along by drugs. It is hard to summarize the youth counterculture because it contains so many disparate strands. At this writing, we are confronted by a variety of what are called "Jesus freaks," whose beliefs range from fundamentalism to political radicalism, all in the name of the true meaning of Christianity. There is a sizable contingent of Nature lovers seeking to return to the earth, now in agricultural communes and now in the image of the self-reliant, individualistic breaker of the prairie. There are advocates of violent revolution and of total withdrawal from social action. Some young people repudiate science in favor of intuitive knowledge, and technology in favor of what comes naturally and organically. Many seek a mindless hedonism without the rationalizations of their elders. One thing is clear, though: substantial numbers of young people are struggling to define a life style that bears little resemblance to the conventions of American culture. And most of them are beset by doubts, contradictions, and conflicts.

Even when we talk about the counterculture of youth, we are still dealing with what may be thought of as "majority" American culture. Those who are members of that culture might bear in mind that there are other significant cultures within the boundaries of the United States. Some of these represent continuations of different traditions, contaminated or diluted in various degrees by majority culture. We have a number of indigenous cultures—Amerindian, Eskimo, Polynesian—and their varieties (hunting, herding, and crop-growing societies tend to have very different ways). Some are imports from Europe, Africa, and Asia; many of the "ethnic" minorities are nowadays clamoring for special recognition. The only truly immigrant American culture, of course, is the one forged by Negroes, which has given us two native art forms, spirituals and jazz, which has contributed a whole vocabulary of hip, cool, and soul, and with which innumerable whites have openly or secretly sought to identify. It is ironic that many black Americans are now turning back to their African heritage (sometimes forgetting that there are as many African cultures as European), when it is precisely their American heritage which is unique and valuable (although the bitter origins of this heritage in slavery make its rejection understandable).

Some universals of culture

Having looked at some aspects of a particular culture, let us go on to discuss some general implications. Any cultural orientation has its own logic, whereby certain conclusions follow "naturally" from a given set of premises. If one "knows" that babies are selfish, scheming creatures who with the slightest encouragement will become monsters of egotism, then it follows, as in fact it does for many people, that one must begin by "breaking the baby's spirit," on the analogy of breaking a wild horse. If one "knows" that heroin transforms human beings into wild beasts, then of course one must protect both society and the users of drugs by banishing heroin. If one "knows" that receiving welfare destroys the recipient's self-respect, then welfare payments must be held to a minimum lest we demoralize the poor by making them feel like parasites. If women exploit men, and men women, it is because each has a cultural version of the opposite sex which makes it less than human and hence fair game. Part of the task of education is to dissolve or transcend cultural preconceptions so that one can perceive and react to people as human beings, with a complete set of human characteristics, including frailties and vices, rather than as specimens defined by a single, conspicuous label (the social psychologist's **stereotypes**): Negro, Jew, WASP, Militant, Rich Man, Astronaut, Movie Star, Undesirable, Welfare Recipient, Playboy, Sex Symbol, Dope Addict, Dropout, Blind Person, Criminal, Cripple, All-American, or whatever. By the same token, cultures can and do convey optimistic and nurturant beliefs: both kinds tend to confirm themselves through the operation of the self-fulfilling prophecy.

Part of the problem in thinking about cultural differences is how to comprehend diversity within unity. For what we are saying is that all people (and peoples) are alike and all people are different. All cultures, no matter how diverse, express a peculiarly human mode of existence of such universality that we cannot be sure whether it is learned or biologically determined. Certainly the human constitution is necessary to the distinctively human things we do. Speaking, as human beings practice it, seems to be intrinsically impossible for apes. Recent efforts to teach chimpanzees to communicate using the sign language of the deaf (Gardner and Gardner, 1969) or plastic shapes standing for words (Premack, 1971) reveal levels of primate ability far transcending those involved in their expressive vocalizations. However, Bronowski and Bellugi (1970) point out a number of limitations on these animals' "language." The most important seem to be that language does not get assimilated as a system for thinking and feeling and there is no evidence that apes can organize "words" into categories and grammatical and semantic relations. For a fascinating, if inconclusive, follow-up of the Gardners' ape Washoe, see Hahn (1971). Also beyond the demonstrated capacity of nonhumans are pictorial representation (although apes do enjoy daubing paint on canvas), the making of fire, and, if not the use of tools, the use of tools to make tools (Simpson, 1966). On the other hand, we cannot predict precisely how a person will behave simply on the basis of his human constitution. Tastes and values and understanding and goals and competences cannot be deduced from normal variations in physique. We know a great deal, for instance, about the structure of the human hand and its ability to grasp,

knead, twist, palpate, and all the rest. But we cannot predict from our knowledge of the hand how a particular hand will be used: to build ham radio sets, to put a coin in a slot, to mold clay into works of art, to carve ivory, to make love, to clean wax out of an ear, or to shape a stone arrowhead. Long fingers may be an advantage to a pianist, but some superb pianists have fingers that can only be described as stubby. The potential functions are manifold, but the realized ones depend on the individual's history within his own cultural setting.

Nevertheless, all organisms with a human constitution share certain forms of behavior. Some of these, of course, have analogs in nonhuman species, while some are exclusively human. All human beings, the occasional hermit excepted, live in groups, and social contact and social learning are essential to the human condition. It takes a long time for the human child to mature to the point of independence, and all societies accordingly have a highly developed **family life**, including quite intricate kinship systems, within which the child is given tutelage in the society's ways. The tutelage goes on whether it is given in the context of everyday activities or in those strange institutions called schools. Babies and children everywhere have the same physical and psychological needs, and every society has selective priorities in its provisions for meeting those needs. How well needs are met is another question, since one can point to societies, primitive and advanced, which produce adults who can barely function well enough to keep the society going.

Central to human social life inside and outside the family is **language**, speaking and listening to speech. Other creatures can make and modulate speech sounds,

John Bryson, Rapho Guillumette

Melvin Konner

A.   B.

Patterns of child care. A. Ghana. B. A Bushman child places herself in a carrying cloth. C. A favela in Brazil.

and all vertebrates have systems of communication for courtship, defense of territory, care of the young, warnings against predators, and so forth, but these, no matter how effective, are always tied to the concrete present situation. That is, to the best of our knowledge, no nonhuman creatures discuss events remote in space or time, or purely hypothetical states of affairs. Although language is a human universal, to find universal features of different human languages is a task that has kept linguists busy and bewildered for many a long year (Weinreich, 1963). It is clear, though, that all languages serve, by whatever linguistic devices, the purposes of factual and mythic and affective communication within a given society. But the utterances of a speaker make sense to his fellows only because they all share a common frame of reference, and one cannot derive the full meaning of an utterance only from what is said. Indeed, we take it as given that speech is used as often to conceal what one is really thinking as to reveal it. The so-called credibility gap in American politics of recent years expresses a widespread conviction that utterances by people in high places bear little if any relationship to the real world.

All people, as we have said, use **tools** of some complexity, whether hammers and chisels and plows and spear launchers or forceps or ultrasonic devices for cleaning the teeth or lasers. All human societies have systems for organizing **time** and **space**. Human beings everywhere share

The infant: two

140

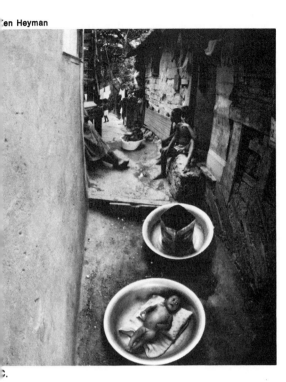

certain **emotions** such as anger, grief, dread, joy, and amusement, some of which seem to be human extensions of feeling states found in many other vertebrates. Even though all people share a number of emotions, different cultures have different rules governing what occasions produce which emotions, how a given emotion is expressed, and toward whom which emotions may be directed. For instance, in the United States, it is considered unmanly to cry, and it is thought improper, outside the pages of certain detective stories, to practice physical violence against a woman. By the same token, physical aggression and coarse language are viewed as unwomanly (or at least not ladylike). All societies have conventions for concealing emotions and for simulating emotions one may not actually feel, as when we enthusiastically congratulate someone for what we inwardly consider an unmerited triumph or an ill-starred marriage.

Since a number of people have fantasies of going to a place where people practice free, untrammeled love, it is as well to point out that all societies have regulations governing the **conduct of sex**—including regulations about how the rules get violated, as in the conventions governing extramarital affairs. Some of these rules differ from society to society, whereas others, like incest taboos, are nearly universal. We do not want to discourage the romantic seeker after Eros entirely, and there certainly are peoples whose sexual practices are far more relaxed than our own, but here again the pilgrim should be reminded that these people too are people, not mere vehicles of erotic gratification. It might also be borne in mind that the free-loving people of the world have a high rate of venereal disease.

Every society has been driven to examine its own existence and the environment in which that existence takes place, and to evolve a **metaphysic,** a general conception of reality, including nonhuman reality, human nature, tribal origins, and the supernatural, together with a supporting **mythology** which in turn implies codes of morals, ethics, good manners, skills (both ritual and functional), and punishments suited to transgressions against the code. The accumulated wisdom of the tribe is often summed up in maxims, aphorisms, and parables. All societies have felt impelled to **ornamentation,** to decorate their bodies, houses, and utensils. While not all societies have developed art as we conceive of it, a distinct activity in its own right separate from those involved in staying alive, all seek beautification. Primitive arti-

The baby's cultural heritage

facts generally represent a blend of the utilitarian, esthetic, and religious. The utility of totem poles and tikis may escape the Western mind, but we have to remember that **magic** plays an essential part in human thinking everywhere. The important thing to see is that even supposedly simple cultures are in fact quite elaborate and that a culture cannot be defined in terms of its quaint folkways, of the sort featured in travelogues, but only by its underlying assumptions about the nature of reality.

For our purposes, it is important to understand how culture is transmitted, how the child comes to think and feel and perceive and act like a Balinese, say, or a Maori or a Navaho or an American or a Greek. This, unfortunately, is a question about which very little is securely known. Whiting and Child (1953), and their followers since, have pointed to some interesting statistical relationships between the economic level of societies and their child-rearing practices, but such studies only hint at the processes of social learning involved. The basic concept is **identification**, taking one's cues to conduct from the behavior of those to whom one is exposed. It has been proposed that identification takes place through **imitation**, aping the acts of one's caretakers. Simple imitation, however, is not a sufficient explanation, since children learn to act in ways consonant with their culture even in novel situations. In the learning of language, for instance, the child learns words from what people say, but he puts them together correctly in combinations to which he has never been exposed. More recently, social-learning theorists have put forth the somewhat broader concept of **modeling**, which means learning to be like the people around you even without imitation of specific acts. There is considerable controversy within the social-learning ranks about what motivates the child to model his behavior on that of others (Bandura, 1971). It has been proposed that the child envies the adult's status, that he covets the resources controlled by the adult, or that the adult simply reinforces modeling, either with concrete rewards or social reinforcers such as smiling and expressions of affection (Bandura et al., 1963). It seems to us that there are at least two weaknesses in the social-learning position. It makes the child much too passive a participant in the learning process, and it leaves out of account the simple notion that a child may want to be like his parents because he loves and admires them. Since social-learning theory does not pretend to deal with cognition, it seems pointless to criticize it for making no mention of values, beliefs, concepts, and thought processes.

Part of the difficulty in describing cultural transmission is that so much of culture seems to be imparted implicitly, without words, in manner and touch and tone of voice, and is learned incidentally, without any immediate behavioral echo, or simply as a corollary of things learned explicitly. For example, if we could gather batches of American readers of this book into one room—as we sometimes do—and ask for a show of hands as to which was better, the natural or the artificial, we would get an overwhelming vote for all that is natural. This is an especially instructive example of the subtlety of implicit teaching and incidental learning, since these admirers of the natural live lives founded on artifice—automobiles, television, record players, air conditioning and central heating, the written word, logic and mathematics, the arts, synthetic fabrics, and provender from the supermarket. Many lovers of nature tend to forget that nature includes tornadoes, hurricanes, earthquakes, volcanic eruptions, droughts, avalanches, mosquitoes, ticks, and chiggers. In this case, the lessons of culture seem to be more potent in shaping attitudes than the evidence of the senses, including the demographic evidence that people who are forced to live close to nature cannot wait to escape it. By the same token, the American or Western value that youth is better than age is not something invented and propagated by young people, but has become a stable cultural tenet transmitted from generation to generation.

The implicit features of a culture are contained in the things its members take for granted, the "of courses." It is because so much of our culture is implicit that it is very hard for us to transcend our ethnocentrism and see our culture as from the outside. It is like coming to know our own bodies, which are simultaneously something to be known and the instrumentality by which we know them. In Heinz Werner's words, one cannot, from within, see one's own eyes. From the standpoint of the majority American culture, *of course* the mother wheels her baby about in a carriage instead of carrying him in a sling against her body or papoose-fashion on her back, of course new highways have to be built to speed the flow of traffic, of course cruelty to animals is wrong, of course beef is good to eat, of course one takes the baby to the doctor or clinic for regular checkups. But from the perspective of other cultures, of course beetles are a great delicacy, of course pork is unclean, of course it is admirable and a sign of great spirituality to stand on one foot for twenty-four years, of course it is bad man-

ners to watch another person eating, so of course one sits with one's back to the feast, of course it is your mother's brother whose authority you must obey.

The present era is unique in that, after centuries of stable continuity, cultures everywhere are changing rapidly, usually in the direction of Europeanization and Americanization (often, as we have said, with disastrous consequences), with European and American cultures themselves in ferment. We can only assume, with some regret, that the rate of change will be accelerated until there is a relatively uniform culture—subject to limits imposed by geography—the world around, putting cultural anthropologists out of business. Meanwhile, there are still recognizably different cultures and, in societies like our own, subcultures.

Most American subcultures were formed by the clustering together of people who separated themselves by preference or were segregated by external pressures from the larger society. Examples are the enclaves formed by groups of immigrants —Chinatown, Little Italy, Little Bohemia, and so on—and based on common language and customs differing from those of the rest of the United States. Some enclaves, of course, are ghettos into which are forced those whom the established society will not allow to live with its members. Harlem and the Negro districts of communities across the country are examples. We even have the phenomenon of the so-called Gilded Ghettos, expanses of suburbia inhabited almost entirely by Jews who are unwelcome in Gentile-dominated suburbs but are able to escape the center city. Back-country communities without modern roads and communications have likewise clung to and elaborated their familiar ways of doing things, with little regard to what was happening in the outside world.

But now, as successive generations of the descendants of immigrants become assimilated into the economic and social life of the country (sometimes through the back door of crime and the rackets), as Negroes refuse to remain disenfranchised, oppressed, uneducated, and poor, as technologically sophisticated factory farming displaces family farming, as suburbs spread into and devour the country, as the rural poor are drawn to the cities, as electricity and bathtubs become more commonplace, as manufactured commodities displace homemade ones, and as radio, television, and magazines spread a common stock of knowledge, ideas, entertainment, and folk heroes, subcultural differences are being remorselessly obliterated. Social class differences remain, but around a shared set of values and assumptions.

Insofar as the spread of uniform culture means the end of ignorance, superstition, xenophobia, moralism, and rigid ideologies, it is probably good. However, it usually also means the weakening or disappearance of local customs, special delicacies, and the skills and competences that get lost when mass-produced commodities replace those made in the home. We can still detect in the United States the differences between southern ways and northern, among east and plains and mountain and west coast, between the rural outlook and the urban, between slums and suburbs, and among ethnic and religious groups, but the rate of change is dizzying.

Social roles

Within any social group or subgroup, individuals play different **roles**, that is, they learn to perform in certain expected ways consonant with their position in life. Within the family, we have the roles of father, mother, wife, husband, son, daughter, brother, sister, and others depending on how the family is organized. At work, we have the roles played by certain specialists—doctor, lawyer, plumber, mechanic —as well as the roles that go with being owner, executive, subordinate, power behind the throne, union representative, and so forth. In the schools, we have the roles of principal, teacher, and pupil. There are roles that go with political office and participation in community affairs. Storekeeper and customer have roles to play. In social situations, people cast themselves, sometimes fleetingly, sometimes consistently, in the roles of virile sportsman, seductive siren, staunch friend, dispenser of sage counsel, and so forth. Indeed, some sociologists would go so far as to say that personal identity consists entirely of the roles a person plays. While most of us are not explicitly aware of role playing, we almost all recognize the special pleasure of those situations which allow us to "be ourselves," to "let our hair down," in sum, to leave off role playing. Every child, at every stage of his development, is being groomed more or less consciously for a particular set of social roles. Within a given society and subculture, each family has its own history, tradition, and values, and provides its own indoctrination, in terms of how it meets or fails to meet needs, the prevailing emotional climate, the games it plays, what experiences it exposes the child to and what it shields him from, what it doesn't know about, and the feelings it attaches to those things to which it exposes the child. What the child learns, we hope it is clear, is not a culture plus a subculture plus a social role, but a way of experiencing the world and himself in relation to it, generalizable or particularizable in these terms. Then, too, the family's general orientation is modified in action both by the child's qualities as an individual, whether boy or girl, whether he arrived at an opportune or inopportune time, whether he is first-born or ninth-born, and also by the meaning that children have for this particular family.

People have children for a variety of reasons. Chief among these, we would like to believe, is the solid pleasure of parenthood, of having a child to share the family's triumphs and tribulations, to be partly a person of the parents' own creation whom they can love and cherish, and whom they can watch grow into a life which he will eventually create for himself. Even when the desire to have a child is extrinsic, or even when pregnancy is unplanned or unwanted, a real live baby, once born, can demolish all his parents' preconceptions and, once they master the mechanics of parenthood, arouse in them a fund of tenderness and protectiveness and delight beyond anything they had ever dreamed of knowing. For some number of parents, the motivation to parenthood is the simple assumption that all normal people get married and then have children. Sad to state, as we know, some people find out after the fact that they did not really want to get married, or at least not now or to this particular person, and some find out—although they are not as likely to admit it, since it is less readily undone—that parenthood was not for them. We may be approaching a time, of course, when contraception is so much the norm that having children will necessarily become a matter of deliberate planning.

Some people want children as a way of perpetuating the family name and fortune —in such cases, of course, role-grooming may be very explicit and sharply defined. In some societies, such as Japan, perpetuation of the family name is so important that, if all the children are girls, one girl's husband is adopted into the family and given its name. For some people, having a child can be a way of projecting into the future the realization of their own frustrated dreams and ambitions, as though having a child gives the parent a second, vicarious chance at life. Sometimes a child is wanted to fill what feels like a vacancy in the parents' lives but may actually be only an emptiness in themselves. Children may be valued as potential contributors to the family economy or because they will look after their parents in their declining years.

For a number of people, parenthood is a necessary proof of their biological adequacy, and a man may need a son as testimony to his virility. Some parents may count so heavily on having a child of one sex rather than the other that, sometimes without realizing it, they only have one name ready. Or they may betray their bias by falling into the habit of referring to the unborn baby exclusively as "he" or as "she." If a child of the wrong sex arrives, they may have trouble adjusting to reality, and in a few extreme cases may treat the child in ways grossly inappropriate to its future sex role. Some children, of course, are valued hardly at all, and are just another mouth to feed, body to clothe, and bottom to wipe. It should go without saying that each of these attitudes has profound effects on the acts and feelings of parents, and hence on their young.

It makes a difference to a baby—and to the roles he comes to embody—whether he comes first in his family or follows other children. A study by Thoman et al. (1970) shows that differential reactions to firstborn and later-born children appear in the neonatal period: inexperienced mothers spend significantly more time with their newborns than do experienced mothers, and although first-time mothers spend more time feeding their babies, the babies get less to eat. The first child typically "breaks trail"—that is, the parents learn about children the hard way, by practicing on their firstborn, who is on the receiving end not only of their fumblings, uncertainties, and outright mistakes, but may also bear the brunt of the excessive anxiety and overprotectiveness expended on a first child. Hilton (1967) reports that first-time mothers, as compared to experienced ones, are "significantly more interfering, extreme, and inconsistent," and that first children are significantly more dependent than those who come later. In spite of the seeming trials and vicissitudes of being first in the family, firstborn children seem to fare somewhat better psychologically than later ones (Altus, 1964, 1966; Ring et al., 1965; Sampson, 1964; Stotland and Dunn, 1962). (In-between children do least well, and the youngest fare second best; if the youngest is born after a long delay, he has much the status of a first baby and achieves accordingly.) These differences may reflect the value of a great deal of adult attention (Rosenzweig, 1966); even if parents have not become blasé about babies, the more children there are, the more attention gets partitioned. Whatever the subsequent outcomes, second and later-born children are handled less anxiously and more casually, with greater reliance on the child's ability to manage some things for himself. Often enough, parents expect a second baby to be just like the first, and are surprised—and sometimes resentful—to find him being his own individual self.

Depending on family variations, some children have to learn their manners early, some are valued for their personalities and others for their symbolic meaning or for their usefulness to the parents, some are initiated from the outset into the forms of religious observance, some are pressed to command and others to compete, or to cooperate or obey or fatalistically accept. Out of their early experience, including the traits of temperament and responsiveness that they bring to the situation, children may come to see the world as looming and ominous, or agitated and bewildering, or lively and exciting, or serene, or deadly dull. The baby's awareness of the world will not take final form for a number of years, but the emotional groundwork is laid down during infancy, so subtly and yet so pervasively that it appears to have been there all along, as though his special way of viewing the world were the only possible one.

It is interesting to note, in passing, that cultural differences among biologically similar individuals are not restricted to human beings. The studies of animal development which we have mentioned show that members of infrahuman species cannot be thought of as having fixed white rat—or monkey or chicken or ant—natures, but that these natures take different shapes in different developmental contexts. Thus, Eleftheriou (1961), studying the physiology of deer mice, found himself hampered by the deer mouse's savage tendency to bite. By the simple expedient of letting deer mice be raised by white laboratory-mouse foster mothers, he was able to secure nonbiting deer mice. Naturalistic observations have indicated that complex behaviors such as hunting are taught to the young of some predatory species such as foxes; we have experimental evidence that mating behavior in white rats or rhesus monkeys cannot be taken for granted as innately given; and that many species of birds sing their characteristic song properly only by virtue of having been exposed to the singing of normal adult birds (Thorpe, 1964; Marler and Tamura, 1964).

Thus, whatever generalizations we make about animal or human behavior, we are obliged to make them with reference to the particular social climate in which development takes place. We must also mention that as the child gets older, he learns a great many things on his own, on the basis of his encounters with people and objects and situations, by solving the problems life puts in his way, and by puzzling out the things that perplex him. But his ways of benefiting from firsthand encounters, and the sorts of solutions he comes up with, are all conditioned upon his cultural experience and the things it has made him able to perceive, feel, learn, and reason about.

Cultural differences extend even to the matter of health care. The British medical profession seems rather more advanced than the American fraternity in recognizing that practices have to be adapted to the attitudes, vulnerabilities, dietary preferences, and folk medicine of various immigrant groups, in Britain particularly West Africans, West Indians, Indians, Pakistanis, and Irish (Carne, 1970; Hashmi, 1970; Parry, 1970). Most recently, of course, the discovery of Chinese acupuncture has caused a sensation.

An example of cultural shaping: sex differences

We cannot hope in this short space to do full justice to the transmission and learning of culture—for one thing, not nearly enough is known about it, although its effects are everywhere to be seen—so we shall dwell in some detail on one aspect of the totality, both as a general example and because of its significance in its own right. This is the way children are made aware of **sex roles** and **sex differences**, particularly in our own society.

Several things need to be said by way of preamble. First, there is the matter of biological differences between the sexes. Obviously, males and females differ in their gross anatomy (leaving out of account the intersexes mentioned earlier). More subtly, there are differences in endocrine balance which can have effects on brain function. For instance, female hamsters without maternal experience perceive hamster pups as something to be eaten, whereas lactating females perceive them as something to be nursed (Richards, 1966). There seems little doubt that having androgens in their bloodstreams makes males more aggressive than females. As S. Levine (1969) points out, there is a circular relation between the central nervous system and endocrines, so that the nervous system altered by hormones reacts in ways that alter hormone production. But the temperamental predispositions associated with biological differences seem slight indeed when we look at the actual variety in sex roles, both vis-à-vis the opposite sex and in the culture at large, around the world.

Second, there is great human variation in sexual mating, in courtship patterns, sexual play, positions during intercourse, and alternate paths to orgasm. Needless to say, a society which did not include somewhere in its definition of the sex act the ejaculation of sperm into the vagina would last only one generation. We cannot take it for granted that sexual motivation arises spontaneously, through simple physical

The baby's cultural heritage

maturation, since animal studies indicate that both drive level and mating patterns depend on early experience for normal development (Altmann, 1966). Nor can it be taken for granted that sexual experience is always defined as pleasant (Church and Insko, 1965). A culture's view of sexuality can weaken the intensity of sexual feelings, it can disguise them from the individual himself, it can intensify them to the point of making them frightening, it can attach bugaboos and sanctions that make sex simultaneously pleasant and disagreeable (athletes are still warned to abstain from sex while in training; there is an ancient Hindu belief that every drop of semen costs the man seven drops of blood), and it can define which acts, objects, partners, and settings produce agreeable sexual feelings, and which disagreeable ones. The culture defines which are permissible partners, which partner initiates sexual activity, the acceptability of homosexual behavior (increasing numbers of people are becoming willing to profess their homosexuality in public and demand immunity from prosecution and harassment), and how private sexual activity should be. It also defines whether one should be made jealous by infidelity, and how jealousy is to be manifested.

Outside the sex act, there can be yet wider variations in the roles assigned to males and females with respect to such tasks as child-rearing (though to paraphrase Clyde Kluckhohn, we know of no society in which the father is expected to bear the children), housekeeping, discipline of children, tending the fields or the herds, marketing produce, managing the budget, handicrafts, hunting, fishing, participation in government and decision-making, and participation in recreational activities. Still

further, there can be great variations among cultures in the traits ascribed to the two sexes: such things as bravery, loyalty, passionateness, deviousness, honesty, perseverance, generosity, cruelty, fortitude, sympathy, emotionality—the reader is invited to supply others. Somewhere on the boundary between roles (prescribed duties and competences) and traits are interests, tastes, and preferences that are assumed to go with being male or female. Thus, we assign different playthings, foodstuffs, activities, occupations, and useful objects to the two sexes, with some overlap. Nobody has yet fully explored and catalogued all the cultural differences in definitions of masculinity and femininity, but a very small knowledge of anthropology is enough to show that they are considerable. Among the Yamana of South America, for instance, swimming is an exclusively female skill (Lowie, 1938). There seem to be some common threads, indicating that biological differences have some determining role, but much of what we take for granted as biologically founded turns out to be what our society is accustomed to think the biological differences mean.

We have already, many times over, changed our conceptions of sex roles, just as we have changed our thinking about human nature (Van den Berg, 1964), and will almost certainly have to change them again. In our own relatively recent history, as we can see in eighteenth-century drawings and paintings, men had long, braided hair (or wigs in the same style) and wore ribbons and bows and long silk stockings. Now, when many young men are wearing their hair long, sometimes braided, or fastened in the back in a bun or ponytail, their elders are likely to feel a sense of moral outrage at a departure from masculine propriety. Similarly, beards are nowadays seen as the mark of the dangerous radical (with connotations of free love and drug use), whereas not so long ago beards were taken for granted as part of adult masculinity—as they still are for certain privileged groups such as explorers. Females are taken to task for wearing "male" attire, for exposing their bodies, and for using zany maquillage.

One of the themes of this book is that children have only recently been discovered as human beings, with characteristics and needs and feelings and rights of their own. But it is only recently that women have begun to be (the process is by no means complete) accorded full human status—competent to vote, to hold office, to own property, to enter into legally binding contracts, to run businesses, to be able to learn mathematics and sciences, to think logically, and to have intense sexual needs and feelings of their own. Many men in our society, but presumably not in the U.S.S.R., still feel uneasy about consulting a woman physician—as do many women. For it must be said that a great many women have been just as conservative as men about accepting a change in the status of women, while others seem to see the liberation of womankind as a chance to revenge themselves for all the slights accumulated during the centuries of bondage and can resist no opportunity to belittle or degrade the male. The war between the sexes has not yet been settled, and both men and women are by no means sure what life style, what role or combination of roles, is appropriate to the female of the species. But by the same token, a change in the female role calls for corresponding changes in the male role, and it still has not been settled how the male role is to be defined. A further ramification is that parents are increasingly

uncertain what sex-related values they should be conveying to their children, boys and girls.

In any case, all parents recognize the importance of sex differences. Note that the first question parents ask, if the obstetrician hasn't already made haste to tell them, is "Is it a boy or a girl?" When they know the answer, and not before, there is language available to talk about the baby—up to now, whatever their hopes, the baby has been an ambiguity, an *it*. Once they know the sex of the child, the appropriate set of attitudes comes to the fore—and the baby's role begins to take shape. Indecision aside, how are these conceptions of masculinity and femininity transmitted to an infant who doesn't yet know that he exists, let alone that he has a body which places him forever in the category of male or female? (We shall take up in Chapter 13 the matters of transvestism and homosexuality, which involve identification with the opposite biological sex.) These conceptions are transmitted not as intellectual knowledge but as dispositions, attitudes, feelings. Parents treat boys and girls differently because they, the parents, have acquired from their own upbringings a set of expectations, of inclinations to respond to and stimulate boys and girls differentially. Rothbart and Maccoby (1966) find that fathers are more tolerant of little girls' aggression and dependency than of little boys', whereas mothers are more permissive toward boys. Kagan and his coworkers (Levine et al., 1967) report that upper-middle-class American mothers, at least, treat infant boys and girls differently, particularly in responding with more vocalizing to baby girls' vocalizations. Thus, usually without knowing it, they express their expectations through manner, through the things they do,

The baby's cultural heritage

Sex differences at thirteen months. At left, the girl separated from her mother by a wire-mesh barrier reacts
by crying. At right, the boy struggles to get past the
barrier.

through the sorts of objects with which
they surround the baby and toward which
they direct his attention and feelings. In
short, they enclose the baby within a
material, social, and emotional environment
which tells him or her what his or her
capacities for action and feeling are. In
some respects, they operantly condition
(see pp. 186–187) the baby into a sex role,
reacting with delight to "sex-appropriate"
behaviors and withholding rewards when
the baby behaves "inappropriately."

More concretely, American boys get blue
things and girls get pink ones. Friends and
relatives give the boy tiny trousers to grow
into, and the girl frilly frocks. Boys get the
playthings labeled masculine, girls feminine
ones. This difference is not so marked in
early infancy, when both boys and girls
are given, for instance, stuffed animals to
cuddle, but it already exists, and it becomes
even more pronounced when babies become able to manipulate objects. From

**The
infant: two**

150

toddlerhood onward, many parents forbid little boys to play with "girls' things," as though masculinity were a fragile state of being easily undermined by any deviation from the ideal. Boy babies can be handled boisterously; with girls one tends to be gentle. One takes pleasure in the delicate contour of a daughter's mouth; in a son one takes delight in how vigorous and husky he is. Some mothers have even reported that they find it less disagreeable to change a girl's dirty diapers than a boy's. Goldberg and Lewis (1969) report that mothers of six-month-old girls touch their babies more than do mothers of six-month-old boys. They offer a catalogue of some specific sex differences found in these same children at age thirteen months: girls played more than boys with blocks, toy animals, a pegboard, and two toys at a time; boys played more than girls with nontoys (e.g., the tape used to cover the electrical outlets) and spent more time banging toys; confronted with a barrier blocking access to mother, girls cried whereas boys tried to move the barrier aside; the girls showed greater dependence on their mothers than did the boys.

It should not be necessary to labor further the point that boys and girls grow up in different, culturally determined emotional atmospheres from the beginning. As they become able to act for themselves and to move around, their initiatives meet with quite different responses, whether indifference, amusement, tolerance, anger, sympathy, punishment, or alarm. It requires no great powers of observation to conclude that it may make a difference whether, as a little boy, it is the female parent who shows great indulgence, or, as a little girl, the male parent. (In the next chapter, we shall have something to say about possible

sexual components in the relations of parents and children of opposite sexes.) All the far-reaching implications for feeling and behavior that go with being male or female require years of elaboration, but it is as a baby that one receives one's first lessons in being a boy or a girl. Perhaps the strength of parental attitudes toward the sex of their child can be seen in these lines from Ogden Nash's "Song to Be Sung by the Father of Infant Female Children":

My heart leaps up when I behold
A rainbow in the sky;
Contrariwise, my blood runs cold
When little boys go by.
For little boys as little boys,
No special hate I carry,
But now and then they grow to men,
And when they do, they marry.
No matter how they tarry,
Eventually they marry.
And, swine among the pearls,
They marry little girls.*

*Implications
of cultural shaping*

It is an uncomfortable notion for many people that they would have been quite different individuals had they grown up in a different family or subcultural or cultural context, yet the conclusion seems inescapable. In the first place, there is no escaping the process of cultural learning. A child can develop only in contact with adults during a long apprenticeship, and there are no culture-free adults. As long as a mother is reacting to a child, whom she inevitably perceives in ways at least partially dictated

The baby's cultural heritage

by her cultural outlook, they are linked in a circuit of interpersonal exchange in which the mother is imparting and getting information about herself, the child, and the world in general.

All cultures work, at least until they disintegrate. But not all work equally well in producing members who are fully human and humane. It is perfectly clear that some cultures shape people in ways that produce endless social frictions, that set individuals at odds with each other, and that set up internal conflicts and dissatisfaction. Most cultures rely on tradition and precedent for solving problems, instead of encouraging inventiveness, innovation, and fresh approaches. A culture may warp or stultify or stunt our humanity. But the answer does not seem to be to do away with culture, even if we could. We have the dire example of what happens to "primitive" peoples when Europeans, sometimes with the best of intentions (or ingenious rationalizations), destroy established cultural forms without providing time, opportunity, and tutelage for the development and assimilation of new forms. In our own country, we have the plight of Negroes uprooted from Africa, held in slavery, where family ties were systematically destroyed, and then emancipated into prolonged lack of identity with either the old or the new way of life; of the American Indians, the Chicanos and Latinos, the Eskimos, and the Polynesians of Hawaii and Samoa. Large numbers of all these people have been condemned by the white man to personal and social rot. This is not, however, to say that these people are culturally deprived. Some members of all these groups have assimilated the majority culture and found a place in society. Black people have evolved a culture of their own which has worked very well in enabling them to survive in a hostile environment. The others have managed to preserve, live by, and find satisfaction in some of the old ways. But we are now, in this generation, for the first time ever, in the unique position of coming to understand how culture operates, how we might remake culture, designing a new version of human nature and rearing our children in approximation of an ideal. Those most entrenched in our present majority cultural orientation, the most ethnocentric among us, are secure in the conviction that what we have is both right and inevitable—the product of human nature rather than its shaper. For these people, all else is destructive subversion, to be resisted as unrealistic Utopianism. It seems to us, by contrast, that the evidence suggests a great deal of plasticity in the human organism, and that we have at least a beginning understanding of what to do—and what not to do—if we are to raise our children to be humane, decent citizens of the planet. This is not to say that it would be easy, but that it is possible.

Unfortunately, we know more about how to change human nature than about how to change the framework of social institutions within which human beings have to operate. And the more human human beings become, the greater the contrast between their humanity and the inhuman and dehumanizing institutions to which in most modern societies they are expected to adapt. Perhaps the best we can do at this stage of social evolution is to concentrate on producing autonomous, intelligent, compassionate, cooperative young people with a sense of humanity, and hope that they will in time reshape the society they inherit. It is going to take a lot of hard work and hard thinking, but there is room for hope. The anthropologists have taught us about ourselves, and we have the opportunity and responsibility to make wise use of their teachings.

4

developmental
principles
and
approaches

The study of human behavior and development is not merely a search for facts. It also involves finding a pattern in the facts, general principles that will enable us to understand the development we have already seen and what is still to come. In the first three chapters, we set forth a great many facts and suggested, at least by implication, a few key principles. It is now time to make the principles explicit. We begin with some general developmental laws, starting with those on which there is wide agreement and working our way to some which are more controversial. These will be followed by a brief account of the application of scientific methods to the study of psychological development. In the final section, we compare a number of theoretical orientations, all of them the subject of sharp debate, but illustrating the ways psychologists have thought about behavioral development. Logically, of course, it might seem that this chapter should open the book. We feel, however, that without some of the substance of development to refer to, the reader would find the materials of this chapter rather empty formulations. The reader now has enough facts in hand that, before we follow the baby into toddlerhood and beyond, we can begin looking for ways to order the facts in keeping with principles and theories.

Principles
of Development

Growth gradients

The first pair of principles to be discussed has to do with the directional flow of physical development. In higher animals, growth invariably proceeds in two related directions, or **gradients**. The **cephalo-caudal** (head-to-tail) growth principle refers to the fact that the head end of the organism develops first, in prenatal growth, with the lower portions taking shape at later periods. This same principle seems to apply to postnatal human behavioral development, in that the baby's head becomes functional before his hands, that is, he uses mouth, eyes, and ears before he grasps; and his hands before his feet, that is, the baby is a skilled manipulator with his hands before his feet come into focus as playthings, prehensile instruments, or, later, things to walk with. Similarly, like the legendary ostrich, the baby at first seems to consider himself invisible as long as his head is covered, as in a game of peek-a-boo.

The **proximo-distal** (near-to-far) growth principle says that growth proceeds outward, from the central axis of the body toward the periphery. The proximo-distal gradient is most conspicuous prenatally in the development of the limb buds from the trunk and, in turn, of the still more remote hands and fingers and toes from the limb buds. Postnatally, the child uses his whole hand as a unit before he can control his several fingers. In general, somatic and functional development seems to grow like an inverted tree, downward from the head and outward from the trunk, organized around the internal branchings of the nervous and circulatory systems and digestive tract.

Differentiation and functional subordination

The principle of **differentiation** states that development proceeds from the simple to the complex, from the homogeneous to the heterogeneous, from the general to the specific. From a single-celled zygote there develop by differentiation an immense number of cells of highly varied structure and function. The first cells formed by division of the zygote are all of the same kind, differing only in their position with respect to each other. As differentiation proceeds, the cells change in character, forming different kinds of tissues with **specialized** functions: nerves, skin, bone, blood, muscle, and so on. In turn, differentiated structures and functions become integrated into new, more inclusive, emergent patterns, yielding a simplicity with many components. Because the differentiated components are submerged in the new organization, losing their separate identities, we have called this process **functional subordination**—that is, the part-functions are subordinated to the emergent whole-function. (Other writers, notably Werner, refer to the same process as **hierarchization** or **hierarchic integration**.)

We can see the themes of differentiation and functional subordination running through all of behavioral as well as physiological development. At first, the baby cries with his whole body; later, his crying becomes more circumscribed. His distress reactions are initially all of a kind, whereas later they take on greater specificity, so that he has distinctive cries for hunger, pain, anger, and loneliness. The innumerable perceptual discriminations the baby learns represent differentiations of self and world. When the baby begins to walk, the more differentiated gaits like striding, hopping, trotting, galloping, running, and skipping all lie ahead. Walking is at first a sufficient occupation in its own right, but later becomes subordinated to the end of getting from one place to another. Soon after he begins to walk, the baby or young

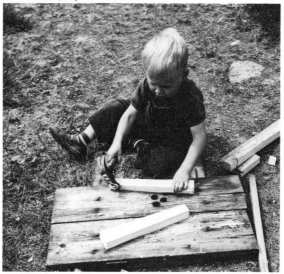

An example of functional subordination: hammering for its own sake becomes hammering in order to make something. Since many readers have concluded that this is a definition rather than an example, you are urged to consult the text for more on this major developmental principle.

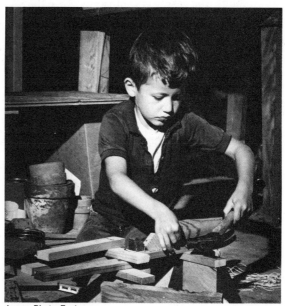

toddler loves to carry things as he walks, but not until later with a view to conveying something to a particular location in order to use it. Speaking begins with single words (or word clusters), but after a period of speaking in single differentiated word units, the child begins combining words into higher-order sentences. For a toddler, hammering as banging is enough; when, as a preschool child, he becomes able to use a hammer and nails, driving nails is a sufficient occupation; at a more advanced stage, hammering or nail-driving is functionally subordinated to making specific things. We shall return frequently to these principles in discussing psychological development.

Asynchronous growth and discontinuity of growth rate

The principle of **asynchronous growth** summarizes the way the focus of development shifts at successive periods in development. If one imagines a baby the size of an adult, the result is grotesque, for babies are not miniature adults. It immediately becomes obvious that the whole body does not grow at once, but that different regions and subsystems develop at different rates and different times. In looking at prenatal development, we saw how during the germinal period the baby's placental structures came first, while the embryo itself lay dormant in the germinal disk. Later, there was an interval devoted mainly to a preliminary formation of the cranial structures, while the body parts marked time. Thereafter, now the heart, now the limbs, now the respiratory system took the lead. Asynchronous growth after birth accounts for shifts in the relative size of head, trunk, and extremities, and for the underlying

changes in glandular patterns. Voices and faces are different in infancy, childhood, adolescence, and maturity. Consider alone the extent to which the nose is submerged or dominant at various ages. Even during adulthood and old age, body proportions keep changing, as clothing manufacturers know.

What we have just said refers to the growth of subsystems of the body. The subsystems, of course, grow in the context of the whole body, which itself changes in overall size and weight, but in spurts, not in a smooth curve of increase. The fact that the rate of growth changes at different periods is expressed in the principle of **discontinuity of growth rate**. Growth is very rapid in early infancy but levels off gradually through the preschool years and goes on at a relatively slow pace during the so-called middle years of childhood. The beginning of adolescence is marked by a new spurt of growth which levels off in early adulthood.

We are not sure what the psychological equivalents of asynchronous growth and discontinuity of growth rate may be, but it is certain that children do have periods of greater receptivity to certain kinds of learning and thinking, and times of intense preoccupation with one kind of behavior or area of experience, which they then leave to go on to something else. We shall talk more about such patterns shortly in our discussion of competence motivation. There is also some reason to believe that new phases of psychological development may be signaled by periods of disruption and turbulence.

The developmental principles we have set forth so far are largely descriptive and generally accepted. The ones that follow are more inferential and have more to do with the subjective experience of the developing person, and so are more open to controversy and debate. They strike us as useful principles for the understanding of behavior, and necessary if one is going to consider behavior in all its subtlety and variety.

Development toward self-knowledge and autonomy

The principle of **development toward self-knowledge and autonomy** points to the progressive differentiation of self from environment, and of various aspects of self from the totality, and to the integration of self-awareness into an emergent self-image or self-schema. It also points to the child's increasing ability to regulate his own behavior and to think and act on his own. We have already sketched in some highlights of the development of self-awareness (see p. 96). Here we want to make explicit that such development is a general trend (complicated by our tendencies to self-deception), accompanied by increasing autonomy, ability to think, decide, and act for oneself, to consider one's own actions in perspective, and to find original modes of acting. Now it is obvious that some of what we experience as self-determination or "will" had its actual beginnings outside ourselves, in the knowledge and understanding and values that other people taught us. But it is possible also to make other people's teachings truly one's own, so that they cease to be external to oneself and instead are part of one's own equipment for behavior.

The development of self-awareness involves several sorts of differentiation. There is differentiation of self from environment, there is differentiation of self as knower from self as thing known—consider the statement "I am thinking about myself"— and there comes to be a differentiation of private self and public self. Here we have a subprinciple of **duplicity,** of being able to think one thing and say another, to have an inner life, and eventually to dissemble and to lie. It sometimes seems that middle-years children go through a period of deliberate lying, not so much to deceive as to test their powers of deception. Perhaps the first manifestation of duplicity appears in late infancy or early toddlerhood with the child's playful simulation of an emotion, as when he pretends to be hurt so as to be cuddled and soothed, or with his playful adoption of an identity not his own, as when he pretends to be a dog. As we shall see in the next chapter, autonomy—establishing an independent self—is a dominant theme in toddlerhood.

Competence motivation

Psychologists and psychiatrists have too long tended to think in terms of tissue-need motivations, whereby some lack or imbalance must be invoked to account for behavior. However, as thinkers (who are also skilled observers) like Barbara Biber and Gardner and Lois Murphy have pointed out, such a formulation does not account for the fact that children brought up in a warm, supporting, stimulating, and responsive environment show from early infancy a pleasure in exploration, manipulation, and mastery of the new things they encounter.

Robert White (1959, 1963) has suggested the name of **competence motivation** for the child's curiosity about things and what they are like and his drive to acquire and exercise skills in dealing with the world, whether at the level of stacking rings on a peg, learning and using new words, or learning to ride a tricycle, perhaps in the same way that adults do puzzles. Human behavior is not all describable in terms of biological imbalances, or even in terms of need for affiliation with other creatures, but includes in addition something like cognitive needs or striving—needs to know, to find out, to be interested.

White, in line with conventional psychological thinking, locates this motive force inside the organism, as though on the analogy of a physical drive like hunger or sex. Other thinkers, like Donald Hebb, Mary Henle, and Kurt Lewin, have called our attention to the motivating and mobilizing power of objects and their demand qualities, of the kind discussed in Chapter 2, and the way these interact with states of the organism to produce behavior. Whichever way we look at it, we must take account of behavior which does not seem to be activated by physical or interpersonal disequilibrium but by the enjoyment of doing what is near the edge of ability—the ability to be tantalized. Indeed, as we have said, disequilibrium interferes with such behavior. Competence motivation becomes an important developmental principle because the behavior it produces leads to learning, and learning to change. Competence motivation has obvious links to Harlow's curiosity drive. Since much of development is built on the accumulation and integration of knowledge and understanding, what Harlow calls learning sets, or learning to learn (see p. 221), must be considered an important factor in development. Learning sets may also help us understand how children become able to perform perfectly novel, emergent acts unprecedented in their own experience—for instance, every normal child says things that he has never heard said (see p. 218).

Ambivalence, growth ambivalence, and dual ambivalence

We have already mentioned the fact of **ambivalence**, of how one can be of two minds about someone or something, finding it simultaneously or in alternation both attractive and repellent. Often we try to conceal one of these minds from ourselves and admit only to the attitude we consider acceptable. Ambivalence describes our feelings about many of the people and situations we meet in life, and sometimes our feelings about ourselves. It also seems to characterize how children feel about growing up, as though there were considerable conflict between a progressive urge, which tells the child to venture forth, to explore, to try new things, and a conservative one, which tells the child to preserve the status quo, to play it safe, to avoid ventures into the dangerous unknown, or even a reactionary one that lures the child back to still-earlier stages of immaturity. This conflict may be termed **growth ambivalence**.

There is little evidence of growth ambivalence in infancy, but it becomes prominent in toddlerhood, where the child at one moment is all autonomy, competence, and bluster, and the next moment is asking to be babied, to be rocked, petted, and fed. Obviously, the weight is usually on the side of progress, since most people do grow up, but not wholly, which may be why so many of us, even as adults, quail and wobble whenever there is a major decision to be made, even when change is obviously in the direction of improvement.

Now, it is bad enough that the child is plagued by growth ambivalence, but to make matters worse, so are his parents. That is, they applaud every step of his development—his first smile, his first participation in family games, his first walking, his first word—but each such step brings an increasing and disagreeable appreciation that the parents are losing their baby, that the child is moving toward self-sufficiency and defiance, away from innocence and into the harsh reality of the outside world. The combined ambivalences of child and parents about the child's **growth we have called dual ambivalence**. Dual ambivalence reaches an acute climax, as we shall see, at adolescence, when the youngster is making his final move away from the family and into mature independence, but it crops up at every stage and transition. The child's first day at school is a moment of excitement but trepidation for the child, and of pride but regret for the parent.

Maturation, experience, learning, and critical periods

Physical maturation is a fact. The child does go through somatic transformations and metamorphoses which have profound effects on his psychological functioning. It is important to understand how maturational changes arise and what their implications are for behavior. It is obvious, first of all, that all of maturation is instigated (and realized with reasonable environmental support) by the genetic material contained in the cell nuclei, and its capacities for processing environmental information

so as to manufacture an organism. We have seen how, at the plastic, embryonic stage of development, the introduction of abnormal information in the form of viruses, x-rays, chemicals, temperature changes, and so forth, evokes teratogenic expressions of a bizarre kind. Once certain alternatives are chosen, however, they are generally irreversible, so that the organism becomes less and less plastic, in the sense of having fewer and fewer alternative potentialities. We know about some obvious influences on postnatal physical development—diet, fresh air and sunshine, illness, exercise—but the psychological relevance of these is obscure. There is good reason to think that autonomic nervous system and endocrine functioning can be shaped by emotional experience, and through them both the vegetative functions that they regulate—digestion, circulation, respiration, sweating, sex, and so on—and associated patterns of temperament and motivation. At least since Freud, we have come to take for granted the notion of psychosomatic illness, the physical malfunctions and lesions produced by chronic emotional stress. It is possible that normal maturation is in part a psychosomatic effect, governed both by stressful emotions and pleasant ones, and hence by the environmental circumstances that produce them. There is even reason to suspect that dwarfism is sometimes a psychosomatic effect (Apley et al., 1971). It is tempting to think that cognitive-intellectual experience, and the demonstrable residue of learning that it leaves behind, also have psychosomatic consequences. In fact, as we have seen, enriched cognitive experience does alter brain biochemistry in the rat, and C. J. Smith (1959) has shown that the brains of rats raised in "rich" environments develop areas of specialized function,

Principles of development

161

whereas the brains of rats raised in ordinary laboratory conditions do not, acting instead according to the "law of mass action." The findings from animal research are reviving interest in a once-discarded concept, what Wheeler called **stimulation-induced maturation.** We know, because as educators we do it all the time, that we can teach people to make new perceptual discriminations, to perceive new patterns of figure-ground organization, and to perceive previously hidden spatial and functional relations, but we do not know whether we have thereby altered the structure of the sense receptors. We do know, though, that sense receptors deprived of stimulation early in life atrophy and may become non-functional.

The chief effect of maturational changes seems to be to make new kinds of behavior possible. That is, **maturation** and **experience** seem to stand in a circular relationship, each feeding into the other. Thus, it is only at a given stage of maturation that the baby becomes able to roll over, to walk, to control his sphincters. Another way of saying the same thing is that a maturational change brings with it a **readiness** for the appearance of a given kind of behavior. The new behavior may appear almost spontaneously—in Wayne Dennis's term, **autogenously,** that is, self-generated—with a minimum of specific preparation, practice, stimulation, or support. Or it may require special environmental stimulation of some sort, as in the case of learning to talk. Now in general, the mere fact of maturation having taken place does not guarantee that the associated behavior will take place. If, for instance, a seemingly autogenous behavior like walking is delayed artificially beyond its normal time of appearance, as by prolonged illness or an injury that keeps a baby bedridden, walking comes with

greater difficulty than under normal conditions. On the other hand, deprivation of proto-walking activities up to that time seems to have little effect.

A difficulty arises in thinking about these issues because psychologists have placed too much emphasis on the motor side of skills like walking, with too little attention to their cognitive aspects. We have already mentioned, for instance, that the ability to walk depends most fundamentally upon a new orientation to space, particularly the vertical. Blind babies, who suffer no known motor deficit, walk later than seeing babies. The achievement of sphincter control likewise depends on awareness of one's body functions, and not merely a change in reflex reactions to tension in bowel or bladder. The maturational changes of puberty do not automatically bring with them sexual lusts and strivings—experimental evidence suggests that white rats and monkeys which have had socially-deprived prepubertal histories are liable to be sexually inadequate, and anecdotal evidence indicates that many physically normal adult human beings have a low level of sexual drive. Many sorts of learning readiness, moreover, such as readiness to learn to use numbers or to read, seem to depend at least as much on prior experience as on any identifiable maturational states. Obviously, since maturation and amount of experience are both highly correlated with how long a child has lived, it is logically very difficult to disentangle the relative contribution of each to a state of readiness.

The concept of **readiness to learn** is closely linked with that of **critical** or **sensitive periods** in development, analogous to those of the embryonic phase, during which a given function is most responsive to cultivation, trauma, or neglect. That is, readiness can be seen as the beginning of a critical period, but critical periods also have an end, beyond which opportunities for learning are of little more use than those that come too early. Unfortunately, the notion of postembryonic critical periods has been tied too closely to maturation, generating a great deal of pointless controversy. It seems more useful to say that there is a hierarchy of learnings such that there are more favorable and less favorable periods for the cultivation of particular competences. These periods are undoubtedly connected with stages of physical maturity, but, as we have already indicated, the relationship may be circular, making it hard to know what is cause and what is effect. We do not at this point know enough about what brings a critical period to an end, whether some maturational change or a conflicting bit of learning, or just what the consequences are of delaying learning beyond the end of a critical period. We do know or suspect a few things. Such evidence as we have suggests that delaying the formation of close social attachments much past the age of six months may impair the baby's ability to form such attachments, with serious implications for all of later development. There is good experimental evidence that puppies kept from human contact during their first nine to fourteen weeks are permanently unable to become attached to humans (Freedman et al., 1961). The evidence is less good, but there is some reason to believe that chronic bed-wetters may have had their toilet training delayed too long, say past age three. As we have said, the body awarenesses essential to sphincter control may get submerged in the more complex experiencing of later ages. We have likewise already mentioned that interfering with walking during the normal period for its development may have adverse effects. On the other hand, we know that some skills ordinarily acquired early in life, such as reading, can still be learned late in life, although perhaps not so easily or so well. Much work remains to be done to clarify the nature of critical periods and their generality for all of postnatal development.

The notion of readiness for learning carried with it the message to parents and educators that they should not push too hard, that learning would come quickly and effortlessly once the child was ready. The more complicated notion of critical periods, which says both that it is futile and even injurious to try to teach something for which the child is unready and that it may be equally risky to wait too long, lest the readiness pass, has created new anxieties for parents and teachers. The key to the problem is probably that no guidelines are given that will let adults know when a child is ready for a particular kind of learning. While some general indicators can be seen (as we have tried to show with respect to toilet training), the only sure test is to try and watch for reactions. When the child seems refractory, there is a good chance that it is too soon. Premature pressure may actually produce results opposite to what the adult is seeking. In all these areas of learning, two rules seem to apply. First, there should always be abundant opportunities for learning. Second, adults must always be sensitive to the emotional feedback—the language of behavior—that they receive in their dealings with children. And, of course, it always helps to have a general notion of developmental sequences.

LEARNING AND CONDITIONING. Here we must make explicit the usual psychological conception of learning as associative conditioning. That is, a stimulus can come to be the signal for an action or a reaction. Students of conditioning recognize two basic processes. One, called **classical conditioning**, occurs when a previously neutral stimulus is paired with a stimulus which automatically produces a response. The naturally linked stimulus and response are called unconditioned. The neutral stimulus, after repeated pairings with an unconditioned stimulus, becomes able by itself to produce much the same reaction as the unconditioned stimulus. It is then described as a conditioned or conditional stimulus for the response. Thus, in infancy, objects associated with experiences of pleasure, like the breast or nursing bottle, or with pain, like the doctor, can become signals to the baby that something pleasant or painful is about to happen. By extension, all kinds of meanings, some of them arbitrary or inappropriate, can come to be attached to features in the environment by classical conditioning.

The second basic process is known as **instrumental conditioning.** When the organism acts in a way that produces desirable results, the results **reinforce** the action and the organism learns to perform that particular action to produce that particular result. Because it has effects, such a learned act is called instrumental. While classical conditioning deals mostly with things done to the organism, largely in terms of vegetative responses, instrumental conditioning applies to what the organism does to its environment and the effects it produces.

Although classical and instrumental conditioning are thought of as distinct processes, they often go together. Siqueland and Lipsitt (1966) taught babies to turn their heads instrumentally to get nourishment, but they began by classically conditioning them to open their mouths (part of the Babkin reflex) in response to a signal.

The fact that accumulated experience—

learning—and maturation blend so inextricably and circularly into each other poses problems for the usual conception of associative learning. As we shall point out in discussing learning theories, the typical learning experiment studies the acquisition of a single response, with little attention to how the learning fits into the totality of the organism's experience. If we are to understand the role of experience in development, we have to move beyond the usual conceptions of learning and consider how the child's encounters with the world enable him to build up a coherent image of self and environment, including such subtle issues as learning to think of himself as competent and the world as open to exploration and conceptual mastery.

As we said earlier, there is increasing evidence of the importance of early experience for later development. The learning involved in early experience transcends the usual conceptions of learning. For instance, the baby's learning that it is worth responding, his learning about the possibility and rewards of exploration, cannot be expressed in terms of any of the simpler models of specific learnings.

The schematization of experience

A component of development is the acquisition of knowledge, a set of more or less patterned, integrated **schemata** (singular, **schema**). This term has been used by Piaget, among others. A schema is a conception of what something or a group of things is like. We have already proposed that stranger anxiety occurs when the baby has developed a schema of familiar people and places. Ordinarily, schemata are implicit, although they can often be verbalized, and are experienced mostly as vague feelings. It is when our schemata clash with reality that they become most easily perceptible. Such clashes surprise us and can produce laughter, bewilderment, or terror, or various combinations of feelings, depending on the nature of the discrepancy. When the burly male speaks in a piping falsetto, or the wispy female in a booming voice, when the naked savage discourses knowingly on Proust and Ionesco and constructivism, when the magician pulls endless yards of fabric out of a thimble, when the nice young honor student down the block turns out to be a sex murderer, previously implicit schemata are brought into jarring contrast with new ones. Sometimes our schemata are so strong that they interfere with our perceptions; we call such schemata preconceptions, prejudices, stereotypes, or superstitions.

We have already seen how the baby discovers his own body, feature by feature and region by region, and how these discoveries come to be integrated into a body schema. The schematization of the body can produce vivid schematic experience when a limb is amputated, leaving behind a "phantom limb" which, until it gradually shrinks away, feels as though it is really there (Haber, 1958). One can even suffer pain or discomfort in a missing extremity. The parts of our own body are not automatically given to us by virtue of some sort of built-in representation in the nervous system, since phantom limbs do go away, and since people born with an extremity missing, but with intact brains, seem never to experience phantoms (Simmel, 1961; Wilson et al., 1962). Instead, the composition and reach and other knowledge of our own bodies seem to be built up through early experience and feedback to our activities, consolidated as a schema which tells us what our bodies are doing and where they are, both the whole body in space and the various parts relative to each other and to the total schema. Most of the time we know automatically and semiconsciously what our bodies are up to —we do not have to stop and wonder where a hand is before we can use it—but the major surface regions of the body can be brought into awareness at will.

The phantom limb has its schematic counterpart in what the authors choose to call "**phantom environments**," that is, animals and people sometimes go on acting in terms of the way things used to be, apparently unaware that circumstances have changed. In an experiment by Carr and Watson (1908), a maze alley that had previously led to food was blocked off, but rats which had learned to turn into the alley thereafter persistently and interminably continued trying to enter the now nonexistent pathway. Skinner (1948) says that if one encloses a flock of sheep with electrified wire, after a while one can remove the wire and substitute string, and the sheep will continue to avoid the string as though it were wire. People, too, in their thinking about social issues such as sex, birth control, economics, conservation, pollution, transportation, international relations, the reapportionment of state legislatures, racial integration, education, or whatever, often act as though they were living in the phantom environments of bygone centuries. Nostalgia, of course, expresses a yearning for a phantom environment, one which may in fact never have existed. For there is a second kind of phantom environment in addition to the things that have ceased to be but that still influence us. This is the universe of things that have never existed but that people make up out of whole cloth, sometimes innocently and sometimes from ulterior motives. Here we have the spirit world, the domain of imaginary explanatory entities from the caloric to instinct to intelligence, and various bugaboos invented by government officials to frighten people into various courses of action.

Our better-defined and better reality-related schemata are sometimes called "concepts," especially when we can name them and talk about them. Our general schema of reality can be said to include more restricted, specialized schemata such as a spatial schema, a schema of time, and schemata of social roles, causation, life, death, sickness and health, procreation, body functions, esthetics, morality, social organization, human nature, shape, color, numbers and numerical relations, history, and so on through all the domains of knowledge.

As the foregoing implies, not all schemata are formed out of direct experience. Linguistic formulations of reality, our own and other people's, also stay with us as schemata. Here we should point to a more general phenomenon, based on the principle of realism. Words and sentences are usually taken to represent something real, that is, we **reify** or **hypostatize** language. It is reification when we create the phantom entities and situations mentioned above. It is also reification that permits us to enjoy a novel as though we were participating in actual events.

Canalization

One other variety of learning that we have touched on and which does not fit exactly either the classical or the operant-condi-

tioning model is called **canalization**, a term that Gardner Murphy (1958, ch. 5) took over from the French psychologist Pierre Janet. When the organism is in a state of need, there are for many need states a variety of possible satisfiers. Thus, hunger, or even a special appetite or craving as for sweets, in principle can be satisfied by any number of different foodstuffs. Usually, though, a given culture decrees that only a few of the many potential satisfiers are acceptable, and after a while the individual develops a taste for and comes to think of the accustomed satisfiers as the only possible ones, rejecting the others as unfit. That is, he canalizes on what his culture defines as the proper satisfiers of needs. The Eskimo child learns to relish whale blubber, the southern child, hominy grits, the Rhode Island child, johnnycakes, the Philadelphia child, scrapple, the Hawaiian child, smoked fish and poi, the Oriental child, rice, and so on around the world. And the child simultaneously learns not to like various other, equally nourishing foods. Most Americans quail at eating raw fish (although they will eat raw oysters), horse meat, or pickled bees. In a study by Burghardt and Hess (1966), young turtles fed consistently for their first few days on particular foods, all of them part of most adult turtle diets, thereafter consistently chose the specific food each had started with. Our many canalizations amount to a schematization of the familiar as "natural" and "good" and "human," with an accompanying distrust of anything that does not match such schemata as alien and hence "inferior." In the matter of food preferences, it should be noted, the body actually adapts to its accustomed diet so that unusual foods may indeed be inedible. For instance, well-meaning provision of protein supplements to people who live on an allstarch diet may blind or even kill them by depleting their scant supply of vitamin A (Bunce, 1969). Persons who do not regularly drink milk stop manufacturing lactase, an enzyme essential to the digestion of the lactose in milk, and introduction of milk into a milk-free diet can cause severe, and even fatal, diarrhea (Davis and Bolin, 1969). Asians apparently tolerate monosodium glutamate (MSG) very well, but in at least some Americans it causes the "Chinese restaurant syndrome." Thus, we should not dismiss as foolish all aversions to strange foods. More serious is the schematization of people into "our kind" and "them." It is our feeling that parents would do well to give their children early in life experience with highly variegated need satisfiers, including people, to forestall the formation of narrow and rigid canalizations which may prevent openness to new experiences. This is not to speak of occasional atypical canalizations—in the realm of sexuality, for instance, we have homosexuality, in which the satisfier of sexual needs is a person of the same sex, and fetishism, in which objects like shoes or underwear or stuffed seagulls become invested with sexual meaning.

It will be seen that there is a kinship between canalization and both imprinting and cathexis (see p. 179). In Murphy's view, canalization is the more general, inclusive mechanism, with imprinting and cathexis as special instances. Burghardt and Hess, however, in the study referred to above, have completely reversed this relationship and describe food canalization as food-imprinting, and the difference may be merely one of choice of words for the same concepts. Since the authors early imprinted or canalized on the thinking of Murphy, we shall continue from his viewpoint. Imprinting, then, would be canalization of response to the mother (or surrogate) as the gratifier of something like a "need-for-affiliation." A difficulty with this position, of course, is that imprinting takes place before there is any opportunity to learn about the need-gratifying potentialities of the mother figure.

Cathexis likewise is seen as canalization on particular objects out of a potentially large array that gratify erotic needs, and in this respect is closer to standard notions of learning. However, cathexis includes not only the gratifying objects but also the zones and channels—mouth, anus, genitals —of satisfaction and, in addition, the activities—sucking, biting, chewing, expelling, rubbing, thrusting, handling—that bring the person into contact with satisfiers. Thus, to make cathexis a special case of canalization requires broadening of the original concept. To make canalization a general principle of character-formation, we should be prepared to include in it such things as hammock-sleeping, as contrasted with ground-sleeping or mat-sleeping or bed-sleeping, as a means for satisfying a need for rest. Whether such a broadening weakens the power of the concept by making it synonymous with **taste** or **preference** is something the reader is free to decide.

In any event, canalization shares with learning theory and psychoanalysis its dependence on needs as a basis for learning, whereas in our view cultural learning is in large part motivation-free. Let us make clear that we are not rejecting the usual principles of learning, such as those having to do with the pairings of events, reward and punishment, primacy and recency, massed and spaced practice, retroactive and proactive inhibition, schedules of reinforcement, and so on, as these apply to a particular item of learning. Rather, we want to emphasize that there are other

Principles of development

mechanisms for learning as well, and that the point of understanding learning is for its effect on development, the way experience gives us a progressively better-articulated knowledge (called by Tolman a "cognitive map") of the world and of ourselves, and the conceptual and symbolic tools with which to think about the world and thus to transform our perceiving, feeling, thinking, and acting.

Role playing

Yet another way that learning influences development is through the child's imitation of the people, real and imagined, whom he observes and hears about, and who provide models for behavior. Such **role playing**, sometimes in a spirit of travesty, sometimes as outright make-believe, sometimes without his being aware that he is absorbing a model's style, and sometimes in an earnest attempt to find and convey an identity, includes the infant's imitation of simple actions and of adult gestures, expressions, and styles of movement, the toddler's taking on of domestic activities, the preschool child's dramatic play, the middle-years child's playing at pirates or spacemen (but in many cultures taking on serious roles as assistants to men and women), the adolescent's performance as whatever the current version of sophistication may be, and so on to the adult's being Pillar of the Community, or Learned Professor, or Captain of Industry, or Prominent Clubwoman, or pleasure-loving Femme Fatale. One of the more interesting things about role playing is the way middle-years and adolescent youngsters play the role of being their age. One eight-year-old boy, for instance, avidly collected base-ball cards and kept track of games and team standings in the sports pages in accordance with the mores of his neighborhood, even though he had never seen a real baseball game or expressed the slightest interest in attending one.

However trivial or specious role playing may seem, it gives the individual a chance to try on styles of life and the values they contain, and thereby to discover those modes of being that he or she finds most congenial and meaningful. It is worth mentioning that advertisers often play on the wish to try on attractive roles, implying that the buyers of their products will gain access to new realms of being. Opinion-leaders and trend-setters seem to be effective because they offer a role model with which people can identify. In general, as we shall say again, role playing is one of the ways one takes on cultural identity. Obviously, role playing implies that one perceives the role. Mary Ellen Goodman (1965) reports that Japanese urban middle-class five-year-olds were able to describe some sixty social role categories, defined by age, sex, kinship, and occupation, together with typical behavior or traits.

The Scientific Method

There seem to be three main approaches to textbook writing in psychology. One is to treat psychology as subject matter, as an

Modeling and social role learning. Note that even when no model is immediately present, the children's behavior is based on observation of adult ways.

Henri Cartier-Bresson, Magnum

Myron Papiz

Suzanne Szasz

Donna J. Harris, The Merrill-Palmer Institute

accumulation of facts and principles. Another is to teach it as method, the established techniques by which psychologists obtain information, with the subject matter of psychology defined as the problems susceptible to study by the available methods. Third is the treatment of psychology as quest, as an attempt to define the central issues and enigmas of human development and behavior and then to devise methods by which to study these problems.

While the older sciences tend to be taught by the first approach, the methods approach looms large in United States psychology, which, self-conscious about its scientific status, has striven to become an experimental science on the analogy of physics and to stress the description of the scientific process laid down by philosophers of science. So it is that most textbooks of developmental psychology have a chapter or more on the scientific method.

We prefer to touch upon the subject lightly, emphasizing the methods that have special bearing on the study of development. One reason is that many of our readers will already have had an adequate introduction to scientific method, as in psychology or other courses. Another is that actual scientific research, as a number of leading investigators have pointed out (American Psychological Association, 1960), seldom conforms to the ideal set forth in textbooks, and is actually a somewhat disorderly procedure involving curiosity (independent of any particular theory), hunches, intuitions, trial and error, false starts, spoiled trials, lost subjects, concern with practical problems as well as abstract theories, and a large dose of serendipity—the happy accident. (Harlow's discovery of the sexual inadequacy of his

surrogate-reared monkeys came about only when he tried to breed them for the purpose of procuring more laboratory monkeys.) Fine as it is for the study of many problems, the experimental method is simply not suited to many important issues in human development, if only because of the ethical implications of manipulating the fate of children.

There is the further problem that human development is a slow process, and our experimental manipulations and evaluation of effects may take years, whereas the experimentalist is oriented to the short-term study which yields rapid results. Furthermore, all but the youngest human subjects have a complicated past for which it is almost impossible to control except in terms of gross sociological indices such as rich-poor, urban-rural, and the like. It is considerations of ethics and time which have helped make the study of animal development so popular recently, since we can place nonhuman infants in controlled environments and do to them things that would be unthinkable to do to human babies (although, to be sure, some people have expressed misgivings about inflicting physically or psychologically traumatic treatments on the higher vertebrates, most especially dogs, monkeys, and apes) and get information rather quickly. We should note that students of animal development often use a technique, **cross-fostering**, to control for genetic effects. That is, the young are exchanged between mothers right after birth, so that their later behavior can be related to the characteristics of both the biological parents and the foster mother who reared them. Unfortunately, this technique has not yet proved feasible with monkeys (Stone, 1965). Cross-fostering is preferable to the so-called **split litter** method, which assumes that litter-mates have highly similar heredities, whereas in fact there is great genetic diversity within litters, even in inbred stocks. Surgical techniques have even been developed for trading babies between mothers soon after conception. This is called **cross-implantation**.

One can experimentally study the short-range effects of nontraumatic treatments, as in learning experiments, on matched groups of human subjects. One sort of quasi-experimental study using variations not created by the experimenter but seized on by him is the comparison of institutionalized and noninstitutionalized children. More directly under experimental control, and an approach that is becoming increasingly widespread, is the enrichment of experience of institutionalized or otherwise severely deprived children. The scientific purist might be offended by such studies, in which "enrichment" consists of numerous, diverse, and more or less simultaneous treatments (human contact, linguistic stimulation, teaching sensory discriminations, music and art, access to a variety of play materials, and so forth), making it extremely difficult to assess the impact of any one.

When one chooses and compares conditions over which the experimenter has no control, such as age, sex, social class, cultural and subcultural differences, child-care practices, or illness or physical impairment, one is obliged to use the method of the **natural experiment**, the chief method of disciplines like astronomy and geology where intervention is out of the question and simulation applicable to only a small range of problems. But notice that natural experiments can follow the laboratory paradigm, except that it is the real world rather than the experimenter that manipulates the independent variable. The natural experiment is usually concerned with outcomes; with functions and abilities such as perception or intelligence or thinking or attitudes, as they are found in subjects from the different comparison groups. The experimenter provides the stimulus and records the response, but he is mainly interested in the way the antecedent variable mediates the response. Thus, for instance, if a researcher wanted to compare human figure drawings by lower-class and middle-class children, he would supply the paper and pencil and instructions, which would be a constant factor for all subjects, while the variation would come from social class differences over which he has no control, but representatives of which he would have carefully selected for comparison.

A once-fashionable method in child psychology was the **normative study**, the recording by age of those changes in functioning that occur in the course of development. Nowadays, our awareness of the impact of different approaches to child-rearing makes us question the universality of almost any age-normative findings. That is, the age at which a new competence first emerges, and with what intensity or in what quantity, or even whether it occurs at all, seems to vary with the developmental context. This does not mean that normative studies are useless, but only that one has to specify the conditions in which the norms can be expected to apply. Normative techniques can be very useful in comparing the effects of sex differences, cultural and social class differences, and home versus institutional rearing on development.

While the canons of scientific method stress measurement, the fundamental technique of the developmental psychologist is **observation**, watching children in action to see what they do and how they go about it in homes, supermarkets, playgrounds, nursery schools, and other settings. It is through observation, often combined with some variant of Piaget's **"clinical" method**, by which one discusses with a child his thoughts and activities, that one comes to a first intuitive comprehension of what children are like. An astute observer can learn a great deal simply by watching and listening to and talking with children, after the manner of the naturalist observing the behavior of antelopes or ants or baboons. The power of naturalistic observation is attested by a review comparing two compendia of the behavior of primates, one based on laboratory studies and the other on field studies, which points out that the two volumes contain virtually no overlapping information (Altmann, 1965). Observations can be made in free situations or in carefully arranged ones, and can be oriented toward recording behavior in general or only some selected aspect of behavior. We can observe with a view to learning about children in general (the **nomothetic** approach) or to capturing the idiosyncratic uniqueness of a particular child (the **idiographic** approach) (Allport, 1942). The **case study** approach, particularly as it applies to normal individuals, has fallen into neglect in recent years, but there is still much to be learned from the intensive study of individual lives (Church, 1968; Dukes, 1965; Garraty, 1954; Langness, 1965; White, 1966). Investigations which study the same individuals repeatedly at different stages of their lives are called **longitudinal** studies; the longitudinal method is usually contrasted with the **cross-sectional** method, which compares the characteristics of different ages by studying different groups of children representing the various ages but presumably similar with respect to such other important variables as sex, socioeconomic status, and so forth.

Among the special environments in which we observe subjects, whether for idiographic or nomothetic purposes, are those provided by **tests**, which permit comparison of the child's performance with some reference group. There are two main sorts of tests, the **psychometric**, which yield a numerical score, or a collection of scores called a **profile**, and the **projective**, which are scored qualitatively, in terms of the personality traits revealed.

The psychometric instruments include **intelligence tests** (of which more later), **aptitude tests** of special abilities such as arithmetic, mechanical relations, dexterity, clerical skills, and so on, **achievement tests** which tell how much the child has learned following exposure to a course of instruction, and **personality tests** which measure the "amount" a child possesses of various traits such as hostility, anxiety, defensiveness, or whatever. Psychometric instruments can be either of the **paper-and-pencil** variety (once the child is literate), which can be given to a large number of subjects at the same time, or **individual** tests, which may be given orally, but which may also involve the subject's writing or drawing something, or assembling puzzles in a way that the examiner has to record.

Like psychometric tests, projective tests provide stimuli for the subject to respond to, but the stimuli permit a much wider range of appropriate responses, which are not "right" or "wrong" but rather are taken as samples of characteristic behavior or style of thinking and response. The stimuli may have a low degree of structure, as in the case of finger paints or the famous Rorschach ink blots, which invite the subject to supply his own structure; or they may be highly structured, like the dolls and house furnishings of Lois Murphy's (L. B. Murphy and associates, 1956) Miniature Life Toys, which the subject is free to organize in ways that seem meaningful to him. Presumably the use the child makes of projective materials reveals something about his inner workings, but the interpretation of his performance has a large component of subjectivity, and attempts to objectify scoring have not been altogether satisfactory. Projective methods should not be thought of as tests in the strict sense, but as semistandardized settings in which to make observations of the kinds considered below.

Allied to tests are **questionnaires**, inviting the subject to supply information about himself, first used by G. Stanley Hall, one of the fathers of child psychology. We can also get information through **interviews**, a more or less formal or fixed series of factual or attitudinal questions asked orally. The interview gives the subject more scope to elaborate on his answers than does the questionnaire, and also permits the interviewer to explore what look like promising byways. Notice that interviews can be used not only with the child himself but also with parents, teachers, or other people who know the child.

Tests and interview questions give the subject's behavior a focus, but there are also devices that let the subject run free but that sharpen the process of observation. First of all, there are **anecdotal reports** of behavior, which may take such forms as a continuous, narrative **running record** or a more global, summary **impression record**. We can prepare tally sheets telling the observer exactly what items or aspects of behavior to be on the lookout for. When we want to compare the incidence of certain behavior, such as nose-picking, teasing, or sandbox play, from child to child or group to group, we can arrange schedules of observation (**time samples**) such that all subjects will be observed for comparable periods. The kinds of behavior one is interested in studying can be precoded, so that recording can be a matter of punching the appropriate keys, which can then transmit data straight to a computer. We can construct **rating scales** by which an observer assigns numerical weights to behavior in terms either of general characteristics such as kind-cruel or of more circumscribed specific behaviors like crying or asking for help. Notice that ratings of this sort always imply a frame of reference, and it must be made explicit whether a child is being rated relative to "children the rater has known," "children of this age," "boys in general," "girls in general," "the child's brothers and sisters," or other children, say, in this child's preschool class. Parents and older children can make ratings of themselves, of other children or parents, of their own children or parents, of schools and teachers, of TV programs, and so forth indefinitely. Rating scales can also be used in the evaluation of things children do or make, such as maturity of play, masculinity of style, imaginativeness of language, or the quality of paintings.

For the study of group organization we have had such techniques as **sociometry**, by which each member of the group is asked which members of the group he would most or least like to have share in some specific activity. The compiling of such choices gives us a good picture of the group's status hierarchy, who the often-chosen stars are, who the choosing but unchosen hangers-on, who the nonselected outcasts. The patterning of reciprocal choices gives us a picture of group solidarity and reveals the clusterings that are cliques. A way of studying the personality characteristics that go with status in the group is the **guess-who technique**, which gives the child a trait description—for example, "this child is always showing off" —and asks the child to guess which member of the group it is.

With one-way screens, the observer can remove himself from the child's ken, along with his possible interference in the very events he wants to study. Recent technologies which permit us to extend our powers of observation include cameras, binoculars, parabolic microphones, tape recorders, and movie and videotape cameras. The use of recording devices also permits us to observe the same bit of behavior repeatedly for detailed analysis and to check the accuracy of human observers. Such equipment can be used to speed up or slow down behavior in ways that may reveal new patterns.

The ingenuity of the psychologist's observing techniques, whether using the naked eye or telephoto lens, along with his real need to study unselfconscious behavior, raises grave questions about invasion of privacy and just what it is about an individual's (and his family's) life that a psychologist has a right to know—especially if the individual does not realize how much he is revealing or to what use the information is to be put. It is because these are such grave problems, and because we feel that the welfare of the individual has

to come first, that beginning students in our laboratories are repeatedly cautioned to keep strictly confidential what they have learned about particular individuals, and not to convert their privileged knowledge into idle gossip. Children may inadvertently expose not only themselves but also all kinds of family secrets, and the student, researcher, or teacher who is made privy to such secrets has a solemn obligation to see that they stay secret. Publications, it need hardly be added, must always conceal the identity of individual subjects. Research on sensitive questions such as personal relations and attitudes may be stressful, and the experimenter must do everything possible to minimize stress and to assure that any temporary dislocations are set right. This is particularly important where for serious experimental purposes the experimenter in some way misleads or misinforms his subjects.

In closing this section, let us remind the reader that he or she will find abundant examples of research applications throughout this book. Let us also say that many problems are waiting to be studied, and in order to study some of them, we will almost certainly have to find new techniques.

Some Representative Theoretical Orientations

This section describes some particular approaches which seek to make systematic sense of human behavior. We have selected those theories which emphasize development or which can be linked to development. Although all these theories have serious shortcomings, they have both contemporary and historical significance for the insight they provide. Psychologists have for the most part abandoned theory-making on the grand scale. Instead, they construct microtheories: theories of learning, identification, signal detection, or whatever. The ultimate synthesis is yet to come.

Psychoanalytic theories

Let us begin with the explicitly developmental views of Sigmund Freud, who was a major modern contributor to the discovery of human childhood as an area of serious investigation. The reader should remember that Freud had very little direct contact with children and constructed his account of development from self-observations, some observations of his own children, and the reconstructions and recollections of his adult patients—his one famous child patient, Little Hans, was treated indirectly, through Hans's father. Freud's was primarily a dynamic, that is, motivational, theory of behavior, although, as we shall see, it always had cognitive and intellectual components. These were later elaborated on by some of Freud's followers, such as Ernst Kris, Heinz Hartmann, David Rapaport, Erik Erikson, and Freud's own daughter, Anna, all of whom became known as psychoanalytic ego psychologists. Freud acknowledged a wide variety of human motives, or drives, but in the end he concerned himself mainly with two: **libido**, or sexual energy, and the **death wish**, or a drive to destruction of self or others (these two motivational forces have been dubbed Eros and Thanatos, from the Greek words for [carnal] love and death). It should be emphasized that, for Freud,

instinctual drives were **unconscious**, so that what the individual thought or said about his own motives might be very remote from the actualities.

Freud proposed a three-way conceptual partition of the person into **id**, the blind strivings of Eros and Thanatos and the source of all the person's motives and energies; **ego**, the rational, reality-oriented part of the person (whence ego psychology); and **superego**, corresponding approximately to the conscience, the moral and ethical part of the person's make-up. Developmentally, the baby at birth is considered to be pure id, a seething mass of passions governed exclusively by what Freud called the **pleasure principle**, unbridled seeking for immediate gratification. Needless to say, the baby's greedy id-strivings collide almost at once with an only partially yielding reality, and out of this collision of forces and frustrations there develops a layer of ego, constituting the practical strategies and the capacity for delay and detour by which the developing person can take account of reality in the quest for id gratification. The ego, that is, is governed by the **reality principle**, taking account of what is already possible or of the means of making gratification possible. The kinds of thinking that accompany the id-based pleasure principle in its search for immediate gratification, whether in the young baby, in adult dreams, in daydreams or fantasies, or in psychosis, are called **primary-process** thought, whereas the reality-oriented thinking associated with the ego is called **secondary process**. Finally, not in infancy but in early childhood, and in ways that we shall discuss shortly, a portion of the ego becomes further differentiated as superego, imparting an ethical-moral, socially responsible dimension, in

Some representative theoretical orientations

175

addition to the purely pragmatic reality principle, to the search for gratification of the id impulses.

The differentiation of some of the id into ego and of ego into superego can be seen as a process of cognitive development. Side by side with it goes a series of motivational changes in what Freud called the **psychosexual stages** of development. Note that the motivations remain the same throughout life; it is the manner of their expression that changes. Psychosexual development refers to shifts in the channels or zones of the body through which id gratification is sought and obtained, and in the objects which serve as gratifiers.

The first of the psychosexual stages is called the **oral phase**, during infancy, when the main channel of gratification is the mouth and upper digestive tract, and the gratifying objects are the nipple and the mother who provides it—plus, to a lesser extent, the thumb, pacifier, or whatever else the baby puts in his mouth. In the Freudian view, the infant's eating is not merely a matter of appeasing hunger and assuring organic survival, but also a source of proto-erotic satisfaction. Furthermore, since the baby destroys what he has consumed, he is simultaneously satisfying his death wish. Early infancy, before the baby's teeth have sprouted, is called the **oral-passive** period. Later, when he has acquired enough teeth to begin to bite, he enters the **oral-sadistic** period in which the aggressive (Thanatos) component becomes even more conspicuous.

In the period we call toddlerhood, according to Freud, the main channel of gratification, subject to some restrictions we shall touch on later, ceases to be the mouth and becomes the lower digestive tract and anus, and the baby enters the **anal stage** of psychosexual development. This period, in which the baby gains control over the anal sphincter and the process of holding on to and expelling bowel movements, is supposedly marked by preoccupation with anal functions, to the point where having his bottom spanked may be pleasurable to the baby. The anal period was thought of by Freud as a time of inevitable conflict between parents and child over who shall regulate the time and place of defecation, and the baby gets ample exercise of his destructive tendencies in withholding bowel movements when his parents want him to let go, by expelling feces when his parents want him to hold on, and by smearing his feces in an act of defiance.

If all goes normally during the anal period, the source of gratification shifts to the genitals, and the preschool years are described as the **phallic stage**—a designation betraying Freud's male-centered view of behavior. The phallic stage, in which gratification is sought without concern for the feelings of other people, is distinguished from the **genital stage** of adolescence and adulthood, characterized not only by mature sexuality in the usual sense but also by love and a concern for others' feelings.

The phallic stage evolves into and culminates in the **Oedipus complex**, named for the tragic hero of Greek legend, King Oedipus, who unwittingly but in fulfillment of a prophecy made at his birth slew his father and married his mother. According to Freud, the boy (we shall talk in a moment about the girl's Oedipus—or, as it is sometimes called, Electra—complex) directs his phallic strivings toward the mother, putting himself in direct rivalry with the father, whom he ambivalently both hates and loves. The father is seen as retaliating with an open or implied threat to injure or cut off the boy's penis—a threat of castration. This threat is usually viewed as being expressed in the context of punishing the boy's masturbation: in actuality, such threats are made by some parents, and were doubtless even more prevalent in Freud's day. The Oedipus complex, and along with it rivalry among siblings, is supposed to represent an inherited memory (Freud more or less explicitly accepted Lamarck's theory of the inheritance of acquired characteristics, as did Darwin for a while) of a so-called **primal horde**, an original family group in which the sons banded together to kill the father and then began warring among themselves for possession of the mother. Freud saw an analogy here with the behavior of some primate groups in which a coalition of young males topples the dominant male and then battles internally for supremacy.

The child, by now about age five, moved both by fear of castration and love for his father, capitulates, renouncing his claim on the mother's favors and at the same time **repressing** (forcing out of consciousness) all sexual cravings. This renunciation of sexuality brings the child into the stage of psychosexual **latency**, corresponding to the middle years of childhood, which ends only when the physiological developments of adolescence bring a new upsurge of more mature sexual feelings, destroying the quiescence of latency. Furthermore, in capitulating to the father, the son is said to **identify** with him, to emulate his behavior, and to **internalize** or **introject**, to make part of himself, his father's moral values, which form the basis of the superego. That is, the parental prescriptions and proscriptions that formerly came to him as "thou shalt" and "thou shalt not" now speak to him in his own voice, saying, "I must" and "I must not," and arouse feelings of **guilt** when violated. To keep sexuality (and excessive aggression) at bay, the ego brings into play several of the **mechanisms of defense**, one of which is repression, mentioned above, and other stratagems by which one reinforces the repression of dangerous cravings and impulses.

The superego is initially a rigid, tyrannical kind of conscience, which only later becomes more flexible and tolerant (corresponding accurately to empirical findings that children shift from literal to relativistic concepts of morality as they mature), and the ego is hard put to mediate among the insistent clamor of the id, the harsh moralism of the superego, and the realities of the outside world. For Freud, a psychiatrist oriented to disturbed—particularly neurotic—forms of behavior, the defense mechanisms were always defenses against oneself, not the world outside. For instance, the child engages in **reaction formation**, a going to the opposite extreme, as when he rejects not only sexuality but the opposite sex in general—middle-years boys notoriously will have nothing to do with girls or "sissy stuff." By the mechanism of **sublimation**, the id energies are transformed into socially acceptable drives, as, for example, the school-age child's new concern with intellectual, objective learning, which can be seen as sublimated sexual curiosity. Freudians would say that it is the resolution of the Oedipus complex that makes children ready for school, and that some of those children who do badly in school are suffering from an unresolved Oedipus complex.

Some representative theoretical orientations

The **obsessive-compulsive** mechanisms found in adult neurotics (extremes of meticulousness, repetitive hand-washing, and so on) have their counterparts in the **repetition** and **ritual** of the normal child as seen in such activities as counting all the cars of a freight train, having to touch every lamppost, holding one's breath until one reaches the corner, or avoiding the cracks in the sidewalk to the tune of "Step on a crack, break your mother's back"—which Freudians would interpret as a disguised expression of ambivalent hostility (and associated guilt and fear) against the now unattainable mother. Other well-known defense mechanisms are **projection**, whereby one ascribes one's own unconscious motivations to other people, and **rationalization**, whereby one justifies evilly motivated behavior in terms of some virtuous or neutral purpose.

Freud never formulated to his own satisfaction the course of the Oedipus complex in girls, but offered the following sketch. Initially, the girl's Oedipus complex is identical with the boy's: the girl, considered to assume that she has a penis, addresses her attentions to the mother in competition with the father. For the girl, however, the crisis comes not with the threat of castration at the hands of the father but with the dreadful discovery that she has been castrated (and amputated)—presumably her interpretation of the female genitalia. At this juncture, the girl can react in either of two ways. Ordinarily she is seen as identifying with the mother, and competing for the father—seeking a baby from him in fantasy as a substitute counterpart of the lost penis. In the face of reality she then will shift from actual striving for the father's favors to substitute father-figures, repressing her impulses

as she reaches latency. The girl's (less common) alternative reaction to castration is called the **masculine protest**, a persistent if symbolic denial of the loss of the penis and the pursuit of an essentially masculine style of life (whether or not involving the practice of Lesbianism), with a more or less permanent inability to play a feminine role in love or marriage. Such women are called by Freudians "castrating females," possessed by **penis envy**, as though seeking to take away from men what rightfully belongs to women. It is worth noting that Freud's teachings about females have been singled out by the women's liberation movement as ghastly specimens of male chauvinist thought.

Both boys and girls, reaching maturity, are seen as seeking mates with whom (in part) to reenact their earlier Oedipal attachments—"I want a girl just like the girl who married dear old Dad." Indeed, all close attachments, including that formed to the psychoanalyst in therapy (**transference**), are viewed as partial reenactments of the ambivalent relations to the parents formed in infancy and early childhood.

It is worth mentioning parenthetically that Freudians invoke the repression that climaxes the Oedipal drama to explain **infantile amnesia**, the fact that we find it hard or impossible to remember anything from before age five or six except disconnected fragments of events. It is as though the repressed sexual feelings took with them all the associated events, to be recaptured only in the special condition of hypnosis or in the **abreaction**—the reliving process—of psychoanalytic psychotherapy.

We should note that normal psychosexual development requires the enactment by child and parents alike of strictly fixed roles in the psychosexual drama. These roles are thought of as instinctive, and so are considered **biological imperatives**. Any departure from the biological imperatives is believed to lead to more or less serious disturbances of functioning. The presumed importance of the Oedipus complex as a key event in which the father plays a key role has been one influence producing studies of boys who grow up without fathers. The results of such studies strike us as far from conclusive. We do not know why nobody, to the best of our knowledge, has ever studied children without mothers.

Before discussing some of the more common departures from the normal course, we must introduce another Freudian concept, that of **cathexis**. At each psychosexual stage, one's supply of libidinal energy is said to be invested, or *cathected*, in the relevant channel and the important gratifying objects associated with that stage. Thus, in the oral stage of infancy, the child's mouth is said to be libidinized (that is, it has acquired erotic meaning), and the bottle or breast—and, by extension, the mother—cathected (has erotic meaning attached to it). When the needs associated with a given stage are gratified, the child is said to withdraw his cathexes and reinvest his energy in the new zones and objects of the next stage. If, however, inadequate gratification is given, all or part of the child's cathexes may remain **fixated** at that stage, that is, the child may still go on seeking the gratifications appropriate to a stage which he is supposed to have outgrown. Paradoxically, fixation can be produced both by insufficient gratification, which leaves him ever hungering, or by overgratification, which leaves the child so well satisfied with his present mode of existence that he is, so to speak, reluctant to move on. But assuming that a child has

found satisfaction at one level and moved on, if he then encounters excessive frustration at a later stage, he may **regress**—that is, go back—to the last earlier stage at which he found satisfaction, so that the baby who finds the demands of toilet training in toddlerhood, say, too taxing, may revert to the clinging helplessness and orality of infancy.

Now it is clear that total fixation at or permanent regression to childhood patterns of behavior would be a rare and profoundly pathological style of life. However, the Freudians have a system of adult character types said to express partial fixations at early levels of psychosexual development. Thus, the adult "oral character" is marked by infantile, dependent, demanding behavior, and by a preoccupation with oral gratifications: eating, gum-chewing, smoking, nail-biting, drinking, pencil-chewing, garrulous talking, and whatever. Oral sadism, deriving from the second oral stage, would be shown not only in a literal tendency to bite but in the symbolic biting expressed in harsh words. Fixation at the anal stage might be expressed in either the "anal-retentive character," who seems to have learned too well the lessons of control, orderliness, and regularity associated with bowel training, and whose behavior is marked by stinginess, the accumulating and collecting of money or other valuables, rigid adherence to forms and routines, suspicion, legalistic ways of thinking, and what has been described as "emotional constipation"; or the "anal-aggressive character," who seems still to be fighting the battle of bowel control and who expresses his rebellion against authority by extreme messiness in personal habits and grooming, by indifference to routines and schedules, and

Some representative theoretical orientations

179

even by the tendency to "dirty" language, which can be seen as a symbolic befouling or "soiling" of the environment or those around him. The "phallic character" would be one who selfishly exploits others sexually, without regard to their needs, concerns, or feelings—in males, the Don Juan or the sexual psychopath or the rapist, in females, the self-centered nymphomaniac.

A few other features of the Freudian system should be mentioned. For Freud, significant motives and their alterations by defense mechanisms were primarily unconscious, and the true mainsprings of behavior lay deep in organic nature. In the course of ego development, some features of experience enter consciousness, including a certain limited knowledge of oneself and one's motives. The knowledge that is not conscious at the moment but is available to consciousness is said to reside in the **preconscious**, as in the case of all those things we can easily remember. The **unconscious** is thought to contain both those strivings that have never been conscious and those that have started forth and then been repressed, for instance, the Oedipal impulses. The presence of unconscious strivings is inferred from evidence of the operation of defense mechanisms, from self-betrayals in such forms as selective forgetting, making meaningful mistakes and slips of the tongue, and from the content of dreams, which are supposed to be symbolic, more or less disguised representations of all the unfulfilled cravings that come out of hiding during sleep, when the person's defenses are down. In short, people constantly do things for reasons that they do not recognize and may even deny.

Having sketched the formal elements of the Freudian system, let us say that Freud made a monumental contribution to our understanding of human behavior. Certainly we can see something like oral preoccupations in infancy—people sometimes describe the baby as being "all mouth." Certainly we can see Oedipus-like or Electra-like behavior in the preschool years, as when the child lavishes affection on the opposite-sex parent, even inviting that parent to share the child's bed, meanwhile telling the same-sex parent to go away, or turning that parent's picture to the wall. (In adults, we can see persistent Oedipal tendencies in people who marry mother-surrogates or father-surrogates.) Certainly we can see people living at odds with their own motives, practicing self-deception (which may deceive no one else) on a staggering scale, and in general struggling to get loose from leftover problems of childhood, including overinvolvement with parents. Certainly we can see ambivalence, strong hostility as well as strong affection to parents and to others who are very close —and certainly the hostility is sometimes veiled and indirect though indubitably there. We can see Freudian symbolism not only in our dreams (one six-year-old girl dreamed that a raging bull trampled down a fence and gored her in the bottom, but, strangely enough, it was "sort of pleasant"), but in myths and fairy tales. Consider the symbolism of the ogre in "Jack and the Beanstalk," of the oven in which the ogre's wife hides Jack, of Jack's cutting down the beanstalk, and of his using the gold stolen from the slain ogre to live alone with his mother. Irrationality and absurdity are everywhere around us, and Freud has taught us to look beyond face values.

Nevertheless, we feel that Freud's brilliant contribution has serious shortcomings, some of them acknowledged by his less orthodox followers. It accounts much better for pathological behavior than for normality, and almost not at all for what we consider superior styles of life. It is possible that babies born in nineteenth- and early twentieth-century Vienna were turbulent bundles of id—or were made so by parental practices—but the babies we know are not only intent on immediate gratifications and sometimes perverse but also cheerful, curious, playful, often affectionate without detectable undertones of salacious desire, and given to joyously pursuing and practicing mastery of skills and objects. Such babies adapt easily to their family's life styles in ways that make it seem unlikely that they are scheming monsters of lust and destruction.

In general, like most drive or motivational theories, Freud's deals with unsatisfied (and even insatiable) instincts, but, as Robert W. White (1959, 1963; see also Chodoff, 1966) has pointed out, a complete psychology has to deal also with the behavior of organisms which are awake and in reasonable equilibrium, free from the goading of deficiency drives. Indeed, one may say that human beings are at their most human when their basic biological needs are least involved. The behavior of a human being in the throes of asphyxiating, choking, starving, or parching is not much different from that of any other animal. And when biological needs are satisfied, they cannot be invoked to account for love, curiosity, the higher learning, imagination, humor, foresight, symbolic activity, and all else that is distinctively human. Just as the old economics of scarcity, in which there is not enough to go around, must yield, in an age of mechanized production and population control, to an economics of abundance, so in the behavioral sciences must deficiency theo-

ries yield to accounts of the behavior of organisms whose basic needs have been satisfied. For the replete organism, as White says, does not invariably drift off into the blissful Nirvana of semicoma, but looks around to see what there is to do next. (This Nirvana concept of motivation is the psychological extension of the physiological concept of homeostasis—seeking the resting-state.) In White's view (and ours), boredom becomes as great a spur to action as lust or hunger.

In terms of development, Freud laid more stress on the determining power of biology (in his own version of biology), and less on the influence of experience with people and things (except for the preordained acting out of the biological imperatives), than present evidence on the effects of early experience makes tenable. But whatever the flaws in Freud's formulations, we can see them only because Freud himself opened our eyes (in Erich Fromm's phrase, people stand on Freud's shoulders and, because they can see so much farther than he, consider him a pygmy; this is a variant of the usual figure of speech, which has the modern pygmy standing on the shoulders of giants [Merton, 1965]), and he showed us phenomena that any adequate theory of behavior is going to have to include. While it may be that Freud's theory was too intricate and complex to lend itself easily to empirical verification or disproof, he at least tried to deal with the full richness of human behavior as it is known to the dramatist, to the novelist, and to the painter.

Freud was the father of psychoanalysis, but his was not the only analytic school. There are several varieties, most of them founded by former colleagues of Freud's as schismatic movements which Freud himself considered heretical. Carl Jung, of Switzerland, presided over a school which lays much stress on the **racial** or **collective unconscious** (an idea found in Freud, too), the basic patterns or structures which guide ideation. These supposedly universal patterns are called **archetypes**, and, as Jung has shown, are found in many cultures. In this view, life is more a search for understanding (as of the way archetypes shape behavior) than for direct or indirect carnal gratifications. Not too surprisingly, Jungians often show a strongly religious orientation.

Otto Rank originally built his system around the **trauma of birth**, a lifelong attempt to return to the warm, safe nothingness of intrauterine existence, from which the newborn babe is cast into a cold, hostile, and unmanageable world. As Rank's thinking evolved, he became more concerned with **will therapy**, designed to help people know what they really wanted, instead of living with the agony of formless dissatisfactions, and to feel free to want it. Rank's influence is still visible in several current versions, including the **nondirective therapy** of Carl Rogers, which places responsibility for his own psychological welfare on the client rather than the therapist, and, more explicitly, in the teachings of many schools of social work.

Alfred Adler, a Viennese socialist, was far more concerned than Freud with social influences on development, in keeping with his Marxian orientation. To Adler we owe such notions as **sibling rivalry**, the warfare among brothers and sisters for the affection of the parents, with much emphasis on the dethronement of the firstborn child from his place of unique eminence by the arrival of younger children. Adler also gave us the concept of masculine protest,

already mentioned, and of **organ inferiority**, the sense of weakness or inadequacy (beginning with every child's smallness and helplessness) that keeps people striving and drives them to extremes of **compensation** to make up for their real or imagined insufficiencies in stature or competence. Organ inferiority was the basis of Adler's concept of "inferiority complex." Basically, Adler's is a more optimistic, problem-solving view of man than is Freud's.

In the United States, as we have said, a school of anthropologically and sociologically oriented psychoanalysis, much in the tradition of Adler, has developed alongside the orthodox one. The roster of this group includes such names as Harry Stack Sullivan, Karen Horney, and Erich Fromm. Horney and Fromm have been extremely critical of modern civilization and the social and personal ills it begets. Where Freud saw civilization as a painfully and partially attained modification of the violence of the id, in their view, modern society is itself inhuman and dehumanizing, so that development is distorted and those who try to live lives of love and virtue, representing man's basic strivings, will inevitably find themselves in torment. We have already mentioned the work of Erik Erikson, who perhaps comes closest to bridging the Freudian and post-Freudian approaches. Erikson evolved a scheme of considerable use in the study of development, describing the eight stages of man, which are a more generalized statement of the Freudian psychosexual stages. Thus, as we have seen, the oral stage of infancy becomes for Erikson the period for the formation of basic trust or mistrust, which are seen as closely implicated with the oral experience of hunger and feeding but which are also related to the dependability with which other basic needs are met. As we shall see in the next chapter, Freud's anal period of toddlerhood is elaborated by Erikson as the time for the development of either autonomy or attitudes of shame and doubt.

We have spoken of a kinship between psychoanalytic theory and the recent revival of instinct theory. For instance, Lorenz (1966) sees aggression in human beings as an instinct run wild. Montagu (1968) has collected criticisms of Lorenz and related instinct theorists, demonstrating the numerous factual and logical errors, from the standpoint of both biology and anthropology, of such a position, so we are prepared to let Lorenz's teachings in this area wither quietly away.

✳ *Learning theories of development*

The learning-theory tradition, which lays heavy emphasis on the role of the environment in shaping modes of behavior, has two main antecedents. The first of these is British **associationism**, characterized by John Locke's doctrine of the newborn as a **tabula rasa**, a clean slate (literally, a wax tablet shaved clean) on which the world writes or impresses its message. The message the world writes on the individual consists of associations, a set of connections between events that occur together in time and space. Associationism found its scientific expression in the second major forebear of learning theories, Ivan Pavlov's conditioned reflex theory.

The basic tenet of learning theories is that the elaboration of behavior observable in the course of development can be explained, apart from a few concessions to physical growth and maturation, as the continuous formation of connections among stimuli and responses. To expand on what we said earlier, Pavlov, the father of classical conditioning, as is widely known, demonstrated that one can link arbitrary, experimentally manipulated stimuli (called **conditioned** or **conditional stimuli**) to already existing "natural," **unconditioned stimuli** that reliably elicit a fixed, **unconditioned response**. One can, in the laboratory, establish a great many conditioned associations, limited only by the number of unconditioned stimulus-response sequences one can identify. One can make some arbitrary event cause the pupil to contract as though a bright light were about to flash, or the eye to blink as though it were about to be subjected to a puff of air.

Pavlov and his contemporary Bekhterev for the most part studied the conditioning of simple reflexes, the way the organism reacts to having something done to it— secretory responses, muscle twitch or limb flexion to vibration or electric shock, and so forth—many of them describable as vegetative responses mediated through the autonomic nervous system. In contrast to reflex reactions, there are also **instrumental acts**, the things the organism does in response to its own inner states, such as the hungry rat's looking for food in a maze. American behaviorists such as Watson extended Pavlov's classical conditioning model to account for such behavior. Another branch of American behaviorism, as we have said, provides separate accounts for classical and instrumental conditioning. The classical conditioning technique has proved very useful in the study of perceptual discrimination and generalization. For instance, one can sound one

Some representative theoretical orientations

particular tone as a signal for food, and introduce a different tone unrelated to feeding, and the animal learns to react to the relevant tone and to disregard the irrelevant one. As the difference between the tones is reduced, the animal's responses allow us to infer the limits of discrimination. On the other hand, if only a single tone is used in a conditioning experiment, the animal will "generalize" his response to a great variety of tones introduced later on.

The fundamental form of classical conditioning is between a stimulus and a response, but repeated associations of stimuli can lead to stimulus-stimulus conditioning, as when Tristram Shandy's mother formed a connection between the periodic conjunction of her husband's winding the clock and then having intercourse with her, causing her to cry out at a delicate moment, "Pray, my Dear, have you not forgot to wind up the clock?" One can also form response-response connections, as in the habitual sequence of actions by which one gets dressed—here we have the phenomenon of "equivalent acts" which may be substituted in a response-response sequence, so that if the child asks his father to tie his shoes just as the father is about to tie his own shoes, the father may go forth with his shoelaces dangling. Response-response conditioning can be invoked to account for behavior when no external stimulus can be found to explain it. Thus, in the language of associationism, states of the organism such as hunger, thirst, sexual arousal, attitudes, or expectations can be described as responses which in turn stimulate yet other responses.

Associationism has been a potent force in American psychology. In the Pavlovian tradition, Clark Hull and his students, no-tably Kenneth Spence, greatly elaborated on the classical conditioning model to take account of more subtle learning such as the formation of concepts and latent learning.

In this view, **concept formation** means detecting an equivalence among a group of stimuli on the basis of the number of "identical elements" the stimuli have in common. Thus, the concept "man" includes all those beings who share such identical elements as deep voices, facial hair, masculine styles of dress and haircuts, and so forth. (Later in this book [see p. 296], we shall propose a similar view which relies not so much on specific identical elements as on equivalence, first, of global physiognomies and, at a more advanced stage, of logical relatedness: a signal flare and a telephone have little perceptual similarity, but we can recognize that they both are equivalent to the extent of being "means of communication.")

Latent (incidental) **learning** takes place in the absence of any demonstrable motivation or reinforcement (reward), as when the hungry white rat, exploring the maze for food, also learns incidentally where water is to be found in the maze, so that he goes directly to the water when he is placed in the maze thirsty instead of hungry. A great deal of our learning, such as our learning about space and time, about values, and, indeed, the cultural learning we have already described, seems to be of this latent, incidental sort. The fact of latent learning was long used to counter association theory, and for a time associationists denied its very existence. Now, the Hull-Spence position seems to be that latent learning follows the same course as overt stimulus-response learning, except that the motivation, response, and reinforcement are fractional rather than full-blown, so that the somewhat thirsty animal, even if he does not actually drink the water, is nevertheless partially reinforced by the mere sight of it. Hull evolved a whole set of axioms to describe the learning process, including a set of propositions about the strength of drives and inhibitions, habit-family hierarchies (the likelihood that any one of a group of competing responses would be released in given circumstances), and secondary or substitute reinforcers (the tokens that can appease the animal without actually satisfying his physical needs, as a pacifier lessens hunger pangs). The Hull-Spence model (the axioms and the predictions derived from them) gives a fairly good account of some cases of learning, but its predictions have been disappointed in numerous other cases, even after much tinkering with the basic axioms and the adding of new assumptions (such as those used to account for latent learning). The reader who wishes a detailed discussion is referred to Hilgard and Bower (1966). In general, the system has become more cumbersome than the facts it sets out to explain, and so has little utility. Shortly before his death, however, Spence published papers assigning much greater weight to cognitive factors than a strict behaviorism would allow, which may signal a decided change in the classical learning-theory camp (Spence, 1963).

A number of Hull's collaborators, including John Dollard, Neal Miller (whose more recent work has been in brain biochemistry and learning to control autonomic functions), and Robert Sears, have sought to fuse Hullian learning theory and Freudian psychodynamics with a particular view to showing the learned (as opposed to instinctive) basis of motives. Their best-known contribution has been the hypothesis that aggression is always produced by frustration, and, conversely, that frustration always leads to aggression. The hypothesis was fruitful in inspiring research, and many of the predictions derived from it were verified. However, while it can be shown that in certain circumstances, frustration and aggression do go together, the generality of the hypothesis has been mooted by numerous observations. A famous study by Barker, Dembo, and Lewin (1941), for instance, showed that one possible outcome of frustration is regression, behavior at a less mature level than before frustration was introduced. Rosenzweig and Kogan (1949) have shown the variety of reactions frustration may produce. Common-sense observation suggests that one can sometimes react to frustration constructively, as by seeking new solutions to a problem.

E. L. Thorndike placed great emphasis on trial-and-error learning, which evolved into the study of **instrumental learning**, in which things are arranged so that the animal itself makes things happen and is rewarded as an intrinsic result of doing the right thing. Thus, if the animal can learn to work the latch on the cage door, he is rewarded by being liberated from the cage. Thorndike phrased this relationship between the animal's own activity and the rewarding results it produces as the **law of effect**, which says simply that those behaviors that lead to satisfying consequences tend to be repeated under like circumstances. Initially, the law of effect went parallel with another that said that annoyance (equivalent to punishment) as a consequence of behavior tended to weaken and, eventually, to **extinguish** the behavior, but later observations led Thorndike to drop this part of his formulation. Instead, the extinction of behavior is said to occur simply because of the lack of satisfying consequences, the lack of reinforcement.

As we have said, Solomon (1963) has collected evidence suggesting that Thorndike and his followers may have been too hasty in abandoning the principle of annoyance, since it seems to be the timing of punishment that determines whether it inhibits behavior. Thus, punishment given at the very inception of an act thoroughly inhibits its completion and strongly deters repetition, while punishment given immediately on completion of an act is somewhat less effective. The longer punishment is delayed after completion of the act, the less effective it becomes. This might serve to explain why punishment rarely deters criminals (without mention of the ethical problem of subduing criminal behavior without providing sensible alternatives). In fact, the criminal act itself, such as committing a burglary, may be successful and thus gets reinforced, whereas it is behavior later in the total sequence, such as trying to dispose of the stolen goods or confiding to a friend, that gets punished. By theory, then, the burglar would be encouraged to burgle again, but, because of later punishment, to modify his post-burglary behavior. Other studies (e.g., Brackbill and O'Hara, 1958; Meyer and Offenbach, 1962) suggest that a combination of reward and punishment (actually, "right" and "wrong" rather than candy and electric shocks)works best in laboratory tests of learning. To return to Thorndike's views, behavior was essentially formless and random, being produced by diffuse states of disequilibrium, such as those engendered by hunger or fear. Those

components of random behavior that happened to produce satisfying results persisted, while those that did not faded away (extinguished). In this way, amorphous behavior could be given shape and made to appear as though it were directed from within, whereas in fact it was the pattern of effects that was responsible for the new orderliness. In this view, the baby's babblings, for example, get selectively reinforced and extinguished until the sounds he makes come out as intelligible language. (We shall quarrel with this stand in the next chapter.)

Reinforcement can be thought of as effective either because it is rewarding (that is, it satisfies some need and reduces tension) or because it supplies information, akin to feedback, that guides the organism in intelligent action. Estes and his collaborators (Keller et al., 1965) have devised techniques to assess separately the relative contributions of reward and information to the learning process, and it appears, as in Spence's findings mentioned earlier, that information is at least as important as need reduction or pleasure. As we have said before and shall say again, one can also quarrel with the learning theorists' conception of the role of motivation in learning, and of the nature of significant motives. More recently, Estes (1970) has recast instrumental-learning theory almost wholly in cognitive terms, effectively destroying the Thorndikean and Skinnerian assumptions on which it was founded.

Work on the law of effect has been carried forward by B. F. Skinner (whose prescriptions for child-rearing we have already mentioned) and his collaborators. Skinner prefers to speak of operant learning or conditioning instead of instrumental, an operant being a whole class of instrumental acts which may differ in how they are performed but still produce the same effect. Thus, the somewhat different instrumental acts of saying at the dinner table, "Please pass the salt," "Give me the salt, please," and "May I please have the salt?" all produce the same result and so belong to the operant class of asking-for-the-salt. Skinner's radical behaviorism goes beyond Thorndike's also in its doctrine of the empty organism (the ultimate *tabula rasa*), according to which the newborn baby can be described entirely in terms of the capacities for action built into his physical constitution, the reflexes that enter into classical conditioning, and the motivational states (defined objectively, in terms of known deprivations, with no implied reference to how the baby *feels*) that will set the baby in random motion. From there on, the law of effect takes over to give shape to the baby's behavior and can be exploited by the parent or educator to make the child what he will—likewise the trainer of animals. The **shaping** of behavior often is used to lead the individual by small steps to ever-closer approximations of the behavior being taught.

Among the specific contributions of Skinner and his coworkers is the analysis of **schedules of reinforcement**. Instead of reinforcing the animal (usually a pigeon in Skinner's laboratory) every time he gives the correct response, one can reinforce some fixed percentage of occurrences of a particular act, or space reinforcements according to some average time interval. Some interesting findings emerge from this sort of analysis. For instance, if reinforcement is given consistently and then discontinued, the reinforced action extinguishes very rapidly; but if reinforcement has been given only intermittently, extinc-

tion is greatly attenuated. As we have seen, though, this principle does not seem to hold when it comes to extinguishing bedtime crying in young infants. An outgrowth of the study of schedules of reinforcement is the field of **probability learning**, the way the organism comes to terms with two (or more) alternative courses of action each of which carries with it a different probability of paying off. Typically, the organism is given a choice of two levers to press, each of which is set to give a reinforcement on some percentage of presses, say 40 percent on one and 60 percent on the other (the two probabilities do not have to add up to 100 percent). Two clear patterns of response have been found, sometimes in sequence. The first, and less profitable, is **matching**, where the subject presses the 40-percent lever 40 percent of the time and the 60-percent lever 60 percent of the time, which yields reinforcement on 52 percent of the presses (.4 x .4 plus .6 x .6). The more mature strategy is to forget the low-payoff lever and stick entirely with the 60-percent one (in our example), which is known as **maximizing**. In fact, few vertebrate organisms can resist an occasional peck or push at the low-probability lever, as though curious to see what will happen.

Skinner has also demonstrated a phenomenon he calls "superstition": a completely irrelevant act occurring just prior to a reinforced relevant one may also be reinforced and thus be incorporated into the total response, so that the pigeon invariably stretches its neck or pirouettes before pecking the key that brings it food (we do not know of any clear human analogies; the first man to blow on a pair of dice may have been rewarded by a lucky throw, but blowing on dice seems in most cases to be learned by watching other people). Skinner has also shown the possibility of teaching an animal behavioral **chains**, elaborate sequences of acts which bring the animal reinforcement.

Skinner shares with S. L. Pressey the paternity of the teaching machine and programed-instruction movement in the United States. In programed instruction (whether or not presented via a machine) an area of knowledge is broken down into small steps or units which are presented one at a time in logical order, each presentation being followed by one or more opportunities for the learner to apply his learning, as by answering a question, with immediate knowledge of results (usually, knowing that one is right is sufficient reinforcement). Programed instruction has proved fairly useful with some subject matters, such as arithmetic, and with some subjects, particularly children who find it hard to pay attention and to learn in regular classroom settings. A learning program can be attacked in solitude, at one's own pace, away from distractions, and the manipulation of the materials, especially on a machine, provides an additional incentive.

As a technique for total education, however, programed instruction has disappointed the original high hopes of its proponents, at least partly because some of its assumptions about how people learn seem to be in error. Some forward-looking technicians, let it be said, anticipate the day when a whole field of learning, including original documents, pictures, tables, charts, diagrams, and movie footage, can be put on a reel of videotape, or, more flexibly, entered in the memory of a computer, together with a highly flexible program that permits the learner to move about through the material according to his own interests, to be used on the individual's private viewing machine (Nelson, 1965). Advanced systems would allow the student to zoom in and out on pictures and maps, to superpose grids and coordinates, to ask questions, to express doubt or disagreement, to request testing, and to ask for clarification when he makes a mistake (Nelson, 1970). In such applications, of course, the original notion of an empty organism, which learns in bits and pieces, has been left light years behind.

The principles of operant conditioning have been applied with varying degrees of success in the so-called **behavior therapies** and **behavior modification**. These methods of treatment take no account of causes; they begin with symptoms and "shape" behavior in desired directions. Such techniques have been especially useful with children with communication problems, such as the mentally retarded (House and Zeaman, 1958). Staats and Butterfield (1965) used operant methods to teach reading to a delinquent, educationally retarded fourteen-year-old; working for 40 hours over a four-and-a-half-month period, they added 430 words to his reading vocabulary, raised his achievement scores to the 4.3 grade level, and enabled him to function in the classroom without disruption. Perhaps the most elaborate application of operant techniques is in the **token economy**; inmates in a prison or mental hospital are given nothing but the most basic necessities unless they engage in "constructive" activities which are rewarded with tokens which can then be exchanged for various privileges, such as a chair to sit on in one's free time. We reserve comment on the ethics of such arrangements, especially when applied to school learning. It has also been demonstrated that one can instrumentally condition such unlikely involuntary processes as changes in brain waves (Miller, 1969).

Developmental principles and approaches

188

In a recent work, Skinner (1971) has gone beyond the prescriptions of *Walden Two* and proposed that American society as a whole be reconstituted as a token economy. Skinner's theory (or nontheory) as a total guide to a philosophy of man is so preposterous that it does not merit the detailed savagery that Chomsky (1971) accords it. On the other hand, reinforcement principles can serve as a useful guide to social policy in some areas. If, for instance, we are in earnest about controlling population, we should stop punishing those whose behavior helps limit population—the dispensers of contraceptives and abortions, those who practice homosexuality—and stop rewarding, as with income-tax deductions, those who propagate freely. Conservationists have pointed out that we ought to reverse our reinforcement schedule for energy consumption, which rewards the heaviest users and wasters of energy with progressively lower rates per unit. Thus, one does not have to think of applied reinforcement as the manipulation of mindless robots, but as social measures that still leave people freedom of choice.

Whatever its contributions, the learning-theory tradition, in all its variations and expressions, fails in our view as a general account of human behavior and development. This is not because of its environmentalism—our most immediate hope for improving ourselves as a species lies in manipulation of the environment rather than our genes, and learning theory is pushing hard to test the limits of environmental manipulation. Learning theory is weak because it fails to come to serious grips with so many areas of learning. It is concerned hardly at all, or at most programmatically, with knowledge, the broad interconnected system of facts and ideas and meaning and values that school learning is supposed to deal with. It has very little patience with the learning of concepts and relations and principles, with thinking, reasoning, and insight, or with the cumulative consequences of learning—for instance, how the things we learn contribute to being intelligent or honest or sympathetic or friendly or involved, or how learning can serve to make a person less egocentric or ethnocentric. Whenever operant theory does try to apply itself to cognitive learning, of course, it violates its own theoretical premises by conceding that cognitive learning exists. In addition to what operant techniques do not teach, there is also the question of what they may teach unwittingly in the way of attitudes or expectations, such as the relation of learning to extrinsic rewards. Learning theorists sometimes go to extravagant lengths to avoid grappling with phenomena that do not fit their conceptions. One device is expressed in **Maier's Law** (Maier, 1960): if you can't explain it, call it something else. The child's acquisition of his native tongue does not happen in ways that fit the usual conceptions of learning, so it has come to be called what we just called it—"acquisition."

Another area in which learning theories are unsatisfactory is that of unlearning, which is not the same as simple forgetting. The child must unlearn, in due time, such beliefs as fairies or Santa Claus, or that babies come by stork, not to mention the many superstitions he invents or accumulates. Indeed, one of the chief problems of higher education is to discover what misinformation or misconceptions the student brings to college so that they can be untaught. Learning theory remains silent on how, in the first place, one can learn things that are not so, such as a belief in Santa Claus, and all the other phantom entities

Some representative theoretical orientations

189

and forces with which people populate the natural order. Nor does learning theory tell us any more about learning through language, by having things described to us, than it does about learning language itself. In general, learning theorists concentrate on the externals of learning, on the easily measurable atomistic indices, such as changes in skin conductivity, salivation, muscle twitches, bar-pressing, or moving from place to place. When they look beneath the surface, it is usually for mediating processes in the central nervous system, bypassing the subjective realm of knowing, wanting, and feeling, as in the accounts of thinking by Osgood (1963) and by Miller, Galanter, and Pribram (1960), or in the work of Pavlov and his followers. This criticism is not to say that learning is independent of the nervous system, but that the facts of learning transcend our knowledge of nervous system functioning, and even where correspondences can be found, learning still exists on its own level and can be studied in its own right, regardless of what neural processes may be involved.

Let us point out that there are other learning theorists who work outside the Pavlovian and Thorndikean mainstreams, and in some cases even contrary to them. Howard and Tracy Kendler (e.g., 1959) study the role of cognitive or verbal mediation, rather than neural mediation, in learning. Their favored technique is to compare the learning of **reversal shifts** and **nonreversal shifts** (also called intradimensional [ID] and extradimensional [ED]), by which the animal is taught a discrimination and then has to learn a new discrimination. A reversal shift is learning that the same dimension of discrimination continues to be the relevant one, but it is now the previously unrewarded stimulus that

gets reinforced; thus if color is the relevant dimension, the animal is first rewarded for responding, say, to the blue stimulus and not the red, and then has to learn to respond to the red and not the blue. A nonreversal shift involves changing the basis of reinforcement to a completely different, previously irrelevant dimension. Thus, if the animal first learns to respond on the basis of color, he then must learn to respond on the basis of size or shape or whatever. Interestingly enough, white rats, young children, and young monkeys, but not older monkeys and people, find reversal shifts much more difficult than nonreversal (Tighe, 1964). That is, it is harder to unlearn to respond to one end of a dimension than to unlearn the whole dimension and shift to another. The Kendlers interpret such findings to mean that linguistic mediation is the key to reversal shifts. While it seems likely that verbal analysis facilitates reversal shifts, perhaps by making possible the framing of hypotheses about what the rules of the game have now become, it is not the whole story, since nonlinguistic organisms like rats and monkeys do, with however much difficulty, eventually learn to make reversal shifts.

Another pair of students of learning who escape the objections we have entered against learning theorists in general are the Harlows (Harlow and Kuenne, 1949), who study **learning set** (also called learning to learn), the fact that the animal generalizes principles to new learning situations, instead of learning a specific response to a specific stimulus. For instance, in so-called **oddity learning**, the child or animal has to learn to respond to the stimulus that is different from the rest of the set. Having done so, he can then transfer the general principle of oddity to a new oddities problem, as when he first learns to pick the block that is a different color from the rest, and then has to learn to select the block that is different in shape from the others.

The Harlows have also stressed that curiosity (without other reward) is a sufficient motivation for learning (White's competence motivation echoes the Harlow findings), and that solving problems is intrinsically satisfying, and not merely a means to satisfying some physical need. We have already mentioned Harry Harlow's research with surrogate mothers, which had as its original aim to disprove the learning-theory hypothesis that the mother comes to be valued as a conditioned stimulus for the satisfaction of physical needs: the monkeys, it will be recalled, preferred the terry-cloth mother, who did not feed them, to the bare wire mother who did.

Stevenson and associates (Stevenson, 1971; Stevenson et al., 1968, 1971) have concerned themselves with how different kinds of learning relate to each other. They ask the same child to perform a great variety of learning, conceptual, and problem-solving tasks. One important finding is that Jensen's (1969) distinction between associative and mediated learning is unfounded, in that performance on both kinds is significantly correlated, and that both deprived and middle-class children show both sorts of learning.

It is an assumption of learning theory that the basic processes of learning are the same in all animal species, but M. E. Bitterman and associates (Bitterman et al., 1958) have shown that there are qualitative differences among animals of different species in their performance on standard learning tasks such as reversal shifts and probability learning, lending support to the discontinuity hypothesis (to be discussed later in this chapter) as it applies to evolu-tionary differences, if not directly to individual development.

A number of students of learning have addressed themselves to the question of learning by imitation, with findings that go counter to the usual learning-theoretical formulation that imitation itself is learned as an operant out of an accidental coincidence of doing something just after somebody else has done it and then being rewarded for it (this notion is central to the **social-learning theory** of identification, mentioned in the last chapter in connection with cultural learning; some people think that social-learning theory should be considered a theory of development, but in fact it deals only with learning from models). One incidental finding, by Darby and Riopelle (1959; Riopelle, 1960), is that monkeys who learn by watching the behavior of other monkeys learn better from another monkey's errors than from his correct responses, indicating that non-imitation is an important part of observational learning.

Maturational theories

The usual textbook formulation of developmental change is that psychological development is a product of learning and **maturation**. Maturation includes but is not the same as growth, which refers primarily to changes in size. Maturation is the continuation of the prenatal developmental processes which produce qualitative changes in tissues or in anatomical and physiological organization. Thus, cartilage ossifies into true bone, myelin sheaths come to cover the peripheral nerves, new enzymes arise in the digestive tract, the body changes in proportions, the endocrine glands change in relative size and activity,

Some representative theoretical orientations

yielding new organizations. The thymus gland, for instance, atrophies during childhood, and the decrease in thymus activity, long a riddle, is now seen as important to the development of somatic individuality, the idiosyncratic tissue composition that makes tissue grafts between individuals extremely difficult (although progress has been made in circumventing the body's immune response to permit organ transplants, and even in utilizing the immune response to combat cancer). The pituitary gland has periods of greater and lesser activity during development, and the gonads do not mature until adolescence.

There is no doubt that maturation of the somatic equipment takes place and that it affects our capacities for acting and reacting. A whole group of theorists has seen in maturation the chief explanation for behavioral changes in the course of development. While such theorists grant that learning takes place, learning is thought of primarily as the activation of structures that have already taken shape in the given organism. It is as though the nervous system becomes a coded or pictorial replica of the outside world, so that perceiving is a matching of neural structure with object, and thinking a running off in miniature of events in the real world. Since it is the organization of the nervous system that structures thought, for example, language is not a mechanism of thinking but only its largely superfluous accompaniment.

Some of the chief proponents of this viewpoint have been Arnold Gesell, Ashley Montagu, Leonard Carmichael, the great Swiss psychologist Jean Piaget, whose thinking has become highly influential in this country only in the last decade and a half but who began his researches almost sixty years ago, Kurt Goldstein, Martin Scheerer, and Heinz Werner. Characteris-

tically, these writers have been more concerned with cognitive processes than with emotion or motivation, and have postulated sets of polar opposites defining the differences between immature and mature behavior. The progression from immature to mature is usually described in terms of stages, epochs in the child's life characterized by particular themes or modes of operation, as in Freud's psychosexual stages, although the exact age periods differ from authority to authority. We shall give only a sampling of the principles and polarities set forth by these theorists.

Gesell proposed a principle of **reciprocal interweaving** which seems to mean a shuttlelike pattern of movement into the future, as though the child takes two steps forward to gain new experience, and then one step back while he consolidates his gains and integrates them with the past. For Gesell, the child's overt behavior is an expression of reciprocal interweaving in nervous system maturation. Gesell's principle of **epigenesis** was simply his statement of the principle of discontinuity, the idea that the individual undergoes qualitative reorganizations as he develops.

Goldstein is best known for the polarity of **concrete** and **abstract** behavior, which he proposed first in connection with his studies of the effects of brain injury. Concreteness means being bound to the present situation and its sometimes irrelevant dynamics, as when the patient sorts a collection of blocks according to color and then is unable to make a new sorting on some other basis such as shape, or when he cannot gratuitously go through the motions of knocking on an imaginary door, or is unable to name a comb until he actually uses it to comb his hair. Abstract behavior requires detachment from the immediacies, consideration of alternative modes of action, and thinking and acting in terms of general principles and future outcomes. Goldstein's formulation is also relevant to normal human development which can be viewed as a progression from concrete to abstract modes of functioning.

Piaget has contributed such notions as egocentrism, already discussed, and its polar opposite, **relativism**, the ability to shift perspectives and see how a situation appears to someone else. He has given the name **primary adualism**—that is, lack of two-ness, or nondifferentiatedness—to the baby's initial inability to distinguish clearly between events happening inside himself and those originating in the outside environment, so that he experiences dreams as happening in the outside world and acts as though he could control external events by wishing, by sympathetic magic. A major notion in Piaget's system is **equilibration**, restoring cognitive balance when the child finds his ideas out of joint with a new experience. Two contrasting processes enter into equilibration. The more primitive, **assimilation**, represents the child's attempts to reshape new experiences, with however much distortion, to fit his accustomed ways of thinking. **Accommodation**, on the other hand, is a change of ideas to take in and integrate new knowledge.

Piaget has given us a sequence of ways in which the child is supposed to perceive causal relations. The first of these is **animism**, whereby material objects, living or not, are regarded as having an animal spirit that makes them behave as they do. Animism may be implict, as when the child simply acts as though something were alive, as when he shows sympathy to a broken plaything, or explicit, as when the child says that the broken plaything hurts. The next is **artificialism**, according to which all events are regulated by some humanlike

entity, as when the child asks, "Why do they have thunder?" At a more advanced level comes **naturalism**, the acceptance of impersonal natural forces as the governing agent in many events, including some portion of human behavior, as in scientific accounts. We have already mentioned Piaget's notions of the nonconservation and conservation of objects. Piaget has also defined a number of stages in the development of logical thinking, such as the **sensori-motor** stage of babyhood, when all behavior is assumed to be stimulated reflex-fashion from without, and the impulsive **preoperational** stage of early childhood, which is succeeded by the stage of **concrete operations**, when the child can solve problems by manipulating things, which yields to the more systematic, analytical approach of the **formal-operational** stage, in which the individual can transcend the information given in perception. Piaget has embellished his stages with descriptive terms drawn from symbolic logic and esoteric branches of mathematics. In addition, he has supplied a model of brain organization to account for the operations of thought and how they change with age.

Piaget's thinking, even after many decades of study, is still evolving and changing, notably in the direction of giving more weight to learning and of making the learning and use of language and symbolic forms a major component in the development of thinking (Inhelder and Piaget, 1964). His astute observations and ingenious task-setting have worked a revolution in the study of psychological development and made this a significant segment of general psychology. The authors, over the years, have assimilated and accommodated to much of Piaget's thinking, and his ideas are implicit in many parts of this book. We differ from him on a number of issues: we attribute much more importance than he to the role of experience, we assign a more central—indeed vital—role to language, and we feel that he—this may be a sin attributable to his disciples more than to the Master—takes far too narrow a view of cognition, limiting it to the coldly logical. We are equally concerned with the emotional components of cognition and with the irrational—crazy beliefs, illogical thought processes, dreams, hallucinations, and all the rest. We might summarize the differences by saying that Piaget has offered us a (highly valuable) psychology of cognition, whereas we are more interested in a cognitive psychology of all areas of human functioning. For a more detailed treatment of the work of Piaget, see Elkind (1971); and for a still more detailed treatment, see Flavell (1963).

Heinz Werner was dedicated to making the principles of individual psychological development the key to a general philosophy embracing animal evolution, historical change, cultural differences, and psychopathology. Werner incorporated Goldstein's abstract-concrete and Piaget's egocentric-relativistic polarities into his view in addition to several developmental polarities of his own. One such dimension is development from **syncretic** (global), undifferentiated functioning, in which perception and thought resemble what William James called a "blooming, buzzing confusion," to differentiated and articulated functioning. Whenever the child or adult meets a new situation he may have to recapitulate this sequence. Many of us can remember the first time we ever saw the engine of a car. At first encounter, it appears as a syncretic, poorly differentiated, burbling, throbbing, ticking, whirring, faintly ominous metal mass enmeshed in a tangle of wires and pipes and hoses and protuberances—although this description is already too well articulated to convey our first global impression. With experience, we become able to sort out—to differentiate—the visible components: the engine block, the manifolds, the carburetor and air cleaner, the fuel pump, the distributor, the generator, the water pump, the radiator and connections, and so forth. And as we are instructed in the engine's functioning, including the movement of parts hidden from view—the rotor, the pistons and rods, the crankshaft, the camshaft, the valves, the timing gear, and so on—we become able to see the engine as an intelligible, orderly, stable, integrally functioning unit: but this now differentiated and articulated whole is quite different from the global, undifferentiated whole with which we began. In the chapters that follow we will point out a number of phenomena that seem to follow the pattern of differentiation and higher-order, emergent integration expressed in the **syncretic-articulated polarity**.

Two other polarities of development are closely linked in Werner's system. These are development from **rigidity** to **flexibility** of thought and action, and from living in a **labile** world to inhabiting a **stable** one. In the unstable world of the young child, where feelings mingle with objects and the spirit world coexists with the material, where meanings and identities change without warning, and where there are no limits on what is possible, stability can be achieved only by adhering to rigid, habit-bound, and ritualistic patterns of behavior. We find similar behavior in adults who, faced with the flux and complexities and perplexities of life, take refuge in tradition and simplistic slogans and dogmas and formulas. If and as the world becomes more stable, reliable, orderly, and predictable, more possibilities for effective action become apparent and behavior can be increasingly flexible and varied.

Werner also had a special interest in language, in both its factual, descriptive, propositional functions and its evocative, affective, expressive ones, as in poetry and metaphor. Some of his ideas in this area are expressed in the account of language learning in the next chapter.

It might be supposed that psychoanalytic theories, which are concerned primarily with motivation and emotion, and maturational theories, which focus on cognition, could simply be combined to give a reasonably complete picture of the individual and his development. The thought has occurred to quite a few people, for the most part originally of a psychoanalytical persuasion, including Silvano Arieti, E. J. Anthony, René Spitz, Peter Wolff, Ernest Schachtel, and David Rapaport, all of whom have sought to integrate the two approaches, largely in terms of parallels between Freud's primary-process thinking and the primitive (egocentric, concrete, rigid, syncretic) thinking described by maturational theorists. It seems to us that these attempts have been abortive, perhaps because psychoanalysts find it hard to cope with the emergentism of maturational theories, and because neither psychoanalysis nor maturational theory makes sufficient provision for learning and the role of context on behavior. Werner, for instance, talked a great deal about cultural differences, but had almost nothing to say about how one comes to assimilate a particular cultural outlook.

It will be seen that the maturational theories of development have a great deal in common with the **structuralism** (Lévi-Strauss, 1966) that is much in vogue currently. Structuralism is a socio-logical concept, quite useful for describing the interrelatedness of shared belief systems or social institutions, but it produces ludicrous results when transferred to the behavior of individuals. For instance, Chomsky's (1968) attempts to derive psychological principles from grammatical structures, which are deduced from the utterances of many speakers, lead to the absurdity that there are no important individual differences in linguistic behavior. One might also conclude from Chomsky's reasoning that children speak better than adults. We shall have to discuss Chomsky's theories later, when we talk about language development, simply because they are highly influential; for the moment it is enough to say that structuralism does not appear to have much applicability to human psychological development.

Kurt Lewin's field theory

Maturational theories have a close link with **Gestalt psychology**. Where other psychologies tried to analyze psychological functions in terms of their elements, Gestalt psychology was concerned with the qualities of organized things-as-a-whole. The Gestalt psychologist would point out that a square constructed of either dots or lines is perceived in terms of its squareness, which is designated a **whole-quality** (much the same as a physiognomy [see pp. 90–91], except that the Gestaltists were not much concerned with the feelings aroused by whole-qualities), rather than in terms of the particular elements that go to make it up.

It is hard to summarize the Gestalt position because it contains a number of contradictions. On the one hand, the Gestaltists insisted upon the distinctive human qualities of human beings, complaining that associationism dealt with "mere facts" to the neglect of values. On the other hand, Wolfgang Köhler (who, along with Max Wertheimer and Kurt Koffka, was one of the founders of the Berlin school of Gestalt, the one best known in the United States) vigorously denied the possibility of qualitative transformations in the course of either species evolution or individual human development. At the same time, he emphasized the role of **insight** (understanding, often rapid, as expressed in "Eureka!" or the "Aha experience") in learning, and the discontinuous learning curves that result when the organism arrives at insightful understanding of the task. Köhler was a reductionist (see p.197), and sought to explain behavior and perception in terms of maplike representations in the brain. Although much of his work was concerned with perception and the effects of different arrangements of stimuli on perception, Köhler staunchly maintained that the real world is in principle unknowable, holding that what we take to be reality is only something that we infer or reconstruct out of discharges in the nervous system.

Although both Wertheimer and Koffka were interested in research with children, the Berlin school was nondevelopmental in its orientation, but it produced one psychologist, Kurt Lewin, who was at least partly developmental in his outlook and made many studies of children. Lewin's point of view is called **topological field theory**, and is based on his concept of **life-space**. The life-space consists of those selected aspects of the environment which stand out for the individual as psychologically meaningful. For instance, male and female walking together along a row of shops are likely, as we have said, to have two very different life-spaces. Lewin represented the life-space as a potato-shaped region marked off with routes and barriers representing types of activity allowed and available, or prohibited and blocked. The routes in this life-space lead to goal objects with positive and negative valences which indicate whether the objects are attractive or repulsive. The person in the field (which may itself be something thought about as well as the person's perceived world) is moved or immobilized by the action of these valences along the pathways that are open to him, representing courses of action. In this way one can represent a number of classical situations. Frustration, for instance, can be shown as an attractive goal across an insurmountable barrier. Various states of conflict can be represented, as when the person is torn between two competing but incompatible attractions, or when a negatively valenced object lies across the path to an attractive one, or the condition of ambivalence, when a goal has both positive and negative valences. Lewin was avowedly "ahistorical" in his approach; that is, he was less interested in how a life-space comes to be constituted as it is than in its structure at the moment of action. He did say, however, that the life-space becomes progressively more differentiated in the course of development, and, as suggested earlier, he conceived of regression as a de-differentiation of the life-space. And it does not seem incompatible with his views to assume that the life-space also undergoes qualitative reorganizations and reintegrations as development proceeds.

Lewin represented the person in the life-space's field of forces as an empty circle, reminiscent of Skinner's empty organism, so that people are no longer described in terms of their own capacities but in terms of their environments. Thus, instead of talking about stupid or intelligent people, we can talk about stupid or intelligent life-spaces. Or, if we want to drop Lewin's terminology, we can talk about more or less intelligent environments. Thus, intelligence is not a property of nervous systems but of how the world appears to people, its qualities and flavors and meanings and possibilities for action. If we adopt this view of intellectual differences, then the goal of education becomes that of making people more intelligent by teaching them what the environment consists of and how it operates (and how they can interact with it), including the action of forces and agents lying beyond perception, whether x-rays or infrared or molecular structure or ultrasound or viruses or RNA or human physiology or the law of supply and demand. For the life-space changes as we come to understand the principles by which we and the world work, including the fact that different cultures shape the life-space of people in very different ways, including the moral, esthetic, and emotional valences it assigns to things. We shall return at the end of Chapter 7 to the topic of intelligence and how it develops.

Underlying Theoretical Issues

It is our aim in this section to look at some of the broader assumptions about human nature that underlie the psychological theories we have just described. That they are all deficient in various important ways does not make them useless—even an erroneous theory can lead the investigator to new and otherwise unsuspected facts and relations.

Reductionism and mechanism

It used to be that theories were meant to explain phenomena in the sense of saying how they were possible. Nowadays, most theorists have concluded that explanation in this sense is out of the question. As soon as we try to understand how living organisms are different from inert matter, how they metabolize, reproduce, maintain physiological equilibrium (**homeostasis**), move about (in the case of those organisms that move under their own power), adapt to stimulation, and so forth, we are at a loss. And when we move to the psychological level and examine such phenomena as consciousness, attention, love, sympathy, thought, perception, self-knowledge, self-control, and the like, our powers of conceptualization break down. Important as these problems are, psychologists have tended to ignore them.

What most theorists now profess is to have abandoned explanation in favor of description, systematic statements of cause and effect, correlations, and analyses. However, we still find many remnants of explanatory thinking and even of the metaphysics that prevailed before science came into its own. For instance, there are those who still insist upon the existence of instincts, which, since no one is prepared to say what an instinct is, is no more helpful than invoking phlogiston or animal magnetism.

A common substitute for explanation is found in **reductionism**: instead of explaining the phenomena themselves, one seeks to account for them by events at a "lower" —meaning simpler or more physically tangible—and hence more manageable level. In the case of psychological phenomena, this means "explanation" at the level of physiology, anatomy, or biochemistry. Or, alternatively, one can construct a "model," in the form of an analogy or metaphor, a mathematical equation of broad generality, or a mechanical equivalent such as a computer. The hidden motive in such explanations often seems to be to explain away rather than explain, to get rid of the intangible phenomena and with them the uncomfortable notion that in actuality they perhaps cannot be explained. In their desire to emulate the more precise and rigorous physical sciences, many biologists and psychologists seem to fear that admitting the facts of human behavior opens the door to vitalism or even mysticism. Most scientists of behavior seek a naturalistic conception of the facts, without recourse to such entities or substances as "spirit," "mind," "élan vital" (which translates roughly as "life force"), or anything else added on to the material organism which lives and acts.

Here we have the recurring conflict between **dualism**, which says that mind and body are distinct, and **monism**, which says that mind and body are merely aspects of the same organism. The authors are sympathetic to a naturalistic monism which recognizes that the organism has **different levels of functioning**, including the psychological. Our brand of monism sees the psychological level in the organism's congress with objects and their meanings and qualities, including the self as object and the symbolic objects that people construct with words, numbers, and the like.

Reductionism has gone hand in hand with **mechanism**, a more or less explicit assumption that the ideal model for organic and psychological functioning is the machine. According to Mumford (1970), Galileo begat mechanism when he conceived of the universe as a megamachine, with societies and individuals working as mechanical components of the larger order. The mechanistic tradition in physiology and psychology received its greatest impetus from the French mathematician-philosopher Descartes, who conjured an image of a machine-man operated by levers and pulleys and valves and conduits through which pneumatic fluids or vapors could travel. Note that this conception is not wholly absurd: our bones and joints and muscles do operate more or less this way, and who is to deny the mechanical pump-like action of the heart and circulatory system? (Descartes was a contemporary of William Harvey, who discovered that the blood circulates, even if very few people, especially physicians, believed him.) Modern theories of nerve action have simply substituted electrochemical transmission of impulses for Descartes' humoral flow. The absurdity comes when we try to extend this model (which Descartes seems to have meant not as an analogy but as the literal truth, although he had to tread softly lest he offend the religious authorities) to other functions, as in the TV-commercial version of the digestive tract as a series of vats, beakers, retorts, and connecting tubes, with stopcocks to control the flow of gastric juices. Or we have the standard model of perception according to which nerves act like wires bringing information into the brain; once the codified information is in the brain, it has to be decoded, interpreted and made sense out of, to which end the model-makers provide something like a cathode-ray screen containing the decoded image and a homunculus (sometimes acknowledged, more often not) to read off the picture and activate the nerves which carry information to the glands and muscles. This miniature person in the brain is the modern-day descendant of the soul, and seems to be the mechanist's device for handling consciousness or mind. In this case, it would seem, reductionism breeds dualism, or even multiplism. For, as Skinner (1963) has pointed out, the homunculus too needs his own perceptual apparatus to read off the cathode-ray tube display, which logically implies that he must have a homunculus in his brain, and that homunculus another homunculus, and so on without end.

The mechanistic approach has found its most sophisticated modern expression in **information theory**, which seeks to describe human functioning in the language of digital computers (Miller et al., 1960). The information-theory model is sometimes helpful and has given us such concepts as **feedback** and **signal-to-noise ratio** and **reverberating circuit** and **information overload.** In the strict computer sense, feedback consists of a yes or no response to a single operation or part operation. In terms of behavior, it means that any action by the organism has effects which feed back to the organism and serve to regulate the next act, and so on. We have already given the example of how the ground feeds back information to our feet in walking. Similarly, the play of facial expression on someone to whom we are talking can serve as feedback that modifies what we say next—in experimental situations, the experimenter can steer and shape what the subject is saying by reacting in a predetermined, arbitrary way that the subject may have no inkling of (Krasner, 1958). The signal-to-noise ratio seeks to specify how clearly important information—the "message"—stands out from the background or is camouflaged by irrelevant, distracting "noise"—the concept of noise can be applied in any sense modality (it is analogous to visual clutter), and not only to hearing. The reverberating circuit is one way to ac-

count for memory or learning or "information storage" by imagining that events set up continuing circuits of neural activity which can be called upon and combined (by the homunculus?) for purposes of thinking and acting. Information overload refers to the condition of most of us most of the time, overwhelmed by a torrent of events far in excess of what we can reasonably process (Milgram, 1970).

There seem to be at least three things wrong, however, with information theory as a general account of behavior. First of all, the evidence that mammalian (or even vertebrate) nervous systems operate according to the same principles as a digital computer is very slim indeed (Sperry, 1965). Second, the computer model requires that complex acts which occur simultaneously in the living organism be strung out in time, even though it be microtime. For instance, one can teach a two-year-old to recognize the letters of the alphabet at a glance, by their physiognomies. To enable the computer to distinguish letters of the alphabet requires a whole system of explicit analyses in which all the ways letters are composed and differ from each other have to be spelled out and programed into the machine (Gibson, 1970). Generation after generation of two-year-olds continue to recognize letters, geometric forms, people, animals, facial expressions, words, sentences, voices, odors, and melodies, while computer engineers are still struggling to teach their machines the simplest sorts of pattern discriminations. Computers are extremely inefficient, but their inefficiency is compensated for by the phenomenal speed with which they perform successive operations. Unfortunately, they are no good on physiognomies. Third, the computer model leaves no room for perversity or inventiveness or meaningful errors, for values or moods or motivational states which any psychologist has to weight in making descriptions and predictions. Typical of the impoverished thinking of computer enthusiasts was their long-held faith in the possibility of machine translation between languages, which those who knew about language could have told them would come a cropper at the first metaphor. The classic, and perhaps apocryphal, case is the attempt to translate "Out of sight, out of mind" into Russian; it emerged as the Russian equivalent of "blind idiot." Even literal translation may go awry: "Charles was suspended for a prank" comes out, in one Russian version, "Charles was hanged for juvenile delinquency," and in another, "Charles was hanged as a prank." We might note that the products of some human translators are not much better, and we cannot help wondering what Chairman Mao *really* thinks.

The nonvitalistic alternative to mechanism has traditionally been holistic theories (in recent years more commonly called **field theories**), which take their analogies and metaphors from those areas of physics dealing with field effects—hydraulics, electricity, magnetism, gravity—from chemistry with its qualitative transformations (as in John Stuart Mill's "mental chemistry"), and from biology with its notions of growth, homeostasis, metamorphosis, and systems. But note that this approach, while perhaps more intuitively congenial to common-sense understanding of human nature, is still a form of reductionism—it makes no provision for consciousness, self-knowledge, self-control, originality, fantasy, symbolic activity, in short what are regarded as the "higher mental processes."

The philosophical alternative to reduc-

tionism is the doctrine of **emergence**; it seeks to define different levels of analysis or "orders of reality" or complexity, each with its own set of governing principles that transcend the principles regulating the simpler levels. As applied to human beings, the doctrine of emergence would distinguish such successively more complex levels as the behavior of the atomic particles of which we are composed; the chemical and biochemical level, including gene action and functions like metabolism and nerve-fiber action; the macrophysical, including the mechanics of movement and the hydrodynamics of circulation; the physiological, including processes like homeostasis, digestion, sickness and recovery from sickness; the psychological realm of subjective feeling, including thought, emotions, and awareness of body states; the person, with attitudes and goals and values and attachments; and, at still-higher levels, man as an element in a team, a group, or a society; or a society as one element in the stream of history; on the cosmic scale of the astronomer, of course, man disappears from view.

Emergence does not deny that events at one level may be coordinated with events at another. Obviously, we can have a psychological existence only by virtue of our material bodies. It does, however, say that each class of events can be described in its own right, without reference to other levels, and that corresponding events on two levels may each need its own set of principles. For instance, we know that perceived color depends on the wave length of light, but whereas wave length varies continuously, hue varies discontinuously, as in a rainbow. Now it is customary to speak of the biological basis of behavior, which is accurate in the sense that without an organism there would be no behavior, and that the way an organism is constituted sets bounds on its behavior. But we can with equal truth speak of the psychological foundations of biology, in that our physiological functioning is responsive both to internal thought and to perceptual stimulation from without, and in that our personal and social experience can, in time, alter even our anatomy, as seen in studies of the effects of enrichment and deprivation and stress on animal development.

CONTINUITY AND DISCONTINUITY. When we talk about psychological development, the contrasting doctrines of reductionism and emergence go by the names of **continuity theory** and **discontinuity theory**. Continuity theory, which is reductionistic, holds that development is simply an accumulation of skills, habits, discriminations, without anything new appearing in the make-up of the individual. By contrast, the discontinuity view, based on the doctrine of emergence, holds that in the course of development the organism undergoes genuine transformations—that is, reaches successively higher, emergent levels of organization—on the model of biological metamorphosis. Thus, in human development, walking is seen as discontinuous with (but emergent from) creeping, talking as discontinuous with babbling, drawing pictures as discontinuous with scribbling, and so on through a hierarchy of emergent functions. Lewin and, from a quite different theoretical standpoint, Zing-Yang Kuo (1967) have both stressed the transformation of the organism as it takes each developmental step.

We should take a moment to clear up a common misunderstanding. Stage theories, like those of Freud and Piaget, imply discontinuity, in that each stage is differently organized from the one before. The reverse, however, is not necessarily so. That is, one can subscribe to a discontinuity view without also accepting the notion of stages. This is because different sorts of function have their own separate timetables, so that social development can have a series of emergences unconnected with the child's growing command of number, which may have little to do with toilet training, or toilet training with the ability to stand on one foot. Indeed much Piagetian research has assumed that certain cognitive functions are linked in stages, that conservation of quantity goes with seriation (the ability to order things serially) and reversibility (grasping that some logical operations can go two ways; e.g., subtraction reverses addition), although the evidence for the assumption is scarce (Berzonsky, 1971; Kohnstamm, 1970).

These differences are not the mere quibblings of theologians. One's whole view of child-rearing and education depends on whether one takes a continuity or discontinuity position, with very real consequences for what kind of people one perceives or produces. The continuity theorist stresses training, the cultivation of skills and stimulus-response relations, whereas the discontinuity theorist stresses the cultivation of insight, understanding, self-knowledge, imagination, and a broad perspective out of which new organizations of behavior and meaning can emerge.

DETERMINISM AND VOLUNTARISM. Tied in here, as suggested earlier, is a further split between doctrines of **determinism**, associated with reductionism and continuity theory, and **voluntarism** (or the exercise of will), associated with emergence and discontinuity theory. The determinist holds that the individual is helpless to control his own behavior and destiny, that he cannot behave in the present with a view to future outcomes, and that if he has an intimation of self-regulation this is nothing but delusion, since he is in fact a prisoner of the accidents of his past history.

Few emergence theorists nowadays would dare to counter this view with a doctrine of free will, because we know too much about how far our characters and motives and abilities and tastes and outlooks are shaped by events that happen during early periods of our lives when we are essentially helpless. We also know too much about social and natural forces and how these can act without regard to individual plans and wishes. Nonetheless, discontinuity theorists would say that, given favorable rearing conditions, human beings acquire a perspective on the world and on themselves that permits them to some extent to anticipate the future, to think for themselves, to inhibit some forms of activity and to force themselves to engage in others, and above all to reason out their situation so as to frame their own set of ethical and moral principles for the conduct of life, instead of blindly obeying all the rules ordained by their culture. The discontinuity theorist would also have to concede that a great many people, by virtue of less favorable histories, show a low degree of self-determination and seem to lead lives governed by the push and pull of circumstance, or at best grumble against fate or strike out in rage against a world in whose workings they have no say.

To understand this issue fully we need to be aware of the concept of **teleology**— which we are not advocating—which says that natural events move toward a goal or purpose, as though in fulfillment of some master plan. The master plan can be thought of as imposed from above, as by a deity, or somehow coded into life so as to predetermine the direction of evolution, development, and behavior. Now it is one thing to say that natural evolution has a direction, which is not hard to define and describe, but quite another to say that it has a prior purpose or meaning. Unfortunately, though, many of those who denounce this brand of teleology extend their denunciation to deny the possibility of individual human purposes and goals, which is quite a different matter. For there can be no denying, it seems to us, that individuals do formulate designs for living, and work hard to fulfill those designs, or that groups of individuals define and execute social policies, some of which, as in agricultural or conservation measures, can influence natural evolution. As Bruner (1962) points out, man, as far as we know, is the only species in which individuals anticipate their own death. The purposive view acknowledges that people in planning their lives may be deceived about their own motivations, or may think, often, that they are acting autonomously when in fact the whole pattern was subtly laid down for them in infancy, or may come up with some wholly bizarre designs, or that circumstances may change in ways that make the original plan obsolete. It only says that, for better or for worse, people can have an orientation toward the future and are able to adapt present action to anticipated outcomes, and that they can act ethically, taking account of other people's purposes and values as well as of their own.

Nature and nurture, optimism and pessimism

Two more sets of contrasts remain to be mentioned as relevant to the specific theories that have been put forward to make sense of the facts of human development and behavior. The first of these is the ever-recurring **nature-nurture** controversy, the question of whether human behavior can best be accounted for in terms of biologically given structures, motives, abilities, propensities, or instincts, or in terms of those qualities acquired through experience in a particular material, personal, and cultural setting. (Those who uphold the nature side in the controversy are called **nativists** or **instinct theorists** or **genetic determinists**. Those who plump for nurture are called **environmentalists**.)

On this dichotomy and the one that follows, we shall not take sides, preferring to seek a synthesis of nature and nurture. We agree in principle with Anastasi (1958) that the meaningful question is not whether nature or nurture gets the credit or the blame, or even how much each contributes to development, but how they interact in the formation of an individual with thus-and-such characteristics. Since we still lack the means to answer this question, the immediate practical issue is how to arrange the environment to bring out the best in everybody. The two areas in which the nature-nurture controversy has raged most fiercely are those of morality and intelligence. Psychologists have pretty much abandoned the search for biological correlates of virtue or wickedness (although echoes are heard in pronouncements on aggression, schizophrenia, addiction to drugs or alcohol, and criminality), but the origin of intellectual differences is still an embittered topic as seen by the recent storm over Jensen's (1969) article. We shall return to the nature-nurture controversy with respect to intelligence in Chapter 7.

The other remaining major contrast to be discussed is between **optimism** and **pessimism**, between those who have seen human nature as intrinsically virtuous, so that the child comes into the world trailing clouds of glory, and needs above all else to be protected against corruption by a wicked world, and those who have seen the newborn babe as steeped in original sin and pervasive evil, so that the task of child-rearing becomes that of beating the devil out of the child to make room for a socially given morality. To this polarity of good and evil must be counterposed the more modern view of **neutralism**, that the child is neither virtuous nor wicked by nature but can become either—or in various proportions both—according to his experience.

Now, if we combine these two dimensions of optimism-neutralism-pessimism and biologism-environmentalism, we can construct a table with six cells, each representing the conjunction of two positions, one from each of the two dimensions, as shown in Table 1.

It turns out that most major theorists can fairly readily be assigned to one of these six cells. (We could, of course, complicate our scheme by adding the dimensions of reductionism-emergence and determinism-voluntarism, but such a complication seems unnecessary. All these theorists have a more or less reductionistic and deterministic outlook, at least as regards the early years.) The cell at the intersection of optimism and biologism contains such names as that of Jean Jacques Rousseau, with his doctrine of Romantic Naturalism, and those of his modern successors such as Arnold Gesell and Ashley Montagu, the latter of whom finds love and cooperation as basic ingredients of the natural order. The neutralist-biologist cell contains the names—again, among others—of Jean Piaget, Leonard Carmichael, and Heinz Werner. Piaget has studied moral

TABLE 1 A TAXONOMY OF THEORIES		
	Biologistic	Environmentalistic
Optimistic	Jean Jacques Rousseau Arnold Gesell M. F. A. Montagu	John Locke Karl Marx Ivan Pavlov
Neutralistic	Jean Piaget Leonard Carmichael Heinz Werner	E. L. Thorndike J. B. Watson Clark Hull B. F. Skinner
Pessimistic	Sigmund Freud	Thomas Hobbes

development as one aspect of cognitive development, which he sees as dictated by biological maturation, but contemplates morality only with the detached eye of the scientist. Carmichael is an evolutionary theorist who sees a decided progression toward intellectual mastery over the environment but remains largely uncommitted on the subject of good and evil. The outstanding pessimistic biologist of our era was Sigmund Freud, who saw human nature as essentially vile, with some faint hope in the corrective forces of socialization and education, especially as their effects became part of human heredity (bear in mind that Freud was a Lamarckian). Moving to the environmentalist column, the optimistic empiricists include the seventeenth-century British philosopher John Locke, with his doctrines of the *tabula rasa*, the neonate as a clean slate on which experience writes or impresses its lessons, and of the **association of ideas**, according to which those events which repeatedly occur together become linked in thought. Karl Marx, the author of economic determinism and dialectical materialism, was likewise an optimistic environmentalist, as was the renowned Russian physiologist Ivan Pavlov, who gave us the conditioned reflex, a more rigorous statement of the association of ideas. Note that Pavlov's system included an emergent something called the **second signal system**, by which human beings are enabled to learn language and transcend their animal nature. The American associationists, such as Edward Thorndike, J. B. Watson, Clark Hull, and B. F. Skinner, have tended to be neutralist-environmentalists and, in their reductionistic way, have had rather less faith than Marx and Pavlov in human beings' capacity for virtue. One might even doubt that virtue seemed to them a relevant topic for psychological consideration. Finally, if only for the sake of logical completeness, in the pessimistic-environmentalist cell we may place the name of the British philosopher Thomas Hobbes, for whom the environment had to redeem a primitive condition of life, which he characterized in a famous quotation as "solitary, poor, nasty, brutish, and short."

All the theories we have discussed suffer, perhaps inevitably, from the flaw of egocentrism. In each case, that is, the theorist and his fellows have adopted a single perspective on the human condition and assumed that they were seeing it in its entirety, in the round. Now it is perfectly clear that these various perspectives yield information so diverse that it seems hard to believe that all the theorists are talking about the same creature, who is now angelic and now depraved, now a black-box robot shaped by reinforcers, and now a shaper of his own destiny, now devious and involved in a life of self-deception and now straightforward, now lust-driven and now serene, now hardheadedly oriented to solid reality, now adrift in a miasma of ignorance and superstition tricked out as philosophy. And yet we know that man is all of these and that any final theory is going to have to reconcile all these incompatibles, that it will have to account for man at his most heavenly and his most bestial, man the passive automaton and man the striver and doer, man at his most deluded and most penetrating.

The authors do not claim to be ready to accomplish this ultimate synthesis, but, to make our biases clear, we do feel that the study of development will reveal man's plasticity, the way experience can bring forth a variety of human natures, and that a few fortunate individuals can be given the psychological means for reconciling and mastering their own conflicting tendencies and finding a meaning in life. As the subtitle of this book suggests, we are concerned with persons rather than the processes into which persons get analyzed. We are further concerned with the person in his environment, which implies an interest in the phenomenology of how environments are experienced. **Eclecticism** is usually taken to mean a more or less uncritical piecing together of theories or fragments of theories, and in this sense becomes a term of opprobrium. But we are seeking, along with Gardner Murphy, Gordon Allport (1964), and others, a synthetic eclecticism whereby all the seemingly paradoxical aspects of human functioning can be subordinated in an emergent conception of man. We refuse to be committed to any orthodoxy, our only commitment being to the humanity of human beings: we have already clearly emphasized that we are more hospitable to some theories and assumptions and more hostile to others. For perhaps the most important single principle of human development is what Ralph Linton calls the **self-fulfilling prophecy**, which says simply that our children become what we expect them to become, whether our expectations be phrased as hopes or fears, left implicit or made explicit. Especially with our fears, we are likely to adopt a defensive, preventive, punitive approach to child-rearing, and the harder we work to stave off this or that dire possibility, the more likely it is that the possibility will become a reality.

While we have been theorizing, our infant has pulled himself to his feet and toddled into a new stage of development, where we must make haste to follow him —at this age, he is moving very fast.

5

the
toddler

Between the ages of about fifteen months and two and a half years, the child lives a style of life that is called by some toddlerhood. Not all authorities recognize toddlerhood as a distinct period in development, preferring to assign the months before age two to infancy, and the months thereafter to the so-called preschool years. This seems to us a debatable course on several grounds. First, it seems inappropriate to call a child who can talk, often very proficiently, an *infant,* or unspeaking one. Second, even though he has become a walking and speaking baby, he is still a baby, very different in manner and appearance and competence from what he will become around age two and a half. Most important of all, toddlerhood is marked by its own very special emergents: completing the transition from quadruped to biped, the development of psychological autonomy, beginning to speak, and sphincter control. We, along with a lot of other people, object to the cuteness of "toddler," but we have not found a better name. Some writers, particularly the British, speak of the "run-about baby," but this is more cumbersome and does not lend itself easily to a designation of the period—that is, "run-about babyhood"—as well as of the child himself.

Behavioral Development in Toddlerhood

Even before he came to be a toddler, the baby may have been walking for some time, but he had probably done so uncertainly, with arms held high for balance—he was so involved with maintaining vertical equilibrium that his hands could not be used for any other purpose, such as carrying things or scratching an itch, while he was walking. When in a real hurry to get someplace, he was likely to revert to the speed and security of travel on all fours. But now he is truly up and away—exuberantly, doggedly, or timidly, according to his temperament—his legs spread apart but pumping steadily. Many toddlers fall down a great deal, tripping or stumbling or simply losing their balance, but they rarely hurt themselves seriously; this is because they have not yet learned the maladaptive reaction, found in older children and adults, of going stiff when they fall. Instead, they tumble limp and relaxed and resilient. In any case, they haven't far to fall. A toddler's legs are still short, by adult standards, in proportion to his trunk and head, giving him a bottom-heavy look which is further enhanced by the bulky diapers that will soon, in keeping with his new estate, give way to training pants. In appearance, as we have said, the toddler is still a baby, and one can follow his growth in Western homes as his head begins to rise above the top of the dining table until he can see what is on its surface, and as he reaches toward and eventually becomes able to grasp doorknobs. (Readers from cultural settings in which these are inappropriate measuring instruments are invited to devise their own yardsticks.) The toddler's babyish charm is indicated by the fact that he, more than the infant, was the model for the cherubim and cupids of Renaissance paintings. His small size means, of course, that he views much of the adult-scale world in terms of the undersides of things—the bathroom sink, for instance, with its water pipes and drain and the rust and scale and cobwebs that are masked from adult vision.

Olive R. Pierce, Photo Researchers

In much of his behavior, too, the toddler is still a baby. Every new object is seized, inspected, waved about as though to sample its heft and whatever sounds it produces, and as often as not stuffed as far as it will go into his mouth. He may be content to sit on the floor for long—for him—periods banging and tinkering with pots and pans and utensils while his mother goes about her work. He is still a baby, at least in early toddlerhood, in being more motor than verbal in his dealings with people. As in late infancy, the toddler probably takes two naps a day, switching to a single nap before age two. With time out for naps, the toddler's waking now stretches from perhaps five in the morning to as late as eight in the evening. Nevertheless, he manifests new and unbabylike competences.

We shall describe shortly some of the major developments of toddlerhood, but here we might mention some minor acquisitions found in children in United States culture. It is during toddlerhood that the child becomes able to chew gum without swallowing it, to drink through a straw, to eat with a spoon (we have not been able to find out at what age Chinese and Japanese children master chopsticks, but Indian toddlers have learned to use only the right hand for eating), to blow his nose into a handkerchief or tissue held by an adult (he may try to blow his own nose, too, with rather messy results), and to eat an ice-cream cone—a skill best acquired in warm weather outdoors, where the problems of mopping up are reduced. By age two, he may become able to work a simple record player, switching it on, selecting a particular record (which he seems to distinguish by the physiognomy of the label, or even part of the label) and placing it on the turntable, moving the

Like the infant, the toddler may spend moments of solitude clutching his blanket and sucking his thumb.

Pots, pans, utensils, and other household furnishings are both playthings and learning materials.

Burk Uzzle, Magnum

Riding a tricycle is a standard skill of American toddlers.

tone arm into position, and adjusting the volume—he generally keeps it turned low, suggesting that his hearing may be extremely acute. He may learn to ride a tricycle or a pedal-less kiddy car, although on a tricycle he may at first try to push with both feet at once and have some trouble getting the knack of alternate thrusts. Also, his skill may outrun his judgment, and he has to be restrained from riding his tricycle into the street. He will probably not learn to put on and fasten his own clothes until the preschool years, but he early becomes adept at removing them, and a parent busy taking goods from the supermarket shelves may be startled to look down and discover a nude baby. The toddler imitates the superficial actions of grooming, chewing on toothbrush bristles or going through the motions of brushing and combing his hair—we even have a record of a seventeen-month-old trying to trim her nails with a pair of pruning shears (Church, 1968, p. 70). Japanese babies by age two have learned to bow properly to an adult.

The toddler is moving rapidly away from babyhood and toward childhood in many other ways. Most generally, as Erikson says, the toddler is striving for **autonomy**, becoming aware of himself as a person among other people and wanting to do things for himself, with the developmental alternative of **shame and doubt** if conditions favorable to the development of autonomy are missing. The toddler demonstrates his beginning autonomy—and his desire for more of it—in every field: in the mastery of his own body (in walking, trotting, climbing up and climbing down, hopping and jumping, manipulating things, and in controlling his sphincters); in his mastery of objects (the toddler typically wants to push his stroller instead of riding in it, he wants to carry outsized things from place to place and back again, he becomes able not only to dismantle but also to reassemble various playthings, he becomes sensitive to attributes of objects such as their color or shape); in social relations (he learns language, he plays elaborate games, he begins to refuse parental commands and requests and offers of help, manifesting what is called **negativism**).

The toddler's push toward autonomy is by no means absolute and continuous, however. It seems to be greatest in Western societies and least in those cultures where the toddler still is regularly carried by the mother or baby-tender. Growth ambivalence shows up in the child's vacillating between dependence and independence, a conflict that will persist in various guises into adulthood. Out on a walk, the toddler may plunge off in pursuit of a pigeon, or go scuttling into a particularly alluring hallway, only to stop short and come hurtling back into his mother's arms. He may strike out on his own to explore the wonders of a store, and then burst into tears when he realizes the hand he is reaching for belongs to a stranger. When trying some new feat such as jumping from a step, he makes a great show of boldness but still clings tightly to an adult finger. In sum, he is still in the early stages of trying himself out, and it will be a long time before he achieves anything like true autonomy of thought and action. Also, in keeping with the principle of dual ambivalence, his parents, while taking pride and pleasure in each new step forward, both lament the movement away from infancy ("my baby!") and are unsure how much to trust the toddler's seeming com-

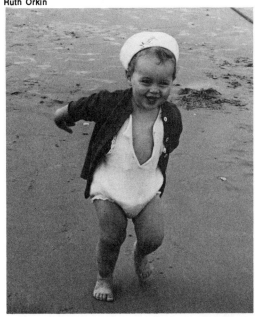

The toddler alternates between daring autonomy and clinging dependence.

petence, when to keep hands off and when to hover or intervene.

*Posture, motor behavior,
and orientation in space*

One of the key transitions of toddlerhood is from creeping to a pedestrian way of life, from quadrupedal to bipedal locomotion. It is true that the child begins walking while still an infant, but toddlerhood is marked by a qualitative change, shown by walking's being the normal mode of travel (although the toddler may still creep in a spirit of play), by the toddler's greater stability, and by his no longer needing his arms for balance, so that he can now carry things with him—as we said earlier, carrying things is a species of compulsion for the toddler. In spite of his new proficiency, the toddler up to about age two may still have to set himself in motion by rocking back and forth from foot to foot (such preludes to action are called **intention movements**, and are seen in a variety of situations, from the dog's circling before he lies down to the pitcher's winding up before he throws the ball).

Before long, the toddler not only walks but trots. In his bare feet, the toddler, like Tuesday's child, is full of grace. His toes are likely to be spread as he runs—and he is likely to run, and to run trippingly on his toes, far more than he is to walk or to use a sedate heel-and-toe movement. Once he has begun to run, he seldom moves in any other way, and one can see the beginning of later preschool styles of action, as in turning a corner—the toddler (and preschool child) typically turns a jog in a corridor by running straight ahead into the wall, bouncing off and changing direction, then resuming his run. He becomes able to hop on two feet, and perhaps to stand on one, although he certainly will not be able to hop on one foot much before age three. He learns to walk backward. He learns to pivot on one foot—at first he had to toddle laboriously around through a change of direction. He "dances" to music, at first by bobbing up and down in place, and then by moving his feet in a crude imitation of adult dancing—but note that children growing up in societies in which dancing is an intrinsic part of life become proficient dancers at an early age. Toddlers also enjoy being danced around in the arms of an adult to the tune of singing or humming or to music from phonograph or radio.

Here once again we must stress the great variety of individual styles, tempos, and temperaments that characterize the toddler's movements, in addition to variations of mood or transitory state. Some toddlers are bold, some are timid, some rough, others gentle, some are darting, some smoothly modulated, some graceful and others clumsy—but before describing a toddler as clumsy, we should make due allowance for the hampering effects of clothing, especially in those climes that demand heavy snowsuits and boots.

In new situations, most toddlers go through an initial phase of cautious quiescence, looking and listening and taking stock and staying in contact with the parent. Then, as they come to feel at home, they are likely to begin a hectic round of impulsive exploration, testing, and probing, pulled first this way and then that by the demand qualities of things and of spatial arrangements. In their familiar settings, by contrast, where the distracting effects of novelty are less potent, many toddlers can spend long periods of time engrossed in a single activity.

The toddler

212

As we have said, toddlers love to carry, shove, haul, trundle, and otherwise set in motion things in the environment, the bigger the better. A toddler would rather carry something big, requiring two hands, than a small thing, and two small things, one for each hand, than a single small thing. This is the age at which the child trots about pulling or pushing the mechanical ducks or corn-poppers or other such toys that produce a pattern of sound and action. The toddler may try to give his dolls a ride in a coaster wagon and have trouble because the handle and pivoting front wheels are designed for pulling, not pushing, whereas the toddler wants to push so he can see the dolls riding.

Almost from the time he first crept, the baby has been able to go up a flight of stairs on all fours (assuming that his world contains stairs). Going up, with the supporting stairs filling up his field of view, is fine; but when he turns around to go down, the stairs drop away beneath him, he faces the void, and the visual-cliff effect holds him fast and fear-stricken at the top of the stairs (although no amount of visual-cliff effect can guarantee against accidental tumbles). It is not usually until toddlerhood that the child learns how to get back down the stairs in one piece. One expedient is to go down in the same position that he went up, but in the reverse direction, feetfirst. This method entails a lot of hesitation, of easing knees and hands warily from step to step, and of twisting and craning to see where he is and where he is going. Another technique is to sit on the steps and bump downward on his seat one step at a time. Somewhere around age two, the child may be able to walk downstairs clinging to an adult finger—but here, as at other times, he may be overwilling to surrender all his weight to the adult and

Raimondo Borea

Toddlers like to carry things, especially big things.

213

simply dangle helplessly. Perhaps by age two and a half, he walks both up and down the stairs, one step at a time, holding on to a railing. Most children cannot climb a vertical ladder until about age three, at least partly because, apparently out of a fear of falling, they cannot release their grip to move their hands one by one in concert with their feet. (It would be interesting to know at what age children manage ladders in societies where, as in Manus, houses are set high on stilts.) By late infancy, the child can be taught to slide down feetfirst from a bed or couch or coffee table, and the toddler has no trouble descending in this manner from surfaces no more elevated than, say, his own head; even so, he still has to be watched when he is off the ground.

In early toddlerhood, the child has to climb up not only onto a full-sized chair but equally onto a toddler-sized one, by sprawling or kneeling on the seat and twisting himself around until, finally facing in the right direction, he gets his feet down and is triumphantly seated. This approach to small chairs, like his cautious feetfirst descent of a staircase, indicates that space behind the toddler is less stable and differentiated than the visible space in front of him. The same ambiguity of rearward space is shown in the way he seats himself on a stool or low bench, which differ from a chair in not having a back to hold on to while climbing up and turning around. The toddler has to aim himself toward the seat, edging backward and peering either over his shoulder or between his legs until he is in place, then letting himself down onto the seat. By late toddlerhood, the baby can, like an adult, plump confidently and casually down on a seat.

However, the toddler does not, by con-

Exploring space.

▼

Amy Stromsten, Photo Trends

trast, climb onto an adult lap, but offers himself to be drawn onto the adult's knees. Sometimes, of course, his frequent lap-sittings may mean that he wants to be snuggled and cuddled and petted and babied. As often as not, though, he is a very active lap-sitter: he seeks and delights in jiggling, bouncing, and dipping outward into space while lightly encircled by the adult's arm or firmly held by the hands. The adult has to do most of the work, but the activity originates in the toddler.

In all this activity and movement we see the toddler's increasing familiarization with and mastery of space and its possibilities. He knows by heart the layout of familiar regions, and may even cry out in protest when, on the way to Grandma's, his mother makes a left turn where she customarily makes a right. He knows where things are kept, including taboo things like medicines. It is important to try to understand in what sense the toddler knows a segment of space. He does not know it as one portion of a larger totality. He shows no surprise that one region of space adjoins or flows into another, but he seems to have no idea which regions are contiguous with which, or along which boundaries, or that other, unknown regions lie just out of view, awaiting discovery. Rather, he seems to know a great many specific locations, and a great many routes linking locations, without any notion of their overall organization. In this respect he is like many so-called "space-blind" adults, who learn to navigate from point to point but are incapable of inventing an alternate route or of drawing a coherent map. Nor does the toddler yet appreciate that one object cannot be in two places at the same time. For instance, the family of one two-year-old had a rather unusual automobile. One day, while out driving in it, they passed another car just like their own, provoking the father to remark jestingly, "Look, somebody stole our car." The two-year-old responded by bursting into tears, unmindful of the "obvious" fact that their car was still safely in the family's possession. The toddler's orientation to space can be summarized by saying that he lives in an **action-space**, defined less by its formal relationships and coordinates than by its possibilites for movement, the dynamics that push and pull and steer and channel the toddler's active migrations. These dynamics are strictly equivalent to the demand qualities or the valences of objects, mentioned earlier.

His growing mastery over both the larger space in which he moves about and also of the spatial relations between objects or parts of objects is shown in his manipulation of playthings. Now, he not only takes things like cooking utensils apart but begins to put them back together as well. He becomes able to screw back on bottle caps of a size that he can manage. He can stack pierced blocks on a peg, but if they are graduated in size he cannot yet arrange them in the "right" order. Nor can he, much before age two, fit together a series of nesting boxes or "eggs." He perceives gross differences in size, but cannot yet reliably distinguish smaller ones, as seen in his stubborn attempts to put large things inside small ones. Also, when fitting together anything except circular forms, he has trouble aligning the forms correctly. He can, however, balance a stack of things, as related in this account:

[Debbie, seventeen months, two weeks] now stacks several objects (two to five of them), then stoops or squats, picks them up gently at the base of the pile, and proceeds to carry them elsewhere.

The note continues:

Refuses, however, to have anything to do with her small blocks, and either ignores them or flings them out of the box with fine vigor (Church, 1968, pp. 70–71).

Here we see the continuation from infancy of the toddler's preference for sizable playthings, such that one could postulate an inverse correlation between age of baby and size of playthings. Friends and relatives usually err in giving the baby presents of miniaturized bits of reality, which may well appeal to older children but whose charm is usually lost on the vigorous action-oriented younger one.

When, as sometimes happens, the toddler stays in one place, his posture is very different from that of younger and older children. As in the account above, when he wants to pick something up from the floor, he drops into an easy squat. He may sometimes stay squatting to play with toys on the floor, but more characteristically he sits with his legs straight out in front of him, with a book or plaything either on his lap or on the floor between his thighs. A typical toddler pose is to stand with legs straight and slightly spread, and to bend double at the hips and waist so that his head rests on the floor and the child can look out between his own legs at an upside-down world. One twenty-two-month-old girl of our acquaintance could edge herself forward from this position right into a somersault. Notice a difference, though: the toddler apparently finds it highly enjoyable to be upside down in relation to the world, but he finds it disturbing when

things—such as a photograph of his father —depart from their familiar up-down orientation in space.

When the toddler is keeping an adult company, he characteristically leans limply against the adult's knees or shoulder (depending on whether the adult is sitting in a chair or on the floor), so limply that he may slide into a heap on the floor. This draping of himself against adults may continue into the school years, although past toddlerhood the child maintains better muscle tone and keeps his balance better. When the toddler is not directly engaged with other people, he is likely to treat them less as people than as things: as obstacles to be shoved aside, as drums to be thumped or kicked, as climbing apparatuses, as resting places. In general, the toddler's posture and movements are marked by symmetry, a limited differentiation of the two sides of the body, so that when he beats time or kicks his heels against the side of a box on which he is sitting, both arms or legs move as one—indeed, if he gets a Band-Aid on one finger, he may demand another for the matching finger on the other hand.

The Beginnings
of Language

While the child's new powers of bipedal locomotion may be the most striking manifestation of toddlerhood, probably more important psychologically is his beginning to speak in his mother tongue. We must stress that use of language is not an isolated skill, like eating with a spoon or riding a tricycle, but brings with it an all-pervasive transformation of perceiving, feeling, thinking, and general intelligence. We might insist that it is only by becoming a linguistic organism, by understanding speech and by speaking, that the child gains access to full status as a human being (Church, 1966). On the side of being able to understand language, the child becomes open to endless verbal instruction; he can learn vicariously, through the words of others; he can enter realms of knowledge, such as history, that he can never know at firsthand; he can dwell in the virtual realms created by writers of stories and poetry; and he can learn accessory means of expression and manipulation like drawing and arithmetic. On the side of coming to speak, the child can convey his thoughts and feelings and wishes to others; he can think and reason and make sense of and order his own experience; he can make original statements; and he can concoct fantasies, jokes, and works of imagination.

There are several general things to be said about learning language before we describe the actual stages of speaking that the child goes through. As the gifted amateur linguist Benjamin Lee Whorf (Carroll, 1956) pointed out, the range of concepts or relations contained in the language we learn may impose a limit on what we are able to think about and on how effectively we think about those things we do think about. In other words, according to Whorf, a person's thought processes and perceptions can be no richer or more precise than the language he learns. We have already spoken of how the vocabulary of a language can be replete with explanatory constructs that invite reification (p. 166)—the miasma, poltergeists, and the rest. Words come to have emotional associations that are not contained in their strict factual meanings. At a much deeper level, however, are the subtle but potent cultural assumptions that shape our thoughts and feelings and the way we talk about the world. Some portion of these culturally bound styles of communication is captured in Basil Bernstein's (1960, 1964) distinction between **elaborated codes** and **restricted codes**. In Britain and the United States (Hess and Shipman, 1965; Hess et al., 1969) and to some extent in Israel (Ortar, 1966), these two styles can be identified in the way mothers of different social classes communicate with their children. Educated mothers tend to speak in elaborated code, which tries to explain how things are and why certain courses of action are desirable. Less educated mothers speak in restricted code, which emphasizes authority and tells the child how to behave without giving him the reasons. Needless to say, these parental styles are echoed in their child's use of language, and children growing up with restricted codes are less able at verbal problem-solving, at least of the kind posed by psychologists.

Note that the emphasis, in the Whorfian view, is on how language and culture limit thought and restrain innovation. However, simply to recognize the problem of language-embedded thought implies that we have partly transcended it. That is, there are linguistic forms, such as oratorical slogans, catchwords, and scare-words, that impede clear thinking, and there are others that liberate us and make us capable of new insights and perceptions and ways of talking about them. It is obviously a task of education to impart language in its liberating forms, as in the language of science, rather than in its constricting forms, as in the language of tradition and dogma. We can tell from the growth and change of a language like English that people keep breaking out of the old forms and finding new means of expression, especially in the sciences. The child himself gives evidence that he is not wholly bound by Whorf's hypothesis. While on the one hand the child lives safely within his linguistic means, in that he can always understand more than he can put into words, he also lives beyond his active-linguistic means, saying words that he cannot pronounce, as in baby talk, making up new words or stretching old ones to cover new situations, and finding ways to group words into sentences well before he knows the standard rules of composition.

Stages in learning language

We know that babies vocalize a great deal from an early age, and it seems probable that preverbal vocalizing plays its part in readying the child to speak. Table 2, adapted from a doctoral dissertation by Sanger (1955), traces the development of some key features of prelinguistic behavior. This table merits detailed study because it shows a regularity of preverbal behavior that most theorists of language learning do not recognize. Beginning at a very early age, the human voice, other people's and the baby's own, is a potent instrument. An interesting aspect of Sanger's observations is that a number of behaviors increase to a peak and then dwindle away—see, for instance, the entries for conversational babbles which are very prominent at eight to ten months, for vocalizing when alone, which has its peak at six to eight months, and for vocal accompaniment to nonsocial action, conspicuous between eight to twelve months. Note, however,

that these infant vocalizations are not language in the usually accepted sense of the conventional symbols by which people in a society communicate with each other, including the special provisions for baby talk.

The baby's learning of true language, the linguistic conventions with which people in a community talk to each other, begins underground. That is, the baby starts to understand what other people say to him before he himself begins to use words. We know that this is happening because the baby responds appropriately to simple commands ("Please give me my socks"), to words or phrases associated with routines ("Bath time"), or to words connected with games ("Pat-a-cake"). The baby's understanding of things said to him is called **passive** or **receptive language**. His actual speaking is designated **active** or **productive language**. "Speech" is used ambiguously; sometimes it simply means talking, but other times it refers to the shaping of sounds and sound patterns. The transition from passive to active language may take several forms. A few babies seem to wait until their listening has given them a good command of linguistic forms, whereupon they blossom forth with complex utterances—we are told that one bright ten-month-old girl's first speech occurred at the dinner table, when she said, "I want a taste." The far more usual pattern is to begin in single words, which may in fact be fusions of two or more words, as in *awgone* (the French toddler's equivalent is *yapu*, from *il n'y en a plus*), *whadda? good-boy, not-in-the-mouth, what-a-pity, enough-is-enough* (sometimes pronounced "enuss-enuss"). Many of the child's first words are in the form of commands or requests. Many children's first attempts to

TABLE 2 PRELINGUISTIC BEHAVIOR: PERCENTAGE OF OBSERVATIONS AT SUCCESSIVE AGES WHERE KINDS OF BEHAVIOR WERE NOTED

Behavior	Age (months)						
	0–2	2–4	4–6	6–8	8–10	10–12	12+
Stimulated nonvocal							
Turns to sound	0	16	18	21	7	11	0
Stops vocalizing to listen to adult	0	10	26	29	26	6	0
Responds to voice alone	20	16	18	21	26	17	7
Appropriate response to verbal cues	0	0	0	0	19	33	53
Stimulated vocal							
Smiles or vocalizes to adult imitation	0	23	26	8	19	22	7
Conversational babbles	0	3	4	4	44	22	13
Imitates a sound	0	0	0	4	26	22	13
Appropriate sound to verbal cues	0	0	0	0	14	33	22
Spontaneous vocal							
Vocalizes when alone	0	25	18	46	11	0	13
Vocal accompaniment to grasping	0	0	9	4	33	28	13
Vocal accompaniment to nonsocial action	0	0	4	29	67	61	33
Calls for adult attention	0	0	0	8	37	33	0
Stable nonverbal sounds	0	0	0	0	4	11	67

Source: Sanger, M. D. Language learning in infancy: A review of the autistic hypothesis and an observational study of infants. Unpublished Ed.D. dissertation, Harvard University, 1955.

go beyond single words into narration or description come out as what Arnold Gesell called **expressive jargon**, a flow of gibberish obviously meant to convey meaning. Indeed, expressive jargon mimics the sounds and cadences of adult speech with such fidelity that it often seems, like the comedian's double-talk, tantalizingly on the verge of being comprehensible. The practiced listener may, in fact, from the context and from occasional real words embedded in the stream of jargon, get a pretty good idea of what the child is saying. Expressive jargon is such a conspicuous phenomenon that we are constantly surprised to find parents who are unaware of it. We interpret expressive jargon as an attempt by the child to leap magically into full-blown language. It is a shortcut of limited utility, however, and most children speak primarily in one-word sentences, or **holophrases** (singular, **holophrasis**). Although such utterances consist of a single word (or word fusion), psychologically they function as complete statements: I want to go "Out!"; Lift me "Up!"; That is "Daddy"'s shoe; Time to "Eat!" (We make no attempt to reproduce the toddler's pronunciation.) Concrete nouns loom large in the toddler's vocabulary, but he also uses a fair number of interjections (*hi, bye-bye, ouch*), verbs (*go, carry, eat*), and adverbs (*up, out, again, back*). Many children learn *hot* quite early, sometimes as a designation for all hot things and often as a general cry of warning. Missing at the one-word stage, at least as we know it in European languages, are most qualifying adjectives and adverbs, and all pronouns, articles, prepositions, and conjunc-

The beginnings of language

tions. At first, there are no inflections designating plurals or verb tenses.

The toddler's holophrases serve a number of functions. Interjections are ordinarily used as greetings, but more than one toddler has been known to bring a visitor her purse and exclaim "Bye-bye" as a clear invitation to depart. In general, the toddler is liberal with imperatives, commands and demands, sometimes, in all likelihood, in imitation of the way he is addressed. Many times words pop out as automatic responses to things and actions. The child often seems to be rehearsing his repertory of labels, going from object to object and saying their names. The child may say the name of an object with an interrogatory ring, as though asking the adult to confirm that he has it right. The child is insatiably word-hungry and seeks the names of things as though compiling a catalogue of his environment. Even the baby who has not yet begun to talk acts as though he wants to hear the names of things. He points to an object and looks inquiringly at the adult; he may even come out with an interrogatory monosyllable, such as "Guh?" When the adult supplies the word, the baby relaxes, apparently satisfied. The child's word-hunger suggests the sense of power over reality that language gives him.

Much thought and discussion have been given to the subject of the baby's first word, on the presumption that this would provide a clue to the understanding of language in general. The reader will recall Frederick II's ill-fated experiment, meant to discover the child's "natural" language, and the Greek historian Herodotus reports a similar venture. Many present-day theorists, from psychoanalysts to learning theorists, are committed to the view that the learning of language must be extrinsically motivated, as a way of reducing tissue needs. Such a view would predict that the child's first words would refer to need states and the things that gratify them. The facts remain ambiguous. Part of the difficulty is in knowing what to count as the first word. For one thing, the boundaries between **babbling**, the infant's preverbal vocalizations, and true speech are not always clear. For instance, *ma-ma* and *da-da* are standard babbles of late infancy —as far as we know, the world around. They are also the standard baby-talk words in many languages for mother and father. The problem is to know when the baby is merely babbling and when he is greeting or calling for his parents as need-gratifiers. A toddler may salute his bath or his bottle with a shout of "Bah!" but if his whole day is punctuated with *bahs,* it is hard to make a case for his speaking. Or a toddler may learn to reply "There!" (pronounced *dzare*) to questions of the form of "Where's the . . . ?" but again it is impossible to decide whether he is using a meaningful word or performing an empty ritual. A second kind of difficulty is to know whether to count as a word those sounds the child says in response to prompting ("Can you say *kitty?*").

The only safe course is to count only spontaneous naming accompanied by pointing to the object named (which automatically excludes interjections, verbs, and adverbs as first words), and we have so few reliable instances of such naming that we cannot support any theory. Our impression, however, is that spontaneous first words may have little to do with need states. It certainly seems to be the case that many babies call their parents *mama* and *dada* only at an advanced stage of speaking. In general, need states move the baby to tears or fussing or concrete action, and not to speech, and words referring to such states as hunger, thirst, fatigue, illness, and pain are very late in appearing. Obviously, both people and animals express their need states and emotions by postures, gestures, facial expressions, and vocal sounds, many of them highly specialized, but these must be considered symptomatic behavior rather than symbolic. From our own observations of children in the process of learning to speak, speaking seems to be intrinsically rewarding and hence self-motivating, and we see no need to invoke outside dynamics.

Once the toddler has a basic stock of words, he begins joining them into two-word sentences, simple statements or questions, usually a noun plus a predicate word, as in "Car, backing up" or "Baby, crying." In the first example, "backing up" seems to have been learned as a unit. In both examples, the comma indicates the laborious piecing together of statements which is characteristic of the toddler's early two-word sentences. As the baby becomes more proficient, his sentences grow in length, but initially still without benefit of articles, pronouns, connectives, and inflections, and in happy ignorance of the "correct" way to form sentences. Miller and Ervin (1964) give the charming example of a two-year-old who, having seen her baby sister bite and break her own balloon, pointed to *her* own and said, "Baby other bite balloon no." In a sequence which no one has yet plotted out, the missing parts of speech begin to appear, words get inflected, and the order of words in sentences comes to approximate that of adult speech.

It is important to see that the child learns language with a minimum of explicit instruction. According to Cazden (1968a), about the only errors that mothers bother to correct are using the wrong word for something. The baby learns language—including not only words but grammatical and syntactical rules and, at the same time, higher-order logical operations of a kind we shall discuss shortly—by hearing it spoken in a concrete context of people, actions, gestures, and feelings. As Donald Campbell (1963) puts it, one cannot teach a child language over the telephone. Cazden (1968a) at first hypothesized that mothers typically "expanded" their babies' utterances: if a child said "Dog bark," the mother would respond by saying, "Yes, the dog is barking." Cazden later abandoned this expansion hypothesis in favor of what David McNeill called **expatiation**, in which the mother carries the discourse forward; in the above example (Cazden, 1968a, p. 134), an expatiation would be "Yes, he's mad at the kitty" or "Yes, but he won't bite."

It is equally important to see that simple, direct imitation plays only a minor part in the child's learning to talk. Instead, it is as though he were abstracting the rules and applying and generalizing them to his own behavior. Here we should not suppose some conscious, rational process, but rather a progressive **schematization** of what sounds (or feels) right. The learning of rules comes out most clearly in the child's errors. Actually, children make remarkably few linguistic errors (factual and logical mistakes are something else again), but the ones they do make are illuminating because they reveal the processes of schematization at work. For instance, many children at first learn the past tenses of irregular verbs correctly (Cazden, 1968b),

The beginnings of language

and then, when they have begun to abide by general rules, change to incorrect forms. For instance, the child may at first say *brought,* and then switch later to any one of various forms, or sometimes use several interchangeably: *bringed, brang, branged, broughted* (some of these forms persist into middle childhood). A common misapplication of the rules is seen in displaced inflections, as in "He pick it ups" and "I walk homed" (Cazden, 1968b). Several children, from different families, have come up with a system of constructions derived from the adult form *each other:* "We're hugging our chothers," "Are you mad at your chother?" and "They're hitting their chothers." The child transforms a declarative sentence into a question by prefixing it with a single word: "May I can have some?" "Is it is a cat?" To express negation, he cannot pile on too many markers: "No, I don't not have none" (Bellugi, 1971). Double negatives persist, too, to the horror of schoolteachers. In addition to codified rules, children pick up the intonations that express banter, despair, sympathy, exasperation, puzzlement, disdain, disagreement, whatever. They also echo their parents' affectations, as in the special telephone manner that most adults assume. It is often an embarrassing self-revelation to hear a child speaking in one's own voice and turns of speech.

The toddler learning to speak is amazingly accurate in his grasp of word meanings: what kinds of things, actions, properties, and relationships a given word refers to. For, proper names apart, a word (or phrase) can be thought of as a **concept** that designates a whole class or category of related things. One research finding is pertinent here. If adults are given a list of words to memorize and later asked to recall them, instead of repeating the words in the order they appeared in the list, subjects tend to regroup them into logically related categories. This tendency is called by Bousfield (1953) **associative clustering**. Now, a study by Rossi and Rossi (1965) indicates that associative clustering appears as early as age two, suggesting that language may exist for the child in an organized way almost from the beginning. In some sense, the child reacts to the words within a cluster as members of the same concept, even though he lacks a word with which to name the concept. For it is possible also, Whorf notwithstanding, to "have a concept" without words; the preverbal baby recognizes members of the class things to eat, or familiar people and unfamiliar people, or things that roll; the nonverbal infrahuman organism likewise recognizes foodstuffs, potential mates, sources of danger, and so forth, and even "generalizes" the stimuli to which he learns to respond in a conditioning experiment. In general, stimuli which elicit equivalent reactions, as when the chimpanzee reacts to a length of rope as though to a snake, can be considered as belonging to the same unverbalized concept. The toddler can learn makes of cars, for instance, with amazing accuracy. But sometimes he generalizes a word in ways that adults find surprising. For instance, many toddlers learn *heavy* in the sense of "hard to lift," but they seem to apply it to anything entailing strain or effort: easing his way down a steep slope, a two-year-old observes, "This is a heavy hill"; vainly straining to reach something overhead, the two-year-old says, "That shelf is too heavy." Many toddlers use *strong* in exactly the same way, and *strong* and *heavy* interchangeably, as in "Is the ice heavy enough to walk on?" What seems to underlie such meanings is that the word refers simultaneously to the person acting, his action, and the thing being acted upon.

In much the same way, the toddler seems to learn attribute dimensions as a whole before their extremes are clearly differentiated, as shown in the frequency with which he mixes up terms like *hot* and *cold*, *open* and *close*, *on* and *off*, and *up* and *down*. A toddler being handed some water in a glass shouts, "Too much! Too much!" and then, when the adult pours some off, screams in protest. In this case, it seems, *too much* is synonymous with *a lot*, which it is only partially in adult speech. An eighteen-month-old referred to all red motor vehicles as *engine*, which was his word for fire engine. It is interesting that redness was one of the two main organizing dimensions of this concept, even though the child at that time could not name colors or respond reliably to color names. We have encountered several children who referred to the adult's arm and leg hairs as *threads*, apparently not recognizing the kinship with head hair. A boy going on age three saw a covered wagon on television and called it a *mixer-truck*, apparently on the analogy of the cement-mixers that deliver ready-mixed concrete to construction projects (Church, 1968, p. 161). This same boy, apparently lacking a word for bite or sting, told his parents through his tears, "Didja bump your toe on a fly?" (ibid., p. 160). A mother gives this account of a toddler's generalization:

Ruth pinched her finger in a door and I told her to come to Mommy and I would kiss it to make it feel better. She held out her finger to be kissed. The next time she hurt her finger she immediately ran to me and held out her finger to be kissed—I thought she remembered and understood. The next day she got a bump on the head and came runnnig to me—with her *finger* held out for me to kiss. It was just a ritual (ibid., p. 229).

This same little girl also demonstrated on many occasions how the same object could be called by a different name according to the function it was serving. For instance, a pillow on the bed was *pillow*, but balanced on top of her head it was *hat*; she scribbled with a *pencil*, but a pencil in her mouth was *cigar* or *pipe*. Carlson and Anisfeld (1969) report that a two-year-old whose linguistic development they were following converted other parts of speech into verbs, speaking of a "louding" airplane and playfully threatening to "stomach" his mother as he pushed her belly.

Language as a tool and a toy

So far, we have spoken mostly of the processes by which the toddler acquires language and of how language exists for him. To fill in the picture we need to say something about how language is used, what functions it serves and what linguistic mechanisms are available to fulfill these functions. In a later section, we shall have something to say about some broader issues involved in linguistic behavior and its development.

It is commonplace to say that a primary function of language is **communication**, to exchange information about enduring or temporary states of affairs, about rules and procedures and expectations and values, and to share knowledge and experience. In general, presumably as part of a more general urge to social communion, most people have a strong urge to tell other people what they know, to surprise them, to act on their emotions, to make them laugh, and sometimes to tease them, but most basically for the satisfaction of social sharing. Part of the process of communication, of course, is asking questions: What is it? What is it for? How does it work? For what reason? and so forth. Obviously, too, a major form of communication is getting other people to do things, issuing orders of one sort or another, which the toddler frequently and imperiously does. By age two, the toddler does a great deal of verbal communicating, not only with adults but also with playthings and with himself. One special form of communication that should not be overlooked is deception, the giving of false or misleading information, whether playfully or in earnest. The toddler may begin to play simple jokes on his parents, announcing to his homecoming father that "Mommy go store," when in fact she is in the kitchen, or he may be able to lie to the extent of denying some accusation with a vigorous head-shaking "No!" There is also, we should remember, the important issue of self-deception, which begins in the preschool years.

An often neglected form of communication is **self-communication**, talking to oneself. Self-communication has various guises: self-direction, as when the baby verbalizes the steps required in, say, playing a record; self-control, as when the child tells himself "No-no" or "Mustn't touch" as he approaches a forbidden object; and, at ever more sophisticated levels, making one's experience explicit for one's own benefit, as in analyzing, figuring things out, making generalizations, stating relationships, describing things to oneself, and in general giving order and coherence

to one's knowledge. This is the process we referred to earlier as **thematization**, which helps form the schemata that guide thought and action. And we must mention again all the processes of rationalization and justification by which one makes one's own motives acceptable to other people and oneself. All these linguistic functions taken collectively add up to verbal thinking. We must also add reverie, daydreaming, imagining, and wishing to the array of self-communication. In the toddler, most forms of self-communication have to be mediated through an adult. That is, the child cannot think directly to himself, but thinks out loud to an adult, engaging in a dialogue which enables the child to formulate, catalogue, and systematize his experience. In much the same way, toddlers and children at the beginning of the preschool years find it next to impossible to talk directly to children their own age and communicate instead through an adult intermediary. Many adults, too, when wrestling with a problem, seek out a friend to act as sounding board on which to try out ideas that cannot be dealt with in solitude.

The language that a child learns contains a number of **subvocabularies**, referring to special, logically related "domains" of experience. For instance, there is the special vocabulary of number and quantitative relationships. Quite early in his speaking history, the baby learns to count one, two, *two* originally standing for any quantity greater than one. He then goes on to one, two, a lot; one, two, three, a lot. Many two-year-olds can count to five or ten or beyond, but this may be a mere recital of a learned sequence. For one thing, the child may count things correctly up to a point and then improvise: 1, 2, 3, 7, 5, 4. Furthermore, he does not adhere to a strict one-to-one correspondence between numbers and objects; thus, in counting, he may skip objects or count the same one repeatedly, so that his last number bears no relation to the size of the collection. Also, counting and summing seem to be psychologically different operations, with the ability to count coming before the realization that the last number counted is the sum; thus, the child may correctly count five things, but, when asked how many there are, still reply, "Two." The use of standardized units of measurement, like inches and ounces, does not appear until the late preschool or early school years.

Another special vocabulary is that of metalanguage, language that describes language, as in such terms as *word, sentence, punctuation, verb tense,* and so forth. The toddler's metalinguistic vocabulary is ordinarily limited to *word,* a stage beyond which many of us never go until we reach school.

Yet another domain is that of time. It is clear that the baby's early orientation to time far outstrips his ability to talk about it. Even the infant develops a stable sense of the recurring events in his routines, and although he may not anticipate that night will fall, he is not surprised when it does. The toddler knows a number of time-related words, like *day, night, first,* and *now.* He shows signs of remembering past events, as when the mention of somebody's name evokes an association, such as "Baby sick. Poor baby." He can anticipate the near future, as when, having been told that he will visit his grandmother after his nap, he bounces awake shouting, "Now go Nana!" Late in toddlerhood, the baby may use such words as *yesterday, today,* and *tomorrow,* but he mixes them up, cannot tell in what sequence they come, and

is likely to fasten on a single word, such as *tonight,* to designate any point in past or future time. He also parrots the adult's "Not now," "Soon," and "In a minute," to indicate delay. To the adult, the toddler is an exasperating dawdler, since he is blandly unmindful of time pressures, schedules, and the need to be in a particular place at a particular time, so that the grownup has to make generous allowances for luring him away from play and into his outdoor clothes. Even while being dressed, the toddler may resolutely persist in trying to build a block tower or look at a book. By the same token, of course, the adult, wrapped up in his or her obligations and preoccupations, may seem an equally exasperating dawdler to the toddler. The toddler shows some grasp of simultaneity, as when the adult tells him, "You go play while I write a letter," and can play synchronously with an adult, taking turns adding blocks to a pile or handing things to an adult engaged in a work project.

We have already mentioned the toddler's orientation in space, his mastery of familiar spaces such as his home, his knowing where things are kept or have been left, and his knowledge of often-traveled routes, such as the way to the park, to the doctor's, to the market, or to Grandma's house. We might stress, however, that his knowledge of extended routes is essentially passive; he watches them unroll with a sense of rightness, but he cannot himself lead the way. If, on a walk, he decides to go around a clump of bushes as though to rejoin the adult on the far side, he is likely to become disoriented and panicky as soon as he loses sight of the adult. His spatial vocabulary expands to include such words as *up* and *down, on, over* and *under, in* and *out, forward* and *backward, beside, next to, far away, against,* and *around.* He is very sensitive to the car's going *up the hill* and *down the hill.* On the other hand, he does not spontaneously perceive that a toy car will roll down a board propped at an incline, and he delights in having this spatial relation demonstrated to him. For reasons we do not understand, toddlers have difficulty learning the meaning of *corner,* whether of a block or a room.

The toddler begins learning the special vocabulary of shape, and can recognize and name such standard forms as cross, triangle, diamond, crescent (called *moon*), heart (called *Valentine* by many children), and star. But notice that his recognition is physiognomic in nature, that is, he does not know how these figures are composed. He does not know that a triangle has three sides or a star five points, he cannot draw these forms, and he cannot yet fit any but the simplest cut-out forms into a formboard. It is interesting that the toddler learns such seemingly obvious shapes as square and circle relatively late, probably because he sees them as concrete things, like ball or window, rather than as general designs corresponding to nothing special in the world of objects. Also, the toddler who grows up among written symbols learns very early to recognize letters and numerals as special classes of forms, as shown by his pointing and asking, "What's this *a*?" and "What's this *1*?", with *a* at first standing for all letters, and *1* for all numerals.

By age two, favored middle-class babies have learned the names for the standard colors, including black, white, and gray, and in many cases such special colors as pink, beige, and aquamarine. Color names are a domain in which there are striking cultural and subcultural differences. So-called culturally deprived children in our society may be greatly retarded in learning colors. Our chief system for coding colors is the solar spectrum (although surprisingly few people are aware of this organizing principle), but in other societies color names may be derived from the colors of the desert, from the plumage of birds, or whatever, and colors that to our eyes look wildly dissimilar may be given the same name. No one has yet found a satisfactory answer to whether distinct colors given the same name are perceived as being the same, or whether the person sees them as different even though he labels them identically. The most promising technique for finding out, it seems to us, is to condition an emotional reaction to one color and then see whether the reaction is generalized according to spectral relations or labels—or, conceivably, both.

One other major conceptual domain is that of causal relations, of how things work. The toddler, out of his experience, learns endless pragmatic sequences: he can turn lights on and off, he can work faucets, the radio, the TV set, and his phonograph, he knows that the cat scratches if you pull its tail, he knows how to tease his parents, but his vocabulary of cause and effect is minimal. He can say such things as "Make the car go," or "Make it work," or "Fix it," but he simply accepts the workings of things without surprise or curiosity, as though they were all to be taken for granted as the natural order of things. It is only later, in the preschool years, that he begins to wonder how the people get inside the television set, or where the musicians are hiding that he hears playing on the phonograph. We can think of only one exception to this general passivity. Two-year-old boys (but not girls in the sample observed by our colleague Dorothy Levens), when they sit in a small rocking chair with a chime fastened under the seat, react by getting up and tipping over the chair to see where the sound is coming from. It is conceivable, of course, that we could elicit more such investigatory behavior by arranging situations in which the child's learned expectations were violated. Bower (1964) and Charlesworth (1968) have proposed that such a procedure be the standard test for learning, with the child's surprise or disappointment as an index of expectation. The idea dates back to Tinklepaugh (1928), who found that monkeys exhibited great distress when they looked in a place where they were accustomed to find a special treat like a banana or peanuts and found instead an uninteresting bit of lettuce. In general, however, although events may startle the toddler, as when the jack-in-the-box pops forth, they do not stir him to wonder. Late in toddlerhood the child asks "Why?" but this query—when it is a genuine query and not just a way of maintaining contact with the adult or teasing—seems addressed not so much to explanations of how things work as to motives and justifications: "For what reason?" or "On what grounds?" rather than "By what means?" or "In accordance with what principles?"

Among the numerous other domains of language and experience, some of which we shall discuss later, are: personal and group origins and history; birth; death; the workings of the body, including sickness; body sensations such as those of hunger, thirst, fatigue, pain, need to eliminate, and sensual pleasure; masculinity and femininity; morality, questions of right and wrong; emotions; manners, codes, and procedures; family relationships; authority and obedience; and the whole realm of hypothetical events, which the preschool child typically enters by playing the game of "What if?" ("What if Daddy died and we didn't have any money?" "What if you had wings and could fly?" The list is endless and heavily fraught with possible disasters.)

Notice that very little time is spent teaching the child language as such, getting him to say words or telling him correct phrasings. Rather, people talk and he listens, or half-listens, and on the basis of his listening he becomes able in turn to talk. But since he learns language in the practical context of people's linguistic dealings with the world, he simultaneously learns from what they say or imply a notion of how the world is, how things might be, how they ought to be, and what can and cannot be done about it. Likewise, what people say contains abundant implications about the child himself. Thus, the language he hears instructs him in how his culture views and values reality, and becomes an important instrument of cultural transmission.

Language, as we have said, consists not only of words and standard word-combinations, plus grammatical and syntactic rules for using words, but also a system (usually unformulated, but overlapping in part with grammatical rules) of logical *operations* by which we represent real or imagined states of affairs (Church, 1971). The two sorts of operations the toddler first uses are imperatives and naming, or *denomination,* the simple act of labeling objects—"Baby." His two-word sentences are acts of *predication,* that is, of posing the existence of something and then designating one of its permanent or ephemeral attributes—"Baby crying." We know that the toddler becomes able to perform, at least in a rudimentary way, the operation of *counting*. We know, too, that the operation of *locating events in past or future time* becomes possible for the toddler, even though he may lack the standard tense forms. Here our knowledge about the order of emergence of operations ends. We know only that over the next several years the child becomes able to do such things as *summate* his counting, *evaluate* things, *compare* things along a number of dimensions such as size and color, *draw contrasts, contradict, brag, make rhymes, alliterate, tease, joke, lie, talk nonsense, make emphatic assertions* ("I am so!"), *make believe, make contingency statements* ("If it doesn't rain, we'll have a picnic"), and eventually statements of double and multiple contingency ("If it doesn't rain, and if Daddy doesn't have to work, and if we get home in time, then . . . "), *hypothesize, define words, draw inferences* ("She's a big girl, [therefore] she must go to school"), *find analogies, describe things,* and so forth. The various sorts of questions a child can ask also can be classified as embodying different sorts of operations —where, what, and which questions, for example. The things a child is asked to do on an intelligence test, such as to say in what way two things—for instance, an apple and a banana—are alike, are in many cases tests of his ability to perform well-defined operations.

We feel obliged to stress a few general principles which are often overlooked when dealing with the vital topic of learning to talk. First, it is obvious that all the words a baby uses, a few neologisms (invented terms) excepted, are in some sense imitations of words he has heard. But simple imitation is not enough to explain the acquisition of language. In the first place, we have no ready way to explain imitation itself, which as we have seen begins very early in life: the fact that an external stimulus gets translated into a series of internal motor events that produce a more or less accurate copy of the stimulus. Second, imitation may be long delayed, so that when a child first uses a word we may have no idea when he heard it originally. Furthermore, imitation is selective and relevant—the child imitates the right word for a given context and, for the most part, uses it aptly. Then again, it is hard to say what it is that the child is imitating when he applies an unspoken grammatical rule. In many cases, his learning requires a transposition of what he hears: the adult, speaking to the child, uses *I* to refer to himself and *you* to refer to the child, whereas the child must learn that he in turn uses *I* and addresses the adult as *you*. In general, learning the rules and learning to transpose imply an intelligent learning that is anything but a simple parroting. As we mentioned, even the child's errors tend to be intelligent errors—as in creating past tenses. We must note also the way the child drills himself in the use of language; Ruth Weir (1962) has given us a charming account of the bedtime soliloquies of a two-year-old, many of which seem to be a quite conscious ringing of changes on standard linguistic forms. Finally, let us repeat that there seems to be no need to invoke extrinsic motivations for the learning of language—not only is speaking intrinsically rewarding, but a great deal of language learning seems to take place by unconscious absorption of words from the surroundings. It is conceivable and even probable, as Mowrer

(1960) has said, that the language some children hear is so heavily freighted with disagreeable content—taboos, scoldings, threats—that the whole idea of speaking becomes repellent, but this negative motivation tells us very little about the usual process of coming to speak.

It is because words have such power over reality that it is so much fun to play with language. Language play of a sort begins, as we have seen, with the babbling of infancy. In toddlerhood, some of the child's expressive jargon is a form of word play. The child spouts nonsense, partly for the sheer pleasure of hearing the sound patterns come out but partly also in a spirit of deliberate silliness, as though recognizing the absurdity of what he says: "Lig a loggie, dig a poggie, a la boggie poggie boggie" (Woodcock, 1941). Toddlers are not so likely to appreciate adults' verbal humor; if the adult, for instance, changes the wording or the sense of a favorite story with some idea of entertaining the toddler, he will probably encounter fierce indignation. It is not until the child has attained the relative sophistication of the preschool years that he can feel sufficiently master of his language to move on to the next stage, where sense and nonsense are consciously intermingled.

The toddler's language often accompanies and punctuates his other play, as mood music, as narration, as commands to himself and his playthings. As his play becomes more social and less solitary, true conversation plays an increasing role in it. His jokes are usually amused commentaries on events and incongruities— "Johnny pants off"—and do not yet include the banter, verbal teasing, and deliberate surprises and manufactured incongruities of which the preschooler is capable. When he does happen upon something that is funny, such as getting his overshoes on the wrong feet, he will repeat the joke, including appropriate expressions of mock dismay, until something new intervenes to break the spell. As we can see, the toddler's growing language skills are assimilated to everything he does; in addition, though, they open new realms of activity to him, in learning and thinking and in the social interchange that will come to occupy an ever-increasing part of his still-narrow existence. Meanwhile, he moves from the verbal music of infancy toward the still-egocentric poetry of the preschool years and the communicative but often barren prose of adult discourse.

Theories of language and language learning

People intent on explaining human nature have focused in recent years on language, the most distinctive feature of human behavior. Skinner (1957) proposed that language has no special character, that it is learned through operant conditioning like any other function. Skinner thought of this process as the selective reinforcement of sounds and sound combinations, to the neglect of sentence construction and meaning. The sounds were thought to be uttered either spontaneously, at random, or imitatively. Unfortunately, Skinner's account overlooked the primacy of passive language, where nothing reinforceable occurs, the creative functions of language (as in jokes and poetry and philosophy), and the fact that learning to speak through the reinforcement of speech sounds would be an extremely laborious process quite unlike what actually happens, where words and grammatical rules are simply absorbed from the language the child hears.

Chomsky (1968), by contrast, has taken the radical stand that learning plays an insignificant part in the acquisition of language. Instead, the child is born into the world with a **Language Acquisition Device** (LAD) prewired with several sets of grammatical rules, all of them variants on a presumed grammar common to all languages. The actual speech to which the child is exposed activates the set of rules that matches what the child hears, and the child begins to speak his native tongue. There are problems in the Chomskyan position, so some supplementary concepts are called into play. All languages have in common designations for time and space (although some languages assign them to a common domain), causation and motivation, agents and actions and objects, and attributes of things and actions, but it is far from clear that this implies a universal grammar. Since, in any case, as anybody who has ever studied a foreign language knows, there are grammatical gulfs between languages, Chomsky invokes a contrast between **surface structures**, in which languages differ, and **deep structure**, which all tongues share. However, since deep structure does not· manifest itself, it remains a hypothetical construct which one must take on faith. In principle, one might be able to perform grammatical analyses of a number of languages and show that they could all be derived from a common set of rules, but this has not been done. Indeed, Chomsky and his followers have not yet come up with a satisfactory description of English grammar, never mind the innumerable dialects of which English consists. There is the additional complica-

tion that we have no reason to think that there is a strong correspondence between grammatical categories and psychological ones; as soon as one takes account of semantics, or meaning, grammar seems far from being the whole of language. Another contrast is made necessary by the fact that children, even after the LAD has been set operating, are such imperfect speakers of their native dialect. This leads to a Chomskyan contrast between **performance**, the child's actual speech, and **competence**, what he would be capable of saying if only the right circumstances were to draw him out. Competence, again, is a hypothetical construct which cannot be directly observed. There are attempts to equate it with receptive language, but the child's inability to understand a great many constructions (e.g., the passive voice—*the cow was kicked by the horse* rather than *the horse kicked the cow*) is severely limited in a way that is embarrassing to a theory that it is all there, awaiting the right moment to appear. Chomsky has played down individual and group differences in the adequacy with which people use language, perhaps because he would have no way of accounting for these differences except to say that they are biologically determined.

In fact, though, children learn at first to talk precisely in the style of their parents. As they move out into the peer group, they then begin talking the language of their peers. As they grow older, they are exposed to still other linguistic influences—books, actors and actresses, teachers, public figures—and their language is further modified. As we shall see, language learning is not something that happens between ages one and three (Lenneberg, 1968), but goes on life long. We do not pretend to have a theory of how the child learns to talk, which does not keep us from wishing that those who construct such theories would trouble themselves to observe the process in action. All in all, it strikes us that the field of psycholinguistics is a bastard discipline, neither psychology, to which one can relate the behavior of individuals, nor linguistics, which seeks to plot the structures of various dialects in all their dimensions without regard to individual speakers and their idiosyncrasies.

All this is not to deny that there are universal features of language. However, these shared characteristics are on a far more general plane than the specifics of grammar. All babies babble, it is a feature of the human condition that we are able to learn language, and spoken language is common to all societies (although some societies have auxiliary signal systems, such as whistling or drumming). The baby is especially alert to the human voice, struggles from an early age to "answer back," and begins with only a little experience to make language his own. All languages are vehicles for ideas, thinking, and expressing feelings. All languages recognize, as we have said, some key domains. But they also represent very different conceptualizations of time and space, causation, and the rest.

More promising, it seems to us, are anthropologically oriented accounts of language learning which begin with the development of communication and thinking (Church, 1966; Hymes, 1968), as in the study of the emergence of logical operations. In this approach, grammatical mechanisms are interesting in terms of how they serve higher-order semantic ends. In other words, one begins with what it is the person says, and then considers how he goes about saying it.

Play and Activities in Toddlerhood

A goodly proportion of the toddler's day is taken up by the mechanics of life—eating, napping, being bathed and cleansed and changed, dressing and undressing—but even so he still has several hours a day free for other sorts of activities which we generally call play. The sustenance-producing or otherwise useful activities of the adult are considered serious work, whereas the activities of the child are viewed as frivolous play. This distinction is in part a residue from the days when hard manual labor, or drudgery, was the price of sheer survival. In part it is a remnant of the Puritan ethic that man redeemed his essential sinfulness through work, and that to play was to flirt with the devil. Such a conception disregards the fact that in many societies, and increasingly in our own, no sharp line is drawn between work and play, so that one can perform life's chores in a spirit of good cheer and mix one's daily labors with other, intrinsically enjoyable activities. Furthermore, mechanization and automation have taken much of the drudgery out of life and have given us large amounts of leisure, and education has given us more scope both in choosing the kind of work we do and in using our leisure to good advantage. On the side of the baby, furthermore, his play is not exclusively frivolous. He works hard at mastering and perfecting new competences, and even those forms of play that seem aimless to the adult feed into his growing awareness of self and world. Notice that the baby is not oriented to achievement. He has no sense of any future benefits to be gained from his play here and now. Such benefits are incidental by-products. Nor does he, in his working toward mastery, feel any need to have final products as monuments to what he has done. The toddler (and older child) can abandon a project midway—he may abruptly abandon the doll he was putting to bed, or drop the crayon with which he was scribbling, or let the tune he was humming trail off—in a way that adults can find frustrating. But for the toddler the activity itself is what counts, not the completion of a total task.

It has been said earlier that the toddler prefers large-muscle activity to small-muscle, that he would rather deal with large things than small ones, that he would rather send his whole body hurtling through the channels and over the obstacles of action-space than engage in the sensitive manipulation of complex playthings, and in general this is true. In the park or on the nursery-school playground, he loves the spring of a jumping-board under his feet (but he wants to hold an adult's fingers), the swooping movement of a swing (but not too high), the tug and jounce of riding in a wagon, the unwieldy weight of big objects to lift and haul and shove. He likes to hammer and pounds tirelessly at his pegboard. He trots about pushing or pulling a roll-toy. He revels in splashing in water, he explores tunnels and tries out—very tentatively when coming down—ramps and catwalks, he learns to ride a tricycle and to pull himself up a rung or two on a jungle gym. He digs in a sandbox, drifts about aimlessly, stares wide-eyed at other children at play, often moving empathically in rhythm with them, sets off in pursuit of a rolling ball, closes doors that he finds open or ajar and, when

he is tall enough to reach the knob, opens closed doors. He squeezes into narrow crevices, steps up and down on large hollow blocks, and clusters with his fellows around every new activity.

But this is only part of the story. The toddler has his quiet moments, when he squats down to follow the progress of a beetle or an ant, or savors the feel and taste of snow, or listens to music (although he usually will bounce as he listens), or scribbles (it is a good idea to give the toddler drawing instruments only when there is an adult free to watch him; otherwise his experiments are likely to overflow to floor, walls, and furnishings), looks at picture books, spends long minutes in the examination and exploration of a new object, or relishes his food. By the time he is two, the American toddler may sit quietly hypnotized for a while in front of the television set, or trot in from the next room for a favorite commercial. There can be no doubt that the toddler finds certain sounds and images fascinating—he memorizes jingles from an early age—but there is reason to question how much sense television programs make to him. We even know of one two-year-old for whom watching television was a comfort device, and who, when he wanted to be quiet, sat on the couch, put his thumb in his mouth, and stared at the blank and silent television set.

The toddler, as the saying goes, is "into everything," and some part of his day is likely to be spent emptying toy-boxes, closets, and cupboards, sometimes with a view to playing with the contents—as when

The toddler

Toddlers exploring the qualities and possibilities of the environment.

232

John Fay

John Fay

Ruth Orkin

Annan Photo Features

Vivienne

Early dramatic play. The African child is laying a fire, an activity he has observed many times. Note how the American child combines dishwashing with sense-pleasure play with water.

Melvin Konner

he drapes himself in oddments of clothing and parades around the house or admires himself in the mirror—but as often as not just for the inherent pleasure he finds in each step of the process, each novelty, each familiarity. From the time the child is a year old until almost school age, reasonably permissive parents must be resigned to a daily cleaning-up chore in which the whole world seems to have disintegrated into minute fragments, which must be collected, retrieved, sorted, reassembled, cleaned, and put away. The child may help, but his contribution is likely to be capricious and ineffective, and, if the adult is not vigilant, the child may take things out and apart faster than the adult can put them away. The toddler plays with his dolls, trundling them in their carriage, feeding them, petting them, admonishing them, wiping their noses, putting them to bed, and so forth. Let us stress that playing with dolls and stuffed animals, and taking one or more such to bed at night, is a part of the normal play of both boy and girl toddlers. Many parents—and aunts, uncles, grandparents, and neighbors—are aghast to see a little boy playing with his dolls, as though his very masculinity were in peril. As far as we know, there is no such danger; quite the contrary, it seems most important to give boys access to the social themes of dramatic play with dolls (of which more in a moment), and to encourage the development of feelings of tenderness, care, and protectiveness that dolls call forth.

In the toddler's play with dolls, we see one of the beginnings of **dramatic play**, the imitation or acting out of scenes and events of everyday life, in which the child tries out roles and identities drawn from the models he is exposed to. The first dramatic play of the toddler is likely to be episodic, confined to simple, unelaborated themes from domestic life: telephoning, answering the door, rocking the baby to sleep, shaving (little girls as well as little boys go through a pantomime of removing whiskers, and little boys as well as little girls may be observed "shaving" their legs and armpits), driving the car, drinking tea, smoking (more than one eighteen-month-old has been found with a cigarette or pipe or cigar shoved deep into his mouth and trying valiantly to strike a match), or fixing the car. In addition, he may trail his mother about the house, either playing on his own or imitating her activities, or even pitching in as best he can to help her with her chores. In some societies, of course, the child is expected actually to participate in family duties, and not simply to play at them.

Over the next few years, the child will weave such simple themes into more complex, sustained dramas. His reenactments tell us much about the things that stand out for him in his world, and about the affective significance things have for him. Common domestic matters, which are recurrent, simple, and easily grasped (at least in their externals), and which give him his first inkling of adult ways, are prominent, with the mother's activities taking precedence over the father's. The child's later dramatic play reaches ever further afield for its subject matter, into the realm of the filling station, the market, the construction project, the railway station and airport, the seashore, the circus, and, at still later stages, into the doings of cowboys and Indians, cops and robbers, spacemen, and, eventually, fairy tales and specially composed plays.

What we have said so far about play patterns in infancy and toddlerhood leads to a twofold developmental classification of play. The first classification is in terms of the **content of play**, what the child does. A classification in terms of content includes: **social-affective play, sense-pleasure play, skill play, dramatic play,** and **ritual** and **competitive games**. The second classification is in terms of the **social character of play**, who it is that the child plays with and the nature of their relationship. This classification of the development of play gives us these categories: **play with adults, solitary play, parallel play, associative play,** and **cooperative play.** Now let us examine these two classifications in more detail.

The content of play

As far as we can tell, play begins with **social-affective play,** taking pleasure in the manipulation of social relations and feelings. Such play begins with the adult, when he talks or croons to the baby, tickles him, works his hands and feet, nuzzles his belly, and generally acts in a way designed to elicit a positive emotional response from the baby. (Let us, however, signal a cultural difference. Caudill and Weinstein [1966] report that such stimulation is the norm in American families, whereas Japanese parents typically soothe the baby and avoid stimulating him.) The baby in turn learns to arouse parental emotion in a spirit of play, by simply smiling at the adult, by calling for attention, by initiating a particular game, by showing off his skills, by pretending not to hear when called, by feigning distress so as to be petted and reassured (adults do this, too, pretending that the baby has wounded them grievously, so that he will give them solace), and by teasing. American parents tease their children, but the teasing they practice is much milder than that found in numerous other societies, where teasing verges on the destructively malicious. Social-affective play implies the universal satisfaction found simply in being in communion with other people, but it also implies that there is a less benevolent pleasure just in getting a rise out of somebody. And, since we can observe teasing in primates, dogs, and other vertebrates, such behavior may be something of a biological imperative among social animals.

Quite early in life, the baby begins to enjoy nonsocial stimulation which produces something akin to early esthetic experience. We have called this kind of enjoyment **sense-pleasure play**. As with social-affective play, sense-pleasure play originates outside the baby, in the patterns of light and color and movement and sounds and rhythms and tastes and odors and textures and consistencies which attract his attention and give him pleasure. Later, in his explorations of object qualities and of his own body, the baby himself can govern his own sensual and esthetic experience. His play with raw materials—water, sand, mud, foodstuffs, whatever—can be viewed as sense-pleasure play, as can masturbation, swinging, bouncing, rocking, scribbling, humming, listening to music, and smelling flowers and other aromatic things. We can assume that the pleasure the toddler gets watching television comes largely under the heading of sense pleasure, more on the analogy of watching clothes tumble about in a drier than of watching a plot unfold. All the forms of play we are talking about can be combined —the toddler's lap-sitting, described earlier, seems to be a fusion of social-affective and of sense-pleasure play.

Once the baby has begun to reach out, to grasp and manipulate, we see the beginnings of **skill play**, consisting of the persistent exercise of newfound abilities, from making a doll dance by hitting it, to removing and reinserting the nipple of his bottle, to dropping things from his feeding table, to walking, to carrying things, to piling blocks, and so on through his differentiating repertory. Obviously, there is often an element of sense pleasure in skill play, but there are abundant instances where the only point of an activity seems to be the practicing of a new ability—sometimes, in fact, with grim determination, as when a seven-year-old comes home at the end of the day a mass of scrapes, bruises, contusions, and tear-streaked dirt, but triumphantly at last master of his two-wheeler. We are not saying that the child has any notion that his mastery of a skill will be beneficial to him or even that he is motivated to become competent; he seems to be moved by the intrinsic fascination of the just-barely-able-to, which acts on people of all ages.

We have already described **dramatic play** as one of the emergents of toddlerhood, and need only add that it seems to be a vital ingredient in the child's process of identification, of learning to be a member of his family and society. After toddlerhood, in terms of the content of play, the child learns **formal games**, initially of a ritualistic, self-contained sort, like ring-around-a-rosy and London Bridge, in which there is no score, and eventually **competitive** ones, from parlor games to baseball. Here again there are cultural differences. In western Europe, winning at soccer may be a matter of life or death, but in the home, a friendly game of poker or Monopoly goes on indefinitely, since no one is allowed to lose.

The toddler

236

It should not be necessary to point out that all these kinds of play extend into adulthood. Social-affective play is found in banter, teasing, practical jokes, flirtation, and the game of love. Sense-pleasure play has its counterparts in adult esthetic experience, in the enjoyment of art or music, in dancing, in the appreciation of spectacles, in the contemplation of natural beauty such as a sunset or a vista or waves breaking on a shore, or in watching the flames in a fireplace. The adult version of skill play can be seen in physical exercise, in practicing golf strokes or fly-casting, in maneuvering one's car adroitly through traffic, in whatever is done to gain or maintain proficiency. Dramatic play is most conspicuous in amateur and professional theatricals, but it also appears more subtly in the role playing of much of domestic, business, social, and community activities. Games, of course, have had an important place in adult life in every society we know of, although it is our impression that women have often been excluded from participation in formal games.

The social dimension of play

The second major line of development in play is the social dimension. Most of the baby's early play is in interaction with an adult, and adult playmates continue to be important for some years. The toddler often wants the adult to be with him simply for company, and not necessarily for the sake of any interchange. Increasingly, the baby becomes able to play alone, or to play in a self-contained fashion as long as someone is near. When the toddler plays in a room by himself, he keeps the door open, and he periodically trots in to where the adult is, as often as not giving the adult's knees a fervent hug before returning to his solitary play.

At first, there is no play with **peers**, other children of the same age. Babies are curious about other babies, and will examine them carefully, with much poking, pinching, stroking, and pulling, while the other baby tries to do much the same, but with no observable recognition of kinship. Young toddlers circle each other warily, sometimes reaching out an investigative hand, but do not really make social contact. Late in toddlerhood, the child may suddenly show a wholesale affection for all other young children, hugging and kissing strange children on the street or in the store, as though in final recognition of a bond.(L. J. Stone's observations lead him to suspect that such recognition is accelerated in the special circumstances of kibbutz life.) At about this time (two or two and a half), the child makes a transition from solitary play to what is called **parallel play**, two or more children playing side by side, obviously taking pleasure in each other's companionship, but without any real exchange, unless it be a grim, silent tug-of-war for some coveted plaything.

The next step after parallel play, in which the activity of one child is unrelated to that of the other, is **associative play**, in which all the children are doing the same thing, such as telephoning or cooking or playing in the sandbox or swarming around the slide, but separately, still without any interchange. In a young nursery-school group, one can watch an activity spread like an epidemic, as when one child decides to dress up and in no time at all the entire group is parading around in various getups.

In the preschool years, usually after age three, children move on to **cooperative play**, in which they can discuss and assign roles necessary to a joint venture, as when two children take turns pushing each other on a swing, or a group playing house decides who is to be the mommy, who the baby, and so forth. As we mentioned earlier, toddlers and young preschool children find it difficult to talk directly to each other, and prefer to have an adult act as middleman. When children do begin to converse, it is in the form of what Piaget calls **dual** or **collective monologue**: the children speak in turn, each apparently listening to what the other has to say, but each talking on a different topic, with little or no relevance to what the other is talking about (see p. 265). Again, if one listens carefully to adult conversations, they, too, often seem to be collective monologues.

Autonomy and Self-awareness

Autonomy

In Erikson's scheme of developmental alternatives, as we have said, the crisis in toddlerhood is between **autonomy**, the wish and, in a limited sense, the ability to be independent, and **shame and doubt**, feelings of worthlessness and incompetence. Out of his experience with people and things, the toddler is developing an ever more refined awareness of himself as a separate person, with his own budding wants and sensitivities and capacities. As he becomes aware of his new abilities, he wants to exercise them for himself, without help or hindrance or coercion from other people. Objectively, we know, the toddler has certain competences and certain limita-

tions. The toddler himself, however, is an extremist: he seems to cherish a conviction of omnipotence, which may crumble totally when he comes up against overwhelming situations—or sometimes for no discernible reason—and give way to feelings of despair and impotence. Just as the toddler is most vigorously asserting his autonomy, he may suddenly want to be helped or carried, to be babied and cuddled and protected.

Perhaps the most dramatic manifestation of the toddler's growing autonomy is his intermittent **negativism**, variously expressed by "No!" (most toddlers learn to say *no* long before they say *yes);* by going rigid all over; by going limp all over; running away, kicking, biting, and scratching; and by temper tantrums. It seems to be a rule that strong parental upset in reaction to negativism acts as a reinforcer, increasing the likelihood that more negativism will be forthcoming. Most of the time, the toddler cooperates cheerfully with adults, automatically and casually, but negativistic behavior can erupt in the midst of conformity. Sometimes, as when the adult tries to do something for the child that the child would prefer to try on his own (signaled by a cry of "Me!"), negativism is real and intense but short-lived. Once the child has either acted for himself or satisfied himself that what he wants to do is indeed beyond his powers, normal relations can be resumed. Sometimes, of course, a real battle of wills emerges, in which case the adult has to be prepared to carry through with full authority, as when the child persists in trying to do something dangerous or destructive. In the aftermath, though, the adult has to be careful that the child does not suffer a damaging loss of face—which is possible at a very early age—and should ease the sting of authority with extra affection, a period of play, and the offering of a substitute activity. But many times the child's protests are little more than play-acting designed to find out how it feels to say no, and a parent who continues unperturbed to dress the child or tuck him into bed may well find the child still cooperating through a refrain of verbal resistance. If a parent fails to detect the playful quality of the child's negativism or disobedience, an actual crisis of authority may be generated where none existed before. Negativism is a normal and even essential part of development and, unless it is inflated into a major issue between parent and child, is soon assimilated to the more constructive aspects of autonomy. In general, if the toddler has ample opportunity to explore and to practice things on his own, balanced by the support he sometimes needs and by a few necessary regulations, he will emerge from toddlerhood with a sound sense of his own abilities and a readiness to tackle the new problems of later ages.

Erikson's scheme of developmental alternatives is derived, as we have said, from the psychosexual stages of Freudian psychoanalysis. Thus, the crisis of autonomy versus shame and doubt corresponds to the anal stage, in which the battle between child and parents for control over elimination was the key issue. Freud, as we know, grew up in the Victorian era, when, in keeping with a widespread emphasis on public order and morality, such biological functions as elimination were thought of as "dirty"—disgusting, anxiety-producing, and perhaps even tinged with immorality. From which it flowed logically that toilet training was to be instituted early and accomplished quickly, with no questions asked and with whatever coercive or puni-

Nancy Rudolph

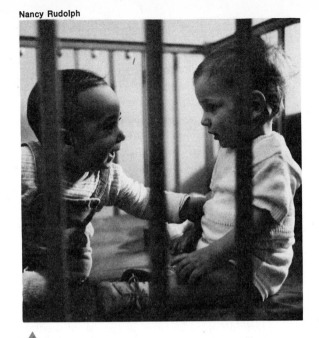

Babies prod and poke each other, without apparent recognition that they are both the same kind of organism.

Toddler negativism.

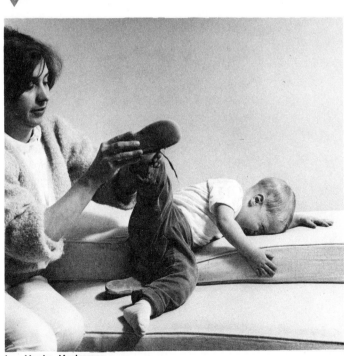

Lew Merrim, Monkmeyer

tive measures seemed called for. It is small wonder, considering what we now know about the timing of developmental innovations, in keeping with the idea of critical periods, and about the child's own stake in finding autonomy, that toilet training so often became a battleground of wills, with the repercussions of unresolved conflicts reaching into adulthood, perhaps in the form of anal character traits (see p. 179). There are still residues of Victorian moralism in thinking about toilet training, but in general nowadays people are more inclined to take a pragmatic, less emotional approach, minimizing stress and conflict and making learning easier. With the tension removed, even the subject of toilet training can become a theme of social-affective play, as seen in the following account by a mother of the behavior of her daughter, age fourteen months, three weeks:

My mother must have told Ruth to say "Ach" when she was having a bowel movement. For a few days when Ruth had a bowel movement in her diaper, she'd say "Ach." One day she said "Ach" but she was clean so I put her on the toidy. She had a bowel movement there, pointed to it, and said "Ach." Since then she tells me "Ach," I put her on, and nothing happens. It has become a game, and Ruth knows how to get my attention (Church, 1968, p. 227).

When we consider, too, that during toddlerhood several important functions are developing at once—notably language and bipedal locomotion in addition to bowel control—and that all these developing functions collectively feed into the child's feelings of self-worth at this stage, then it is easy to imagine that a disturbance in any of these areas would lead to an impairment

of these feelings, or shame (as regards his value) and doubt (as regards his competence).

Self-awareness

Now it is time to look in somewhat more detail at the ingredients of the self-awareness that is so central to the toddler's autonomy. Let us begin with some of the ways the toddler, when focused on things outside himself, can egocentrically forget his own existence and his own role in situations. He seems, for instance, to have little awareness of his own weight, as when he flings himself about in the arms of an adult or tries to walk up a piece of cardboard propped up against a wall. He seems to have no notion of himself as an obstacle, and does not move aside to let others pass. He even seems to have no idea of himself as obstacle to himself, since he will toil heroically to pick something up without realizing that he himself is standing on it. He often seems not to recognize that something is wrong with him, or if he does, to know what it is. Even when he clearly feels pain, as in the case of an insect bite, he cannot localize it accurately. Early in toddlerhood, the child may not be aware, even while it is happening, that he is wetting or soiling himself—or, afterward, that he has wet or soiled himself. It is interesting that he begins to localize seeing in the vicinity of his eyes, but when he is invited to peer through a cardboard tube, he plants it squarely between his eyes, as though in the center of a single Cyclopean orb (Church, 1970). When we stop to think about it, even adults ordinarily experience the visual field as a unitary whole, and the toddler's attempt to look through the tube probably reflects the same unity of visual experience. What is interesting also is that this "Cyclops effect" persists after the child can say that he has two eyes, indicating that knowledge at the verbal level is not always perfectly coordinated with knowledge at the level of concrete experience (Halpern, 1965; Maccoby and Bee, 1965).

It often seems as though the toddler's bodily integrity were easily threatened, since he may react quite violently to breaking things or finding them broken, and may refuse ever to play with a broken doll, even after it has been repaired. Here we see evidence of a close empathic identification with the things he deals with. Toddlers often manifest what looks like an almost compulsive neatness and cleanliness. Although he may enjoy dabbling in cereal or mud, the toddler afterward wants his fingers wiped clean. The Freudian theorist would say that the child's smearing of mud or milk is disguised play with his own feces, and that his desire for cleanliness expresses guilt. It seems simpler to assume that dirty or sticky fingers interrupt smooth communication with his playthings, and that the child wants the impediment removed.

In spite of gaps, the toddler has progressed far beyond infancy in self-awareness. His growing mastery first of defecation and then of urination, entailing recognition of the need to eliminate, the ability to restrain elimination by an act of will, and then to let go or actively expel, implies an expansion of bodily awareness. The toddler can name his major facial features and body parts (with only some confusions, as in the case of a two-year-old girl who, asked if she could point to her body, spread her legs and pointed to her genital region—some such confusions, of course, are induced by adult euphemisms or ignorings), and becomes able to follow such instructions as "Let's see you open your mouth" or "Let's see you close your eyes." A few toddlers may be able to answer such questions as "What do you smell with?" and "What are your eyes for?" although verbal knowledge of sensory functions is more likely to appear in the preschool years. Furthermore, the child can begin to direct and instruct himself, to keep up a running commentary on his activities, and to regulate his own behavior verbally in terms of parental commandments and taboos, indicating a dawning conscience (even though the toddler—or older child—doesn't always obey himself).

Toddlers show a variety of reactions to being caught in some forbidden activity. They may, with fair individual consistency, burst out crying in either woe or anger, run and hide, feign sweet innocence, tense up and tremble, try to hide what they were doing, proffer the forbidden object to the adult, make a great display of affection as though to divert the adult, or even hurry to finish the activity before the adult can intervene. Many toddlers are vividly aware of ownership, may spend a large amount of time labeling objects with the names of their owners, and fiercely resist use of any object by someone who is not its owner. Such possessiveness may apply to other people's belongings before the toddler begins to defend his own against encroachment. Many parents with an altruistic bent try to bring up their children in a spirit of openhanded sharing, and are disappointed when a toddler seems to be selfish about his own possessions. It seems to be the case that almost all toddlers and young preschool children go through a period of possessiveness, which may be an important step in the definition of an identity and the articulation of relationships in the outside world, and which cannot be rushed.

Notice that two processes are at work in the formation of the toddler's self-awareness. First, there is the awareness that grows out of action, out of doing things and the feelings that go with particular activities. When he meets and masters a problem, he feels strong and competent and good. Second, there is the self-awareness that comes with other people's reactions to what he does. We have an example in the behavior of our articulate friend Ruth, just before her second birthday:

I was telling Ruth how proud of her I was for going on the potty. She said, "Sometimes I wet my diaper and sometimes you are not proud of me. Now you are proud of me." She thought for a minute and added, "And I am proud of myself, too" (Church, 1968, p. 284).

Thus, an atmosphere of affection and applause (and when parents literally clap their hands in praise of the toddler's accomplishments, he joins in, too) fortify a sense of self as worthwhile and deserving of love. By contrast, an atmosphere of unrelenting reproach, disapproval, and exasperation keeps the toddler off balance, cripples his exploration, and reflects back to him an image of himself as unclean, inept, and beyond loving.

Let us emphasize that we do not advocate abandoning adult authority. The child who is loved and respected and valued can tolerate restraints and reproofs, and can even benefit from them in defining an identity. Once again Ruth, just under age two, gives us an illustration: "[She] got a scold-

Possessiveness.

▼

Ruth Orkin

242

ing and started to cry. In the midst of her crying, she asked, 'Pick me up, please. I want to cry in the mirror'" (ibid.). For the child on the road to sound autonomy, the deformations of his self-image are temporary. Even as adults, we have moments of shame and embarrassment when we feel swollen and lumpy—or when, in dreams, we find ourselves walking agonizedly naked in a sumptuously attired crowd—but such feelings pass, leaving us at home with a body which, for all its shortcomings, is not such an unpleasant vessel to inhabit. In the same way, the toddler, triumphant in his growing array of skills, causing his parents to laugh affectionately at his cute sayings, discovering in the world around him the new and fascinating wonders that are the external counterparts of his burgeoning sensitivities, soon forgets his setbacks in a larger sense of competence and self-esteem. And just as the toddler's self-respect depends on the world's respect for him, his esteem for others is contingent on his own self-esteem. Hostility, viciousness, and evil seem to originate in one's own sense of worthlessness, and whether one is caught in a vicious circle of hatred or a benign circle of love, we cannot escape the circularity of development.

The Regulation of Behavior in Toddlerhood

In talking about the major behavioral manifestations of toddlerhood, we have inevitably touched upon problems of authority and control. For the now-active toddler, in his pursuit of autonomy, by definition collides with the people and things around him. Collectively, the behaviors that parents try consciously to teach their children are known as the process of **socialization**—such things as good manners, eating in the proper way, speaking with respect to elders, chewing with one's mouth closed, modesty, and skills such as managing clothes. The explicit teachings of socialization are contrasted with the often unconscious transmission of culture. Before we discuss some of the specific major areas in which parents have to make decisions, a few general principles are worth mentioning.

First of all, many libertarian parents find the very idea of authority repugnant, as though to regulate a child will cripple his emotional freedom, deaden his creativity, and make him forevermore an abject puppet. The toddler represents in microcosm the perpetual problem of the individual versus society, of the way one person's striving after gratification or fulfillment can conflict with another's, and the need to find a *modus vivendi* with one's fellows that does not unduly stifle anybody's individuality. Among adults, we look for a certain degree of self-control and self-sacrifice, ability to postpone gratification, accommodation, give and take, cooperation, and a search for shared gratifications and fulfillments. The toddler, of course, is not an adult. Until he can exercise judgment, his parents have to exercise it for him. Furthermore, in keeping with the principle of growth ambivalence, the toddler dreads freedom almost as much as he resents restraints, and parents have to find a balance between, on the one hand, imposing limits that give the toddler a sense of stability and security and, on the other hand, encouraging exploration and venturesomeness. And parents who regret the necessity for control can console themselves that the most original, creative people have invariably been highly disciplined, not in the sense of being beaten into line, but in the sense of disciplined to take account of how things are. But just as there is danger in no control at all, so is there danger in overcontrol. At all stages, parents have to trust their children, and they have to be prepared to take the risks that go with freedom.

A second important consideration, implied by the first, is that of developmental **timing**. It is futile, and hence frustrating for parent and child alike, to expect of a child behavior of which he is not yet capable. Sometimes the child's readiness or unreadiness is a matter of motor control or proficiency, sometimes a matter of how much and how well he can understand. Although developmental readiness is a necessary condition for learning certain things, two points should be emphasized. Sometimes the only way we can find out whether a child is ready is to try to teach him, being prepared to desist if it becomes evident that the child is not ready. A corollary of this point is that our attempts at teaching, if carried out in a relaxed way, may be what induces the readiness necessary to learning. The second point is that, from toddlerhood on, we must beware of the contrary tendency, holding the child back and denying him the experiences necessary to his development, overprotecting and "babying" him— the psychiatric term is to **infantilize**.

Another general principle is contained in the doctrine of **gradualism**. Babies tend to be conservative, to resist innovations, and in introducing something new, the transitions should not be unnecessarily abrupt, nor should we expect quick results. This does not mean that parents should be hesitant, which would be at odds with the principle that follows, but that they should watch the baby for feedback and adapt their tempos to his reactions. It is all right and probably even beneficial to push a little, as long as one knows when one is pushing too hard. In child-rearing, one makes haste slowly, in the sense that too hurried an approach to anything may defeat itself by the extreme resistance it provokes. Even the most cooperative of children need time to get used to new ways of doing things.

A further general principle is that of **parental self-confidence**. Parents must be able to act decisively, secure in their own maturity and wisdom and love for their child, and without undue concern for what The Neighbors will think. There will be times, too, when parents have to disregard to some extent what the child himself thinks. As we have suggested, there is a distinction between **needs**, which have to be met in the interests of sound development, and **wants**, which can sometimes be indulged but which sometimes have to yield to other considerations, of health, safety, parental convenience, or whatever. Parents who try to satisfy all a child's wants may soon find themselves at the mercy of a small tyrant who is no happier about his power than they are. There is still another aspect of parental self-confidence that should be mentioned. Parents should not be so afraid of losing a child's love that they hesitate to do anything that might antagonize him. The toddler cannot help getting angry when we thwart him, and parents have to accept the consequences of their decisions, without becoming dejected at the thought that the baby may cease to love them, and also without becoming indignant because he dares to react. An incidental feature of parental self-confidence is that it helps parents be relaxed, and not always on the alert for everything that might go wrong. For it is an important matter that parents should not create problems by seeing dread portents in everything the child does and reacting to the supposed portents as though the problem had already arisen. For instance, the mother who is afraid of having a "feeding problem," like the mother who feels it is her duty to fatten her child, puts so much emotion into every meal, and reacts with so much dismay to any balking on the child's part, that she spoils his appetite and manufactures a feeding problem. Here is one more instance of the self-fulfilling prophecy in development.

A final general principle in the care and rearing of toddlers is **avoidance of moralism**. That is not to suggest that parents should be indifferent to morality. But morality, like the rest of the child's psychological equipment, is something that develops, and there are appropriate and inappropriate moralities for different ages. The central core of any true morality, awareness of and concern for the feelings of others, has its beginnings early in life in the parents' love and respect for the child and for other creatures in the environment. The parents' attitudes are conveyed to the older infant and toddler both in their manner and in such words as "Gently" or "Easy" applied to the manipulation of vulnerable objects, whether pets or bric-a-brac. Toddler morality cannot extend far beyond this first stage, and it will be some time before such moral issues as generosity and selfishness, truthfulness, modesty, and so forth, can be meaningful to the child. With these general principles

in mind, let us go on to examine some of the specific practical issues faced by parents of a toddler.

Physical safety

Although both Freud's and Erikson's views of toddlerhood have their origins in the conception of the anal period, with its attendant matters of control, we prefer to begin our discussion of particular issues with questions of physical safety. For no matter how vital the proper resolution of successive crises, the child's first job is to survive in one piece. The toddler is a relentless explorer and tryer-out of things, and his enthusiasm and curiosity far outstrip his prudence. This is partly because his perceptual capacities and knowledge are still limited, and partly because he may egocentrically forget about himself as an object of harm. He may be so absorbed in watching the car backing out of the driveway that he fails to realize that he himself is in its path. In general, the toddler simply does not see the menace in speeding cars and their capacity for mangling flesh and bone. He loves water and has no idea that pond or ocean can engulf him and fill his lungs with unbreathable liquid. He does not sense the jolt of electricity lurking in a wall outlet or empty socket, or the incisive potentialities of a knife, or the toxicity of medicines or household chemicals. Adults, who adjust automatically to the changing field of forces inside a moving car, do not realize that the passive toddler may be flung across the car when it turns a corner, or sent hurtling against the windshield by a sudden application of the brakes.

Dangerous things and substances must be kept where they will not tempt the toddler to experiment. Their storage places —the medicine cabinet, the kitchen cabinet where the cleansing compounds are kept, the shelf for paints and solvents—have to be strictly taboo. Taboos are best conveyed by a bark of "No!" fortified, where necessary, by a slap on the outstretched hand; usually, though, the parent's tone of voice is enough. But since the toddler's still-immature conscience is easily lulled, and since forbidden fruits are always the most alluring, a number of repetitions may be necessary. Also, the toddler is learning to tease, and he may continue to reach for proscribed objects, watching out of the corner of his eye for a reaction from the adult. When this happens, it may be well to remove the child from the site of temptation and get him started on something more constructive. As the toddler's vocabulary and understanding increase, other, more precise words can be substituted for the original *no*, words like *hot*, *ouch*, and *cut*. Let us add that, the stronger the bonds of affection between parent and child, the easier it is to make taboos stick. Two additional points need to be made. Once the major hazards have been removed from the child's environment, parents should try to relax and not hover protectively over the child. In the first place, they do not want to make the child fragile-feeling and fearful. In the second place, he needs some scope to make mistakes and to learn from them, to tolerate a certain number of minor bumps and bruises and scrapes.

Toilet training

It is obvious that children in our predominantly urban-suburban society must learn, sooner or later, to use toilets. In some vil-

lage or rural settings, when the weather is favorable, one can go off behind a convenient bush, and even in the city it is not unusual for slum children to relieve themselves in an alley or between two parked cars; but by and large it is mandatory that our children stop soiling and wetting themselves and use the elegant plumbing put at their disposal. There is a component of maturational readiness for **toilet training**, but maturation alone will not do the job. The parents must teach the child. This need not imply, however, a grim struggle for supremacy. The negativistic toddler may be on and off in his cooperation, but once he gets used to the idea and knows what is expected of him, he is usually willing to try out the process, if only because he wants to be like his parents.

Bowel and bladder training differ in both their timing and their methods, and so have to be discussed separately. **Bowel training** usually comes first, and control can often be established early in the second year. Training can be complicated, however, by the fact that many babies have their only bowel movements when asleep. Apart from this difficulty—which seems to go away without anything being done about it— bowel training can be effective when movements come on an approximate schedule and when there are advance warnings of which the baby himself seems to be aware. Even in late infancy, parents can see—and sometimes smell—a bowel movement approaching and, tactfully, put the baby on the potty-chair in time. (A potty-chair is recommended, rather than a seat that fits over the toilet, since the toddler can get into it himself, without help, and since quite a few children are frightened by the altitude of a toilet seat or by the turbulence of a flushing toilet.) But it is in toddlerhood, when the child can recognize the significance of certain interior stirrings and can perform the actions of holding on, relaxing, and expelling, that voluntary control becomes possible. Once the toddler is willing to try, further progress is more a matter of parental attitudes than of techniques. A casual, cheerful manner throughout, a concern for the child's comfort—like his elders, he may want to have something to "read" while sitting on the pot—a reasonable amount of praise when he does well, all contribute to the success of what should be a cooperative enterprise. Anxiety, prolonged confinement, strain, disgust, haste, and punishment or moral outrage when the child falters merely prolong and complicate the process. We should say, though, that an occasional child masters bowel control and then, satisfied, cannot be bothered to use the pot until some later age when he recognizes the inappropriateness of defecating in his clothing. It may be a good idea to let the child use his pot without the chair occasionally. This is because children sometimes fasten on one particular set of familiar conditions as appropriate to elimination and cannot function when these conditions are changed. One well-trained little girl, for instance, on a camping trip with her parents, was quite unable to eliminate, in spite of an obvious need, when supported comfortably on her mother's forearm. Next time, her parents took along her toilet seat, which, although it had to be held by an adult, was sufficiently familiar to permit her to move her bowels. To forestall such rigidity, in the interests of being free to take trips, it is sound practice to vary toilet conditions.

Bladder control comes in two stages, waking control and sleeping control. Waking control usually comes first, somewhere around age two, while sleeping control may lag some months behind. Since urination occurs more frequently than defecation, the opportunities for learning are greater. On the other hand, the premonitory feelings seem to be less distinct, and the mechanisms of muscular control more elusive. However, the baby's readiness becomes evident in his staying dry for ever-longer periods, and when he has not urinated for a while, parents can invite him to try. In the West, at first, both boys and girls urinate sitting down. In the case of boys, this means that the penis must be held pointed downward, especially if, as is often the case just before urination, the boy has an erection. Both boys and girls, when they have a chance to observe their parents in the bathroom, may want to try to urinate standing up, the way Daddy does. Explanations to the boy about his short stature relative to the height of the toilet, and to girls about anatomical differences, will probably have little effect, and both boys and girls may have to learn from sad, wet experience before they are willing to sit down again.

We should note in passing that bladder control appears somewhat earlier in girls than in boys, in keeping with the advanced developmental pace (including physical growth and maturation) set by females up to adolescence. As we might expect, bladder control is seldom established all at once, but takes time to become stabilized. There are occasional children who abruptly train themselves. One child, remarking spontaneously apropos of a baby sister that babies certainly wet a lot, thereafter stayed virtually dry. A little girl on a motor trip was fascinated by filling-station rest rooms and, after insisting on frequent visits to them, became completely trained. These, however, are the exceptions. Ordinarily, bladder training has to follow its on-and-off course while parents give the child ample opportunity to use the toilet—the light clothing of summer weather helps—but without making it the principal feature of his existence, offering praise for success, and taking accidents in stride. Even after the child has good control over his urinary sphincters, he may suffer brief relapses when tired or engrossed in play—all children seem reluctant to take time out to go to the bathroom—or more prolonged ones if he is sick or otherwise upset.

Nighttime bladder control follows almost automatically—but with some lag—as a consequence of daytime control. It appears that the child's practice in controlling his urinary sphincter reverses the reflexive response to bladder tension, from relaxation and expulsion to contraction and retention. It seems to make no great difference in establishing bladder control whether the child imbibes reasonable quantities of fluids at bedtime. It may help the process to awaken the child before the parents go to bed and allow him to urinate—in the case of a boy, the pot can be brought to his crib—but it is probably better not to do this unless it seems that nighttime control is becoming excessively delayed. In general, as in other areas, the less fuss, the easier the learning. Parents must expect occasional lapses, even in children who have good control, especially in times of illness, special excitement, or unusual strain. Even older children subjected to severe stress may revert to bed-wetting. During the evacuation of London during World War II, school-age children separated from their mothers were said to wet their beds in such numbers that, as one

observer put it, "half of England was awash."

An occasional child, of course, is unable because of some physical irregularity to control urination, and in such cases medical intervention may be necessary. Sometimes persistent emotional disturbances interfere with normal control, and parents have to do what they can—sometimes with professional medical or psychological help—to remove the causes of such disturbances. An occasional child seems to wet the bed for no reason except that he sleeps so deeply that normal controls are lost. Commercial devices are available for the treatment of chronic bed-wetting, that which persists beyond age four or five. Such devices seek to establish a conditioned response between bladder tension and awakening. When the child begins to wet, the urine bridges an electric circuit, causing an alarm bell to ring or giving the child a mild electric shock, thus waking him up. After a few repetitions, the need to urinate is supposed to act as a signal to awaken and go to the bathroom. Eventually, as control improves, it is enough that the child wake up only enough to tighten his sphincter but otherwise sleep on. We have heard of some successful use of these devices, and also of some failures, so we can recommend them only tentatively, and then only in serious cases where other means have been tried and found wanting.

Sibling rivalry

Another area in which problems may arise during toddlerhood is that of **sibling rivalry**. There is a traditional belief, dating back to the story of Cain and Abel, and made into a formal psychological concept by Alfred Adler, that there necessarily exists among siblings—children of the same family—a spirit of competition, jealousy, and hostility. For instance, an older child, and especially a firstborn one who for a while was an only child, may feel that a new baby has deposed him from his reigning position in his parents' affections. A younger sibling, on the other hand, may feel resentfully envious of an older sibling's size, strength, and privileges. Adler and others have plotted out what they believe to be the typical patterns of sibling rivalry that go with particular birth orders (or positions in the "family constellation"), modified according to the sex of the siblings, but for our discussion here we need be concerned only with the particular circumstance that a toddler may be upset by the arrival of a new brother or sister.

Experts have proposed various ways of forestalling or minimizing a toddler's jealousy toward a new baby. If the toddler is old enough—two and a half rather than one and a half—he should be told in advance so that the baby does not come as a total surprise, although not so far in advance that he forgets about it or that it becomes unreal with the slow passage of time. Within his restricted competence, the toddler can be given a share in the preparations for and care of the newcomer, so that he can feel that the baby is in some sense his—or the family's—as well as his parents'. Most important, the parents should not become so engrossed in the care and appreciation of the new baby that they lose sight of the toddler's continuing need for affection and attention—the friends and relations who come to admire the new baby can help in this respect, too. It is doubtful whether these and allied measures, no matter how assiduously and skillfully prac-

ticed, will altogether prevent the older child from becoming jealous of the new intruder. Nor is it certain that all jealousy should be prevented, if we want children to know a full range of emotions. We might also note in passing that the family dog or cat may exhibit a certain amount of jealousy toward a new baby as well.

A toddler may show jealousy of a new sibling in any of several ways. He may **regress**, turn back to more infantile ways of behaving. He may begin to whine or cry easily, he may cling to his parents, his speech may become more babyish or even disappear, he may lose control over his bladder. Such behavior often indicates that the toddler feels left out; it is as though he had concluded that the only way to get attention is to be a baby. If the toddler shows signs of regression, it may be necessary to give him an especially generous ration of love, together with whatever hints are possible that he can safely act his age. Another way in which the toddler may show his jealousy is by trying to injure or get rid of the newcomer. He may suggest to the parents that they somehow dispose of the baby (slightly older children have been known to propose flushing it down the toilet as a promising expedient), or that it is now quite time to return it to the hospital. Sometimes the toddler will try to take matters into his own hands with the sincere intention of doing away with the usurper. Here is one mother's account of the reaction of a seventeen-month-old boy to the arrival of a baby sister:

When I came home with Jenny, Mark stared at me at first as though I were a complete stranger. He cried bitterly when his father carried Jenny from the car to the house. He was somewhat aloof for several hours. I was

Suzanne Szasz   Robert Leavitt

▲

Sibling relations. Note that rivalry and jealousy are not always dominant.

prepared to see some jealously in Mark, but somehow I thought it would be subtle, or directed against me. Not so at all! The first chance he got, he went right for the baby, with the most agonized expression, and tried to sock her. He looked grimly determined to smash this little bundle of trouble, and yet he was obviously terribly upset by his own impulse and sobbed, "No, no," even as he went for her. . . . The ice finally broke one day perhaps a week after Jenny and I came home. I was diapering Jenny, and Mark was watching from his grandmother's arms. Jenny made some little noise. I imitated her and said to Mark, "Doesn't that baby make *silly* noises?" Suddenly Mark smiled broadly and said, "Silly!" It must have been a revelation to him that I was on his side. Here we all were together, laughing at the baby. From then on, there was almost no more trouble. Gradually we let Mark loose in Jenny's presence, and it was practically no time before he was admiring her "tiny toes," kissing her, and patting her **The toddler** ("Gently, gently," he would remind himself).

Sometimes, of course, a peaceful solution such as this does not work, in which case the toddler must continue to be restrained from injuring the baby. But there need be no suggestion that the toddler is wicked or depraved. A formal, inflexible, categorical, and even angry prohibition can be imposed in full understanding of how justifiable the toddler's feelings are. Just as one can love a toddler—or any other person—and yet not approve of everything he does, so can one disapprove of something the toddler does, or wants to do, without ceasing to love him. As in all of discipline, the emphasis must be as much as possible on the act, and not on the toddler's worth as a total person. Especially in the matter of jealousy, an excessively moralistic approach can reinforce the toddler's conviction that he has been displaced. There are bound to be times when the new baby has to be given a disproportionate share of attention, as when he is sick, and when the toddler will inevitably feel that he has taken a second place in his parents' affections. But such temporary strains, as

250

long as they are the exception rather than the rule, will probably do as much to strengthen as to weaken the bonds between toddler and parents. It is when the toddler is consistently relegated to second place that he comes to think of love as something that has to be earned or stolen or fought for—or regressed for—rather than as something that is given as a matter of course in a free exchange. Sibling rivalry may be peculiar to small, nuclear families of the kind Europeans take for granted. In large, extended families, or in communal societies where the children belong to everybody, sibling rivalry may not develop or may take very different forms.

Eating

An area which used to be of more concern than it is now is that of **eating**. On the practical side, parents, aware of the toddler's need for nourishment for growth and energy, sometimes are alarmed about whether the child is getting enough of the right foodstuffs. Their anxieties can be quite impervious to fact. They may consider that the child is wasting away, whereas he is clearly full of bounce and energy, and, as the pediatrician's records show, is growing normally and is no more subject to illness than the next child. But in addition to the practical aspects of eating, eating is closely bound up with cultural values as well. Some of us are heirs to the Puritan tradition that there must be no waste and that a clean plate is somehow a mark of virtue. In the same tradition, eating itself is not thought of as pleasurable, and dessert is frivolous and hence permissible only after the grim drudgery of meat and potatoes and spinach has been disposed of. In the Continental tradition, where food is to be enjoyed in its own right and good nutrition is incidental, the child who does not eat heartily is seen either as unhappy or as bearing a grudge against the provider of food. In some societies, from Germany to Italy to Greece to Polynesia, the bulk that comes with heavy eating is a sign of health, of prosperity, and therefore of prestige, of happiness, and sometimes of beauty, and is moreover a tribute to the mother as loving and to the father as a good provider. As far as we know, parents everywhere tend to worry far less about overeating and possibly obesity—at least in the early years—than about lack of appetite, "fussy" eating, and the possibility that the child will become scrawny and debilitated.

Parental fears that the child will not eat enough of the right things are usually groundless and can be harmful. If the toddler has ample opportunity to choose from a varied and well-balanced diet, he is almost certain to get enough to eat, even if his intake appears to approach zero. We must remember that there are individual differences in metabolism, in need for particular nutrients, and in food preferences, and be prepared to make allowances for them. If, on the other hand, his mother becomes anxious and applies pressure, urging and cajoling and trying to force-feed, she can in her agitation make eating altogether disagreeable and create a true feeding problem where none existed. If it seems important that the toddler eat at mealtimes rather than at odd moments during the day, or if between-meal snacks throw his diet out of balance, he can do without snacks. If he then surprises his parents by turning ravenous at mealtimes, he can be fed a little early. Many toddlers and older children suffer a drop in blood sugar late in the day, giving rise to irritability and lack of concentration. This can be countered with a glass of juice, a bit of chocolate, or a lump of sugar, usually at no cost to the toddler's appetite.

Setting limits

Finally, we come to the problem of **setting limits**, which is closely related to the topic of safety with which we began this section, but with this difference: here we are less concerned with the toddler's physical welfare than with the rights of others, with parental convenience and the preservation of property because of its economic, esthetic, or sentimental value. Inevitably, some household objects have to be forbidden to the toddler because his competence is unequal to his curiosity and because he is blind to the values that adults see as obvious properties of objects. However, since a constant stream of "No!" and "Don't touch!" bewilders and paralyzes a child, and eventually loses all force,

it is as well to reduce prohibitions to a necessary minimum. If fragile and precious objects are not needed for everyday use, they can be put safely out of the child's reach, and those that are needed can be grouped in a few locations, so that a few wholesale taboos can do the work of many specific ones. The knowing visitor can guess the age of the family's children by the "high-water mark" above which breakable possessions are kept. But there are two ways in which these prohibitions can be more flexible than those having to do with safety. First, the child can satisfy his curiosity about some objects by being allowed to handle them under supervision, holding them in his own or an adult lap to prevent breaking, and being given the caution of "Gently" or "Carefully." Second, some activities can be tolerated occasionally but not always. For instance, a tired mother can perfectly well decide that today is not the day for the toddler to empty out the bureau drawers, even though such behavior might be perfectly permissible another time. It should be clear that prohibitions work best in a context of freedom, so that the toddler has places he can go, things he can play with, times and places he can make a racket and run off steam. And if he is not allowed to tear up the first editions, there is no reason that he cannot have a collection of old magazines and telephone directories to do with as he will—he is perfectly capable of making and abiding by the discrimination. But the mother of a toddler learns to recognize long silences, which may at first seem blessedly peaceful but which become increasingly ominous and may end with a loud crash and a scream of distress.

When it is necessary to set limits, these should be firm and definite. The toddler has little comprehension of subtlety or tolerance of ambiguity, and finds comfort and security in clearcut guidelines. Tentative, hesitant admonitions invite the toddler to test the limits, to keep probing to see how far he can go and what he can get away with, behavior that is as trying for the toddler as it is for the adult. There is little place for "reasoning with" the toddler. Indeed, "reasoning" may be far less satisfying for the toddler than an abrupt command. The latent menace of much of the adult's reasoning is conveyed in a preschool child's tirade against a contemporary: "I'll hit you! I'll cut you up in little pieces! I'll—I'll—I'll *explain* it to you!"

Although parental definiteness can eliminate much resistance, testing of limits, and teasing, the child's striving for autonomy will not let him accept all authority passively. Sometimes the answer is in distracting the child, by changing the subject or introducing a new and attractive activity. Not every issue must be resolved, or every moral drawn, and we must remember the danger of the child's losing face. Sometimes a conflict of wills, or excessive pressure on the child, will result in tantrums. But even these are not always as serious as they may seem. Witness our friend Ruth at age fifteen months:

Ruth has tried tantrums to get her way. She lies on the floor and cries. If I ignore her and leave the room she stops crying, comes to the room I am in, lies on the floor and screams. I go into another room and she follows. When she discovers she cannot get any attention this way, she comes over to me, puts her head in my lap and puts her arms around my legs and says, "Hug" (Church, 1968, p. 233).

In general, adult excitability tends to breed tantrums, which can make for a vicious circle where adult and child feed the flames of each other's passion, escalating to the breaking point. By contrast, tantrums that go unrewarded in terms of anger or dismay or surrender—or later moralizing—tend to subside more rapidly. If tantrumlike behavior persists in a given situation, the adult can only keep his head and carry on; if need be, a small and very angry child can be carried under one arm, his legs flailing behind the adult, without injury to either party. But as long as the bonds of basic trust are there, and if the adult respects the toddler's autonomy and makes allowance for differences of tempo, life with a toddler can be surprisingly serene. It is those adults who douse the toddler with cold water, or threaten him with loss of love or abandonment, who stoke the fires of tantrums.

6

the
preschool
child:
one

Between the ages of two and three, the child moves out of toddlerhood and becomes a preschool child. We can quarrel with the designation in two ways: not all preschool children attend preschool; nor is there any reason to think, in the case of the child who does attend school, that either he or the school is "pre-" anything, any more than they are "post-" something else. It is true that every age period is marked by anticipations of things to come, just as it bears residues of what went before, but at the same time each period needs to be recognized in terms of its own identifying characteristics. However, the label "preschool" seems to be firmly fixed to the years from two and a half to five, and until a better one comes along, we can only try to disregard its irrelevant connotations.

Until a very few years ago, the preschool years were the most intensively studied segment of childhood. As we have said, from the time the newborn baby left the hospital until he appeared at nursery school, he used to be hidden away from the greedy clutches of the psychologist. When he enters the first grade, he is once again barricaded behind the requirements of the school curriculum and the understandable reluctance of school administrators to have psychologists invade the classroom and disrupt routines—besides which, school-age children who have served as subjects for psychologists go home and tell their parents about the strange things they have been asked to do, and in less than no time the principal's phone is aclamor with demands for explanations. Thus, when the nursery-school movement got started in the United States in the 1920s, for the most part under college and university auspices, psychologists

rushed to exploit the new pool of subjects thus made available. In recent years, the picture has come into better balance as psychologists have become more willing to leave their home base and study infants and toddlers in collaboration with pediatricians and public health nurses in pediatricians' offices and well-baby clinics, and even to go into the babies' homes. However, while a few communities and school systems have become more tolerant of psychological research in the schools, the study of school-age children and adolescents is still a difficult business, and psychologists on more than one occasion have met with embattled resistance from the community.

In this chapter, after a general description of the child, we shall talk first about the child's relations with other people—adults and, more and more, other children. We shall discuss his play patterns and how these reveal his orientation to a world compounded of reality and magic. We shall talk about his growing mastery of concrete and symbolic materials, and the emerging self-image that reveals to him his own vulnerability and mortality.

An Overview of
the Preschool Years

The study of preschool children is rewarding not only from a scientific but also from a personal standpoint. For children of this age are, in the authors' biased view, delightful to work with and to know. The charm of this age may be evident even to harassed parents. The professional worker sees the preschool child as one who, not yet having learned the duplicity and guile, the masks and disguises and evasions of later ages, wears his personality on his sleeve. His thoughts and passions are instantly translated into words and deeds. His behavior is often colorful and sometimes violent, and, because of its transparency, easy to observe and record. His growing mastery of language and materials makes communication with him less demanding than with a toddler, but his very competence makes clearly evident his limitations, the gaps and misperceptions and miscomprehensions and erroneous assumptions that make his thought processes fascinating to follow, if somewhat baffling. But since his thinking is not restricted by adult considerations of logic, his utterances may have a quality of vivid imagination and even of refreshingly penetrating insight.

But let us add a caution: we are describing the child of parents who have time and energy and the inclination to talk with and listen to the child, who surround him with books and pictures and music and raw materials to be shaped as he sees fit, who can take him on excursions to places of interest. The child of this age from a "deprived" background is likely to give quite a different picture. In pointing to such differences, we are not reflecting on the child or his family, but on the society that has short-changed them both. We should also point out that not all children from what seem like deprived backgrounds suffer the psychological consequences. Some families manage to battle through unspeakable adversity and raise children who are emotionally and intellectually robust. Furthermore, the picture of the child of deprivation is one gleaned by psychologists and educators with whom the child may interact in anything but a spontaneous way, in nursery-school settings which may feel wholly alien to the child in terms of his accustomed experience. But we cannot ignore the psychological reality of rats and hunger, of being protected from an ominous outside world by being sequestered in a dim room with only a television set for company, of having to share a bed, wet and dry, with many others, the lack of privacy, and a climate of pervasive violence. There is little chance for a poor household to be child-centered, which carries both drawbacks and advantages for the child.

Our experience with the limited sample of poor children who find their way into preschools shows us, in general, a child who is fearful and inhibited, passive but explosive. He speaks grudgingly and with difficulty and, because he lacks words for many things, vaguely (we shall say more about linguistic differences in the next chapter). His play consists mostly of formless rough and tumble. He eats voraciously but without relish and is loath to try unfamiliar foods. Of course, remembering what we said in the last chapter about physiological adaptations to one's regular diet, he may be right. His regular diet, unfortunately, may leave him malnourished, his skeletal development is likely to be inadequate, even his baby teeth may suffer serious decay, and he is highly vulnerable to an array of infections. We should remember, too, that malnutrition can begin before birth, as a reflection of the mother's inadequate diet. His sleep patterns are in many cases irregular. These conditions are most pronounced in remote valleys and in cabins on abandoned southern farms, where outright starvation is far from uncommon, but they exist side by side with affluence in the cities and suburbs. Poor children do not score well on conventional intelligence tests, and they may grow up without acquiring some standard competences, but they develop a stubborn capacity for survival and, once communication has been established, turn out to be interesting and enjoyable people. Superficially, however, poor children are very different from middle-class children, and it is important to bear these contrasts in mind as we talk about, for the most part, the happy, mischievous, vitamin-fortified, energetic, bright, imaginative, voluble, knowledge-hungry American middle-class preschool child.

During this period, the child's growth rate is leveling off from the first spurt of infancy. In his first two years, the "average child" added 14 or 15 inches (35 cm.) to his height; in the next three years he grows 9 or 10 inches (25 cm.). Nevertheless, somewhere between ages two and three the child reaches half his adult height. In his first year, the baby gained some 15 pounds (7 kg.), tripling his birth weight; thereafter, his annual rate of gain drops to about 5 pounds (2+ kg.) by age five. Indeed, growth in height may be nearly counterbalanced during this time by the loss of baby fat (although his belly will stay rounded and his waist all but invisible) so that he seems not to be gaining weight at all. His proportions are changing. His legs grow faster than the rest of him: at age two, they account for 34 percent of his length; by age five, 44 percent, which approaches the half-and-half proportions of the adult. (Note that the figures for length and weight are essentially meaningless, even within the United States, since subgroups differ so greatly, but the data on proportions are approximately valid for

all children getting reasonable nourishment.) As the child's legs lengthen and his head growth slows, he loses the top-heavy look of infancy and toddlerhood. His full set of twenty baby teeth is usually completed by age two and a half, roughly the beginning of the preschool years. Similarly, the end of this period coincides more or less with the loss of the first of the baby teeth. As the cartilage and bones of the child's face develop and the fat pads in his cheeks dwindle, his countenance loses its babyish cast and becomes better defined and more like his adult self. Sex differences in rate of growth are not very pronounced during the preschool years, although, as we shall see, boys and girls tend to follow ever more widely divergent paths of psychological development.

Along with changes in size and proportion go changes in posture and locomotion and manipulation. Now, when the child sits on the floor to play, his knees point forward but his forelegs are bent back along his thighs, and his buttocks rest on or between his heels. He loses his toddler ability to bend double, legs straight, and rest his head on the ground. The high-stepping toddle of age two becomes a free-swinging stride. Over a period of several years, his one-stair-at-a-time approach to staircases yields to a continuous movement of ascending or descending, and he learns to scale ladders and jungle gyms and trees with low branches. When he wakes up from sleep, he may bounce to his feet, kick

Sitting positions. A. Infant propped sitting. B. Infant sitting unsupported; note typical lotus position of the feet. C. Toddler squatting. Another toddler posture is to sit with legs thrust straight forward. D. Preschool child with forelegs folded back. E. The school-age child sits in a great variety of positions.

A. John Fay

B. Phoebe Dunn, DPI

C. Robert W. Young, DPI

D. Michael Heron, Monkmeyer

E. Marion Bernstein, Editorial Photocolor Archives

his feet out from under him and land seated at the edge of the bed, and, by straightening his body, allow himself to slide to the floor. (American middle-class children generally move from a crib to a bed around age three, although in other settings the child from early babyhood sleeps on a mat on the floor, in a hammock, or whatever.) The preschool child may still, as when he was a toddler, turn a corner by bouncing off a wall, or he may learn to hook his inside hand on a wall or piece of furniture and swing himself through the turn. He learns to spin about in one place to make himself enjoyably dizzy. When running along a smooth floor, he may stop to play with a toy by dropping abruptly to his knees and sliding to a standstill. In ordinary circumstances, he may move about with much swooping and twirling, flailing and flopping and tumbling, until his parents wonder if he can possibly walk in a straight line. Actually, when the child does have a chance to clamber about on a rocky hillside, he may show surprisingly agile sure-footedness—which does not mean that he need not be watched and tended. The preschool child is still likely, just as when he was a toddler, to snuggle up to an adult knee or shoulder and gradually drape himself limply against the adult. Now, however, when he is carried, he takes some responsibility for holding on, wrapping an arm around the adult's neck or clamping his knees around the adult's waist, and plays some small part in keeping the child-adult totality in balance. From the people around him or from television, the child may pick up the idea of doing exercises, and perform a marvelous travesty of physical culture. He tries to do somersaults, sprawling sideways at the top of his turn. Similarly, he picks up styles of

dancing, from ballet to ballroom to teen-age steps to tribal forms, and executes them in ways ranging from wild burlesque to smooth competence.

In the sphere of manipulation, the preschool child goes from clutching spoons and banging kitchenware to manipulating mechanical toys or hammers and saws. His use of materials is increasingly subordinated to making replicas of the world around him, and the making of replicas to their use in dramatic play. The blocks and boxes he likes to carry become building materials to be fitted into intricate and delicately balanced structures. With paint brush or crayon he progresses from scrawls and scribbles to lines and swirls and dots and cross-hatchings and color masses. Where first he used single colors arbitrarily selected, he goes on to single colors chosen with care, to combinations of colors kept well separated, to many colors freely intermingled, to colors used to identify specific areas. From the welter of his early experiments with line and form and color there emerge depictions of recognizable objects and activities. With a pencil or a ball-point pen, perhaps because they offer less opportunity for "abstract" explorations, the child is more likely to make an attempt at representation.

The preschool child's linguistic skills are expanding and elaborating. He acquires, at his own level, some of the skills of the contemplative philosopher. He brings language to bear on his busy taking in and digesting of the world—its color and flavors and textures and implications. He enters the realm of vicarious experience provided by written literature; he listens to and discusses stories and goes through the motions of reading, "saying" the text as he turns the pages. Indeed, quite a number of preschool children learn to recognize many printed words and may even in fact read. Some children are helped in learning to read by television, particularly the commercials with their many repeated conjunctions of printed and spoken brand names and slogans. The children's TV program "Sesame Street" has sought to capitalize on the commercial technique to teach children letters, words, and numbers, with how much success (particularly with its supposed target, poor kids) we are not sure. In general, research on the impact of TV on children has encountered formidable problems of methodology. Nevertheless, Meichenbaum (1971) has made an interesting proposal to incorporate into "Sesame Street" some instruction in problem-solving based on the modeling research of Bandura and Walters (Bandura, 1971).

The preschool child has fewer internal limitations on his ability to formulate his experience than when he was a toddler, and knows fewer external, socially directed restraints than he will in the years ahead, which makes this a time of maximum spontaneity. In his openness, he often gives us striking insights into his own world and even ours—provided, of course, that we in our turn are prepared to be openly receptive to what the child has to tell us. All too often, we adults, instead of looking and listening and comprehending, laugh or admonish or shrug off or are seized with moral indignation.

As an infant and toddler, the child found an identity as a member of his family. Although the family continues to be his primary base and frame of reference for some years, now he begins the slow process of finding his place in humanity at large. He is exposed to more new things—real and imaginary—more new situations, more new

Preschool competence in dressing. Note that the heel of the right sock does not match the child's heel, and that the shoes are left tied, since most preschool children cannot tie their shoelaces.

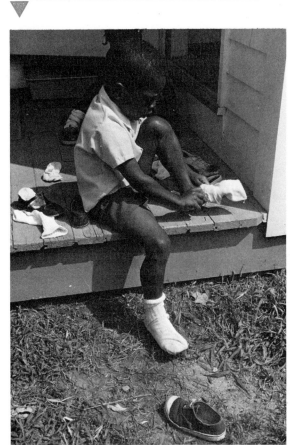

Philip A. Biscuti, Connecticut College

people, more new roles, enlarging and complicating the possibilities for identification. He becomes aware of other children as people like himself and so becomes able to communicate with them directly, exchanging information and feelings and ideas. In his play with his peers, he moves from the parallel play of toddlerhood toward integrated and elaborate cooperative play projects. As his awareness of his body becomes more stable and better defined, so does his awareness of his own vulnerability, so that the preschool years witness the development of new fears about intactness. Fears also increase as the child learns about the many menaces lying outside his ordinary experience, surgery and gangsters and war and kidnappers and ghosts and hobgoblins. During the preschool years, the child's personal style becomes more sharply articulated. Some styles can be defined fairly objectively in terms of traits or orientations such as leader, follower, participant, onlooker, outcast, or lone wolf. We can invoke such dimensions as energetic-sluggish, bold-timid, talkative-reticent, hostile-friendly, independent-demanding, imaginative-pedestrian—the list goes on and on.

The preschool years do not lend themselves to a summary in a simple phrase of the kind we employed for infancy ("basic trust") or for toddlerhood ("autonomy"). For one thing, development goes on in too many directions at once. For another, the broad range of individual and group differences apparent at this age make generalizations shaky. Although Erikson has defined a set of developmental alternatives for this age (**initiative** versus **guilt**), just as he has for all the eight stages which he considers descriptive of the life cycle, he himself says that the preschool years are a time of rapid

At bedtime, the preschool child is revealed in all his tender immaturity.

▼

fluctuations, between overdependence and eager independence, between competence and ineptitude, between maturity and infantilism, between boyishness and girlishness, between winsome affection and sudden antisocial destructiveness. But just as the child is not all of a piece, neither are the preschool years themselves. Age five is a far cry from age two. Just as the toddler may retain many of the ways of an infant, so is the young preschool child in many respects still a toddler. Half-undressed for a nap, sucking his thumb or a pacifier, clutching a teddy bear or a frayed strip of blanket, he is revealed in all his tender immaturity. The young preschool child may still be incompletely toilet-trained. Observations by Roberts and Schoellkopf (1951) indicate that at age two and a half, some 40 percent of children have occasional daytime "accidents"; the child's sphincters are even more likely to betray him during sleep. By contrast, the five-year-old seems sophisticated, competent, and self-assured —and is twice as old.

Meeting People

In the young child's eyes, his parents are the repositories of all wisdom and strength and virtue, but during the preschool years his social horizons gradually broaden to include, on somewhat lower planes, people outside his immediate family. True, he has visited and been visited by numerous people during his early years, but, to judge by his behavior toward them and his later recollections, they have existed for him largely as curious, transitory apparitions without solid identities. Often, all the chil-

dren he meets in a strange household are assumed to belong to the same family, and whatever adults he meets are assumed to be the parents of all the children. Now he begins to form genuine attachments to new adults such as a teacher, and then, through the teacher, to his contemporaries until, perhaps around age four, he can operate for fairly extended intervals in the company of his peers—although he still needs to have a familiar adult nearby to turn to in moments of perplexity or distress or crisis, or just because he wants some petting and cuddling. Some children, from babyhood on, have a variety of adult caretakers—grandmothers, neighbors, aunts, nursemaids, teen-age sitters—in which case it may be easy to accept new adults. Similarly, some children spend a good bit of time in the company of siblings close in age, cousins, and neighborhood children, and are likely to show a temporary advantage in social skills over children with less experience.

If the two- or three-year-old goes to nursery school, it is desirable that he be weaned over a period of some days from his mother to his teacher. As he becomes convinced that the teacher too is a human being, and that his mother will indeed return for him at the end of school, he can safely turn his attention first to the play materials and then to the other children. It is, of course, an individual decision whether a given child should go to nursery school and when he is emotionally ready to go, and if anxiety over being separated from his mother continues more than a week or so, the decision may have to be reconsidered. It is perhaps worth digressing to point out that there are special difficulties in establishing nursery schools for underprivileged children, as is now happening on a large scale under federal auspices. The poor child, whose early training is likely to include great stress on independence, may find it easier than the middle-class child to leave his mother. He may, however, find it very hard to accept his new teacher, who may have the handicaps—from his point of view—of the wrong color skin, unfamiliar accent and speech patterns, and a general behavioral style that he finds alien and unsettling. Moreover, he may have trouble coming to terms with the whole new world of possibilities and assumptions. The very abundance of a well-equipped preschool may be hard to take in, and the idea that things are there for *him* to use may surpass credibility. These difficulties can be overcome, but they require an extra ration of patience and understanding.

As we noted in the discussion of toddlerhood, young preschool children may at first treat each other like mere things. Before long, however, a reciprocal curiosity appears, manifested by a staring examination and a hesitant reaching out to touch each other's faces and bodies. Once the children have inspected and identified each other and learned each other's names, usually from the adults, they can exchange affection and play together. Their first play, of course, is likely to be of the parallel variety, in which there is little or no overt interchange—one child may hand the other a plaything, or take him by the hand to lead him to the swings or sandbox—but there is obvious satisfaction in the company of the other child. The children at first find it very hard to talk to each other except in imperatives, negatives ("No!" "Don't!"), and possessives ("Mine!"), and their first attempts at sustained conversations are likely to take the form of dual monologues. When the exchange of information or explanations are needed, the children are likely to call on an adult to act as their go-between.

Later on, the children begin to do things in bunches (**associative play**): a flock may congregate in the sandbox, or crowd into the rocking boat, or swarm over the climbing structures, shrilling together in an expression of shared feeling. Such behavior illustrates what the social psychologist calls **behavioral contagion**, the spread of an activity or a mood or an impulse through a group. Such contagion is a commonplace in the nursery school, where one can witness epidemics of telephoning, silliness, grotesque lurching about and collapsing to the floor, water play, tricycling—no sooner has one child begun something than everybody wants to do it. There is a growing willingness to look and admire—as when the teacher calls attention to somebody's new shoes or to the special plaything a child has brought from home—without, as yet, any need to compete for the center of the stage. Perhaps this is the place to say that there are qualities of children and their behavior that the printed word cannot fully convey, and that it is important for the student of human development to see and hear the activities of living children. If the student does not have access to a laboratory school, films and recordings may give some of the actuality that we can only suggest. Much can be learned, too, through discreet observation and eavesdropping in the playground or supermarket.

In their quieter moments together, young preschool children are likely to engage in "conversations" which seem to have as their aim less the exchange of information and ideas than the pleasure of affective communication. Such conversations, as we have said, are called **dual** or collective monologues, in that what one child says bears no relation, not even a tangential one, to what the other child says, the other's utterance serving simply as a springboard for a new line of thought. The following example of a dual monologue is between two four-year-olds, who are past the age at which such exchanges are common. Their teacher describes them as sitting cozily side by side, swinging their feet, waiting politely in conversational style for their turn to speak, and enjoying a feeling of "comfortable togetherness":

Jenny: They wiggle sideways when they kiss.

Chris (*Vaguely*): What?

Jenny: My bunny slippers. They are brown and red and sort of yellow and white. And they have eyes and ears and these noses that wiggle sideways when they kiss.

Chris: I have a piece of sugar in a red piece of paper. I'm gonna eat it but maybe it's for a horse.

Jenny: We bought them. My mommy did. We couldn't find the old ones. These are like the old ones. They were not in the trunk.

Chris: Can't eat the piece of sugar, not unless you take the paper off.

Jenny: And we found Mother Lamb. Oh, she was in Poughkeepsie in the trunk in the house in the woods where Mrs. Tiddywinkle lives.

Chris: Do you like sugar? I do, and so do horses.

Jenny: I play with my bunnies. They are real. We play in the woods. They have eyes. We *all* go in the woods. My teddy bear and the bunnies

Nancy Hays, Monkmeyer

Preschool children revel in the movement of a swing.

A preschool conversation.

Robert M. Sachs

and the duck, to visit Mrs. Tiddy-winkle. We play and play.

Chris: I guess I'll eat my sugar at lunch time. I can get more for the horses. Besides, I don't have no horses now.*

Not all preschool conversations are of this kind. Many times the child is earnestly trying to get or give information, to communicate, and *non sequiturs* of the sort that occur in a collective monologue would be frustratingly infuriating. Even so, the preschool child's communication is far from perfect, although a sympathetic and patient adult can often divine what the child is driving at. One problem is that of egocentrism: the child simply does not recognize the need to provide the information necessary to understand what he is trying to say. Another problem is that he may provide too much irrelevant information, so that his message is drowned in distracting "noise." Finally, he may not be able to maintain a single line of thought, so that he goes off on a succession of tangents. We recall a three-year-old boy who, having bowled over a little girl as he charged across the playroom, turned to her and said, "You should watch where you got what was coming to you!"

Needless to say, imperfect communication is not restricted to the early years of life, as the misunderstandings, cross-purposes, and confusions of many adult interchanges demonstrate. It is worth emphasizing that many adults are guilty of egocentrism, both in the cognitive sense of being unable to adopt another's point of view and in the emotional sense of giving such high priority to their own concerns and preoccupations that those of other people fade into nothingness; it is for this reason that many seeming conversations are in fact nothing more than collective monologues. But during the preschool years, children begin to be able to shape their thoughts to other people's, to describe events coherently, and to use language to coordinate group activities in pursuit of some agreed-on goal, lapsing less often into blind self-assertion. The adult who wishes to establish communication with a preschooler will find himself frustrated if he tries such gambits as "What did you do today?" The child has been living his life, not keeping a mental record, and is at a loss to answer. But if the adult simply makes himself available, speech will sooner or later come pouring forth from the child, perhaps in intolerable volume.

There are three other aspects of social relations with peers that emerge during the preschool years—sympathy, aggression, and leadership. As traits, though seemingly contradictory, these appear most clearly in the same individuals (Murphy, 1937). Studies of the development of competence by Burton White and his associates (Ogilvie, 1969) suggest that the three-year-olds deemed most competent were able to be either leaders or followers as the circumstances warranted. Competent three-year-olds took pride in the things they made, could show affection to peers or ignore them, could use peers to get help, and, without clinging, knew when to turn to adults. Three-year-old competence seems to be related to maternal competence as defined earlier (p. 109).

At least from toddlerhood, the child is

---

* Most of the quotations from children, unless otherwise credited, were recorded at the Vassar College Nursery School. We are grateful for astute observations by Dorothy Call, Dr. Miriam F. Fiedler, Susan Fry, Cornelia Goldsmith, Agnes Griffiths, Dorothy Levens, Eveline B. Omwake, Lucretia Williams, and many others.

capable of **sympathy** toward members of his own family: the toddler may soothe an unhappy parent or offer one of his toys to an ailing sibling. But the toddler's or young preschool child's first reaction to the distress of an unrelated child his own age, if he reacts at all, is likely to be to burst out crying himself. Such crying is probably less a matter of sympathy than an act of empathic participation, reflecting poorly articulated boundaries between other people's feelings and his own. It is as though what hurts the other child hurts or threatens him, too, just as the adult can feel a jolt of pain when he sees someone fall down. Such reactions are another form of the behavioral contagion referred to above.

Sympathetic, as contrasted with empathic, reactions to age-mates begin when the child pauses in his play to stare at another child who is suffering. Later in the preschool years, we can see behavior akin to mature sympathy. One child will console another, or run to fetch the teacher to deal with an emergency, or rebuke a child who has been unkind. Of course, as Murphy has pointed out, the child's motives may be less than pure, and his sympathy may be tainted with elements of patronizing superiority, guilt, anxiety, or disguised hostility. Observe, too, that children are not necessarily consistent in being sympathetic, and a child who acts compassionately in one situation may behave quite cruelly in another; this is particularly likely to be the case when the mob spirit takes over and children gang up to taunt and abuse a victim. Other times, a usually sympathetic child may simply not understand another's distress, as when he witnesses a tumble.

Authentic sympathy implies understanding of other people's feelings, both posi-

tive and negative, and it is perhaps for this reason that sympathy and leadership go together. At this age, though, group organization typically shifts from moment to moment, making sustained leadership difficult. Moreover, the child acting as leader is liable to lose interest and slip out of his role. In spite of these impediments, a number of preschool children do show consistent leadership in one form or another. Some children impose their will by sheer force of muscle or character. Some become "bossy," identifying successfully with adult authority—this is different from the futile officiousness of the insecure child who is trying in vain to win the respect of his fellows. Some preschool children can play on the group like an organ. Some, remaining inconspicuous or aloof, can nevertheless exert a quiet but still-potent authority as arbiter, adviser, or model.

It seems likely that it is leadership that mediates the coexistence of **aggression** and sympathy in the same child. Children who have strong feelings and are also responsive to the feelings of others, so that they know when to yield, to adapt, to be flexible, probably make the most effective leaders. Successful leaders, child and adult, must know how to listen as well as command, or they soon find themselves leaders without a following. Needless to say, sympathy and aggression do not always go together. Some children who display little aggressiveness are capable of considerable sympathy—most of all, perhaps, in those situations where they themselves feel imperiled. Other children are aggressive in ways that show no component of sympathy and in fact appear quite heartless. Some aggression, of course, expresses serious psychological disturbance.

Regardless of their source, the preschool child's passions run high, even if, like sum-

Marlis Muller

Myron

Donna J. Harris, The Merrill-Palmer Institute

Nancy Hays, Monkmeyer

Ruth Orkin

mer squalls, they come and go quickly. For a young child, apparent acts of aggression may be more an exploration than an outburst of hostility. Yet in a flash of rage, if his strength were equal to his feelings, there is little doubt that he would kill without hesitation. But at this age, enmities are as unstable as friendships, so that, a moment later, the child may be showering endearments on the person he was just prepared to annihilate. Although as a rule friendships and enmities shift and change rapidly, in any one nursery-school group there are likely to be one or two children who are universally liked and admired, and another one or two who are just as pervasively disliked and shunned or picked on.

Like other forms of social behavior, children's quarrels and combats show developmental changes. To the best of our knowledge, there have been no recent studies of preschool children's fighting, but the findings from a classic study by Dawe (1934) are probably still essentially correct. Although for many purposes we do not have to concern ourselves with sex differences during the preschool years, boys and girls show very different patterns of conflict after age three. Most notably, boys become increasingly combative between the ages of three and five, after which disputes fall off. Girls, on the other hand, quarrel less and less after age three. Boys engage in physical combat more than girls, who learn early to use their tongues as weapons, and both sexes try to settle property disputes by snatching and fleeing with the disputed article.

In general, combats develop from grim, wordless tugs of war over a contested plaything, typical of toddlers and young preschool children, to physical violence punctuated with angry cries and shouts, to violence displaced upon an enemy's property, as when a hat is trampled into the dirt, upon neutral objects, or upon weaker scapegoats. And physical clashes give way in turn to more "civilized" verbal ones. At younger ages, preschool children quarrel mainly over possessions. Then, unprovoked physical attacks, and retaliation, become common. Late in the preschool years, as at subsequent ages, social difficulties become the main source of conflict; who will play with whom, what they will play, who will take which roles, who will be included and who excluded, and who likes or dislikes whom. Note that four-year-olds are already adept at teasing and insults, and many a fight begins with a slur on a child's character or competence.

If we watch and listen carefully, however, we will discover that a lot of what looks and sounds like aggression is in reality nothing more than a part of the preschool child's constant role playing. We quote a lunch-table conversation which reveals a half-playful aggression reinforced by the four-year-old's love of language for its own sake and by a species of cooperative competition in which each child builds on the others' ideas in an effort to surpass them in outrageous fantasy:

John: We'll cut off his arms.
Ellie: We'll saw off his legs.
Don: Let's hang him up in a tree and tickle him.
John: Let's poke him full of black and blue marks.
Ellie: Let's cut off his hair and put it in the sandbox.

Meeting people

Don: Let's cut out his grunties.

John: Let's smear him all over with grunties.

Ellie: Let's make him eat lots of grunties.

John: We'll wrap it up in some paper—not cellophane—some yellow paper, and then tie some string around it.

Two other preschool themes stand out in this passage. First, there is the large dose of **scatology**. Children very early learn the shock value of certain words, sometimes from having produced them accidentally in the course of making up nonsense words, and sometimes from hearing them used by older children in a tone of voice that conveyed their secret power. The child may have little or no idea what the words mean, but he knows very well that he can agitate his parents by saying them. Later in the preschool years, many children become temporarily addicted to "toilet talk," generously using words whose meaning they know quite well. Observe, though, that the middle-class preschool child's "bad language" deals only with superficial anatomy and with elimination; it is only in the middle years that the child begins to appreciate and exploit the special vocabulary of sexuality and its feelings and varieties, usually, of course, in its four-letter forms. Needless to say, the slum child comes into contact with and adopts a far richer vocabulary of scatology than does the middle-class child. Preschool children also pick up from the people around them such forms as *hell*, *damn*, *goddam*, and *son-of-a-bitch*, which they ordinarily use aptly, as expressions of displeasure, if ignorantly and, to the adult ear, jarringly. In general, adult outrage at the child's use of certain words only intensifies their value for the child, and they are best dealt with casually—

their occurrence is more an esthetic abuse than a moral one. Some restrictions may be necessary, but these can be couched in terms of the times and places and audiences suited for such expressions.

The second theme is that of mutilation. As we have already noted about the toddler and as we shall see later, when we discuss self-awareness in the preschool child and the fears and conflicts he may have to deal with, body intactness is often of great concern to him. One way the child has of mastering his concerns about his body is to make sport of them in his play, just as the medical student affects an air of toughness or plays macabre jokes to help control his squeamishness about the sometimes sickening things he has to do.

The preschool child's social behavior, like much of his waking life, revolves around play. It is now time to examine in more detail what his play consists of, what it means to the child, what it tells us about him and his world, and what it tells us about *us*.

Play, Reality, and Fantasy

As we said in connection with toddlerhood, "play" is the term we use to describe whatever young children do that cannot be classified as the serious business of life—sleeping, eating, eliminating, getting

In other societies, children acquire practical competences and assume serious responsibilities at an early age.

Ken Heyman

Melvin Konner

Paolo Koch, Rapho Guillumette

Dramatic play, modeling, and identification.

dressed or undressed, getting washed, going to the doctor or the dentist, doing small chores. In the preschool years, though, play patterns change in at least four ways. First, play becomes more playful, to the point where the child makes a game of everything he does: he eats with the handle of his spoon or fork; he wants to wear his clothes turned front to back, or to wear his shirt as trousers; the boy, urinating, traces curlicues and arabesques in the toilet bowl (and sometimes, alas, outside it); he feigns hunger at bedtime and fatigue at the table; he "forgets" how to do things and makes "mistakes" so that he has to begin a project over again; he experiments with strange combinations of foodstuffs—one four-year-old boy invented a concoction he called (for reasons unknown) "Mexican soup," consisting of milk, chocolate ice cream, and mashed potatoes. Second, through the playfulness there seems to be a new earnestness in the preschool child's play, as though he is seriously trying on roles as a way of learning and experiencing the life styles they represent. Third, al-

Nancy Rudolph

panding emotional range and his ever-greater knowledge and skill in thinking give him new powers of imagination, both in the sense of playing with ideas and possibilities and of imagining entities and situations unlike any he has actually experienced. As we have said, his play becomes more and more social, collaborative, and, late in the preschool years, cooperative.

The preschool child continues unabated his earlier activities of sense-pleasure play, skill play, and social-affective play, and various combinations of these, but the dominant motif of the preschool years is dramatic play, the taking on of roles and the acting out of themes drawn first from domestic life and then increasingly from the world at large, including the world of fantasy. There is evidence from research by Singer (1966, ch. 6) that a capacity for fantasy is one important way in which normal children differ from children who act out their every impulse, including impulses to violence and destruction. It is our further conviction that dramatic play is an important vehicle for learning, for identification, in the sense both of learning about other people and how to be like them and of coming to know oneself. But from the child's point of view, the satisfactions of dramatic play seem to lie in the magical sense of power and participation that are not yet his in the larger world. Let us remember, though, that we are talking about American middle-class children. We do not know how highly elaborated dramatic play becomes in other groups; certainly in many "primitive" societies, actual participation and apprenticeship in adult roles—as beggar, dancer, food-gatherer, cook, nursemaid, and so forth—begins at an early age.

though the child can lose himself in his play to the extent that, for instance, he becomes angry with another child who will not play his part properly, or he actually tries to eat the mud pie he has fashioned, he nonetheless recognizes that playing—making believe or pretending—is a realm distinct from the real world in which genuine power is exercised and irreversible consequences follow from actions. He by no means understands how the real world works—he has no idea, for instance, of where money comes from and how it functions—but he knows that it falls very little under his influence. Fourth, the child's ex-

In dramatic play, the child puts himself —sometimes literally—into other people's

Play, reality, and fantasy

shoes. We see children dressing up in adult clothes, playing mother or baby or doctor, serving tea, acting the role of fireman or groceryman, pretending to be a rabbit or a tiger, and simultaneously being pilot and airplane, or steam shovel and operator. Roles which involve visible and clearly functional activities seem to appeal most to the child. The jobs of housewife, librarian, filling station attendant, carpenter, or bulldozer driver can be grasped instantly, at least in their externals, and emulated. Although it may chagrin the white-collar or professional father, it is not surprising that the child finds the role of office worker or attorney drab and unappealing. The child's literal adherence to the externals of a role, with little comprehension of its essence, shows up in the sometimes amusing mistakes he makes. For example, a child turns to his teacher and announces, "You know, I'm really desperate! Tell me how to play I'm desperate." Or a three-year-old girl, playing doctor with a doll as patient, says, "Now I have to test her knee-flexes." Or a boy, four, reports, "I'm afraid I have to tell you that I took out Jimmy's tonsils. It's all right, though—I put in some new ones." A five-year-old explains, "When my mummy hasn't any money my daddy runs and catches a check for her" (Miller, 1959).

In group dramatic play, young preschool children change roles rapidly, with no sense of strain, sometimes to meet the demands of the game and sometimes simply because they tire of a given role. The Baby may clamber out of his carriage and announce that he is going to be the Mommy; the erstwhile Mommy may then make herself comfortable in the carriage, or perhaps decide that she will be the Daddy, provided a third child will agree to be the Baby. Note that the children at first feel no need to adhere to roles of the same sex as their own. At age three, children are only beginning to be aware of physical differences between the sexes, but they are learning that there are socially defined roles for the two sexes. Observations by Fagot and Patterson (1969) indicate that "teachers consistently reinforced feminine-type behaviors more than masculine behaviors, and reinforced boys but not girls when they performed opposite-sexed behaviors. Peers, on the other hand, reinforced mostly same-sex peers."

Reflections of the adult world in play

Since so much of the child's dramatic play is modeled on the behavior of familiar adults, we can often gather from his reenactments the special qualities and meanings that the adult world has for him. It can be a revealing and chastening experience to have our gestures, postures, mannerisms, affectations, foibles, and turns of speech echoed back to us through the play of our children. Needless to say, we sometimes encounter reflections of parental tenderness, humor, good sense, and compassion. But the most striking insights come when we find ourselves projected as a scolding or whining voice, as a monument of pomposity, as a pettifogging tyrant, as a sleeping ogre who if disturbed snarls and gnashes his teeth. Much of the child's play is an unconscious caricature of adult ways, but a caricature that may be closer to the truth than we like to admit. Sometimes, of course, the parody becomes conscious, as in the following exchange between two four-year-olds perched atop a nursery-school jungle gym and convulsed by their own cleverness:

Jack: It's *lovely* to see you!
Danny: I'm so happy to see you!
Jack: How *are* you? How have you been?
Danny: Sorry I have to go so quick.
Jack: I hope you have a good time falling down and bumping your head.

The caricature is less conscious, but no less telling, in a speech by Alice, age four and a half, as she tucks her doll into bed: "We like to have her, but I just want her to stop the nonsense. She wets the bed all the time. You *wicket* girl! You bad, *wicket* girl!" Another time, at age four years eight months, Alice, having been excused from naps, was alone with her teacher and decided to play school:

"I'm going to be the teacher and I'll teach you how to write." *Takes pad and scribbles. Goes off across room to discipline a very noisy class (imaginary). Bawls out one child after another, ties them to their desks with long, long ropes so they can't get out, shuts the door firmly on them so she can't hear them crying. Throws arms around teacher's neck, kisses her, says,* "You're very, very good. Pretty soon you can go out and play with those recesses. That's really hard. It's really for older children."

Let it be noted that Alice was not necessarily mimicking the behavior of particular adults. In some cases, dramatic play is a fairly faithful copy of actual events, but in other cases it seems to reflect the child's perceptions of the adult world at large.

One thing that the child seems to be sensitive to in the adult world is the relative importance of different roles. It may be painful but illuminating to fathers to realize how often the mother, by virtue of her central role in household affairs, which of course is the area most visible to the child, assumes much greater prestige than the father, so that boys and girls alike may compete to take the part of mother in organized dramatic play. The behavior of a four-year-old girl with marked leadership qualities toward a boy whose standing in the group was low shows some of the status attached to particular roles in suburban society. The boy had been persistently trying to intrude on a game of house in which the little girl was Mommy. Finally, with subtle skill, she let him in and expelled him again in one smooth movement: "O.K. You be the Daddy. Finish your breakfast and I must drive you to the station. Here's your briefcase and you must get on the train. G'bye!"

A striking contrast in the role perceptions of slum kids emerges in the following record made by Barbara Frederick of two four-year-olds in nursery school:

James had been strutting around the now somewhat cluttered housekeeping corner, reveling as usual in his masculine role of "head of the house." Now he sat holding a baby doll in his arms and rocking, while discussing the "baby's" health with Honey, his "wife." When Honey asked for money to take the sick baby to the doctor, James stopped rocking. His previously relaxed, almost benign expression changed into a scowl. His large eyes narrowed to slits as he hunched forward in the rocking chair. Still clutching the doll, he shouted at Honey, "Did you spend all them quarters I give you? Well, shit, you ain't gettin' *no more*! You wanna run me, woman?"

Honey met this attack with a defensive air. Although not submissive, she was made cautious by James' violent manner. Her arms folded across her chest, her set face expressing determination, Honey mumbled under her breath, more to herself than to James (who was now leaning back in the rocking chair, rocking slowly and intently watching Honey's face): "You only give me *two* quarters, and I need 'em for dinner. If you don't like it, I ain't cookin' *nothing else!*"

Some revealing glimpses into the child's-eye view of the adult world come from the experimental or clinical use of toys which invite the child to construct scenes from family life. In his dramatizations, and in the very arrangement of the toys, the child may convey his conception of the relative significance of members of his family, the things which frighten children or disturb adults, or the weight of adult controls and impositions. He may depict himself hemmed in by threatening creatures or adrift in isolation, he may act out themes of sibling rivalry, or fantasy the revenge he would like to take against parental discipline.

Reality and fantasy

Much of the play we have been describing can be viewed as a product of the child's fantasy life. Such a view, however, would be only partly correct. It assumes that reality and fantasy are two distinct realms, which is not altogether the case for the preschool child, for whom fact and fancy are likely to be interchangeable. The line between the two realms becomes more sharply defined during the preschool years —as when a four-year-old was heard to say to a playmate, "Let's pretend we're not playing pretend," or when another four-year-old asked his father about a cutout paper boat, "Would this *really* float on *pretend* water?"—but feelings, thoughts,

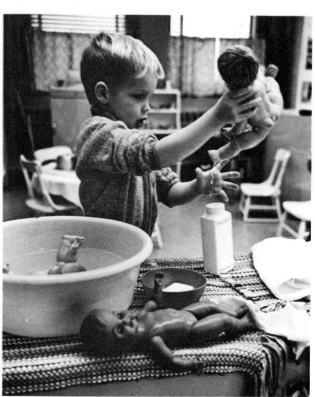

Even boys are likely to identify with the maternal role because of its high visibility in their lives.

Myron Papiz

and wishes continue to flow out into and influence the objective world, animating and coloring and shaping it in ways that adults may find surprising. Let it be said that in some respects the preschool child is in perfectly satisfactory contact with our "objective" world: he recognizes people and places and limits, he appropriately uses the tools and playthings available to him, he observes certain safety precautions, and so forth. But around and between and within objects all sorts of magical potentialities lurk.

To the preschool child, dreams are real events taking place in real space—a child may even balk at sleeping in his own room, on the grounds that it contains too many dreams. Stuart, a preschool child from whom we shall hear more, expressed puzzlement about dreams on highly realistic grounds: "How can I see the things in dreams unless my eyes are open?" Preschool children believe that the people they see on television are quite literally located inside the set, although it is not much before age four or five that it occurs to the child to wonder how they got there. And cartoon characters on TV are endowed with the same reality as the living people whose images he sees, and the activities and transformations seen on TV—like the metamorphosis of pumpkin into coach in "Cinderella"—are taken as possible and actual. Similarly, at some point the preschool child is likely to examine a radio or phonograph in search of the orchestra he hears playing.

The preschool child may nourish a firm conviction that he can magically influence events by an application of his will, just as he sees an adult "making" the car go. Observe that, as mentioned before, such a conviction is not too far removed from the "body English" that an adult exerts to steer or to propel a billiard ball or golf ball. This sort of conviction can also engender great guilt if, in a moment of anger, the child wishes somebody harm and that person subsequently suffers a mishap. Professional magicians are said to find preschool children an unresponsive audience. This seems to be because, in the child's own magical scheme of possibilities, there is nothing more remarkable in sawing a woman in half and then reuniting her than in the unanalyzed wonders of everyday life. For much the same reason, adults are far more likely to be entertained by *Alice in Wonderland* than are very young children.

Fantasy is related to, but different from, both humor and lying. The preschool child's humor is mostly a matter of burlesque, playing tricks on people, and talking nonsense, but it sometimes takes the form of pretending something that is not so, as when the child playfully denies his own identity and assumes another. Such a playful change of identity is quite different in character from the imaginary identities discussed below. It is worth noting in passing that adults' attempts to amuse the preschool child may be wasted or may backfire. For instance, one father thought it would be entertaining to tell his children that when he went to get a flu shot—which is briefly quite painful—he tried to run away, kicked and screamed in protest and had to be restrained by two nurses, and then fainted from the agony of the shot. This account was highly enjoyed by a school-age child, but the family four-year-old became seriously distressed, oblivious to the note of playful histrionics.

Lying does not appear in elaborated form until after the preschool years, but because the child's world is a mélange of the real and the fantastic, he may seem, to adults uninstructed in his ways, to be playing free and easy with the truth. In general, if the child's wishes conflict with reality, reality has to yield. For instance, a four-year-old looking for a particular television program brought the schedule to his father to find out when and where the program would be shown. Told that there was no mention of the program, he proclaimed, "They [i.e., the newspaper] ought to be punished for saying wrong things!" He tried again later in the day, and this time decided, "They must be crazy if they don't list it." Preschool—and older—children may become quite angry at a parent for not making the car go, even after it has been pointed out to them that the way is blocked by other cars.

At first, the lies a child tells seem to be an effort to remake reality so as to conform to a more desirable state of affairs. However, at least by age four, the child seems really to be trying to deceive his parents. He denies that he has performed certain misdeeds, such as using his mother's fountain pen to punch holes in cardboard, or claims that he has executed certain tasks, such as washing his hands for dinner, or he may displace responsibility to a sibling, the family cat, or persons unknown. By the end of the preschool years, he may be able to make up accounts of behavior designed to gain special merit for himself or to shed discredit on another, in at least a half-serious expectation of being believed.

When the child lies, though, or simply keeps his own counsel in hopes that he will not be discovered, or when he tries to keep a secret, he is at a double disadvantage. First, he is likely to feel that his thoughts, even the unspoken ones, are perceptible to adults—perspicacious adults can in fact often guess what the young child is thinking—and that it is only a matter of time before some all-seeing adult will notice. Second, like other people, the preschool child feels a potent urge to share all his knowledge and ideas with someone—in the case of guilty knowledge, to confess and so to rid himself of a burden—and secrets are liable to come spilling out. ("You know what, Daddy? I have a secret. . . .") Even when the child does lie, it is probably good practice for parents to restrain their moral outrage and to treat the matter casually, indicating that they have some doubts, that they favor telling the truth, but that they have a general faith in the child's veracity. Certainly the preschool child's exaggerations and fantasies are not a moral issue, and parents have no reason to be concerned about them except in the rare, extreme case where they seem to threaten the child's grip on the real world. In the same way, it is only when the child's lying becomes so constant and pervasive that he seems to have lost trust either in his parents or in himself (as in mendacious bragging) that parents need become seriously concerned.

By the late preschool years or early school years, it becomes the child's turn to be morally outraged by adults' white lies, in ways that may be embarrassing when the child screams at full volume, "You're telling a lie, Mommy!" If truth-telling is represented as an absolute good, it is hard for a child to understand the distinction between lies told for personal advantage and those told to shield the sensibilities of other people. The child is as "realistic" in his morality as in his perceiving, and takes no account of motivation or extenuating circumstances. Piaget has devised several tests of moral realism for use with school-age children, in which the child is asked to judge which is the worse of two acts. These can also be used with four- and five-year-olds. If one asks the preschool child which is worse, the boy who, in trying to do a favor for his mother, smashes a stack of twelve plates, or the boy who, in stealing a cookie, breaks a single dish, he, like the young school-age child, is almost sure to censure the boy who broke the greater number of dishes. Such moral realism seems to be spontaneous although influenced by the absolutism or flexibility of parental attitudes.

Between the ages of two and five, the child increasingly demands realistic props for his fantasy play. For the young preschool child, a block can serve as a doll, a train, a building, or a cow. For the five-year-old, a block is strictly building material, and he wants some approximation of a real airplane to land at and take off from the airport he has constructed. The three-year-old can people a universe with sticks and stones and paper and rags—although he makes little effort to shape them into representational images. The four-year-old, to be a successful cowboy, wants some key accessory—a broad-brimmed hat, a cap pistol, or a neckerchief. For him, one element can stand for the whole configuration. The five-year-old is likely to feel dissatisfied in his role playing unless he can wear the full regalia of his part.

In older preschool children, there is also a striving after logical consistency in whatever roles they play, as though such consistency, like the use of props, is necessary to buttress their belief in their own fantasy. For example, the child playing the role of cowboy may not be able to go swimming until he has ascertained that

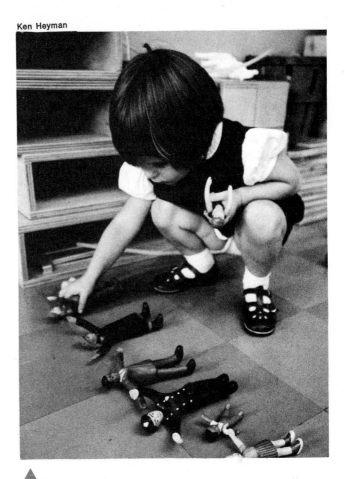

The preschool child is not bound by everyday considerations of reality in his play.

cowboys sometimes shed their standard costume in favor of a bathing suit. A little girl playing a male role asks, "When I grow up to be a big man, will I have a penis like my Daddy's?" By age five, the child may be able to shape raw materials to make his own supporting props. He can lay out boxes and blocks to make a space ship, cut out pieces of wood and nail them together to make boats and airplanes, and improvise a costume out of oddments from the rag bag.

It is during the preschool years, especially at ages four and five, that **imaginary companions** most often appear. (We use the term generically to include not only imaginary playmates, animal or human, but also imaginary realms, identities, and playthings, as well as real playthings which seem to be treated as though they have an autonomous psychological existence.) One of the more careful studies, by Ames and Learned (1946), indicates that some 20 percent of children may have imaginary companions of one sort or another. Our own inquiries, for the most part among female college students, suggest that the incidence may go as high as 50 percent. Most imaginary companions seem to have vanished by age ten, although it is not unheard of for adults to have imaginary companions, and not only such fictional characters as the rabbit "Harvey." The authors know of an instance in which a military detachment at an air base during World War II shared an imaginary dog who, after the war, returned home with one of the men and became the pet both of his family and the neighborhood.

Imaginary companions are often experienced with all the vividness and solidity of real material objects, and children's families may find themselves making extrava-

gant adjustments to the invisible (to them) visitor, taking care not to kick him or sit on him, and setting a place for him at table. Imaginary companions are sometimes born of a special need in a child's life, for a friend, a scapegoat, an extra conscience, a model, or an escape from either too stressful or too dull a reality. Frances Warfield's autobiographical account of her imaginary friend, Wrinkel, provides an excellent description both of the phenomenon itself and one of the many functions an imaginary companion may serve. Wrinkel's behavior expressed the resentments and frustrations of a well-behaved hard-of-hearing girl who was afraid to acknowledge her handicap and therefore could not ask people to speak louder:

Wrinkel came along at this time [*age six, according to her recollection, slightly beyond the preschool years*]. I wanted a close friend. Also, in my world of aunts and sisters, a boy was interesting.

Wrinkel was invisible and inaudible, which left him free to do and say whatever he wanted. The first time he entered a room he found the exact center of the ceiling and drove in a large invisible staple. He tossed an invisible rope ladder through the staple, festooning it over the tops of pictures, curtain poles, and chandeliers, and climbed over people's heads, listening to their talk and making nonsense of it.

Wrinkel was smarter than anybody—smarter than my sister Ann. For one thing, he was a boy. For another thing, though he could hear as perfectly as Ann could, he didn't care whether he heard perfectly or not. He chose to hear, and to act on what he heard, strictly as he had a mind to. . . .

When people talked and talked and Wrinkel didn't make sense of what they said, that wasn't because he didn't hear it. It was because he liked to make nonsense by weaving his own name in and out of their sentences. . . .

He killed people off for me all the time. He killed off all the ones I didn't like—the ones who cleared their throats pointedly or raised their voices at me, as if they thought I might not hear them. He killed off deadpans, when they mumbled some question at me (Warfield, 1948, pp. 8–9).

Not all imaginary companions, it should be said, are as pleasant for the child to have around as was Wrinkel. Sometimes they are distinctly unwelcome, like the invading hallucinations of a schizophrenic, and seem to be the incarnation of some deep-rooted dread or guilt. For instance, while in some children a companion who acts as a conscience may be gently reproachful, in others such a companion can castigate the child into a frenzy of terror. On the other hand, imaginary companions need not serve any apparent motivation or embody a special problem. They simply appear on the scene, do what they do, and depart—sometimes fading away, sometimes dying a melodramatic death in a car crash or at the hands of pirates.

Other Activities of Preschool Children

It should not be supposed, for all this, that preschool children spend all their time in dramatic play or the exercise of fantasy, though they slide readily in and out of each. Children from favored families spend time with their parents, in conversations, in trips to the park or the zoo, in playing rough-and-tumble games, in sledding or in sliding on the ice (some preschool children are able to skate or ski), splashing at the beach, building sand castles and digging tunnels in the sand, mock-wrestling, working around the house and yard, looking at books and being read to, listening to stories the parent makes up, studying leaves and stones and insects and birds' nests, working mechanical toys, and just observing and taking in. Some conversations with adults are serious and deal with such topics as tastes and preferences, feelings, age, geography, shared adventures, the existence and nature of God, elimination and other body functions, accidents and sickness and surgery and death, animals, Santa Claus (we are reminded of one four-year-old's account of all the things Santa Claus was going to bring him, after which his six-year-old brother shook his head in a mixture of pity and condescension, saying, "Oh, Richie, if you only knew what I know")—in sum, a huge array of things real and unreal. We must not forget that children love to confront their parents with hypothetical situations introduced by "What if": all the world were covered by water, people could fly, there were only men in the world, and so forth ad infinitum. Some conversations are built on frank absurdities—the nursery-school director's spanking machine, for instance, or the child's deciding that he will play the role of adult.

Some four- and five-year-olds, once they have learned to count, can play simple board games such as Parcheesi with parents and older siblings. Notice, though, that the preschool child hates to lose and will cheat, fudge, stretch the rules, and demand endless exceptions and opportunities to change his mind when he has made a mistake. Sometimes one or more preschool children will play in a group with older children and be involved in such advanced games as cops-and-robbers (the small children are invariably cast in the role of victim, which often means being flung into jail or roped to a tree)or putting on a play or circus. (Staging a performance of this kind involves interesting subsidiary—but still far from functionally subordinated—activities such as making posters, selling tickets, and arranging scenery.) With peers or by himself, the child builds with blocks, draws and paints, cuts out and pastes, looks at pictures, saws and hammers, blows soap bubbles, listens to records, sails toy boats, and thinks about things.

The mastery of materials

In all his activities, the preschool child is interacting with things in the world, and we can see a steady progression in the direction of increasing appropriateness, ingenuity, imagination, and mastery in the way he uses the things and substances available to him. This is in keeping with a more general trend from impulsive activities under the control of the environment and its demand qualities toward planned, internally directed occupations. Of particular interest is the way the child uses raw materials to shape new products, from manipulating the materials for their own sake to the functional subordination of materials into emergent constructions. The child finds raw materials everywhere: cleaning tissues are not merely something to blow one's nose with or to wipe up spilled liquids, they can be bunched together and secured with rubber bands to make a doll, they can be wrapped around a doll to make clothing, they can be spread over a doll as blankets. Paper clips, pipe cleaners, cotton wool, gummed reinforcements, cellophane tape, paper bags, metal foil, ad-

hesive tape, rags, drinking straws, toothpicks, water, clay, and lumber are all grist to the preschool child's mill.

In shaping materials, the child uses such tools as scissors, saws, hammers, nails, drills, and staplers. He can make some limited use of screwdrivers and wrenches. With adult inspiration, he makes abstract collages of old wallpaper, leaves and twigs, and sculptured library paste. He makes constructions out of empty matchboxes, cereal boxes, cleaning-tissue boxes, and folded paper, decorated with sand, buttons, sea shells, junk jewelry, spangles, and so forth. Here we are put in mind of Guilford's (1967) **Unusual Uses Test**—designed as a test of creativity—which requires the subject to tell all the ways he can think of to use, say, a common brick. Goodnow (1969) has shown that kindergarten children give significantly more unusual uses when they are allowed to manipulate the objects than when they are allowed to see, but not handle, them.

One of the more interesting lines of development is in the child's drawing and painting, which tells us less about his perceptual processes than about how his world is organized emotionally, in terms of significances. It makes a difference in how the child operates whether he is using paints, crayons, a pencil, or a ball-point pen. With a coarse medium, such as poster paint laid onto large sheets of manila paper with a wide brush, the child is likely to engage in experiments in pure form and color, in the spirit of sense-pleasure play, without any concern with depiction of objects. Indeed, at this age, it is only the most tactless of adults who would ask the silly question, "What is it?" On the other hand, one can perfectly well ask a child to "Tell me about your painting." Even when he does begin to paint pictorially, accidental effects may suggest new possibilities and divert him from his original purpose, so that what begins as a picture of a horse may midway become a picture of a house, which may then be transformed into a boat or may revert to an abstract exercise in design. Thus, what may look like an unrecognizable jumble of forms and colors may actually be a composite of many superimposed intentions. By age five, many children paint elaborate scenes containing complex events and activities set against detailed backgrounds of grass, trees, buildings, fences, animals, sky, clouds, and sun or moon or stars.

By contrast, with a fine medium, like a pencil or a ball-point pen, the child is likely to attempt pictorial representations, most typically first of people. The child's first drawings of people ordinarily consist of a roughly circular line enclosing marks standing for eyes, nose, and mouth—these may be in almost any position relative to each other. Even before he goes on to further elaboration, the child may draw an upturned or downturned mouth to indicate happiness or sadness. The next step comes with the addition of ears and hair, the latter in the form of a scribble at the top of the head or a series of loops more or less encircling it. Next, stiff, sticklike arms sprout straight out from the sides of the head, ending in a club of a fist or a sunburst of fingers (if they happen to number five, it is probably accidental). Then legs grow downward, either directly from the head or from the arms near the head; the legs, too, are jointless and end in a ball of foot. The torso is likely to appear first as a disconnected whorl between the legs—to the oversensitive adult eye, this may look like an attempt to represent the genitalia,

The preschool child experiments with line, form, and color.

but in fact it seems to occur to very few preschool children to draw the sex organs. Then the torso takes shape as a crude oval or rectangle with the legs appended. For a while, even after the torso is represented, the arms may continue to grow out from the head; then they are attached to the torso, but only approximately in the shoulder region. Head and torso are likely to remain for some time juxtaposed, without an intervening neck. Implied action may be contained in the figure from an early age, but it usually has to be inferred, either from the inclusion of some additional form such as a shovel or car, or from the child's verbal description; to represent walking or running or sitting overtaxes the child's skills. Clothing and scenery may appear by age four. By age five, arms and legs, as well as the torso, may be represented by enclosed spaces.

Some children depict the complete human figure as an assemblage of discrete parts, like a piece of machinery, while others come to draw it as an ameboid whole. In general, heads loom disproportionately large, and people tower over trees and houses. Even though one figure overlaps another, both are usually shown in their entirety, as though the near figure were transparent. When the child first draws a house, he strives mightily to show all four walls, and usually ends up settling for three.

These are the stages that seem to characterize the figure drawings of middle-class American children given liberal access to paper and pencils and encouraged to scribble, trace, color, and draw. Our observations of twenty-eight lower-class four-year-old children indicate that their ability to represent people is, by comparison with a middle-class sample, significantly lower (although eight of the twenty-eight lower-class children made drawings as elaborate as those of the middle-class controls). Valid comparisons of drawings by children from different cultural backgrounds may be hard to make, since in some societies only a very few children may be given much opportunity to draw, and these few may be inducted early into a highly formalized system of representation and decoration.

Similar patterns of development can be observed in the use of other plastic materials, from modeling clay to building blocks. In his block play, the three-year-old is more concerned with problems of balance and shape and how big a structure he can erect than with combining blocks to make a particular *thing*. (Let the reader not be misled by our use of *he*—girls play with blocks, too.) The four-year-old functionally subordinates his use of blocks to make things, but his structures are usually sprawling, amorphous, loosely hung together, and easily toppled. By age five, the child can build highly integrated, tightly balanced block structures that may reach to phenomenal heights and are often baroque in their intricacy. His block constructions are in many cases functionally subordinated to dramatic play which may continue over a period of days.

The kind of block play we have been describing depends, of course, on the child's having lavish quantities of blocks at his disposal, in a variety of sizes and shapes, as in a well-equipped nursery school, to a degree impossible in many homes. The preschool child's carpentry develops in much the same way: the three-year-old takes pleasure in simply cutting and nailing pieces of wood, the four-year-old hastily slaps together crude and ramshackle airplanes and boats, while the five-year-old plans, measures, carefully joins together, and smooths and paints, returning to the same project, if necessary, again and again.

The competence in the use of materials found in middle-class American children dwindles into ineptitude by contrast with the skills found in many primitive societies. The old ways are changing, of course, with the ever-wider spread of Western practices and commodities, but one can probably still find relatively intact communities in which three-year-olds build functional traps to snare fish or birds or rodents, or in which five-year-olds can be trusted in their own canoes on the waters of the lagoon. Notice that the "primitive" child's situation is very different from that of the middle-class American child, whose life is culturally deprived by being tied into the market economy of the larger society. In the tribe, or in any small, self-contained setting, little girls participate early and actively in the woman's duties of child care, cooking, cleaning, weaving mats, and so forth, and little boys, in hunting, fishing, making traps and weapons, gathering food, or whatever else may be the man's role, and it is hardly surprising that they develop a precocious competence in the skills of their society.

Awareness of Self

The description of self-awareness in infancy and toddlerhood was a relatively simple matter. We could speak of self-discovery, of abilities, of playfulness, of role playing, of basic trust and autonomy and negativism. By the preschool years, however, all the components of adult self-awareness (see p. 96) are in operation, if only in a preliminary sort of way. Traditionally, adolescence is the time for shaping an identity, a sense of who one is and what one believes in, for defining values and goals and meanings. Many writers have spoken, with justice, of the preschool years as a first adolescence, a time for a first identity formation in preparation for moving away from the family into the world of school and peers and practical achievement. It should be remembered that the child's developing self-awareness is almost a special case of his developing awareness of things around him, particularly other people. His awareness both of himself and of the environment increases as he becomes psychologically more differentiated from his surroundings, as he comes to distinguish between external events and internal ones, and as he learns to suspend action in favor of contemplation, thought, and feeling.

Some musings by the child Stuart, whom we quoted earlier, at intervals during his fifth year help give the flavor of developing self-awareness in the preschool period.

What is my back like, Miss Williams? (Nice, like other backs, etc.) *No!* Different. *Mine!* (Yes, but most backs are alike.) Like Mr. Stone's? Wide? (Like his and other people's.) Oh. (*He is thoughtful and slightly dashed.*)

You can't see your own face, can you?

These observations remind us that in knowing one's own body one must coordinate two perspectives, one given from outside through sight and hearing and the other given through inner experience. The comments, occurring over a span of three

▲

The preschool child is still learning about his own body and its functions.

days, of another boy, age four years and two months, give further insight:

(In the barber's chair) Can you see your hair when you're not looking in the mirror? *(Next night in bed, calls father into room)* When I yawn [*opens mouth wide*] I can't sing. Why? *(In bed the next night)* When I hold my nose and close my mouth [*demonstrates*]—see, I can't breathe. But when I hold my nose and open my mouth, then I can still breathe.

The preschool child: one

One would suspect that certain regions of the body are much more important for the child than others. For instance, when he washes his face, he washes only the frontal surface, and when he washes his hands, it is only the palms. We should also mention that older preschool children become very modest about exposing their bodies, even when their parents have set no particular example in this regard. One four-year-old girl, seeing a painting of a nude, asked, "Isn't she embarrassed?" It is in the school years, however, that modesty and privacy become a real issue. Now back to Stuart:

(Inspecting his abdomen as he dresses after nap) You know a thing? There is something funny about my skin. It fits all smooth mostly, but when I do this, there are extra skin in crumples. What is that for? (It's loose so you can move and stretch, etc.) No, it is not loose or it would show. It would hang down. It would be too big. (Like a rubber band.) Would it break if you pulled it too much? (Can stretch a lot.) I had this same skin when I was a baby. It fits very nice. It is me.

was there. It is funny—I could not see it. . . . It is funny, it was *my* pain in my throat. Why could I not see it? I could feel it, it was mine, mine pain. . . .

Observe that Stuart's experience of pain in both synesthetic and intersensory. Pain produces a synesthetic effect of color, as it apparently did too in his description of the dentist's office (see below) and it seems to exist for him as something solid and potentially visible. This seems comparable to the infant's looking for the piano chord or the handclap, and is like another child's description of an electric shock to his hand: "It feels like a bone in your arm." We see the same tendency in Stuart's musings about speaking.

Why have you a long head, and me a little round one?

Sometimes I wonder about the blood in me. Inside me it is all wet and blood and moving and lots of insides, but outside is all dry and careful and you would never know about the inside part by looking at the outside part. Not unless you got a hole in you and some of the blood came out. All the people are like that. Their skins keep them in, but underneath their skins is such a lot. . , . Your insides never stops. . . . It is so funny to think of you being all wet inside and all dry outside. Everybody is like that. I am. Why, Miss Williams, *you* are (*laughs*). Did you ever think about it? (*Teacher offers to show him anatomical picture.*) A picture that would be for you would be for me, too? Then we are alike. You and me are alike.

Your insides is like if another person lived inside your skin.

Did you ever have a red pain in your throat? The pain it was there. I could not see it, but it

A voice is a fast thing, isn't it? Are other sounds voices of things? [*The reader is urged to dwell a moment on this insight.*] Is the day got a voice, a sound? Where is your voice? It comes out of your mouth? *Does it, is it, in* your mouth? (*Here Stuart begins to elaborate his idea half in play, half in earnest.*) Are all the words stored up some place in your mouth? How can you get food in if all those words are in your mouth? How much space does a word take? Words are thin little things. But some of them make a big noise. A sound—is it bigger than a word?

Stuart's growing awareness of common experience, including the recognition that adults not only have the same kind of bodies but that these towers of omnipotence and infallibility have feelings, doubts, and frailties akin to his own, is not limited to the human sphere and does not automatically lead to clarification in adult terms. Thus, on other occasions, Stuart wanted to know how it feels to be an earth-

Awareness of self

worm and whether it hurts the ground to have holes gouged out of it.

Stuart's comments bring us back to another important strand of self-awareness, the problem of intactness of the emerging self. The more the child becomes aware of himself as an autonomous individual distinct from his surroundings, the more he is obliged to question his own identity and the more concerned he becomes about body integrity and intactness. This concern is not an altogether new development, but it becomes particularly acute late in the preschool years. Stuart, at age five, objected strenuously when his teacher appeared without her accustomed glasses and hence incomplete or damaged or deformed. These further quotations show how a visit to the dentist, blended with anticipations of a tonsillectomy, seems to have stirred up some of Stuart's feelings about staying intact:

Once there was Stuart with a tooth and in it was a hole. So it was fixed. The man had many little streams there, very nice. There was a pain, a bright pain. It was bright when he pushed with a noise and a bar. But there was no blood. No blood. . . . Can I get a hole in my hand like the hole in my tooth? Will it have to be filled with a loud noise? . . . The queen was in the garden hanging up her clothes, there came along a big thing to snap off her nose. . . . Her nose was not. It bled and bled and she died. Humpty Dumpty did die, too. He fell off and couldn't put together again. . . . When I have my tonsils out—what will happen when I have my tonsils out? Will it bleed? Will I be dead? [*Another four-year-old, not faced with a tonsillectomy but trying to make sense of things he heard, asked, "You can't live without tonsils, can you?"*] Being blood is being dead. Why do I have my tonsils out?

I do not like myself not to be myself, and

that is what will happen if even my littlest tonsils is taken away from me.

. . . Sad it was to have a nose taken off. So it will be sad to have a tonsil out. Blood, blood, blood. When the nose—the tonsil is out (Stone, 1966).

Fears

The sense of vulnerability that accompanies growing self-awareness is often expressed in specific fears at ages four and five. A classic study by Macfarlane and associates (Macfarlane et al., 1954) shows how patterns of fearfulness change with age and how widespread fears are in the late preschool years. Just as cognitive development depends on affective involvement with the world, so does fear develop out of knowledge of one's own vulnerability and an understanding of the potential dangers inherent in the environment. Note that fears need not be realistic. It is as easy to be afraid of ghosts or witches as of cars and ocean currents; kidnappers, though real, are rare, but this does not reduce the child's fear that he will be abducted. Moreover, the specific fears that a child may have may merely express a more general sense of menace. The swaying curtains in his room may take on monstrous aspects, and unnamed terrors may lurk under beds or in closets. It is for this reason that children may need to have a light left on when they go to bed. On the school playground, a child who snarlingly declares himself to be a tiger, or who pronounces his undulating arm a snake, may provoke genuine panic in his fellows. Their fright may be tinged with skepticism, but they would rather not take a chance on finding out. Freudian writers, of course, find in the fearfulness of the late preschool years an expression of Oedipal conflicts and castration anxiety.

Among other things, the child may develop a fear of death. This fear is not rooted in an abstract knowledge that all men are mortal, and that he himself will some day grow old and die, but simply in knowing that people do die and that something could happen to him—not eventually, but now. What dying means is likely to be uncertain and variable. At first, the child whose contact with death is likely to be a matter of dead insects or a mouse or frog found in the street may simply say that death means that "you put it in the garbage." In games, death is reversible: "Bang! You're dead. O.K., now you must be alive again."

Children find it hard to grasp the blank finality of death—as do older people who, in self-pity, imagine themselves as able to witness the remorse of others when they themselves are dead. One child asked, "If you woke up one morning, and you were dead, would it hurt?" Stuart put it in these terms: "Being dead is like being blind, only *all* the time and the same feeling all over, everywhere, like blind in the eye." While the best analogy in life to death may be that of a continuing sleep, the child who is told this may become terrified of going to bed at night. Awareness of death as a threat to himself may come much later than a fear that one or both parents may die, and the child may violently resist any separation from a parent, lest it be final.

Middle-class American adults especially are inclined to shield young children from knowledge of death. This shielding is made easier by the separation of generations, so that many children never get to know their grandparents or other old people well, and so have little contact with dying. Not only do people put their elders in nursing homes or otherwise out of sight, but old people themselves collaborate by taking up residence in "retirement homes" or colonies for the aged. The general improvement in health has meant that relatively few children or young adults die any more—automobile accidents kill more people than any of the major diseases. Thus, parents may even deny the fact of death ("Grandpa's gone on a long trip"). They may try to disguise their own feelings (it is doubtful that even devout believers feel the supposed joy conveyed in "Grandpa is happy now in Heaven"). The child, however, with his acute emotional sensitivity, is not likely to be fooled. The unusual behavior of the adults, the air of mystery and exclusion, and the macabre atmosphere with which our society surrounds death will tell him that something is seriously wrong. And his piecing together of fragments of knowledge may produce fear and bewilderment far greater than he would feel in response to simple frankness about what has happened and how his parents feel about it.

The tendency to conceal death from the child rests on the same assumption of childish innocence that leads adults to try to insulate the child from other realities—sex, money, disagreements and animosities between adults, insanity, depravity, and the hard facts of power. In all of these areas, in the authors' view, children benefit from being given as much information as they can understand and manage, rather than inventions and evasions that needlessly confuse and complicate their feelings. This does not deny to parents the right to say, "I'll tell you more about it when you're older." As we have said before, parents must be able to judge the timeliness of information.

Awareness of growth and continuity

A further aspect of self-awareness is the child's growing recognition of himself as changing with the passage of time. Time is beginning to move—as we know, it slips away with ever-greater velocity as we grow older—and the child begins to sense the transitory nature of his experience; as Stuart remarked, his birthday had come and gone and there was nothing left, but he was older. It sometimes appears that the child senses fleetingly that growing older brings with it not only competence and privileges and freedom but also responsibility and loneliness, which might explain otherwise seemingly unaccountable spells of babyishness, sulking, clinging, whining, and weepiness. The penalties of growth may be made especially prominent by the birth of a sibling, but even children without siblings show a certain amount of growth ambivalence, as when they play at being baby or ask the adult to "feed me" or "dress me." The child of preschool age delights in looking at the family photograph album, most of all at pictures of himself in earlier incarnations. Similarly, he likes to be told stories of his own now-dim past. This is not to say that preschool children do not remember anything. They can vividly recall isolated events or details of events that have escaped their parents, to the point where parents can use their children as memory storage machines, capable of recalling the name of the man who bought their car or what kind of dress Mrs. Jones wore when she came to tea. But their memories are spotty and lack continuity and organization. A three-year-old boy, passing a familiar landmark, comments, "Sally Smith cried and cried," recalling an event from six months before, but he can-

not remember that the occasion was a trip to the beach. Or a three-year-old girl, seeing a sample of wallpaper with a splatter design, observed, "Egg man"; the following week when the egg man made his delivery, her parents for the first time noted that he wore a tweed coat remarkably similar in coloring to the wallpaper sample.

One way children cope with the problem of an ever-changing identity, as we have seen, is to assume a new one, to become somebody else. Our friend Stuart, for example, spent a number of months, when he was four, earnestly, doggedly, and skillfully being a particular nine-year-old boy whom he had heard of but never met. There is no evidence that he ever convinced anybody else that he was anyone but Stuart, but he nevertheless managed for a time to awe his peers with his patronizing manner and references to the school he attended, where they had real "lissons." Part of the temporal dimension of identity lies in the ability to do something now in anticipation of a future reward (Mischel and Metzner, 1962). In experimental situations in which the subject can choose between an immediate small reward and a delayed larger reward, preschool children already show ability to delay gratification. Delay of gratification, however, is much more likely to be found in middle-class children than in lower-class ones, perhaps because poor children have little reason to believe that the future will be an improvement on the present.

Preschool children know the names for all the major external parts of the body, although there are striking social class differences in this respect. Poor children are at a special disadvantage when it comes to naming joints, such as wrist and ankle, and such adornments as eyebrows and eye-lashes. The middle-class four-year-old can usually say, and the slum child usually cannot, that he smells with his nose, tastes with his tongue (or mouth), and touches with his fingers; that his eyes are to see with and his ears to hear with. The four-year-old has some vague idea of digestion but he seems not to take seriously the notion that food is transformed into feces. He is more willing to accept that the fluids he drinks are discharged as urine. As suggested earlier, he knows about the air and breathing, and about the beating of his heart. As a study by Gellert (1962) has shown, young children have little or no knowledge of their inner organs, how they are arranged, or how they function. The four-year-old may know that germs cause illness, but he doesn't know what a germ is.

It is interesting that, although the preschool child obviously is aware of himself and other people, he has a hard time keeping both kinds of awareness in mind at the same time. Asked how many people there are in his family, he may neglect, because he is counting from his own standpoint, to count himself. Asked if he has a brother, he will (assuming it is so) answer yes. Has his brother a brother? No. Is he his brother's brother? Yes. Has his brother a brother? No. The reader will not fail to notice the principle of egocentric thinking at work.

7

the
preschool
child:
two

In this chapter, we begin with cognitive functioning in the preschool years. We then go on to discuss the schools that are increasingly being provided for children of this age. Finally, we examine the whole complex issue of intellectual differences among children which become clearly visible during the preschool years.

The Preschool Child's Thinking and Perceiving

In this section, we shall try to deal systematically with how the world exists for the preschool child and how he thinks about it—in other words, with his **cognitive,** functioning. In older, classical psychology, functioning was partitioned into the three areas of **cognition** (knowing, including perceiving and thinking), **affection** (feeling and emotion, including attitudes and values), and **conation** ("will," or, as we would now express it, motivation). We now realize that these areas are far from distinct. The way a person cognizes the world necessarily includes his motivational states and his attitudes and feelings toward the things cognized. Feelings are closely implicated with drives and motives, and are always directed toward cognized objects of some sort. Perception, learning, and feelings are essentials in the development and arousal of motives.

It follows, then, that the topics we have already discussed, such as play patterns, the mastery of materials, and self-awareness, can also be seen as aspects of cognitive functioning. In fact, our discussion in this chapter has an implied aim of showing how cognition may be the basis for integrating all of behavior and experience, that emotion and motivation can be seen as components in the way the individual cognizes objects and situations, including the self as object, and symbolic or imaginary situations. Notice that cognition was for many years an outlaw topic in American behavioristic psychology (see the highly derogatory treatment by Verplanck [1957]). Even the study of learning, which one would think has something to do with knowing, was in large part dedicated to showing that learning did not require cognition, that learning was a supremely noncognitive process. In recent years, thanks in part to the belated discovery of the work of Jean Piaget, Heinz Werner, and their collaborators, cognition is once more respectable.

Let us note that our emphasis, in the discussion that follows, will be on shortcomings in the preschool child's cognizing, not with the idea of holding him up to ridicule but to make graphic both how far he has come and how far he still has to go. Furthermore, those who have to deal practically with preschool children should appreciate how the child's still-primitive grasp of reality may make communication difficult, and how necessary it is to take account of situations as the child views them.

Mastery of language

Cognitive development is closely bound up with progress in the mastery of language and symbols, bearing in mind that language as it is handed down to the child may liberate his thinking but may also constrict it by embalming experience in stale formulas and cliches, by providing false or nonexistent conceptual entities and explanations, by shunting certain interesting topics like sex and death off into the realm of euphemism or the unspeakable, and by deceiving him into thinking he has understood something just because he has labeled it and catalogued it. At its best, though, language can free the child's thinking by providing him with useful forms and operations.

Here we must pick our way into the contentious area of social class and subcultural differences in language. We mentioned earlier (p. 217) Bernstein's and Hess's distinction between restricted and elaborated codes. Hess and Shipman (1965) introduced the idea of asking mothers to teach something specific, like how to operate a gadget, or the rules of a game, or how the child should cope with his first day at school, to her own child. Her instructions were then analyzed in terms of linguistic style. Some experts have objected that such designations imply that children growing up in disadvantageous circumstances are learning a debased, fragmentary version of English, whereas in fact they are learning a distinct dialect. Bee (1969) has proposed that the difference between middle-class and lower-class mothers in the way they talk to their children is not a linguistic difference but a difference in teaching strategies. Lower-class mothers, by contrast with middle-class ones, are less willing to let the child make mistakes and perhaps learn from such mistakes, they are overspecific in the help they give the child, and they are less encouraging. Brophy (1970) draws a distinction between what he calls **proactive** teaching strategies, associated with the middle class, in which mothers try to point out in advance the nature of the task and how to go about solving it, and **reactive** strategies,

associated with the lower class, in which mothers give little advance instruction, reacting instead to what the child does as he goes along. It might be pointed out in passing that the Hess tasks were not culture-free, and the mothers (and children) might have performed differently with tasks closer to their own lives. Cazden (1970) points out, following Labov (1969), that lower-class children may seem linguistically deficient when talking about a subject remote from their own experience but become remarkably proficient when talking about their own personal doings. Hidden in this debate is a fundamental issue of values, whether the dominant middle class has any right to impose its culture on those members of society who are born into a different culture. Members of the middle class are ethnocentrically inclined to forget that the practical situation of the lower class necessarily gives it a very different perspective from the middle class on welfare workers, policemen, landlords, earning a living, and the host of social institutions which preserve the way of life of the well-to-do. It is obvious that poor people have a right to their own perspective, but it is doubtful that many want so badly to pass along a familiar life style that they are willing on that account to let their children stay trapped in poverty. It seems to us that the dilemma can be solved only as we devise a new culture that transcends anything we now have. A more advanced, more humane culture will call for some new approaches to education, about which we shall have more to say.

The first steps in learning language have been accomplished by the early preschool years, and the three-year-old who comes from a reasonably stimulating background is a fluent talker. We have to remember, though, that language learning is a lifelong process, and can never be said to be complete. We keep on learning new words, and we learn more about the scope and limits and the shadings and complexities of meaning of the words we already know. We learn to read, and to read at higher levels of sophistication as we learn about metaphor and imagery and allusion and reading between the lines. We learn to read skeptically and critically, carrying on a running debate with the author. We learn to talk about painting and poetry and politics, and we learn the special vocabularies, syntaxes, and logics of such fields as mathematics, chemistry, and economics. Much of our school learning is by necessity vicarious, through words that tell us about long-gone events, distant places, the adventures of fictional people, and forces lying beyond direct perception. Even operations that seem wordless, as when we make or look at pictures, or shape raw materials into a meaningful pattern, or react emotionally, are conditioned by language.

The quotations we gave in the last chapter illustrate the ways in which the preschool child's mastery of language is less than perfect. Some linguistic weaknesses persist well into the school years, not to mention the errors (and crudities) that schoolchildren teach each other. Phonetically, the speech of many preschool children shows residues of baby talk. Sounds and syllables are likely to get misplaced, as in *aminal, hangerburg,* and *pisghetti.* On the semantic side, the English-speaking three-year-old may still have trouble with pronouns and their shifting relativism. Even four-year-olds may mix up *he* and *she,* not because of any failure to distinguish the sexes but because they forget which pronoun goes with which sex. *We* may be learned as the first person

plural but in addition function as a collective designation for the parents, who so often speak to the child in this form. Like the earlier difficulty with *you* and *I,* this one arises out of a too-direct reflection of what the child hears. Thus, "Are we going out tonight?" is likely to mean "Are you and Daddy going out tonight?"

Designations of time gradually become more precise, and by age four or five many middle-class American children know the days of the week, the seasons of the year, and some of the key holidays that fall in different seasons. Clock time ordinarily eludes the preschool child except for a few hours that mark turning points in the day's activities. One boy, age three years and four months, translated his mother's statement that she was going out for a short while, only a couple of hours, into "Mommy's going out for a couple of whiles." Some especially verbal children may be able, by age five, to define words, particularly concrete nouns and usually in terms of action qualities: *car*—"You ride in it"; *banana*—"You eat it." Some five-year-olds can specify, at a primitive level, the defining attributes of a class of objects: an orange and a peach are alike "because they're both juicy"; a suit and a dress are alike "because they keep you warm." Even earlier, children can specify how two things are different, as in "Doggie bark, kitty meow." Needless to say, the child's ability to specify differences and similarities is far from absolute and depends on the nature of the contrast or resemblance—he may even have trouble with such a seemingly obvious difference as that between bread and cake.

EQUIVALENCES AND CONTRASTS OF MEANING. Some writers use terms like *abstraction, generalization,* and *concept* to describe the way people take note of similarities and differences among things. We prefer to reserve such terms for some precise technical applications and to speak instead, following Klüver (1936), of **equivalences**; it seems enough in speaking of the behavior of preschool children to say that they react to the members of certain classes of things as roughly equivalent, and are increasingly able to put into words the salient features of objects, actions, and relationships. Note that many equivalences appear without language, as when the male stickleback fish accepts a rounded block of wood as equivalent to a female, whereas others are wholly dependent on language, as when we say that coal and a muscle are both sources of energy. In fact, it appears from classical conditioning and other studies that human and infrahuman subjects "assume" equivalence until experience teaches them otherwise. The child's equivalences may surprise the adult. One toddler, having heard the label *windmill* given to a large, shingled, grain-grinding windmill, went on to apply it to a rambling, shingled house, a water-storage tank, a television antenna, and a small, skeletal, water-pump windmill.

As we have said, children from an early age accurately differentiate the sexes, but on the basis of hairdo and clothing rather than anatomy (we do not know what effect today's unisex styles are having on the preschool child's perception of sex differences). Even a five-year-old, looking at a photograph of a naked girl with a boyish hairdo, may identify it as a boy. In the era when boys' hair was worn short, many children, unbeknownst to their parents, took it for granted that Christopher Robin was a girl. We have the account of a four-year-old girl reporting that a new family had moved in across the way, and that the newcomers had a baby. Asked whether the baby was a boy or a girl, she replied, "I don't know. It's so hard to tell at that age, especially with their clothes off."

Sometimes the preschool child compensates for his linguistic deficiencies by stretching known terms to fit new situations—we have seen this at work in the use of *strong* and *heavy* (see p. 222)—or by inventing new terms. A three-year-old girl hoped that the new baby would be "a boy-girl. You know, a girl with a penis." Children may invent antonyms to describe a contrast: "It has an upper part and a downer part"; "They're sure not slow-pokes, they're fastpokes!"; "Sometimes nobody eats with me, and sometimes lots-of-bodies." Having spotted a berry and then being unable to find it again, a four-year-old remarks that he "must have undiscovered it." For some preschool children the very reasonable opposite of *O.K.* is *Nokay.* Observe that such drawing of contrasts comes well in advance of being able to learn to supply antonyms on demand, which typically appears at age seven but is found in bright children at age five or six (Kreezer and Dallenbach, 1929; Robinowitz, 1956). A precocious boy, not quite four, observed a Jules Feiffer cartoon consisting of a series of profiles of the face only and accompanying text and asked "What does this say?" Before his parents could reply he gave his own answer, "It says, 'If there aren't any heads, make them as good as you can,'" and then took a pencil and filled in the missing parts of the profiles. It appears that this obscure-sounding utterance was meant to say two things: "Those drawings look like the exercises in my older sister's schoolbooks," and "The task is to complete the drawings."

Preschool children come up with such inventions as the assertion of good behavior, "I am so being hāve" (we are reminded of a notice on a gate: "Be ware of dog"). In general, the verb *to be* has a dual existence for many preschool children, a duality formalized in some languages, including Spanish and the Scandinavian tongues. When describing an action, the child says, "He bēs quiet"; but to describe a state or attribute, he says, "He is sad." Some inventions are downright poetic: "Rounder is wider than longer"; "You don't look like you are"; one little girl liked to "secret around in the night"; held up in traffic, a boy complained to his mother, "Look at that old truck busying up the street so we can't get through." Sometimes the emotional meanings of a term dominate the strict semantic ones; for instance, one child climaxed a torrent of spluttering invectives with ". . . you—you—you wrong number!" In spite of the metaphorical quality of these formulations, children of this age cannot grasp metaphors and other figures of speech, just as they miss irony and sarcasm (although they can certainly detect emotional tones of voice and expressions of feigned emotion). Analogies, however, may occur to the child, as when a four-year-old watching a cow being milked commented, "It's like a water pistol," or when a three-year-old girl, watching her mother hold some garment against Father's body to see if it was the right size, asked, "Is Daddy a paper doll?" Children, like adults, can get trapped in their own analogies. A Russian child asks, "Mommy, the nettle bites me?" The mother replies, "Well, in a way . . ." and the child continues, "Then why doesn't it bark, too?" (Chukovsky, 1963). Alice, age four and a half, produced this joyous combination of words and sounds, worthy of Lewis Carroll himself:

"There's nothing true about that so don't be so glee." "I'm not full of glue, I'm just appearing to." Thumbly, thumbly, glantering damously. Clitter clatter, sing the clitter clatter and the violins some time over. . . . Sing the songs of meener, with the doors of the clitter and the marches too in the dark of the pleasantly opter.

Late in the preschool years, one finds the beginnings of philosophical wisdom, as when a four-and-a-half-year-old observes, "It doesn't matter, just the way it doesn't matter which sock your foot goes into."

DESCRIPTION, NARRATION, AND MEMORIZATION. Preschool children's description and narratives are rambling, loose-jointed, and circumstantial; they include endless detail, relevant or not—although they may omit key information—so that it takes a nicely attuned listener to disentangle the central theme and direction of what the child says. Beginning late in the preschool years and continuing well into the school years, we find accounts of movies or television dramas consisting of fragments linked by the all-purpose connective " 'n' then." The sequence of the narrative may correspond hardly at all with the actual sequence of events.

Young children memorize things in wholesale bunches and not in a systematic, organized way. Understanding is by no means necessary to memorization, as illustrated by the well-known hymn "Gladly the cross-eyed bear," the refrain of "Three chairs for the red, white, and blue," and the Pledge of Allegiance: ". . . to the Republic of Richard Stands . . . one naked individual. . . ." (For the benefit of readers outside the United States, the original reads "to the Republic for which it [the flag] stands" and "one nation indivisible.") Preschool children learn yard after yard of nursery rhymes, fairy tales, and advertising jingles, but they cannot paraphase or summarize their undifferentiated knowledge. They can only recite it, and if they are interrupted in the middle of a recitation, they may find it impossible to resume where they left off, and so be obliged to go back and start all over again.

Perception

To move from language to perception, we get clues to the child's perceptual experience from his explicit verbalizations, from his concrete behavior with objects in the course of the day's occupations, and from his behavior in specially contrived test situations. The child gives voice to such discoveries as that distant objects look smaller than near ones, as shown by his ability to mask a person at a distance with his finger, or that his fears about being sucked down the bathtub drain are groundless because he is too big to fit. A five-year-old girl asks of a stained-glass window brightly lighted from behind by the setting sun, "Would it burn you if you touched it?"

We know further that some "obvious" properties of matter are by no means obvious to the preschool child. Both everyday observation and formal experiments make it clear that young children cannot reliably predict whether a cube of wood or iron will float or sink when placed in water. Once they have discovered empirically which will do which, the explanations they invoke may be wildly irrelevant, such as that things sink or float because they are dull or shiny. Nor does the child anticipate that

to put an object in a full glass of water will cause an overflow. One of the best everyday indicators of the child's perceptual development is his progress in drawing, not only of people but of cars, houses, trees, and animals. His ability or inability to solve jigsaw puzzles and the way he uses blocks to build structures also give us information about how the child perceives.

Now let us look at some formal approaches to the study of **perceptual development**. Inhelder (1953) has shown that if a young child is asked to draw a line representing the water surface in an outline drawing of a beaker, he draws it parallel to the bottom of the beaker, no matter whether the beaker is upright or tilted. Standard sensory illusions, such as the Muller-Lyer illusion, have been studied in children of various ages. The evidence from such studies with young children has been conflicting, partly, we suspect, because the magnitude judgments required are too fine or perhaps even meaningless to children of preschool age. However, Robinson (1964) found that preschool children of high intelligence show the size-weight illusion (the size of an object influences our judgment of how heavy it is) and showed that two-year-olds could be taught to make weight discriminations which abolished the illusion. O'Reilly and Steger (1970), by contrast, concluded that children younger than six could not make stable weight comparisons. Stevenson and McBee (1958) have found that preschool children make form discriminations more easily if the forms are solid cutouts than if they are simply printed on paper (rats do better with three-dimensional shapes, too [Kay and Oldfield-Box, 1965]). It should be remembered that although two-year-olds can learn the names of abstract geometric forms, it is not until age three or later that they can match complex cutout forms to the spaces in a form board. And even when they clearly match form to hole, they may have trouble orienting the form so that it will go into the space. Experiments by Ghent (1961) and by Wohlwill and Wiener (1964) have shown that four-year-olds are sensitive to the up-down orientation of abstract forms and show consistent preferences for one particular orientation of such forms. Furthermore, the preferred orientation for many forms is reversed between ages four and eight, with the change beginning around age six, perhaps, since some of the shapes used resemble letters of the alphabet, in association with learning to read. Cairns and Steward (1970) report a sharp decline in reversals of letters after age four, especially in children who knew the names of the letters and had a well-defined knowledge of left and right. Gibson and her associates (Gibson, 1970) have found that most four- and five-year-olds from favored backgrounds can distinguish cursive script from scriptlike scribbles, and block letters from letterlike nonsense shapes.

The authors have made some observations on perception in three-year-olds with a view to testing the relevance of the Gestalt laws of perceptual organization, which describe the conditions under which objects and groups of objects cohere perceptually (the so-called **autochthonous laws**). The Gestalt psychologists assume, for example, that the chromatic kinship between adjacent hues on the solar spectrum, such as yellow and orange or orange and red, is innately given, so that the child would be expected to group colors spontaneously in the order of the spectrum (red-orange-yellow-green-blue-purple or its

reverse). Three-year-olds do not, and neither, surprisingly enough, do many educated adults. Another perceptual task is to trace a looping line. Most three-year-olds do not follow the line across its intersections with itself but change direction and detour around the loop. Given the task of completing a geometric figure, such as a square or triangle, with a corner missing, children up to five do not supply a corner but instead draw a single line joining the ends of the break. If one substitutes pictorial equivalents for the abstract forms, the results are the same. Given the task of coloring a cross composed of one oblong overlapping another, some three-year-olds disregard the lines that separate the oblongs and color the cross as a single mass. Those who do see the division apparently do not see the partially masked oblong as continuing out of sight behind the uninterrupted one, since they are as likely as not to color the two exposed ends different hues, as though they were unrelated shapes. These observations conflict with conclusions reached by Bower (1969), who claims that many Gestalt laws operate in early infancy.

We still do not know as much as we should about the genesis of the child's perception of pictures. Since pictures are a major medium of communication and education in our society, it is important as well as interesting to know what aspects of pictures the child responds to and how he makes sense out of them. We know that picture recognition begins in late infancy, and that toddlers recognize pictures of things and of particular people, and gross pictured emotions such as happiness and sadness. We have not been able to find out whether toddlers recognize real things, such as animals in the zoo, on the basis of having previously seen pictures of them. Toddlers can recognize pictures of familiar objects, like a horse or a particular make of car, taken from an unfamiliar angle, such as looking down from above. A study by Hunton (1955) indicates that children may at first be indifferent to the inversion of pictures. Awareness of inversion may come in two stages: at first, the child may not see it as an upside-down picture of an upright object, but as an upright picture of an upside-down object.

We do not know very much about developing awareness of pictured actions, relationships among people and things, and overall themes and meanings. We do not know enough about perception of size and distance in pictures, although Wohlwill (1962) has shown that children's awareness of size and distance in pictures can more easily be changed by varying the amount of information contained in the picture than can adults'. And still to be explored in the child's perception of pictures are the effects of color versus black and white, natural color versus arbitrary color, photographs versus drawings, line drawings versus chiaroscuro, naturalistic versus stylized, and so forth along all the possible dimensions of depiction.

An issue that has not been settled is whether there is a regular developmental pattern in children's preference for form or color in making perceptual matches. The standard procedure (Brian and Goodenough, 1929) is to show the child a pair of stimuli alike in shape and color and to ask him to choose a third stimulus for the set from two others, one matching the pair in shape but not color, and the other matching it in color but not shape. It appears from a study by Gaines (1970) that children of a given age may respond either to color or form, and that training in color discrimination or shape discrimination reverses some children's original preference.

Elkind and Weiss (1967), using arrays of pictured objects which children are asked to name, showed that there is an age change from the preschool years to school age in the scanning patterns of children. Young preschool children dart unsystematically from picture to picture however they are arranged, older preschool children follow the structure of pictures arranged in rows or in a triangle, and first-grade children use a consistent left-to-right scanning strategy. Kugelmass and Lieblich (1970) found a tendency in Israeli children learning to read Hebrew, which goes from right to left, to use a right-left scanning pattern, although this disappeared at later ages.

Weir (1964) has found a complex development of probability learning between ages three and a half and eighteen. The reader will recall (p. 187) that when confronted with two levers that deliver rewards on different percentages of presses, the way to maximize rewards is by sticking with the lever that delivers the greater percentage of payoffs. On a lever that paid off 66 percent of the time, 70 percent of three-year-olds maximized, 66 percent of five-year-olds, 20 to 25 percent of children ages seven to fourteen, and 50 percent of eighteen-year-olds. We suspect that this is one more instance in which older or brighter subjects reject obvious solutions and go looking for nonexistent complexities.

As we said earlier, there is continuing debate about whether the closely related operations of conservation, seriation, and reversibility can be taught to preschool children, or whether preschool children who have been taught conservation have

The preschool child's thinking and perceiving

301

really learned. We remain skeptical of research in this area, pointing out only that some children as young as three show seemingly sound conservation, and that the interesting research question is to find out what kinds of experience makes them so different from their age-mates. We should also point out that conservation of volume is by no means perfect in adults—two six-ounce (186-g.) containers, like a frozen fruit juice can and a wasp-waisted soda bottle, may look widely different to the adult observer.

Shantz and Watson (1971) have confirmed observations on spatial egocentrism made some years ago by Piaget and his associates. The child (between ages three and a half and six and a half in Shantz and Watson's sample) is shown a model of a landscape and asked to indicate, by choosing from an array of photographs, what the landscape would look like from vantage points other than his own. Preschool children do very badly on this task. Shantz and Watson found some relationship between success at this task and the ability to remember a spatial layout after the child himself has changed location, and also with the ability to recognize that the layout had been surreptitiously altered.

*Social and subcultural
differences in cognition*

Responses on a number of cognitive tasks tell us both about preschool children in general and about social class and subcultural differences. For instance, there are again significant differences in favor of middle-class children, as compared to "culturally deprived" children, on the task of completing a geometric figure with a piece

missing, mentioned earlier. In addition, it appeared that some deprived children could not recognize the pictures.

Some other tasks on which middle-class four-year-olds perform significantly better than deprived children are: knowing color names, both in the passive sense of responding correctly to requests such as "Show me the *red* block" and in the active sense of being able to answer "What color is this block?" or "What color is the sky?"; copying geometric forms and block capital letters; drawing a picture of a person; "running" paper-and-pencil mazes; naming body parts; knowing sensory functions; selecting the odd member from a set of three or five things, and verbalizing the nature of the oddity. Our investigations (Church, 1969) suggest that deprived and middle-class four-year-olds do about equally well when it comes to knowing the left and right sides of the body (only a few in each group made the distinction), dealing with such spatial terms as near and far, top and bottom, and on and under, and knowing relative size terms. Schmidt and Nzimande (1970), using the color-form preference test, show that color is overwhelmingly dominant for Zulu children, but those Zulus who go to Western-style schools eventually show a shift to form preference. Hansley and Busse (1969) report that lower-class American Negro children lag well behind middle-class whites in the development of mature scanning strategies.

Potentially useful techniques for studying age changes and cultural differences in cognition include jigsaw puzzles of appropriate levels of difficulty; describing pictured situations; and Guilford's Unusual Uses Test, mentioned earlier. It is clear that established intelligence tests offer a skimpy array of materials which do not take account of our growing knowledge of the child's perceptual and cognitive range. We shall return to this point later in the chapter.

The concrete basis of abstract thinking

Most formal measures of cognitive functioning ask the child to detach himself from the personal, the emotional, and the pragmatically relevant, and to turn his attention to the abstract, logical, formal, analytical properties of things. Most of his life, however, is rooted and enacted in terms of personal relations, particularly family ones, and human behavior is the concrete prototype of all his understanding. Thus, when the child is given a formal classification test consisting of blocks that offer a number of abstract principles for grouping—color, shape, size—he may ignore all these and instead base his arrangement on the intimate, concrete scheme of his own existence and group the blocks into families, large ones being the "father" and "mother" and smaller ones the "babies." Here the child relies on the attribute of size, but size tied to emotionally important human relations. Nor should it be supposed that the child has any intellectual understanding of family organization. We have already said that he takes it for granted—equivalences again—when he visits a strange household that all the people assembled under one roof constitute a family. A four-year-old who meets his teacher's husband is likely to ask, "Mr. Jones, are you Mrs. Jones's daddy?" and the next moment, with no sense of paradox, "Mrs. Jones, are you Mr. Jones's mommy?" A mere adult cannot really know, of course, whether the child is using *mommy* and *daddy* in the conventional sense or whether, lacking the words *husband* and *wife*, he is trying to ask something like "Are you the daddy in the family in which Mrs. Jones is the mommy?" Less ambiguous is the indignant retort of a five-year-old to the assertion that people in the same family cannot marry: "They can, too! My mommy married my daddy!"—though this involves the problem of time perspective and the virtually unimaginable time when mommy and daddy did not even know one another. (A further complication here, of course, is the possible Oedipal theme implied in many children's expressed intentions of growing up to marry the parent of the opposite sex.)

Children wrestle hard to understand the relationships implied in *grandfather, grandmother, uncle, aunt, cousin,* not to mention relatives-by-marriage, at least partly because they find it so difficult to realize that their own parents were once children. We must remember too that even the people the child knows well may not have a constant identity for him in changing circumstances. We have the case, all too poignantly familiar to nursery-school teachers, of a child's failing, until prompted, to recognize his teacher one weekend when he met her on the street; the following Monday, after some deep and puzzled thought, he approached her and asked, "What's your name with your hat on?" This is only one instance of a general phenomenon known to adults: we may fail to recognize the corner storekeeper or policeman when we see him away from his familiar setting and wearing an unaccustomed costume.

Older preschool children are somewhat better able to detach their thinking from personal and affective considerations and to deal with the objective properties of things. In a classification test of the kind just mentioned, the five-year-old can sort blocks on the basis of such attributes as size, color, and shape—although he may not be able to make explicit what he is doing—but he cannot use these attributes consistently and systematically. Thus, he may produce groupings of the kind called a **cluster**, in which one key block serves as the point of reference, the other blocks being related to it in terms of some point of resemblance, but without any regard for how they may be related to each other. For example, if the key block, A, is a large red triangle, then block B may be attached to it on the basis of triangularity, C on the basis of redness, and D because it is big.

Another kind of grouping intermediate between the family and the formal is the **chain**, in which each successive block is related to the one that went before, but without regard to the overall organization. Thus, B goes with A because they are both squares, C with B because they are both blue, D with C because they are both small, and so forth. As we have said, the available research findings are ambiguous about whether the child will prefer form or color or size as a basis on which to pair stimuli, and about age changes in such preferences. The ambiguity may be produced by group differences, individual differences, intra-individual differences, differences among test stimuli, and differences in instructions. Only research which controls all these sources of variance—and perhaps others— can answer this question. Our findings with respect to the ability to select the odd block from a set of three, tested with middle-class three- and four-year-olds and deprived four-year-olds, suggest that color is an easier basis of discrimination than size

or shape, but this is by no means conclusive. Inhelder and Piaget (1964) report that their subjects rarely attempted any sort of classification before age five, instead using the blocks to make designs ("graphic collections"); the first attempts at classification used shifting criteria, like the chain arrangements mentioned above.

Causation

We have already touched briefly on some central areas of cognitive organization, such as time, space, and causation. It is now appropriate to look at each of these more closely. We have pointed out that young children do not inquire closely into causation, but seem to accept cause and effect as given—obviously, children may be angered or amused by departures from expectation. The child asks about motives— for what reason?—but not about processes —by what means did this come to pass? To turn on a television set and watch the screen light up into a segment of life complete with sound effects, to hold a piece of ice in one's hand and watch it melt, to trust a knife to the support of a magnetic holder, to follow the budding of a flower, these are not effects in the realm of physics or biochemistry but simply how things are.

According to Piaget, the child's first perception of causal relations is **animistic**: things are seen to move, act, and react in terms of their own built-in thoughts, feelings, purposes, volition, moral judgment, and power of spontaneous movement and change. It seems clear, from the love and care that the child can shower on dolls or stuffed animals, the worry or compassion he can feel for a broken plaything, and the anger he can show toward some inanimate thing that will not do his bidding, that the child often perceives things animistically.

A number of anthropologists have questioned whether animism is a universal of childhood or whether it appears in Western societies as a result of adult tutelage. It seems clear that we do much to make animism explicit, whereas in other societies animism as such remains at the implicit level of the dynamism we spoke of earlier (p. 96). Older children and even college students (Dennis, 1953) often are willing to say that they think of things like fire or the moon as being alive. Every society we know of has a mystique of certain inanimate things like fire, the moon, the sea, the wind, and nature in general. Thus, it is less important to know whether animism as such is a universal than to understand the dynamism and magicalism resident in universal human experience. The child's animism—in our society—is unstable: he shifts back and forth between an affect-charged animistic orientation and a materialistic and pragmatic one, just as he does with respect to reality and fantasy. A doll may at one moment be an animate, sentient participant in his play, only to be indifferently tossed aside, lifeless and inert, a moment later. Stuart conveys something of the animistic outlook when he speaks of "discouraged songs" and "tired songs" and "happy houses," when he asks what it feels like to be a stick of wood, whether it hurts the ground to have holes dug in it, and when he tells how the hands of his clock move in response to changes in his activities. Looft and Charles (1969) tried to combat animistic thinking in seven- to nine-year-olds by showing them a movie explaining the biological concept of life. The technique worked well for some subjects, while others were unaffected, and some merely became more confused.

According to Piaget, animism is succeeded in the child's perceiving and thinking by **artificialism**, the assumption that all events are to be explained by the action of some humanlike agent or entity or force which wills things to happen in fulfillment of some purpose of its own. Thus, the child's early causal questions—the animistic attitude does not lead to questions—are likely to ask about personal agents and motives or reasons: "Who did it?" "For what reason?" "Why that way?" For example, a child seeing the ground blanketed with pine needles asked, "Why did they put these here?" making quite clear the assumption of a conscious, purposive agency. Chukovsky (1963) cites a child who wants to know, "Why do they put a pit in every cherry? We have to throw the pit away anyway." In general, as we have said, children perceive purpose and meaning in everything and find it hard to view occurrences in terms of accident, coincidence, or the action of material, impersonal forces. But let us note that Western adult society does little to convey a naturalistic view of the world to the child. Some parents and nursery schools introduce the child to scientific ideas, but most of what we explicitly or implicitly tell the child is couched in the language of dynamism, artificialism, and moralism.

If **dynamism** is the basic mode of perception, so that we naively experience space and the objects that occupy it as held together and activated by a nameless general energy, we can understand how perceptual development consists of the progressive differentiation of objects, attributes, and relationships, and their integrative schematization according to various principles which may or may not be articulated and which may or may not correspond to the realities. The role of language in perceptual development then becomes that of a device which focuses attention on this or that aspect of the world, differentiating it and integrating differentiated features. It is the dynamistic substructure of perception that allows the child to accept the world's marvels without surprise or wonder or any seeking for detailed, systematic explanations. De Vries (1969) did a study in which she disguised a cat with dog and rabbit masks; three-year-olds accepted the seeming transformation as real, while older children were skeptical but frightened. Chukovsky (1963) gives a couple of quotations which illustrate the young child's acceptance of the possibility of magical metamorphoses: "Daddy, when you were little, were you a boy or a girl?"; another child, trying to feed cabbage to chickens and having been told that chickens do not eat cabbage, explained, "I'm giving it to them so that they may save it for after they become rabbits." It may be dynamism that makes us mistake contiguity for causation: a boy struck a utility pole with a stick at the exact moment of a power failure, and was thoroughly and guiltily convinced that he had blacked out the city. Many scientific principles are simply articulated and quantified dynamisms. We can sum up the action of gravity in a formula, we can state Newton's laws of motion, we can describe the release of nuclear energy, the replication of a DNA molecule, phosphorescence, and so forth, but the exact causes of these events elude us. This may be why, of course, people find mechanistic explanations appealing, since the pushes and pulls and frictions of mechanical systems are so easy to comprehend.

The Belgian psychologist Michotte (1946) has constructed an apparatus for studying the perception of causality. Two squares of different colors are set in motion relative to each other (the "squares" are in fact the exposed portions of solid lines traced on a revolving disk), and by varying the temporal relations between the movement of the squares, one can produce the impression that one square is acting on the other in various ways. One can produce such effects as **launching**, where one square sets the other in motion the way a golf club does a ball; **triggering**, where one square seems to release a power of autonomous motion in the other, as though it had tripped a switch; and **carrying**, as though one square were pulling or pushing the other, so that one square seems to be moving actively and the other passively.

To the best of our knowledge, Michotte's techniques have never been used with preschool children, but Olum (1956) has used them to study causal perception in seven-year-olds and finds two main effects never reported by adults. She describes these as **mutual approach**, where the stationary member of the pair is seen as moving to meet the other, and **passing**, where the moving square is seen as going behind or in front of the stationary one, even though such a passing never in fact takes place. It would be interesting to take such observations down to still earlier ages, although we can foresee some difficulties in getting younger children to make intelligible reports. In the same area, we might mention in passing Heider and Simmel's (1944) film of "apparent behavior," which shows geometric shapes in motion in a way that conveys almost inescapably an impression of purposes, attitudes, and emotions. Again, as far as we know, no one has yet studied young children's reactions to this film.

The preschool child is still in transition toward the more systematically organized world of adulthood. A predominantly dynamistic outlook permits the creation of the phantoms and hobgoblins that befuddle serious, rational thinking about human affairs and social problems, and so must be outgrown. It is obvious, though, that adults never fully grow out of the magical world of childhood. The authors like to think that this is as it should be. Most of our verbal play requires that we be able to straddle the worlds of magic and reality, as the child is beginning to do when he deliberately toys with the idea of growing up in reverse, starting as an adult and becoming a baby, and even when he collaborates in the prefabricated fantasies of an animated cartoon. For the adult, music and art and literature and love, and even science and mathematics, have no meaning without magic. Without magic, we are cut off from our roots in universal human experience and wander forever homeless.

Time

Time is a dimension in cause and effect, but more generally it provides one of the frameworks within which we orient and organize and coordinate our lives. We regulate our behavior according to clocks and calendars and schedules, we remember and anticipate and plan. But we also have a **personal time** which is only partially correlated with formal time schemes, as when time drags or flies, when we feel relaxed or under pressure, or when we feel that we are losing time, wasting time, saving time, or using time wisely. Personal time is closely related to our sense of our own mortality, and we have already mentioned how having a sense of a goal or direction

is an intimate part of our self-awareness. In our experience of personal time, we dream of time machines, fountains of youth, getting a fresh start, perpetual-motion machines (solar batteries and radioactivity-powered machines give us a fair approximation), and eternal bliss or damnation in an afterlife. We try to capture time in such images as Old Father Time, the Grim Reaper, and relentlessly flowing rivers.

We must remember that our familiar ways of partitioning and ordering the passage of time, no matter how logically self-evident they seem to us, are not the only possible ones. The Balinese, for instance, have, or had a few years ago, ". . . a complex cyclical system of days, grouped into concurrent weeks. . . . And of these weeks they have a complete series from a two-day week to a ten-day week" (Bateson and Mead, 1942). Unless a Balinese knows where he stands with respect to all these weeks at any given moment, he feels badly disoriented, just as we do when we suddenly discover that today is actually Thursday, whereas we have been acting as though it were Friday. Unlike us, the Balinese have little regard for keeping track of elapsed time. They know precisely when, in terms of their several calendars, a child's birthday falls, but they are not likely to know, or care, exactly how old he is. (Needless to say, they know what general age period a child is in, that it is time he was weaned, or that it is no longer appropriate to carry him, or that he is old enough to run with the other children, or that he is about ready for the transition to adulthood, but these are not tied to particular chronological ages.)

There are pronounced cultural differences in the value assigned to time. In our highly scheduled society, punctuality and regularity are esteemed. In other societies, though, an appointment is kept only if the parties thereto are so inclined, work patterns are casual and impulsive, and the spirit of leave-it-to-the-morrow prevails. As E. T. Hall (1959) has pointed out, attitudes to time may reflect status relationships, as in who is allowed to keep whom waiting, and for how long. Obviously, in such settings, children's time concepts and the role of these in their thinking will be different from those found in our society. Even when non-European peoples adopt the European time scheme, they are likely to modify it in unexpected ways. For instance, we have a calendar from India in which the horizontal rows consist not of weeks but of fortnights, and it requires a conceptual wrench to be able to use such an arrangement. We must also note that our system of seasons assumes the changes that take place in the earth's temperate zones, whereas in the tropics or the frigid regions people may get along very well with no seasons or only two. The tenacity of cultural time orientations is illustrated by the Australians, who celebrate Christmas in the full heat of the summer with a traditional heavy meal of goose or turkey. Even well-educated people may have a conception of historical time in which eras and events and personalities are hopelessly jumbled, in which Napoleon may trade remarks with Charlemagne on the eve of the Battle of Hastings.

The young child, who has no knowledge of history, whose clearly remembered past can be measured in hours, and whose future is a vague abstraction he has to accept on the word of adults, may understandably have some difficulty coming to terms with the formal time schemes of his society. Even when he has learned some key words, these may not yet have their conventional meanings. One four-year-old insisted, for instance, "It is not today! My mommy said it was Monday!" An understanding of the sequence yesterday-today-tomorrow may be delayed until the school years, although we know of one preschool child who announced to her dumfounded parents, "Today is yesterday's tomorrow." Most four-year-olds, as we see in their play patterns, are very much creatures of the moment, whereas by age five, many children can engage in planned projects extending over many days.

As we said in connection with the child's self-awareness, many preschool children are entranced to learn of their own unremembered past and beg their parents to tell them about "when I was little." Let us point out that, in our view, past eras in one's own development are lost to memory not because they are repressed, but because they are assimilated and submerged in new organizations of knowledge of one's self and world, such that we become new versions of ourselves capable of recapturing former modes of being only in special circumstances—dreams, hypnosis, or in response to associative cues, whether the taste or odor of some bygone substance (witness Marcel Proust), an old photograph or letter, a visit to the haunts of our childhood, or the rediscovery of a once-cherished plaything (witness the powerful film *Citizen Kane*). Which is one reason people write and read books about child psychology.

Children, as we have said, have a hard time conceiving of their parents' ever having been little, and seem to entertain two quite paradoxical notions about their parents' past. On the one hand, the parental past seems to reach into prehistory, as implied in the often-heard request, "Tell me how it was in the olden days," as though the parents had known dragons and giants. On the other hand, children find it hard to accept that the world was ever essentially different from the way it is now, and listen incredulously when a parent says that he or she remembers the introduction of the jet airplane, commercial television, transistor radios, and the picture window, or, to go a little further back, zippers, cellophane, and commercial radio. A statement by one four-year-old suggests that he planned to grow up backward in time so as to join those who were already mature: "Pretty soon this will be the olden days and I'll be a man." Numerous children, as we have said, expect to catch up with their parents and marry them. Chukovsky (1963) quotes a child who asks, "Mother, who was born first, you or I?"

The preschool child is far more aware of his own growth than of changes in adults, if only because parents celebrate the child's alterations in size and competence, while trying their best to ignore or conceal their own changes. Just as his parents' lives stretch endlessly into the past, so do they promise to extend changelessly into the future, even though the child may know, but without much conviction, that his parents will someday be *very* old. It follows, then, that catching up is possible. Disillusionment on this score came to Stuart as early as age five, and we are fortunate to have a record of the very moment when he first realized that time is the same for everybody:

It would be funny if I was big and you were little. I wouldn't pay any attention to you and I'd make you do things you didn't like to. [*Here Stuart is playing a favorite game of the preschool years, reversing the roles of child and adult, and, in the process, giving us yet one more glimpse of how grownups may appear to preschool children.*] But I guess I won't ever be able to do that to you 'cause I won't ever be able to catch up to you. I won't ever be able to be the same as you at the same time.

Closely tied in with the child's awareness of time in relation to growth and change is, of course, his awareness of his own and his parents' mortality, again perhaps tempered by a sense of immortality.

Space

Our civilization's ways of organizing space —at least on a terrestrial scale—are quite simple, even though some people have trouble with geometry or road maps. For large segments of territory, we use compass bearings and coordinates of latitude and longitude—bearing in mind that the impossibility of mapping a spherical surface on a flat plane, together with habits of thought left over from the days when surface travel was the norm, may leave us with outmoded forms of spatial thinking: it is difficult for many people to grasp that the shortest route east or west may in actuality be north or south, over the poles. For shorter distances, we are used to dealing in routes, the particular pathways, cues, and landmarks ("Bear left at the broken-down stone church"), and the behavior involved in getting from one place to another. In dealing with concretely perceived space (as contrasted with space that unreels a bit at a time as we navigate through it), we have a vocabulary of adjectives (high, low, outer, inner), adverbs (here, there, where), and prepositions (on, under, around, behind). Such indicators are tied to the pull

Terrace

▲

FIGURE 1. A five-year-old's spontaneous map of the house in which he had lived a year and four months; on the right is the actual floor plan of the house. Both drawings are somewhat simplified; the child's original drawing includes the location of furniture.

of the earth, to the polarities of our bodies, and relations among things and locations. Some spatial relations, like up-down, are fixed (until we take off into interplanetary travel), while others, after the manner of first- and second-person pronouns, may be tied to the standpoint of the observer—if two people are facing each other, what is left for one person is right for the other, and what is in front of one person may be behind the other.

Simple and obvious though these notions seem, other societies may organize space quite differently and assign different values to spatial relations. The Balinese is as strictly oriented to space as to time, and cannot act without knowing how he is facing with respect to the cardinal directions

and such key reference points as temple and graveyard and, within the home, kitchen and latrine. To sleep, one must align oneself just so. In Bali, as in most island cultures, a key organizing principle is the dimension of inland-seaward. Around the periphery of the island, directions refer to settlements or distinctive terrain features, so that the reference points change as one moves. The Eskimo child of eastern Canada, who lives in a world of ever-changing landmarks, learns to navigate over long distances seemingly on the basis of a few stable terrain features and also on the basis of wind directions and temperatures, and perhaps even qualities of humidity and the smells characteristic of particular regions (Carpenter et al., 1959). Needless to say, non-European cultures provide versions quite different from our own of what the earth as a whole is like.

We have already seen how, in infancy and toddlerhood, spatial relations are linked to the baby's own actions and migrations, with only a beginning notion of how things and places are related to each other. The preschool child develops a considerable vocabulary of concrete spatial relations, but he moves slowly away from an orientation in what we call **action-space** toward a more organized **map-space**. Maier (1936) performed a classical experiment in which children learned all the particular routes within a swastika-shaped maze and then were tested for their grasp of the layout of the maze as a whole. It was not until the late preschool years or early school years that children formed an inclusive "map" of the maze. We can see the contrast between the child's practical command of space and his knowledge of spatial relations at about age five when he spontaneously or on request tries to draw maps of familiar areas such as his own house. Figure 1 is a map by a five-year-old, together with the actual floor plan, of a house in which he had lived just over a year. Dart and Pradhan (1967) use mapping ability as an indicator of readiness to learn scientific ways of thinking. Mapmaking is very difficult even for adolescents in non-Western cultures. One would judge that they are too concretely tied to action-space to be able to picture the complex relations involved in mapping.

Beyond map-space lies **abstract-space** of the kind involved in geometries of two and more dimensions. Such notions are completely closed to the preschool child, and for the most part to the school-age child, but it is interesting that many adults are perfectly able to deal with abstruse geometries without ever having mastered the rudiments of map-space. All of us know people who are "space blind," who get lost whenever they depart from familiar pathways and who find it almost impossible to find their way to a new location alone, even with the help of elaborate and specific directions. We find it curious that such people need not be handicapped in their dealings with abstract-space.

In general, then, preschool children are largely tied to action-space, with a beginning awareness of map-space. Even so, they may be able to grasp the notion of the world as round, as shown in this quotation from Stuart, at age four and a half, trying to disentangle a temporal idea which he has understood as spatial (note that the vocabularies of space and time overlap, as in *before*, *after*, and, in the present instance, *end*):

Miss Williams, what is the end of the world? . . . I don't see how it is a *place*, because my mommy says the world is round, and so there could not be any end where the world stops, or where you could fall off. It goes around, and then when you get to where you start, it goes round again.

As Stuart himself added, the problem again boils down partly to making sense of adult vocabularies: "I wish the grownups would say the same thing so I could know."

In this section, we have been talking about three-dimensional space, the space in which material beings exist and move and exert causal action. Earlier, in talking about perceptual organization, we touched upon problems in two-dimensional space, perceiving meanings and relations in designs traced on a flat surface. Note that the experimental psychology of perception has dealt almost exclusively with the perception of two-dimensional arrays, as though such perception were basic. In fact, however, it is three-dimensional perception which is fundamental, with the ability to comprehend two-dimensional patterns coming later, and sometimes not at all. A study by Hochberg and Brooks (1962), using a single subject who was not exposed to pictures for the first two years of life, sought to demonstrate that pictorial perception was as "natural" as the perception of voluminous space. Unfortunately—from a scientific standpoint, not the individual's child's—there seems to have been no attempt to shield the child from all the other two-dimensional patterns that are commonly found in middle-class settings—wallpaper, fabrics, book covers, and so forth.

The behavior of disadvantaged children seems to suggest that they find little meaning in two-dimensional patterns, such as pictures. It is not that the children cannot see such patterns, but that they fail to perceive the message they contain. It is our belief, subject to further empirical study, that it requires practice to see the meanings and the spatial relations in two-dimensional representations and designs. This is not an abstract theoretical argument, but one that has serious implications for understanding the effects of deprivation and what one has to do to counteract such effects.

Notice, too, that ideas of size and quantity can be viewed as special cases of spatial extent and organization, whereas ordinal numbers—first, second, last—can refer to temporal organization, spatial organization, or simultaneously both, as when children line up in the order in which they will have a turn at pinning the tail on the donkey, or when turns in a table game are dictated by the clockwise spatial disposition of the players. But measurement, expressing size and weight and duration and velocity in terms of conventional standards, is beyond the preschool child. The child says that something is very

heavy or very light, or that something is going very fast, but pounds and miles per hour—and dollars and cents—are not part of his cognitive repertory.

A School for the Preschool Child

The idea of providing for the daytime care of children too old to be treated as babies but too young to be admitted to regular schools had diverse origins. Many of the first preschools and day care centers were inspired by considerations of social welfare, to take poor children out of the slums and off the streets, to shelter them, warm them, feed them, and keep them constructively occupied. Maria Montessori, who founded a whole movement in education, wanted to go further and salvage the intellectual abilities of poor children. Ironically enough, in the United States, until the last few years it was primarily a few children of affluent parents who were taught by the Montessori method. American nursery schools have by and large developed in a different tradition, and have grown independently of the more formally organized, less child-development-oriented public-school kindergarten movement. However, there are indications of change in the kindergartens, and in the grades as well, and the nursery-school tradition may be having an influence.

More recently, preschool education has been given a major thrust by the Head Start program, with its so-called children's

Not all children attend a preschool. ▶

Ken Heyman

Henry Monroe, DPI

Ken Heyman

centers, and the day care movement, both of which we include as preschools. In spite of some scattered educational successes, the Head Start program has tended to suffer because of conflicting goals and approaches, inadequate planning, insufficient and erratic funding, and ill-prepared teachers; Head Start's main achievements have been as a community enterprise and health center (Kirschner Associates, 1970). As a knowing observer like James Hymes (personal communication) pointed out at the outset of Head Start, in his concern over inadequately prepared teachers, the program threatened to "give poor children poor schools." "Evaluations" of Head Start have erred in lumping together both effective and ineffective programs and discussing the resulting "averages." What is needed, rather, is an analysis of what works and what does not, discriminating between routine programs and those of high quality. Thus, the spate of unimpressive or even negative findings (see Westinghouse Learning Corporation, 1969; Hellmuth, 1970), viewed in the context of a few consistently stunning successes, seem beside the point. In criticizing Head Start, we are not joining those who, in Edward Zigler's (Rowan, 1970) phrase, are "crucifying the children of this country on the cross of IQ," as a later section will make evident. We earlier voiced some skepticism about day care on a mammoth scale, and we favor great caution lest some of the mistakes of Head Start be repeated.

In the past, preschools on the nursery-school model have taken on a variety of shapes. Some, more or less in the naturalistic tradition of Jean Jacques Rousseau, have viewed themselves as vehicles of social reform, whereby children's natural virtue was to be let flower uncorrupted by the values of adult culture. In urban set-

tings and in a context of small, nuclear families, many educators have seen in the preschool a chance to give the child access to space, time, and things offered in an earlier day in rural life and the extended family. Other preschools seem to have existed mainly to provide a pool of subjects for psychological research. Many preschools have functioned largely as baby-sitting services or parking lots so that mothers would be free to work or to spend their time otherwise than in child care. In general, facilities for preschool children have catered either to the poor or the well-to-do (in small numbers in either case), but rarely both together. The parent-cooperative nursery school represented an attempt to make the benefits of preschool available to the middle classes. In the big cities and in prosperous suburbs, certain nursery schools are seen as training grounds for the better colleges, and competition to get one's child enrolled is as keen as for admission to the more prestigeful institutions of higher learning.

In recent years, for both rich and poor children, the preschool has often become a place for early coaching in intellectual skills in preparation for the formal schooling to follow. It is our opinion that much of the intellectual force-feeding and pressure to early reading that goes on in certain nursery schools today is irrelevant, poorly managed, and potentially a menace to sound intellectual development. We particularly deplore the attitude that the child has to be prepared to enter conventional schools. No amount of intellectual cultivation in the best preschool can stand up to the deadening effects of the usual public school. At the same time, these new rigidities have their counterparts in traditional ways of thinking about preschool children. All too often, preschool educators, in the interest of protecting children against forcing, may underestimate the intellectual capabilities of a young child and block him from learning things within his capacities but outside the accustomed province of the preschool. The resistance of some preschool educators is epitomized in the cry that one can never—or must never—teach a four-year-old to read, ignoring the ones who do read. Such teaching, it is sometimes seriously claimed, may wreck the child's nervous system, or turn him into a bookworm who neglects social participation and physical exercise, or, *horribile dictu,* destroy the traditional curriculum of the early school grades, as though these represent the organically right sort of education for all children. Such views are founded on the assumption of biologically fixed and universal timetables for the maturation of learning abilities, an assumption which is at best very fragile, and leads to the equally untenable view that everyone who has not learned to read by the age of seven is some sort of lost soul. Moreover, it seems to overlook the distinction between forcing formal learning and permitting and encouraging genuine curiosity and discovery.

We take the stand that preschools should concern themselves with all aspects of development, including intellectual development, fostering but not forcing and with full sensitivity to each child's interests and status. We further believe that, for most preschool children, formal learning should proceed from the child's concrete transactions with people, other living creatures, things, and materials, and should be taught as occasions offer rather than as organized group "lessons." At the same time, a good teacher can make sure that some occasions for learning come to pass, by sound planning, shrewd choice of materials and activities, and alertness to the child's reactions. Ordinarily, we think of preschools in terms of the way they serve the educational needs of children, but a good preschool also maintains close liaison with parents and can serve as a valuable source of parental education—and parental education of teachers. It is often possible, too, for parents to participate directly in the classroom work of the school.

Let us try to straighten out a current terminological confusion. When one speaks about "new" or "innovative" trends in grade-school education, the image is of a liberalized approach akin to the authors' version of an ideal nursery school; "traditional," by contrast, refers to teacher-dominated, stay-in-your-seat and do-as-you're-told classrooms. This distinction seems to have been reversed when applied to preschool education. The kind of preschool we shall be talking about is nowadays described, pejoratively by some, as "traditional." What is called "modern" or "innovative" in preschool education are classes dominated by teachers, routines, drill, group recitation, and clearly defined lessons, much like the "traditional" grade schools.

The kind of preschool we shall be talking about should be understood as an ideal —an ideal sometimes but not often enough approximated in actual schools. It is our point that, unless one has the resources and ingenuity and determination to work toward an ideal, preschool education is not likely to be of any special benefit to the child.

The raw materials of a preschool

We will not linger over the need for a preschool to have a sound, safe building

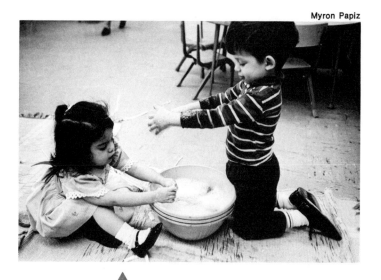

Myron Papiz

Natural raw materials like water, mud, and sand are vital elements in preschool experience.

Nancy Rudolph

with furnishings and equipment scaled to the children's size and proportions—adults visiting a nursery school for the first time may have the sensation of entering a Lilliputian universe where everything, including washbasins and toilets, is in miniature —with areas set aside for domestic play, for music, for water play, for painting, for tabletop activities, for block-building, for carpentry, and so forth; and to have protected play yards with a proper complement of swings, slides, jungle gyms and other climbing apparatus, pits to dig in, wagons, tricycles, large hollow blocks, boxes, and all the rest. Sometimes indoor space for climbing, jumping, and tumbling can also be provided. All these facilities and materials are important, but their importance lies in their contribution to the school's more general educational functions of meeting children's needs and providing scope for emotional, social, and cognitive development. (We should also point out that when children move out of the family and into the larger world of school, whether at age two or age seven, they encounter a whole array of unaccustomed bacteria and viruses, and the more vulnerable may have bouts of sickness, although in the long run, they develop solid immunities.)

First on our list of basic ingredients come the **human qualities** of teachers and age-mates as the child works his way into a broader pattern of social relations. It seems to us desirable to mix children and teachers of diverse cultural, ethnic, and economic backgrounds, so that they can learn from each other about the varieties of the human condition. It also seems desirable to include, as the opportunity presents itself, some proportion of handicapped children—those with motor difficulties or with sensory disabilities like impaired vision and hearing—for their own sake and for the sake of the physically normal children who may thus learn early to accept the handicapped as fellow human beings. There is evidence, as from a study by Chesler (1965), that the handicapped constitute a minority group against which the majority is prejudiced. However, lack of prejudice is not an automatic consequence of early exposure; careful explanations are needed, and active intermixing of the children to help the normal child overcome any spontaneous distaste and also any vulnerabilities that get stirred up by the sight of abnormalities. Obviously, children with major impairments need extra care and attention, and a school should be staffed accordingly.

Second come **space** and **time**, free space and free time to move about in freely, but also articulated space and time to provide a stable yet variable framework which gives the child a sense of order and organization.

Third come **learning materials**: play equipment, blocks, plastic materials (paint, water, clay, dough, lumber, cooking ingredients, and so forth, and all the tools, utensils, and instruments that go with them); props and dolls and figurines for dramatic play, especially on domestic themes, and clothes and accessories for dressing up; a wide array of books and pictures and charts; Montessori-like "educational" playthings such as puzzles, picture lotto, mosaic design kits, and science materials like magnets and dry-cell batteries; musical equipment ranging from percussion blocks through melodic instruments like xylophones, autoharps, and pianos, to record players and records; pet animals (birds and fowl, fish, frogs, guinea pigs, rabbits, tur-

tles, and, in season, tadpoles); the foods and beverages served at lunch and snack time (too often, in our preoccupation with vision, hearing, touch, and kinesthetic experience, we neglect the cultivation of taste and smell); and the resources of the actual community—visits to farms, ranches, factories, stores, firehouses, railroad stations and airports, docks, fish hatcheries, woods, brooks, and lakes.

Fourth and finally, and involved in all that we have been saying, is language, the formulation and elaboration of experience in words and numbers which become a part of the child's working equipment for understanding and ordering events and in logical and imaginative thinking. In programs for deprived children, the emphasis on symbolic formulations has to loom proportionately larger than in programs for children from rich verbal environments. Two sharply contrasting approaches to linguistic enrichment can be found in the work of Minuchin and Biber (1967), who favor an elaboration of traditional nursery-school practices, and that of Bereiter and Engelmann (1966) who put great emphasis on drill and recitation in the correct forms. We find much to respect in the work of Blank and Solomon (1968, 1969), who, in individual tutoring sessions, encourage the child to give voice to his thoughts and feelings. Two recent surveys (Cazden, no date; Parker et al., no date) give some idea of the numerous and diverse efforts going on in the area of linguistic and cognitive education for young poor children.

The resources of the preschool are not used singly or haphazardly, but are woven into a curriculum. But before we go on to discuss their organized patterning, let us look more closely at their individual importance. In its use of free time and space, the preschool gives children an all too rare scope to wander and explore, to follow their own thoughts through, whether in conversation or alone, to be aware and to be made aware of changing vistas and the changing lights of days and seasons, to watch events unfold and to follow them from origin to conclusion. Needless to say, freedom of space in a preschool should always be freedom within limits: the yards have to be stoutly fenced, gates and doors and windows must have child-proof latches, stairways must be protected, there should be things to climb but they cannot be sky-high—although they may well seem so to a three-foot (90+ cm.) child. Too free a space, apart from exposing children to physical dangers, leaves them disoriented and anxious. Outdoors, space is structured by fences and gates, by walkways and trees and grass and dirt, by the contours of the ground, by the fixed play equipment, and by equipment sheds and playhouses. Indoors, the spatial organization of shelves, partitions, equipment, and furniture sets up fascinating mazes whose mysteries the children can unravel and wonder at. Spatial arrangements define areas for particular kinds of activities. In buildings not excessively "modern," there are corners to which a child can retire and feel snugly alone. Systematic and stable arrangements of space invite children to discover for themselves the many polarizations of space into up and down, forward and sideways and backward, over and under and around, and so on. By structuring time into dependable but unhurried schedules and routines, the preschool gives a sense of recurrences and stability and predictability.

The preschool tries to treat space and time as a city does—or should—treat its parks, leaving some areas in their wild state, trimming and formalizing others, and clearing or paving still other areas for specified purposes such as bridle trails, athletic fields, and playgrounds. However, there is one fault with our analogy. When one paves a tennis court, it is lost to nature. But when a preschool sets up a schedule, it can do so provisionally and revocably. A flexible preschool can sets its schedule aside to capitalize on a mood or an idea, to take advantage of a snowfall or a large patch of ice, to witness a special event; in short, a good program leaves room for surprises and improvisation and spontaneity.

The human resources of the preschool, as we have said, include both the teachers and the other children. A good preschool needs teachers in great plenty, for it is to them that the child must shift some of his family attachment before he can form relations with his peers. The teacher, however, is not a substitute parent—save for occasional crises—nor is he or she (we would like to see broken the stereotype of preschool teaching as an exclusively female function) simply a warder. The preschool teacher has a special relationship with the children. He or she must be an involved participant, and not an aloof bystander on the lookout for crises. Dealing with children so young, the teacher must be prepared to give affection freely, but without infantilizing the child or intruding on him. The good teacher is attuned to the preschool child's vacillation between assertive maturity and clinging babyishness, and can respond in ways that seem suited to this child at this moment. The teacher has to perform such maternal functions as helping the child with his clothes, eating, toileting (and toilet accidents), and naps. The teacher has to protect the child from aggression by other children, from impersonal dangers, and sometimes, from his own impulses. The preschool child's passions, as we said earlier, can become violent, so violent indeed as to frighten even himself; when his passions threaten to run rampant, the teacher has to intervene to comfort or soothe or restrain, to help the child understand and control the forces that rage with him. The teacher has to be clearly in charge. A weak and vacillating teacher invites disruptions that test the limits of authority. A harsh and scolding teacher destroys the atmosphere of creative exploration. Punitive discipline, at home or in school, breeds fear, hostility, and potential violence. Effective control calls for self-confident teachers, who are firm but relaxed, strong but warm, compassionate and gentle and encouraging even while setting well-defined limits, at all times working toward eventual self-control (Galambos, 1969, 1970). Perhaps above all, the teacher is a source of ideas, knowledge, hypotheses, and comment, and a model for curiosity and compassion. What is called free play in the preschool is in fact play guided by the teacher, materials, and other children, in ways that contribute to growth.

The experience of cooperative nursery schools, college laboratory schools, and the best of the Head Start groups has shown that aides and students and volunteers, under the supervision of well-trained teachers, can extend and enrich a program. One reason for the success of some Head Start centers, even when staff and facilities have been less than ideal, appears to be the assignment of a teacher, a paid aide, and a volunteer to each group of fifteen children. In our experience, the chief problem in the indoctrination of untrained assistants has been to help them overcome fear that the children will get out of control, and learn not to react moralistically and punitively to the children's childish ways.

The other children of his own age give the preschooler an introduction to social adaptation. Preschools in general have tended to group children in narrow age bands, a practice which has some virtues. It means that older children do not have to be stopped from picking on younger ones, or younger children protected from older ones. With children at his own level in size and strength, the child can safely fight out minor battles. He can try out his feelings and ideas on people who think the way he does. Among his peers, he can learn to cooperate and to share—not only material things but sympathies, antipathies, fears, interests, enthusiasms, and thoughts as well.

But, as we have said, a preschool with a mixed population teaches the child simultaneously that humankind is all one while being infinitely diverse. Thus, one can also make a case for more experimentation with grouping together children over the whole range of the preschool years, or beyond, family style, so that the older children can share their knowledge and know-how with the younger ones, and can themselves benefit by taking a protective and helping role with the little ones. (There is some reason to believe that children in certain institutions benefit from such groupings.) It is possible, of course, to combine groupings of both sorts, segregating the ages for some kinds of activities, such as outdoor play, where older and younger children need quite different equipment, and mixing them for others, such as (some) story-telling, singing, and meals.

A school for the preschool child

Marlis Muller

Hanna Schreiber, Rapho Guillumette

Raimondo Borea

Michael Carlebach, DPI

The learning materials of the preschool can be infinitely varied. Books provide the children with vicarious emotional experience, with ideas, with experience in the possibilities of language, factual information, and opportunity to exercise creative imagination. Stories read aloud to a group provide a fine occasion for shared feelings, for getting to know each other as well as what is in the story. The skilled teacher reads so as to allow children to respond and question, to look at the pictures and chime in. With three-year-olds, reading groups should be small when possible, as few as two or three children; with four- and five-year-olds, larger groups are possible. Here we note an irony: the literature available to preschool children has been so superior in content, style, and quality of illustrations and design to what, until recently at least, children were likely to encounter in standard school textbooks, that for children who have been to a good nursery school entering the grades in schools which tend to limit the child's reading to those texts is an intellectual and esthetic step backward.

Listening to music, making music (however crudely), moving to music, and singing together are an essential part of preschool life. Plastic materials such as paints and clay and specially mixed and colored dough—and sticks and stones, and dirt, mud, sand, and snow—have a double importance. At first, the child likes to explore and manipulate them for their sensory qualities alone, without any thought of making anything with them. Later, he learns to shape and combine and

Music in the preschool.

Preludes to reading.

decorate them to give solid external expression to his thoughts and feelings and perceptions.

The domestic play corner, with its dolls, toy furnishings and kitchenware, and a rack of men's and women's clothes for dressing up, provides the settings and materials for many of the ever-recurring themes of dramatic play. Domestic play can be given a realistic turn by letting the children take part, at their various levels of competence, in cooking projects. The youngest children can shell peas and squeeze oranges with a fair amount of adult help and supervision. Slightly older children can make fruit gelatin and puddings. Still older children can try their hands at scrambled eggs, meat balls, fruit salads, cookies, and perhaps even birthday cupcakes. (We should make it clear that the nursery-school teacher has an obligation at least to go through the motions of sampling the results of the children's cooking; while it would be less than humane on some occasions to expect her to eat them, and she may resort to a promise to save them for home, usually such simple enterprises produce distinctly edible products.)

As themes drawn from the outside world begin to emerge in dramatic play, blocks and boxes and formal toys such as trucks and bulldozers, rubber animals and people, and real, functioning stethoscopes take on increasing importance as props. Animals kept in the school invite observation and curiosity; they may supply a lesson in procreation and animal maternity, if not paternity, as in the laying and hatching of eggs, or the litters of guinea pigs, and in growth and development, with chicks and tadpoles as subjects; and they can be used to teach gentleness and compassion. The use of animals seems especially important in en-

Preschool children undertake quite ambitious cooking projects.

Nancy Rudolph

richment programs for disadvantaged children: urban poor children seem to know animals only as vermin or as something to be feared, and to help them come to terms with a parakeet or white laboratory rat or hamster seems to give the children a whole new set of emotions. In this matter, of course, the educators of nursery-school teachers may have to battle some deeply ingrained prejudices, since a great many citified people feel that any animal other than a dog, cat, horse, or cow is a loathsome object and find it unthinkable that anyone could pick up a horned toad or pet mouse, never mind a beetle, earthworm, or garter snake.

For a preschool in a rural or semirural setting the natural surroundings, manicured or left wild, provide spaces to traverse, things to climb and swing from, and places to run and hide and look. In addition, the leaves that fall from the trees in autumn, the squirrels busily gathering nuts and seeds, the rabbits and pheasants that leave tracks in the snow, the sap rising in the trees, and the woodchuck emerging from sleep in the spring, all are the stuff of a first venture into natural science. In spring, the children can plant their own flower and vegetable seeds and watch them grow. (Readers from very different climes will have to rework these passages.) Even in city schools, glimpses of nature are available in parks, and field trips to farms and open country can often be arranged. What city schools lack in raw nature can be compensated for by rich materials available for social sciences. If the country child can see food being grown and harvested, the city child can see it being marketed. Older preschoolers can also visit the gas station down the street, the museums of art and history and natural history, the

Suzanne West

At all ages, male adult models are important.

▲

Learning activities in the preschool.

garbage trucks, even the dynamos humming in the local power station. They can observe snow plows and pavement mending and seasonal changes of uniforms and store windows.

Running through all the child's encounters with the living and inert materials of the preschool is the flow of words. The teacher, as interpreter, is telling the child about things, supplying names for events and objects, answering his questions and stimulating him to ask more, and the child is taking in and digesting information, asking questions, and trying out his own formulations and hypotheses. This calls for a model of teacher behavior very different from the folded-arms bystander who merely oversees or referees. Out of the child's observations, his movements through space, his successes and failures

in trying to make things happen, and out of the flow of human communication, factual and whimsical, speculative, imaginative, systematic, emotional, he begins to form ever more integrated conceptions of what reality as a whole is and how it works, and of ways of thinking about it and acting on it symbolically and concretely. The teacher's phrasing of reality is of considerable importance, both in terms of the information (and sometimes, alas, misinformation) she conveys and in terms of the attitudes and values she expresses, including prejudices and assumptions which she may not realize she holds.

Curriculum in the preschool

The resources we have discussed are not merely made available to the child to use at odd moments, as the impulse takes him, and neither are they flung wholesale at the

The preschool child: two

Donna J. Harris, The Merrill-Palmer Institute

child with the expectation that he will pay full attention and take in and retain everything. The use of materials is planned and scheduled in keeping with the children's receptiveness and interest and maturity, in ways that provide variety both from day to day and within a given day, and in ways that promise to link separate experiences and make them part of a meaningful whole. We have to remember, in thinking about the organization of a preschool curriculum, that the child may be bursting with physical energy at one moment and with ideas the next, that he now feels sociable and now craves solitude. In general, a plan of activities tries to balance listening with talking, action with contemplation, application with relaxation, regulation with freedom, and boisterous with quiet play, and must be flexibly responsive to the situation and state of the children.

The preschool's curriculum is built around its routines, the stable sequences, known to the child and dependable, that punctuate the daily cycle: outdoor time, juice time, music time, bathroom time, story time, lunchtime, bathroom time, nap time, bathroom time, free play time (to paint, build with blocks, play with water, and so forth). Except for the times set aside for such biological necessities as eating, elimination, and rest, the pattern of activities can vary.

Let us say, though, that we are of several minds about how long a preschool day can or should be. Through age four, if the child has a functioning home to go home to, we favor a morning program, dismissing children right after lunch. We see lunch (which is an expensive option) as an integral part of a preschool curriculum, both for the sake of educating taste and smell and because it is often a time of easy sociability when ideas flow freely and experiences can be compared. For children on substandard diets at home, of course, breakfast and lunch can be important nutritionally as well. However, the school day may have to be lengthened for children of working mothers and for children from unfavorable home environments. The essential thing is that a long school day not be allowed to deteriorate into a daylong dreary custodial operation or one in which the children become surfeited with too many planned and organized activities, or—particularly in northern winters—a mere holding operation as the shades of night start closing in.

We also have to remember that good preschool teaching is grueling work, and too long a day will take its toll on teachers, who may have family responsibilities of their own and who certainly have to have time to attend to administrative chores. In a college or university setting, preschool teachers are often teachers of college stu-

A school for the preschool child

325

dents, too, and the preschool schedule has to allow time for teachers to meet with students. Our ideal of preschool education seems to work best when parents can be involved, as welcome visitors or as participants, and time must be provided for parent conferences and for the writing of meaningful reports for parents and for the record. In general, then, the younger the child and the longer the school day, the more complicated life becomes, the more elaborate the provisions which have to be made to make such complications bearable, and the larger the available staff must be.

It is important for all education to be individualized. It seems particularly important in the preschool for teachers to be able to take account of individual needs or shifts of mood, to respond to individual queries or insights at the crucial moment, and for the child to know the benefits of sustained communication with an adult who takes him seriously. There are several ways in which a stable curriculum can be adapted to meet the individual needs of children. Sometimes it is a good idea to divide the group among several activities. A teacher or student teacher or aide may take small groups on excursions: a walk, a visit to the school kitchen or boiler room, an outing to watch a construction project or to see the tree-trimmers at work. Seldom, of course, are all the children in a preschool class doing the same thing at the same time. Even when some whole-group activity, such as musical games, is in progress, some stalwart individualists may continue with a block-building project, or ask a teacher to read a story, or blow soap bubbles in the washroom, or even sit on the sidelines, thumb in mouth.

Obviously, if nonparticipation seems to be too much the rule for a given child—

because of pervasive homesickness, because he lacks interest in his fellows, or is afraid of them, or is an outcast—ways must be found to draw him into contact with the others. Operant conditioning methods, long used unlabeled by skillful teachers, have proved useful for this purpose, a favored adult "reinforcing," via expressions of affection and approval, any moves the child makes toward involvement with his peers. In most cases, once the child has begun making contact, peer relations prove to be intrinsically satisfying and adult reinforcement is no longer necessary. Sometimes it is a matter of deliberately forming small groups, including the solitary child, to read or to carry on a particular enterprise, on the grounds that it may be easier for him to form one-to-one attachments before venturing into the group as a whole, and that it may be easier for the other children to be friendly when the competition is reduced and in the context of a special and enjoyable project. This, too, is part of the curriculum.

Holidays, birthdays, or perhaps only an unusually festive spirit may call for a departure from routines. With the youngest preschool children, a minimum of planning and anticipation is possible. By age five, however, children can embark on long-range undertakings that may supersede the regular schedule. The Christmas party (now often combined with Hannukah celebrations, sometimes to the dismay of both Christian and Jewish purists), a puppet show, a play based on a favorite story are among the possible enterprises. Older children may initiate a sustained play proj-

Preschool activities.

ect such as the building of a block city or, outdoors, a playhouse or network of canals. It is a good idea, when feasible, to let children pursue such inventions to a logical conclusion, even if it means encumbering a playroom floor area with semipermanent block structures or carving up a section of the playground with gaping trenches. A certain amount of mess and clutter is inevitable in a lively program. Field trips are also likely to interrupt routines. Such outings may be suggested by a story or by one child's experiences, or it may simply occur to the teacher that a particular trip would be especially relevant at this juncture. Field trips are valuable because they give substance to things the child may know about only verbally. Then, in discussions after the trip, the child is stimulated to further verbal elaborations. From such discussions may come ideas for still other field trips.

For all this flexibility, however, the basic framework of routines has to be there. It is both educational and reassuring to preschool children, who need stabilizing landmarks to which they can orient themselves. Amidst the round of activities and projects, children need relatively static periods of digestion, recapitulation, repose, and just plain enjoyment. The varied curriculum should be seen as an introductory survey of the universe, and not as a collection of lesson units that the child is supposed to retain. The value of the curriculum lies in the delight of knowing—if only for a fleeting while—that such things exist; it is in the raising of questions that the child can ask his teachers, his parents, and himself; it is in the orientation to learning and knowing and understanding as one of life's great satisfactions.

Premature demands that specific learning be retained may spoil the delight and ad-venture of learning. This does not mean that one never reminds a preschool child of something he has known and forgotten, or never encourages him to apply past learning to the solution of present problems, though with no implication or tone of voice of chiding. It does mean that one understands the value of preschool experience in the child's own terms, and in the perspective of all the long years it will take him to arrive at a mature grasp of the world he lives in. As Bruner (1960) has pointed out, we can not only settle for half-learnings and half-comprehensions but value them, secure that the child will cover the same ground time after time, each time at a more sophisticated level of understanding and expertness.

A teacher for the preschool child

What we have said so far implies that the preschool teacher—certainly the head teacher for each group—needs extraordinary personal and professional qualifications. It is our conviction that if we could put our very best teachers into the preschool and early grades, learning could be made functionally autonomous (that is, self-motivating and self-sustaining) so that later schooling could be organized around the library and the laboratories and the discussion table, instead of being the dreary, regimented, syllabus-bound thing it has so largely become, even at the college and increasingly at the graduate level. Pending Utopia, let us talk about what we can hope for in the teacher of preschool children. Since it is almost impossible to arrive at any objective weighting of virtues, the order in which we discuss them does not reflect an order of priority.

It is certainly important that a teacher—at whatever level—like children. As a human being, she (we yield, for the time being, to the facts of contemporary life) will not like all children equally, but she will not let the children become too aware of the fact. As in any occupation, one works best when one's job brings pleasure, and the surest way to enjoy teaching is to enjoy watching children in action. But enjoyment and effectiveness in teaching, as in parenthood, are vastly enhanced when liking for children is coupled with a thorough and differentiated understanding of how they operate. Again, though, as in parenthood, understanding does not mean that the adult relinquishes adulthood to become once more a child. It is important to be able to share the child's wonder and confusions and grief, but from a secure standpoint in adulthood where one can help the child straighten out and manage his feelings; to enjoy his growth and his discoveries and even some of his mistakes.

Teachers have to understand the special ways of children if communication between adult and child is to take place. But teachers also need a great fund of information about things in general. Furthermore, it should be information that they have made their own, and not merely facts and formulas parroted from textbooks. If the teacher is going to deal with the cosmic questions her pupils raise in a wide-open preschool curriculum—about God, Santa Claus, death, and life—she must be prepared in advance. Apart from metaphysics, she will have to cope clearly and honestly with such issues as where Mommy has gone and when she will return, why people are different colors, what is a cocoon, what makes lightning, what is a fever, what happens when you flush the toilet, tell me about when I was a baby, can I look under your dress, and a host of others impossible to predict but vital to anticipate. The teacher not only conveys knowledge, but with it orientations to knowledge, that learning is exciting, or that grownups are stupid, or that the world is full of fascinating mysteries, or that curiosity is dangerous and the child had better learn to keep his ideas and questions to himself. The teacher needs to be an alert observer, but a participant observer who can interpret and clarify the child's intellectual and emotional experiences, and who capitalizes on the fortuitous occasions for learning which arise.

Middle-class teachers trained in middle-class institutions have to develop special sensitivities in working with disadvantaged children, for whom the preschool and the teacher are alien and sometimes threatening. Such teachers have to learn not to overwhelm the child, to be receptive and let the child do some of the approaching, to be aware of dialect and cultural differences and possible misunderstandings. As we have said, special efforts may be needed to overcome the young child's already deeply ingrained fears, suspicions, and expectations of exclusion. At least initially, the poor child's chief problem may be excessive passivity, inability to reach out and speak out.

It is evident that the teacher needs more than intellectual qualifications. She needs physical stamina. Keeping pace with a pack of preschool children can be strenuous work, especially at those moments when they decide to scatter in all directions at top speed. Like athletes, many preschool teachers burn out early (or, as in other fields, find that the accretion of years does not bring a corresponding growth in in-

come) and move on into administration, library work, or teaching the less mercurial children in the older grades. The teacher must be prepared, as we have said, to suppress her fears and revulsions when children hand her their beloved pet frogs, snakes, or other fauna, or pieces of them. She must be more or less shockproof, but this implies neither moral neutrality nor lack of emotion. She will have occasion to become angry, but in an adult fashion. She will inevitably be moved to delight and also to occasional laughter, but a sympathetic laughter that children can share, not a derisive or contemptuous laughter that humiliates. She will have her irritable days and her depressed days, but without imposing her moods on the children or expecting them to be especially sympathetic or considerate. Unlike a mother, the preschool teacher as a general rule has to subordinate her feelings and needs to the children's. Even while a preschool is helping its pupils mature, it remains more child-centered than any home could healthily be.

It would seem, in sum, that the central qualification of a preschool teacher is maturity, but a special form of maturity responsive to childhood and its magic. The preschool teacher can react appropriately to both sides of the growth ambivalence expressed by Stuart:

Being big is the best, best thing, isn't it? . . . But sometimes I wish I didn't have to grow big. NOW! That's why you must take care of me and we will pretend I'm a little baby and have a long time to wait till I grow big.

The varied roles of the preschool teacher.

As early education spreads, under government auspices, as in Head Start, Home Start, and day care, our concept of it has to expand. Not only do we need specially trained teachers, but we have to recognize that the needs of poor children and their families are not exclusively psychological and pedagogical. Early-childhood centers have to be able to provide medical and dental services, social work, advice on practical problems, and often a significant part of the child's diet. Above all, as recent history tells us, they have to be responsive to the wishes and desires and ideas of the communities they serve.

Intelligence, Intelligence Tests, Intellectual Differences, and Intellectual Development

Now, when the child has moved out of the natural environment of the family into the seminatural habitat of the preschool and is on the threshold of formal school, seems an appropriate time to talk about intellectual diversity, the fact that some people are smarter or dumber than others. The fact of intellectual diversity is not to be disputed. The debate centers around the ever-persistent nature-nurture controversy, the question of where intellectual differences come from. This is an important practical issue. One's willingness to invest large sums of money in education—and what kind of education—depends on how much faith one has that cognitive functioning can be changed for the better. One's attitude toward racial integration depends on the extent to which one accepts the debased social and intellectual status of Negroes—or of the poor in general—as a product of inferior biological endowment or of the degrading conditions in which they have been forced to live. A proper scholarly discussion of the nature-nurture issue would require a book in itself; indeed, over the years, it has been the subject of numerous volumes, such as Hunt's (1961). Let us remind ourselves that Americans have always been simultaneously optimists, with great faith in the power of schooling to raise the mass intellectual level, and Social Darwinists, convinced that things are the way they are because thus it is biologically ordained. Hunt represents the environmentalistic side of the American mentality, which has prevailed in the dominant behaviorism of American psychology—let it be noted that although the behaviorist view of human nature is neutralist, behaviorists have put more stress on ways to improve human functioning than on the things that pervert it.

In recent years there has been a resurgence of biologism, with each theorist stressing a single theme in human behavior. Lorenz (1966) has given us instinctively aggressive man; Ardrey (1966) has given us instinctive territoriality as the basis of aggression; Tiger (1969) tells us that sex differences are biologically fixed; and Tiger and Fox (1971) seem now to be offering their own version of the territorial instinct.

Closer to home, we have had a number of recent statements on the genetic determination of mental illness such as schizophrenia, and Jensen (1969) and Herrnstein (1971) have spoken out for a biological view of intellectual differences. We wish to take a stand against this position. Our stand, however, is a difficult one, because

it does not deny the possibility of strong genetic influences in intellectual development. What it denies is the possibility of coming to any firm conclusion on the subject on the basis of available evidence (Scarr-Salapatek, 1971b); and particularly the evidence which is said to show that large human groups (rather than individuals) differ in intelligence on a genetic basis. Both Jensen and Herrnstein give the impression of arriving at a conclusion and then trying to make a case for it. Both are guilty of logical errors, errors of fact, errors of imagination, and a strange detachment that leads one to suspect that all their knowledge comes out of books, probably phrased as numbers.

Neither author seems to be aware of the distinction between biology and genetics. Not all of biology, as we have said before, is genetically fixed. Even the newborn baby has a nine-month history during which his genetic equipment has been interacting with environmental influences, good and bad. The child of a malnourished mother, for instance, is particularly vulnerable to impaired development of the brain, and there is reason to believe that such impairment affects intellectual functioning. More important, Jensen and Herrnstein overlook differential learning opportunities, although one of the best-established facts about human biology is that we are eminently learning animals.

Particularly in the case of Jensen, who tries to make a case for the genetic superiority of whites over blacks, there seems to be an odd misunderstanding of what is meant by race. In Jensen's discussion, a Negro is a Negro is a Negro, although in Africa the term applies equally to Pygmies and the Watusi. In the United States, of course, it is impossible to treat black and white dichotomously, since racial mixing is the rule rather than the exception. We know of only one recent study that has set about seriously studying racial mixture (Willerman et al., 1970). For reasons that will become clear, we have reservations about the findings of this study as of any other in the field, but the results are interesting because they show the complexity of the matter. All the subjects were four-year-old children of Negro-Caucasian matings, but the investigators also took account of which parent was of which race, whether the parents were living together, and the sex of the child. These three dichotomous variables (race of mother, Negro or Caucasian; marital status, married or unmarried; and sex of child, male or female) yielded eight groups of children. The average IQ's of these groups were as follows (remember that the average IQ of the population as a whole is assumed to be 100): sons of unmarried white mothers (and black fathers), 94.7; sons of married white mothers, 100.8; sons of unmarried black mothers, 67.5; sons of married black mothers, 88.4; daughters of unmarried Caucasian mothers, 100.3; daughters of married Caucasian mothers, 103.8; daughters of unmarried Negro mothers, 88.6; and daughters of married Negro mothers 105.1. If one is going to take such studies to heart, one must be prepared to accept the clear fact of female biological superiority in intelligence.

Neither Jensen nor Herrnstein takes a developmental view of intelligence. They seem unfamiliar with the literature on non-human animal development (p. 105) which demonstrates the profound effect of variations in early experience on physiology, emotionality, and problem-solving ability. They seem unable to imagine the developmental implications of being poor, although a survey of the literature by Neff (1938) found that economic status was the most powerful correlate of differences in intelligence-test performance, regardless of race. Thus, the kinds of intelligence-test scores that Jensen finds characteristic of American blacks are equally characteristic of poor white children who are isolated from the dominant culture in urban and rural slums, in Appalachia, in the Scottish Highlands, or on the canal boats of England. Jensen and Herrnstein seem to forget that successive waves of immigrants have been stigmatized as biologically inferior—Irish, Italians, Poles, Japanese, Chinese, and all the rest—by the guardians of racial purity. They overlook a crucial distinction between Asian and European immigrants and those from Africa: the Africans were involuntary immigrants whose native culture was ruthlessly and systematically destroyed by the slave-owners. Jensen, in asserting that Negroes are capable of only low-level associative learning, overlooks that Negroes everywhere learn to speak grammatically (never mind that the grammar of Negro-English dialects departs from that of "standard" English), a process which by definition cannot happen through mere association. Furthermore, as we have said, there is direct evidence from the work of Stevenson and his associates (Stevenson, 1971; Stevenson et al., 1971) that associative learning is positively correlated with cognitive learning, and, in fact, that middle-class children do rather better at associative learning than do disadvantaged children. In general, Jensen and Herrnstein seem not to comprehend the concept of culture, and the profound way in which culture shapes our perceptions, thought processes, and capabilities. Herrnstein and

Intelligence, intelligence tests, intellectual differences, and intellectual development

Jensen are themselves excellent exemplars of this fact—they apparently have no suspicion of how thoroughly ethnocentric their views are. Seemingly, they do not know that one component of the dominant American culture is **test wisdom**, knowing how to do well on tests by outguessing the test-maker, a skill acquired by practice in taking tests and pretty much independent of the content of particular tests.

Those familiar with tests and testing have long known that tests are culturally biased—a point to which we shall return—but attempts to create culture-free or culture-fair tests have not prospered, presumably because culture permeates everything so thoroughly. It is odd that Jensen takes no note of cultural bias because he himself has done research on it (Jensen, 1961). One could interpret Jensen to be saying that because American Negroes do not share the dominant culture, they have no culture and can therefore be regarded as less than human. It is lamentably true, of course, that the disruption of Negro cultures continues today, helped along by the migratory patterns and a welfare system that breaks up families, so that few American Negroes have a sense of family and group tradition comparable to the rich oral history of their African cousins or to that which is written down for people from Asia and Europe.

Our main quarrel with the Jensen-Herrnstein position, though, centers on the instruments by which intelligence is assessed and the conceptualizations which underlie them. Herrnstein, whose own work lies outside the field, hails the mental measurements movement as one of psychology's most glorious achievements. Anastasi (1967), who is one of the country's most eminent psychometricians, takes a more modest view. According to her, mental testing has developed in isolation from psychology as a whole and has contributed very little to it. In our opinion, mental tests as they exist and are being misused are a blight on the psychological and educational landscape in that they give psychologists and others the illusion of talking about something real instead of about numbers which may or may not stand for something. Examined closely, intelligence tests are pathetically flimsy tools with which to study an important topic like intellectual ability. Numerous writers (e.g., Anastasi, 1967; Church, 1966; Fowler, 1962; Hunt, 1961; Sigel, 1963; Spiker and McCandless, 1954; Stott and Ball, 1965; Tyler, 1963) have faulted the tests on a number of grounds: lack of independent validation other than school performance, which emphasizes the same content and skills as the tests; inadequate standardization; cultural bias; conventionality of content; errors of mathematical logic; lack of any theory or even a good definition of what it is they are supposed to measure; instability of individual performance from one testing to another; and untested assumptions about how intelligence is distributed in the population. It is a curious and disheartening bit of intellectual history that the tests have marched bravely ahead without any serious attempt to respond to the damning criticisms that have been made.

To understand how fundamental the criticisms are, we must look at how intelligence tests are constructed. Since the pioneering days of Alfred Binet early in this century, the process has begun with the collection of a large miscellany of single test items which presumably have some bearing on intelligence. From there on, test construction is a highly pragmatic procedure, with little regard for theory or even logical coherence. The pool of test items is given to a sample of the population for which the test is intended, and is then boiled down to those that work best. (In practice, the makers of newer tests have borrowed heavily from the items on older ones.) The test-maker retains those items that show a gradual increase of passes with what is presumed to be increasing brightness within a sample all the same age, or with increasing age in a mixed sample. The age at which either 50 percent or 75 percent of children (the criterion varies from test to test) pass an item establishes its position on an age scale. Here we must introduce the notion of **mental age**, as distinct from chronological age, the time that has elapsed since birth. Mental age is a score on an intelligence test expressed in terms of the age level of the items passed (on the Stanford-Binet test, each item stands for a given increment of mental age). William Stern introduced the further notion of **Intelligence Quotient** (IQ), obtained by dividing a person's mental age by his chronological age and multiplying the result by 100 (to get rid of decimal points). Thus, a person who scores at the average level for his age would have an IQ of 100; a score above his age would yield an IQ greater than 100, and below, less than 100. More recently, test-makers have adopted the notion of the **deviation IQ**, determined not by calculating an actual quotient but in terms of where the individual falls on the distribution curve for people of his age. Either way, a person's intelligence-test score always expresses his standing relative to the comparison group of people his own age on whom the test was standardized. It thus becomes a vital issue that the standardization group be representative of the same population from which the individual comes. In practice, this requirement is seldom met. What most nonspecialists do not realize is that intelligence-test-makers have long since abandoned any pretense of measuring intelligence in the raw. Instead, they seek to infer intelligence from what a person has learned. The assumption is made that the people being compared have all had equal learning opportunities but have benefited differentially from these opportunities because of different endowments. This, as we have tried to show, is an untenable assumption, in terms of both the differing concrete environments in which babies and children develop and the differing interpretations of the environment supplied by different cultures and subcultures.

The actual test items call either for bits of knowledge or the exercise of skills. Test items may be grouped into subtests supposedly drawing on related skills or areas of knowledge, or left in their miscellaneous state. The kinds of areas tested are typically arithmetic, vocabulary (which may include either word knowledge, skill in defining words, or both), copying geometric forms, using colored blocks to reproduce a pattern, memorizing brief stories or strings of numbers, using a code, interpreting common (or what used to be common) proverbs, assembling jigsaw puzzles, knowing certain facts, understanding social conventions—the list goes on and is potentially enormous, although any actual test should require no more than about half an hour. As is apparent, the person's actual score is a summing or averaging of performances on items representing very different sorts of mental functions. It follows that a given score can stand for a great many different patterns of performance. (Extremely high

and low scores necessarily stand for homogeneous performances, but those in between the extremes ordinarily represent a
mixed pattern.) While the items or subtests
are treated statistically and practically as
interchangeable, they clearly are not. Let
us imagine a test having three subtests
(ten is the usual number, but some have
fifty-odd). An IQ of 100 on this test could
mean that the individual scored at the
same level on all three subtests, or that he
scored high on analogies, average on arithmetic, and low on spatial relations, or very
high on one and below average on the
others, and so forth. Thus, anyone who
thinks that an IQ of 100 tells him something about a person's ability is guilty of
symbolic realism, since widely discrepant
patterns of abilities may be masked by a
common label. Note that the subject may
be given equal credit for knowing about
antonyms or for being able to repeat several digits after the examiner, although the
operations involved are hardly equivalent.
Ability to do arithmetic is very largely
determined by experience (but children
who fail miserably on intelligence tests of
mental arithmetic may have no trouble
figuring gambling odds), vocabulary is obviously a matter of experience, and all so-
called verbal tests and many so-called performance tests are loaded with vocabulary.
Thus, the Information subtest of a Wechsler test may ask you not only to identify
the author of *Romeo and Juliet* (hardly key
figures for slum children) but also to define
a lien and the Koran.

Needless to say, if the tests are to be
"objective" measuring instruments, the
items must have only one correct answer
each. Thus, the tests test only for what
Guilford (1967) calls convergent thinking,
thinking that moves toward a fixed end,
and cannot test for divergent, original

thinking, or for attacks on problems which
have no known answers. We propose that
some future intelligence test include the
item "Discuss the nature and origin of
intellectual differences." Not only do intelligence-test items always have a "right" or
"best" answer, but the content is often
banally conventional and the "right" answer remote from the real world. The
Wechsler scale asks the child what one
should do if one finds an unmailed letter.
The correct—or pious—response, of course,
is to mail the letter, but a truthful poor
child who recommended examining the
letter to see if it contained money would
lose credit. The Binet test asks the child
how to respond if a stranger asks for directions. The right answer is to guide him
on his way or to refer him to someone who
knows, but what the slum child knows is
to steer wide of strangers.

One further note is in order on the selection of test items. It is often held that
the biological nature of intelligence is revealed by the fact that intelligence is normally distributed, that is, the scores of a
great many people form a frequency distribution similar to that of the bell-shaped
normal curve. In fact, though, the test-
makers select items and item combinations
so as to yield a normal distribution, discarding those that introduce peculiarities
in the distribution. In fact, we have no way
of knowing how intelligence is distributed.
In practice, one could make up an "intelligence test" to yield any kind of distribution curve imaginable. For instance, one
could make up a test consisting of a single
item. This would produce a completely discontinuous distribution of those who knew
the answer and those who didn't. By making the item easier or harder, one could
shift the cutoff point either way.

We mention only in passing that a subject's performance can be significantly affected by the sex or race of the examiner or even by individual differences between examiners of the same sex and race. In spite of their strivings for objectivity, the test-makers have given us items which produce endless scoring problems, so that unsuspected biases can creep into the superficially simple matter of marking a response right or wrong.

Some test-makers have taken an approach somewhat different from the one described here. Recognizing that traditional intelligence tests combine performances on very different kinds of functions, they have sought ways to tease out these different abilities (called **factors**) and measure them separately. As it has worked out, the technique of factorial analysis has given us a magnificent demonstration of the self-fulfilling prophecy in action. Those factorial theorists who believe that intelligence consists mostly of a general, all-purpose intelligence (designated g) plus some specialized abilities (called s) extract from their factor analysis a large g and a number of puny s's. Those of an opposite persuasion, who feel that g is of minor significance while s's are what count, find ways to chop up other people's g's into numerous s's. The way one demonstrates a factor is to hypothesize its existence, find or invent some items that seem to belong to that factor, and then intercorrelate performances on these items as compared with unrelated items. The method never seems to miss, although some observers find in it a demonstration of the analyst's ingenuity in putting together related items and not of a structural component of intellect. In viewing the sophisticated manipulations of the factor analyst, however, it should be remembered that the data all derive from the same initially defective test items.

We must also point out that, according to the biological argument, intelligence, barring some physiological disaster, should remain relatively stable. In fact, repeated measurements on the same individuals show rather wide fluctuations in scores, and the farther separated in time two testings are, the less resemblance there is in the results (see Tyler [1965] for the work of Bayley, Macfarlane, and others). The meaning of such variations is further obscured, however, by the fact that different test items representing different kinds of abilities are used at different ages, so that we are not really comparing the same person at two points in his life but how at point a he deals with one kind of material and at point b with another.

We should be aware that psychologists outside the psychometric tradition have developed numerous tasks for the study of cognition and cognitive development which could be very useful for the study of intellectual differences. However, by a quirk of history, cognition and intelligence have come to be treated as two distinct realms of psychological functioning. In any case, it should be apparent that Jensen and Herrnstein are hardly justified in drawing conclusions about biological differences on the basis of intelligence-test performance (Scarr-Salapatek, 1971a).

What we have said should not be taken to mean that existing intelligence tests are useless (Dyer, 1961). With groups similar in background to the standardization sample, some limited comparisons can be made. If we consider it the task of education to teach children the prevailing culture, then intelligence tests can be used to evaluate the effectiveness of such teaching. In theory, one could even use tests across cultural boundaries as a way of studying cultural differences. Some skilled examin-

Intelligence, intelligence tests, intellectual differences, and intellectual development

337

ers know how to use tests diagnostically, to help understand a particular child's ways of learning and thinking, and to note possible disturbances.

Whatever the merits of the tests, we still must talk about research evidence pointing to a hereditarian view of intellectual differences. This evidence would include Tryon's (1940) selective breeding of maze-bright and maze-dull strains of rats; comparisons of the intelligence of identical twins reared apart from each other with the intelligence of identical twins raised together, of identical twins with fraternal twins and nontwin siblings; and comparisons of the intelligence of adopted children with that of their true parents and adoptive parents (Tyler, 1965).

The findings from all these studies have met with environmentalist criticism. For instance, Searle (1949) concluded that the difference between Tryon's two rat strains is a difference of temperament rather than intelligence. McGaugh et al. (1962) found that the difference between the two strains disappeared when their maze-learning schedules were changed. Wild rats and mice are vastly brighter than their laboratory-reared brethren (we mention only in passing that the evaluation of intelligence in animals is as confused an undertaking as in humans). We must also note that most animal studies omit the vital control of cross-fostering, whereby newborn litters are swapped between mothers of different strains to insure that the behavior of the young is due to genetic causes rather than to being raised by their own mothers (see p. 170). When the data from the most famous of the twin studies (Newman et al., 1937), which compared identical twins reared apart, are regrouped, as we have done in Table 3, to take account

TABLE 3 COMPARISON OF IDENTICAL TWINS RAISED APART IN TERMS OF DIFFERENCES IN IQ AND DIFFERENCES IN EDUCATIONAL AND SOCIAL ADVANTAGES (DESA)

	Large DESA	Small DESA
IQ differences<10	1, 4, 7	1, 1, 1, 2, 2, 5, 6, 8, 9
IQ differences>10	10, 12, 12, 15, 17, 19, 24	—

Source: Adapted from Newman et al. (1937) and Johnson (1963).

of psychological similarity or dissimilarity between the physically separate environments in which the members of twin pairs were raised, it appears that environment did in fact exert an influence on intellectual development.

Decreasing similarity in IQ's as we go from identical twins raised together to identical twins reared apart to fraternal twins to siblings in general can be seen to be associated with decreasingly similar environments. Even fraternal twins, because of their differing stimulus characteristics, can provoke quite different reactions from people around them and so in principle can inhabit very different psychological environments even while living in the same physical one. The critic has no ready answer to the finding that foster children often (although by no means invariably) are more like their real parents than their adoptive parents in measured intelligence, except to say that nobody has yet sufficiently studied the psychology of adoption and the possible problems of identification involved. In addition, those who are interested in possible environmental influences on intelligence point to positive evidence of the kind discussed in the next paragraph.

Most of our knowledge of environmental effects on intelligence comes from studies of infrahuman species, like those already cited. However, Wellman conducted a still-controversial series of studies which indicated that nursery-school experience of the right sort could markedly raise a child's IQ, and we have Skeels's (1966) follow-up study of institution children "adopted" by the inmates of another institution (pp. 104-105). The returns from Head Start have been mixed, but the best programs have had a considerable impact,

which is likely to be obliterated quickly when the children are put in the dreary environment of most elementary schools. The impaired intellectual functioning of institution-reared children could also be used to show the effects of environment, except that, unlike Skeels, we have no possible way of knowing that such children would be brighter if brought up in more favorable circumstances. Sayegh and Dennis (1965) found improvement in institution children given only three weeks of extra stimulation.

The reader is reminded that we are not trying to make an environmentalist case. We merely want to convey that any conclusions are premature. Unfortunately, the study of intelligence and intellectual differences has become locked in by past errors, which get perpetuated by an imagined need for "comparability" of research findings. We would propose that psychology should begin again, not from scratch but from the perspective of past mistakes. As Cole et al. (1971; Cole and Bruner, 1971) point out, it may be time to stop studying isolated variables and begin studying people in the world. The anthropologists have almost given up on the study of cultures, so maybe there is room for the psychologist to move in. One final point should be made before we leave the nature-nurture controversy. Even if it were to be proved that genetic endowment plays a major part in intellectual endowment, this still would leave open the possibility of major environmental influences. What we already know tells us that experience can modify intellectual ability. The question that remains is whether we have to accept that the present spread of abilities will always be with us, even though the average is moved upward, or whether we can offer hope that, with the proper variety of educational means, everybody could aspire to high intellectual development. Obviously, we do not need a theory to find out. The pragmatic search for educational means can and should go on regardless of theories, just as people will find their way in life regardless of what intelligence tests tell them.

Nevertheless, it is unsatisfactory, if only because we want to advance our own understanding, to be totally atheoretical in our thinking about education and intelligence. We would like therefore to propose a different way of looking at things, one that deals with beliefs as well as knowledge, with feelings as well as sheer reasoning, with the person as a whole in congress with his real and imagined surroundings. Out of this view there may some day emerge a measuring instrument, but for the time being we are more concerned with understanding than with assessment. We believe that much of the confusion in this area comes about because people have tended to localize intelligence in the organism, or even more narrowly in the central nervous system, as though it were some kind of mechanism or structure. Instead, following Stoddard (1943), we would like to propose abandoning the noun "intelligence," which invites reification, the translation of a convenient hypothetical construct into an entity, and substitute the adjective "intelligent" as a characteristic of organism-environment relations. In this view, it makes just as much sense to talk about more or less intelligent environments as about more or less intelligent people. Intellectual development in this view becomes the progressive discovery of reality, and the task of education to give the child an intelligent—differentiable,

thinkable, manipulable—environment. Here we are returning to our somewhat modified version of Kurt Lewin's field theory (see p. 195).

Our transactions with the environment —which includes, let us remember, the natural and man-made physical world, animals, people, things, institutions, and symbols, and all the meanings, sounds, odors, and demand qualities that emanate from them—are obviously conditioned on the way our environment appears to us, the way our personal life-space is constituted. Out of our cultural learning and our personal experience we come to perceive the world in diverse ways, so that different individual life-spaces have different organizations of what stands out as figure and what blends into the background, different possibilities for action and manipulation, different casual dynamics, and, in sum, different patterns of meaning. The unintelligent life-space is the sphere of primitive experience into which we are all born and which is perceived egocentrically, dynamistically, phenomenalistically, and magicalistically, activated by psychic and spiritual forces of a kind unknown to science. The psychologically primitive environment permits full play to superstition and is populated with imagined beings and entities, from poltergeists to the miasma to "intelligence." Such an environment is phrased in tradition-bound formulas, platitudes, axioms, precepts, taboos, myths, and slogans. All action has a moral component and must be accompanied by the proper ritual observances lest it misfire. The primitive environment invites acceptance and submission and discourages invention and innovation.

By contrast, the more intelligent life-space is one in which primitive forces are subordinate to more orderly and manageable ones, as generally known in the educated parts of our society, so that magic gives way to science, we look beneath the surface of things to see what makes them tick, and we evolve sets of principles applicable to various domains of reality. We learn to distinguish between moral and morality-free spheres of action and to emphasize the pragmatic rather than the ritual. We invent new—and sometimes better —ways of doing things, we learn to exploit natural forces, we let machines do our work for us (including a certain amount of our thinking). In the arts, we experiment with novel combinations of lights and sounds and words and meanings. We search for new, largely secular formulations of the meaning of it all. We invent new social doctrines. Most radically, we look for ways of altering and improving human nature, through child-rearing practices, education, drugs, surgery, and psychotherapy.

Let us note that even the most emancipated of us are still hobbled by superstitions, dogmas, irrational convictions and intuitions, rigidities, and some imperviousness to evidence, but we have moved away from the Stone Age and the Middle Ages, from witch trials and public executions, from mass manias and holy crusades. We still have a considerable way to go, as one can read in the headlines, but we have made a beginning. In this interplay of person and environment, the part that seems to remain most stubbornly as a property of the person is language and symbols, and the environment can be no more intelligent than the symbolic systems with which the person can manipulate facts and relationships intellectually, in thought.

If, as we propose, we now consider education to be a process of giving the child an intelligent environment, one whose workings and possibilities and impossibilities he understands, we must take account of our society's profound ambivalence about intellectual development and education. For it is only some small fraction of the community that has worked its way into the light of modern understanding, and that fraction is none too well represented in the seats of power. On the whole, many parents are more interested in whether the child is "doing well," in the sense of getting good marks, than in what and whether he is learning and whether he finds learning exciting. This duality is also expressed in the contradictory attitudes communicated implicitly to boys and to girls. Boys are expected to do well, but it is assumed that they will find intellectual activity unmanly and will dislike school. Girls are conventionally expected to be more docile and to accept the schooling process, but they are assumed not to be capable of serious intellectual achievement, which in any case is viewed as irrelevant and perhaps even inimical to their eventual feminine role. In fact, girls do learn better in school than boys, partly at least because the schools are run by women and offer an effeminate, prettified curriculum.

Equally important is the distinction that can be drawn between safe and unsafe areas of learning. We can see the various school subject matters as a spectrum running from the skill subjects (reading, writing, and arithmetic) through the physical sciences, the biological sciences, the social sciences, the arts and humanities, to philosophy and metaphysics. Branching off from this array are the applied fields: engineering, agriculture, medicine, social work, and so on. We encourage the child

Intelligence, intelligence tests, intellectual differences, and intellectual development

in mathematics and the natural sciences, particularly if he is a boy, just as we welcome new knowledge in these fields. We smile upon the learned technologies, such as engineering and medicine, but as we move away from this region of the spectrum, learning and logic begin to clash both with established social doctrines and with our emphasis on what is practical, manly, and uncontroversial. Even the generally esteemed, not to say revered, field of medicine becomes controversial in such areas as birth control and surgical abortion, organ transplants, and the prolongation of dying. The applications of chemistry and biology in agriculture become controversial when they raise economically important questions about pollution and depletion of the natural environment. In biology itself, the hypothesis of evolution still arouses distrust and antagonism and the last legal prohibition against teaching it was repealed only in 1969. Sex education is taught in many school systems, but most courses stop short of the psychology, sociology, and ethics of sex. Conservatism and conventionality restrict thinking in many fields, and it is extremely easy for the child to acquire a conventional outlook, beginning in the preschool years. Even when young people realize that the adult world has not dealt with them honestly—as when adolescent disillusionment sets in—they lack the knowledge necessary to arrive at reasonable formulations of their own.

As educators, we have to bear in mind that intellect is not purely intellectual. We sometimes become so preoccupied with the symbolic tools of thought that we neglect the factual substance of knowledge, including the reaches of human virtue and evil, reason and stupidity, nobility and petti-

ness, plasticity and fixity, sensibility and opacity, passion and prejudice. As a rule, schools do not discuss the ethical demands of modern life. Since most children, prior to entering school, have grown up among adults who live in a twilight zone between primitive and sophisticated thought, some part of an intellectual education has to be devoted to reeducating children out of the errors they have learned, to divesting them of the clichés, the slogans, the platitudes, the dogmas, and the unspoken assumptions that dominate much of conventional thinking. A free and rich preschool education—whether in school or at home—which encourages questioning and deliberately avoids dogmatism seems to be a vital part of the total span of intellectual development.

We are proposing that the life-space be thought of as a system of conceptual domains—space, time, number, the body and its functions, social roles, physics, chemistry, politics, economics—each with its own subdomains. These domains, insofar as they are distinct from each other, would be our substitute for factors in thinking about the variety of ways in which people can be bright or not so bright. That is, most people know some domains well and others less well. Within each domain we could probably chart the development of understanding, from the child's discovery of his feet to earning a degree in medicine. Thus, if we had to measure someone's intellectual ability, we would investigate his grasp of the workings of relevant domains. Obviously, there are some skills, like reading, that embrace all known domains, but each domain demands its own special reading skills.

Notice that a key domain in intellectual development is the self, and the child cannot have an intelligent life-space without an intelligent view of himself. For every differentiation and higher-order integration of external reality implies a corresponding differentiation and integration of the person himself, a greater freedom to think, to act, to know himself, to become involved, to care, to be committed, and to wonder. This, in sum, is what we mean by being intelligent.

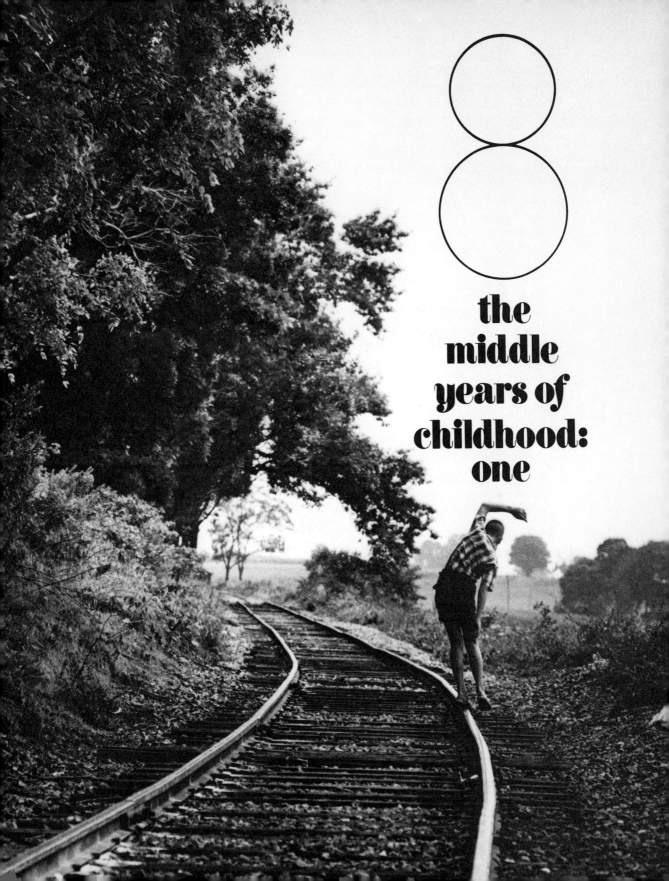

8

the middle years of childhood: one

The period of life from age six to age twelve-plus has been given a number of labels, each pointing to an important characteristic of development. The **middle years** are a period of relative tranquility between the turmoil of the preschool years and the tumult of adolescence. To label this period the **school years** is to point out that the child is now capable of a kind of systematic learning more or less akin to what goes on in schools. The designation of the **gang age** refers to the cardinal importance of affiliation with one's age-mates—the gang. Psychoanalysts call this period **latency**, a time of supposed sexual quiescence between the Oedipus complex and the eroticism of adolescence. The middle years begin with the loss of the first baby teeth and end at about the time the permanent teeth (except for the wisdom teeth of late adolescence or early adulthood) are all in, so that we can call this the **age of the loose tooth**. For some observers, this period is noteworthy for its **literalism** of thought, and for others, for the strong **ritualism** to be found in children of this age.

An Overview
of the Middle Years

The middle years are perhaps the age adults know least about. One reason is that children of this age turn their backs on adults and unite in a society of children. Parents, caught up in their own concerns, tend to be satisfied to let these newly competent children go their own way— which the children do, clustering into same-age and same-sex groups drawn from the pool of neighborhood and school acquaintances. At this age, the values of one's peers become considerably more important than those handed down by adults. What is more, school-age children learn to keep their thoughts from adults. They stop thinking out loud and, besides, practice deliberate guile and deception. To fortify their sometimes hostile, sometimes bland taciturnity toward adults, together with their peer-group solidarity, they form secret societies. Although a given club may last no more than days or weeks, it may be protected by mortal oaths and covenants, binding for life and countersigned in blood (or perhaps red ink). Another factor in adult ignorance about the middle years is that adults take this age for granted, as though it had no secrets. Adults are concerned with how to civilize or educate their middle-years children, but it seldom occurs to them to wonder about what their children are like, what the children themselves think about and are concerned with.

Yet, when we stop to think about it, the middle years can be an open book to adults. It is at this age that people begin to have organized, continuous memories rather than the piecemeal, episodic ones of the preschool years. We learn some of life's most basic lessons as babies, but we cannot recall the events that taught us. We can bring back snatches of early childhood, but the special flavor of that life is gone. But our school years are our own and can be evoked readily by the proper cues: the way one worked a loose tooth about with one's tongue, the reluctance to break the last thread that held it in place, putting the now-fallen tooth under one's pillow for the tooth-fairy to take in exchange for a gift; the pungent and unchanging smell of chalk dust and disinfectant in a schoolroom; the memory of the books one read;

the recollection of the jokes, riddles, and rhymes of childhood; or, in the case of a Marcel Proust, the flavor of biscuit dipped in herb tea. When parents of older children reminisce, it is about their children's preschool years; but when adults harken back to their own childhoods, it is to their middle years.

The middle-years child himself recognizes the special qualities of this period. When asked what the best age is to be, preschool children and adolescents yearn either forward or back; the school-age child, by contrast, likes his own age period best. At no other age has he as much freedom and as few responsibilities. Middle-years children may aspire to be teen-agers, and in many respects today's middle-years children are the teen-agers of just a few years ago: they listen to rock-and-roll and folk-rock music, they wear their hair in the teen-age fashions, they emulate teen-age dress and slang, they do the more advanced dance steps, they watch teen-age programs on TV and go to teen-age movies (and some, as we know, get hooked on drugs), but they reject the heterosexual entanglements of adolescence and the worries and burdens of adulthood. Indeed, adult life seems incomprehensible to the middle-years child. He cannot understand why adults, with all their power and freedom, do not gorge themselves on ice cream and candy, or perpetually watch television, or otherwise exploit the good things of life instead of being the fretful, trouble-ridden creatures they are.

We must once again make explicit that we are talking primarily about contemporary middle-class American and western European children. All middle-years children show many of the same tendencies, but these get dampened or modified in various ways in different societies or different segments of our own society. According to Aries (1962), childhood itself is a relatively recent invention. In earlier times, children past age seven or so were expected to act like adults—we doubt, however, that this expectation was fulfilled very often. Slum life imposes a precocious maturity on some children. The work responsibilities given to children in primitive settings place limits on the time they have for play (although the boundaries between work and play are less sharply defined than for Europeans [Leacock, 1971]). In western Europe, potent pressures for academic achievement are often at odds with the childish spirit. In the Soviet Union (Bronfenbrenner, 1970) some proportion of children are organized to be each other's socializing agents in the image of the New Soviet Man (and Woman).

With all these variations, the school-age child spends as much of his time as possible in the company of his peers, from whom he learns firsthand about social structures, about in-groups and out-groups, about leadership and followership, about justice and injustice, about loyalties and heroes and ideals. But even as he becomes a member of the distinct society of children, with its own roles and rules and folkways, he also, sometimes unwittingly and sometimes grudgingly, learns the ways and standards of adult society. It is possible that this dual social learning is the basis for many of the strains and conflicts that arise in adolescence, when the youngster is at war both with the adult world and with himself. Among his friends, the middle-years child lives in a special culture with its own traditional games, rhymes, riddles, tricks, superstitions, factual and mythical lore, and skills, transmitted vir-

An overview of the middle years

Ysbrand Rogge, Rapho Guillumette

Ken Heyman

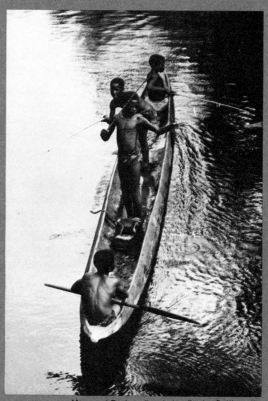

Marc and Evelyne Bernheim, Rapho Guillumette

tually intact from one childhood generation to the next, sometimes over a period of centuries, with no help from adults and often in spite of them. The peer group corrupts the child's linguistic practices, and he learns to speak reasonably proper English (or whatever) at home and an agrammatical, scatology-laden jargon with his contemporaries. In the group, middle-years children jabber constantly, but they seem to have very little to say. There was a recent vogue for walkie-talkie radios, and the messages that came through the crackling static seemed to be exclusively of this order: "Can you read me? Over." "Yes, I read you loud and clear. Can you read me? Over." "Yes. I'm over in Charlie's yard. Can you still read me? Over."

As we shall reiterate, adult society and middle-years society intermix spatially, but with no more attention back and forth than between the sparrows and squirrels feeding side by side. Middle-years children are everywhere. They ride their bikes all over town, they explore woods and fields and ponds, or junk yards and construction sites, they scale fences and take shortcuts through yards and alleys, they play on the sidewalks and in the streets, they erect clubhouses in vacant lots and tree houses where they can, they set up refreshment stands and stage shows and hold exhibits. They congregate at all events and spectacles, shinnying up lampposts to see a parade, sitting on the edge of the platform during a political speech; they turn up at fires and smash-ups and to watch the drowned body brought ashore. They go to the movies in pairs or packs. They sprawl

◄ Competence in non-Western settings. The Macao children are assembling strings of firecrackers.

During the middle years, children play in same-sex groups. Note how the girls are here relegated to spectator status. They seem to be responding to the photographer rather than to the antics of the boys.

▼

Nancy Rudolph

in front of the television set (and even television-watching becomes a social activity), consuming endless snacks. They play games like poker and Monopoly, they toss a ball back and forth, and sometimes they even do solitary things like reading or putting their stamp or baseball card collection in order.

As with other age periods, we have to point out that the middle years are not a single steplike unit. We find it convenient to distinguish three subdivisions of the middle years, corresponding roughly to the American school divisions of primary (grades 1 to 3, or six- to eight-year-olds), elementary (grades 4 to 6, or nine- to eleven-year-olds), and junior high school (grades 7 to 9, or twelve years plus). The six-year-old retains many babyish characteristics, including a taste for silliness and a tolerance of or even a desire for cuddling. He is likely to be but a fringe member of the gang, imitating its ways with literal dead seriousness and doing the bidding of the older children, and still likely to blab its secrets and activities to adults. He still, in these early school years, cries easily. By age nine, the child is sparing with his affections (particularly if he is a he and not a she), an active member of the gang, and skilled in its ways. He has learned to bear everyday buffetings and disappointments stoically, and if he has to cry he does it away from the gang. By age twelve, with exceptions and variations, he has developed a cocksure air, is controlled and competent (although his table manners may have deteriorated steadily throughout this period), scorns all things he considers childish, and is fiercely independent. Girls by age twelve have outgrown the long-legged, knobby gawkiness of the early school years and often merit the description of "womanly"—although they may be on the threshold of another awkward age.

Our scheme does not fit boys and girls equally well. Girls change much faster than boys during this period, and many sixth- and seventh-grade girls have entered puberty. It is at this point that one feels the shock of anomaly in watching a full-bosomed young woman playing tag or jumping rope. Class photographs of the seventh grade show how the young ladies tend to tower over their male classmates.

Children's rate of growth slows down during the middle years. They continue to grow, but at a slower pace than earlier and later. The average six-year-old is slightly over 3½ feet tall (about 105 cm.) —Oriental children are slightly smaller on the average than their Caucasian and Negro age-mates but are fast catching up. By the time he begins his adolescent growth spurt (average age eleven for girls, thirteen for boys), he is crowding the 5-foot mark (about 150 cm.). During this same period the child's weight doubles, from 40 to 80 pounds (18 kg. to 36 kg.). Most boys double in muscular strength during this period, while girls lag somewhat in this regard.

Striking changes come about in the child's physiognomy, the cast of his facial features. From birth until adolescence, the brain case takes the lead in growth over the face, so that babies and children have a small face crowned by a high forehead. In the neonatal period, facial features are indistinct and typically neonatal as much as clearly individual. Fat pads fill out the baby's cheeks, giving him a round-cheeked, full face. The fat pads dwindle during toddlerhood, and by the later preschool years the child's face is comparatively lean. It is the successive losses of baby teeth and the appearance of permanent ones that distinguish the changing face of the middle years. The baby teeth go approximately in the order in which they came, beginning with the lower front teeth and moving symmetrically back. The six- to seven-year-old is noted for his gap-toothed grin. When permanent teeth come in to fill the gaps, they loom disproportionately large, and the eight-year-old is distinguished by his outsize, "tombstone" front teeth. It is only in adolescence, when the nose and jaw come into full flower, that the face at last catches up to the teeth in size. Later losses of baby teeth during the school years are not so conspicuous, since they occur farther back, but the shedding of old teeth and the eruption of permanent ones go on until age ten or twelve (the four so-called wisdom teeth may not grow out until late adolescence or early adulthood and sometimes fail to appear at all).

The middle years are the time for the acquisition of many major and minor motor skills, related to the climate and the culture. Although some children learn earlier or later, the typical (northern) American middle-years child learns to ride a two-wheeler, to swim and dive, to roller-skate and ice-skate, to hang by his knees and to skin-the-cat, to play baseball, football, or whatever other sports his culture favors, to cross his eyes, spin tops, to jump rope (which is mainly a pastime for girls, but boys too jump rope when away from girls), to snap his fingers, to wink one eye, and to whistle. Boys play mumblety-peg, and girls, jacks.

Boys and girls mature at different rates during the middle years, and, what is more, questions of masculinity and femininity become prominent. Boys associate

D. Tucker Hood

Social role learning.

more—and more ostentatiously—with boys, and girls with girls, each sex pursuing its own separate interests and identities until communication is cut to a trickle. In adolescence, of course, the sexes will suddenly find new reasons to come together again, but this time in the new guises they will have meanwhile assumed.

Having thus sketched in a picture of traditional childhood, let us qualify it. It is not that new research has revealed formerly hidden truths, but rather that middle-class childhood itself seems to have changed considerably. Urbanization, affluence, mobility, and a spreading social awareness have brought changes, some of them reflected in the schools. Whether because of the schools or in spite of them, children are brighter than they used to be, not merely in the sense of doing well academically or scoring higher on standard tests, but in the sense of being more alert and sensitive to their surroundings and asking more logical and penetrating questions.

Children, if one can believe accounts like Joyce Cary's *House of Children* (1955), or the authors' own memories, used to drift through life in a misty, half-focused, dreamlike, dissociated state, but no more. The children of yesteryear used to harbor endless superstitions and beliefs, were prone to dread and terror, and were genuinely moved by ghost stories and horror movies. Today's children laugh at myths and superstitions, and horror movies have become satirical and farcical. Boys used to be dirt-streaked ragamuffins; many now choose and display their wardrobes with care, emulating teen-age grooming, though they may still dislike bathing and their clothing becomes easily disarrayed. Yesterday's twelve-year-olds used to hammer

or rope together makeshift rafts which constantly threatened to disintegrate in midstream; today's twelve-year-old fits together a well-joined skiff, tightly caulked and waterproofed, and makes it work.

Through the mass media, children come to an early awareness of sex, and boys, in the words of one observer, learn to leer before they have learned to giggle. The schools, the mass media, the teen-age world, and commercial interests all exert tremendous pressures to precocity, and flat-chested little girls in the late middle years wear beginner bras and discuss questions of feminine hygiene; the commercial world offers children junior bridge, and boys are given junior dinner jackets. Children may dance the latest steps at mixed parties, which may also encourage crude ventures into necking and petting, and in some families they are served nonalcoholic cocktails before dinner.

Most generally, parents have moved in on child life, often with a wish to give their children every advantage but sometimes, we suspect, in an attempt to recapture their own childhood—ironically, at the cost of their children's. The result, for large numbers of children, is a highly organized and tightly scheduled round of music lessons, dance lessons, horseback-riding lessons, visits to the orthodontist, Little League and medium-sized leagues, and other activities, with mother cast in the role of chauffeur. All these doings, together with school and homework, quite effectively fill the child's day. Even in summer, and especially if the mother works

Activities of middle-years children. The photographer had to stop taking pictures of the parachutists, because his attention spurred them to blood-chilling feats of daring.

Robert L. West

Wayne Miller, Magnum

Ken Heyman

Bonnie Freer, Photo Trends

Myron Wood, Photo Researchers

and so has to be out of the house much of the day, many children go to summer school or camp. Many camps, too, are no longer places where one swims or hikes or communes with nature, but have become either specialized schools, as in the case of music camps, or general academic ones in rustic settings. The plight of the contemporary middle-years child has been amusingly set forth in Robert Paul Smith's *"Where Did You Go?" "Out." "What Did You Do?" "Nothing."* (1957). Smith makes that point that today's child no longer collects butterflies or rocks or sea shells, but buys collections already classified, mounted, and labeled. According to Smith, childhood lore no longer gets transmitted from child to child, to the point where Smith himself has felt impelled to write a book (1958) telling children all the things they used to tell each other. We do not know how childhood is faring in other lands, and it certainly is not a wholly lost way of life in the United States, but the things we will have to say about this period must be interpreted in the light of the changing reality.

The Society of Children

It is only during the middle years, as we have said, that the child surrenders to and revels in his status as a child, aspiring neither backward to babyhood nor forward (with some exceptions, which we will come to) to adolescence and adulthood. Although the school child lives within adult society, he seems to pick his way through it, preoccupied with the concerns of childhood. One of the most striking characteristics of the middle years in our own and many other societies is that children have a special, separate subculture with traditions, games, values, loyalties, and rules of its own. The culture of childhood shares many of the attributes of primitive cultures. It is handed down by word of mouth, it includes many rituals and magical formulas whose original meanings have been lost, it is hidebound and resistant to alien influences and to change.

In one sense, the immersion in being a child and the strong peer-group affiliation of the middle years seem like time out from the process of development. From another standpoint, though, they seem necessary and valuable in the process of finding an identity. The preschool child takes his identity from his parents. The middle-years child, with this much of a foundation, is now ready to begin the quest for an independent identity and existence. As he has grown in stature, he has become able to see his parents more realistically, to know their frailties and imperfections, and has begun to realize, however dimly, that he must find stability in himself. This "time out," then, represents an essential moving away from the parents toward a genuine separate sense of self.

But the school child differs from the preschooler in more than independence. He is also becoming less egocentric, more able to view himself with a certain detachment and objectivity. He begins to see himself in terms of the labels society applies to him —male or female, age six to twelve, white or colored, rich or poor, smart or dumb— and all that these connote. The gang, too, has its set of labels by which it knows the child and he knows himself. The gang is quick to seize on any idiosyncrasy of constitution, manner, skill, or whatever, and thereafter to treat the child in terms of this trait. The stereotype which the gang holds of the child is often expressed in his nickname: Skinny, Fatso, Four-eyes, Dopey, Professor, Limpy—the total frankness, especially of boys, often startles adults. Most children wear their nicknames proudly, even opprobrious ones, as a badge of their belonging, of having an identity for the group. Any recognition, even contempt or mockery, is preferable to being ignored. The outcast or scapegoat would rather have the gang persecute him than act as if he didn't exist, and even the label "Stinky" means that he has an identity. The child's sense of self comes largely from the way others, adults and children, treat him, but it also comes from actual accomplishment and a feeling of competence. As he gets older, it increasingly depends on knowing that he has a role to play, that there is a place for him in society, and particularly that there is a place in which he can do something useful. All this implies further that the child becomes able to criticize himself according to the standards of other people, and, increasingly, to measure himself against abstract standards, a set of ideals.

Child society is a proving ground where the child learns to function apart from adults, but it has its dangers as well. The child's declaration of independence is not merely a withdrawal from adults, it is also in some part a turning against them. But because the child cannot stand up to adults by himself, he is doubly dependent on the gang for support and reassurance. The child's independence may thus turn into a new slavery, complete subservience to the group (Asch, 1940; Berenda, 1950). (The conformity of this age is expressed in an eight-year-old's lament that "Everybody in my class has poison ivy except me!") Such subservience contains two dangers. The first and immediate one is that pressure from the gang may force him, against his own better judgment, into dangerous, foolish, or immoral deeds. We are not speaking here of such minor immoralities as trying out smoking, or stealing apples, or sexual exposure or sexual play, which, however adults may view them, are a normal part of gang activity and appear to have no ill effects on the child. Rather, we have in mind the serious acts of violence or degradation into which the mob spirit sometimes leads children's gangs, particularly boys' gangs.

The second, long-term danger of submission to the group is failure to grow out of it, to be able to think and judge and behave independently, even in the face of social pressures. This is not a hazard for most children, who, it should be remembered, are simultaneously learning several sets of cultural norms: the parents', the gang's, the school's, and perhaps those of a much larger culture as embodied in stories, poetry, and works of art and music. The child of highly educated parents, who may entertain values quite different from those of society in general, may have to juggle yet another conflict in reconciling what he has learned at home with what he encounters in his school classmates and their families. However, some children grow up to be people who feel threatened and disoriented if obliged to take a stand without knowing the "right" way of thinking as set by group opinion, and doubly so if they sense that their feelings run counter to the group's. It is perfectly normal to experience some discomfort or anxiety when one is ignorant of or in conflict with group standards, but a mature identity permits us to know what our opinions are and to stand by them confidently even in opposition to the group. Let us note a contrary danger. Some children, meeting persistent rejection by the gang, may too quickly take refuge in an inappropriate identification with adults. The "'good boy" or the "good girl," who may appear to adults as a model for childhood, may be missing out on an important part of experience, with possible repercussions to come. Such a child's estrangement from his peers may be made worse by adult acceptance and approval, as he or she gets to be known as a "goody-goody," "Mama's boy" (or girl), or "teacher's pet." In sum, the tensions that go with the usual multiple identifications of the middle years, even though sometimes painful, are probably all to the good in the long run of development.

For the child does assimilate the several adult cultures to which he is exposed. He may argue against parental precepts one day and be overheard the next passing them along as his own convictions. Sometimes his conversion comes after the fact. In one case we know of, the girls in a fifth grade had ganged up on one of their members and were making her life a torment. When word reached the parents of one of the ringleaders, they commanded her, to the accompaniment of tears of resentment mixed with guilt, to be friendly toward the scapegoat and to invite her home to play the next day. In no time at all, the former victim had been reintegrated into the group and stood high in its esteem. As most adults realize, many of their preachments sound fatuous to the children they are meant to influence, but parents ought not on that account to abandon their no-

tions of conduct and morals. The way children continue to take on adult values even as they resist them implies also that little pitchers have big ears. Just as the child may seem deliberately deaf to parental strictures, so he may simulate casual deafness to things that are not really meant for his ears, and which parents believe they are keeping to themselves.

We should note that the gang spirit does not necessarily die out with childhood but may extend well into adulthood. The outlaw gangs of the horse opera show many of the same traits as children's gangs, as do rebel bands roaming whatever forest or jungle. Military units often have gang-like qualities, as do adult fraternal organizations, lodges, and clubs, especially those that live on rules and rituals, with content left largely undefined.

Later on, we shall talk more about children's contacts with adult society, how they resist it, take it in, and conflict with it. For the present, we want to look at middle childhood where it is purest, in the peer group: kids moving in packs and doing things in packs.

Childhood tradition

The children themselves form the society of children, but the beliefs they profess and the lore they practice are its culture. This culture is seen in the group codes of solidarity, stoicism, prowess, conformity, and the like, but shows forth perhaps most vividly in the ancient tribal rituals. We do not say "ancient" lightly. While historical research is impeded by the gulf between adult and child, and by childhood culture being a spoken rather than a written one, it has been possible to trace many still-common games and chants back to the Middle Ages and beyond to Roman and Druid, and perhaps Sanskrit, sources. This body of culture has been handed down from generation to generation, but from generations of almost-adolescent elders to the generations of younger brothers and sisters whom they initiate. As we said, though, this chain of cultural transmission is being attenuated, and the culture itself is losing out to commercial and urban pressures as a living thing. We should therefore be grateful that the Opies have set down a large part of the vanishing heritage in their charming compendium, *The Lore and Language of School Children* (1959; see also Withers, 1948).

Adults, looking back, will realize that childhood culture is a world that closed behind them and which they do little or nothing to communicate to their children. Grownups may teach children their prayers, but children teach children counting-out rhymes. Adults may teach children baseball, but children teach children stickball and keep-away. To recall the games and chants and rituals of the middle years is, like the evocative loose tooth, another effective passport to our own childhoods. And when, comparing recollections, somebody offers a minor variation in the wording of a rhyme, we feel a thrill of indignation at this intolerable unorthodoxy. Such indignation is a further clue to the relative fixity of this culture and to the unthinking way we learn it as a given. To add one more accent to the feat of transmitting a culture virtually intact down through the ages, we might point out that it takes only three or four adult generations to span a century, but there are perhaps fifteen childhood generations per century. This remarkable cultural durability depends in large part on children's love of ritual for its own sake and on their (mostly unspoken) sense of magical power in the literal repetition of forms having the character of rites and incantations and spells. Hence, any violation of the strict formula is felt to nullify its potency, or implies that one is tempting fate.

GAMES AND CHANTS. Breughel's sixteenth-century "Children's Games" and a 400-years-older Chinese painting, "100 Children at Play," show children at already venerable pastimes, yet much like those one can see on any contemporary American playground, centuries, languages, and nations away. Among the more durable of children's games are hide-and-seek, marbles, tag, hopscotch (observable in India as in Indiana and called *Klassike* in its Russian version), blindman's buff (often rendered "bluff" and now played mostly by adult prescription at the birthday parties of young school-age children), Red Rover, dodge-ball, jacks, London Bridge (along with ring-around-a-rosy, increasingly the province of preschool children)— the reader is invited to supply his own favorites. London Bridge is believed to date back to the medieval custom of entombing someone alive in the foundations of a bridge to propitiate the river spirits, just as the bottle of champagne smashed against the prow of a new ship is a libation offered to Neptune. Many children's traditions preserve early forms of adult culture. The metal forms used in jacks are derived from the knucklebones or vertebrae used in a similar game in Roman times. Notice here that we are talking only about games, which do not cover the full range of children's activities. Such other pastimes as playing catch, making snow-

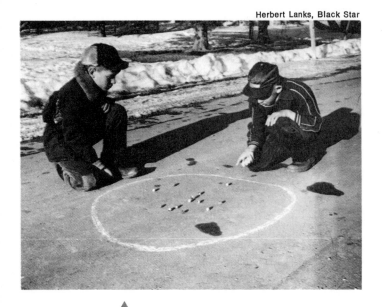

Traditional games of childhood. The Aboure children of the Ivory Coast are playing a form of checkers which requires skill in counting and reasoning.

men, swimming, bicycle riding, and kite flying are widely engaged in but do not qualify as games with stable sets of rules.

Many games go on to the accompaniment of **ritual chants**, like those that go with London Bridge and ring-around-a-rosy, with skipping rope ("Mabel, Mabel, set the table"), and with ball-bouncing ("One, two, three, a nation"). Closely allied are the counting-out rhymes: "Eeny, meeny, miney, mo," "One-potato," and so forth. There are rhymed guessing games: "Buck, buck, you lousy muck, How many fists have I got up, One, two, or none?" This particular specimen has been traced back to Nero's day: *Bucca, bucca, quot sunt hic?* One decides who will go first by "Junk and a po," the outcome being decided in terms of paper, stone, and scissors. Some chants are reserved for special occasions: "Ladybird, ladybird, fly away home," "Last one in is a rotten egg," "I scream, you scream, we all scream for ice cream," "It's raining, it's pouring, The old man is snoring," "No more spelling, no more books, No more teacher's dirty looks" (this last is still a compulsory recital even by children who love school and their teachers). Some are magical incantations: "Rain, rain, go away." Others are taunts: "Susie's mad, and I'm glad, And I know what will please her," "Roses are red, violets are blue, If I had your mug, I'd join the zoo." Many favorite chants are burlesques on standard songs ("Here comes the bride, Big, fat, and wide") and may or may not be attached to specific occasions.

Even though the words of children's sayings are often empty of literal meaning for the child, the charm of saying them and the need to say them accurately are there. Much of the charm seems to stem from the sense of participation in group ways and from satisfaction that one is in the know, that one has the key. The sense of fraternitylike membership is well demonstrated when two children catch themselves saying the same thing at the same time and instantly fall into the ritual of hooking their little fingers together, making a silent wish, and then exchanging the prescribed phrases before they break the hold with a ceremonial flourish and remain mute until a third person speaks to one of them and so breaks the spell. If they forget and speak without this release, the wish is lost. All the other children are aware of their role in the rite and of their power to enforce silence until they choose to free the main participants. The point is the shared character of such rituals, and the obligation on each person to play the required part. One assumption of the game is that the principals should not be liberated too quickly, and if anyone speaks too soon, this is felt as a gratuitous and offensive destruction of a magical moment, to be greeted by the indignant and almost equally ritual cry of "No fair!"

Young school children play their games, just as they recite their sayings and perform their rituals, according to ironclad formulas that permit of no variation. Later in the school years, this initial absolutism mellows somewhat in favor of a degree of relativism. Piaget (1948), in his investigation of children's concepts of rules and morals, found definite changes with age in the way rules are conceived (we shall have more to say on the subject of moral development in the next chapter). Early in the school years, they are accepted as *given:* timeless, immutable, and inherent in the game itself. If it is pointed out that children in the next county, say, follow

slightly different rules, this departure from The Right Way may be viewed as pitiably ignorant or verging on the sacrilegious. When a child enters a new community, he is often made to feel somewhat ashamed of the incorrect rules he used to follow. When, in the middle of the middle years, the child begins to realize that the rules come from somewhere, he may conceive of them as the work of some obscure Rule-maker who fixed them for all time. Still later, minor changes in the rules are permitted, provided everyone agrees—there arise what adults would call local ground rules. Finally, late in the school years, children can grasp the fact that rules are arrived at by consensus and serve merely to define the conduct and purpose of the game in an orderly way.

It should be noted that this development in the conception of rules runs parallel to a change in the kind of games children play. Increasingly, during the middle years, children engage in competitive games which do not simply run their course like London Bridge or farmer in the dell, but have an outcome, a score. Nevertheless, ritual predominates for most of the school years, in the compelling nature of rules, in the self-contained quality of games, in the inflexibility of sayings, and in the conservatism of children's attitudes.

OTHER CHILDHOOD RITES. In addition to communal rituals, there are solitary ones which are nevertheless defined by the child culture and carry strong group sanctions. Among these are the superstitious observances (not walking under a ladder, turning back if a black cat crosses the path ahead); obsessive humming and counting (including counting repeated things, like freight cars, counting by fives or by tens, and counting backward); avoiding or stepping on sidewalk cracks; touching every lamppost, and so on without end. Many children invent private rituals as well. One adult recalls how he had to be in bed and under the covers before the door swung shut, or else the (imaginary) mice under the bed would bite his toes. A woman recalls how she had to get upstairs before the basement toilet stopped flushing lest she be captured by some obscure bogey; it is interesting to note that this ritual was taken over, in modified form, by each of her two younger siblings in turn. In general, such rituals serve to ward off some threat, nameless or specific.

There are yet other forms of behavior in the middle years which, though less ritualistic than those we have described, are still closely bound up with traditional childhood culture. There are the ever-recurring **jokes** and **riddles**, which seem wholly threadbare to adults but which come as revelations to each new wave of children and are for them the essence of sophisticated wit: "Why do firemen wear red suspenders?"; "Waiter, there's a fly in my soup." Some of these are standard, but others may come and go in cycles, which seems to be the case with the knock-knock jokes and the little-moron stories, while others, like the more recent elephant jokes and sick jokes, may have a brief vogue and then vanish forever. Traditional children's humor is still with us, but is being fortified with adult-manufactured humor of the kind found in *Mad* magazine, TV cartoons (which nowadays tend to the satirical), and in the person of various culture heroes such as TV and rock-'n'-roll figures, and in slogan-bearing buttons.

There are the **stunts**, the tricks one learns to do with one's body, control of which is extremely important at this age and which has so many peculiar and unexpected potentialities. School-age children learn to make themselves cross-eyed, to see double, to contort their faces into horrendous shapes, to rub their bellies while patting their heads, to snap their fingers, to whistle, to turn somersaults, to skin-the-cat, to perform exercises in double-jointedness, to cross their arms and clasp their hands and be perplexed as to which finger is which. Late in this period, a fortunate gifted few will be able to wiggle their ears. Children learn to slide needles through the upper layer of skin without hurting themselves. They ink themselves with mock tattoos. A verbal counterpart of stunts is found in the perennial **tongue-twisters**. The learning of body stunts goes along with learning such **physical skills** as jumping and vaulting over barriers, swimming and diving, skating, playing ball, and all the rest. Some skills involve the manipulation of external agencies, as in riding a horse or sailing a boat. And, of course, the child's practical competences feed into his total sense of identity.

Still another characteristically ritualized way of dealing with reality at this age is the making of **collections**. In the early school years, at least, collections should more properly be called aggregations: pocketfuls and drawerfuls of the incredible and often unspeakable miscellany that every mother of a school-age child has to cope with. Later in the school years, collections tend to become more homogeneous and orderly: stamps ranged neatly on the pages of an album, dolls propped

Tricks and stunts of childhood.

Michael D. Sullivan

Robert L. West

Jerome Wexler, Photo Trends

Annan Photo Features

Marlis Muller

Robert J. Smith, Black Star

neatly on a shelf. But no matter how disorderly or even repulsive the child's accumulations appear to adults, to the child every length of twine, every scrap of cheap jewelry, every broken model, every thumb-eared comic book, every faded sea shell deserves the designation "very valuable." Often, in fact, the objects that the child collects take on highly charged magical or talismanic properties.

The child masters the magic of reading, writing, and arithmetic, and then goes on in the middle middle years to **coded talk and writing**. The child's codes, ciphers, and secret languages emphasize both communication with the in-group and exclusion of the out-group. Again, their function is largely ritual—the child who has mastered a code is hard put to think of anything to say in it. They contain a touch of the magic found in the special priestly language of many societies, and even the most commonplace message takes on a mystical tinge when couched in Pig Latin or Op, or laboriously transcribed into code or cipher.

The world of the middle-years child is highly differentiated but it is far from being integrated into a coherent whole. This time of life is full of joy and abandon, of delightful discoveries and surprises, of wonder and amusement, but it is likewise full of dreads, terrors, anxieties, uncertainties, and worry. The child is touched with a sense of his essential human isolation in a vast, powerful, unpredictable, and largely uncontrollable world. His childhood culture as expressed in shared group activity gives him the emotional strength to carry on. His culture as expressed in

skills and rituals and collections gives him a magical dominion over an otherwise unmanageable reality. Without the devices of his culture the regressive components in his perpetual growth ambivalence might overwhelm him. But, as we have said, the culture of childhood is a crutch to help him through a stage of development, and if he does not gradually free himself of it, it becomes a millstone.

The peer group

Having looked at the highly formalized traditions in the culture of childhood society, it is now time to look at the actual society of children, at children functioning in groups, how such groups are organized, what they do, and what their activities tell us about children of this age. The gang may have many degrees of organization, from a loose cluster of children playing in the schoolyard or the street, to well-defined pairs or groups of friends, to clubs for the sake of having clubs, to special-purpose clubs such as ball teams or delinquent gangs. It seems to be the case that children can play in pairs or bunches, but not in threes. When three children play, two of them almost inevitably band together against the third.

Let us stress the psychological separateness of the world of kids and the world of adults. It is fascinating to walk down a city block—ideally, after the evening meal in summertime—and to observe the child and adult societies carrying on their activities in and around each other but reciprocally oblivious except when they collide. Children step aside for cars without breaking the rhythm of their game. The driver of the car slows down for the kids, but with-

Middle-years children develop endless motor skills.

out really noticing what they are doing. Strolling adults are unaware that they walk through a game of stickball at a crucial moment, while the children barely pause to let the invaders pass. The conversations and greetings of the adults mingle in the observer's ear with the shouts, chants, and jeers of the children, but the two sets of sounds do not interpenetrate each other. And along the shifting boundaries between these two societies are strung the younger children, the toddlers and young preschoolers the responsibility of the adults, the older preschool and young middle-years children the province of older brothers and sisters, who keep watch on them with a bored but remarkably efficient eye. Some of the children on the fringes are making the transition to the gang. Instead of hanging back and keeping out of the way, they begin to move in around the edges, watching, listening, taking in, imitating doggedly, and participating when allowed to, gratefully accepting whatever roles or crumbs of attention that come their way. For children in the early middle years, somewhat older children are invested with enormous authority and prestige. In many ways, the children who have arrived in gang society appear more grown-up and knowledgeable to them than do adults. By age eight or nine, the transfer of affiliation and loyalty from the adults to the gang is nearly complete.

Parents are often distressed to find that their erstwhile loving child now seems to have lost his affectionate and confiding nature and become a stranger to his family. He is likely to be taciturn, sullen, and insolent. He affects odd mannerisms, gaits, and postures. When he does speak, his speech is likely to be slurred and careless.

He uses the special, restricted language of the gang. He praises things with "keen," "swell," "cool," "a fun thing." "Oh, wow" serves either to praise or deride. Currently popular pejoratives are "junk" and "queer." The child uses the scatology of the streets liberally, partly to shock his parents and partly to demonstrate his sophistication. The argot of the middle years is often the teen-age slang of yesterday.

The group-oriented child seems to live only for the moment when he can tear from the house and join the other kids, leaving, if he can get away with it, chores and lessons undone. Parents, seeing their child draw away from them, may be moved to become more demonstrative or possessive, to quiz the child about what is ailing him, or to storm at him for lack of filial devotion. Such measures are more likely to drive the child deeper into the gang than to win him back to the family. The child is taking a necessary step on the road to maturity, he is filing his private Declaration of Independence—an independence, let us remember, that is in fact merely submission to a new set of controls. Furthermore, we cannot take the child's behavior at face value. Much of his behavior is role playing, doing what is expected of him, and this applies to all the kids in the gang. If the child turns strongly against his family, it is probably a measure of the strength of the bonds that tie him to it and have to be overcome. If he is all bravado and self-assertion, it is because he has to cover up his doubts and anxieties.

It is not from his parents alone but from the adult world in general that the child declares his independence. On the lips of school-age children, "the grownups" is a term of derogation. The teacher who invites the children to identify some miscreant will meet a wall of silence which masks outrage that the children should be asked to violate the code against snitching. In schools where adult policies and conduct give the children little to resent, it sometimes seems that the children will invent issues just to test themselves against adult authority. In such cases, of course, some of the children may half-humorously half-recognize that they are inflating a trivial matter out of all proportion. Commonly, the child invokes gang authority to counterweight parental authority: "Gee, Mom, all the other kids..." (are going on a particular outing, have later bedtimes, travel after dark without an adult escort, watch a forbidden television show). Sometimes gangs, especially of boys, do things that seem expressly designed to arouse adult retaliation just so that they can outrun or outwit it. It is a lot more fun to steal apples from an orchard or a pushcart if you are seen and chased. Adults who view such behavior either disapprovingly or indulgently ("Boys will be boys") may be missing the psychological point: I can stand up to adults and survive.

The extremism of the child's declaration of independence reflects the fact that every middle-years child is more or less in the position of what Margaret Mead (1942) has called the "immigrant personality." The child of immigrant parents in the United States typically finds himself ashamed of his parents' foreign, old-fashioned ways and strives feverishly to be as unlike them and as like members of the host culture as possible. So it is with the school-age child, whether or not the child of immigrants. In his case, of course, the host culture is the subculture of childhood. And his parents, no matter how solidly American, are no longer the source of

Playgrounds.

all wisdom and power. Indeed, they may appear all too contemptibly weak and mundane and merely human. By this age, the child has overheard too many parental quarrels, witnessed too many episodes of worry and panic, been too often the butt of arbitrary adult authority, ever again to believe in the omniscience and omnipotence of adults. This is the age at which some children spin "**foundling fantasies,**" suspicions, often reaching the point of profound conviction, that the child is of exalted birth and by some dreadful mischance has fallen into the hands of baseborn foster parents.

In our society, the attitudes of both immigrant and native-born parents abet the immigrant-personality syndrome in their children. In the case of immigrants, no matter how firmly they cling to the old-country customs and values, parents are likely to feel ashamed of their ignorance and differentness and to take pride in their children's successful Americanization. Even native American parents share with their children the assumption that the younger generation will outstrip the older in both attainment and wisdom. As Mead has pointed out, parents are aware that the world their children are growing up in is in fact radically different from the one they knew as children and will be still more radically different by the time their children have grown up, so that many of the established precedents are becoming outmoded. The children know this, too, and feel their parents belong to an alien era, just as the children of immigrants feel that their parents belong to an alien place. Children have always retorted that "Times have changed" when parents launched upon a lecture beginning "When I was a boy" (or girl). In times past, though, the

parents have always felt secure in the belief that there were eternal verities transcending the fads and foibles of the moment. Now, by contrast, they realize that the eternal verities have been left behind by the political, economic, moral, social, scientific, technological, and philosophical revolutions of the century. Unfortunately, this realization has tended to weaken the parents' confidence in their own authority. How prescribe for life in a world transformed beyond recognition? As we shall see later, parents must somehow continue to find strength to be parents, but meanwhile let us return to the child and his gang.

We have already pointed out that social organization changes during the school years. Probably the first real coalition of young school children consists in the sharing of a secret and the formation of best-friend attachments—which may change from day to day, and which may inspire the announcement, "You know what? I have four best friends!" Genuine affiliation and stable group membership, and the climax of love for the secret society, are found in the middle middle years. By the later middle years, clubs and gangs are less likely to exist primarily for the sake of belongingness or for the formal rites they practice, and are more likely to be organized around particular kinds of activities and functions. The older school child is likely to be involved in and handle easily (although not without conflicts) multiple memberships and affiliations. The fact that he is moving closer to adult society and its distinctions and discriminations is also evident in the composition of the groups and

Social relations in the middle years. ▶

Robert Smith, Black Star

Eileen Christelow

Marlis Muller

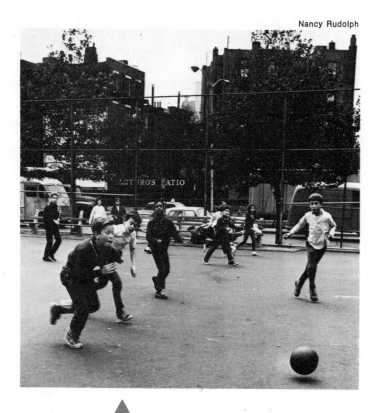

Kickball in Greenwich Village.

cliques to which he belongs. Within a given sixth grade, there is likely to be a clearcut social hierarchy (or two hierarchies, one for boys and one for girls) with very little contact between adjacent strata. The patterning of social organization during the middle years reveals the same principles of differentiation and functional subordination as other aspects of development. For instance, the gang spirit differentiates out of the totality of fellow feeling and at first is valuable in its own right, so that just being with the gang is satisfaction enough. Later, the value lies in the things the increasingly better integrated gang does.

Depending on the number of children available, the neighborhood play group, with its unannounced but regular meetings before and after supper, may either include a variety of kids playing together or break down into subgroups divided according to age and sex. In some areas, there is direct continuity between childhood play groups and adolescent street-corner society, or even adult-sponsored delinquent gangs. Some urban delinquent gangs maintain their organizational activities intact while successive generations of youngsters pass through them. In rural areas, and to some extent in the suburbs, children's friendships depend on family friendships and contacts made in school. Play groups are likely to include perforce a wider range of ages, although boys and girls still tend to play separately. In cities, affiliations are usually made within the home block. Outside "our block," one is in alien or even hostile territory. Notice that possessiveness toward and readiness to defend the home "turf" have something in common with the territoriality of many nonhuman species, observable most clearly in birds during the mating season (Scott, 1958). To say this, however, is not to elevate territoriality into a major determinant of human behavior, as some writers have sought to do (Ardrey, 1966).

Since geographical divisions in many American communities correspond very closely to ethnic and economic divisions, neighborhood affiliations may help perpetuate in children's society the same segregation and prejudices that prevail in adult society. (Needless to say, specific indoctrination in prejudice also plays its part.) However, children's groupings along geographical lines in the cities are partly counteracted by other influences: schools that draw children from several neighborhoods (although "ability" groupings within the school may simply mirror neighborhood groupings), adult-fostered visiting relationships, the chance to meet children in formal after-school programs and at summer camp, the common experience provided by the mass media, and the telephone, which is fast becoming as important a medium for school-age kids as it is for adolescents. (The younger school child transacts his business and hangs up; older children hold protracted, often whispered and furtive exchanges.) In the suburbs, the school, adult-organized activities, the family car, and considerations of which friendships are socially advantageous for "my child" become powerful determinants of affiliation patterns.

Certain individual children—usually the best-looking, the biggest, the strongest, the most physically mature, in some circles the brightest, the most energetic, the wittiest—acquire a great deal of popularity and, with it, some power of leadership. However, children of this age are in many respects hard-headed pragmatists, and when it comes to engaging in particular activities—a game of baseball, say, or staging a play—they look for leadership to those children competent in that activity (Hendry et al., 1944). Popularity may weigh heavily in choice of activity, but once the decision has been made, practical considerations take over. The technique of sociometry (see p. 173) reveals how leadership shifts from one undertaking to another.

Let us repeat and emphasize that group membership has two faces: belongingness and exclusion. Just as six-year-olds love simultaneously to share a secret and to define its secretness by keeping it from someone else, ten-year-olds, in forming a club, can experience a sense of "we"-ness only by leaving out "them." Something of the flavor of a school-age club, apart from the ceremonial aspects, is well conveyed in the following quotation from *The New Yorker*:

The rules of a secret society of nine- and ten-year-old girls in a certain community on Long Island that shall here be nameless are as follows:
1. Do not tell a white lie unless necessary.
2. Do not hurt anyone in any way.
3. Do not hit anyone except Ronny.
4. Do not tell a black lie.
5. Do not use words worse than "brat."
6. Do not curse at all.
7. Do not make faces except at Ronny.
8. Do not be selfish.
9. Do not make a hog or a pig of yourself.
10. Do not tattle except on Ronny.
11. Do not steal except from Ronny.
12. Do not destroy other people's property, except Ronny's.
13. Do not be a sneak.
14. Do not be grumpy except to Ronny.
15. Do not answer back except to Ronny.*

* By permission, copyright, 1954, The New Yorker Magazine, Inc., September 18, 1954.

The society of children

Usually, a number of children are left out and they in turn form an equally exclusive club of their own. Notice that such clubs commonly have an overabundance of officers, codified rules, ceremonies, oaths, and vague but portentous secrets. The members enunciate ambitious if ambiguous goals, but the underlying, unspoken motivation seems always to be to formalize and solidify belongingness. Sometimes, however, a child gets left out or is deliberately excluded from all memberships. Such children often are cast in the role of scapegoats on whom children higher in the pecking order can vent all their hostility and antipathy. Rejection by the entire group points to the despotic nature of majority rule. The minority of one experiences a strong, if perhaps temporary, inner conviction that the group must be right and that there must be something wrong with him. Herein lies the tragedy for the permanently or repeatedly excluded individual, whether the exclusion be on personal or ethnic grounds.

Every child who comes into a new neighborhood is at first a minority group member as he faces the bristling outside of in-group feeling. We can be thankful that middle-years group organization is unstable, offering, during periods of reorganization, openings through which the excluded individual can slip inside—provided, of course, that his exclusion was not on ethnic grounds. Notice that ethnic and racial prejudices work both ways. It comes as a shock to many white Americans that their skin is a signal for dislike. A fascinating series of studies by Sherif and associates (1961) has shown how one can produce and undo prejudice experimentally by varying group composition and goals and by putting goals in a competitive or cooperative framework.

The sex cleavage, sex roles, and sex differences

The tendency for the sexes to go their separate ways begins in the late preschool years and reaches a peak at about age ten. First- and second-graders invite both boys and girls to their birthday parties (or whatever other occasions are thus celebrated), but by age eight the idea of including the opposite sex in any kind of formal social arrangement becomes unthinkable (or so it used to be). This cleavage of the sexes is partly a matter of different interests and activities, but at a more basic level it is built into the childhood culture, probably a vestige of ancient adult cultural views on the inferiority of the second sex. Girls continue to play house and games like hopscotch and jacks, while boys roam farther, play rougher, wrestle, and learn baseball. The institutionalization of the sex cleavage, such that one must actively profess disdain of the opposite sex, suggests that here, as in declaring one's independence of adults, one must go to extremes to assert one's boyness or girlness.

Virtually all boys go through a period when they reject the female sex (with the possible exception of their mothers), loudly announcing vows of total, permanent celibacy. Notice that the knightly ideal, which found its ultimate expression in the cult of the Virgin, depicts womankind both as a fragile vessel to be placed on a pedestal and worshiped from afar and as a Delilah who, given half a chance, will castrate the male and drain him of his manhood. The knightly ideal is perpetuated in the rhetoric that surrounds Mother's Day (Father's Day is a pallid afterthought), in the teaching given to athletes and military personnel, and in the traditional cowboy movie, which no longer gets filmed but which nonetheless haunts late-evening television. Middle-years boys experience a mixture of puzzlement, outrage, and contempt when they see their just-older heroes, who until now have shared, and perhaps even taught them, their misogyny, beginning to tolerate and even seek out the company of girls. In one sixth grade, the boys who formed a committee to choose a class play informed their teacher that they would produce Jean Genet's *The Death Watch*. The startled teacher asked why they had settled on that particular play and was told, "It's the only one we could find that didn't have any girls in it."

Girls, by contrast, although expressing a complementary disdain for boys, nevertheless carry along a romantic vision of domesticity in which they picture themselves as brides and even as mothers and housewives, but mated to misty figures bearing no resemblance to the grubby, uncouth boys they know in real life. In the same vein, girls of this age may enjoy "love" movies, whereas boys are volubly disgusted by them. It should be stressed that many mature young women enter marriage in the spirit of the young girl's daydreams, with almost any presentable male cast in the role of groom, and with the focus on an elaborate nuptial ceremony and reception, with what comes later left in the vague realm of "happily ever after." It is also worth stressing that the mothers of girls may begin playing the marriage game when their daughters are hardly out of the cradle, arranging circumstances and encounters that will guarantee the girl an early and socially satisfactory marriage. Such mothers may themselves be thoroughly disenchanted with the institution of marriage, but they have not been able to shake loose from the idea that marriage is the ideal state for women. The women's suffrage movement early in the century aimed to win for women the right to vote, and, in addition, sought to emancipate women from the bonds of matrimony. In the 1940s and 1950s, a reaction set in, expressed in what Betty Friedan has scathingly described as *The Feminine Mystique* (1963), and the homemaker role for women was actively glorified. Now, perhaps as a product of increased education, women are once again seeking to define a new role and a new image for themselves, in which love, sex, marriage, and parenthood can each be considered in its own right rather than as part of a package deal in which one cannot have one without all the others. Unfortunately, and in part because of some of its spokeswomen, the women's liberation movement has come to be identified for many people as a Lesbian crusade or as an antimale campaign, or as a repudiation of childrearing.

The sex cleavage shows up too in attitudes toward pets. Boys and girls both love animals, but with a difference. Girls typically love puppies and kittens, which some would interpret as an expression of a maternal instinct, and such relatively inert creatures as guinea pigs, rabbits, fish (the heroic measures some girls will take to keep guppies from eating their young are a wonder to behold), and parrots in all their varieties. Boys, by contrast, like dogs, who can serve as companions and stunt artists. Boys used to like horses, perhaps in identification with cowboy heroes, but seem to have transferred their affections to motorcycles and motorcars. Girls, on the other hand, love horses to the point of mania, collecting pictures and figurines and begging for riding lessons. Girls have been known to select a college because it had its own stables. Some psychoanalysts have interpreted the girl's affection for horses as an expression of the masculine protest and an accompanying penis envy (see p. 178). In this view, control over such a powerful creature would be a symbolic subordination (and perhaps castration) of the male.

The sex cleavage is not, however, absolute. Brothers and sisters sometimes play together, especially when there are no other playmates available. If there are few children in the neighborhood, boys and girls intermingle. Late in the middle years, boys engage in sham-hostile invasions of girls' play groups, girls stand around making fun of the boys at play, and in the neighborhood play group, games of tag, catching, and mock-wrestling go on between the sexes, signaling the breaking down of the barriers in anticipation of adolescence. With the approach of puberty, though, girls are likely to turn their attention to older boys—and sometimes to develop crushes on older women or men—rather than to make peace with their male contemporaries.

Whether they play apart or together, boys and girls do many of the same things. Nonetheless, there is a distinct bifurcation of tastes, interests, and activities during the middle years, some areas of play being entirely feminine and others almost entirely masculine—a few girls are likely to participate in predominantly male pursuits, but practically no boys ever openly engage in what are thought of as purely female ones. However, as our culture changes, and as girls get bigger and stronger and thus able to compete with boys on a more nearly equal physical basis, it seems likely that the interests of the two sexes will become more similar. Unfortunately, there are no up-to-date findings on sex differences, and the older research is unreliable both be-

cause children have changed and because they engage in a different array of activities nowadays. In fact, the older lists of games contain entries like Salvation Army and Pound the Back that the authors are at a loss to recognize.

In general, boys tend to be doers and girls talkers. Boys tend to be oriented to things, with a special emphasis on things mechanical, and girls to people and social relations. Girls engage in sports (including touch football), but boys in addition read about them, idolizing the heroes and clustering in search of autographs around the hotel where the visiting team is staying. Girls like to ride bicycles, but boys also enjoy taking bicycles apart and putting them back together. In school, girls perform better than boys in the early years but later slip back into second place.

Girls think about love whereas boys are curious about sex—and, in the gang, exchange endless sex lore and sometimes engage in sexual experiments, including simultaneous masturbation, reciprocal masturbation, or even fellatio and other sexual acts. Obviously, many a school-age girl and boy have engaged in reciprocal sexual inspection ("I'll show you mine if you'll show me yours"), but heterosexual exploration at this age, to the best of the authors' knowledge, rarely goes beyond this. Apparently it does not spontaneously occur to middle-years boys and girls that they can stimulate each other's genitals other than by coitus, and their occasional clumsy attempts at intercourse are almost certain to meet with frustration, if only for reasons of anatomy and mechanics. In tribal societies where there are many opportunities to observe adult sexual behavior, prepubertal simulations of sex are likely to be tolerated. Middle-years girls may have powerful sexual fantasies, but they apparently engage in homosexual activities only when these are initiated by an older woman, such as a tutor or governess. It is possible that boys' homosexual experience in the gang arouses or expresses a streak of latent homosexuality in American males (as the widespread homosexuality in the British public schools—attested to by many autobiographical and literary accounts—seems to produce a great deal of practicing homosexuality in upper-class male adults; as one observer put it, "It is more than the old school tie that binds the Establishment together"), which might help account for the adult American male's ambivalence toward women, his liking for all-male activities, and his sometimes frantic assertions of masculinity, as when he projects an image of himself as the fearless, two-fisted frontiersman or makes a great compensatory display of sexual prowess.

Boys generally identify more strongly with the gang and peer culture than do girls, who remain parent-oriented even while identifying with their peers. Indeed, the male peer culture is very different from and in many instances at odds with the standards of adult culture, while the female peer culture, although distinct from that of adults, is very much like it. Not all boy groups, of course, are preoccupied with physical action. Some, perhaps the more bookish, like to relive the Robin Hood or King Arthur legends, or invent private countries or planets or historic events which they can draw or write about or stage in makeshift but no less heroic dramatizations.

The differing interests and activities and attitudes of boys and girls can be thought of as expressions of their sex roles, their assumptions, spoken or tacit, about what

Social-role learning in a violent culture.

Jesse Miller, Nancy Palmer Agency

Leonard Freed, Magnum

Charles Harbutt, Magnum

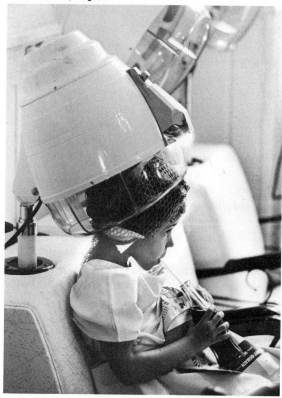

▲

Sex-role learning in the middle years.

it means to be a girl or a boy. Since conceptions of sex roles differ greatly from culture to culture, it seems safe to conclude that sex roles are in some part learned. Some explicit teaching of sex roles ("Big boys don't cry," "It's not ladylike to sit that way") is done by adults, older children, and age-mates. A considerable portion of the learning of sex roles, however, takes place after the manner of operant conditioning, by virtue of the rewards and punishments—the feedback—one gets for

acting in appropriate or inappropriate ways (as defined by the culture). Then, too, a certain amount comes to pass as a result of deliberate or unconscious imitation of the models, real and fictional, that one is exposed to and who exemplify masculine and feminine styles of life. One can speak of a sex role as a set of social expectations, the way people expect other people of a given anatomical sort to behave. The ways sex roles are taught and learned are called collectively **sex-typing**. In the learning of sex roles, there seems to be a learning set, or snowball, effect. Thus, once the child has taken on certain aspects of the masculine or feminine role, he or she is then

The middle years of childhood: one

more open to the incorporaton of further aspects of that role, so that masculinity breeds further masculinity and femininity, femininity.

The anthropologist Ruth Benedict (1938) described cultural differences in **continuity of sex roles.** In our society, sex-role continuity seems to be greater for girls than for boys. If we assume that the female adult role is that of wife, parent, homemaker, and participant in local school and community affairs, then we can see how even the childhood culture of the girl prepares her for such a role. By contrast, the boy's childhood culture teaches him to be a hunter, woodsman, warrior, roustabout, and free-swinging playboy, which is quite at variance with the life he faces as husband, father, citizen, and good provider who will earn his living at desk or workbench. (Let us note that there are occupations more or less continuous with boyhood culture, like being a forest ranger, but only a few of these, such as the military and the construction industry, employ large numbers of people; and even if the boy grows up to enter such an occupation, it is usually combined with a domesticity for which boyhood has prepared him hardly at all.) The girl's role continuity is further enhanced by the fact that child-rearing, at home and at school, is largely in the hands of women. In one respect, though, we feel that there is some disadvantage for girls as well as for boys in having so much of their upbringing taken care of by women. Just as boys may lack male models to identify with at firsthand, so may girls lack males to relate too. A further complication is that women are looking for a new image of themselves, and there are very few models to tell them what this new image might be. The girl's female preceptors expect her to be like them, or at least like the ideal selves that they aspire to.

The situation for boys is also difficult but in a different way. The boy's female preceptors expect him to meet their standards of decorum, yet if he fails to exhibit a certain amount of rebellious spirit, of aggressiveness, of boisterousness, and even of ruthlessness, adults—women and men—become perturbed and feel that "something is missing." The role expectation for boys includes the parts of both Little Lord Fauntleroy and Tom Sawyer. The boy is taught obedience, generosity, and kindness, but if he does not stand up for his rights he is scorned as a sissy. Besides meeting adult role expectations, of course, the boy has to measure up to the rather different role expectations of the gang. Conflicts apart, boys are expected, perhaps in anticipation of their later responsibilities, to be ambitious and to strive for tangible achievement. Let us remember, however, that adults do not realize they are teaching their children to play sex roles but believe, rather, that they are simply witnessing, now with trepidation and now with satisfaction, the natural unfolding of male and female development.

The accomplishment-oriented role expectations for boys, plus the conflicts in expectations, plus the lack of adequate models, may account for the fact that boys are consistently more prone than girls to minor and major emotional, scholastic, and behavior problems (although mortality statistics suggest that boys may be biologically more vulnerable than girls). Boys are more likely than girls to stutter, to have reading disabilities, to wet the bed, to develop tics, to be rowdy and undisciplined, to become schizophrenic, and to run afoul of the authorities. The most central male diffi-

The society of children

375

culty seems to be control of aggression, and it is in this area that role expectations are most ambiguous, with conflicting and subtle pressures to act out one's feelings in some circumstances and to restrain them in others. But the incidence of misbehavior in the two sexes is not simply a matter of what children do; it is also a matter of how adults judge what children do. Research has shown that girls' misbehavior is judged more leniently than boys'—partly because boys, with greater available energy, make more noise in the course of misbehaving—which suggests that the greater frequency of misdeeds by boys may be an artifact of greater adult sensitivity to its occurrence (McClelland, 1961). A similar tendency may be at work in the fact that girls get better grades in school, whereas boys score higher on academic aptitude and achievement tests. And we must not forget that the people who judge behavior and give school marks are very often women.

The long-term effect of education and of a sophisticated culture in which there is less demand on sheer muscle is to make males more feminine and females more masculine. Historically, as the level of education rises, men become capable of greater tenderness, take an interest in domestic affairs, consider women their partners rather than their chattels, and take an interest in esthetic matters. At the same time, women become less flighty and capricious, become more analytical and logical, assert their right to sexual equality, and enter traditionally masculine occupational fields. These changed patterns are transmitted culturally in the educated classes, whereas the children of uneducated parents move in this direction as they rise through the educational system. This is not to say that in the future all sex differences will be

It is among his peers that the child gets his first introduction to many of the facts of life.

Annan Photo Features

376

abolished. It does imply that, as parents, teachers, and social engineers, we can see through the artificiality and even perniciousness of some of our sex-role expectations. We brutalize boys when we expect them to be cave men living in a technological, educated, humane society, and we brutalize girls when we expect little from them in the way of intellect and creativity, and when, on the other hand, we expect them to be passive, docile, accepting, and cast in traditional roles. In Freudian terms, we cultivate the boy's id and superego, we cultivate the girl's superego, and neglect the ego development of boys and girls alike.

Home
and Family

In order to make various features of the child's behavior stand out, we have to exaggerate them, and in the process we tend to distort and caricature them. Thus, both the child and the authors overdo his declaration of independence from the family. In fact, home and family continue to be important emotional refuges and sources of learning, entertainment, and companionship throughout these years. To begin with, some of peer-group life is lived within the home. Singly or in small groups, children visit each other's abodes, becoming involved in kite- or model-building projects, sometimes grandiose in conception and hurried in execution, in jewelry-making or embroidery, in writing and staging plays, in table games, in drawing pictures, in sharing marathon feasts in front of the television screen, sprawled in remarkable postures which may indeed be genuinely restful but are at the same time part of middle-years role playing.

But the child has siblings as well as friends, and we should take a moment to look at his dealing with his brothers and sisters. Granted that every family and every relationship is unique, we can still risk some generalizations. If siblings are fairly close in age and are all within the middle-years age band, their contacts at home are likely to be marked by baiting, bantering, bickering, battling, belittling, and bedlam, interspersed with some joint activities, some comparing of notes on school, people, activities, tastes and preferences, and, lest we overlook it, some more or less harmonious sharing in whole-family enterprises and in chores. (We should observe that many poor families have no all-family activities, not even whole-family meals.) If there are two siblings of the same sex and fairly close in age, the older often takes the role of mentor to the younger. Sometimes this is welcomed and accepted, sometimes not. When the siblings are in different periods of development, as when a school child has preschool or adolescent brothers and sisters, the gulf is likely to seem unbridgeable. The post-pubertal elder is inclined to be particularly critical of the grubby, noisy, ill-mannered, sassy younger child. He sometimes expresses this in open rage, occasionally through slaps and blows, and sometimes in elaborately haughty doubts as to their common parentage. The school-ager, in turn, shrewdly hacks or picks away at the adolescent's new and precarious dignity. A preschool brother or sister, on the other hand, is seen by the middle-years child as constantly underfoot or tagging along, disturbing and wrecking his property, and receiving favors and indulgences from the parents such as he was certainly never granted in the long bygone days (and since parents tend to be more indulgent toward successive children, he may be right). The elder child is highly jealous of the hard-won prerogatives of his age, while the younger resents them as preferential. If the younger child is much younger, an infant or a toddler or young preschooler, and so not in competition with the middle-years child, he is likely to be treated affectionately and indulgently—if sometimes as a nuisance. Occasionally, a new baby comes into the family after the first crop of children has reached adolescence. In such cases, the adolescents often seem to pitch into the role of assistant parents with great zeal.

Parents, all too aware of the turbulent aspects of sibling relations at home, are often thoroughly startled to learn how the children close ranks in family solidarity outside the home when one of them is threatened or abused. The terms "kid brother" and "big sister" may be used disparagingly, but they also carry considerable affection, which is supposed to be masked from the gang. It should further be pointed out that lower-class middle-years children, rather more often than middle-class ones, are likely to be put in charge of their younger brothers and sisters, who play on the edges of the group while the games go forward. It should be noted, too, that this responsibility for the younger kids is usually coupled with real authority over them. It is possible that the wielding of such authority is intrinsically satisfying in its own right, fits in well with the child's drive for independence, and enhances identification with the parents and their segment of society. Such responsibility is very common in many other cultures.

For all their insistence on freedom and privacy from adults, for all their sassiness and rebelliousness, and for all the fault they find with their parents and parental ways, children do not suddenly stop loving their parents. Indeed, as in displays of sibling solidarity, the same children who criticize their parents freely will not tolerate the slightest slur on them from outside the family. Parents cannot hope to remain high on a pedestal, but if they can bring themselves to climb down gracefully, they will find that there are other bases on which to be parents. And let us stress that there is no sight more pathetic than a father or mother trying to be a "pal" to son or daughter (not that there is any lack of things that they can enjoy doing together). There are plenty of peers around to serve as pals, and the child needs his parents as parents, which means as adults and not as pseudochildren. He needs them to turn to when he feels cut off from the gang in one of its periodic realignments, when he is sick, or at other vulnerable moments; he needs them as consultants on ethical and moral problems, and simply at times when he wants to be a member of his family, trading news and jokes and confidences, asking for information and advice and help with homework. At bedtime, he is likely to welcome a frolic, being read to (even though he is a perfectly proficient reader), and cuddling (those boys who have been taught that demonstrations of affection are unmanly may reject cuddling, but we suspect that they crave it nonetheless).

The child boasts of his parents' achievements to the gang, perhaps partly in hopes of gaining prestige but also because he is identifying with his parents, no matter how grudgingly. The child's conscious models are the gang and the gang's heroes: cowboys, nurses, athletes, movie and television stars, and other glamorous luminaries. It is mostly when one's father happens to be in an interesting and visible occupation—plumber, fisherman, garbage collector, fireman—that direct and conscious identification takes place. The case is more difficult for mothers, whose domestic activities by now form so accustomed a background of the child's life as to be all but invisible, or, when the child has to help out, are experienced as drudgery pure and simple. (In emergencies, such as a maternal illness, the children may pitch in with real enthusiasm.) Even if she has a career, it is unlikely to meet the double specifications of glamor and visibility.

Whatever the manner of the child's identification, he continues to need regulation. He may need parental backing to maintain his own values in the face of group pressure. Just as he expects privileges—a growing allowance, later bedtime, more freedom to roam, as he passes various developmental milestones—in keeping with increasing maturity, so is he able to accept increasing responsibility. When the child shares in family prosperity or hard times, in its triumphs and disasters, when he contributes by picking up in his room at age six, by making his bed and doing dishes and hanging up laundry at age ten, by shoveling the driveway or raking the yard at age twelve, when he has an appropriate part in family decisions—whether to acquire a pet, where to spend a vacation—he is becoming aware of the bonds of reciprocity that tie together a family, and, eventually, the world. It is worth noting that the democratic privileges accorded to children are still limited and subject to adult authority. Children in the school years are not usually ready for full demo-

Vivienne, DPI

Children and their parents.

Ken Heyman

cratic self-determination. But sound authority, even when it hurts them the most, is on their side and is aimed at producing sane, rational, sensitive, humane adults.

Even though adults must be strong, their authority with children of this age cannot be absolute. Parents have to recognize children's commitment to the peer-group mores and understand the importance of the group for the child's growth toward independence. Obviously, adults have to combat the gang's more pernicious teachings, but in full awareness of the constructive functions of group affiliation. The peer culture is a mixed blessing, but we do not know of any substitute for it or shortcut to the benefits it brings. Here, as at all ages, parents must be prepared to let the child try out some enterprises that the parents know to be foredoomed, to let him make some mistakes and, we hope, to learn from making them. And it is the job of parents to support the child through the pain of failure and to help him learn the lessons it teaches—without rubbing it in.

Sexual Latency and Growth Latency

Earlier, we defined Freud's concept of **latency** as a hiatus in sexual interest and activity beginning with the resolution and repression of the Oedipus complex and ending with the urgent reawakening of sexual desires associated with puberty. In Freudian terms, the sex cleavage of the middle years, accompanied by a lavish show of indifference and even animosity toward the opposite sex, would be a reaction formation, a going to the opposite

extreme, in order to keep sexual impulses repressed. The upsurge of intellectual curiosity observed in school children would be sublimation, a transformation of repressed sexual energies, and also a disguised sexual curiosity. The child's rituals, chants, and rigid adherence to rules and formulas would be viewed as magical devices for controlling impulses and feelings, including the anxieties and hostilities brought on by the traumatic climax of the Oedipal drama.

In point of fact, the collective and individual rituals of school-age children bear a marked resemblance to the behavior of adults burdened with what psychiatrists call an **obsessive-compulsive** neurosis. Obsessions, which do not always accompany compulsions, consist of the thoughts one cannot get rid of, like the snatches of melody that run unwanted, mindlessly and maddeningly, through consciousness. Obsessive humming, recitation, and counting are common in the school years. Adult compulsions are an irresistible need to perform some useless act: to wash one's hands repeatedly, to check the door locks over and over again before leaving the house, an incessant taking stock and tallying of things and arrangements, arranging one's work materials neatly over and over again before starting work, and other senseless but obligatory rituals, such as rubbing one's hands together three times, that precede any action and that sometimes become so protracted that the action itself is never begun.

There are two ways of looking at compulsions, and perhaps two types of compulsions, both relevant to behavior in the middle years. The first sees compulsive rituals as a way of giving order, meaning, and manageability to a world in flux, and so of finding security and certainty. Compulsive preparatory rituals are a way of making sure that everything is in place so that one can safely act, or perhaps even a device for postponing indefinitely a secretly undesired action. The second perspective on, or type of, compulsive behavior is as a disguised symbolic enactment of an impulse or past event that is too strong to be wholly repressed but too threatening to be admitted directly to awareness or acted on. Thus, compulsive handwashing might be interpreted as expressing feelings of uncleanliness generated by one's unacknowledged "dirty" cravings. Analogously, the child's rituals may be seen as a partial expression of imperfectly repressed Oedipal urges.

However, Freud's original notion of latency as an asexual time out has had to be modified in the light of what we now know about sexuality in the middle years. Sexual interest and play are not snuffed out, but are simply hidden from adult attention. It is worth noting that whereas Freud had to combat the popular belief that there was no infantile sexuality to become latent, the post-Freudians have to combat Freud's idea that there is a gap in the chain of overt psychosexual development. A possible reconciliation, not inconsistent with psychoanalytic theory, is that it is only attraction to the parent of the opposite sex that is repressed, making possible attention to other sexual objects.

Children, regardless of any theory, are eager to acquire forbidden information and to pass it on to other children. We have already mentioned some of the actual sexual behavior that goes on during these years. By the middle school years, there is a steady traffic among children in off-color stories, which may be poorly comprehended but are sure to elicit titters and giggles. Children likewise giggle together over the dictionary in which they look up words referring to sexual or excretory functions, or over the Bible, in which they look up references to fornication. The doctor's child is guaranteed popularity by allowing his friends to consult the plates in medical texts. One outcome of the child's researches is his discovery that sex is a general human phenomenon, and not just something peculiar to him and his group. Notice also that sex and toilet functions are poorly differentiated at this age. We should also note the sexual component in the teasing and tussling between boys and girls of this age, and in the bodily discovery and mastery underlying the physical skills and stunts the child practices.

It is not always easy to tell, of course, the extent to which the child's sexual behavior is motivated by real, internal lusts and cravings, and to what extent by simple curiosity, especially curiosity about the unknown and forbidden. It is our guess, however, that spontaneous lust rarely arises much before the end of this period, and that sexual feelings have to be externally stimulated or, once the child has learned about the possibility, self-stimulated. But whatever the motivational basis of their sexual curiosity and behavior, children know that such things are frowned on by adults and the mere mention of them will meet with explicit threats (some of our children are still being told that masturbation will stunt their growth, or cause mental deficiency or insanity, or cause disease, or cause the penis to drop off), reproaches, or, at best, a strained reserve and a sense that one is in taboo territory. As a result, most children experience some anxiety and guilt in connection with their sexual investigations.

Sexual latency and growth latency

Sex education

Children are further made aware of adult ambivalence about sex and of the ambiguity of taboos, including adult violations of taboos. Indeed, in this area as in such others as honesty in money matters (including income tax and traffic fines), generosity, telling the truth, levels of competence and importance, adult hypocrisy becomes plainly evident to children of this age. The parents themselves, who grew up under even more restrictive conditions, can be pardoned if they feel that sex is a highly sensitive topic about which it is hard to talk to children. Yet most parents feel that they want their children to know the facts of sex, to understand them, and to grow up to enjoy sex wisely and thoroughly. Their first problem is to know for themselves what the morally and psychologically relevant standards are for the conduct of adult sexuality. This is something that they have to decide for themselves, since the culture today provides answers ranging all the way from total sexual license, whereby it would be rude and selfish to refuse just about any prospective partner, to a harsh puritanism which says that sex should be enjoyed minimally, and then only in the narrow context of procreation, disarranging one's nightclothes as little as possible.

The second problem for parents is to know what to tell children and how and when. To take the last question, that of timing, first, the school-age child, with his greater wariness about expressing his feelings and his awareness of adult taboos, is less likely than the preschool child to cue his parents with specific questions. All the same, the parents can be sure that the child is picking up information and misinforma-

tion—and attitudes—from his contemporaries, and if the parents wish priority for their views, they should begin giving information sooner rather than later. As with the preschool child—to move to the what and how part of the problem—this is never done once and for all; it must be taught and retaught at increasingly complex and concrete levels. Certainly in dealing with children in the later middle years, there is no reason a girl should be left to experience her first menstruation as a shocking and perhaps terrifying surprise, as so many girls still do, or why boys, for that matter, should not have some factual knowledge of the menstrual cycle instead of deep ignorance or a dim awareness, fed by Biblical or other sources, of some great, dark female secret. The principle of early timing applies not only to anticipating events or rival information, but is important also in giving information while it is still primarily of informational interest, before it gets mixed up with the emotional storms of adolescence.

The question of how to impart knowledge may also be one of who imparts it. Frank discussion of sexual matters between parent and child may imply an intimacy that both find very trying, and it is possible that somebody else should do the job. As one insightful ten-year-old observed to her teacher, "My parents are very understanding and all that, but there are some things it's easier to talk about with other people." The "somebody else" may be a book designed for young readers, of which there are several excellent ones available (e.g., Johnson, 1965; Child Study Association, 1965). It may be an uncle or an aunt, a family friend, a physician, a clergyman, a recreation-group leader, or a teacher, although none of these positions guarantees that the person has the requisite knowledge, skill, sensitivity, and wisdom for the task.

The teacher who sets out to impart sex information must feel secure herself, must have already won the confidence and respect of the children, must have some sort of understanding with the children's parents (some proportion of parents simply do not want their children to know about sex, although how they can keep them from finding out that there is such a thing eludes us), and must deal with small enough groups of children so that she can discuss rather than lecture, maintaining a one-to-one relationship with each child (the tittering bystander changes the whole tone of the situation). Under such optimal conditions, the teacher can deal with mixed groups of boys and girls. However, if she —or he—makes tactful opportunities for it, she is more likely to be approached by individuals or by small same-sex groups seeking enlightenment.

Formal programs of sex education for schools have recently been devised and widely adopted. They have met with enraged protests from some groups and individuals who seem to equate sexual knowledge with sexual activity, and both with communism. Ill-prepared teachers have indeed sometimes botched the job badly, but it seems clear that future education will routinely include information about sexual functions.

The what of sex education has to include more than where babies come from, and cannot leave children with the sense that sex is one more pleasant activity along with eating sweets, watching television, playing children's games, and going for outings with the family. It is not enough to say that sex is beautiful or that it occurs in a context of love. The parent or other instructor has to convey, preferably before the upheavals of adolescence begin, some idea of the urgency of sex drives, of the ecstatic pleasure of erotic experience, sex differences in sexuality, the varieties of sexual experience and stimulation, and, more subtly, of the place of sex in temporary as well as in more profound and lasting relationships between people. From this point of view, we consider it desirable, when parents are comfortable in communication, for the boy to get some sex truths and views from his mother and the girl from her father—if only inside warning of the wiles and ploys of the other sex. The parent who has been frank in these respects will find it easier, as the need requires, to convey the role of sex in mature love, and the desirability, in terms of such later relationships, in terms of one's own feelings of personal integrity, and in terms of enjoying sex in all its fullness, of accepting restraints on and postponements of gratification.

The authors are not prepared to say when the right moment comes for which kinds of sexual experience. It is clear that many school-age children are seduced into one kind of sexual activity or another, by other children, by adolescents, or by adults of their own sex or the opposite sex, for the most part without apparent harm. The ultimate meaning of childhood sexual experience has to be judged in terms of how it influences the individual's self-image relative to other people, and this, in turn, has to be judged in the context of the values and disvalues assigned by the culture to various forms of interpersonal relations. We strongly suspect, however, that the child's sexual taste and discrimination will be learned less from parental admonition

Sexual latency and growth latency

than from the concrete behavior of the adult world. Above all, it is the child's parents who provide a model of adult love and affection.

Growth latency

While the notion of sexual latency seems to be at least partially contradicted by the facts, there is another sense in which the concept of latency is quite applicable to the middle years. We have chosen to call this **growth latency**, referring to the slower pace of physical development than in the periods preceding and following the middle years. The school-age child is on a plateau of growth between the first spurt of infancy and the one that introduces puberty. Physical growth and reorganization continue during these years, but at a slower pace, without the abrupt emergences of earlier and later phases. A number of workers in this area have developed the notion of **growth ages**, providing separate measures for the various asynchronous aspects of growth. Thus, the child's chronological age can be compared with his Mental Age, Reading Age, Height Age, Weight Age, Grip Age (the strength of his grip), Dental Age, Carpal Age (bone ossification as determined by x-rays of the hand and wrist), and so forth, yielding various "indices" of growth. (Such research relies heavily on the use of x-ray studies of the interior of the body, and has become much less common as people have become aware of the perils of exposure to ionizing radiation.)

Within the general framework of the growth latency pattern, any number of individual growth patterns are possible. Some of the more characteristic growth pathways are represented in the so-called Wetzel grid, on which an individual's growth indicators can be entered to see if he conforms to any of the standard growth patterns. If he does, fairly accurate predictions can be made of ultimate growth status. Such predictions may bring realistic reevaluation both to the shrimp who feels that he is forever doomed to be dwarfed among giants and to the erstwhile giant whose growth has slowed down and who sees the former shrimps shooting past him. However, so many factors of health, diet, exercise, and endocrine function enter into physical growth that individual predictions have to be made with considerable caution.

Growth latency may be the physiological counterpart of the psychological phenomenon of the middle years as a period distinct from all the rest. It is the psychological stability of these years, between two periods of turbulence, that make them seem, at least in retrospect which may be misguided, the "halcyon days of childhood" which many adults look back on with nostalgic longing.

the
middle
years of
childhood:
two

Cognitive Functioning
in Middle-Years Children

Thus far, we have mentioned only in passing that the school-age child goes to school. Leaving aside for the moment the nature of the schooling available, formal learning is a singularly appropriate thing for children of this age to do. A major shift in cognitive functioning takes place somewhere around the beginning of the school years. In Piaget's terms, the child enters the stage of **concrete operations**. This means that the child **conserves**, that is, he recognizes that certain properties of the world, such as the volume of liquid in a flask or the number of buttons in a box, cannot be changed simply by altering their disposition in space. It means that the child is capable of **seriation**, putting things in a sensible order, on the model of numbers. It means that he can grasp the notion of **reversibility**, that certain logical operations can go two ways, as subtraction undoes addition or division undoes multiplication; hydrogen and oxygen can be combined to produce water and water can be analyzed into hydrogen and oxygen. It means that the child can **classify**, sort things into categories on the basis of shared attributes. More generally, the child has developed various readinesses—reading readiness, number readiness, and so forth, including the emotional readiness to put aside his immediate concerns and preoccupations and pay attention to facts and ideas outside his everyday experience. The child's increased self-awareness shows up in his growing capacity for field-independence (see p. 72), both in the sense of responsiveness to internal bodily cues and in the sense of having and hewing to opinions and ideas of his own. It used to be as-

sumed that readiness for school was largely a matter of physical maturation, but we have come to know too much about the effects of early privation and enrichment on school learning to accept so simple a view. There may indeed be maturational differences between those who learn easily and those who do not, but we do not know what they are or to what extent they are the product of differences in emotional and cognitive stimulation. We know that it is very hard for a child to pay attention in school if he is hungry, if he does not get enough sleep, if he has some acute or chronic illness, if he is afraid to go out on the streets, if he is afraid to come home, if he has problems of family identity, or if he cannot see the point of what is being talked about in class. Thus, the cognitive maturity supposedly characteristic of the middle years can be complicated by a host of physical, emotional, and motivational factors.

Assuming conditions favorable to the development of learning readiness, we see that the middle-years child characteristically turns his attention away from family involvements and outward toward the world at large. He begins to substitute a naturalistic view for a magicalistic one. He learns to appraise human behavior objectively as well as affectively. He learns—slowly—to try to take other people's points of view. He comes to turn away from an exclusive preoccupation with human affairs (in which we would have to include the child's dealings with domestic animals) toward the analysis of the living and inert nonhuman sphere. He becomes able to think about things distant in time and space. He wants to know about the mechanics of things, how they work and how they are made. Make-believe is no longer blended hit-or-miss with his reality. He has not abandoned magic and make-believe, but they are more private than before, and the line between being and pretending is sharply drawn. He is learning, however imperfectly, to think systematically, in terms of organizing schemes and principles like the taxonomies of biology and the characteristics of numbers. But above all else, he wants to know.

He wants both knowledge and know-how. He wants information (although, at this age, he does not discriminate well between information and misinformation), and he wants to catch on to the skills and tricks and competences and procedures that are the mark of the initiate. Many kindergarten children seem to have the half-formulated belief that simple enrollment in first grade will magically confer such skills and membership. Even at a slightly higher level of understanding, abilities like reading or playing the piano seem to the child to be a matter of knowing the right trick—one reason why practicing palls when the trick is not immediately forthcoming. Thus, the same forces that move him to embrace the rituals of childhood partly govern his approach to school learning and give to it some of the other's ritual flavor. Even late in the school years, the child may consider it an achievement to memorize the Gettysburg Address, even though he knows little or nothing about its occasion. At the same time he asks, "You know the Gettysburg Address? 1270 Elm Street, Gettysburg, Pennsylvania."

Symbols

At the heart of the school child's cognitive status is his increasing mastery of symbols. The preschool child is caught in word

A field trip to buy a pumpkin for a Hallowe'en jack-o'-lantern.

Nancy Rudolph

realism, such that words and statements are as real as anything else and are easily confused with the things they stand for. Notice that word realism is never outgrown. It is this attitude toward words that makes some topics unspeakable, that drives people to euphemism, whereby an unlovely subject is given a safe name; to hints and allusions, whereby people never really say what it is they are talking about; and to circumlocution, whereby they define a topic by talking all around it without giving it a name. Part of the job of educators and writers is to put into words things that their students and readers cannot or dare not say for themselves. We have rather often heard from lecture audiences that the views we have expressed on values, divorce laws, abortion, and other touchy topics, were things that they had always thought but had never put into words. Needless to say, we have also received some abuse for daring to say such things. It is verbal realism, too, that enables one to participate vicariously in stories, to respond to oratory and to poetic evocation, and to accept as fact the often false pronouncements of public figures. For those who can read, the written word carries even greater power—who can doubt the authority and accuracy of something that has appeared *in print*?

Nevertheless, the school child has begun to sense that words and the concrete things or actions or attributes they may refer to belong to distinct orders of reality. This differentiation of levels gives the child greater freedom to manipulate symbols, as seen in the delight he takes in playing with symbols and meanings. Middle-class middle-years children typically are fascinated by rhymes, alliteration, anagrams, codes and ciphers, foreign words and

phrases, onomatopoeia, and puns (including double entendre—but not yet metaphors). They like to play with the ambiguities of language, as in "I simply can't bear it. It's much too heavy," or "You want me to take my vitamins? O.K., I'll take them to my room." They play with negatives, as in the poem about "The Little Man Who Wasn't There." That symbols have not been completely differentiated from the rest of reality is shown, however, by children's literalism: their unquestioning acceptance of the words of chants and rituals without wondering what they refer to, and their inability to detect sarcasm or irony, where one often says the opposite of what one means.

They do comprehend broad travesty and burlesque, and a favorite occupation is to compose playlets satirizing television commercials. Sometimes they make the connection between words used in a variety of senses, as in *bear-bear*, or to tell a *lie–lie down*, and sometimes they do not. Asch and Nerlove (1960) report that children may understand the meaning of *a sweet person*, but deny any connection with the sweetness of sugar. They love big words and use them globally, without really knowing their meaning. Werner and Kaplan (1950) carried out a study of age differences in ability to deduce the meaning of a word from its use in various contexts. The child would be given a series of sentences containing the same made-up word and asked to guess the word's meaning. Some characteristic responses were that the word means the whole sentence (the response to the word *bordicks* in the sentence "People talk about the bordicks of others and don't like to talk about their own" was "People talk about other people and don't talk about themselves, that's what bordick means"); that the word means itself (that *contavish* means "You know, like contavish"); or that the word stands for some condensation of the sentence (the response to *bordick* in the sentence "If you are smart and work hard your work will not have a bordick" was "Bordick means smart so you won't get a D").

Indeed, for many young school children, language seems to be only partially differentiated into single words, which may be a factor in beginning reading difficulties, since the divisions of words on a page may not correspond to the sound groupings the child hears and uses. (Even among college students, we find such undifferentiated terms as *anotherwords, infact, alot, alittle, inspite, outloud, otherhand, motorability*.) In reading, the child may have further difficulty with analysis of words into phonetic elements, and some number of children read at first simply by memorizing the words that go with certain letter combinations. Notice that this process initially goes in only one direction: the child knows that *c-a-t* on the page in front of him spells *cat*, but he himself cannot yet spell *cat*. Traces of immature language persist throughout this period, as in double negatives and the past tenses of irregular verbs ("Harriet baby-sitted with us over the weekend"). In general, though, children of this age become increasingly able to dominate language, to make it do their bidding, and, as at other points of near mastery, they practice their skills indefatigably. As they progress in reading, the mechanics become functionally subordinated to meaning, so that it takes an effort to see the letters themselves. The Stroop color-word technique, for instance, employs color names printed in ink of a color different from the color named. The better children

can read, the harder they find it to name the color of the ink (Comalli et al., 1962; Sichel and Chandler, 1969).

Among the particular symbolic skills that appear early in the middle years—given the proper stimulation now and at earlier ages—are the ability to define words, to supply antonyms on demand, to find similarities between related things (that is, to make explicit the nature of equivalences), to detect and specify absurdities and incongruities in pictures and stories (as when the child is presented with sentences like "They looked out and saw that the sun was shining, so they took their raincoats with them"), to count indefinitely, to count by twos, fives, and tens, to count backward (although even four-year-olds nowadays learn from television the refrain "10, 9, 8 . . . zero, blast off!"), and to add and subtract (like many primitive peoples, some children find it hard to grasp that one can use the same number system to tally qualitatively different things).

Such skills do not emerge full-blown, but develop over a period of a year or two in a fairly regular progression. When it comes to defining concrete nouns, for instance, the child may at first give a partial definition in terms of a single characteristic or function, which, while accurate enough, is insufficient to describe the class of things under consideration. Thus, *bicycle* may be defined as "It's got pedals" or "You ride on it." At a slightly later stage, a bicycle becomes "Something that you ride on [for want of the word *vehicle*], and it's got two wheels, and these pedals that you push, and handlebars to steer with." Notice that this sort of definition is far less egocentric than the earlier ones in that it supplies the information necessary for understanding.

Cognitive functioning in middle-years children

391

Observe, too, that the more advanced style of definition implies a detached, gamelike, abstract attitude to the task, since the child knows that the examiner knows what a bicycle is and that the examiner is asking the child not for the sake of the information gained but to see how well the child can convey information.

A somewhat similar pattern of development can be seen in the way a child attacks the task of finding similarities. The five- or six-year-old may misconstrue the task and, asked in what way a cat and a mouse are alike, reply simply that "The cat chases the mouse." At a more advanced stage, he seizes on peripheral, nondefining characteristics of the two things, as when he says that a cat and a mouse "Both have whiskers," or "Both have four legs," or that an apple and a peach are alike "Because you eat them both." At a still more advanced stage, the child is able to name the class of things to which the two specimens belong, and can make explicit that cats and mice are animals, that apples and peaches are fruits, and that bicycles and cars are both means of transportation. Notice that the ability to define words or to give similarities is not some generalized mental mechanism that develops in the child. His level of competence depends very much on the characteristics of the materials he has to deal with. It is easier to define concrete nouns than abstract ones like *justice*, and it is easier to define nouns than adjectives like *proud*. It is easier to say how a bicycle and motorcar are alike than to specify the similarity between *salt* and *water*, *25* and *36*, or *first* and *last*, so that the child who can say that an apple and a peach are both fruits may still respond to the pairing of *salt* and *water* with "They make salt water," or to the pairing of *coal* and *paper*

with "Paper is white and coal is black," or "You can write on paper with a piece of coal." The child may have special difficulty dealing with the similarity between opposites like *first* and *last*; it requires considerable sophistication to appreciate that, in order to be opposite, things must belong to a common domain.

One way of finding out what words mean to the child is to ask him to define them. Another is to infer the meanings of component words from the way he interprets whole statements such as common proverbs (Richardson and Church, 1959). It is only late in the middle years, as we have suggested, that the child begins to sense the metaphorical meanings of many proverbs. When he does begin, he fails to see the need for any logical parallels between the proverb itself and the more general idea it is meant to express. As a result, his first attempts at a metaphorical interpretation reveal the physiognomic, global way in which he apprehends the proverb. For example, a nine-year-old boy defined *An ounce of prevention is worth a pound of cure* as "Well, if something is too heavy for an old person, you could help him carry it"; an eleven-year-old girl defined *Every cloud has a silver lining:* "There's a blue cloud in the sky." Some interpretations, however, show common misunderstandings of particular words. A nine-year-old defines *Absence makes the heart grow fonder* as "It makes your heart grow weaker, I guess." Now the primary misunderstanding here is not of the word "fonder," but of "absence," which to this child, as to many others, means "sickness," by a process of you're-absent-from-school-because-you're-sick.

Sometimes emotional associations or moral considerations distort the child's understanding. Many middle-years children are taken aback by *Revenge is sweet*, and may even refuse to try to define it. When they do try, children are likely to change the meaning of the statement, even to the extent of forcing words out of shape, as in "You don't revenge too hard," or even "It means the same thing as 'forgive.' " We can see the way personal, subjective matters intrude on the thinking of children in a typical nine-year-old interpretation of *A stitch in time saves nine:* "Like if you had a broken hand, you stitch it, like if someone got hurt, say, like a nine-year-old, he needed stitches."

Two well-known techniques, the **word association test** and the misnamed **semantic differential**, seek to get at the feeling tones associated with words rather than at their content. The word association test requires the subject to say the first thing that occurs to him in response to each of a series of stimulus words. Although originally meant as a device for locating sensitive areas of a person's experience, the word association test has proven at least as useful for studying systematic developmental changes in the organization of associations. The young middle-years child is likely to respond with concrete, contextual associations drawn from everyday life, as in *dog*—"barks" or *eat*—"dinner." (Notice the analogy to such similarities responses as "The cat chases the mouse.") Such responses are called **syntagmatic**, in that stimulus and response form a statement. Some young children give rhyming responses, as in *table*—"Mabel," or **Klang responses**, where the response word bears a global phonetic resemblance to the stimulus word, as in *baggage*—"language." With increasing age there is a shift from contextually related responses to formally,

logically related ones such as synonyms, antonyms, and logical coordinates (*chair*—"couch") or subordinates (*gem*—"diamond"). Such responses are dubbed **paradigmatic**, in that they fit a formal scheme, or paradigm. Paradigmatic responses belong to the same grammatical part of speech as the stimulus word, whereas the typical syntagmatic response combines a noun and verb or a noun and adjective. Studies by Koff (1965) and by Jenkins and associates (Jenkins and Russell, 1960; Palermo and Jenkins, 1965; Jenkins and Palermo, 1965) indicate that the patterning of children's word associations has changed in the last half century, with today's eight- to twelve-year-old children giving far more formal and fewer contextual responses than their counterparts of yesteryear. While these findings may indicate that today's children are more mature than children of an earlier day, a secondary finding is that the modern groups agreed more in their responses than the early samples, which may imply a lessening of diversity over the years. The semantic differential (Osgood et al., 1957) scales (which elicit only a small part of the semantic content) require the subject to rate "concepts," words or phrases such as *mother* or *wild strawberries*, on antonymic dimensions such as hot-cold or strong-weak. The scales as they now exist have numerous logical deficiencies (Weinreich, 1958) and they have been little used with children (an exception is Maltz, 1963), but they offer some promise as a research tool in understanding the meanings words have for children.

Later in the school years, the child becomes capable of such advanced symbolic manipulations as multiplication and division, and translating back and forth between words and numbers. Indeed, we consider the one almost unqualified success among recent attempts at curricular reform in the grades to be the introduction of New or Modern Mathematics, which begins with the logic of numerical relationships and brings the child early to such algebraic operations as finding unknowns, generalized formulas, factoring, and finding roots and exponentials. The chief reservation we have about the New Math is in its teaching. The derivation of shortcut methods of calculation is too long delayed in most schools, leaving the child to solve problems by perfectly logical but unnecessarily cumbersome roundabout techniques.

Children also learn to make and use maps and the special concepts of geographers. Middle-class urban and suburban children do not, however, characteristically orient themselves to the points of the compass in the way children living in the country learn to do. Children also learn to understand charts, graphs, and diagrams, and can translate simple blueprints into material objects. Notice, too, that the world is full of diverse symbols (some of which are better described as **signs**, conditioned signals for particular reactions): the policeman symbolizes authority, the expensive new car symbolizes high status, the trademark symbolizes the company or the product, money symbolizes work and buying power, the flag symbolizes the social or political group, and so forth. There has been little formal study of the way children come to react to such signs and symbols.

General information

In his transition from an egocentric, personalized, subjective orientation to an objective, relativistic view of the world (which, obviously, is never complete), the child builds up a framework of expectations. It is this framework, which must be constantly revised, that enables him to marvel, to wonder, to be curious, and to organize—however primitively—the facts he accumulates. He locates himself in time (although his early years have been largely erased from memory) and recognizes, if with little personal conviction, that the world existed before he entered it and that it will survive his passing. He meditates upon what it means to be age ten or twelve or twenty. He ponders the mysteries of life, birth, and death. He becomes aware of the processes of his own body—respiration, circulation, digestion, the senses, the hiatus of sleep. He learns about germs and viruses and disease and may have bouts of hypochondria. When the city child first learns where meat comes from, this may be quite disturbing, and a number of children go through a period of partial or total vegetarianism (which is becoming an article of faith for many teen-agers). The child is interested in causal sequences to the extent that he wants to know how to do things, but he remains largely phenomenalistic and realistic, and hence fatalistic, in his outlook. Nonetheless, his framework of regularities makes some new relationships stand out for him. He sees the burst of the fireworks display and notes that it takes a second or so for the sound to reach him. The concept of gravity comes to him with the force of revelation, and the idea of weightlessness becomes a new field of fantasy. Children are fascinated by space travel and space exploration and, more recently, have discovered the world beneath the sea through snorkeling, scuba diving, and the undersea adventures of Cousteau.

As times change, many of the groups of

middle-years children we now see seem to be increasingly pragmatic and decreasingly romantic. As they read more and travel more, they are less inclined to glamorize the frontier and warfare, and show more concern with social issues and human relations. And, as we have said, the movies and television shows they prefer stress the sardonic and the satirical even when dealing with traditional themes like mystery and adventure and cowboys and Indians. Like yesterday's children, today's are very much moved by questions of justice and injustice, especially with regard to themselves. The child, with his magicalism and artificialism, finds it hard to accept that it is the accident of rainfall or competing parental obligations that causes him to miss out on some treat, and instead looks for some malevolent agency to account for the injustice. Increasingly, though, children seem able to deal with general principles of justice and to see how these apply to problems like poverty and prejudice. There is already evidence that today's middle-years children have a social awareness far exceeding that of past generations, and they help swell the ranks of peace marches, ecology campaigns, and various liberation movements. They do not think very clearly about the issues, but they display humane intuitions.

The middle-years child's growing objectivity and skepticism have other consequences than in the realm of factual knowledge. The child becomes able to judge his own performance by stable, external standards, enabling him to comment, "Isn't this a junk drawing?" or to compare his athletic skills with those of his classmates. Middle-class children come to feel at home with the "objective" test, whether of how far one can throw a ball as compared to others of the same age and sex, of ability, or of achievement, and they take their scores on such measures as seriously as do adults. Another by-product of the child's new detachment, his new ability to stand off from things and eye them critically, is that he turns the tables on adults. Previously, he was a transparent object of adult appraisal. Now, he can return the adults' scrutiny and do his own appraising, a gift that they may find unsettling.

Thinking and reasoning

As we have said, the middle-years child's growing mastery of symbols and his ever-broadening fund of general knowledge permit him to think in ways that come to approximate those of adults. Indeed, in some areas, the child may know a great deal more than his less educated parents and so be able to think more rationally than they—parents typically complain that their children's homework demands more knowledge than they the parents can muster. But however adroitly he can deal with certain circumscribed topics like doing proportions, batting averages, interplanetary travel, and the habits of starfish, his everyday thinking on matters of personal concern is likely to be muddled by emotionalism, confusion of levels of discourse, magicalism, facts invented *ad hoc* to substantiate his point of view, *non sequiturs*, superstition, misinformation, and the murk of ignorance. To the best of our knowledge, no one has ever applied a systematic logical analysis to the spontaneous reasonings of school children, but it seems likely to us that children are abundantly guilty of every logical fallacy known to philosophers.

One common form of thought in chil-

▲

Scapegoating in animals, as studied by Nathan Azrin. When the animal receives an electric shock alone in his cage, he freezes into immobility. When he has a cage-mate, however, he attacks ferociously, as though the companion were responsible for the shock.

▼

dren and adults is **scapegoating**, the venting of one's frustrations and resentments on some convenient person, animal, or thing, sometimes explicitly putting the blame for one's misfortunes on the scapegoat. Azrin (1967) has demonstrated scapegoating in a variety of nonhuman species. An animal given a painful electric shock when alone in its cage responds by freezing into immobility. However, when there is another animal in the cage (of whatever species, including stuffed toys), the animal reacts to shock with a vicious attack upon his cage-mate, as though that helpless creature were to blame. When the child puts the blame for some disappointment on his parents or the Almighty, he is scapegoating. In general, it is very hard to convince children (and many adults) that some events just happen, that no one is to blame, or that an action or a state of affairs can be multiply determined, with no single person or agency responsible. But scapegoating seems to be only one form of a more general process by which one seeks out an object on which to fasten one's feelings. Many school-age children suffer a certain amount of diffuse anxiety or even dread, and the child has to find something to be frightened of—he seeks a fear-goat, so to speak, for his fears. In general, children of this age attach their fears to real things—animals, kidnappers, burglars, and the rest—but fears of imaginary entities—ghosts, witches, punitive forces—persist throughout. And even when the child is afraid of real things, he fears them out of all proportion to their actual menace. We can see further analogies to scapegoating and fear-goating in the love-goating of the older middle-years child's crushes and hero worship and in the adolescent's eager search for someone to fall in love with. This general process seems to work both as a means of handling emotions and also as a way of identifying and giving shape to otherwise elusive feelings. Notice, too, that such emotion-goating has much in common with the private, compulsive rituals we talked about earlier.

MORAL JUDGMENTS. The child's logic, as we have said, is colored by his knowledge and ignorance and by his emotions. One special dimension of his feelings about things is the moral meanings he attaches to them. The preschool child has a conscience, but in terms of responsibility for his acts he must be thought of as amoral, a view shared by most theologians (with due provision for the cleansing away of Original Sin). The middle-years child, by contrast, is moralistic. He learns and applies the rules of right and wrong in a harsh, rigid, absolutistic way that, early in this period, makes no allowance for good intentions and extenuating circumstances. Having been told that he lives in a free country, he cannot understand why he cannot always do just as he wishes. The battle cry "It's not fair!" (nowadays often phrased as "It's cheat!") expresses the child's detection of a departure from the rules as he construes them. Piaget (1948) has proposed that the two main characteristics of the child's moral judgments are **moral realism**, the assumption that moral rules have an existence in their own right, analogous to the conception of Natural Law, and **immanent justice**, the sense that misdeeds carry within them the seeds of their own punishment. Milton Senn (personal communication) gives an interesting example of immanent justice in a twelve-year-old boy who violated hospital rules to sneak in and visit a relative who had a broken leg, then himself was in an accident in which he broke his leg, and was profoundly convinced that his injury was a punishment for his transgression. In this case, the boy's sense of immanent justice was exacerbated and compounded by a nurse who told him that if he did not cease his cries of woe, the doctors would be obliged to cut off his ailing leg. Not too surprisingly, the boy screamed harder and more persistently than ever.

Children judge each other much more stringently than would adults, and are likely to suggest summary execution or a session on the rack as appropriate remedies for minor infractions. We suspect that such harshness—as in the Freudian reasoning about the compulsive traits of latency—represents the child's concern about keeping his own impulses in check. It may also be an attempt to give order to shifting reality by putting the world into rigid compartments, with the result that any injustice or untruth threatens the still-precarious stability of the universe. It may appear to adults that children flout every established moral tenet, but when we look closer, we see that children are regulated by codes (especially those they impose on each other in the gang) more binding than adults could tolerate.

Obviously, children do violate their codes, and, like adults, they find devices for avoiding guilt. They become masters of denial (which often seems to include actual loss of memory for the misdeed), rationalization, and self-justification. In general, the defense mechanisms against guilt consist in using the magic of words to change the meanings of an act so as to make it fit the person's conception of right and wrong. This process is greatly facilitated by the child's literal-mindedness. The letter of the

Cognitive functioning in middle-years children

rule is more important than its spirit. He will argue legalistically and litigiously for the narrowest possible interpretation, so that his behavior falls outside the letter of the law: "You said not to run. I was galloping." Later in the school years, children relinquish much of their absolutism in favor of tolerance, flexibility, and relativism, just as they learn to be more dispassionate about the gang's codes and the external fixity of the rules of games. Adults, too, find themselves coming in for censure. A casual expletive, such as the child himself would delight in using in the gang, on the lips of an adult may provoke real moral indignation.

Kohlberg (1963) has elaborated Piaget's account of the development of moral judgments into a system of six successive stages:

1. Obedience is the norm and disobedience meets with punishment.
2. Pleasure-seeking and the avoidance of pain are the chief guides to conduct.
3. One acts virtuously to gain or maintain the approval of others.
4. Faith in authority.
5. Reciprocity with others and a common law established by consensus.
6. Conduct should be governed by individual principles of right and wrong.

Stages 1–4 go with the middle years, 4–6 with adolescence. Kohlberg's stages seem to apply in a number of societies (Kohlberg, 1964), although they have not been tested in non-Western settings.

Philosophers have wrestled for centuries with the meanings of *good* and *bad*, and almost all agree that the moral dimension of *virtue-evil* is relevant. Other dimensions on which people pretty regularly evaluate things are the esthetic, or *beautiful-ugly*,

the pragmatic, or *useful-injurious*, the *rational-irrational* dimension, and the dimension of emotionally *pleasant-unpleasant*. It seems to be characteristic of school-age children that their evaluative judgments confuse these dimensions, so that to denounce something as "queer" or "crazy" is also to question its morality, beauty, utility, and emotional qualities.

Middle-years children do learn to echo adult judgments of sunsets, vistas, and works of art or music as "beautiful," but this seems to be more a learning of which objects fall in the esthetic realm than any ability to make autonomous esthetic judgments. Formal studies of children's evaluations of works of art are still in their beginnings (Machotka, 1966; Shesh, 1966), but everyday observation of which things children own and treasure, and the things they aspire to own, not to mention their preferences in food and music, suggests that their taste is at best vulgar and at worst atrocious. It probably does little good to try to cultivate the "right" tastes in a child since the end result is likely to be simply a narrowing of enjoyment to the conventionally accepted finer things in life. The child who, in time, develops his own tastes is likely to arrive at sounder, more meaningful esthetic evaluations, and to be more receptive to esthetic innovations, than the child who has learned to accept and reject on the basis of ordinary standards.

EIDETIC IMAGERY. As far as we can tell, children at first think and remember in images, which may be so vivid as to compete with reality itself. Such naturalistic, hallucinatory images, which may be auditory, tactual, olfactory, gustatory, and proprioceptive as well as visual, are called **eidetic** images (something like what is popularly referred to as a "photographic memory"). The sometimes fantastic (but spotty) memory of the preschool child seems to reside in a capacity for evoking eidetic images. Haber and Haber (1964) found strong eidetic imaging in 8 percent of a sample of eight- to twelve-year-old children, although a large number showed some degree of eidetic ability. Some people retain their eidetic capacity throughout life and are able to recall effortlessly and with uncanny accuracy such details as the contents of a drugstore window or the costumes in a street parade. Eidetic imagery seems to be important for specialized talents like drawing, arithmetic, and music, and many musicians report that they can look at a score and hear the music being played. Eidetic imagery is more than mere memorization, since the eidetic subject can spell out from an imaged street sign long foreign words that he cannot even pronounce, or "read off" in any sequence numbers from, say, a five-by-five arrangement of twenty-five digits which he has examined briefly. Most of us retain only a weakened, faded capacity for eidetic imaging, which gets submerged, with experience, in the abstract gist, the symbolic essentials of things, rather than the life-like totality. Except for special purposes, eidetic images are cumbersome tools of thought, and it is probably just as well for the child's cognitive development that eidetic imagery is subordinated during the school years to more abstract, manipulable symbolic thinking.

Other aspects of cognitive functioning

Schnall (1968) and Kasdorf and Schnall (1970) have found age changes in the extent to which subjects, viewing a series of pictures in which each successive picture contains a modification of the preceding one, perceive the pictures as representing change, rather than isolated depictions. The pictures are shown at intervals too great to permit a movielike fusion, which means that the younger subject's perception is more veridical, true to what he is being exposed to, than the older one's. At the same time, he lacks the essential ability to integrate experience, to see connections between things, which the more mature subjects do.

An area of research straddling the border between cognition and personality has to do with what is called **locus of control** (Bialer, 1961) or **attribution** (Weiner et al., 1971). Locus of control refers to the extent to which the individual feels that his successes or failures are due to what he himself does or else to the workings of external forces over which he has little control. Weiner's attribution theory divides internal control into the two factors of ability, which is thought of as enduring, and effort, which is transitory. External control is divided into task difficulty, which is stable, and luck, which comes and goes. Thus, when a child does badly on an exam, say, he can explain it by saying that he didn't really try, or that he wasn't smart enough, or that the exam was too hard, or that he got a bad break. Research in children's attributions is still too new for us to be able to draw any confident conclusions about what different response patterns may signify.

All told, then, the world of the middle-years child includes isolated domains or segments of experience which are logically organized and about which the child can reason in a mature fashion. However, the world as a whole has not yet come to be a coherent, integrated system, and clouds of magicalism surround and sometimes invade the more orderly realms of thought. It is

Cognitive functioning in middle-years children

obviously the work of education to make the world comprehensible, manageable, and manipulable in thought, with the ambiguities and paradoxes and controversies made plain, and it is the topic of schooling to which we turn in the section that follows. The reader is asked to bear in mind, however, that schooling is not always educational, and that education goes on not only in school but also in the family, in newspapers and magazines, on television, in the playground, in the bushes, and in the gutter.

A School for the School Child

We now want to discuss those formal institutions which our society provides for the indoctrination of its school-age young. Foremost among these, of course, is school, but the scout troop, the recreation center, and similar agencies serve many school-like functions, and much of what we have to say applies to them as well. Also, although we are talking about grade schools, our discussion applies in some measure to secondary schools and colleges. In what follows, we want to take account of what schools are, what they conceive their goals to be, what they actually do, the problems they face, and why there may be reasons that schools as we have become used to thinking of them are inherently incapable of providing an environment conducive to sound psychological development.

Let it be said that the authors speak only as observers. Neither of us has ever been responsible for a classroom of children except preschoolers and college students. We

do claim to know something about children, however; we have sat in on (and filmed) a great many classes, we make some inferences from the behavior of college students about what their earlier educational experience must have been like, we have talked to a great many teachers and principals, and we think we have some perspective on society as a whole. What is more, we have seen some good schools at work and working, whether in slums or prosperous neighborhoods. Even in some otherwise dreadful schools, isolated classes may be doing a superior job. Whatever the chances in political terms for a new approach in the public schools, we are confident that new ways of thinking can help us accomplish the task of education, which is, after all, the single most vital collective task of a society.

Trends in the development of American schools

Three main approaches to education have dominated United States schools. **Classical, traditional education**, modeled on old British and Continental practices, has been found in some of our most prestigeful private schools. Such schools characteristically place heavy emphasis on classical languages, French, mathematics, history, and sports, with rather less attention given to natural sciences, social sciences, and such languages as Spanish, Russian, Japanese, and Mandarin. In sum, the traditional

Schools in other settings. A. Learning to count in Tanzania. B. Learning to read in Iran. C. A country school in Bolivia. D. An orthodox Hebrew school in the United States.

A.

Lynn McLaren, Rapho Guillumette

B.

Davis Pratt, Rapho Guillumette

C.

Gerhard Gscheidle, Photofind, S.F.

D.

Leonard Freed, Magnum

Classrooms, traditional and modern.

schools have been subject-matter centered. Another segment of our private schools has been in the forefront of the **progressive education** movement in all its varieties. The progressive schools have tended to be child-centered rather than subject-matter centered, stressing good mental health and emotional development as salient goals of education. Their approach to teaching at the elementary level typically is less concerned with the usual separation of disciplines, and aims at integrated education with facts and skills learned incidentally as subordinate parts of projects and themes. Art, music, and poetry, with the children being urged to be active in these fields, loom large in the usual progressive curriculum. We can see that traditionalism differs from progressivism in what is considered the important content of education and in methods of instruction, with the traditional schools emphasizing the magisterial role of the teacher and the progressive schools emphasizing the discoverer role of the pupil. Strands of traditionalism and progressivism can be found in the public schools, but in general, public education has been dominated by the "**basic education**" approach, which emphasizes fundamental skills like the three R's and training for life's practical problems. This approach can be thought of as social-utility centered.

Historically, the basic education approach seems to have had its origins in the need to Americanize our polyglot population and to guarantee a minimal level of literacy to everyone. The basic education approach found its empirical and philosophical justification in the work of Thorndike and his associates from 1900 on (Grose and Birney, 1963). Thorndike denounced the doctrine of "mental discipline" which was invoked by traditional educators in support of the study of German,

Latin, mathematics, and other subjects that were supposed to teach students a generalized logic. Thorndike conducted a series of studies from which he concluded that there was no generalized transfer effect or that such transfer as was found occurred only between highly similar skills (the reader will recall the principle of "identical elements" in perceiving equivalences, p. 184). The lack of a transfer effect and the futility of mental discipline were duly recorded in psychology textbooks and have been interpreted by educational theorists to mean that the schools should concern themselves with teaching specific, useful skills. In this view, teaching was subordinated to training, on the analogy of the way one trains animals.

It is interesting, in a grisly sort of way, that the doctrine of skill training took the ascendancy despite a good deal of contrary evidence, almost as though it met some culturally given psychic need. Indeed, one can see in Thorndike's work the formalization and glorification of American anti-intellectualism. Harlow's work on learning sets, which imply the transfer of principles rather than of specific elements, even at the nonhuman level (as when the animal applies the principle of oddity from having learned to choose the odd color to choosing the odd shape or size), goes against Thorndike's conclusions. But the most telling argument against Thorndike's position comes from Thorndike's own work. For in fact Thorndike found a transfer effect, even after elaborate statistical manipulations designed to minimize it. It is true that the transfer effects were small, but they were measures of change over only one year. If we consider that similar effects could be gained year by year over a period of eight or twelve or sixteen or twenty years of schooling, they would add up to a very impressive total effect. In any case, it is perhaps more important that the literature on the transfer effect, both pro and con, is pathetically naive and can hardly be taken seriously by anyone concerned with advanced intellectual functioning. (The studies in this area concerned themselves, for instance, with whether a skill learned with the left hand transferred to the right, ability to memorize nonsense syllables, learning to hit a submerged target with a BB gun, paired-associate learning, and so forth.)

For the past fifteen years, the United States has been struggling, at the federal, state, and local levels, with the cooperation of foundations and consultants and task forces, to overhaul its educational system while gearing it to deal with a vastly enlarged population. Great numbers of additional people have been drawn into teaching, new schools have been built, new books have been published, new curricula have been drawn up in mathematics, earth sciences, biology, social science, and so forth, and new techniques and technologies have been devised: ungraded classes, team teaching, teacher aides, programed instruction, teaching via television, language laboratories, science kits, more audio-visual aids, until one may have trouble finding child or teacher in the gadget jungle. Colleges of education have been rehabilitated into liberal arts colleges and even universities, sometimes in fact and sometimes in name only. National figures have taken the time to philosophize and psychologize about the process of education. Preschool education for poor children has come into being on a national scale. The education business has seen a time of boom followed by bust.

The collapse of the knowledge industry has run parallel with a spiritual collapse in the schools themselves. Charles Silberman's (1970) indictment was only a documentation of what numerous observers already knew or suspected. Reading disabilities are rampant, teachers are demoralized, drugs circulate even in the grade schools, vandalism is widespread, truancy is the rule, and boredom is everywhere.

It seems to be the case that vast educational reforms and expenditures have taken place without any attempt to change the framework of dreary assumptions and values that have crippled our schools from the beginning. We have failed to see that to make schooling compulsory automatically pitted the child against the system. We have prescribed a single period of life as being the only fit time for education, and have tried to schedule learning in a way that would blow the fuses on a computer. We have made the schools instruments for sorting people into social and occupational roles, as though the main business of schools is to prepare people to enter the existing economy. Perhaps most fundamentally, the schools have drawn back at the brink of cultivating intellect. Let it be noted that not all intelligent people or people who do intellectual work such as teaching, writing, or other professions qualify as intellectuals. The intellectual is to be recognized by his skepticism, his tendency to criticize, his impatience with traditional solutions, and his moral concern—in Socrates' term, the intellectual is a gadfly. In his role as gadfly or thorn in the flesh the intellectual makes life unhappy for those people who do not want to be bothered with social problems like education, sex, poverty, prejudice, pollution, militarism, imperialism, and overpopulation. And so, as we have said, we go about the business of education ambivalently, teaching rea-

sonably well the safe subjects with obvious practical applications, but dealing out banalities and platitudes in areas of controversy.

The child quickly picks up conventional attitudes to sensitive subjects and conspires gladly in the game of simulated teaching and learning of something without ever saying anything about it. The lower-class child may smell the falsity of it all, but he lacks the words with which to combat it. For the middle-class child, the teachings of the school in the areas of biology and sociology are not so much patently false as ambiguous. Middle-class parents, some because they themselves began life in the slums, others because they have really forgotten about the humanity of poor people, especially poor people of a different race, manage to bring up their children in a middle-class capsule buffered against the bitter realities of poverty. The middle-class child knows about social problems such as poverty and war, but without the immediacy of firsthand experience. He could summon up the words to argue with his textbooks, but he lacks solid knowledge of the facts.

The teacher feels—and not without reason—that he or she should stick to the syllabus and the textbook, and not go venturing forth into untrodden realms. In general, the teacher is not thought of as someone who communicates her own life experience to children; she is simply the mediator between child and prescribed curriculum. Thus, a considerable part of the educational process becomes gamesmanship at which middle-class children play skillfully and poor children less so. If one continues to play the game skillfully for sixteen years, one is rewarded with a degree which entitles one to marry a handsome, well-bred spouse, get a good job, live in a nice house in a nice neighborhood, have nice friends, join the country club, and bear healthy children who will then repeat the cycle.

Meanwhile, some new trends in schooling are emerging which we find congenial and promising.

The liberal school

The schools as they exist are so awful that at least two thinkers in this area (Goodman, 1964; Illich, 1971) have proposed that we do away with them altogether. Illich's argument is that schools are inevitably the instruments by which society maintains the status quo, sorting children into those who will be rich, those who will perform different levels of labor, and those for whom society has no use whatever. To this end, the school uses grades, diplomas, certificates, and similar paraphernalia that determine the young person's future. Goodman's argument is that teaching simply does not work, that effective learning always occurs incidentally, by observing and participating in the activity of others. Goodman, among others, takes as his primary model learning to talk, which occurs, as we have seen, with a minimum of instruction. We agree with Goodman that a great many things can be learned incidentally, but only, alas, if the child is fortunate enough to be exposed to them. What most children learn from their everyday environment is the standard culture and its values, including the implicit Social Darwinism and racism that underlie the kind of schooling that Illich is talking about.

Thus, we are not prepared to abolish schools, but we are willing to think radically about a new order in education. We agree with the radicals that schooling should not be compulsory (the reader may find this hard to swallow, but he should try thinking it through), that a school has to be so attractive and rewarding to the children that they are eager to go. Indeed, in the best schools that we know, the children hate to leave. It is conceivable that some version of the voucher plan, by which parents and children exercise control by paying only for services actually rendered, might be an effective device to get the schools to make themselves attractive. We have some misgivings about the voucher plan, however, simply because we distrust the ethics of the entrepreneurs who would be moved to cut themselves in on the action. The simplest approach is to let the presence or absence of children be a gauge of how well the school is doing. More basic than any gadgets and gimmicks is the kind of attitudinal change that understands what the schools are supposed to be about.

In our thinking about a design for a "liberal" or "modern" school, we want to retain the subject-matter-centeredness, the child-centeredness, and the social-ultility-centeredness of earlier approaches, at the same time giving to each a somewhat different meaning. Our approach is child-centered in that we favor giving the child an education that will be personally relevant and that will contribute to his full development as a person in line with Polanyi's (1958) notion of **personal knowledge**. One of us has summed up the goals of personal education as:

. . . multiplying our perspectives on reality; by informing us about a far greater range of phenomena than we ever can know from personal experience; by teaching us the sets of princi-

Somebody come and
Somebody come and play today
Somebody come and smile
Somebody come and smile
smile ___ ing the songs
___ long
It won't ___
Somebody c___

Raimondo Borea

Philip A. Biscuti, Connecticut College

Nancy Rudolph

Christopher G. Knight, Photo Researchers

Raimondo Borea

ples according to which different realms of knowledge cohere; by teaching us techniques of logical, psychological, and stylistic analysis; and, most centrally, by equipping us with the symbolic systems—verbal, mathematical, diagrammatical, representational, expressive—by which we master reality conceptually and shape new realities in imagination (Church, 1962).

Our approach is not child-centered in the sense, sometimes encountered, of education being a continuous process of individual or group psychotherapy, or in the Romantic Naturalist sense that the child should be sheltered against instruction and left to find his own way. Our approach is, however, child-centered in the sense that we have to take account of how children think and learn, and of the individual child's style of thinking and learning. There is a common subject matter—the world—for all children, but this does not imply that they all have to learn the same things at the same time and in the same way. Thus, we are subject-matter centered in the sense that the child's ego and feelings of self-worth are not at stake, that he is free to pay attention to the demands of the learning task without being distracted by irrelevant emotions. This is not to say that learning should be emotion-free, but that the emotions should originate in the subject matter and the child's feelings about it and not in his feelings about himself. There is also an obligation on the school to teach the world as the best modern minds view it in the light of the best available empirical evidence. We want to teach the actualities of economics rather than the

Activities in the classroom.

dreams of economists. Here we should bear in mind Bruner's (1960) notion of the "spiral curriculum," which says that children can learn at their own level any subject matter at any age, that we can settle for incomplete, intuitive understanding at intermediate stages of learning, and that full knowledge and understanding come with repeated attacks, at ever more mature levels, on the same topics. It is obviously not enough to teach the substance of a subject matter; in addition, one must teach its logic, its organizing principles and the deductions these will or will not permit. Finally, our thinking about education is centered not in utility for society as it exists, but in terms of how one can build a more rational, more humane society than the one we know at present.

As Bruner (1961) has pointed out, education will begin to work only when schools are prepared to tell children the truth—and, we might add, to tell it truthfully, without hiding or playing down the emotions and values involved. The subject matter of social studies, people are often startled to realize, is the world, how it is, how it got to be the way it is, the economic, political, ideological, and psychological forces that keep things moving and changing, and what if anything people can do individually and collectively to make the world humanly habitable. In staying silent on the burning issues and controversies, the schools are communicating attitudes of timidity and impotent acquiescence. If the schools want to engage in liberal—and liberating—education, they have to be prepared to talk about life and death, sex and love and hatred, fanaticism, superstition, corruption, motives, power, propaganda, bigotry, communism and capitalism and their alternatives, and the causes people kill and die for.

The schools have to be prepared to deal with issues frankly, critically, and analytically, with constant appeals to the evidence. Schools have to learn to communicate an ecological style of thought which takes account of the interconnectedness of things, not only in biology but in all of human affairs.

If the school does its work well, we should expect a high level of achievement by all its pupils. For people are likely to think of poor learning as a judgment on the child and, through him, his parents. There will probably always be some number of children who cannot learn in a school setting and for whom special educational provisions have to be made, but we are willing to bet that the number will decline drastically as the schools become more flexible. We are liable to forget that poor achievement reflects on the teacher and the school and their ability to communicate an essentially simple subject matter to children. The insights of the great scientists and philosophers were, in their day, remarkable accomplishments. But, once formulated, the great ideas become obvious and can be assimilated by anyone who is not markedly defective. The problem is one of communication, and often highly individualized communication, and it is here that the genius of the school and the teacher is put to the test. We may some day discover the one right and universal way of presenting the world so as to guarantee comprehension, retention, and the power of generalization to new instances, but until that day teachers are going to have to improvise, diagnose, analyze, and intuit to find ways to open each individual's senses and understanding to the marvels of reality. Since adult understanding is far from perfect, we also have to bear in mind that sometimes the children's discoveries and insights will outrun our own, and we have to be prepared to listen carefully and to learn from the children themselves.

A TEACHER FOR THE LIBERAL SCHOOL. Obviously, this kind of educational process assumes teachers possessing a wealth of knowledge and understanding as well as independence and commitment. In fact, of course, our teachers are products of the same sorts of schools in which they themselves are teaching, and it is unlikely that the schooling of most of them has prepared them to undertake the kind of education we are talking about. Fortunately, the vicious circle of education is not quite a circle, so that each generation of teachers is somewhat better educated and brighter than the one before. In addition, of course, the teacher's educational opportunities are no more confined to the classroom than are the children's, and quite a few teachers manage to learn a great deal in the great outside world. The problem is to convey to teachers the notion of personal knowledge (a term coined, as we have said, by the philosopher Polanyi [1958]), the idea that knowledge is not something external to oneself but something to be absorbed and incorporated into one's own world view.

But the approach to teaching we have suggested requires not only a substantive change in what the teacher is capable of but also in the teacher's image of herself or himself, and in the community's and school hierarchy's role expectations and image of the teacher. The teacher must be, and be accepted as, autonomous (which does not mean irresponsible), free to adapt and experiment and respond, to digress, and to be as creative as she knows how.

The teacher has a responsibility to children, parents, and the community to impart certain conventional skills and key facts, and also some of the complexities beneath simple surfaces. She may choose to do her teaching within the framework of a standard syllabus. But she needs to have some freedom to choose. She also needs time and latitude to invent and to vary and to deal with individual children. She has to be free to teach both convergent thinking, which leads to a verifiably correct solution, and divergent thinking (Crabtree, 1965; Biber, 1959), which is concerned with possibilities rather than testable conclusions. For her first responsibility is to the children, to give them—or help them acquire—skills and knowledge and principles that will be useful to them in understanding the world and where they do or can fit in. She can help them develop zest and spirit and curiosity and imagination and originality. But she has to be trusted as a professional who knows her job and her children and who comprehends the ethical restraints that go with dealing intimately with immature—but maturing—human beings.

This means freedom from bureaucratic control and endless petty regulations. It also means freedom from endless chores, paper work, clerical duties, and nonprofessional assignments like playground duty and corridor duty. It means a humane working schedule so that education can go on at a pace suited to the child's capacity to absorb things and mull them over. The hectic tempo of the average teacher's day is one that no assembly-line worker would tolerate. Teachers need time not only to teach, to prepare lessons, to read and think, but also to go to the bathroom, to have a relaxed lunch with colleagues, and to participate in the planning and thinking of the school as a whole (Kreutter, 1966). The teacher needs time to take courses, attend lectures, take part in professional meetings, and do whatever else enhances her professional competence. Somehow, education has become infected with the business ideal of efficiency, and the teacher is expected to perform accordingly. Some teaching and learning can be efficient, and it is our hope that children will not go on very long painfully deciphering each printed word or toiling laboriously over every simple calculation. But thoughtful, serious learning in the substantive fields takes time, and time is a commodity in short supply for teachers and pupils.

DISCIPLINE AND AUTHORITY. Liberal schooling requires great freedom of movement and expression for children, which horrifies those who are used to thinking of children as anarchic animals always ready to explode. The traditional view of school discipline has been that the children would erupt into chaos if adult controls were even momentarily relaxed, and proponents of this view could point to the actual behavior of children to support it. What they failed to see, of course, was that the restraints they imposed helped build up the very tensions and hostilities that caused the children to explode. (In the slums, of course, and sometimes in the suburbs, the schools may draw hostility as symbols of a repressive society.) They likewise failed to grasp that the traditional subject matter traditionally presented often induced a boredom and a craving for change and activity that were almost irresistible. By contrast, the more doctrinaire progressive educators wanted to remove all restraints and demands on the child, who, they assumed, left to his own devices and provided with abundant learning materials, would flower naturally into knowledge, wisdom, and humane fellow-feeling. This approach is summed up in the plaint of the cartoon child, "Do we have to do what we want to do again today?" Here we have the contrast drawn by Kurt Lewin and his collaborators (1939) between **authoritarian** adult-dominated, rigidly controlled styles of leadership, and the **laissez-faire** style in which the adult renounced virtually all control. What we propose, again following Lewin, is a **democratic** style in which the adult retains authority but uses it flexibly, with due respect to the wishes, needs, and inspirations of the children. Thus, the questions of discipline, teaching methods, techniques, and materials become subordinate to how one defines, and with what evidence, what is good for the child, in terms of his present and future intellectual competence and in terms of those personal qualities that will enable him or her to be effective as friend, lover, spouse, parent, breadwinner, citizen, and sometimes solitary searcher after goals and meanings. There are times when good order in the classroom is meaningful, when the children should be listening to the teacher or to the child who is making a report, when only one child at a time is allowed to raise a question or make a comment. But there are other occasions when good order rightly gets lost in the play of ideas, in construction projects, in the search for information in dictionary, encyclopedia, reference book, field, or laboratory, as children go questing individually or in small groups.

A modern school in which children are active participants in their own education has to tolerate a reasonable amount of noise and confusion. The teacher must retain authority, but he uses it judiciously, balancing group and individual interests and educational values. The teacher provides as much leadership and allows the children as much initiative as seems educationally wise. But the children's respect has to be based on the teacher's qualities as a person, on his command of knowledge, and on the sense that, even at his most authoritative, he is on the children's side.

The liberal school as a whole is organized, and is perceived by the children, as an institution that helps children learn the truth. This means that it trusts its children who, like their teachers, are free from endless petty regulations and procedures. In too many schools, colleges, and universities, one gets the impression that the school belongs to the administration and is run for their comfort and convenience. The administrative machinery of a school is supposed, rather, to relieve teachers and students of administrative cares and thus facilitate the process of teaching and learning. But all too often, the administrators become the policy-makers, decision-makers, and authorities, who set standards for hiring, admission, promotion (of both teachers and pupils), leaves of absence, and discharge or suspension. The student's record folder tends to turn into a dossier, so that many parents and children come to fear the permanent consequences of "geting a black mark on your record." A student's performance has to be evaluated for the information of his parents, for his own guidance, and for the guidance of his successive teachers. But all examinations ought to be diagnostic, in the sense that they enable teacher and child to understand what he still needs to learn. Marks and diplomas make little educational sense, and might well be eliminated. As much as it may horrify administrators, it really is possible to live without a standardized system of student evaluation (the problem of evaluating schools and teachers is something else again). When it comes time for the child to move on to another school, it proves quite easy to extract a summary of his achievement from his teachers' comments, in general and in particular areas.

TEACHING AND LEARNING IN THE LIBERAL SCHOOL. The astute reader will have noticed by now that the authors' sympathies lie with a somewhat modified version of progressive education. We find many virtues in the British Infant Schools (Featherstone, 1971a, 1971b; Weber, 1971), whose practices have been greatly influenced by the teachings of John Dewey and Jean Piaget. In its American version, the Infant School is coming to be known as the **"Open Classroom"** approach. In what follows, bear in mind that although the teacher operates differently from the way she does in a standard classroom, she is there working hard—indeed, the Open Classroom is far more demanding of the strengths and ingenuities of the teacher than is ordinary teaching. The child is given great freedom to move about and to choose what he will work on from an environment carefully prepared by the teacher to provide opportunities for learning. The teacher seldom deals with the class as a whole, but spends time every day with each child, listening to him read and suggesting new readings, helping him with calculations, admiring and criticizing his art work, and so forth. It seems, as in Blank and Solomon's (1968) studies with preschool children, that a few minutes of individual instruction may be worth hours of group teaching. On the basis of the time spent with the child, reviewing his work and suggesting what steps to take next, the teacher has a detailed knowledge of each child's progress. According to the particular school, great emphasis may be placed on art, music, or dramatics. Perhaps most important, there is a range of ages in each class (typically, five to eight or nine), and the older children help the younger ones with reading and arithmetic, educating themselves in the process. Kids in groups organize dramatic productions and study projects. In Great Britain, the teacher has to deal with large classes and is obliged to improvise many of her own teaching materials. The success of the Infant Schools indicates that these burdens are bearable, at least by people of great dedication, but we think it less than humane to expect teachers to bear them.

We suspect that, if we had to run such a school, we would be tempted, in addition to reducing class size, to supplement the procedures with some of the new technologies. We can see room for the judicious use of teaching machines for certain topics and at the child's wish, and we are impressed by recent work in "inquiry training"—which cultivates the art of noting ambiguities and obscurities and contradictions, and asking questions to clear them up—as a means to cultivate symbolic problem-solving skills, and efforts to foster creativity (Olton and Crutchfield, 1969; Torrance, 1962; Wardrop et al., 1969). These methods can be seen as education in a preliminary approach to scientific methods as suggested in the film *Learning is Searching* (Stone et al., n.d.). We resonate to the question-asking approach described by Postman and Weingartner (1969), in which the teacher is nondirective and leaves it to the student to decide what he wants to learn about, but suspect that it may be too amorphous for primary-grade children.

In keeping with the view that learning should be intrinsically motivated and rewarding, we believe that concrete reinforcers like toys and money, which have had a vogue recently, should be used only as a last resort, and then only sparingly (Mecklenburger and Wilson, 1971). Some of the prefabricated curricula might be useful, and we have a continuing faith in the utility of films. Indeed, we feel that some literary classics, even such standards as *Tom Sawyer*, are couched in a language incomprehensible to today's children, and are accessible only in their cinematic renderings.

A word should be said about learning to read. We suspect that all the learned analyses of the process make reading seem a frightfully difficult thing to do, whereas it should be in fact quite simple. The process is as much a matter of motivation as perception (Stone et al., n.d.). It helps a lot if the child is read to a great deal during the preschool years. In the course of being read to, he grasps the general idea of getting information from marks on paper and also begins to recognize a few words. If he learns the alphabet, this gives him a tool for analyzing and memorizing words. Reading and writing often begin with the child's own name. Experience in drawing and painting helps in the articulation and stabilization of two-dimensional space. For those children who come from illiterate or semiliterate families, the methods that Sylvia Ashton-Warner (1963) developed in working with Maori children in New Zealand seem to be the method of choice. She wrote down stories (often quite hair-raising) dictated by the children, who quite readily learned to read back their and their peers' compositions. A debate is going on about whether children who speak nonstandard English should be taught to read in their own dialects. To do so seems to be of no special help to the child. Studies by Lava-telli (1970) indicate that children who speak one or another Negro-English dialect have no particular trouble reading and writing standard English. Indeed, as Cazden (n.d.) points out, there is only a loose correspondence between spoken and written standard English. Learning to write along with learning to read is becoming accepted practice, which means that we have to be tolerant of the child's early gropings. It is not hard to figure out the meaning of "licwid," although the adult might have trouble knowing, without its concrete context, that "didow shit" is the child's rendering of *ditto sheet*.

If the learning process goes as it should, the child will learn, through his classroom experience, through reading, through observation, and eventually through working in the laboratory, that the world is full of fascinating subtleties, and learning should become self-sustaining. This means that the child must be treated as an active participant in his own education, and not as a receptacle into which the teacher pours her (or the prepared syllabus's) accumulated wisdom. Rather, the teacher should stand beside or behind the child, guiding him toward a reality that exists independent of them both.

The kind of schooling we are talking about would be expensive, especially if it entailed replacing outdated present school buildings with new ones designed with a special eye to educational needs. The country can afford it. Whether we do it depends on where our values and priorities lie. If we do support education on the scale it deserves, we should do so in full awareness of the power of knowledge and ideas to subvert traditional beliefs and practices and lead to fundamental social changes.

Good liberal schools already exist, in

the United States as well as Britain and elsewhere, in slums and suburbs, and they work—up to a point. That point seems to be one reached toward the end of the middle years, when schooling, except for a very few children, seems to become meaningless in comparison with the pull of the real world. It is our hope that the adoption on a large scale of sound educational practices in the early years will motivate increasing numbers of youngsters to stay in school. If so, the high schools will have to change radically to suit a new kind of learner. But we must also face the fact that large numbers of children, perhaps most, will not want to continue in school. For many youngsters, adolescence brings about so drastic a change in outlook as to make improbable any benefits from academic schooling. The young person is so preoccupied with his growth, with the opposite sex, with urges to shed childhood and assert independence, that school is little more than a prison. To anticipate what we shall return to in our discussion of adolescence, this means, as Paul Goodman (1969) has said, that society will have to provide alternatives to the high school and college as we now know them. Most obviously, we will have to change our child labor laws to allow children to work without being exploited. In the home, children must be permitted and expected to take on more responsibilities than they currently are. There must be provisions for apprenticeships in skilled occupations. There will have to be technical institutes in which young people can learn practical skills, from plumbing and computer programing to medicine and the law. Such institutes must tolerate and make provision for the limited initial competence (which, with a different set of expectations, may

be less crippling than we realize) of children and adolescents. There have to be academies of the arts and sciences where students can drop in and drop out of their own volition. There have to be research institutes where those strongly motivated to working on the intellectual frontiers can apprentice themselves to practicing scholars and scientists. There have to be more institutions of liberal arts to which adults can repair when they feel a need to gain perspective on their own experience. Notice that we have discarded many notions about what can best be learned at what period of life, or what the best way to learn things may be. We have also discarded the idea of diplomas and degrees. Admission to the skilled occupations and professions would be by examination, as in fact it now already is in many fields. We are aware that examination practices are often deliberately designed to exclude certain groups, or that they can be administered dishonestly, but these are problems that can be solved.

What we have said about schools applies with equal force to other adult-led childhood enterprises such as recreation groups, scouting, or the rehabilitation of delinquent gangs. While leaders in these situations may need preparation in some ways different from that for teaching, it is still imperative that, like teachers, they have a genuine zest for the activity, a thorough understanding of children, a knowledge of the individual children in the program and their individual needs, an awareness of the forces governing adult society, and how to make the group's ideas and purposes relevant to those of the kids. If the leader of a voluntary program fails to attune it to the needs and values of children, the program will deteriorate or the children go elsewhere. The adult working with delinquents or in a high-delinquency area must likewise understand that he is not dealing with children who are simply wicked, or who need only to have their time filled with wholesome pursuits to keep them out of mischief, but with children facing real and terrible problems who seek magical solutions and ready reassurance through identification with the gang. The defense of the home turf by the block gang is only the psychopathology of nations in miniature. The values of the gang may seem far more meaningful than the respectable, alien ones of the middle class. But even when dealing with middle-class children, the group leader has to take account of the children's own motives and wants, and of the gang's mores, or the program will disintegrate in a cloud of boredom or fisticuffs.

Too many adult-sponsored programs are like child or adult clubs in which the fact of organization takes precedence over actual goals, leaving the membership floundering, or providing ersatz functions, once the opening ceremonies are over. Part of the trouble, as we have suggested, is that adults do not sufficiently trust children to be able to manage their own free time, and so invent a plethora of time-killing boondoggles. We have to provide things for children to do, but we have to be a little more creative about it than in the past. Otherwise the kids would be just as well off watching TV.

10

adolescence:
one

In this chapter and the next, we shall be dealing with that period of life known as adolescence. We must immediately confront a complexity. Earlier age periods, from infancy through the middle years, have universally recognizable growth characteristics. Although the physical changes of adolescence, the pubescent growth spurt and puberty, indicative of sexual maturing, are universals, the years from age twelve or thirteen onward take on very different psychological meaning in different societies. The prolonged postponement after puberty of fully adult status is a relatively recent phenomenon of Western-like societies. Up until a few hundred years ago in Western society, and still today in many tribal societies, the physical fact of puberty, usually marked by a ceremonial observance, meant automatic entry into adulthood. Beginning with the children of the rich, there was increasing acceptance of delay in adopting adult status. As the concept of secondary education for people in general spread, so did prolongation of childhood. As society grew more complex, the number of adult roles multiplied, and the young person, instead of moving in the parental footsteps, had to make a choice. Furthermore, economic change went hand in hand with intellectual and ideological upheaval. Institutions like religion and inherited wealth were called into question, there were revolutions and counterrevolutions and countless new social doctrines. Both socially and ideologically, the young person had to define an identity, who he was and what he believed in and where he was headed. Even where identity was not a major issue, as in the settled middle class of the United States in the early years of this century, there was still great ambiguity about where childhood ended and adulthood began, and this ambiguity generated what was accepted as the awkwardness and self-consciousness of the adolescent years.

Until fairly recent times, these phenomena of adolescence, no matter how widespread, were thought of in terms of the young person's concerns, his inner cravings, aspirations, fears, dreams, and conflicts. Here we have the image of "classical" adolescence, a period of lusts warring with purity, of self-consciousness, identity-seeking, idealism, religious conversion, moodiness and changes of mood, despair, inner turmoil, rebellion, and iconoclasm. Since World War II, adolescence has been taken for granted as a status, the way people are from the time of pubertal changes until that ill-defined moment when they assume the new status of adulthood. Young people accepted this immature status and seemed content to defer adulthood, especially as they could claim new privileges as part of their new status. They were reinforced in their acceptance of limbo by the mass media and the culture they transmitted, and also by adults for whom youth was the great ideal and who themselves were reluctant to grow up and grow old.

In the late 1960s and early 1970s, we are witnessing two somewhat conflicting trends. More and more young people have been finding more and more ways to put off adult commitment—at least partly in mass disillusionment with the adult world. Increasing numbers of young people have been going to college, more college graduates have been going on to graduate school, and more holders of graduate degrees taking postgraduate fellowships. At the same time, there has been growing recognition among young people that adolescence goes on too long, and we hear a rising clamor from college students that they are locked away from life on campus, that their studies are irrelevant to the real world, and that they want to participate in the fateful decision-making that governs their lives. But even as eighteen- to twenty-year-olds were being given the vote, the job market was crumbling and young people were in danger of liberating themselves into unemployment. Indeed, a number of young people who have broken their family ties have been ending up on welfare, which imposes new limits on their freedom. The picture is further complicated in that just when many well-to-do young people, many of whom are in college because it is what is expected of them, are getting turned off by higher education, a new and more serious wave of poor people are working to get into college and stay in.

Thus, the tale of contemporary adolescence is a far from simple or stable one. Much of the empirical research seems dated and remote, so that a fair amount of what we shall say in these chapters is drawn from impressions gained from our contact with young people themselves, from people who work with them, from journalistic accounts, as well as from formal research.

We shall approach the psychology of adolescence roundabout. In this chapter we shall deal with the biology and sociology of this age, with physical growth and puberty, and with the adolescent role as a cultural invention. Within the framework of this construct, we shall look at the young person in the social networks of family, friends, and school. We shall then take up the diversity to be observed among adolescents, including the special variations associated with social class, ethnic background, family values, and ideologies. In the next chapter, we shall look at some of the common psychological themes that appear to underlie the surface diversities—such themes as sexuality, idealism, rebellion, the self, and identity formation. It is worth mentioning that we have gone through a demographic shift. In the early 1960s, thanks to the post–World War II baby boom, adolescents made up the single largest chunk of the American people. The population bulge has now moved into adulthood, but large numbers of adolescents are still with us and highly visible (in 1970, according to the Census, twelve-year-olds were the largest one-year age group in the United States).

They are visible in part because of the worldwide spread of what has come to be known as the youth culture or the counter-culture, marked by certain shared manifestations of dress, speech, and tastes in music and the arts. The youth culture senses itself as a community without boundaries, and its highly mobile members take satisfaction in their ability to recognize each other and to communicate without preliminary formalities.

Periods of Adolescence

Like all the other age periods we have talked about, adolescence is a time of continuing change. We must draw a distinction between early adolescence, late adolescence, and early adulthood. Early adolescence, as we use it, refers to the period from the beginning of pubescence (which, in the individual case, is known only in retrospect) until about a year after puberty, when the youngster's new physiological patterns are fairly well stabilized. Late adolescence is the ensuing period up to driving and voting age or the beginning of college. Young adulthood refers to the period through college and into the early twenties.

We feel it necessary to include postadolescent young adulthood in our discussion of adolescence because the boundaries have become blurred and because much of the adolescent life style has been carried into adult life. Moreover, many young adults continue to be preoccupied with what we regard as the central concern of this period, what Erikson (1963) has called the **search for identity**, coming to know who one is, what one believes in and values, what one wants to accomplish and get out of life. After coming to terms with a new kind of body, with new potentialities for feeling and acting, and rearranging his or her self-image accordingly, the adolescent must confront a whole new constellation of meanings in the life-space. The young adolescent is concerned about who and what he is; the older adolescent has to be concerned, in addition, about what he is going to do with himself for the rest of his life; although some young adults have made career and family commitments, they are still coming to terms with their place in society and with adult life patterns. Relations with the opposite sex in early adolescence are marked by fumbling, often furtive investigations in books, in films, and in real life, too, with intermingling for the most part in groups. In later adolescence there is more pairing off, and more forthright experimentation, but not necessarily for keeps. The young adult feels more confidence in himself or herself as a sexual being (which is not to say that young adults are free of sexual problems) and may have embarked on marriage or a less conventional alliance.

In early adolescence, the youngster seeks independence in new areas like religious beliefs or dating, but very much in the same way as when he was younger: he wants more privileges, more freedom from adult supervision and restraint so that he can follow the dictates of the peer group—the crowd—but with little sense of responsibility for the consequences of his own actions. The young adolescent, perhaps even more than during the middle years, is concerned about his status with his immediate peers; he strives to be as much like the others as possible, perhaps because he feels so much out of step with them. For, almost against his own volition, he is becoming ever more of an individual, with ideas and values that may not match the essentially conservative code of the gang, but his own only half-understood uniqueness is not completely welcome.

The older adolescent shares the younger one's concerns but is, in addition, confronted by the problem of where he will stand with respect to the entire adult world of independence and responsibility—sex, marriage, jobs, military service, politics, parenthood—and must face the chilling prospect of being on his own.

Young adulthood nowadays comes in a number of different versions. There is the traditional holder of a first regular job, blue or white collar. It seems to be the trend that going to work is taken for granted by women almost as much as by men. Other young adults may go on living with their parents. Some of these, even though working, may not yet have achieved social and emotional independence. Others may consider themselves fully independent and be accorded full recognition as such even though they continue to be economically dependent.

Biological Maturing

The physical changes of the adolescent period are often said to begin with puberty. It seems somewhat more precise to say that the adolescent period begins with **pubescence**, the period of about two years immediately prior to puberty and the physical changes during that period which culminate in puberty. The beginning of pubescence is marked by an increase in the rate of physical growth, the onset of the **prepubertal growth spurt**, and the end of growth latency. Along with the growth spurt come changes in facial and body proportions, the maturing of primary and secondary sex traits, and an assortment of other physical changes. (Some writers refer to the period of pubescence as "preadolescence." Psychologically, to be sure, the pubescent youngster is in many respects more of a middle-years child than an adolescent. However, "preadolescence" is a confusing term because yet other writers use it synonymously with the middle years.)

Puberty is the point in life at which sexual maturity begins, marked in girls by the **menarche**, the first menstrual flow, and in boys by a number of signs, the most reliable one probably being the presence of spermatozoa in the urine (detectable under the microscope). In fact, the borderline of puberty is not altogether clearcut for either girls or boys. Menstruation at first is likely to be skimpy and irregular, sometimes with months intervening between flows. Boys may feel strong phallic urges and discover that female propinquity is a potent stimulus to erection, but still be unable to ejaculate. In law, twelve is commonly designated as the age of puberty for girls, and fourteen for boys. There are, however, wide group and individual variations in actual age at puberty. In general, American young people are maturing earlier than they used to (Sullivan, 1971). In 1964–1965, the average age at menarche was twelve and a half years, and the "normal" range (a standard deviation each side of the mean, encompassing about two-thirds of the subjects) was from about ten to fifteen. The acceleration of puberty has been related to improved diets and health. Living at high altitudes, one the other hand, seems to have a retarding effect, since girls in Denver menstruate later than those living near sea level. Frisch and Revelle (1970) relate menarche to a critical point in body weight of about 106 pounds (48 kg.), which might account for the lag associated with altitude, since high-altitude babies are lighter at birth and continue lighter than their sea-level age-mates. As Johnston et al. (1971) point out, this critical weight varies with race; many Asian women, for instance, never get within shouting distance of 48 kilograms. We should not overlook the possibility that increased exposure to sexual stimulation may also speed up sexual maturing; the reader will recall the principle of stimulation-induced maturation. Boys, as a rule, lag about two years behind girls in reaching puberty. There seems to be a similar lag in boys' social development, making for certain dislocations which we shall discuss later.

In general, youngsters sprout up in the

two or so years before puberty, especially in the year which culminates in puberty. This year before puberty is called the **maximum growth age**, or MGA. Puberty marks the *apex*, the peak, of the growth-rate curve. After puberty, the rate of growth slows down, with girls reaching their full height at about nineteen and boys at twenty-one or twenty-two—nobody really knows just when growth stops, but annual increments beyond the ages given are too small to be measured accurately. Changes in body proportions, of course, go on lifelong. During physical adolescence, the child's height increases by about 25 percent and his weight doubles—obviously, weight is less predictable than height. During the period of growth latency, children gain slightly over 2 inches (5 cm.) a year in height and from 4½ to 5 pounds (2+ kg.) in weight. At the peak of adolescent growth, girls grow about 3½ inches (9 cm.) in a year and gain about 11 pounds (5 kg.), while boys grow 4 or 5 inches (11 cm.) a year and put on 12 or 14 pounds (6+ kg.). Boys are somewhat bigger than girls except between the ages of nine and fifteen, when the earlier maturing of girls sends them sprouting past their male coevals. (In Egypt, at no age do girls surpass boys in height, although girls are heavier starting about age nine; in India, girls are taller than boys from age eleven, and heavier from age ten [U.S. Department of Health, Education, and Welfare, 1970].) But let us note that in both sexes there are early maturers and late maturers and a vast number of individual growth patterns.

In the United States, over a forty-year period, fifteen- to sixteen-year-old boys have become almost 2 inches (5 cm.) taller and 10 pounds (4.5 kg.) heavier than their forebears; girls have gained better than ½ inch (1.25 cm.) and 1¼ pounds (.5 kg.). Interestingly enough, seventeen- to nineteen-year-old girls are about 3 pounds (1.4 kg.) lighter than their counterparts of forty years ago, reflecting changes both in diet and in concepts of beauty. These averages conceal socioeconomic differences. The children of the rich are no bigger than their parents. Thus, average size will probably not continue to increase, once the less-favored segments of society catch up.

The maturational changes of adolescence, including changes in both size and physiological organization, are governed by stepped-up activity in the pituitary "master" gland, an endocrine organ recessed in the base of the brain and producing a variety of hormones. Secretions from the pituitary regulate other growth-governing endocrine glands, notably the thyroid, adrenals, and gonads (the testes and ovaries). The functioning of the endocrine glands during adolescent growth provides a nice example of feedback control. Pituitary hormones stimulate adrenal hormones which stimulate gonadal hormones which then inhibit pituitary secretions. But as the pituitary slows down, so do the gonad-stimulating secretions from the adrenals and thus the pituitary-inhibiting secretions from the gonads, and the pituitary once again becomes active. Note, however, that we have no way of accounting for the increase in pituitary activity except to say that it is part of the genetically programed pattern of normal maturation.

In both sexes, the extremities and neck grow faster than the head and trunk during pubescence, which gives youngsters of this age their long-legged, gawky, coltish look. In boys, there is a marked broadening of the shoulders. In girls, the pelvis enlarges—an artist can draw middle-years boys and girls with essentially the same proportions, but as they mature he must take account of very different configurations. Facial proportions also change as the nose and chin become more prominent. Girls more than boys develop a layer of subcutaneous fat that rounds and softens the contours of face and body, whereas boys develop a leaner, more angular and more muscular appearance than girls.

On the surface of the body, the development of the secondary sex characteristics expresses changes in underlying physiology. Both boys and girls develop pubic hair, at first as a downy tuft on the forward face of the pubic mound, and axillary (armpit) hair. Facial hair and chest hair appear in boys, and are considered a mark of manhood. Girls, too, may develop a slight mustache and a sprinkling of facial hair and hair around the nipples, which in no way contradicts their femininity. The pubic hair, or pubes, appears first, whence the name "pubescence." The pubic hair spreads until it surrounds the genital area, becoming in the process darker, longer, coarser, and kinkier. In boys, facial hair comes earlier than axillary hair, appearing first as a darkish shadow on the upper lip. Chest hair—to the despair of young adolescent boys—appears only in late adolescence and continues growing well into manhood, which fact may have given it its special status as a badge of virility—even though the boy may by then be past the peak of sexual prowess. In boys and girls alike, the skin becomes coarser, with larger pores, and the sebaceous glands become more active, producing an oily secretion. As a result, young people become more subject to blackheads and acne. The composition of sweat is altered, and it becomes much stronger in odor. Much adolescent self-consciousness is caused by awareness of the odors of sweat and menstruation, and adolescents are a special target of advertising for deodorants and skin ointments.

The shift in physiological organization is further reflected in blood pressure, in basal metabolic rate (BMR: the rate at which the body in a basal—resting—state consumes oxygen), and in pulse rate, all of which show a rise at about the time of puberty. BMR relative to body size and pulse rate thereafter decline, with girls continuing to have a higher pulse rate and a lower BMR than boys. Prior to puberty, blood pressure is higher in girls than in boys, but after puberty the reverse is true.

The girl's external genitalia enlarge but otherwise change very little, whereas the boy's external genitalia change markedly. To begin with, there is a considerable increase in size. One of the signs of pubescence in the boy is the enlargement of the testicles. As the testes and scrotum grow in size, they become pendulous. Since sperm cells need a fairly constant temperature (below normal body temperature) to survive, an effective thermostat is built into the testicular structures: when the surrounding temperature goes down, the testes are drawn closer to the groin as a source of body heat, and vice versa. The shaft of the penis becomes longer and thicker, the glans (the head of the penis) grows until, in some cases, it emerges completely from the foreskin, and the penis as a whole also becomes pendulous. The penis is capable of erection from birth on, but until pubescence erection is likely to be in response to local stimulation or irritation and carries little sense of sexual urgency. Around the time of puberty, the penis begins to tumesce very readily, either spontaneously or in response to sexually provocative sights, sounds, smells, language, or whatever—the male adolescent inhabits a libidinized life-space where almost anything can take on sexual meaning. Now tumescence is accompanied by strong and unequivocal urges to ejaculate.

The literature suggests that close to 100 percent of male adolescents masturbate more or less regularly, although lower-class culture dictates that masturbation is unmanly and lower-class boys are likely on that account to take less pleasure in the act. In a sample of forty-eight male college students, unfavorable ratings of masturbation effectively canceled out favorable ones, yielding an average rating just below neutrality (Church and Insko, 1965). Boys may also have "wet dreams" (technically, *nocturnal emissions*), ejaculation during sleep, perhaps to the accompaniment of erotic dreams. Perhaps the publicly most noticeable secondary sex trait in boys is the "change of voice" brought about by enlargement of the larynx, the voice box. (In an earlier day, boy sopranos were kept permanently so by castration; without the gonadal contribution to growth, the larynx remained immature.) The change of voice in intact choirboys gives a measure of historical differences in age at puberty. In Bach's eighteenth-century boys' choirs, boys had to be let go, because of change of voice, at an average age of eighteen, except during a period of war and privation, when they matured considerably later; London schoolboys in 1959 had a change of voice at an average age of 13.3 years (Sullivan, 1971). Most boys go through a period when their resonantly baritone voices shift treacherously and instantaneously to a squealing falsetto. Girls, too, have a change of voice, but it is less marked than in boys. Girl's voices become slightly deeper and considerably fuller.

Apart from the growth spurt, the first sign of pubescence in girls may be either the appearance of pubic hair or enlargement of the breasts, or both developments may coincide. The areolas grow larger, become elevated and conical in form, and take on a darker pigmentation. We do not know at what age the nipples become capable of erection. The breasts usually reach almost full size prior to the menarche, the beginning of menstruation. Some boys show a slight and temporary enlargement of one or both breasts during pubescence. There is still a great deal of debate, largely among anthropologists, about the concept of "adolescent sterility," the idea that girls cannot conceive for several years after puberty. In some societies, such as Samoa, the postpubertal years are a tacitly acknowledged period of experimental promiscuity for girls. (Since the explicit culture decrees virginity until marriage, chicken blood is dabbed on the nuptial couch to represent the ruptured hymen, or maidenhead.) It is clear that, in our own society, menstruation is skimpy and irregular for the first few years, and the rate of spontaneous abortion and of fetal and neonatal deaths is decidedly higher for sixteen- to nineteen-year-old mothers than for those in the twenty- to twenty-nine age group. However, enough teen-age pregnancies and parturitions occur to make adolescent sterility less than safe as a method of birth control. Even less is known about when actual fertility begins for boys, since spermatozoa need to be present in considerable quantity for impregnation to take place.

One of the typical features of pubescent physical development is **asynchrony,** which we defined earlier as the way the body's various organs and subsystems grow at different rates and at different times. Asynchrony, or "split growth," is especially evident during pubescence, when arms, legs, nose, and chin may seem suddenly to sprout individually, with no regard for overall proportions and harmony. Indeed, the left and right sides of the body may grow at different rates, although by puberty the various body parts have come back into approximate balance. (Needless to say, people at all ages have some left-right asymmetry, as becomes evident when we piece together a photograph made of two lefts or two rights, with one reversed [Wolff, 1943].)

One of the characteristics of adolescence is a feeling of being out of step, and asynchrony may enhance this feeling. Moreover, any deviation from the group average is likely to make the child feel out of step. The early-ripening girl probably feels out of place among her unripe classmates, and the late-maturing girl is a lost soul among the hips and bosoms that surround her (Faust, 1960). The early-maturing boy, by contrast, is likely to be at a social advantage, although he may suffer the pangs of dethronement as the others catch up and even surpass him. The late-maturing boy may suffer the most of all. The late-maturing girl may be neglected to the point of ostracism, but the late-maturing boy is likely to be made a butt, a scapegoat, and an object of scorn and ridicule (Weatherley, 1964). Interestingly enough, as Mary Cover Jones (1965) has shown, personality differences between early- and late-maturing males persist well into adult life. Following up in their forties a group of men who had been classified in their teens as early- or late-maturers, Jones found that the early-maturers were poised, responsible, successful, and conventional, and the late-maturers were active, exploratory, insightful, independent, and impulsive—all with due allowance for individual

differences. There are growth tables from which one can make fairly good predictions of eventual adult stature, and adolescents might derive some comfort from these and the reassurance they give that most people sooner or later end up, by definition, in the normal range.

Now that we have seen some of the major changes that take place in the adolescent's body, it is time to consider psychological adolescence. We shall return later to how these bodily changes fit into the adolescent's view of himself or herself.

Adolescence as a Cultural Phenomenon

Writers on the subject of adolescence—as far as formal psychology is concerned, beginning with G. Stanley Hall (1904)—have been struck by the young person's agonies of self-consciousness, his preoccupation with who he is and where he belongs. Adolescence has come to be known as a time of inner turmoil, as a period of **Sturm und Drang**, of "storm and stress." Needless to say, this inner turmoil finds external expression, and the adults who have to deal with adolescents come in for their share of turmoil, too. Many writers have attributed the turbulence of this age to the physiological upheaval associated with puberty, and, by implication, to the discrepancy between the adolescent's sexual maturity and mental immaturity.

It now seems obvious that this explanation will not do. For one thing, there are societies, and sections of our own society, in which adolescence is not a time of *Sturm und Drang*, so that although all young people go through the physical changes of adolescence, only those in particular cultural settings show the behavior we take to be characteristic of this age. Furthermore, careful observation shows that the psychological crises of adolescence do not ordinarily begin until a year or more after the period of most rapid physical change; for some individuals, there seems to be virtually no relation between physical changes and typically adolescent behavior. For these reasons, we are obliged to view adolescence as a cultural phenomenon derived from the way people in European societies interpret the fact of physical maturing. (Notice that European, in this sense, includes non-European countries settled by Europeans or strongly influenced by Europe: Latin and North America, the Asian sections of the Soviet Union, Australia, New Zealand, Japan, and the emerging middle class in whatever part of the world. Psychological adolescence, along with concern about mental health and creativity, and along with waste and pollution, seems to be a luxury that only reasonably well-to-do societies can afford.) In sum, adults and the peer group both define roles for the adolescent to play, and in assuming these roles, the young person takes on his adolescent identity.

In primitive societies, there is no equivalent for our concept of adolescence. In some primitive societies, the transition from childhood to adulthood is so smooth that no particular note is taken of the process. More usually, we find that the young person on the threshold of maturity goes through a ceremonial adolescence. The rituals by which adulthood is conferred are variously called **puberty rites**, **rites de passage**, and **initiation ceremonies**. They may be carefully timed to coincide with puberty, children of various ages may be rounded up and initiated, or it may be left to the child himself to decide when he is ready to assume the rights and cares of adulthood or when he feels able to endure what may be a rigorous procedure.

At their simplest, initiation rites may consist of nothing more than a haircut or a change of clothes. More complex rituals may involve elaborate tattooing, periods of isolation or fasting, or a search for a vision or revelation. Some ceremonies are ordeals which serve at least partly as tests of character: circumcision with a sharpened stick, surgical removal of the clitoris, having one's teeth filed to a point, the ability to take torture without crying out, the infliction of lesions which will leave scars considered a mark of beauty. Young men may have to demonstrate their manhood in mortal combat, and the scalp at the belt or feasting on the heart and genitals of the man you have slain may be the ultimate measure. Such *rites de passage* seldom last more than a few weeks (admittedly, these may be highly vivid weeks), and even the longest of them are negligible compared to the approximately seven years that we take for granted as a transition period. We know of only one exception among non-Western peoples. Beginning at puberty, the Masai male assumes the status of warrior, which may occupy ten or more years of his life. While a warrior, he may not marry, but he is allowed to accumulate property, and he graduates directly from warrior to elder (Beals and Hoijer, 1965). In the more usual case, once the puberty rite is successfully at an end, the young person has attained full adult status and apparently assumes it without any lingering sense of ambiguity. The demands and prerogatives of his new role are perfectly clear and other people take it for granted that he will play the role correctly. In most primitive societies, adultlike obligations are gradually imposed on the child, and he and his peers practice the prerogatives, such as sex, on their own, often with adult approval, so that childhood tends to flow continuously into adulthood, with only the ceremonial punctuation of the puberty rite to break the continuity.

It is tempting to go beyond these generalizations about other societies and to detail the diverse ways in which the seal of maturity is bestowed. It would also be interesting to discuss the meanings attached to various practices, and how the young people themselves view them. So detailed an account would take us deeper into anthropology than is appropriate, and we refer the curious reader to his local library, where he will find the pertinent literature, often in locked cases. The essential fact that emerges from a comparison of our culture with others is that psychological adolescence is not a necessary corollary of physical adolescence, but a cultural phenomenon produced by a delay in the assumption of adult roles. That is, the more we prolong the period of subadult status, the more elaborate become the rules that govern behavior. Sometimes the role demands come into being unconsciously or on a wave of social contagion. More and more, adults and adolescents alike are taking thought with regard to the adolescent condition and giving explicit voice to what they understand its role characteristics to be. It is adolescents taking stock of adolescence, sometimes in response to adult teachings, who have proclaimed doctrines of sexual freedom or the glories of marijuana. On the other hand, it is the shrewd poll-takers and promoters who have set forth the notion of the teen-age charge account or credit card, and it is the image-makers who have conveyed that cigarette-smoking and motorcycle ownership are essential ingredients of the adolescent role.

It would appear that as societies become industrialized, the total period of apprenticeship is lengthened, the taking on of adult roles is deferred, and the interval between sexual maturity and adult status gets longer. Indeed, a long adolescence is a relatively recent phenomenon in our own society. It is worth noting that such ceremonies as the Christian confirmation, which requires the individual, once he has reached the "age of discretion," to confirm on his own the religious beliefs he has been taught, and the Jewish Bar Mitzvah, both held at about age thirteen, probably began as puberty rites. We might also recall that Shakespeare's tragic heroine Juliet was only fourteen, and that in colonial times marriages often took place in the early teens. On the law books of many states today, the marriageable age is still twelve for girls and fourteen for boys, although it becomes a matter of momentary nationwide interest when youngsters of this age actually assert their legal prerogatives. The New Hampshire legislature recently defeated a move to change the marriageable age for girls from thirteen to sixteen, and for boys from fourteen to seventeen (Anonymous, June 8, 1971). Nowadays, in our aristocratic social strata the girl "comes out"—implicitly into the marriage market— at age eighteen. In the more plebeian segments of society, the girl makes her debut somewhat earlier, at a "Sweet Sixteen" birthday party, although both these rituals seem to be on the decline. (The idea of a debut is alien to members of some ethnic groups in which marriages are arranged be-

Adolescence as a cultural phenomenon

tween families by a marriage broker or go-between; and in the middle class, dating provides the way to get to know prospective mates.) The important point here is that the former symbols of adulthood—financial independence from the parents, completing school—are being postponed to ever-later ages. Also, in our society there is no one event or criterion that marks off immaturity from maturity. The adult world gives the adolescent ambiguous information about his status, reinforcing his own ambiguity about himself.

Our culture contains numerous micro-*rites de passage*, some written into law and others simply part of the folkways, but no single one a true indicator of adulthood. Indeed, as we have suggested, these micro-rites may be in conflict with each other. Even the law is inconsistent, from state to state and from one area of functioning to another. The age of consent for girls may be anywhere from age twelve to age eighteen—but while the law specifies the age at which sexual intercourse without marriage may take place, in most states and localities it prohibits or penalizes extramarital sexual intercourse. (Although we ordinarily think of statutory rape as applying to girls, the laws have sometimes been invoked against older women who seduced boys who had not reached the age of consent. There is a further instance of a group of seventeen-year-old boys being charged with statutory rape for having relations with a prostitute just below the statutory age of eighteen [Sherwin, 1966].) Depending on which one of the United States he lives in, the individual may be allowed to drive a car at fourteen or not until he is eighteen. Up to age twenty-five, the American male must pay an extra premium on his car insurance. Employers must pay a

higher rate for accident insurance if they employ minors, further complicating the already difficult picture for the would-be adolescent worker.

The adolescent suffers from two kinds of technological unemployment. First, automation reduces the need for production workers. Second, the conditions of our society reduce the need for unskilled workers. A third consideration is that adolescents are reluctant to enter occupations which are accorded low status in our value system, even though there may be plenty of openings and even though the actual work may be highly useful: barbering, plumbing, auto repairing, and so on. (It is interesting that the craft unions, like the medical profession, conspire to keep workers in short supply in order to enhance their market value. In the process, they have discriminated in favor of their friends and relations and against other minority groups.) The child labor laws, while serving the perfectly admirable purpose of keeping children (all except newsboys and farm workers) from being exploited economically, may incidentally deny adolescents the chance to get practical experience and, with it, a sense of growth, accomplishment, and independence.

The age at which the young person can buy alcoholic beverages may be set at eighteen, nineteen, twenty, or twenty-one, which makes for very real problems as in the case of New York State, which permits drinking at age eighteen, so that adolescents from adjoining states drive in, tank up, and then drive drunkenly in the direction of home. Quite a number never make it. Seventeen-year-olds may enlist in the military, and nineteen-year-olds can be drafted (very few people welcome the draft card as a badge of maturity). But while teen-agers have long been considered old enough to kill and be killed, they may not be considered old enough to drink, only recently have they been given the right to vote, and at various times people get very agitated about making the boys' military surroundings more homelike, both to ease the shock of transition and to provide a wholesome moral atmosphere—in other words, draftees should still be treated like children. The platoon sergeant is cast in the dual role of Fagin and house mother.

In the past, our society's views of when one should stop being a child and become an adult have been very much influenced by transitory conditions. During the Great Depression of the 1930s, for instance, there was considerable pressure to keep young people out of the overcrowded labor market. They were urged to stay in school, and those out of school were organized into "youth groups," many of whose members were fully mature people, if not middle-aged. When World War II came along and reversed the manpower picture, the pressure on young people was to get into either the armed forces or the production and distribution of war goods.

Things are in flux in the seventies, and any attempt to capture the complexity is bound to fail, but we will do our best. The 1950s were an era of complacency, of conformity, of seeking individual fulfillment. The mood of the time was "privatism," a lack of concern with larger issues. The 1960s were marked by a new idealism and activism sparked initially by black discontent and accelerated by the Indochina war. It was a decade of civil rights marches, urban riots, campus teach-ins, antiwar demonstrations, communes, drugs, campus takeovers, and trashing and bombing. The young people grew their hair long, adopted

A rock festival in 1970.

new forms of dress and adornment, and were called flower children, hippies, crazies, and freaks—the last a term many still cherish. The mood of the 1960s exhausted itself in frustration and despair, and among older adolescents and many young adults there has been, in the 1970s, a revival of privatism. Some of the well-to-do young people are abandoning school in quest of "alternate life styles," notably life in urban or rural communes. Communal living is also being fairly widely practiced by young adults holding conventional jobs. Low-budget travel abroad is highly favored, and many youngsters work at part-time jobs to finance next summer's vagabondage. More poor youngsters than ever are staying in school and going on to college, some in pursuit of economic betterment and some in hopes of an understanding of the political process that will enable them to exercise power. The relatively affluent young people who stay in school are more serious students than those of a generation ago, struggling with ideas instead of plugging for grades. Violent revolution of the anarchistic sort, prominent in the late sixties, seems to be in abeyance for the moment, although there is evidence that there are young revolutionaries biding their time, organizing, debating aims and strategies, and sniffing the currents of events. Almost all young people have to some degree been radicalized so that what were once controversial topics, like American foreign policy, the environment, and business morality and immorality, have become the "of courses" that one doesn't bother to talk about. Moriarity and Toussieng (1970), in a follow-up study of subjects studied as babies and young children by Lois Murphy and associates, found that even the offspring of conservative Kansas parents,

although not activists, showed strong sympathy with those working for change.

Although we have been speaking of older adolescents and young adults, many of the same trends can be seen in younger adolescents. In addition, of course, these youngsters are still involved in some of the more traditional concerns, such as relations with the opposite sex. Dating is less frequently practiced than in years past, although it is still fairly common in the suburbs and small towns. Early dating produces some anomalies, as in the case of a thirteen-year-old boy about to meet a girl at the movies for his first date, who asked his mother, "Do you suppose I could tell her to meet me inside? That way I wouldn't have to pay for her ticket." "Going steady," much talked about in the fifties and early sixties, seems to be a vanishing institution. In general, congregating in the park, the hang-out, or somebody's home, or going to the movies in batches is now the way young people get together. There is a new freedom about striking up acquaintances with strangers who are perceived as members of youth society, through the common coin of dress, speech patterns, and attitudes and values.

The earlier maturing of young adolescents appears in the increasing frequency with which they too work part-time, whether at baby-sitting, doing the neighbors' chores (some enterprising youngsters borrow or save capital with which to buy a power mower or snowplow), or even founding a business such as a neighborhood newspaper or a truck garden. Such activities are, of course, a throwback to a still-earlier era when it was taken for granted that young people earned extra money around the neighborhood. In between, there was a period in which both parents and children accepted incompetence and parasitism as the norm.

Many of the milestones by which young people once measured their progress toward maturity no longer exist. Girls no longer wave their hair (indeed, those with curly hair may seek ways to straighten it), parents and children no longer battle over the use of cosmetics, there is no urge to emulate the adults who wear high heels (perhaps in part because today's adolescent girls are so tall that minimizing height is more of an issue than emphasizing it), and even on "formal" occasions any variety of dress may serve. Neither are there any age distinctions nowadays in the clothing worn by boys once they have left the preschool years. About the only remnant from the old days is the boy's first razor, and since many young men never shave at all, this too may be on its way out. The current signs of maturity are the driver's license, the passport, the high school diploma, and working papers, which are more the province of the state than of parents and older friends and relatives. The last two years of high school are likely to be a time of especially painful waiting for the older adolescent—he may not know where he is going or what he wants to do, but the petty controls of school and parents are becoming intolerable.

To some extent, this pushing of milestones toward the beginning of the adolescent time scale seems to be an upward diffusion of lower-class practices into the middle and upper classes. In general, mature status is granted relatively early in the lower classes, and children higher in the socioeconomic scheme of things (especially boys) have always envied the freedom of their lower-class counterparts. Upper-class parents used to resist their children's clamor for various privileges with the argument that certain things were "vulgar" or that "there's plenty of time yet for that." Now, with the extensive homogenization of our culture (including a certain amount of affluence even among those who on other measures might be called plebeian), vulgarity is much less of an issue. As for time, parents nowadays are inclined to share the adolescent's feeling that time is running out and that he must hurry to taste life's pleasures before the world goes smash or, an equally dread alternative, his capacity for enjoyment is vitiated by adulthood. Also, psychologically, time does slip away from children and adolescents faster than it used to, because we fill their days with so many demands and activities, and filled time passes much more quickly than empty time. On the other hand, filled time is later recalled more vividly than empty time, which may be one reason that adults who have had an active adolescence look back so fondly, whereas those who were bored as adolescents are glad to have left this period behind.

Although adolescence seems to have arisen almost by accident out of the evolving pattern of our society, it has become solidly institutionalized as a period when the individual is no longer a child but is not yet an adult, and it has been bound about with rationalizations. Our key rationalization is that the manifestations of adolescence are natural and inevitable, that adolescent behavior is rooted in the adolescent's incomplete maturity. We should like to make the point, anticipating later discussion, that the immaturity of adolescents is largely a product of the way we treat them, that interactions between the adult world and the adolescent world too often

**Adolescence as
a cultural
phenomenon**

431

form a vicious circle, a positive feedback loop in which every reaction produces a more intense counterreaction, bringing out the worst in everybody. It is our contention that much of the strife between adolescents and adults is useless and destructive and could be eliminated to everybody's benefit. Some conflict between the generations may be inevitable, and some kinds of conflict may be beneficial, but much of it is simply the reciprocal discharge of frustrations. Life in a complex society such as ours may indeed require an extended apprenticeship, but, as Robert Nixon (1962) points out, this should not mean enforced immaturity, and we can question whether the apprenticeship we provide is adequate on either psychological or economic grounds. One difficulty may be that adults, in their fervent pursuit of youth, fail to offer young people models of mature behavior. The mass media, too, offer a confusing image of adulthood.

The Adolescent
and His Parents

If the adolescent's central problem is to define an identity independent of the authority of his or her parents, it follows that the young person has to break innumerable ties to his family based on authority, affection, responsibility, respect, intimacy, money and material goods, immaturity (on both sides), possessiveness, and just plain habit. In this section, we shall deal primarily with how the adolescent and his family work toward and at the same time resist this painful series of ruptures, and the stresses engendered in the process. Here again, we lean to the side of exaggeration and caricature (although reality sometimes defies caricature) to make the important features salient.

We should begin by saying that adolescents and their parents spend some part of their time getting along with each other very nicely, sharing discoveries and fresh looks at experience, exchanging banter, talking over plans and problems, and simply enjoying each other's company. It is also important to note that some adolescents grow up with essentially no conflict with their families beyond the frictions that go with living together. Such adolescents, who are more likely to be girls than boys, show an early and thorough identification with the family's values of whatever kind, whether upper-class or lower-class hedonism, the super-respectability of the static lower middle class, prosperous middle-class self-satisfaction, upwardly mobile ambition and acquisitiveness, or the values that go with living by thievery.

The family of such adolescents lets go easily, confident they will continue to be emotionally close and that the youngster "has got the right stuff in him" to enable him to make his way. The general rule, however, seems to be that the adolescent grows away from his family, both in spirit and in body, until home sometimes seems little more than a rooming house where he eats, sleeps, drops his clothes to be picked up and laundered, looks at the sports and entertainment pages (or, if a girl, at the advice columns) and comics, watches television, and makes and receives phone calls. Chores are likely to be executed in a straw-boss–convict relationship rather than as a shared work experience, which deprives them of most of their value. The adolescent's own room, if he has one, or the privacy of a hotly contested bathroom, serves as a refuge where he can study and register his own growth, where before the mirror he can experiment with, practice, and perfect the masks he wears, the styles and images he wants to project. Mealtimes, in those families which eat together, are perhaps the only remaining opportunity for real exchanges with his family. And although the dinner table may serve as a forum, it can also become an arena. A substantial part of the time the adolescent spends with his family is likely to be colored by feelings—on both sides—of frustration, outrage, humiliation, sullenness, resentment, and dramatic (or melodramatic) despair.

Underlying a great many conflicts are the allied states of ambiguity and ambivalence. Ambiguity haunts the young adolescent especially with regard to his own body, such that he is not sure whether he should be acting like a child or an adult. He tends to repudiate his childish self, but hardly with assurance or without regrets. He feels perfectly self-confident up to the moment that he confronts the task of demonstrating his competence. He demands privileges but views their corresponding responsibilities as onerous. From the parents' point of view, of course, the ability to bear responsibility is as much a mark of maturity as is having privileges. To the child, by contrast, responsibilities are imposed by adults and so are degrading tokens of his inferior status. The parents do not share the young adolescent's ambiguity about where he stands. He is clearly still a child, but a child big enough to help out.

It is primarily with reference to the older adolescent that parents experience ambiguity, uncertainty about where he stands and how he should be treated. The older adolescent looks very much like an adult and sometimes even acts like one, but his occasional slips and even blunders betray the child who lurks within. The older adolescent feels little ambiguity about his grown-up status. His problem is growth ambivalence, an urge to take the final step into adulthood coupled with a sense that to do so is to step into the void. His growth ambivalence, moreover, is shared by his parents, leading to an intensification of the pattern of **dual ambivalence** whereby parents and child are at war with each other about his status and each side is at war with itself. To complicate the pattern further, father and mother may have somewhat different patterns of ambivalence, which can set them at war with each other. Further, there may be a triangle of back-and-forth emotional ambivalence in which love and devotion war with resentment and hostility.

One source of the older adolescent's growth ambivalence is the fear of failure. Every time he reaches for adulthood, he puts himself on trial. Consciously, of course, the adolescent refuses to acknowledge the possibility of failure, but it repeatedly crops up as a chilly, threatening presence. Another source of growth ambivalence for the young person is that adult privileges themselves hold half-sensed terrors. The adolescent is by no means sure that he wants to liberate and indulge the new forces at work within himself. He has not yet learned to sense these forces as truly his own, he has not yet integrated them into his self-schema, and he is not sure whether he can control them once they are turned loose.

Thus, protest and grumble though he may, he sometimes feels a secret relief when his parents add the weight of their authority to his own uncertain controls. Into the bargain, it is likely that the vehemence of his protests is in direct proportion to the anxiety he feels, and the protests are partly against his own uncertainty. Even if his parents did not already share his growth ambivalence, it would still put them into what Bateson et al. (1956) call a double-bind situation, in which they are damned if they do and damned if they don't, and so cannot win. For if the parents exercise control, they are snoopy and domineering; if they let the youngster decide for himself, they are neglectful and uncaring. An early version of the adolescent's dual attitude is seen in a composition by a high school sophomore who says, "The parents should make it their job to see to it that their children do their homework" (which, it is promised, will insure "less juvenile delinquencies") and, in the next breath, "Parents should treat boys of fifteen years of age as grownups and not children" (Stone, unpublished).

This parental double-bind does not mean that what parents do is of no importance. Parents still have to provide limits and guidelines and values, and if the child fights them, this has its developmental importance, too. For if the young person is going to find a set of durable values that he can call his own, he will probably have to begin by contesting the established values of his parents. And parents, if they expect the youngster to listen, have to react with something better than moral indignation.

Parents, of course, are eager to have their children grow up. Indeed, when parents criticize an adolescent it is likely to be on the grounds that he is acting childishly. But although parents urge the young person toward adulthood, they often act as though his reaching the adult state is still in the comfortably far-off future. It is said that readiness for adulthood comes about two years later than the adolescent claims, and about two years before his parents will admit. As often as not, parents, without knowing it, retard development, even though they may show no open regret over losing "my baby." There seem to be several possible roots for parents' unwillingness to let the child grow up. For one thing, they know their own child too well and are all too aware of his weaknesses and inadequacies. They are overaware, also, of the perils and pitfalls of the great outside world. They fail to see, however, that the only way the youngster can overcome his weaknesses and cope with the problems of an independent life is by actually moving into the world. No one is ever fully prepared in advance for adult life, and every developmental step has its risks—letting the child walk by himself, cross the street alone, sending him off to school, letting him run with the gang, letting him go out unchaperoned, letting him use the family car—each requires a fear-provoking wrench that has to come. A recurring if unspoken theme, of course, is the fear of sexual involvement in adolescence. In keeping with the double standard of our society, the fear is greater in the case of girls than boys, but it applies in some measure to both. Let us stress that the ambivalence is there for the young person as well as his or her parents. Many parents, nowadays, are concerned about hard drugs (though more and more, however much they disapprove, have resigned themselves to experimentation with marijuana, as with cigarettes and alcohol), but, from published accounts, large numbers seem fearful to confront the issue head on.

At a still more hidden level of motivation, the youngster's growing up may be threatening to his parents. By a process of reverse identification of parent with child, it may reawaken the unresolved fears and conflicts of their own adolescent pasts. It may bring home to them with new and frightening force how the years and dreams have slipped away, leaving them members of an aging generation. It may even breed a species of jealousy over the pleasures that still await the adolescent, perhaps tempered by a wry recognition that youth is wasted on the young. It may simply coincide with or it may provoke the later crisis of identity that many adults go through, women at age thirty-five to forty and men at forty-five to fifty (see p. 490). It may imply the end of the parents' usefulness, that their mission in life is at an end, or it may spell a lonely life in a house that has suddenly become too big. Parental resistance to the child's growing up may stem from unwillingness to relinquish authority built up over a decade and a half.

Parental resistance may be greatest for a firstborn child, who in this area as in so many others has to break trail for the other siblings. In general, parents, like everybody else, resist change, they are unwilling to surrender old habits and adopt new ones, to let go. As we have said, the growth ambivalence of parents dates back at least to late infancy, and if the adolescent is not so well prepared for adulthood as he might be, it may be because of an intermittent, if loving and well-intentioned, sabotage of his autonomy by parents over the years.

With dual ambivalence as the background, conflicts between the adolescent and his parents can arise on almost any subject. Much of the passion attendant on these conflicts is probably generated by both parties' need to drown out their own feelings that contradict what they are expressing. Among the favorite topics of dispute are dating, friendships, dress, time schedules, chores and duties, money, automobiles, school marks, future schooling, morals and manners, access to the telephone, religious observances and beliefs, politics and economics—not necessarily in this order of prominence or importance. In all these matters, the adolescent wants to be free and unconfined, but at the same time he is coming to realize that he is enmeshed in a network of reciprocity that inevitably restricts his freedom of action. Often, indeed, it is this very inevitability which he is fighting, rather than the specific restriction he is made to observe.

It is worth pointing out that the inescapability of reciprocal responsibilities may add another dimension to the adult's ambivalence as well. When the parent rages to the child about responsibilities, his wrath may be in direct proportion to his own secret wish that he could repair to a tropical isle, slough off his duties, and live a life of anarchic selfishness. No matter how well adults—particularly males—have adapted to a life based on social reciprocity, they cannot restrain a twinge of sympathy for those who refuse to yield. The adolescent is often shrewd enough to detect this source of ambivalence and to be outspokenly aware of his parents' departures from their own professed standards. It is quite common to hear adolescents call their parents "hypocrites." While this allegation may have some truth, some part of parental hypocrisy may be an attempt to help the adolescent make a better life for himself than the parents'. Parents often try to give their youngsters the "benefit of their experience," to teach the lessons which they had to learn the hard way, from life itself, sometimes too late for it to do them any good. But it seems to be the case that the adolescent cannot learn these lessons. He simply does not know enough about the workings of the world for the lessons to make sense, he is too much wrapped up in his immediate personal concerns, and he feels that his parents are fundamentally ignorant of his situation and are living in the past. Again, let us remember, both generations agree that times have changed.

Let us look at some exceptions to this pattern of dual ambivalence. We have already said that many young people identify early and thoroughly with their parents' ways and values, and slip easily into the roles for which they have been preparing. In upwardly mobile families, parents and children may work hard and cooperatively to launch each child in turn toward a level of achievement beyond that of the parents. In the lower classes, the pressures are rather consistently on the side of rapid maturing and early assumption of adult roles. There may be conflicts, but they are not the conflicts of dual ambivalence. While the lower-class child is more likely than his middle-class or upper-class counterpart to leave school early and get a job, there may be pressure from his family to stay at home and contribute his earnings to the family. Here, too, then, we often find friction about freedom and money. The situation is further complicated when the family belongs to an immigrant or other minority group, with traditions of strong parental authority, entailing additional problems in identification and conflicts between mores. This is especially true in the case of female offspring who, in the old culture, were expected to be submissive and subordinate. For many young males nowadays, the possibility of being con-

scripted adds one more complication. It is also a fact of our times that many young people leave school, are rejected for military service, and cannot find work.

On farms and ranches, where the youngster's life is necessarily centered in the home and home place (although fast cars and private airplanes and helicopters have done much to break down the former isolation of country people), and where he participates directly in a relatively self-sufficient family economy, there tends to be less of a gap between the generations. In the present era of factory farming, the parents are even likely to be college-educated. The parents are inclined to welcome and accept the child's growing up, and he in turn finds it easy to demonstrate his competence in the terms by which they measure maturity. It is largely in a market economy of specialized services centered outside the home that conflicts are most likely to arise. It has always been said that farm children learn the facts of life early, from watching the animals, but we know of no evidence showing that farm children have either more or fewer problems than city children in coming to terms with their own sexuality.

Just as the presence of conflict is not always bad, lack of visible conflict is not necessarily a sign that all is well. One way to achieve a seemingly idyllic order of peace is through authoritarian and repressive methods of child-rearing. The effects of an authoritarian upbringing can be seen in a composition written by a fifteen-year-old girl:

I'm glad my parents are people who know what is best for us to do and know how to go about making us do it. There are many parents today who do not know how to handle their children. As a result of this the children become too independend [sic]. Then the parents wonder why they do not get good marks in school. . . . When [my mother and dad] say no once there is no use asking a second time, because they will not change their minds. Mom says she wants us to grow up and get a good job and be respected by other people, if nothing else. . . . It makes me proud and happy when I think about how my parents have protected me from becoming a junvenile [sic] delinquent (Stone, unpublished).

We can see that the writer's parents have accomplished their goal of indoctrinating her with their values. Paradoxically enough, however, one can produce the same sort of dogmatic authoritarianism by following the opposite course of giving the child a minimum of direction. The child who is left to find his own values is very likely to seize upon the most conservative, traditional, orthodox ways of doing things, probably because the lack of guidance makes him so insecure that he is forced to grab for the obvious. Thus, one is obliged —assuming that one wants to produce a child who can truly think for himself—to steer a middle course, not in some abstract pursuit of the Golden Mean, but because it is what works.

Democratic-minded parents also want to impart values to their young. But they distinguish between basic, humane values and superficial, merely conventional ones, and between moral and moral-free spheres of action. They know that the way to teach values is not in terms of external, rigid rules of behavior, but by getting the child to think about the consequences of his action. They know that there is room for differences of opinion about how values are translated into behavior, that in real life one sometimes has to choose between values, and so do not try to map out in detail a "correct" way of thinking for children. Such democratic practices by no means preclude adolescent rage—even at what is perceived as parental wishy-washiness.

One can produce authoritarianism either by browbeating the child or by leaving him to his own moral devices. But one can also obtain essentially the same result by various more subtle manipulations. One can, without saying a word, teach values by the equivalent of operant conditioning methods, simply in terms of the emotional feedback one supplies to the youngster's deeds and utterances. One can "explain" with sweet reasonableness why one course of action is better than another, and that by clinging to his own wishes or convictions the child is willfully hurting the parent. Since the adolescent's feelings are often ill-formed and elusive, one can even convince him that he really wants something quite different from what he thinks he wants. The adult, with his greater command of logic, can stack the cards to persuade the young person that he is behaving irrationally. Thus, while adults can manipulate the child into reaching the parents' point of view as though it were his own, an adolescent so manipulated is even more helpless than the browbeaten one. He no longer knows what he really feels or wants or believes in, he always is vaguely at odds with himself and senses an uneasy and irrational guilt no matter how he acts.

If some parents use these various techniques of indoctrination, it is perhaps because they have long since stopped thinking about the issues involved. But we cannot take values for granted, especially if, as in our society, we espouse two—or more—sets of conflicting values. It would seem to follow that reasonable parents, who do think seriously about values, would have no trouble communicating them to their offspring. This, however, is not the case. The young person, with his limited experience, simply cannot share the perspectives of those who have been around twenty-five or thirty years longer than he has. In times that change as rapidly as ours, there is bound to be a gap between the generations, exemplified in the remark of a young teen-age girl who, preparing blissfully for her first formal dance, turned to her helpful mother and asked, "Did they have parties like this when you were alive?"

The Adolescent's Activities and Associates

Like the school-age child, the adolescent shuttles back and forth between two cultures, that of adults and that of his peers. Now, however, the situation has changed radically. For the adolescent peer group no longer, as in middle childhood, thinks of itself as a childhood society, but as a new kind of adult society, the wave of the future. To this end, there is a conspiracy of silence among adolescents about their own and each other's pasts. The very thought of their recent immaturities is too agonizing to bear, and they firmly block out any possibility that such immaturity could still be part of their nature. This emphasis on being grown up—"sophisticated"—does not, of course, lessen friction with the world of chronological grownups. Indeed, much of the separateness is imposed by adult disdain or fear. It is only the occasional adult who represents an ideal, or the one who, like the athletic coach, flatters the adolescent by treating him bluntly and without reserve, who the adolescent feels is an exception to the alienness of the adult world. It often seems that parents are barred from direct dealings with their offspring by a need to play the parental role as defined by others. Even the direct expression of love may be blocked as incompatible with the lofty exercise of authority and the preservation of adult dignity.

It used to be that adolescents hurried toward adulthood, with a view to bringing into being their own version of Utopia. Nowadays, they are held back by various forces. The idealistic ones suspect that, far from taking over and transforming the system, they will become its slaves (Friedenberg, 1959). Many adolescents shy away from the involvements and responsibilities of adult life. The adolescent culture, both spontaneous and insinuated from without, and epitomized by the cult of the guitar (or whatever talisman succeeds it), has become so powerfully institutionalized that for many adolescents it has come to seem a permanent way of life—indeed, the middle-aged ski bums, surf bums, and hippies that we see give the impression of perpetual adolescence. As larger numbers of adolescents discover that they can have such benefits of adulthood as sex and money without the annoying clutter of careers, spouses, children, mortgage payments, and political participation, adolescence seems an increasingly attractive and perhaps permanent way of life. Here again, adults may offer little in the way of adequate models. The rock musician's image of perpetual youth may be the one to identify with.

Adolescents have always been groupminded, but today's teen culture seems more self-consciously communal and community-minded than ever. Young people talk less than those of a generation ago about the importance of popularity, but it is obviously vital to be widely liked. It is likewise important that one be abreast of the latest trends.

There are loners, male and female, but most adolescents seek the safety, warm companionship, and reciprocal reinforcement of the group. Some are kept in the group by pressure from their contemporaries or even from misguided parents or guidance counselors who worry unduly about the boy or girl who "doesn't have enough friends." During adolescence, the cliques into which young people form become ever more homogeneous and stratified by social class and academic achievement level. Increasingly, individual friendships are based on common tastes and interests. As adolescents become more mobile—by age sixteen or seventeen many of them have, or have access to, a car—they can maintain friendships over an ever-wider geographical range. As they travel about the country, driving or hitchhiking, or journey abroad, they help to cement today's world-wide youth culture.

Let us point out that adolescents are diverse individuals so that our generalizations about them, and about what we see as the chief styles of being adolescent, do not apply to all adolescents equally, and to some hardly at all. Also, much of what we say applies only to outward behavior, and may not do justice to the adolescent's actual feelings—indeed, in later sections, we shall see how inner feelings may be very much at variance with what outward behavior would lead us to believe. Here we are mostly concerned with adolescents in groups.

As we have seen, the adolescent spends less and less time at home, and very little

A major activity of young people is hanging around.

Laurence Fink

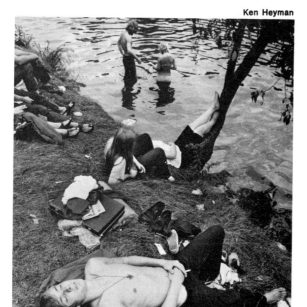

The Woodstock Festival, climax of a bygone era.

Horsing around.

of the time he spends there may be family-oriented. He may even do his homework at a friend's house, or he may prefer to spend his evenings at the public library, where he can study among his friends or, in nice weather, hang around the library steps smoking and chatting. A major portion of the adolescent's time, at least until the minimum legal school-leaving age and probably well beyond, is spent in school. It seems safe to say that, for most adolescents, the academic side of school and college seems merely the price one has to pay in dull drudgery for the privilege of being an adolescent. And, to anticipate future discussion, let us say that what we know of most school and college programs leads us to feel that the young people are often right.

All too many adolescents—and schools—are anti-intellectual, and even those who find their studies attractive are inclined to conceal the fact, lest they gain fatal reputations as grinds. It is socially acceptable to get good grades, since otherwise one cannot get into the right colleges where one makes the right contacts and acquires the credentials needed for the right jobs—and perhaps find a mate—but it is widely taken for granted by school and student that what the adolescent gets from his education are some socially and vocationally useful skills and, in those institutions that have liberal-arts pretensions, a veneer of culture.

But even if schooling is only a purgatory to be endured on the way to adulthood, school is still important as the source of friends (and, decreasingly, as the site of certain shared activities like dances, athletic contests, plays, and special-interest clubs). The primary social life of the standard American high school is that which erupts when the bell signals the end of the hour. This is at least partly in response to the degrading tyranny practiced by some administrators and teachers. At its extreme, the commotion in high school corridors is enormous, partly as an explosion of pent-up energy and partly for display. (We mention only in passing that in too many high schools the commotion includes seething racial hostilities.) The boys show themselves at their most masculine—many adults mistakenly conclude that the free-form attire, long hair, and gentle manner now in vogue among adolescent males are a badge of emasculation, but a stallion's heart can beat strongly regardless of externals. The styles vary with social background, but the girls find ways to make themselves vivaciously or coolly alluring. And no matter how interested in their own group the clusters of boys and girls seem to be, they are really proclaiming and radiating how interesting they are—it makes a considerable difference in their behavior whether anyone worthwhile is watching. In a sense, they are all like politicians running for office, cultivating the esteem and acclaim and recognition that will tell them that everything is all right.

These patterns persist even in an age when young people are thought to be preoccupied with making love and revolution. As this is being written, an economy that has been booming, with only minor interruptions, for over a quarter of a century has turned gray and soggy, and this fact is almost certain to have an effect on young people. One thing that has divided adolescents and their parents in this generation is that parents have memories, if only from their own childhoods, of depression times, when food and shelter could not be taken for granted, whereas young people, even

those who had no part in the general prosperity, have never had occasion to question the availability of wealth. Recent economic strains seem to have brought back some of the same feelings.

In their search for popularity and status, adolescents are more selective on a number of counts than are school-age youngsters. Some American high schools, of course, are highly homogeneous in their make-up, but most are sufficiently variegated to allow a predictable social hierarchy to emerge. In most large schools, the chief social division is into **sets**, the major blocs into which the students distribute themselves. Many of these parallel adult social patterns. Sets may be based on orientations to the future, social background, or personality type, or on some combination of these. Since sets form spontaneously and not by decree, they defy systematic classification. The important thing is that they are psychologically real, and the adolescents know to which they and other people belong, even though in a large school some people in the same set may not know each other. The other important fact about sets is that they overlap virtually not at all. Even though, technically, one might qualify for several sets, one gravitates to the set that seems most suitable. Within a given set, distinct, rather exclusive friendship groups—"crowds" or "cliques"—take shape, usually on the basis of common tastes, interests, and styles. Nowadays, with the growing idealism of young people, there is often a conscious effort to break down adult social separations and to seek out friendships from different backgrounds. Such linkages, unfortunately, are more likely to thrive within the walls of the high school than outside. Personal friendships of the one-to-one variety usually develop within a clique, although a shared consuming interest—in amateur radio, in hot rods, in writing, in chess—can draw together people from several cliques or even sets. Some individualists cannot be assigned to sets and refuse or are unable to align themselves with cliques, and may have a lonely time of it within the standard school structure. Where the middle-years child's peer group was peopled with friends, best friends, and faceless strangers, the adolescent has a wide circle of casual acquaintances as well. One of the adult social skills he is acquiring is the ability to exchange flip, breezy greetings with people he knows only slightly, and the number of such exchanges is a measure for himself and others of how near he is to his goal of popularity, about which we shall say more shortly.

Thus, the pattern of teen-age associations is quite intricate, based as it is on group (set and crowd) identification, arbitrary class lines, personal likes and dislikes, tastes and interests, and keen attention to the overall popularity hierarchy within the school. In thinking about joining a club, the adolescent may be far less concerned about the club's theme and program—travel, photography, dance, art, hiking—than with who its members are and where he stands in relation to them, or where he wants to stand. Status motivation is strong, since status determines dating patterns, whom you hang around with in and outside school, whom you emulate and whom you despise, and the adolescent keeps checking his status by other people's responses to him and to the rest of the group.

The irony in the whole system of judging oneself by the company one is allowed to keep is that everybody is in the same boat and feels it necessary to keep up his or her defenses. The mask of self-assurance worn by the campus leader is as false as the mask of independent aloofness worn by the outcast, and the poses and postures fool everybody except the one who assumes them. Adolescents are too self-involved to be able to see deep into other people's feelings. They see that adults, who play a somewhat different game by different rules, hide behind a facade, but they do not know what it is they are hiding. But when dealing with their contemporaries, whose opinions are so all-important, they may not even distinguish between mask and reality.

Now let us take a moment to trace the development of this pattern of adolescent social organization. In the junior high school, as we have said, there is a spectacular mismatching of the sexes. The average junior high school is populated by young ladies and male children, with most of the girls well launched into adolescence and most of the boys still in the middle years. This works some hardships on the girls, who are ready for male companionship, but hardly of the kind to be had from their classmates, and who find it almost impossible to penetrate the social order of the high school. They are usually forced to make do with the materials at hand, and a school dance, back in the days when dancing was cheek to cheek, was likely to be characterized by the young ladies towering over and dragging around grudging and grubby escorts who would rather be playing baseball. The junior high school years are a kind of limbo for many girls. Around the sophomore year of high school, boys begin to catch up to girls in maturity, and the interests of the two sexes, while not identical, now better complement each other. Boys give up their bicycles and, for the most part, the neighborhood games, and become increasingly oriented to social relations at the verbal level, with physical activity taking second place. Boys and girls begin playing the game of status, with the assumption that status determines dating and mating and that dating also helps decide status. With status the key, the football game itself is less important than whom you go with and how you conduct yourself while there.

The school, however, is only one focus of adolescent social life. Another is the **hangout**, the gathering place. It is permissible to go to the hangout alone, but it is preferable to go with a few other people of one's own sex, hoping and expecting to meet and mingle with a bunch of the other sex, without the formalities or financial responsibilities of a date. Steadies, of course, may meet at the hangout by prearrangement. Some community centers serve as hangouts, occasionally as deliberate substitutes for unsavory commercial establishments. The ones that succeed best are those which reproduce most clearly the atmosphere of the neighborhood hangouts and allow the youngsters to feel comfortable in the tentative amorousness of early adolescence. More commonly, though, the deliciously dangerous—but outwardly blasé —encounters between sexes take place on the premises of those drug stores, candy stores, diners, shopping centers, drive-in restaurants, dime stores, or, in warm weather, on favored stretches of beach, which the kids view as hospitable. In the case of the drug store or sweet shop, being hospitable to adolescents often means sacrificing the magazine display and, usually, adult patronage.

Adolescent social life goes on around as well as within the hangout. Boys cluster near the entrance, appraising and commenting on the clusters of girls who stroll casually by and then back again, ostensibly bound on some errand or absorbed in shop-window displays, but tinglingly aware that they are being scrutinized. Just as with adults, the openness of the mating calls and the amount of wolf-whistling and hip-twitching vary with group traditions, but the basic phenomena remain the same (although the women's liberation doctrine is spreading that girls should not exploit their bodies). Notice that, unlike school, where sets and crowds are mixed together in the same building (although they may segregate themselves by patterns of courses of study), the hangout usually caters only to a single set.

In much of America, car ownership by adolescents is a powerful determinant of the physical structure of their society. The kind of car one owns is a symbol of status, although the relationships are by no means simple. Sports cars, old or new, are high in status but low in convenience, although there may be a special merit in packing six people into a two-seater. Old touring cars carry much cachet, especially when the hood conceals a supercharged engine. Family sedans are for squares, and probably the most successful combination of assets is the mock sports car which combines racy lines and high performance with commodious and comfortable seating. Dune buggies and snowmobiles have been very popular, but they are meeting fierce opposition from conservationists, and it is to be hoped that the ecology-minded young will abandon these modes of transportation. But any car is better than no car, and, failing a car, a motorcycle or motor scooter is better than walking or being dependent on

The adolescent's activities and associates

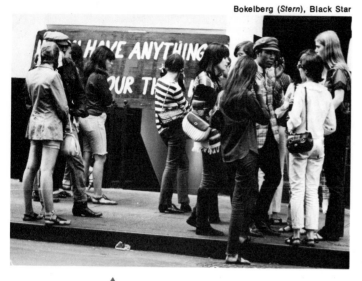

Street life.

Much of adolescent life is lived on the telephone.

the charity of others or, most humiliating, having to ride the bus. In some circles, of course, the motorcycle is the key to social organization, and status is correlated with size, power, and gleaming complexity—motorcycles are groomed with the care once lavished on horses.

In their cars, adolescents go to drive-in movies, sometimes on dates (often, to bolster their courage, on double and triple dates), sometimes in same-sex herds which jockey from space to space looking for a car loaded with an opposite-sex herd with which to intermingle. Sometimes they prowl through the entertainment district looking for action. If a group of boys can gather a like number of girls, they may go drinking and dancing, or they may seek out a lovers' lane in which to pet. The drive-in theater itself may be a petting ground, but wandering security officers keep the expressions of passion in check. The car is thought of as a setting for sexual intercourse, but again surveillance by highway policemen may make such an outcome unlikely—one may, of course, wonder about possible motives of voyeurism and sadism that impel policemen to sneak up on a parked car and suddenly shine a bright flashlight into the interior. Sometimes cars are used in drag racing, sometimes in chicken racing, and often just as transportation.

The most usual pattern is just riding around, headed nowhere in particular, sometimes at high speed but often at a leisurely pace, watching the scenery go by, shouting and whistling at girls, and just idly talking. It is only in special conditions of emotion or intimacy that one finds shared convictions and concern with such profundities as life, death, human nature, religion, war and peace, and the meaning of it all. We should point out that the enormous prestige that attaches to cars, plus the pleasures of riding around in them, accounts for some 90 percent of car thefts—the youngster (or, more often, a bunch of youngsters) simply rides around for a few hours, parks the car, and walks away. It should further be noted that motor vehicles are the greatest single cause of death between the preschool years and adulthood, and that motor vehicle accidents account for almost two-thirds of deaths among eighteen- to nineteen-year-old boys. Motorcycles are especially lethal.

Dances and dancing seem to be fading out of their former prominence in adolescent culture. Rock concerts and festivals flowered for a while, but the scene turned sour and the festivals are withering away. Movies are currently favored. Sometimes the herd goes to church socials, sometimes on hay rides, on bus trips to the big city, sometimes on outings to the seashore or ski slope or just hiking. Perhaps the most important part of herd life, however, takes place when the herd is dispersed to its various homes and the telephone is brought into play. On the phone, friends can have intense, confidential discussions impossible in the public eye of the herd itself. It is worth noting that the protracted phone calls that drive parents to a frenzy—and have driven many families into becoming two- and three-telephone families—are usually between members of the same sex. The opposite sex is still pretty much of an enigma to the adolescent, and although the youngster may yearn toward it, chaff with it, neck and pet and perhaps even have coitus with it, talking with it comes almost as hard as talking with a speaker of an alien language. At least until late adolescence, phone conversations between a boy

and a girl are likely to be brief and to the point—indeed, almost curt and abrupt. Superficially, talking seems like the simplest and most innocuous form of human communication. In psychological fact, however, to talk to somebody means to let down one's guard and be prepared to reveal oneself, and the telephone does not permit one to do much besides talk. With the herd, one fills up time with scuffling, catch-phrases, comments, wisecracks, banter, snatches of song, a few chords on the guitar or the blast of a record player, a sip of soda or a drag on a cigarette, a dance step, all devices that replace saying something, but which are only the incidental stuff of telephone communication. Some youngsters, we are told, spend hours playing records to each other over the phone. In special circumstances, of course, the talk may flow more freely. At a recent New Year's Eve gathering of tenth-graders, three boys and two girls, the topics of a nonstop conversation included the personalities of their classmates and teachers, smoking and drinking, sex and sex education, money and jobs, events in Bangladesh and the George Harrison–Ravi Shankar benefit concert, torture, the movies, personal feelings and reactions, celebrities, parents, and a field trip they had taken to the mountains.

Our description of herd life has elements of caricature, but it is essentially true. However, as we have said, it is not equally true for all adolescents, and even to the extent it is, it does not deal with the inner concerns we shall be talking about soon. Some youngsters participate very little in herd life, some because they have overriding interests and some because the various herds will not let them. Sometimes both forces are at work. Because the herd has rejected him, the adolescent casts about for a hobby or interest. In some suburban areas, there are cases of young people who are isolated from the herd and who fill their hours with drugs and television. Solitude is not the only alternative to herd life, however. Some young people dislike the mindlessness of herd activity and prefer more direct, individualized friendships. The youngster who does his homework conscientiously has very little time for herd life except during holidays. Some adolescents alternate periods of intense study with periods of group life, but few can combine them. Some youngsters like to read a great deal, or take solitary walks and daydream. Some have parents who strictly limit group participation. Poor youngsters have a group life, but it cannot range as freely as do the more affluent hordes. It is lived more on the streets, since there is nowhere else to go in the slums. Finally, a fair number of adolescents nowadays use their free time to make money, perhaps by tending counter in the hangout, although jobs are not as easy to come by as they were a few years ago.

Popularity and conformity

The dependence of the adolescent on peer-group standards and values is, if anything, even more slavish than that of the middle-years child. The greater the wall between adolescents and adults, the more elaborate the peer culture becomes and the more the adolescent has to turn to it for support and identity. He seizes upon and displays all the trademarks of his kind, so that nobody can possibly miss them. Rigid conformity is the rule, extending to matters of dress, adornment, hair styles, tastes in foods and music, posture, gait, vocabulary, and intonation. The individual and his crowd are ever eager for innovations, but the kind of innovations that fit the established framework of teen culture.

When an adolescent wishes to assert his individuality, he is likely to do so by carrying whatever fad is prevalent one more step toward its ultimate utterness. Partly because he wants to stand out, and partly to reassure himself of the solidity of his new culture, he is always striving for vividness and extremes, as in his slang. Note, however, the forced, strained, artificial quality of much adolescent behavior—even when he plays the role of hip teen-ager well enough to fool his fellows, adults can sense the synthetic character of his performance. Fads and crazes propagate rapidly among teen-agers, so that we have the fascinating spectacle of very rapid change within a highly conservative framework. We shall talk in a moment about some real changes that seem to have occurred in adolescence in recent years, but the basic traits of adolescent culture yield slowly to social pressures.

As we have said, much of adolescent culture originates in the fertile brains of adults —magazine and newspaper columnists and the publishers of teen-age periodicals, composers and musicians and music publishers, clothing manufacturers, the makers of novelties—who skillfully gauge the adolescent *Zeitgeist* with the help of opinion polls and informants and panels, and who plant or pass along ideas for new fashions in dress and decoration, new kinds of parties, new turns of speech, new record-

The adolescent's activities and associates. ▶

Diane Koos, Black Star

Gordon Baer, Black Star

Laurence Fink

Hella Hammid, Rapho Guillumette

A current style of adolescent attire.

ing stars, and so forth. The teen-age market has come to be recognized for the potent force it is, and we have evolved a whole new subeconomy catering to the tastes of adolescents. More recently, many young people have themselves become manufacturers (usually of sandals and junk jewelry, but sometimes of high quality goods) and merchants, sometimes in stores but more often on the streets, trying to dodge the police. These young entrepreneurs draw some of their trade from adults who identify with the youth style, thus reversing the pattern. Resort hotels and cruise ships have parallel programs of entertainment for adults and for their teenage children. One day's program at a Catskill resort included the following activities for teen-agers: ice skating, ping-pong tournament, a choice of dance lessons or a coed volleyball game, a shuffleboard contest, a splash party, a swimming meet, a joint teen-age and adult cocktail party, and, finally, at 10 P.M., a "Coke-tail" party. Thus, adults connive with young people in the construction of a separate culture, even though they may bemoan its existence and influence. But while teen-age doings may strike adults as inanely or perniciously juvenile, to adolescents they are part of the swinging new adulthood that will replace the drab one of the oldsters. And since so much of the time the adolescent does not have a great deal that he wants to do (he craves action and excitement, but is vague about where to find it), cannot have the things he wants the most, and isn't sure that he really wants them anyway, he uses passing fancies to fill up the vacancy of waiting and to preserve group solidarity until the days of waiting are over.

The young person's dependence on

group belongingness to tell him who he is, and his submissive conformity to group ways to guarantee that he belongs, can produce highly injurious results. In the street gang, the youngster (male or female) may have to prove himself in combat or by taking part in a murderous assault on some arbitrarily chosen victim. Characteristically, young people arrested for violent assault claim, in a convincing sort of way, that they did not want to take part but felt that they had to lest they be thought "chicken." The chicken race (for example, racing two cars to the edge of a cliff) by which adolescents tested their manhood seems to have gone out of fashion, but it is far from inconceivable that it will re-emerge, particularly in the bloody times we live in. The girl may be forced by group pressures into promiscuity, and in some cases into sex acts before an audience. A high school nurse, who tries to avoid confidences but receives them anyway, reports that there is tremendous peer pressure to engage in sex, and that many succumb to the pressure. Those who do, end up feeling severely guilty or unclean. Obviously, these consequences need not follow intrinsically motivated sex. The use of alcohol and drugs may be in response to group pressures. It is not enough to say that young people should have sufficient moral character to resist group pressures; failure to conform can produce feelings of guilt and inadequacy as severe as going against one's own conscience. Thus, the group can place the adolescent in a double-bind situation such that either of the courses open to him will lead to painful consequences. What is interesting is that not only can a single strong leader sway the group to act against its own better feelings, but in some cases no leader is needed; that is, each individual in the group can be opposed to a course of action and yet sense a group demand so strongly that he follows the course anyway.

The dependence of the adolescent on group approval is so severe that it has been labeled the "popularity neurosis" (to which American adults are not always immune). It is only late in adolescence that some young people define abstract standards of virtue against which to measure their own behavior. Meanwhile the adolescent acts primarily in ways that he thinks will make people like him. His concern about having a "good personality" is often less a search for inner strength than for the tricks that will win acceptance by others— being an athletic star, playing a musical instrument, developing a sense of humor, augmenting his vocabulary, being active in things. The devices are legion, and again the adult commercial world has moved in with stories and articles on how to be popular: what to say on a date, how to refuse a boy's advances without antagonizing him, how to obey one's parents without losing face, how to get rid of or conceal the blemishes that make one feel a pariah. And for those who cannot buy popularity at any price, there is an abundant literature providing fulfillment in fantasy.

The need for popularity stems in large part from the lessons parents teach their children. It is important to get along with people, to have people like you, to be well-adjusted, to harken to the voice of public opinion. But it becomes particularly acute in terms of the intermediate stage of the adolescent's self-knowledge. The adolescent cannot be satisfied with what he thinks about himself; he needs someone out there to tell him that he is all right. Nor can he judge his own worth in terms of what he produces—jokes, observations on events and people, the product of a special talent, the physical appearance he creates—unless it meets with special acclaim. And the louder the acclaim, the better. The adolescent is not one for subtleties (except his own, which he treasures), and unless his audience is noisily appreciative, he may doubt the sincerity of its applause. But again we come full circle to the consideration that the vigor with which one adolescent applauds another may itself express a seeking for the applauded adolescent's approval. The self-involved adolescent usually fails to recognize that everybody else feels out of step, too. Ironically, the occasional adolescent who is indifferent to popularity and goes his own way may find that his peers flock around him as a tower of strength. The adolescent's parents are as anxious as he is for him to be popular, but they are likely to disapprove of the particular people he courts. This is because they are blind to the group standards of whom it is important to be in with and whom it is better to keep at a distance. To parents, almost every adolescent other than their own looks like a potentially bad influence; parents want their youngsters to be popular, but they may be hard put to say with whom.

Social Class Differences

We have already said that adolescence may be very different for lower-class youngsters from what it is for those from the middle and upper classes. Before we go on to point to some of these differences, one thing should be made clear. The recent rediscovery of poverty in the United States has made us keenly aware of the social and economic injustices that have been perpetrated on Negroes, to the point where many people come to assume that all Negroes are poor and that all poor people are Negroes, neither of which is true. A larger proportion of Negroes than whites is poor, but there are a goodly number of well-to-do and rich Negroes. Because prosperous blacks are usually forced to live in segregated communities, many white people are unaware of their existence or numbers. There are also a great many poor white people packed into urban slums or dispersed through rural ones. We should also bear in mind that there is some socio-economic spread among American Indians, Americans from the Latin countries, Polynesians, Orientals, Micronesians, and Eskimos. The interesting, if perhaps depressing, thing is that people of racial minorities take on middle-class ways of thinking as they rise economically, and, while not forgetting the hardships of their former existence, tend to lose all sense of identity with their origins.

One point of difference between the classes is that lower-class adolescents may be systematically excluded from participation in middle-class activities. They are treated as second-class citizens by teachers (who may themselves be in the process of escaping from a lower level of society and overidentifying with the middle class), employers, the police, the courts (the middle-class transgressor may be let off with forfeited bail, a fine, or a rebuke, whereas the lower-class one may go off to jail), welfare agencies, housing authorities, and middle-class contemporaries. Tied in with second-class treatment is psychological exclusion, so that even those areas of participation that are theoretically open to all comers—school, school-sponsored clubs and activities—are cast so strongly in middle-class terms that they are meaningless or even repellent to lower-class youngsters. Here we have the vicious circle of the self-fulfilling prophecy. Like any out-group member, the lower-class adolescent may come to accept the in-group's view of himself and in so doing conform to the middle-class stereotype of the lower-class personality. Thus, he both "justifies" middle-class rejection and increases his own alienation from the majority society. It is only the extraordinary lower-class adolescent—the athlete, scholar, or artistically gifted, the extremely ambitious or ruthless one—who can move into the middle class. Notice that the change from lower-class to middle-class status involves more than a change of financial circumstances. It means, as *Pygmalion* and *My Fair Lady* have indicated, a change of speech patterns, of personal attire, of tastes, attitudes, and life style.

Although there are obvious disadvantages to being a lower-class adolescent, it has its compensations. Lower-class parents are more willing than middle-class ones to acknowledge and accept their children's adulthood. The lower-class youngster may be spared the stress on academic and material achievement that bears constantly on the middle-class one (although some upwardly mobile parents bring strong pressures to bear on their children for the good school grades that will give them a better life). In a limited sense, sexuality is taken more freely for granted in the lower classes, especially for males (Friedenberg, 1959). Indeed, many middle-class youngsters may envy the lower classes their greater apparent freedom, and envy may lead to emulation. We usually think of culture as spreading downward in society, but in fact there is a steady upward spread of culture

from lower to middle classes, largely by way of adolescents. The middle-class boy may date a lower-class girl in hopes of finding her sexually compliant, or he may join a crowd of lower-class boys in order to share in their sexual adventures. Middle-class youngsters may romanticize the lower classes, as eighteenth- and nineteenth-century painters romanticized peasants and milkmaids, and adopt the externals of their way of life. The Mod look in clothing, jazz and rock-and-roll, and a great deal of slang began in the lower classes. When middle-class youngsters take over lower-class slang, they often do so in response to qualities of toughness, vividness, and daring, but without any exact understanding of the rich and often scatological metaphors involved. (They do, of course, understand perfectly well the four-letter words they now spout so freely as an indicator of emancipation.) It is interesting to note that members of racial or ethnic minorities, particularly in low-tension areas, are often accepted on their own merits by their adolescent contemporaries—as long as they are in school. Outside school, where the in-group members feel themselves exposed to adult eyes, they are likely to become cool and distant. We should note that not all the impediments to assimilation of ethnic and lower-class out-groups come from the middle-class white North European Protestants. Out-group members themselves form strong group identifications to which they may cling tenaciously. The Black Pride and Black Power movements reflect this trend among Negroes. A report by Wayne Dennis (1968) tells us that human figure drawings made by eighty black college students in 1957 included not a single one that was recognizably Negro. By contrast, 18 percent of drawings collected similarly in 1967 were of black people.

11
adolescence: two

In this chapter, we first look at some different versions of adolescent life style beyond the mass phenomena we have been discussing. Then, with more regard for the person within the role, we shall talk about the development of the self, coming to terms with sexuality, and the idealism which often reveals the world as a hard place to live in and may make the adolescent hard to live with, but which also gives hope for the human condition.

A Taxonomy of Adolescence

One can recognize a number of styles among adolescents, and it is now our task to try to specify some of the main variants. Subject to revision and without benefit of much research, we think we can distinguish four main types with a number of subvarieties: **conventionalists, idealists, hedonists,** and **psychopaths.** These categories are not as mutually exclusive as strict logic demands, but they provide a convenient framework for discussion. The introspective adolescent is likely to find himself in all of them. All these types have their adult counterparts, although we cannot assume a straight line of development from adolescent type to adult.

The conventionalists, to judge by a values test to be described in a minute, are probably the most numerous group. They are the ones who have never seriously questioned adult values and whose main goal in life is to fit in and get along with society as it exists. They may aspire to rise above their parents or wish simply to repeat the pattern of their parents' lives, but they have no misgivings about the estab-

lished order and consider it their job to find out how best to adjust to things as they are. The conventionalists produce the bulk of the early marriages. The domestic life of such couples may look like an awkward game of "playing house." The family shopping basket is piled high with chocolate milk, soft drinks, frankfurters, potato chips, bread, cupcakes, and sugar-coated cereals. Parenthood may come as a rude surprise, although they may enjoy having a live doll for their house play. Early marriage, however, is not the rule, and may even be on the decline. The conventionalists may go through the motions of teenage culture—they believe in "having fun" —but they never feel really shut off from the adult world. Moreover, the conventionalists, and to a lesser degree the idealists, supply most of the volunteers who work on hospital wards, teach retarded children, and provide companionship for the aged, infirm, and emotionally disturbed. They are likely to be active in junior-grade social, civic, and business organizations. There is one subvariety of conventionalists who are such avid pleasure-seekers that they might be dubbed **transitory hedonists** —transitory because their ultimate return to the fold is certain, no matter how many wild oats they sow along the way. All adolescents are likely to be influenced by the mass media, but these perhaps more than most. But whereas the ordinary conventionalist grownup looks back on youth as a lost age of innocence, the transitory hedonist looks back on youth as a lost time of splendor and gaiety and perpetual fun and games.

The test of values mentioned a moment ago consists of five incomplete sentences (Essex, unpublished) to which students are to supply the endings. The sentences are: "I like children who . . . ," "I dislike chil-

looking at yourself

dren who . . . ," "When I was a child I liked adults who . . . ," "The most important thing for a child to learn is . . . ," and "I wish my parents had . . . ." The responses to all five sentences are interesting, but the key statement is the one dealing with what is most important for a child to learn. Overwhelmingly (and by now we have used this technique with thousands of students from Poughkeepsie to Honolulu) students enjoin conformity: children, they say, must learn to accept authority, to obey, to be good, to have nice manners, to be well adjusted, to get along with others, to accommodate, and similar themes. A fair number stress love as an essential of human existence, and quite a few emphasize independence, but seemingly less in the sense of being able to think for oneself than of not being a burden to others. Relatively rare are such themes as originality, creativity, self-knowledge, and autonomy. Religious beliefs and practices are seldom mentioned, although most of our subjects profess some creed. This is in keeping with findings from a study of a Dutch sample by Mönks (1968), who classified adolescents in terms of their attitudes to the future, and who found little spontaneously expressed concern with religion in general, and even less with formal, organized religion. This may be changing, of course, as religion comes to be of increasing concern to young people. Our findings have two limitations. They are a couple of years old, and, as we said earlier, radicalization has been spreading like wildfire. Also, our subjects have been predominantly (but far from exclusively) female, and males, at least in the past, have been more likely than females to stress deviant or defiant styles.

Idealism, as we shall see, is a component in most adolescents, but here we want to talk about those for whom it is a dominant theme. The idealists, obviously, are those who express profound dissatisfaction with the state of the world and either work hard to change things or withdraw. The withdrawal may be into a private world centered upon personal fulfillment or into a Utopian subsociety, such as the occasional Walden Twos or the religious or agricultural commune. The idealistic adolescent corresponds most closely to the classical image of the iconoclastic, moody, romantic rebel portrayed by Goethe (1774), Alain-Fournier (1913), Joyce (1917), Salinger (1951), and other novelists. There seem to be three main ways in which idealism is manifested by those of today's young people who do not withdraw.

First, we have the **revolutionaries**, who are convinced that injustice and repression have gone beyond the point where reform is possible, making violence necessary. From South America to Seattle to New York, the young revolutionaries are setting fires and detonating bombs. So far, their violence has been visited primarily on property symbolizing exploitation, but enough people have been kidnapped, maimed, and killed to assure us that the revolutionaries will go as far as they feel they have to. Many have accepted the principle of robbery (the current term is "rip-off") as a legitimate revolutionary tactic. However sympathetic we may be to their causes, we believe that nonviolent means are available, if slower, and the revolutionaries we have talked to often strike us as rigid, moralistic, narrow, and overperfectionistic, unwilling to make any concessions to human frailty. Moreover, their designs for remedies seem to have been drawn up in total incomprehension of history, sociology, economics, and psychology. But one thing must be conceded: they are idealistic,

Bruce Roberts, Rapho Guillumette

Arthur Tress, Photo Researchers

Bob S. Smith, Rapho Guillumette

Ken Heyman

Christa Armstrong, Rapho Guillumette

however uncongenial we may find their ideals. It is a moot point whether right-wingers who practice violence, from Klansmen who burn school buses to policemen who club demonstrators, should also be considered idealists gone astray. Certainly, as we shall see shortly, there is a right-wing idealism, but it appears to us that the idealism of preservers of the status quo is of a shallow, unreasoning kind not incompatible with the psychopathic orientation below.

The less revolutionary idealists can be called **radical reformers**, exemplified by the civil rights and peace movements and the campus protest and political movements. As Paul Goodman (1966) has pointed out, the campus movements include both left and right wings. These are united in their populism, faith in ordinary people (although how much young college students know or understand about ordinary people, whom they idealize in the mass and shun in the individual case, is another question) and distrust of government and authority, with an all but anarchistic belief in freedom of individual self-determination. There are, however, with an exception to be noted in a moment, fundamental and important differences. Conservative reformers view human nature as fixed, and social differences as biologically (and maybe even divinely) determined (Social Darwinism again). In the conservative scheme of things, fixed human nature tends to be vile, selfish, and competitive, but the pursuit of selfish ends will "naturally," through the workings of a fully competitive free-enterprise system, produce the good of the

whole. But without the spur of economic want, people will stop working and relapse into animality. The conservatives have great faith in tradition and believe that we have simply wandered from the right, natural path and need only to return to it. For all our shortcomings, the evidence of our national prosperity shows that we are still God's chosen and should feel free to coerce and subjugate inferior people in the interests of keeping the system going, which is ultimately for their own good. They believe that the disorder and unpredictability of capitalism are a creative ferment which leads to an orderly, harmonious society. Those who fail to benefit from the system are the victims of their own defective character, but large-scale social disorders are produced by interfering with the free workings of the system and will disappear automatically when we allow the system to return to its natural state. Recently, a group of young people calling themselves libertarians (Lehr and Rossetto, 1971; Tuccille, 1970) have broken away from the conservative movement on the grounds that it has betrayed true conservatism by endorsing governmental intervention in business and private conduct, as in the draft. A recurring theme in the libertarians' plea for individualism is the right to possess and cultivate the wilderness, although to the best of our knowledge the only uninhabited (by humans) wilderness left is the ocean.

The **progressive adolescent reformers** have been studied by Keniston (1968), who finds strong identification with progressively oriented parents. The younger generation pushes parental ideals into action and, by contrast with the conservative, sees the present state of society as the predictable outcome of free-enterprise capitalism,

---

Adolescents come in a number of varieties.

which in their view intrinsically moves toward monopoly, vested interests, and a powerful establishment which manipulates and exploits ordinary people, often by manipulating the government itself. From this standpoint, tradition is a guide to what not to do, what dreadful errors to avoid; it tells us that what is needed are new, creative solutions to our problems. This view assumes a plastic, morally neutral human nature and says that the way society is now organized brings out man's most brutal, rapacious, inhumane potentialities. The progressive adolescents believe that a rearrangement of society in which economic and political considerations were subordinated to humane ones would enable people to develop the capacity to love, cooperate, explore the full range of human feelings, and find meaning and satisfaction in work that is done because it is useful and not just for the sake of making money. They believe in self-sacrifice for the common good, but they are by no means anti-hedonistic. However, apart from the intrinsic pleasures of useful work, pleasure for them is to be found in inner experience and in human contact and shared experiencing rather than the possession of material pleasure-stimulants. Notice that many young people of this breed do not work directly in the movement but are inclined to enter professions like teaching or medicine, as doctors or nurses or technicians, or the law, with a view to practicing in the "community." Others enter the crafts and find satisfaction in renovating—sometimes illegally—decaying or abandoned dwellings.

The third main type of idealist is exemplified by the worker in government- or foundation-sponsored volunteer programs such as VISTA (many idealists who joined the Peace Corps have become disillusioned or have been forced out for pursuing their idealism too energetically), the young person who actively works in direct contact with people to redeem mankind. The radical reformers resonate sympathetically or empathically to the motives of the volunteer workers, but question whether it makes any sense to remold people without at the same time reshaping the framework of social institutions that impoverished and brutalized them in the first place. In short, the more radical idealists of the left see those who accept government or foundation support as "tools of the establishment."

There may be a growing fourth group of idealists. These are the young people who take religion seriously and may even live in religious communes. Others may prefer a solitary quest after an individual faith.

All adolescents have a healthy streak of sensuality, but there is a small number who make it into a way of life. The hedonists are those young people who devote themselves, for as long as they can manage it, to a life of pleasure. Their life is a search for kicks, often centered around a surfing beach or ski slope, but with generous helpings of alcohol, drugs, sex, travel, or whatever else holds the promise of thrills. They support themselves by begging, petty thievery, casual homosexual or heterosexual prostitution (they sometimes attach themselves to a wealthy older person), as beach boys or ski instructors or sidewalk artists or strolling musicians, by selling their blood to blood banks, and even, when times are tight, by odd jobs. They have their gathering places around the world, some of them the spas and pleasure spots frequented by the idle rich, movie stars, and homosexuals, others the locales where living is cheap and drugs are easy to come by (although many governments are less than hospitable to young hedonists and their alien life styles). Some hedonists are young people of good education and good looks, with nice manners and a kindly outlook on their fellow man, and they seem to have little trouble maintaining themselves and finding sources of pleasure. We have no information on how many hedonists maintain their style indefinitely, die, or settle down to more or less conventional ways.

Outwardly, the *psychopaths* (a small but highly visible group) have much in common with the hedonists, but they affect a cold-blooded, brutal, exploitative approach to other people (which may actually be a cover-up for fearfulness), and may even find gratification in brutality. But where the hedonist really seems to enjoy life, the psychopath is a restless, dissatisfied grasper after ever-elusive thrills. The kicks never come through with full pungency, the laughter is always a little hollow, the sexual partners are never quite as beautiful or responsive as one had hoped, people are never quite intimidated enough by one's appearance, one's motorcycle reaches top speed just below the threshold of ecstasy. The periodic resort riots are probably started by conventionalists out on a group spree, but the riots turn nasty when the psychopaths get involved and cut loose. Characteristically, the psychopath lacks humor. Although he lives outside society, or leaves ordinary society behind as soon as he can shed his working clothes and don his uniform, he is thoroughly conventional in his outlook and will tolerate no slur on Motherhood, Capitalism, and the American Way of Life. Indeed, the psychopaths have aligned themselves with their former enemies, the police, to practice violence against idealists protesting war or oppression. One of the more bemusing paradoxes of our day is to hear right-wing spokesmen extolling the virtues of the black-leather-jacket contingent, virtues which, a few years back, they might have found it hard to define. The motorbike gangs have been trying lately to change their image to that of Friend of the Community, although a number of deadly feuds have made the new image hard to maintain. Again, notice that many individuals who live the psychopathic life are probably not themselves psychopathic personalities, but are seizing on a culture that offers them an identity they could not find on their own. It is easy to find the psychopaths at stock-car races, demolition derbies, and similar events. After the races, they terrorize their fellow motorists by maneuvering their bikes or high-power cars through traffic at furious speed. Needless to say, the psychopathic style of life is not confined to the young. We must, however, take pains not to libel the psychopaths, since all indications are that they will inherit the earth.

Since no system of categories that we can think of is going to capture all adolescents in all their wondrous·variety, we ought to mention those who seem to have no peer-group affiliation. There are those whose shyness keeps them apart, who feel more comfortable with younger children or adults, and who watch the antics of their contemporaries with a certain amount of envy without knowing how to become part of the herd. There are those youngsters who go through adolescence in a state of bewilderment, who seem to have no idea of who or where they are or of where they are going or why. There are the solitary romantics, who read novels and drink in the glories of nature and write poetry and contemplate suicide and dream of heroic adventures and form crushes on older people—again, much as in the images of "classical" adolescence. But even those who rejoice in the clamor of Babylon keep listening for the final blast.

The Adolescent Self

Having looked at adolescents in masses and submasses, we return to the individual and to what we see as the central psychological theme of adolescence, finding an **identity**, a sense of self in relation to the world at large. The adolescent's self-awareness is in great part expressed in self-consciousness, a concern about how well he measures up. The adolescent worries about where he stands on a number of measures—how much money he has to spend, how good-looking and attractive he is, how intelligent he is, how witty and how daring, whether he can meet the demands of his moral conscience. A key concern, however, is with his progress toward physical maturity.

To the adult, it seems that the physical changes of adolescence go on at a rapid pace, from which we might conclude that the main problem of the adolescent is having to come to terms with his successive incarnations. This is partly true. Certainly the fast-growing young adolescent often seems not to know what to do with his gangling arms and legs; new internal stirrings and impulses may take him unawares; and boys find it hard to control the vagaries of their voices and are panic-stricken lest a suddenly taut phallus be visible through their clothes. It is not for nothing that this has been called the "awkward age." It is equally true, however, that the adolescent's growth is almost always subjectively experienced as excruciatingly slow, no matter how objectively fast or slow, early or late, it may be. The boy may daily fondle the fuzz on his lip or cheek, wondering if it is yet time to shave it off, or he may watch anxiously the slow growth of a hair on his chest. Having learned about ejaculation, he may masturbate furiously, wondering if he can yet make it happen. The girl may measure her height or her bust once a week, anticipating the time when she will reach some magical ideal—as she approaches it, of course, she begins to worry about when and whether she will stop, or instead shoot on to a new record. A few years ago, before the current no-bra fad, she might have hopefully laid in an anticipatory supply of brassieres. Or she may equally well resist acknowledging the changes that have come over her body.

Whether maturing takes place too fast or too slowly, it can be a source of agonized self-consciousness. The simple awareness of new and still-elusive potentialities for feeling, acting, and being acted upon can be unsettling. Equally important is the way physical changes and their psychological implications get reflected back from the environment. This mirroring happens at all levels: the tightness of his clothing tells the youngster that his body has grown; the realization, especially in a girl, that her style of dress is no longer appropriate; the way adults tease boys about the change of voice, about how often they have to shave, and about taking an interest in girls—an imputation the pubescent boy may welcome but vehemently deny; a girl's becoming aware of the appraising stares men direct at her—or they may even approach her; the realization that one has outgrown certain playmates, or been left behind by others, not only physically but in terms of interests; the new meanings that emerge in what people say and do, or simply in the way things look and taste and smell and sound.

This is a time of painful sensitivity, when one's fragile self is raw and bleeds easily. Girls may feel that they cannot bear to be looked at. They may adopt a hunched or cringing posture to minimize their height or their breasts. They may wear voluminous and somewhat bizarre clothing to conceal their bodies. They may be prone to fits of seemingly unprovoked weeping. Girls may have several quite different attitudes toward their menstrual periods. Some feel a warm, quiet satisfaction at this manifestation of mature femininity, some feel polluted, some are frightened by it, and some take it matter-of-factly.

Boys are traditionally less modest about their bodies than are girls, but at this time they may find all manner of excuses and devices not to expose themselves in the school locker room or shower room, for fear their development differs grossly from that of their fellows. By the same token, the adolescent boy snatches furtive glimpses of his mates' anatomy in search of standards of normality (such checking up should not be thought of as homosexual leanings, although, obviously, these body awarenesses are closely tied to sexual feelings, which we shall treat separately in the next section). Here we want to stress the out-of-stepness, the need to check up on oneself relative to one's contemporaries. Let us remember that markedly early or

Much of the adolescent's search for identity takes place before a mirror.

late maturing, of which we spoke above, has both practical social consequences for how the child fits in, and psychological consequences for how he views himself, objectively as measured against age-mates, and intersubjectively in terms of how he perceives their perception of him.

But self-awareness is only in part a matter of body awareness. And body awareness is only partly a matter of maturational status. It is also a matter of having a male body or a female body, a sickly or healthy or strong or weak body, a beautiful or plain or ugly body—and such self-judgments are often a hopeless mélange of objective and subjective. That is, a person who in other people's eyes is altogether comely can nevertheless experience himself as homely or physically loathsome; he can accept the odors he radiates as normal or intolerable; he can ignore facial blemishes or regard them as total disfigurement. Beyond body awareness is awareness of self as a person at various levels of competence, virtue, self-direction and self-control, importance, and orientation in time. Some young people acquire a sense of going somewhere, while others drift aimlessly or flounder in agitated despair. Some feel that their best years lie behind them and live on past triumphs, while others feel trapped by past disasters. Some people learn to experience themselves as possessing an immortal soul which will survive the death of the body and go on to a new life in other realms.

This differentiation of layers of self, and, with good fortune, their eventual integration into an identity, develops out of a sense of ambiguity. The ambiguity of early adolescence is beautifully expressed in Phyllis McGinley's "Portrait of Girl with Comic Book" (1952):

Thirteen's no age at all. Thirteen is nothing.
It is not wit, or powder on the face,
Or Wednesday matinees, or misses' clothing,
Or intellect, or grace.
Twelve has its tribal customs. But thirteen
Is neither boys in battered cars nor dolls,
Not *Sara Crewe*, or movie magazine,
Or pennants on the wall.

Thirteen keeps diaries and tropical fish
(A month, at most); scorns jumpropes in the
   spring;
Could not, would fortune grant it, name its
   wish;
Wants nothing, everything;
Has secrets from itself, friends it despises;
Admits none to the terrors that it feels;
Owns half a hundred masks but no disguises;
And walks upon its heels.

Thirteen's anomalous—not that, not this:
Not folded bud, or wave that laps a shore,
Or moth proverbial from the chrysalis.
Is the one age defeats the metaphor.
Is not a town, like childhood, strongly walled
But easily surrounded; is no city.
Nor, quitted once, can it be quite recalled—
Not even with pity.*

The perspicacity of McGinley's observation is borne out by interviews with thirteen-year-old girls and with their parents. The case of early adolescent boys is less clearcut. They certainly seem subject to ambiguity, but they seem able to function with less emotional waste motion than girls. It is possible that the adult world and the peer group are more accepting of the boy's burgeoning sexuality than of the girl's, allowing him to be more at ease about it. The boy seems to encounter more

Adolescence: two

462

ambiguity later in adolescence when it comes time to match concrete competences with the role demands of adulthood.

Filled as they are with ambivalences, few adolescents feel really in control. They tend to be trapped between impulses that are not really a part of themselves and what often seem like unreasonable or capricious adult constraints. But lack of control also carries the hidden blessing of lack of responsibility, and adolescents become masters at the mechanisms of defense. Like adults, they learn to rationalize their behavior with all the guile of an expert lawyer. They project blame either onto motives beyond their control or onto an environment that does not understand the real, interior adolescent. (One teen-age girl to another: "So I said to him, 'How do you know this is the real me you're talking to?'") They play tricks of memory, prettifying and justifying their own role in past events and downgrading that of others. The younger adolescent spends hours before the mirror trying desperately to read off from his own features the secret of who he is, and, incidentally, of what he looks like to other people—which for him, at the moment, is more or less the same thing. The older adolescent spends hours before the mirror trying out hair arrangements and facial expressions and postures, worrying a pimple on his chin, trying to gauge how best to achieve maximum effect —that is, to reveal his True Self. It should be noted that the perpetual solitary self-appraisal of the adolescent is more emotional than objective. He (or she) is able to see himself only through the haze of an ideal image. An unhappy adolescent will focus on the ways in which he fails to meet this ideal, and appear to be quite unaware of his assets. Another adolescent,

less prone to self-disparagement, will equally unrealistically blot out of consciousness any unsightly features (as opposed to blemishes), lingering intently over any that seem promising.

We have stressed how the adolescent escapes from the adult world into the peer society. We can now see how he is also escaping from himself, how the roles the peer culture offers him are a refuge from the doubts, ambiguities, and ambivalences that confront him in solitude. The peer group, of course, is not a perfect refuge. It makes demands, too, and these demands may violate the adolescent's self-image. Just as we maintain a zone of sensitivity around our material bodies, so that we leave a margin for error in our adjustment to space, so do we maintain a zone of personal privacy. This zone is not uniform around all regions of the body: we shake hands freely, but an embrace is more special; the girl may tolerate the boy's hand on her arm, or his arm across her shoulder, or even a slap on her buttocks, but his hand on her breast or thigh may be an encroachment on the zone of privacy. Group life entails endless invasions of privacy, and there may be powerful pressures to act contrary to conscience. But the group does offer an identity, in terms both of acceptance and of the roles it defines. Many authors speak of "finding one's identity," but it is as much a matter of constructing an identity as of discovering who one already is. Perhaps one reason that adolescents avoid self-knowledge even as they seek it is a vague sense that once one acknowledges traits and motives, they crystallize as permanent features and so obstruct the formation of a superior self.

In his role playing, then, the adolescent can be seen as trying on ready-made identities to see how well they suit him. Some of these roles are modeled on particular people, movie and television stars and heroes of the day, others are based on fictional characters from literature or the mass media, and some are based on culturally defined "types": the tough guy, the sweet young thing, the gay young thing, the woman of the world, the man's man, the bored sophisticate, the esthete, the clown, the revolutionary urban guerrilla. Those youngsters who are actually moving toward particular careers begin to play the roles, to affect the mannerisms, associated with occupational types—the role playing of young people aiming toward medical careers is a marvel to behold, and so is that of youngsters who have identified with business careers, journalism, the law, teaching, whatever. We take the adolescent search for identity so much for granted that we tend to forget that it is peculiar to cultures in which there is a fair amount of social and economic mobility. In societies where the adolescent has no choice but to fit into a predetermined niche (which is coming to be the case in our own society as it stabilizes and ossifies, so that the offspring of public servants go into government, actors' children grow up to be actors and actresses, and psychologists' children grow up to be psychologists), the problems are different.

It can be seen that the adolescent, like the preschool child playing cowboy, tends to seize on the externals of a role and may miss its essence. This concern with outward appearance sometimes verges on the magical, as when the adolescent chooses a new name to be known by. The choice is made with earnest care, and only after much weighing of alternatives, since it must express in pure form the very inner-

most ideal self, it must project the perfect image. A similar force seems to lie behind the new and ornate handwritings many adolescents adopt, especially girls. The adolescent is seeking to capture the style of his role portrayals, a style conveying one whole approach to life which he can sense forcefully but not put into words. He is discovering what various styles of life feel like to him and also what sorts of reactions they produce in others. These reactions have to come mainly from peers —in early adolescence from peers of the same sex, and increasingly in later adolescence from peers of the opposite sex. Teachers may sometimes play along with adolescent role playing, but parents make a most unsatisfactory audience. When, in the course of quick changes of role, the adolescent girl decides to try out a new hair style or color, or to speak in a lazy, insolent drawl, or to wear a saintly appearance, or when the boy decides to wear his shirt casually unbuttoned to the waist, or to greet with a cynical, sneering grunt whatever people say, or to assume an air of unaccustomed humility and submissiveness, parents are likely to respond by asking, "Who are you being today?" The adolescent is taken aback when adults fail to recognize that the new self now on display is the true and final one. The adolescent easily forgets that earlier role incarnations were equally valid at the time, and when reminded of them he repudiates them wholly and contemptuously: "That was ages ago! I was only a baby then!" Indeed, he may be guarding against the realization that his present self is as ephemeral as past ones, and so cannot tolerate any reminders of what he once was. To have his baby pictures shown—above all to his peers—brings him to the depths of mortification. Through it all, of course, the adolescent manages to remain recognizably his own personal self.

In short, every new personality is assumed totally and cannot be questioned—this week—and every old one is remorselessly buried. But even here there is a hint of ambivalence. The adolescent, adrift as he is, may have a private urge to recapture the continuity of his life and may secretly welcome reminders (in private) of his forgotten past. By late adolescence, the young person may, with luck, be able to reintegrate the various selves he knows—his body, his public personality, and the private core of feeling that is the "real me," his past, his present, and an image of the future—into a single functioning schema that he can take for granted without endless embarrassment, introspection, and anxious reading off of other people's reactions.

Adolescent Sexuality

A major part of adolescent self-awareness involves the further sexual awakening that comes with the approach of biological maturity. For many adolescents, as we have said, the world becomes libidinized, sexualized, so that the most innocuous objects and events take on erotic implications. In Freudian terms, pubescence spells the end of latency and the beginning of adult genitality. The task of this age, according to the psychoanalysts, is to master (to inhibit, control, and direct) sexuality in the service of mature love, and to sublimate surplus sexual energies into productive work. As Freud pointed out, sexuality affects and is affected by behavior in every sphere of activity. Even if one does not accept Freud's thesis that the sex drive is the basis for all constructive action, it is still necessary to acknowledge its pervasiveness and importance, particularly in adolescent behavior.

We have to begin by pointing out that sexuality is not the same for adolescent boys and girls. This is not an assertion of a biological absolute, but a description of our recent and current society. If present trends continue, with increasing acceptance of female sexuality, it is possible that girls will become more like boys in their sexual feelings, and indeed have sexual appetites far exceeding those of the young male. As things are now, male sexual desire is highly specific and is clearly centered in the penis. The boy can be easily aroused by a variety of external stimuli—words, pictures, random thoughts and associations—or he may deliberately arouse himself by self-stimulation or by seeking external stimulants. Sexual desire in boys is urgent and aims toward rapid discharge of tension in orgasm (even so-called oral and anal erotics seek orgasm). According to Masters and Johnson (1966), males are more distractible during the sex act than females, and are likely to detumesce if something interrupts them.

Among girls, at least in terms of today's culture, there is a much wider range of normal individual differences. Some girls experience desire in much the way boys do, and a few are avid for constant experience to the point of nymphomania. Many others may not know direct sexual urges until later in life, and some apparently never do (although Freudians would want to know the reason). It is interesting that many a twenty-year-old girl can talk about sex as though it had nothing to do with her. College instructors are sometimes amazed at the bland "sophistication" with which female students can discuss erotic literature. What the instructor may not realize is that such literature may simply have no libidinal impact on such students. For most adolescent girls, however, "desire" or "lust" is not the correct description, and we might do better to speak of "sexual stirrings." These, unlike male desire, are diffuse and not as clearly differentiated from other feelings: romantic yearnings, maternal cravings, mild intoxication, enthusiasm, pity, sensual feelings such as come from having one's back rubbed or one's hair combed, or even such emotions as anger and fear. Many girls find, in fact, that sexual arousal occurs only in the midst of a general state of tension, excitement, or agitation. For most girls, specifically sexual arousal must be brought about by direct stimulation of the body, particularly of the erogenous zones. Female sexual arousal seems to be less climax-oriented than male desire—that is, it is experienced more as a state to be maintained indefinitely than as the prelude to orgasm (although there is every reason to believe that most girls are capable of orgasm).

The lower intensity and specificity of sexual feelings in girls than in boys may be related to several factors. On the cultural side, it may derive from the double standard which says that girls are supposed to be less highly sexed than boys, and that manifestations of female sexuality are to be met with disapproval and repression. If this is the case, females should become more like males in the nature of their sexual cravings as the climate of values shifts toward greater permissiveness. Biolog-

ically, the difference may correspond to the lesser degree of anatomical differentiation of the female genitalia. Even the fact that the girl's genitals are less visible to her than the boy's to him may reduce the clarity of genital sensations.

In addition to differences between boys and girls in the nature and strength of sexual feelings, there are important differences in developmental timing (Kinsey et al., 1948). For boys, the peak of sexuality—measured by the frequency with which orgasm is sought—comes a year or two after puberty, at sixteen or seventeen, after which there is a slow but steady decline. In girls, the peak comes much later, often not until age thirty or beyond—the actual timing seems to depend a great deal on the amount of sexual experience. Again, as attitudes and self-attitudes change, as exposure to sexual stimulation through advertising, literature, movies, and television becomes more common, it is possible that girls will be moved to a full sexual awakening at ever-earlier ages.

Simply because sexual desire in boys is a distinctive state, unlikely to be confused with other feelings, we should not assume that it is uncomplicated by other feelings. It becomes involved, first of all, with the universal adolescent fear of embarrassment. We have already mentioned that the boy may be alarmed lest an erection be noticed by others. He may furthermore be afraid that he will let slip some of the illicit thoughts that are so often with him. Because of the many conflicting ideas about sex that he has picked up, he may be unsure about how he should act. A special source of confusion is his ignorance of how girls feel about sex—the folklore, after all, paints them as both monuments of purity and Jezebels. Notice that girls themselves embody this duality. They expose their bodies, paint themselves alluringly, sing siren songs, sit, walk, and writhe lasciviously, and lash out viperlike when boys "go too far." European males in the United States find American girls very confusing, since they seem to be inviting intimacy but in fact are saying only that males should find them interesting and attractive. The boy may have doubts about his own sexual adequacy, from questioning his appeal to girls, to worrying about premature ejaculation, to wondering if he simply wouldn't wither at a crucial moment. He may have been told that sexual indulgence weakens men—athletes are still warned that girls will undermine their manliness, although certain swinging heroes of the sports world are fast eroding this assumption. Sex may appear dangerous merely because it entails such violent feelings. The boy may have been frightened by descriptions of veneral disease—some of the anti-V.D. instruction given by the military perhaps unwittingly makes girls a conditioned stimulus for loathing; this in addition to religious training that may tell the boy that sex is sinful and unclean. American boys take it for granted that their first sexual experience should be with girls their own age or slightly younger, whereas in European societies it used to be assumed that an older woman would initiate the young male into the mysteries. In well-to-do families, a maid was often hired with this tacit assumption in mind. It was considered uncouth for a young man to enter marriage without the knowledge necessary to instruct his bride. Notice that this kind of cultural arrangement was rather more congruent with what we know about sexual development than is the American one.

For boys, sexual cravings are initially quite separate from notions of love. Although a boy, when aroused, would prefer a sexual partner of his own age and of his own or higher social class, he may not be too discriminating and may be willing to settle for masturbation or a prostitute. The homosexuality of middle-years childhood goes underground in adolescence except for occasional adventures instigated by older homosexuals, and except for adolescents who seem committed to the path of homosexuality. But when a girl does invite a boy's favors, even though she yields herself only up to a sharply defined point, he finds it very easy to fall in love with her. Many male adolescents carry about a free-floating amorousness that settles readily on a convenient love-goat. But this love is quite different from what he will feel as a mate and a father. It is more an amplified form of the affection he feels for his male friends and seems to be compounded of delight in shared intimacy, the freedom to let down one's guard, and the glow that comes from being accepted, all in the heated atmosphere of sexual desire. Needless to say, he attributes to his love-goat those qualities he hopes to find, regardless of what she may actually possess. Love-goating works the other way, of course, with females falling in childish love with convenient males, but the purely sexual components may be muted, diffuse, or missing. Mature love, we presume, includes a measure of objectivity in viewing the beloved object, which makes for rather less disillusionment as the relationship evolves.

For girls, love has traditionally taken a decided priority over sexuality, although this, too, may change with increased sexual freedom for women. The love-goating of girls comes in part from the adolescent cultural climate, which says that falling in love is the thing to do. But it also seems to be motivated by some notion that attachment to a male is the way to an identity. It seems that the passivity built into females by the larger culture may impede identity formation by requiring a merger with someone stronger. This may mean, to both the girl and her partner, sexual surrender, but its more basic origin seems to be the need for identity. This may be why girls are attracted to physically powerful males (much to the despair of the less powerful). If the girl vacillates about surrender, it is perhaps in part because surrender both promises an identity and threatens its loss. For the point of belonging to a male is really to possess him, to make him a more potent extension of the self. This notion is a vestige of the knightly ideal, that the man becomes a slave to the love of the empedestaled virgin, who remains virginal in spirit even after she has rewarded the man with her favors. By the judicious manipulation of her favors and favor, she can make the man her puppet. This pattern, too, may be changing as the status of females shifts toward equality on all fronts.

We can see how, in girls, romantic feelings centered about a possessive surrender point straight to domesticity. Partial surrender becomes a highly effective device for keeping the male's motivation at fever pitch. Total surrender risks "losing the man's respect" and thus the man himself. Sometimes total surrender permits the girl to manipulate the male by playing on guilt feelings, but this is obviously less satisfactory than the manipulation of sexual drive. When the game is played right, the young man comes to accept that marriage is the price he has to pay for sex with a "nice" girl. We should repeat that many mothers encourage their daughters to play the game of husband-catching, and are fairly explicit about the rules—"Never go all the way." They begin, early in the game, a painstaking cultivation of the mothers of eligible boys. In sum, when adolescent girls become "boy crazy," it is evident that sexuality may play only an indirect and minor role in this phenomenon.

We should note that while our culture's attitudes toward sex are often ambiguous and inconsistent, and may stress sexual adventure rather than meaningful relations, they are more liberal than those of some other cultures. For instance, in a study of values by Church and Insko (1965) in Hawaii, Caucasian-American undergraduates showed significantly more favorable attitudes to items dealing with aspects of sex than did Japanese-American subjects, and males gave significantly more favorable ratings than females. A subsample of Chinese-American female subjects gave slightly more favorable ratings than Caucasian-American females. The contrast among groups shows up clearly if we consider the number of subjects who gave a favorable rating to premarital sex: 18 out of 24 Caucasian-American males, 9 out of 24 Japanese-American males; 8 out of 24 Caucasian-American females, and 1 out of 24 Japanese-American females. We have received some limited reports that tend to confirm these findings; it appears that in marriage Japanese and Japanese-American women submit obediently to the wishes of the male, but with only simulated pleasure. There were cultural differences, too, in which aspects of sex were favored or disfavored. Masturbation had the highest rank among items for

▲

Adolescent "romance."

Japanese-American females, and tied for first place with petting for Chinese-American females, whereas it ranked third or fourth with the other groups. There is reason to think that masturbation by Japanese women may not be for the sake of sexual stimulation and discharge, but instead serves as a technique of self-soothing.

Intellectual curiosity about sex continues to be a component of adolescent (and adult) sexuality. Boys and girls are voracious seekers after sexual information and get it from whatever sources they can. Some of the frustrations of this age come from not even having a vocabulary with which to talk about these vital matters. The youngsters know all the four-letter words, and use them liberally in other contexts, but to use them in discussions of sex cheapens the topic. Curiosity in adolescence, of course, goes way beyond a craving for anatomical and physiological knowledge and extends to "What do you do?" "What is it like?" "Does it hurt?" "What happens when?" and "Is it all right if you . . . ?" One of the difficulties is the sense that there must be something more that one does not know about. Even adolescents with a fair amount of sexual experience are likely to feel vaguely baffled and cheated. Their experience somehow never quite measures up to the promise of the erotic episodes they read about in books or see in motion pictures. Many adolescent discussions of sex, and much reading of erotic literature, have as their unspoken theme the search for the "something else" that presumably lies beyond. Young people's craving for knowledge is not merely a desire to find out what sex does or should feel like to them but equally what it is like for the opposite sex. Girls understand the potency of male urges, but unless the girl has equivalent feelings, their special sexual quality is likely to elude her. Male ignorance about female sexuality is amazingly great. Males may project their own sexuality onto women, they may see women as essentially frigid, indifferent or

Adolescent sexuality

hostile to sex, or they may see them as emasculating Delilahs. Boys are uncertain which, if any, version of female sexuality to believe. In general, according to a study by McCreary-Juhasz (1967), young people know a lot less about sex than they think they know, and females are decidedly more ignorant than males. Recent newspaper accounts indicate that young people are quite ignorant about effective contraceptive techniques, and a large proportion of sexual encounters risk pregnancy.

From what we have been able to learn by talking to young people, many feel profoundly ambivalent about sex, and even those who practice it regularly, but without forming close human relationships, may get little satisfaction from it. Under these circumstances, on the male side, the pleasure of orgasm is, as one young man put it, like using a woman to masturbate with. The chief pleasure sex seems to bring young men is the satisfaction of triumph, of being able to boast of his conquests to his fellows, or of describing the unusual circumstances of a liaison (like deep in the icy water of a lake). But even these pleasures are marred by the sense of being cheated, by guilt, by fear of pregnancy (young men report that they do not use contraceptives—assuming that they know what to do—because it would seem disrespectful of the girl; the spreading use of contraceptive pills may make this concern obsolete), by worry about venereal disease, and by doubts whether a girl who would sleep with him is worth sleeping with. Since most male adolescents are not masters of the art of love (and it is likely that the girl would reject the practices involved as "unnatural," "abnormal," or "dirty"), the girl may be denied even the simple fleshly pleasures. In addition, the fear of pregnancy, for obvious reasons, is considerably greater than for the boy. Although the double standard is fading, it is still true that many males feel strongly that the woman they marry must be chaste, and the girl who gives in knows that she is reducing her value on the marriage market. She also knows that if she is found out, censure will fall more heavily on her than on the boy, who is expected to sow his wild oats pretty much where he can. Indeed, the girl in a rape case or a paternity suit can expect to find herself portrayed in court as a slut or a whore (Sherwin, 1966).

The authors are frequently asked for their view of what the revolution in sexual attitudes is doing to the morals of young people. Whatever revolution there has been began with a simple willingness to talk more openly about sex and progressed to a greater willingness to sleep with the person you intended to marry (Freedman, 1966). By now, it may have gone even further, as witnessed by the rapid spread of venereal disease. (Notice that in Okinawan society the young man moves in with his fiancée immediately after the engagement has been announced [Maretzki and Maretzki, 1966]. Scandinavian society is not too different.) Girls are the key to any sexual revolution, since, if we can believe the data, most boys are ready to engage in sex at every opportunity—if ambivalently. There are boys who seem not to experience strong urges, and others who observe a single standard that says that males as well as females must remain pure before marriage, but both of these are a decided minority. Some of the social class differences noted by Kinsey (1948; Rainwater, 1966) still seem to apply. Lower-class boys are less likely than middle-class ones to practice masturbation, are more likely to engage in homosexual practices (without becoming committed full-time homosexuals), and, as we have said, have easier access to heterosexual intercourse.

Although the American culture's proclaimed sexual values are rapidly disintegrating, this does not mean such values are useless. Increasingly, though, values are going to have to be individualized to suit persons and situations. It seems to the authors that sex is most meaningful and satisfactory when one has reached a stable degree of emotional and social maturity. It seems to us that the young woman ought to beware of impulsive sex generated in a moment of unthinking passion, because when the passion is past, she is liable to feel disgust and self-disgust. It may seem cold-blooded and antisexual to say that one should enter a sexual relationship open-eyed and clearheaded and after a certain amount of deliberation, but the alternative is likely to be psychologically damaging. Sex at its best is too marvelous a thing to be attained casually and indiscriminately. It requires full openness and intimate fusion between two persons, and one does not want to be that intimate with just anybody. But without the intimacy and openness, sex becomes a matter of sensations which can be induced as well by self-stimulation as by contact between bodies. It is our contention that it is this intimacy which constitutes the "something else" that adolescents find missing from sex. And in general, still-unformed adolescents simply do not have this capacity for opening themselves freely to another person. The campus clamor for "free sex" overlooks that the restraints on free sexual expression lie as much in the immaturities of adolescents as in adult controls. And the proclamation that "sex is beautiful" is likely in adolescence to be more an article of faith than a statement of verified fact. Thus, without invoking any of the traditional moralities, one can find good psychological reasons for going slow and waiting for adulthood—if not necessarily marriage—before looking for sexual fulfillment. Adulthood, of course, is not strictly a matter of chronological age.

However, if girls are going to exercise restraint, they may have to learn to stop provoking males to lust by tricks of dress (or undress), gait, manner, voice, and partial surrender that promise more than the girl is willing to deliver. Girls early acquire an elaborate provocativeness that probably has little to do with sexual feelings. In preschool or middle-years girls, provocative behavior often resembles the ritual mating patterns of nonhuman species, movements that appear spontaneously in the right releasing circumstances and which, stimulated by the proper reciprocal behavior in the male, culminate in sexual receptivity. Such evolutionary remnants probably enter into the sexual dances of many societies, which are so effective that they can bring the participants up to and even into climax (Danielsson, 1956). It is conceivable that Americans could return to tribal sexual patterns, but it seems more likely that, as part of the burden of civilization, we will move on to the cultivation of a highly developed eroticism based on a special relationship between two persons. As it is, American girls behave—in many cases unconsciously—in ways as sexually stimulating as those of the Tahitian maiden, but they don't really mean it. In terms of playing the marriage game, such promising and then backing off works to lure the male into the trap, but we cannot help questioning whether this is a psychologically sound approach to a mature relationship between a man and a woman.

It seems to us that people can get to know each other, fall in love, decide to have sexual relations, to live together, to get married and raise a family, without the maneuvering and manipulation that go into the marriage game. But it may be Utopian to think that men and women can learn to treat each other as human beings who can talk openly and honestly and who can get to know each other before embarking on a sexual adventure. It seems sad that it is only in the marriage bed that many men and women find that they do not really like each other so very much after all. But, in principle at least, a new understanding and the end of exploitation between the sexes may lead to a discovery of the glories of real sexual fulfillment (Kirkendall and Libby, 1966).

Adolescent Idealism

Like the preschool child, the adolescent is full of contradictions. These contradictions, however, seem to be simply diverse expressions of the central theme of finding and constructing an identity. Since much adolescent behavior strikes adults as offensive, infantile, and even bizarre, they may find it hard to see that, underneath the superficial manifestations of fads, costumes, slang, wisecracks, poses, posturing, and role playing, a thread of idealism runs through much of their behavior. (Idealism, as we shall see, is found in all varieties of adolescents to some degree, and not just in those we labeled *idealists* in an earlier section.)

In this section, we want to emphasize the side of the adolescent that we do not see when he is with groups of his peers and which he may conceal from all but his closest friends. Indeed, when he complains that his parents do not understand him, he is often saying that they fail to see this side of him. The adolescent is busy losing old illusions and building new ones to take their place. At times, he becomes convinced of the hopelessness of all illusions and lapses into cynicism or despair, no less genuine for the melodramatic display he makes of them. The air of bored sophistication he sometimes affects is meant to say that he has seen through the flimsy pretensions of the world around him and feels above its pettiness and corruption. His occasional apathy and lack of involvement express feelings of futility about the state of the world. But even though his disillusionment is often grist to his histrionic mill, it means at heart that he is really searching for an ideal and decent world for his ideal and decent self to respond to. When he lashes out at adults, it is often in protest against the sick society to which they acquiesce and in punishment for its lack of idealism. Needless to add, his idealism is often at odds with his own animality, the sordid cravings and weaknesses that threaten to undermine his purity from below. Adolescent boys, especially, may be quite poignantly conscious of and troubled by a sense of duality, a split between their carnal and spiritual natures. And through it all, of course, the adolescent tends to enjoy his suffering for the romantic picture it gives him of himself and for the emotional workout it affords.

A great part of the adolescent's idealism

probably stems from his resistance to growing up. Particularly in early adolescence, he wants to enjoy his new powers in total freedom uncontaminated by the practical demands of life. Furthermore, very little that he sees around him matches the glory he senses in his new powers. By comparison, the world of everyday adult activities, the world of political machinations that he reads about in the papers, looks tainted and shopworn. The young adolescent, viewing himself largely from the inside, experiences himself (when he is not embarrassed, despondent, or self-accusing) as pure spirit, and the only worthy external counterparts of this experience are to be found in the majesties and austerities of religion, in the beauties of nature, in certain idealized public or fictional personalities, in poetry or music, in political abstractions—in short, in reality seen from a great distance.

As long as the adolescent is less than totally disillusioned, as long as he can hold on to the conviction that virtue and decency are possible, that there exist external counterparts to his ideal self, he can keep going, often on a plane of high elation. But when, perhaps in response to some minor personal setback such as being refused permission to use the family car, or having been stood up on a date, or having been forbidden to wear one's new bikini, the adolescent feels alone and helpless in a vast, unresponsive, hostile world, he is prone to depressions of the sort that the Germans have aptly named **Weltschmerz** —world pain. It was this phenomenon that most impressed early European writers on the subject and which we find memorialized in the writings of Goethe, and perpetuated in the quest for sincerity and good faith of Huckleberry Finn and Salinger's Holden Caulfield. It is when enveloped in *Weltschmerz* that the adolescent takes long, solitary nocturnal walks (preferably in the rain), composes long, melancholy poems, or toys with the idea of suicide—a special kind of suicide following which the disembodied adolescent can still stand by and witness and savor the remorse that people will feel "after I'm gone." Although contemplating suicide is for most adolescents an emotional self-indulgence, enough actual or attempted suicides occur to keep us from making mock of the subject. Teicher and Jacobs (1966), among others, have studied adolescents who have tried to commit suicide and have found some characteristic patterns. Sixteen is the most dangerous age. Poverty is an important factor. About twice as many girls as boys are suicide-prone. Girls are made vulnerable by a recent fracture in the parents' marriage (separations and divorces at earlier periods of life seem unrelated to suicide), by a recently broken romance (especially if the girl is pregnant), by isolation from her family and friends (to which a love affair may contribute), and by repressive and intrusive discipline. Boys, by contrast, are made suicidal by very early disturbances of relations with the mother, particularly if there is not a strong father figure in the home.

It is in times of *Weltschmerz* that the adolescent may first become attuned to the miseries of the world's downtrodden and to the social ills, inequities, injustices, anomalies, and absurdities that generate great quantities of misery. Needless to say, those adolescents who have grown up in conditions of misery have known about them all along, but adolescence may bring a planetary awareness of and identification with other people who share a similar fate. The

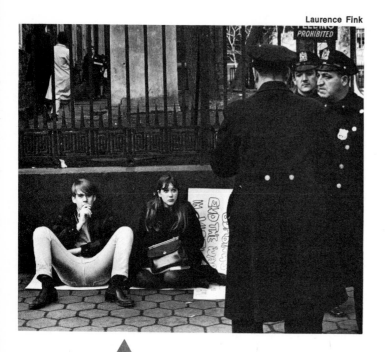

The confrontation.

How you react to your own ideal self.
– don't know yourself well enough
– highly emotional stage

474

social concerns of the adolescent may mark a new stage of fellow-feeling for humanity at large, to the point of advocating instant revolution.

Some adolescents find the answer to their idealism in religion, embracing it seriously for the first time, intensifying the beliefs they have always held, or converting to another, more promising faith. For some number of adolescents, religion as it is practiced exemplifies the worst in hypocrisy and corruption, and religious belief the most debased of superstition, and these idealistically leave their faith, often with great difficulty, as depicted by James Joyce. Different religions may appeal to the adolescent in different ways. He may be enthralled by the ornate pageantry and symbolism of one, by the puristic austerity of another, by the militancy of another, or by the castigations of yet another. Whatever religion he chooses is a vehicle by which he can project himself beyond mundane reality and into the heady realm of the ideal absolute. His concern with religion is, of course, part and parcel of his concern with the nature of the world into which he is moving; and the nature and existence of God, and the need for and the possibility of faith are among the topics endlessly debated in adolescent bull sessions—which, incidentally, provide adolescents with one of their best opportunities to find out how other people feel and to try out their own opinions. For some adolescents, faith is a source of comfort and gives assurance that their individual lives have some meaning. It provides order in a disorderly world. For some, faith provides an escape from concern about the state of the world, since everything by definition is for the best and particular events are only the working out of the inscrutable divine will. Some faiths promise an apocalyptic resolution of human vice and stupidity, which many adolescents find a grimly appealing prospect. A number of adolescents, while rejecting religion and established faiths, espouse a diffuse, generalized belief in some vague divinity. Some adolescents see in the promise of an afterlife a reward for whatever torments they may have to suffer in this world.

It is important to understand that even delinquent and destructive behavior like that attributed to the Weathermen and the Panthers can be an expression of a disappointed idealism. We may wish that all disillusioned young people would follow nonviolent paths, and we may sympathize with civil rights workers and protest demonstrators as idealists on the march, but we must remember that some portion of young people are in basic revolt against all the assumptions and doctrines and ideologies and values of our society, and that some of these know of no other way to express their loathing except through acts of destruction and violence. The adolescent conventionalist may feel that the world as it exists is already an approximation of the ideal and so is unaware of any basic contradiction in becoming part of it. The conventionalist may express his idealism in volunteer work for worthy causes. Even the psychopath, as we have said, subscribes to conventional ideals, and may furthermore experience his psychopathic life style as conforming to the knightly ideal—notice the names that street gangs assume: the Dukes, the Barons, the Black Knights, the Dragons—of chivalry and valor.

A few youngsters carry their idealism beyond adolescence and find careers which give it some practical expression: political

Hare Krishna celebrants.

Perry Ruben, Monkmeyer

Shooting up. Drugs are a serious problem among bored young people, in suburb as in city.

organization, work with civil rights groups and peace groups, the arts, a religious vocation, teaching, social work, work with the handicapped or deprived, scientific research, and so forth—although it should not be assumed that everyone working in these fields is an idealist. Most youngsters, however, by late adolescence have pretty well come to terms with things as they are —in the words of the idealists, they have "sold out"—and have given up on working any major changes in the social, political, or economic structure (although in later years they will contribute a certain amount of time to "good causes" and crusades for "better schools"), or in the culture's value system, and are trying to find their place in society as it is given to them. This is the time when they have to weigh the advantages of further education against the appeal of getting directly to work and settling down, when they have to balance their actual skills and capacities against their often grandiose ambitions, and their preparation and ambitions against the economic realities (Crites, 1965). On these and other adolescent themes, see the research reported by Douvan and Adelson (1966).

This is often a stressful time for the adolescent on two counts, omitting the stress of abandoning or compromising his ideals. First, the variety of possible occupations has become so large as to be bewildering. Indeed, despite the almost total vocational and geographical mobility theoretically open to the young person, the choice of a career is usually settled by accident: whom one knows or whom one's family knows, what one happens to hear about or stumble upon, what is available locally. Second, the thought of having to measure up, on his own, to the rigorous standards of commercial competition is likely to provoke one more upsurge of ambiguity and ambivalence amounting to panic. All his life the child is asked, "What are you going to *be* when you grow up?" Now the question suddenly and alarmingly becomes, "What are you going to *do* after you finish school?" Nowadays, of course, the choice is often, for the moment, between school and military service (or, for some, prison or exile), which does not relieve the panic, and the youngster who hopes to dodge the draft by getting married and siring a child while still in school may find that he has put himself in an extra financial bind. The young person's panic may obliterate his dreams, ideals, and ambitions and send him rushing into the best job he can find in a hurry, giving up on sailing to the South Seas or painting in Paris or regenerating the world. The pressures and seductions are many, and it is a rare and admirable young person who can hold fast to his ideals in this turbulent transition.

12
becoming
mature

12

Helping the Adolescent into Adulthood

The quantities of knowledge that a person needs to make his way in a complex civilization like ours is reason enough for the long apprenticeship that we call adolescence. But we may question whether the apprenticeship we provide is the best one for adolescents and for society as a whole. At best, we prepare adolescents to go on living in a world that is a forward projection of the present one, and at worst, to live in a long-vanished phantom environment. Since we know that the world will either have to change radically or go smash, and since it is out of the question that the direction of change can be toward a bucolic "good old days," we obviously are teaching adolescents wrong (Platt, 1965). They have their own answer, of course, in the perpetuation of teen-age culture into adulthood, but inasmuch as the teen-age culture is inadequate even to the needs of adolescents, we can doubt whether it will work for adults.

We cannot achieve preparation for adulthood in adolescence alone. It must begin in infancy. But it is in late adolescence that the preparation reaches its culmination, when the ambivalences must be resolved in favor of growing up into independence. We have so far left open, just as our society does, the answer to the critical question of when adolescence ends and adulthood begins. The young person passes many milestones, but there is no single marker that tells him that he has left childhood behind. The best we can say, then, is that the individual is grownup when his society tells him that he is—

that is, when adults, other than his parents, begin more or less consistently to treat him as one of themselves. Parents may be the last to detect and acknowledge the adolescent's changed status.

It is in the behavior of teachers, parental friends, uncles and aunts, employers, and especially strangers such as waiters, taxi drivers, and barbers that the young person can read his adulthood. These people, less biased than his parents, will be reacting to something in his appearance and manner that betoken maturity. As we suggested earlier, there is a strong element of circular reinforcement, of positive feedback, in this process. The sooner people begin to take the young person's adulthood for granted, the sooner and more easily he assumes the role, and the easier it is for others to react to him as adult. Early in the process, there may be some irony on the part of adults, and some self-consciousness on the side of the adolescent (it may be a long time before the young person can refer to himself or herself without awkwardness as "Mister" or "Miss"), but even as a semiformal game, recognized as such by both parties, it serves the adolescent as a way into adulthood. The interesting thing is that the adolescent, for all his straining for acceptance, usually passes into adulthood without immediately being aware of the fact. At some point, he realizes that he no longer half-expects people to challenge his adulthood, that he himself is no longer bluffing or merely playing a role, and, looking back, that he has already crossed the threshold that he has still been half-anticipating.

The basic theme of this section is that, in addition to providing a rational society for him to grow up to, adults can best help the adolescent into adulthood by treating him, at least in public, as much as possible like an adult without, however, throwing him so completely on his own that he is overwhelmed by anxiety. In elaborating this theme, we have to remain on a level of some generality to allow for all the diversity that exists among families and individuals. In the things we say to parents, the underlying principles of parent-child relations are the same ones that we have outlined all through these pages, with the changes of emphasis made necessary by the special character of adolescence.

Parents

Parents find it hard to be consistent in their treatment of adolescent offspring, at least partly because the adolescent is far from consistent in maintaining his maturity. It is probably the case that adolescents are least mature when dealing with their parents—analogously husbands and wives, too, let down their public propriety in the intimate atmosphere of home. One day parents may acknowledge the youngster's maturity, responsibility, and independence, and the next day express impassioned doubts that he or she will ever make the grade. And acknowledgements of maturity are often coupled with a reproach, a command, or a stricture which automatically negates the young person's maturity: *"Since* you are grow up, I expect that . . . ," or "I'm surprised that . . ." Adolescents, whatever their individual differences, unanimously bristle when parents offer adulthood with one hand and take it away with the other. Parents, obviously, want to teach their children lessons, at the levels of fact, principle, and ethics. What they may not realize is that, by late adolescence, the time for such teaching is past, that from now on the young person is going to learn his explicit lessons elsewhere, from books, contemporaries, teachers and other preceptors, employers and bosses, fellow workers, and in meditation. However, there remain many implicit lessons that the adolescent can derive from his ventures into independent action, sometimes directly from the consequences of action and sometimes indirectly, from the way his parents react to the consequences. But even when parents are reacting with dismay or anguish or anger, they can still convey a basic respect for the adolescent, for his sometimes fragile dignity, and for his need to preserve his self-esteem. Parents can thus play an important role in encouraging and restricting independence and in mediating between the youngster and the results of what he does. Sometimes parental respect will be tinged with amusement, but it is probably not a good idea to let it show. On the other hand, it often helps if the adolescent can laugh at himself.

The key lesson for parents to learn is how and when to let go and not to let go. But adolescence is too late to begin to learn this lesson. From toddlerhood on, children and parents have to practice letting go of each other; like other kinds of weaning, this one is better done gradually. Prior to late adolescence, however, the child has needed the assurance that he was not letting go for good. Adolescence, by contrast, is an exercise in really letting go and a preparation for a new kind of relationship between parent and child based on reciprocal respect between older and younger adults. Parents generally feel, and sometimes announce, that they would gladly sacrifice themselves for their child.

Helping the adolescent into adulthood

481

Come late adolescence, they have to make good; but it may come as a shock to discover that the sacrifice consists not in giving themselves up but in giving up their child. Furthermore, considering the adolescent's own ambivalence, they must likewise help him give them up. This two-sided giving up may be especially difficult when the adolescent is a girl. We take it as normal that a young man, even though single, may find a job and go out on his own. The girl, by contrast, may find that marriage is the expected escape route from the nest. Until marriage, even though she may be working and perhaps having affairs, there are internal and external pressures to remain at home in a grown-up little girl sort of status. As we have already remarked, this too may be changing.

One of the advantages of partial independence is that it permits the young person to make mistakes. Obviously, parents have to stand firm against clearly disastrous courses of action, but the young person is going to try things that his parents do not know about in advance, and there will be various ambiguously risky enterprises where his parents will simply have to hope for the best. Even if the young person lands in jail or the hospital, finds himself stranded penniless on some remote shore, or finds himself in danger of becoming a father, or if she discovers that she is pregnant, or when he or she finds it impossible to cope with debts, parents have to help salvage the situation and try, in genuine cooperation with the young person, to analyze what went wrong. Obviously, according to what one reads in the newspapers, a certain proportion of young people are doomed. However, we must beware of self-righteous moralizing, of "I told you so," and of giving up too readily.

Even in less consequential matters, such as letting the adolescent choose his own costume or imposing a family curfew, too many parents are likely to rescind a privilege the first time the adolescent abuses it, intentionally or mistakenly. We have to expect occasional regressions and blunders as part of the developmental process and the adolescent cannot be penalized every time he goes astray. In adult life, major mistakes carry their own major penalties, but in adolescence the young person's feelings of guilt, shame, embarrassment, and inadequacy may be sufficient corrective penalty, without his necessarily having to take lifelong consequences for foolish acts. As things now stand, of course, the fewer the family's financial resources and the less its influence in the community, the more likely it is that the young person can get himself into a permanent bind with a single rash deed. The poor family is less likely than the well-to-do one to know what community resources are available to help in times of crisis. Fortunately, though, most adolescents do not get into major trouble, even though parents may feel constantly threatened by the possibility. If they can have faith in their child's basic soundness, they can be truly on the side of growth and freedom and can ride out whatever crises arise.

The most reasonable of adolescents will sometimes lash out and rail and rage. Parents have to be able to discern the issue and to know whether it is a real issue, on which they have to stand firm, or a sham issue that simply needs clarifying or that represents a psychological rather than a practical need. Sometimes the adolescent demands freedom of self-determination because he really feels ready for it, and sometimes as a way of finding out whether indeed he is ready. Parents have to exercise judgment, knowing that in some cases to give the adolescent what he insistently claims he wants (drowning out his own doubts and misgivings) may drive him to renounce it forever. Furthermore, no matter how perverse it seems, the adolescent may feel that his parents have betrayed their responsibility to him when they yield to his demands.

In times of anger, the adolescent may denounce or belittle his parents, but such denunciations need not be taken literally. In the heat of the moment, the adolescent means them with all his heart, and wants them to hurt. But they spring less from a sweeping rejection of his parents than from a need to assert himself as autonomously individual. In some ways they resemble the toddler's negativism and the preschool child's "I hate you!" Neither the preschool child nor the adolescent expects his parents to take such outbursts as a final statement of how he feels. Also, in the language of adolescent ambivalence, "I hate you" may mean "I'm afraid I love you too much." Such attacks do not call for retaliation, nor need they trigger lectures on the ingratitude and insolence of today's children. If an adolescent wants to be independent of his parents, it is because they have taught him autonomy as a value, no matter how hard they find it to let go. The conscious gratitude comes later, when the young person has achieved a certain amount of stability and perspective and can appreciate that his parents did a better job of preparing him for life than he realized at the time. Or it may not come until the adolescent, now grown up, has children of his own and can share a parental view of things.

Some writers have suggested that con-flicts between the generations are not only inescapable but essential to the process of growing up. Without necessarily espousing this view, we feel that a complete lack of conflict may indicate that the adolescent is in a bad way. He (or she) may have evolved fancy techniques for lulling parental concern, and outside the home does exactly what suits him. If such a youngster gets into trouble, the results are likely to be especially devastating. On the other hand, there are adolescents who have been beaten, cowed, or brainwashed into abject submission to the dictates of their parents and who seem wholly unable to think for themselves. On a scale of authority which runs from complete lack of adult control through ineffective or erratic control to absolute control, we can locate a point where the final decisions are up to the adult but the youngster has wide latitude to try things out and make mistakes.

Adults must be willing to mean it when they invite the adolescent to make his own decisions and not feel betrayed or snatch back the freedom if the decision is not the one they would have made. This is particularly important in the domain of ideas and ideologies. If the young person is to be someone who can think and act for himself, who defines his own code of values, then he needs an opportunity to try on and oppose all sorts of doctrines and convictions. Adults who try to suppress deviant patterns of thinking in young people may be troubled by misgivings about how well their own assumptions would stand up in the marketplace of ideas. It is a proper function of parenthood to challenge the youngster's more wild-eyed notions—although the odds are very much against his ever trying to put them into practice—but on a plane of tough-minded fact and reason, treating the youngster's discoveries and inventions as something worth discussing seriously and respectfully. An adult can find ways to demolish a child's line of argument without demolishing the child. Sometimes, of course, the child's hare-brained notions happen to be correct, whether or not he can defend them rationally, and parents have to be ready to lose a few debates.

One thing that parents might be aware of is the hidden topics in many debates. That is, the ostensible issue may be politics or economics or continuing in school, but beneath the surface may be raging unresolved issues left over from earlier years. The young person may still, for instance, be fighting the battle of basic trust, or autonomy, or feelings of guilt about his body and its functions, he may have met social rejection in the middle years, or he may secretly be worried about his parents' relations with each other. Parents, too, as we suggested earlier, may be fighting battles that have little to do with the issues at hand: their own lost youth and idealism, ambivalence about their own sexuality, feelings of inadequacy related to work or community standing. Sometimes the adolescent's behavior breaks down in response to the pattern of pressures and weak spots, and professional intervention may be called for. For the most part, however, crises have to be worked out the hard way, in the crucible of the everyday world. What happened when the child was two or five or ten cannot be undone when he is fourteen or seventeen or twenty, but must be dealt with in terms of the new person he has become. Short of the near-redoing of intensive psychotherapy—about whose efficacy we have little assurance—his problems can be solved only at their new levels

and in their new forms. To recognize their buried sources, however, is to understand them better and to avoid the trap of taking immediate issues too literally.

Sexual attitudes and behavior are the key to many conflicts between the generations. In the matter of sex education, as in other areas, parents must build on earlier foundations. Factual education about sexual matters should be virtually complete before puberty. During adolescence, sex education must be addressed to the meaning of sexuality, to the meaning of the youngster's own body experiences, to answering his doubts and allaying his anxieties. In spite of all their knowledge, many children feel that they are sexually abnormal in some respect, and the only way of reassuring them about this is to let them know what people in general are like. The sexuality of boys is taken for granted, even though parents may find it disagreeable to contemplate in detail. But what is overlooked is that both boys, with their high level of overt sexuality, and girls, with their high level of latent sexuality, need instruction to make sense of these matters. They need to know about the differences between the sexes, and especially about the greater diversity of sexual responsiveness in adolescent girls than in boys, at least in European cultural settings. They need to learn that sexual activity does not automatically imply pleasure or satisfaction, that conquest in itself is meaningless except insofar as the girl can truly participate or the young man can truly reveal to her the delights of full expression; they need to know that masturbation is neither morally wrong nor a mark of depravity, nor yet the equivalent of full sexuality; they must realize that intermediate forms of gratification are possible and acceptable.

Both young men and young women should understand that social pressures to make the girl acquiesce in sexual intercourse contrary to her own feelings are psychologically harmful, and that a girl who lacks strong urges during adolescence is not on that account frigid. On the other hand, the girl who finds sex repugnant, rather than merely uninteresting or dangerous, may have more general problems of openness and intimacy. The Freudian enlightenment has had one unfortunate consequence in that a great many people have come to believe that sex is or should be the *summum bonum* in life, and young people need to learn that, whatever its joys, sex is only one strand in the fabric of life. Sex is not something to be exalted, almost like a new deity, any more than it is something to be locked up in the dungeons of the unconscious. The pursuit of the orgasm has become almost a way of life for some women, an elusive Holy Grail or Bluebird of Ecstasy, to the point where the woman who has never known orgasm, or who experiences it only occasionally, feels both biologically inadequate and cheated by her lovers.

We have to accept the fact of sexual urgency in some individuals, male and female, and we also have to accept with equanimity the fact that some people lack urgent drives and are largely unresponsive to sexual stimulation. The unresponsive ones should be free to try, but they should not be made to feel guilty if it does not work. Pro-sexual moralism is as foolish as antisexual moralism. But the answer to moralism is knowledge, and young people cannot bring sex into functional subordination to a total scheme of life unless they understand its diverse workings.

We must also bear in mind that a number of people, male and female, learn to use sex as a way of dominating and exploiting other people. Sex used in this way is incompatible with true maturity. True sexual morality is not to be instilled with threats and warnings. It is learned in day-to-day living with one's family. And a family in which the adolescent learns that the opposite sex is to be regarded as prey or as a natural enemy is not going to teach morality. Hence, as in other areas, morality arises from a sense of self-respect and respect for other people, and it is this that parents can impart to their adolescent children.

Throughout, of course, sex is confounded with love. Love is what the adolescent thinks he or she is in, or has just been in, or wants to be in, and which parents view as premature. In fact, adolescent attachments are only provisionally permanent, and the adolescent's feeling that they are eternally enduring is premature. But the adolescent's falling in and out of love is a vital preparation for mature love, for generously giving and receiving affection and for being able to live with a member of the opposite sex in a spirit of understanding and cooperation in a context of good communication. Thus, either to combat the adolescent's falling in love or to encourage it as a charming example of "puppy love" is irrelevant. And it is both irrelevant and injurious to try to relive one's own adolescence through the affairs of the heart of one's children.

Although parents may be favorably inclined to the idea of their child's falling in love, he almost always seems to them to fall in love with the wrong person. In fact, as we have suggested, the adolescent falls in love primarily with himself, projecting his romantic idealism onto almost anyone who offers the slightest encouragement, real or fancied. Needless to say, parental apprehensions about love between adolescents are based on fear of sexual involvements. However, love and sex are usually quite separate until late adolescence and even then may converge only in a setting of an anticipated durable liaison. For the adolescent boy, love is idealized, and he feels his sexuality as almost antagonistic to love. For the girl, her still diffuse sexuality is decidedly secondary to love. Falling in love may increase the probability of her yielding to a boy's advances, but reciprocal love is likely to reduce, at first, the intensity of the boy's advances. However, a goodly proportion of unwed mothers, or girls who are forced to marry because they are pregnant, are "nice girls" who yielded in the throes of adolescent love—the promiscuous girl ordinarily takes precautions. The bulk of unwed mothers, of course, are lower-class girls who acquiesce not out of pleasure or desire but as a response to social pressures and need for acceptance, and who know little about the facts of procreation and even less about how to prevent it; in some groups, of course, marriage is not expected or by custom follows getting pregnant.

Unless they are dealing with an overly docile child, parents will find that they can make little headway in either cultivating or suppressing a particular attachment. They can try to expose their child to what they consider suitable love objects, and they can speak frankly about what they consider unsuitable ones. The very rich can ship a son or daughter to a distant clime to "forget," but in general to try to forbid contact is worse than vain, since it will only increase the strength of the feelings, and to keep a child locked up, away from school or work or the hangout, is impossible for any length of time. If parents can think back to their own adolescent pasts, they can at least recognize and sympathize with the youngster's feelings, whatever they may think of the objects to which these feelings get attached. The time to talk such matters over is in the interludes between attachments. It is perhaps in such quiescent periods that one can best try to make clear the differences in the way the two sexes fall in love.

Family, school, and society

So far in this section, we have spoken frankly but essentially in conventional terms. We have, in effect, taken it for granted that youngsters stay at home through the high school years and then get a job or go to college. If they go to college, then (if the draft doesn't intervene) they get a job, with marriage and children following. But, as we have seen, this pattern is changing and in fact may already have become obsolete for many young people. For better or for worse, times are changing, and new ways will have to be found for adolescents. We have already suggested, toward the end of Chapter 9, some of what we see as possible new ways.

Adolescents have to be given more options—to work, to study, to combine or alternate work or study, or even at times to do nothing. We cannot foresee the precise shape society will be taking in the years ahead, but there will probably be different patterns of work, if only to take the pressure off the natural environment. Young people will have to have opportunities to do meaningful work, although it seems likely that some kind of laws will still be needed to prevent exploitation of young workers.

The one thing we should not think about doing is continuing the schools as they are. Most adolescents consider schooling as a form of penal servitude, pointless except as an initiation ceremony. Teachers sense the pointlessness, too. Many of them do not really understand their own subject matters or have any real idea why it would be to the student's advantage to learn what they have to teach. It is simply their job to try to make the student learn it. And even the best of secondary-school teaching collides with the fact that the student is there involuntarily, with his real interests in the world outside. This is why we say that young people have to be given a chance to grapple with the real world. The lucky ones will come to realize that science and literature and art and philosophy have useful lessons to teach. But this realization almost always comes after the fact—with maturity, not in anticipation of it. Indeed, students nowadays show themselves at their most ingenious not in mastering the curriculum but in circumventing it. The clever young person reads not the assigned "classic" but a crib designed to help him pass an examination on the unread text, one more sample of academic gamesmanship at work.

Thus, the adolescent needs schools that he can drop in and out of, and he needs a variety of schools and learning opportunities. We strongly approve the trend to extramural, do-it-yourself education. If necessary, skilled workers should be paid to accept young apprentices. The young person should have access to vocational schooling, academic schooling, and an apprentice relation to scholars or scientists. The adolescent also needs sources outside school and family that he can turn to for information and advice, and for personal and vocational counseling. Counseling is now for the most part the responsibility of the already overburdened school, and it might better be quartered elsewhere, as in a special agency or in neighborhood centers. The younger adolescent may need someone he can turn to who can tell him what is happening to him in terms of bodily, emotional, and social growth, what course it will follow, what people expect of him, and what he can do about it—many parents simply do not know enough about these matters to be of help to the young person. Some of this counseling may become one function of the newly emerging category of child development specialist. The adolescent may want advice on family problems, and parents themselves may need someone they can consult. The older adolescent often needs vocational guidance, not merely in terms of what he is fit for but also in terms of the variety and scope of existing occupations, including areas the adolescent may never have heard of. He needs to be helped to be aware of changing patterns in the job market (many young adults now rue the day they were sold on glorious careers in engineering), what new specialties are likely to come forth, and what preparation is needed. He needs help in planning both imaginatively and realistically. Many idealistic young people nowadays want help in making a career out of working for social change. Not everyone can be a Nader's Raider, and we may need a number of equivalent new organizations, including frankly political ones.

Girls especially need help in breaking out of the sex-role stereotypes that get bred into them from birth on. Fair employment practice acts increasingly forbid job discrimination on the basis of sex, and women are working in just about every occupation known to the Census Bureau. This is not to say that girls should not aim at being a teacher or housewife; rather, they should know about the whole range of options and make a genuine choice. Good counseling can help a girl, if she so desires, find ways to divide herself between parenthood and further education or a career, timing things so that she can be with her children at the points where they need her most. What is more, the young woman who wants motherhood and a role outside the family should make sure that her mate understands that he will have to take on a bigger share of parenthood and housework than used to be considered standard. It is becoming a fairly common pattern, for instance, that a woman takes a medical degree, then has children, and then, when the children have reached a degree of self-sufficiency, returns to take her internship or residency. Many doctor-mothers also join a shared practice, which permits a regular working schedule, part-time if it seems desirable, and guarantees certain hours free for family life. If working is going to become the norm for women, employers will obviously have to find ways to be flexible, as in part-time and maternity leave arrangements, and in letting female employees do work at home.

What all this adds up to is this: adolescence is a cultural invention which provides few psychological satisfactions for young people and poor preparation for adulthood, so why not uninvent it or at least redesign it? That is, the young person would move more directly than at present from childhood into adulthood, but at a time and pace that he sets for himself.

He would be free to assert as much freedom and responsibility as he cared to. This kind of change would require changes in institutions, like schools, attitudes, and laws that limit the freedom of choice of young people. If it is too radical to ask for an end to compulsory education, we could compromise by moving the school-leaving age down to thirteen. The child labor laws would have to be greatly modified (what we need more than child labor laws are laws that protect all workers from exploitation, such as that visited on large numbers of migratory farm workers and their families). The age at which people are allowed to drive cars would have to be lowered (although they would still have to demonstrate a mature level of competence before being licensed). We would have to set the age of consent and marriage lower. But if young people are going to be free to marry, they must also be free to undo mistaken matings. Indeed, marriage and divorce as the concern of the state may be an obsolete notion. We would have to make it legal for young people to buy alcoholic beverages—those who find the idea shocking should remember two things: youngsters who want liquor can always find ways to get it, and they are less likely to want it once the aura of forbidden fruit has been removed. If marijuana were to be made legal, it would have to be legal for everyone beyond child's estate.

It may seem a contradiction that we suggest abolishing adolescence in a context of numerous support services for young people. In fact, though, we have in mind that these opportunities for learning, training, counseling, and the rest should be at the service of all adults. Multiple careers are becoming the rule, and early retirement means that many vigorous people want to resume their educations or work in public service. Liberating young people should go hand in hand with opening up new possibilities for young and old alike. It is only in middle age that some people begin to find themselves as artists, philosophers, or novelists.

Thus, the community center should cater to everyone. We need an expanded vision of what such centers should consist of. At present, they seem to be pitched to too low a common denominator of passing away the time. The ultimate curse of our present styles of adolescence and old age is boredom. Young people escape their boredom in drugs or promiscuity or vent it in vandalism and, sometimes, riots. Old people just cave in; those who can afford it blunt the wasted hours with alcohol. Besides the recreation rooms and arts and crafts facilities common to most neighborhood centers, such places need libraries and reading rooms, study counselors, and perhaps a continuing forum under believable and uncondescending adult leadership (or a system of rotating leaderships) on such topics as sex, marriage, parenthood, religion, politics, war, economics, careers, and values. We suggest this last with some trepidation, for the people who organize "rap sessions" on college campuses seem to us all too often to be spreading misconceptions and misinformation. Their evangelical fervor is sometimes all out of proportion to the substance of their ideas.

We believe that opening up the world of adulthood to young people, so that they can function side by side with people of various ages, may help to restore the sense of community that present social divisions have tended to destroy. For instance, our overprivileged youth needs to learn about the realities of working-class life. Young people need to be reminded that practical competences do not come by magic but have to be acquired by long and diligent application. They need to be reminded that older people, if their skills have not been automated out of all utility, often have knowledge and know-how beyond that of young people. Young people need to learn, as it is almost impossible to learn in the family, that people do not lose their humanity as they get older, but find new and satisfying versions of humanity proper to different stages to maturity.

A Definition of Maturity

Development does not stop when one reaches adulthood. One can even recognize such developmental periods as young maturity, middle maturity, old age, and senescence. While such periods are fairly well defined physically—in terms of stamina and vigor, sexual potency (which declines in the male even as desire increases in the female), sensory acuity, speed of reactions, loss of head hair in some males, the graying of hair in both sexes, a tendency for the waistline to bulge and the shoulders to hunch, creases and puckers in the skin—their psychological meaning is by no means as clearcut. There is, obviously, a progressive change of roles, and not only in terms of whether one is climbing the ladder of success or is on the skids. Most people become, in turn, spouse, parent, grandparent, and oldster. Even if one's life appears to be at a standstill, the changes that are happening in other people's lives mean that one's position relative to them changes, too. Friendship patterns change, recreational tastes change, and the life-space is repeatedly transformed.

Many young people, and not a few adults, see adulthood as a slipping away of all that is dear, a series of renunciations, an exercise in loss and doing without, a resigning oneself to the inevitable. In fact, our culture almost guarantees such a pattern. Young parenthood is often a time of mature delight, but for many it is only adult doll play and for still others it is a time of considerable resentment caused by the constant and inescapable burdens of child care. For some young people it may mean giving up youthful freedom for dreary responsibilities. Many young males become preoccupied with the pursuit of success or embittered by its elusiveness or unattainability, in either case to the neglect of the joys of fatherhood, husbandhood, and domesticity, the last being regarded as the preserve of bored young females.

Both men and women have a crisis of middle age, like that of adolescence probably related only in part to physical changes. If a young woman marries at age twenty-two, has one child when she is twenty-three and another, final one at twenty-five, by age thirty-five her most intensive maternal functions are largely over, the routines of housekeeping are easily disposed of, her husband is busy outside the home, and massive boredom may set in. It is bored women in the thirty- to forty-five age group who become alcoholics, turn promiscuous, "take courses," go into psychoanalysis, engage in Good Works, or become chronic shoppers. Age forty-five to fifty and the menopause may bring life to a climax of boredom and frantic pleasure-seeking. Crises of this kind

may be the prerogative of the affluent. The woman who lives in poverty may be ground into despair early in adulthood. Moreover, new life styles for women may obviate the problem. While many women meet the crisis of middle age quietly or constructively, some of the prosperous ones of this age travel around the world, endlessly shopping for bargains in Hong Kong or Marrakech, lavishing money and favors on gigolos and beach boys. The less affluent shop at home and visit the neighbors, seizing on newcomers and spilling their medical or psychiatric autobiographies to anyone who will listen—usually to another woman in similar circumstances, who will reply in kind. The chronic players of bridge, Mah Jongg, solitaire, and similar time-killers (including beauty parlor going) are prominent in this age group.

The crisis of middle age comes somewhat later for men, characteristically in association with—and with the awareness of—the physical changes of ages forty to fifty (the French call it *la crise de la quarantaine*): graying and balding, gaining weight, presbyopia, and so forth. In both men and women, middle age may bring on severe depression, sometimes called **involutional melancholia** from the involution, or regression, of the womb (the changes of middle age are called the **climacteric**, including the female menopause, but just as the female menopause need not mean the end of sexual enjoyment, so the male climacteric need not mean the end of potency). Fear of loss of potency may be a factor in the middle-age crisis of a number of men, leading to an extravagant pursuit of sexuality as though either to deny the decline or to harvest as much pleasure as possible before the end. A sizable number of men, according to Masters and Johnson (1966), react unnecessarily to declining virility by simply giving up sex. Equally often, though, the crisis centers on work. High hopes may have turned to ashes, early resignation to mediocrity or to one's place as a cog may have become bitterness, the postponement of achievement may have gone on too long until it now seems too late to begin. For some men, disillusionment comes with the discovery that they can succeed in work but in nothing else—that they have failed as husbands, lovers, friends, fathers, community leaders, and founts of wisdom. Ironically, the man who has attained success may in middle age feel a need to work even harder, as though to prove to himself and others that his powers are not flagging. However, it appears to be increasingly the case that men of forty-five to fifty who have laid by some wealth are willing to retire, or go into semi-retirement, and devote themselves to the pursuit of pleasure, sometimes in company with their wives and families, sometimes not. The crisis of middle age often seems to go with a ruptured marriage, although it is hard to say what is cause and what effect.

Old people are generally regarded by themselves and their families as a useless burden, to be filed away in a retirement colony or nursing home until the liberation of death. Even well-to-do old people may prefer the secure limbo of a retirement home to an active life in the community. Those who have done research in colonies for the aged report that the inhabitants typically cut off contact with and interest in the outside world and preoccupy themselves with the minutiae of everyday life (Bennett and Nahemov, 1965). They both let go and give up with a vengeance. As Kalish (1965) points out, suicide and homicide apart, we exercise more options about death than we usually recognize: where, when, how, in whose company, and even whether, since medical care is rationed. In some societies, of course, a "no work, no eat" philosophy prevails, and those who are too old to earn their keep are simply let starve. We, by contrast, tend to keep our old people alive, but grudgingly and on tiny pittances, and the physical and psychological isolation of the aged seems to hasten their decline and demise.

It is our thesis that maturity—all of postadolescence—can and should be a time of fulfillment, of continued growth and repeated discoveries and insights, of ever-renewed enthusiasm, of fresh understanding and solid wisdom. One has a choice. He can spend maturity and old age looking wistfully back on the good old lost days or he can, more than at any other period, relish the joys of the moment, savor the zest of things, and look forward to the excitements of the future. He (or she) can keep physically fit and vigorous, or he can strive foolishly to preserve the powers of youth, or he can cave in and go to seed; he can choose to spend old age as either a fossil (or a vegetable) or a sage. We want to try to describe the kind of maturity that represents a culmination rather than a downgrade, in which curiosity and the capacity to learn continue undiminished and even grow long after the body's tissues have begun to fail. Maturity in this sense does not come to everybody, and we know of no way to guarantee that it will, but we personally know enough exemplars of true maturity to feel confident that it is possible.

Many models and goals for maturity have been offered. The authors are not happy about most of them, and have some feeling that it is hopeless even to try to

A definition of maturity

define this special kind of maturity. Nevertheless, they are inclined to go ahead, in full recognition of the risks. The first risk is of committing the "psychologist's error," which is a variety of ethnocentrism. Most psychologists—even, paradoxically enough, reductionists—have a strongly human-centered, individual-centered orientation and attach great value to verbal skills, social skills, social consciousness, intellectual attainments, and scientific and artistic creativity. They are inclined to overlook other styles and areas of achievement. They may praise the mechanic's craftsmanship, the clerk's conscientious thoroughness, the businessman's acumen, the athlete's strength and agility, but their ultimate ideal generally turns out to be Socrates or Einstein. A second danger is found in the fact that many models for maturity seem to be largely reflections of their author's own idealized personalities, saying in effect, "See how wonderful I am" or "This is what I wish I could be." A third risk is that criteria for maturity may degenerate into a set of pious preachments which clothe in toplofty sentiments moralistic imperatives addressed to lesser men. Finally, standards for maturity are all too likely to seem to force everybody into a single, narrow mold, doing violence to the diversity that we have been talking about and extolling throughout this book.

The authors will try to avoid these pitfalls and offer a description of versions of maturity that takes into account man's frailties and imperfections and the variety of individual tastes and traits and endowments. Our procedure has been, first, to think of and to generalize about persons, historical and contemporary, who, in our view, have gone furthest toward effective functioning in all spheres of life—at work and at play, in relations with the world at large, with neighbors, co-workers, superiors, subordinates, with friends and families, and with themselves. (While some of these individuals might agree that we did well to select them, we have not consulted them and we feel sure that those still living would prefer to remain anonymous.) Second, we have borrowed selectively from those authors who have dealt with the nature of maturity, relying especially on the work of Maslow (1950) and Goldstein (1939). The result inevitably will reflect the authors' personal tastes and philosophies. In point of fact, however, there seems to be a good deal of agreement on this subject among various writers, whether theologians, psychologists, healers, or philosophers.

If an individual is going to grow toward the kind of maturity we are talking about, he will find it helpful to have secure developmental, preadult underpinnings—he should not have to deflect his energies into refighting childhood battles or nursing old hurts. Maturity can only be built on sound foundations. Unless the child has been able to establish basic trust, his world is quicksand. Without basic trust, he cannot establish autonomy, the trust in himself that enables him, by successive stages, to separate his identity from his parents and then from his contemporaries and stand on his own two feet as an integrated—internally and to the saner aspects of society—individual. The starting point of maturity is reached when, without rupturing his basic emotional ties to the environment, the individual is nevertheless free to move about within the framework they provide, when he no longer has at every moment to question his own identity, his own wishes and aspirations, when his freedom is no longer something to strive for but something to count on and to use responsibly. It is necessary to point out, however, that many people do survive and recover from developmental setbacks along the way, sometimes with therapeutic help and sometimes on their own. But they must somehow get beyond their childhood conflicts. While the task of maturity is made harder for such people, they occasionally do especially good, if delayed, jobs of growing up. Adversity, although hardly to be recommended, does sometimes seem to have a strengthening effect. We should make clear that growing out of childhood does not mean abolishing one's past. Apart from the pleasure that childhood recollections can bring, or the relief one feels in looking back at a closed chapter of turmoil, having sound foundations means that one can carry into adulthood those childhood qualities of freshness, enthusiasm, and emotional involvement that stand a person in good stead throughout life.

When a person can live with his past without being bogged down in it, he remains adaptable, **capable of continued change**. It is important to specify, however, what kinds of further change are and are not possible in adulthood. At birth, the individual, subject to constitutional limitations, is capable of following a great many developmental paths. Psychologically, at least, he could equally well become a Kaffir, an Eskimo, a Japanese, or a proper Bostonian. By the end of infancy, however, he is already irrevocably committed to a particular line of development (still, however, with many possible branchings). If he has started off as an American, he can never go completely back and get a fresh start as a Samoan. While he might successfully live in Samoa, he could never think

and feel and act exactly as a Samoan does. Similarly, as the effects and acquisitions of each stage of development are consolidated during childhood, certain doors are closed behind the individual and new vistas open up ahead. The only way the individual can "go back" is via a pathological regression, and this does not mean a return to early plasticity. By the time he has reached adulthood, the individual's choices are strictly limited by his past experience, but they are nevertheless incredibly rich in terms of the new varieties of experience that will become available to him. It is important to note, too, that as the individual matures he has an increasingly greater say in what further lines of development he chooses to follow. His early development depended on an accident of birth and the play of circumstances, but as he moves toward personality integration he develops a species of **self-determination**. He becomes able to accept or refuse the choices offered to him, and, what is more, to invent new lines of development independent of immediate circumstances. He becomes, within certain inescapable limits, the master of his own destiny. Here we take issue with Skinner (1971), who advocates repudiating the delusion of freedom and surrendering to benevolent control. We believe that Skinner errs in concluding that because there can never be absolute freedom, there can be no freedom at all. We concur rather with the existentialist concept of a determined freedom, which at its highest development forces one to be autonomous.

Another characteristic of becoming mature is the development of **wisdom**. The individual does not merely know things, but is able to apply his knowledge. He does not learn as voraciously as he did earlier, but

A definition of maturity

493

this is due less to a decline in capacity than to greater discrimination about what is worth knowing. Also, he learns at a level of increasing generality and decreasing specificity. However, he becomes more aware of gaps in his knowledge, and is better able to define his own ignorance and learn what he needs to. His accumulated experience gives him new insight, sensitivity, understanding, and tolerance. Out of his experience, he builds up a broad perspective which permits him to see his own and other people's problems in a larger context. His emotions become more stable, and, while remaining strong, are tempered, controlled, and integrated. His enthusiasms are more focused and less volatile, so that he can plan and act in long-range terms. As he loses in primitive plasticity, he gains in mature flexibility. He has habits, in the sense of automatic responses to the mechanical demands of life, but he is not bound by habitual ways of thinking. He is always willing to take a fresh look, to consider new evidence, and to have his assumptions challenged. He can change with the times, and shed values and principles made obsolete by the march of history. If he remains enthusiastic, it is certainly not always about the same things. He outgrows his old tastes and interests, he may even outgrow friendships and careers. He can make such changes and still hold fast to such fundamental values as esteem for human feelings and integrity.

We should not give the impression that wisdom always means assuming the role of philosopher—or at least not of the contemplative philosopher. The mature individual can be ribald or genteel, sweet or acid, jolly or glum. The important point is that he be alive, with vigorous interests that make him interesting to be with. But

no matter what his tempo or temperament, it will probably find some of its expression in **humor**. This is not the same as being good-natured. The individual on his way to maturity can be a curmudgeon or a pessimist, and his humor can be bitter, sardonic, or ironic as well as frolicsome, earthy, or subtle. In any event, one of the stigmata of the maturity-bound person is that he both enjoys wit and is able to give his own original twists to his observations of the human comedy.

An important characteristic of the individual who becomes mature is that he is **at home with reality**. This does not mean that all mature people see reality in the same way. They will share a common body of facts governed by more or less fixed principles, but they will differ as to which facts are most important, what meaning to attach to them, and what opinions to hold about them. Being in touch with reality has two sides, being at home with oneself, and being at home with conditions in the outside world. The individual has to accept the stubborn reality of things as they are, without retreating from them or being overwhelmed by them. Obviously, he doesn't like everything that he sees, and he certainly need not leave well enough alone. Because he cares about the state of the world and its inhabitants, and because he wants to have some say in what happens to him and his fellows, he wants to act on reality. But he acts within the limits imposed by practical principles, and does not try to transform reality by magic or wishful thinking, and he acts within the framework of respect for other people's integrity and of awareness of his own fallibility, so that he is unlikely to use force except in self-defense—and not in anticipatory self-defense against some imagined future aggression. Knowing the limits on his own powers and the inertia that dwells in reality, he is not impatient for all change to take place right now, even though certain crucial situations may call for emergency measures. And he does not get so involved in trying to influence his surroundings that he has no time for the simple but fundamental pleasures of life—love, conversation, food and drink, sunshine, exercise, catching up on chores, or pursuing hobbies and crotchets. And even while he is strongly committed to a set of values, he can remain sufficiently detached to maintain perspective, to see alternative points of view, to keep from suffering a personal destruction every time his values encounter a setback, and to be able to laugh at himself when necessary. The more in touch he is with reality, the more he becomes aware that it is full of rampant ambiguities, questions to which there seem to be no fixed and easy answers, and he has to learn to tolerate such ambiguities without taking refuge in dogmatism.

But, as we know, the individual cannot look outer reality in the face unless he is prepared to look himself in the face, too. He is **at home with himself.** He knows his own weaknesses and limitations, and, while he would like to change them for the better, can tolerate them as well as he does the shortcomings of outer reality—and, as we have suggested, he can laugh at his own foibles. Perhaps even more important is his ability to acknowledge and accept his inner needs, cravings, and impulses. The individual must bring his feelings to consciousness and give them explicit shape before he can master and control them. The alternative is repression. The distinction between modulated control and rigid repression corresponds to the distinction between relaxed spontaneity and unpredictable impulsiveness. The person who has made his feelings truly his own does not have to be on constant guard against them—he knows where they are and what they are doing—and can act freely without being afraid that some hidden force will take possession of him. The person who tries to avoid or deny his own feelings must, by contrast, perpetually keep watch lest they spring out unexpectedly. This vigilance not only restricts his freedom to act but, what is more, is often in vain. While he is patrolling his defenses in one area, the caged enemy is liable to erupt as an uncontrolled impulse someplace else. The integrated person can without dismay entertain notions which, if translated into action, would land him in prison or a mental hospital. Such eventualities might serve to restrain him from acting on his fantasies, but the really important deterrent lies in his knowledge that to carry out his more primitive impulses would probably bring harm to somebody else. Because he is human, it costs him something to keep his thoughts to himself, but far less than the person who has to fight with unknown forces. Being used to his own feelings, the individual is better able to recognize and formulate creative insights when they occur. Most important, a knowledge of his own feelings gives him insight into the feelings of others, and in addition is the surest guarantee we know of against projecting his own feelings onto the environment. It should be made clear that the person headed for maturity is not immune to guilt and anxiety. But he can keep them within bounds, accept them as part of his human nature, and even utilize their motive power instead of harboring them as free-floating energies.

A definition of maturity

It follows that the mature individual has to be able to live comfortably with his own body, whether it be strong or weak, handsome or ugly, healthy or failing. This does not mean that he fails to groom it or to tend to its ills, but that he can be at ease about it, not wasting his time in futile laments or hypochondria. He can use it as his means of contact with the world, as the vehicle of his feeling and sensation. And just as the individual can never wholly separate himself from his concrete standpoint in time and space and society, so he is always to some extent the captive of his own body. This means that he experiences it both from the inside and the outside, that it is both his and an organism with an existence of its own, that his self-knowledge can never be absolute but contains the same ambiguities as his experience of outer reality. The individual who would become mature has to learn to tolerate ambiguity in himself as well as in the outside world, not in a spirit of futility but in one of forging ahead regardless.

If the individual's growth toward maturity is rooted in the positive emotional bonds of early infancy, **human relationships** are going to have a high priority for him. In his own life, he may be concerned either with the people closest to him or with people en masse, or even with the fate of unborn generations, but he cannot help having a sense of affiliation with humanity at large. He feels this way in full recognition of human stupidity, perversity, weakness, and evil. Indeed, knowing his own nature as he does, he is likely to know that human beings are a mixed lot but, all in all, worth bothering about. Needless to say, he will not esteem all people equally, and recognizes gradations of affiliation, from profound involvement with those

closest to him through less acute fellow-feeling for those at a distance to real hostility for those who threaten humane principles. But whether or not his existence is centered in family life, he needs and seeks close human attachments. He will be able to give and receive affection freely, without embarrassment or fear for his own integrity. He learns to adapt to various kinds of human relationships and roles: of lover to lover, of spouse to spouse, of parent to child, of man to woman or woman to man, of friend to friend, of student or of teacher, of employer and employee. He will find out that close personal involvements cost something in emotional wear and tear, in responsibility for those he is involved with, in loss of freedom, but he gladly pays the price. Most important, in his relations with people he will become better able to react to the people themselves, and not to some image of them formed out of his own needs and character. Similarly, he will want to be close to them for the sake of what they are, and not merely for the sake of the way they reflect him back to himself. When he can truly perceive people and be aware of their awareness, he will learn a respect for their integrity—or a compassion for their lack of it—that will forever restrain him from frivolous or selfish meddling with other people's lives. He will not have to go looking for affection. Because he is at ease with himself, because he is open to experience, because he has opinions and enthusiasm, people will want to be with him, to share in his excitement of life. Because he respects himself and other people, other people will respect him.

The person equipped with the human sensitivities that make for maturity will usually have a powerful **concern with so-**

cial problems and ways of alleviating them. This does not, however, necessarily imply that he engages directly in working for a new order on either a collective or individual scale. There are other approaches to advancing human welfare than working in the field of social reform or education or mental health, or than performing the functions of a "good citizen," such as voting, or joining the P.T.A., if his temperament inclines him away from these particular activities. One of the most effective forms of good citizenship is to be a sound person, part of a sound family, a good neighbor, and an influence for human charity on the level of personal dealings. An honest businessman—or an effective craftsman—can often accomplish as much, simply by being what he is, as a host of petition-circulators. Or he may function both ways.

For all his social-mindedness, for all his savoring of human relationships, the maturing individual is not dependent on always having company. Typically, he not only is able to tolerate but requires a certain amount of **solitude** in which to think his own thoughts and enjoy his own company. Furthermore, he likes to devote a certain amount of time to unsocial activities: reading, listening to music, gardening —whatever his tastes dictate. This capacity for entertaining himself, for drawing on his own resources, in fact contributes to his social life. It means that he has something to offer people. His wit, his freedom from pretense, even his occasional idiosyncratic crankiness, all the qualities that make him good company are the reflections of the qualities that enable him to be self-sufficient.

The kind of person we are talking about, with his sensitivity to other people's feelings and his respect for other people's integrity, is almost inevitably committed to a **democratic code of ethics**. But he is democratic in a deeply personal sense, and not merely ideologically. He has a sense of humility balanced by self-esteem, and he knows that there are satisfactions to be gained and things to be learned from almost everybody. One of the things that make him interesting to other people is the fact that he is himself interested in what others have to say. And these other people are not only the accepted authorities and pundits. The person headed for maturity is not going to be impressed by high estate or repelled by a low one. Neither, however, will he automatically and perversely disdain the high and espouse the low. Just as the small child judges people less by their station in life than by their emotional warmth, so our subject judges people by their vitality, their strength, their flexibility, their emotional richness, and their honesty—in short, by the virtues he himself strives for—rather than by their objective attainments and social position. Indeed, his own social position may be rather humble—enough admirable people have lived in slums and slave cabins to demonstrate that maturity is not a prerogative of the privileged few.

It is apparent that the person who is becoming mature **does not accept values ready-made**. He is likely to be quite unconventional in his opinions, or to hold them for unconventional reasons or in unconventional combinations. He is looking for a rational, consistent, humane, and realistic system of values, and is not likely to be happy with codes that represent the accretion of habits, traditions, superstitions, or prejudices, of outworn assumptions about human nature and the structure of reality. To look for a set of values of his own means, in effect, to try to extricate himself from his own culture, is his goal. This can be done only to a limited extent, of course. If the mature American finds fault with American values, beliefs, and practices, he does it in an American sort of way. He may become an internationalist, but he can never wholly become psychologically an Englishman or a Swiss. Even people who live abroad and come to feel completely at home in their new surroundings present to the natives no problem in recognition as outlanders. Nevertheless, the mature individual may be able to bring a fresh view to standards and assumptions that other people take for granted, and in any case he will be willing to challenge the obvious. And a liberation of this sort is an important part of mature flexibility, creativeness, and the humor that make life worth living.

On the other hand, his original ideas about values are likely to bring the individual into conflict with his society. Most mature individuals want to live within society, even when its goals conflict with theirs. To keep their integrity, they must be prepared to take nonconformist stands. But they will not waste their time and energies in pointless nonconformity. The individual has to learn when nonconformity is likely to be productive, when to speak out and when to remain silent. His values must be so structured and scaled that he can distinguish between what is central and inviolable and what is peripheral and expendable—or at least postponable. He has to balance his beliefs against his natural wish to lead a quiet, comfortable life, doing his work and enjoying his family and friends. Mostly, of course, among one's friends one can freely express opinions which, stated in print, might look dangerous and subversive. This is because

friends see the individual's opinions in the context of their own awareness of his sincerity, decency, humor, balance, and humaneness. Nevertheless, there is always the possibility that the person who tries to think for himself will run seriously afoul of public opinion and be forced to choose between recanting or suffering the consequences of his folly. Since the individualistic individual finds life pleasant, he will not enter upon martyrdom lightly. Nevertheless, he will by definition be committed to certain principles—religious, political, intellectual, ethical, or whatever—that take precedence over his own existence. Obviously, if he can live and struggle for his principles, he would rather do so, but if there is no choice but to abandon them or perish, he may well be willing to die for them. Mature people, in their everyday affairs, are probably brave and timid in about the same proportion as everybody else, but they generally have in common a streak of stubborn moral courage that appears when the chips are down.

To live realistically (which by no means forbids the conscious exploitation and enjoyment of fantasy) means to live in **consciousness of one's own mortality**. If this becomes a morbid preoccupation, it is no better than pretending that one will live forever. But held in perspective, the ability to face the certain expectation of death, of a final limit to one's period of achievement, lends a valuable urgency and importance to what one does, and helps keep one's values in focus and proportion. The older one gets, the greater the likelihood that people to whom one feels close will die. Bereavement brings with it special trials, and the mature person must learn to endure bereavement without repressing or otherwise blurring its impact. In general, the mature person has a healthy respect for danger, without being panicked into fleeing from commitments and involvements.

Obviously, we have not been painting a design for happiness, or at least happiness in the sense of surcease from turmoil and travail. There are built-in pains and penalties in becoming mature, a few of which we have already mentioned. The individual knows that certain things lie beyond his power of decision or influence, and that he simply has to tolerate them. But as an active person he would prefer to make decisions wherever he can, instead of merely letting things happen. Because he wants to weigh the evidence and the outcomes, he may find some decisions hard to make—which can be trying for other people as well as for himself. Nevertheless, he knows that he has to go on choosing between alternatives, that each alternative costs him something, and there are things he will never be able to do and experience. He also knows that there are things he will never be able to do again, that he can never recapture his youth or relive his first encounters with certain experiences. He knows that his integrity is continually threatened by practical demands, by seductive temptations, by concessions and compromises, by conflicting values, and can be preserved only at the cost of some psychic strain. If his ideas are too much out of joint with the temper of the times, he may feel lonely and cut off from companionship.

In spite of these drawbacks, he knows that the only real rewards of life come with continued growth, and that there is no room in the one material life he has for major regrets. As Solon pointed out, one can only judge whether a man is happy when he dies. Too many people come to the end of the line with a sense of "Wait! Not yet! I was just going to begin!" The individual who has approached maturity can know that he has loved and been loved, has done his work, has made his mark on people, and, although he wishes there were more time, that he has made the most of what there was.

In sum, the adult with a capacity for true maturity is one who has grown out of childhood without losing childhood's best traits. He has retained the basic emotional strengths of infancy, the stubborn autonomy of toddlerhood, the capacity for wonder and pleasure and playfulness of the preschool years, the capacity for affiliation and the intellectual curiosity of the school years, and the idealism and passion of adolescence. He has incorporated these into a new pattern of simplicity dominated by adult stability, wisdom, knowledge, sensitivity to other people, responsibility, strength, and purposiveness.

**A definition
of maturity**

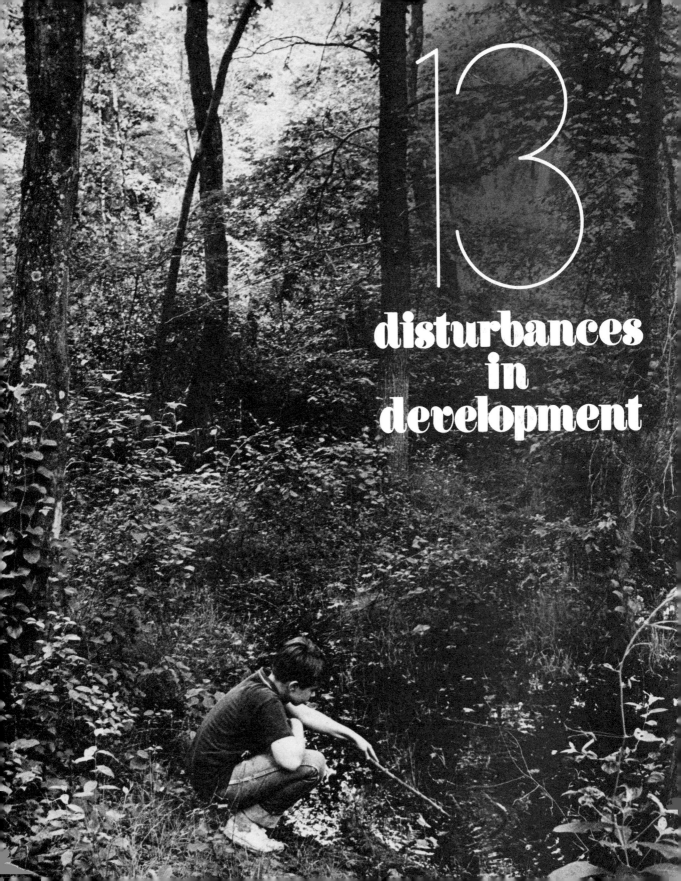

13

disturbances in development

This book is about normal psychological development, the way people with reasonably sound constitutions grow up in reasonably favorable environments, including the normal "problems" that large numbers of parents and children have to face. Sometimes, however, the developmental process goes seriously awry, and this book would be incomplete if we failed to mention some of the major aberrations that occur in childhood, along with what we know or suspect about their causes and remedies. The study of abnormal development is important for practical purposes, in hopes of relieving human misery, and also for theoretical reasons, again in hopes that our theories will lead us to increased understanding of normal as well as disturbed development. It is in abnormal development that one can often see most vividly the subtle interplay of constitutional and social-environmental forces, sometimes to the point of total indistinguishability.

A Conception
of Abnormality

In discussing deviant patterns of development, we shall follow the same chronological formula adhered to throughout this book. It is our general view that most psychological abnormality can be understood as a failure of identification. As we have seen, normal development involves a series of indentifications: with parents, with peers, with adults outside the family, with society in general, with institutions, with principles and values, with styles, and with humankind at large. Identifications at each

age set the stage for those to follow. Notice that some identifications may seem undesirable. A pattern of paternal brutality toward sons may be handed down through the generations, just as may primitive ways of thinking. But if the alternative is no identification, then even quasi-pathological ones become desirable. Defective identification may be rooted in organic impairments which interfere with the full apprehension and orderly schematization of reality, including identification figures and their behavior; in the lack of appropriate models and stimulus conditions; and, often enough, in the back-and-forth interaction of such conditions. For instance, parents may react to a child's being a cripple in a way that breeds intellectual retardation or neurotic self-loathing, even where neither is a necessary outcome of the child's condition.

Speaking broadly, we can say that defective identification is expressed in either defective functioning, such as general retardation or more specific blocks to learning, or emotional disturbance—even though intellectual functioning may be normal or superior—severe enough to interfere with normal living. Let us make explicit that we are skeptical of the "trauma theory" of psychological disorder. In our view, sustained privations and deprivations seem to be the key, with traumatic episodes becoming seriously traumatic when there are no compensating influences in the child's life. But in many cases we are at a loss to understand the causal history, the **etiology**. Even where we can demonstrate organic brain damage, animal studies suggest that it can be effect as well as cause (see p. 108).

Most troubled or inadequate children show aberrant functioning most prominently in some one particular area, although closer examination usually reveals that other areas are involved as well. Thus, neither diagnosis nor treatment can properly be focused on a single symptom, although parents' (and other adults') worries are often phrased in terms of a single problem—bed-wetting, thumb-sucking, stealing, tantrums, reading problems—and "what to do about" it. As we have seen, at every stage of development there are ways of behaving which may seem odd or ominous to adults but which are perfectly normal at that age. Indeed, any adult who acted in the way a child does would be a prime candidate for the mental hospital or the lock-up. But in this chapter we shall not elaborate further on such behavior, confining ourselves rather to those manifestations of genuine disturbance which parents or teachers may become aware of and which they have good reason to be troubled about.

We cannot hope, within the compass of a short chapter, to cover the whole field of behavior pathology in childhood, and those who wish to explore further are referred to more inclusive sources such as Jane Kessler's (1966) excellent treatise. We shall point out only a few of the more common or most intensively studied conditions that arise during childhood and adolescence. We shall deal only summarily with treatment procedures, partly for lack of space, partly for lack of expert qualifications, and partly because there are still so many unknowns. Therapies for children and adults are proliferating furiously (Parloff, 1970), and we cannot even pretend to keep up with each movement.

We are also skirting several other issues. One is what we mean by "normality." If one defines normality according to what most people are like, then we can only conclude that normality may be very hard to distinguish from psychopathology. The mere absence of overt pathology is hardly an indication of normality. Some thinkers speak of "creative mental health," defining normality in terms of positive characteristics found in only a small percentage of the population. We mention only in passing that, as our society is organized, there is great blurring of the boundaries between psychological disturbance and criminality; that is, someone declared to be "mentally ill" can be locked up, even if he has never been accused of any actual misdeed. We partly agree with Szasz (1961) that the very concept of mental illness as a disease akin to measles or tuberculosis is obsolete, although we are more prone than Szasz to recognize that there are some chronic behavior patterns that express a severely disordered outlook on the world. We agree with George Albee (1970) that psychologists for too long have slavishly followed the model provided by medicine and the treatment of physical illness in our thinking about disturbed behavior. However, we are not yet prepared to elaborate a purely psychological theory of abnormality. The way we think about psychological disturbance is closely tied to how we think about treatment. In evaluating the worth of any course of treatment, we must bear in mind two related phenomena. In the field of physical illness, we have the **placebo effect**, the fact that some proportion of sickness is cured or ameliorated by sham drugs of zero curative value; and in the domain of behavior, we have the **Hawthorne effect** (Homans, 1941), whereby morale and performance improve in response to anything that gives the individual reason to believe that people are interested in and care about him. The individual's suggestibility can be turned against him, as in the sale of nostrums, but suggestibility may sometimes be all we have to work with for individuals in distress.

The Neonatal Period and Infancy

A number of abnormal physical conditions are apparent or detectable at birth (the reader is reminded of the assessment techniques mentioned in Chapter 1). Certain of these congenital (present at birth) disorders have clearly hereditary origins, as in the case of the numerous enzyme abnormalities discussed earlier. It will be recalled that certain of these can be diagnosed prenatally from the chromosomes found in cells from the amniotic fluid, and abortion can be induced to prevent further development of some of the more serious conditions. There are also various inherited patterns of mental deficiency, some of which are signaled by characteristic physical stigmata.

Other conditions are thought to be associated with genetic anomalies produced by the action of viruses or radiation on the ovum before it is fertilized. One such condition is **Down's syndrome**, or **mongolism**, linked to either an extra number 21 chromosome or to a translocation (part of a chromosome breaking off and attaching itself to another) involving a number 21 chromosome. Mongolism was originally named for one of its more conspicuous stigmata, an extra fold of skin over the eyelid reminiscent of that seen in Asian peoples, but in fact it is an affliction of the total organism with a whole pattern of related somatic abnormalities. (It should not be necessary to say that the presence of the mongolian fold in Orientals says nothing whatever about their intellectual capacities.) Some of the other physical components of Down's syndrome, including some that do not appear until after infancy, are short stature and slight build; a skull flattened in back; late-appearing, irregularly spaced teeth; a thick, protruding, stubby, fissured tongue; general motor retardation; and various physiological abnormalities including permanent sexual immaturity. Most mongoloids show severe mental deficiency, but the spread of intelligence reaches up to the normal level, so it is not safe to infer serious mental impairment on the basis of physical symptoms alone. Classically, mongoloid children are described as placid, cheerful, and easy to manage, although irresponsible. In point of fact, however, some mongoloids are mischievous and irritable, and many of them are inveterate show-offs. Mongolism used to mean an early death, but medical progress has worked to the advantage of mongoloids as well as of other people, and a number of mongoloids live a long life. New techniques are being tried for the education of mongoloids with some degree of success, and there is hope that chemical therapies can be found to undo Down's syndrome as a somatic condition. Other conditions associated with chromosomal anomaly are intersex (incomplete differentiation into male or female), various deformities (whose origins cannot always be known for certain), and some forms of cancer. While these conditions are genetic, they are not inherited in the usual sense, and although they are in principle heritable, they are usually associated with inability to reproduce.

Other abnormal conditions detectable at

birth are the product of environmental insults to the developing embryo. We have already mentioned in Chapter 1 such prenatally influenced conditions as the **thalidomide syndrome** and the blindness or deafness or deformity that can be caused by **rubella** in the mother early in pregnancy. (An interesting sidelight is that newborn babies whose mothers have had rubella during pregnancy are themselves highly infectious, sometimes for a year or more, and need to be quarantined from the rest of the nursery.) Some conditions, such as **cretinism**, a pattern of stunted growth and mental retardation produced by inadequate functioning of the thyroid gland, have largely obscure basic origins, although some cases are due to insufficient iodine in the maternal diet. Fortunately, cretinism, if diagnosed early, can be cured by continued treatment with thyroid extract. One other potential source of early abnormality, as pointed out in Chapter 1, is **incompatibility of blood type** between mother and child, as when an Rh negative mother bears an Rh positive baby. We have also mentioned the danger that a protein-deficient diet in late pregnancy and the early postnatal months can lead to restricted brain development. Here is one way that poverty can have an impact on the baby even before he is born. The importance of maternal diet for sound prenatal development has led many obstetricians to modify former practices aimed at holding the mother's weight gain to a minimum.

The birth process itself contains such hazards as the risk of mechanical injury or of oxygen deficiency (**anoxia**) while the neonate is making the transition to independent breathing. Injury to the motor centers of the brain before birth or at

A child with Down's syndrome, also called mongolism. Most cases of mongolism are associated with an extra chromosome 21, as shown in the karyotype in Chapter 1.

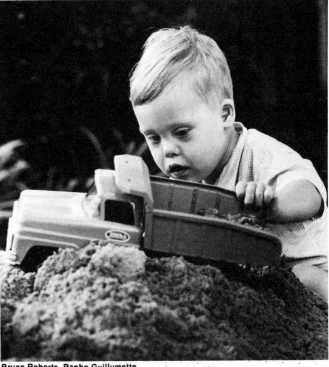

Bruce Roberts, Rapho Guillumette

birth can produce **cerebral palsy**. Characteristically, the victim's muscles are innervated in conflicting and uncoordinated patterns, so that he has great difficulty in walking, speaking, eating, and fine manipulations. His body may be racked into twisted attitudes by muscle tensions, he may involuntarily grimace a great deal, and he is likely to make a great many superfluous movements, sometimes in fixed, repetitive patterns. Because of their sometimes grotesque behavior and appearance, which to the ignorant often connoted insanity or feeble-mindedness, many cerebral palsied children used to be hidden away from public view. Cerebral palsy often has secondary effects beyond the primary one of motor impairment: perceptual disturbances, epilepsy, mental deficiency, and so forth. However, these secondary effects are by no means inevitable. Some victims of cerebral palsy reach a high level of achievement, and many lead a normal life including a job, marriage, and parenthood. The cerebral palsied child's poor motor control may make assessment of his intellectual abilities especially difficult, but special techniques for this purpose have been devised (Haeusserman, 1958). The physical and intellectual problems of cerebral palsy are often further complicated by emotional ones. Both the child and his parents may suffer considerable embarrassment and frustration, and in assessing the child's functioning it is not always possible to sort out the contributions of motor impairment, cognitive limitations, and emotional disturbances. Cerebral palsy, like other forms of brain damage, can produce either a generalized cognitive deficit or a special impairment such as difficulty with language. Nowadays, the cerebral palsied are no longer locked away from sight or

relegated to the scrap heap. Educational and training procedures have been devised that show great promise of letting cerebral palsied people lead normal lives.

Abnormal deliveries are said to produce what Pasamanick (Pasamanick and Knobloch, 1963) calls a "**continuum of reproductive casualty**" ranging from cerebral palsy and epilepsy to elusive disturbances of functioning whose precise physical origins are hard to specify. Graham and associates (1962) found that children who had suffered anoxia at birth and were followed up at age three showed, as a group, some impairment of functioning, but that a goodly number of individuals apparently escaped any serious consequences. A number of other investigators, notably Pasamanick and Knobloch (1963), conclude that minor birth injuries to the brain are responsible for subtle effects that do not show up until later in life. These effects include poor motor coordination, hyperactivity, and impairments of symbolic functioning. Studies of children with known birth abnormalities show a higher incidence of such difficulties in later life than is found in the children of normal births. Similarly, retrospective studies of children with various academic and behavior problems show a higher-than-expected frequency of difficult or traumatic births (Kawi and Pasamanick, 1959). The use of high forceps to speed delivery carries a risk of brain damage. Heavy sedation of the mother during labor, as we noted in Chapter 1, produces sluggishness of some days' or weeks' duration in the neonate.

Even when actual injury to the brain cannot be demonstrated, there is some reason to suspect the presence of what is called **minimal brain damage** or **minimal brain dysfunction** (MBD) as a factor in various disturbances of behavior. Prechtl (Touwen and Prechtl, 1970) has given us the concept of "optimality" of functioning, and reports that any departure from optimality at birth foretells lasting effects. Notice that MBD, at this writing, has the status of a hypothetical construct, an idea invoked to explain behavior when no other obvious causes can be found. Whether MBD proves to be a useful explanation will depend, it seems to us, on devising accurate methods of differential diagnosis and distinctive treatment methods, medical or educational or both, specially suited to children who show the symptoms. Although they do not explicitly relate their findings to MBD, Bell et al. (1971) observe that children who are extremely reactive as neonates tend to be unusually low in responsiveness as preschool children.

Premature birth has it hazards, including those, mentioned earlier, associated with isolation. Prematurity may bring with it lasting impairment (Drillien, 1964), and occurs most often in conditions of poverty. It carries the threat of anoxia and also of excessive oxygen used to combat anoxia. Pure oxygen given in large quantities to premature babies can cause **retrolental fibroplasia**, changes in the internal structure of the eye which cause blindness. Since the discovery of the relationship between overgenerous use of oxygen and RLF, doctors are inclined to use oxygen sparingly with premature babies, and the incidence of RLF has declined following a brief (1940–1955) period of increase. However, the physician sometimes has to choose between the risk of RLF and the risk of the baby's dying, and a certain incidence of RLF may be inevitable. We should remember, too, that the practice of putting premature babies in isolation has come under attack. It is not impossible that the increased stimulation given premature babies may improve their oxygen intake and make oxygen therapy less necessary.

Blindness from other causes and deafness may also be present at birth. It should be remembered that there are many degrees of blindness and deafness, causing various degrees of disability and calling for different sorts of remedies. There is even some evidence to suggest that the use of hearing aids in early infancy can overcome some congenital deafness or partial deafness (Griffiths, 1966). As we have said, the psychophysical techniques used to study neonatal perception may prove to be valuable diagnostic instruments for the early detection of sensory impairments (which also include color blindness and defective taste, smell, touch, pain sense, awareness of hot and cold, balance sense, and proprioception from the muscles and joints). There are, of course, various other physical disabilities that may be apparent at birth or shortly thereafter, some with psychological consequences: crippled limbs, heart malformations, harelip, cleft palate, and so forth. Fortunately, the total incidence of such conditions is quite low. Furthermore, surgery and the use of prosthetic devices, coupled with new educational techniques, are doing much to counteract even severe physical impairments.

Severe **mental retardation**, sometimes associated with demonstrable physical deficiencies and sometimes without known cause, may become apparent only during the course of infancy. Severely retarded infants are usually characterized by poor muscle tone and physical inactivity, emotional unresponsiveness, and greatly delayed development, so that they may still be lying helpless while their counterparts

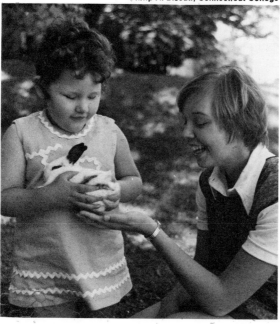

▲

A blind child being given special tactile experience.

A deaf child learns to feel the muscular vibrations and breath changes of normal speech.

▼

are scuttling about on all fours or even toddling. Moderate and mild degrees of mental retardation are extremely difficult to detect in infancy and may be reflected not at all in the baby's physical, motor, and emotional development. We must also bear in mind the wide range of normal development among infants, and parents should not rush to the conclusion that slower than average maturation means that their baby is mentally retarded. Many normal and even superior babies develop slowly early in life but, in their own good time, catch up.

Baby tests may indeed detect severe impairment, but otherwise are worthless for predicting later intellectual status. In general, if a baby is reasonably active and alert, responds emotionally to people and situations (and fear and rage are perfectly normal responses to some stimuli, including doting visitors who move in too fast), and if his pediatrician is satisfied with his progress, he is probably normal. Unvarying apathy seems to be the most important single danger sign. Gaze aversion, even to the mother, and failure to smile are sometimes serious indicators, as may be the baby's not reaching out his arms to be picked up. It is becoming evident, though, that the effects of emotional deprivation, stimulus deprivation, and cognitive deprivation take hold in infancy, and some unknown number of physically normal babies has almost certainly been made retarded by the lack of appropriate attention, vocal and verbal stimulation, play, and playthings. It used to be taken for granted that mentally defective babies should be whisked off to the nearest institution and forgotten. Nowadays, with the realization that putting a baby in an institution can be a premature entombment, and that much can be done to help flawed babies, there is a far greater tendency to keep them at home and to give them as nearly normal an upbringing as possible.

Pediatricians and child psychiatrists have come to recognize a condition called simply **failure to thrive**, marked by deficient physical development in the absence of any organic impairment (Leonard et al., 1966). Failure to thrive may be associated with a number of different specific symptoms; feeding problems, chronic vomiting, diarrhea, constipation, distended bowels, sleep disturbances, and chronic crying and irritability are among the most common. Failure to thrive seems to be caused by disturbed relations between the baby and his parents, who show serious inadequacies in their personal functioning, as parents and otherwise. It greatly resembles the effects of institutionalization. Another possible sign of infantile psychopathology is chronic and severe body-rocking, crib-rocking, or head-banging, analogous to the stereotyped, repetitive movements to be observed in some zoo animals. Less intense rocking or banging, however, may occur in perfectly sound babies. We have already mentioned, in Chapter 3, the **battered child syndrome** as one manifestation of disturbed parent-child relations. As more public attention is given to brutality toward children, the more widespread physical abuse seems to be.

Toddlerhood and the Preschool Years

By the end of infancy, any severe hereditary or congenital physical defects are likely to have come to light (although a few rare inherited conditions like Hunting-ton's chorea, a degenerative disease of the central nervous system, do not appear until maturity). By early childhood, more distinctly psychological problems sometimes appear. One such problem may be that of intermediate mental inadequacy, which may show up in greatly delayed language development or in failure to make normal progress from infantile speech to more mature forms. Mental inadequacy may, of course, have a physical basis, but we are often at a loss to account for it. In the absence of gross physical signs, however, special education of the kind pioneered by Samuel Kirk (1958, 1962) can do a great deal to improve the intellectual functioning of seemingly retarded children, especially when begun early. In general, as the child gets older, he has to solve increasingly complex problems, and as life gets more complicated, lesser degrees of intellectual inadequacy become evident. On the other hand, slow learners do learn, and, given sufficient opportunity, many retarded people eventually reach a respectable intellectual level.

Some toddlers and preschool children—and even an occasional infant—live in a state of **chronic, diffuse emotional strain** which hampers their functioning and development and may foreshadow more serious disturbances to come. There are a number of signs which can tell parents or teachers when a child is suffering in this way. These are not signs for which adults need go looking, but to which they can be sensitive and recognize when they do occur. They are not signs of serious psychological disturbance, but of distress to be relieved. The reader should remember that no *single* sign need be cause for alarm; it is when they appear in combination that action may possibly be called for. One of the most sensitive barometers of a child's emotional state is the quality of his voice. A child whose voice is too consistently shrill, or harsh, or muffled, or flat and toneless, may—barring specific hearing defects—be having trouble with his emotions. He may be feeling emotions too strong for him to manage; he may be bottling up his feelings without any channels of direct discharge; or—even more serious —his capacity for emotional responses may have been muted or deadened. Chronic emotional distress often shows up, too, in the psychosomatic evidences of autonomic imbalance of an acute or chronic nature, as on a child's skin, in the form of rapid and seemingly unprovoked flushing, paling, and sweating—and the fair-skinned reader should know that dark-skinned people also flush and go ashen, if not pale. Similarly, emotional strain can even provoke or contribute to the appearance of eczema. Chronic distress can sometimes be seen in the qualities of body movement, whether tense jerkiness or flaccid sluggishness. It may be revealed in constant sighing or yawning or swallowing. It can show up in digestive upsets such as frequent vomiting or urination without adequate physical cause. Sleep disturbances, including frequent nightmares and strong bedtime fears, may betray a more pervasive state of strain. The child who spends *long* periods doing nothing, the one who *constantly* plays with his genitals, or the child with *persistent* tics and twitches may be having emotional difficulties. In overall behavior, chronic stress may be expressed in either agitated restlessness or in dull listlessness —notice again that flattened or missing emotion is as much an indicator as emotional pyrotechnics. We should emphasize that emotional upset in children in this age range is directly and intimately tied to body functioning, an anticipation of the hysterical and psychosomatic manifestations we shall talk about later.

The stress signaled by symptoms of these kinds can often be relieved quite simply, by giving the child more overt affection or a little more freedom, by setting limits more definitely or by scaling down the standards he has to meet, by simplifying his environment or diversifying it, or, if he is old enough and if it can be done tactfully and sympathetically, by helping him talk about his feelings and by reassuring him about them. The important point is to try to understand the particular sources of the particular child's unhappiness and to rearrange things accordingly. Sometimes nothing can be done short of removing the child from his family, and since we are woefully short of good child-care facilities, this is hardly a solution. Sometimes, too, we cannot unravel the causes of a child's distress, and sometimes, even when we can, his reaction patterns have so solidified that easy solutions are no longer possible. In some cases, adults may be completely unaware of how their own behavior affects the child—a mother who screams at her children wonders why the children scream so much; or the father who whips his children or constantly ridicules and belittles them cannot understand why they show him so little affection or respect; or parents of both sexes are puzzled when their attempts to breed self-sufficiency in the child make him cling harder than ever—and a certain number of parents seem incapable of learning that it is their behavior that produces in the child the very symptoms that they worry about. Various forms of psychotherapy may be helpful with young children, although more often it is the parents who need help in understanding themselves in relation to the child. The professional can sometimes help by explaining to parents what children are like (remember that people lived with children a long time before anybody began to notice their special characteristics), how differently they operate from adults, and how different their life-spaces are.

More profound psychological disturbance may appear during this period in the form of **childhood schizophrenia**, an early form of the disorder which we shall discuss more fully under adolescence. In addition to the fairly classical, adultlike schizophrenia (which we, along with Szasz [1961], prefer to think of as a characteristic style of behaving rather than a disease entity) found in occasional young children, a special variety has been recognized, described, and studied just within the last three decades. Kanner (1944) has labeled this disorder **early infantile autism** and considers it a condition distinct from schizophrenia. We shall discuss autism in some detail because it is an easily recognizable pattern and, although uncommon, seems to be on the increase. The apparent increase may be simply a product of improved diagnosis which distinguishes autism from mental deficiency, although the picture has become obscured by the introduction of the concept of minimal brain dysfunction (see p. 506) to account for some cases of what formerly would have been called autism. Certain features of autism are simply exaggerations of normal childhood behavior, but exaggerations so gross and so rigid that they become qualitatively different from the normal.

Autism may develop gradually, from early infancy onward, or it may appear almost abruptly, often between ages two and three, following a seemingly normal course of development. Parents report of the autistic infant that he does not call forth the ordinary parental sentiments, perhaps because he himself seems unresponsive to human stimulation. He may be described as "a very good baby," content to lie isolated in his crib without yelling constantly for attention. He may not smile, or he may smile at things rather than people, he may be indifferent to cuddling or even withdraw from it, he may never hold out his arms to ask to be picked up. Some—but not all—autistic children are hyperactive and hypermotile; some are expert escape artists and defy all parental efforts to confine them to crib, room, house, and yard; and some on the loose scale fire escapes and rooftops. They seem to have little sense of personal danger and repeatedly suffer severe injuries with no loss of the drive to keep going. Indifference to pain is thought by some psychiatrists to be one of the outstanding features of autism. Some autistic children show remarkable mechanical ingenuity, learning to operate latches, knobs, locks, and light switches, and to take things apart and put them back together at a very early age.

When autism appears after age two, parents may first be made aware that something is wrong by the child's failure to talk. Even more generally, autistic children fail to show the ordinary imitative behavior found in most babies. Quite commonly, the autistic child comes into professional hands initially as a case of suspected deafness. Some autistic children eventually learn to talk, in some cases very well, but their speech is likely to show certain abnormalities. One feature prominent in the speech of many autistic children is **echolalia**, a compulsive parroting of what they hear. Instead of answering a question, the child may simply repeat it, sometimes at great length. Such children appear to have unusual difficulty in making the transition to the use of the first person singular pronoun, simply referring to himself as he hears others do. Or the child may pick up a phrase, a name, a snatch of song, or even a long verse, and repeat it endlessly, sometimes as a reply to something addressed to him.

The most central and pervasive feature of autism is the lack of human contact, physical, visual, or verbal. The child may seem emotionally intense, but his emotions do not fit the usual qualitative categories of anger, fear, amusement, and so forth. His feelings seem to be bound up in inanimate—preferably mechanical or physically manipulable—things. The autistic child is fascinated by rhythmic, repetitive patterns. Not only does he memorize and repeat songs and verses, but he can spend protracted periods switching a light on and off, flushing a toilet, watching a record-player turntable spin, lighting matches, or operating a mechanical toy. Some psychiatrists have sought to capitalize therapeutically on the autistic child's mechanical preoccupations by having children communicate with a computer that asks the child questions (via tape) and then asks further questions depending on how the child replied to the one before. There is reason to wonder, of course, whether this approach may even further reinforce the child's attachment to machines to the neglect of people. The child himself may like to spin or twirl or roll, machinelike, or he may adopt ritualized, perseverative gestures or mannerisms. Like the fictionalized Jordi (Rubin, 1960), many autistic children carry with them at all times a "jiggler," typically a toy

tied to the end of a string so that it can be taken out and jiggled in moments of tension. Autistic children show little interest in sex and rarely masturbate. They often do very well in unambiguous school subjects like mathematics, and some can perform prodigious feats of memory, analogous to those of the idiot savant (who may indeed have been, in some cases, an unrecognized autistic), such as being able to say on what day of the week any date over the past hundred years fell. The autistic child is not likely to have highly elaborate delusional ideas, although he may hate, for instance, to walk past an open garbage can for fear it will swallow him up. In general, it would seem that the autistic child has identified with the nonhuman world and treats other people—without hatred or malice—as though they are only another kind of thing. At the extreme, we may get the child who seems himself to have become a machine, as in Bettelheim's (1959, 1967) case of Joey the Mechanical Boy.

Autistic boys outnumber autistic girls four to one. Typically, the autistic child is a firstborn, but some autistic boys have an older sister or brother. All reports agree that he is usually the child of intelligent but rigid and undemonstrative parents who may not comprehend the special needs of babies and who may even find it distasteful to minister to so messy a creature as a young baby—or perhaps only this particular baby. Rimland (1964) has proposed that autism represents genetically high intelligence that has somehow been flawed, as by a disturbance in the gene system. In most cases, we find more plausible the hypothesis that autism develops when the environment fails to provide the usual props of emotional development, leading to severely defective identification. On the other hand, we must acknowledge a residue of cases for which environmental explanations seem not to hold.

As in all nature-nurture discussions, of course, no absolute answer is possible simply because we cannot hold the variables constant, and most especially when we have to deal with retrospective data. Although it might appear from the autistic child's unresponsiveness that he is emotionally inert, close observation suggests that emotional responsiveness may simply have withered from lack of feedback, leaving him with emotions that are poorly differentiated as well as largely unexpressed. Away from home, the autistic child is prone to panic, indicating that he may have a stronger attachment to his family than we realize. Fear of strange situations might also account for his good behavior in school and for the fact that he seems rarely to get to know his classmates. Autistic behavior often seems to resemble an attempt to find refuge, order, control, predictability, meaning, and feeling in relations with things or with human beings reduced to the thing level. Ignorant of the meaning of human emotional relations, the child can find satisfaction in the play of empty sensory patterns. His adoption of rigid and repetitive behavior patterns can be seen as a way of preserving a fragile integrity and also as a defense against boredom.

About a third of autistic children are reported to grow into reasonably normal adulthood, although Kessler (1966, ch. 11) questions whether the once-autistic child could ever hope to form true friendships and love relationships, or to establish meaningful communication beyond routine formulas and procedures; she also points out, however, that we have had no follow-

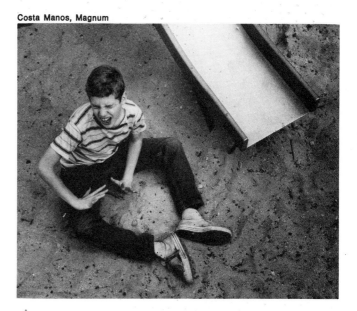

Childhood psychosis.

up studies that would give us this information. According to Eisenberg and Kanner (1956), the best predictor of recovery is the acquisition of language by age five, and the most important factor in making recovery possible is acceptance by an understanding teacher at school—an acceptance made difficult by the child's conspicuous abnormality and the sometimes disruptive effects of his occasionally tangential behavior. The usual therapies seem to be of little avail. There is some evidence that autism or at least some of its manifestations may be amenable to "behavior therapy," based on the principles of operant conditioning, in which desired forms of behavior (or approximation thereof) are promptly reinforced and undesirable forms ignored (Wolf et al., 1964; Hewett, 1965; Grossberg, 1964; Krasner, 1971). Behavior therapy seems to work quite well for many simple conditions, particularly those marked by a single symptom. It appears that a widely discussed case of protracted sneezing was kept going partly by reinforcing effects of the attention it attracted; the sneezing stopped when sneezes met mild punishment (electric shock to the finger) instead of concerned attention.

Returning to more common types of disturbances in this developmental period, we saw in Chapter 6 that the self-awareness of the preschool years often brings with it a number of **fears**—of death and bogymen, of bodily mutilation, of terrors hidden in the darkness, of being orphaned, and so forth. Sometimes these are expressed openly, sometimes they are denied; sometimes a child forms a fear of some specifically threatening object, and sometimes he projects a nameless or unacknowledged dread upon some real or invented menace (such a projection is called a **phobia**). If the child's phantoms are poohpoohed, or if they fail to take explicit shape, his fears may be more diffusely expressed, in a generalized shrinking timidity, in somatic symptoms, or in nightmares. When the child is basically secure, specific fears, especially if they can be formulated and dealt with sympathetically and realistically, come and go and do not constitute a major problem. It is only when the child becomes obsessed with some particular threat, amounting to a phobia, or when he is too pervasively and inexplicably anxious about everything, when his nightmares come too often and too terrifyingly, that his fears become symptomatic of real personality disturbance.

Late infancy, toddlerhood, and the preschool years are an especially unfavorable time for **hospitalization and surgery**. This is the period when children can least tolerate prolonged separation from their parents, and when body integrity, the focus of many fears, becomes a major issue. The best opinion seems to indicate that elective surgery should be deferred, wherever it is medically possible, at least until age three and preferably to age five or later. Very young infants seem to tolerate surgery well, especially if their mothers stay with them in the hospital. Past infancy, the important factor is being able to talk to the child about what is going to happen and prepare him for what might otherwise be a seriously disorienting experience. No matter at what age the child goes to the hospital, he should be told the truth; hospitalization is doubly traumatic if the child has been led to believe he was going to the circus, or to visit friends (Levy, 1945; Robertson, 1970).

Obviously, conditions arise which make it imperative to operate on or hospitalize young children. When this happens special measures are needed to prevent secondary effects. In the matter of surgery, for instance, many doctors, recognizing the importance of emotional as well as surgical considerations, have learned to establish a relationship with the child, to let him cooperate in preliminary procedures, to avoid forcible handling, and to let him know as clearly and unthreateningly as possible what to expect. They have learned to give the child sedation in his own room before he is taken to the operating room. Preferably, a parent should be with the child both when he is put to sleep and when he comes out of the anesthetic. As for hospitalization itself, especially if it is prolonged, the main secondary effect to be feared is lassitude and apathy or sustained and generalized anxiety. One countermeasure is the hospital play program, where professionals and volunteers work to give pediatric patients the individual affection and stimulation necessary to normal functioning, and for which overworked doctors and nurses may not have time. A perhaps more radical measure, adopted by a few far-seeing hospitals, is to allow mothers to stay with their sick children, or to visit them at any hour or for as long as they wish. Not only does this work to the psychological benefit of young patients, but mothers can assume many routine nursing duties—trained nurses being in short supply—and lighten the hospital's administrative load. Sometimes, of course, it is the mother who has to go to the hospital, and the dangers of separation are still there.

In the preschool years, when language is being elaborated and consolidated, **speech defects** may be noted. Certain of these may have their origins in defects of the speech apparatus, making articulation difficult. The great majority of defects of articulation are due simply to immaturity, and the child straightens out his own pronunciation as he grows. Sometimes, though, these defects linger beyond their appointed time. When the child continues using baby talk long after his contemporaries have left it behind, it may be a sign that his parents are encouraging it by talking baby talk to him, or by overmothering and overprotecting him, or by making babyhood too attractive. When the child first begins to talk, of course, parental baby talk is almost inevitable. Once the child is well launched in speaking, however, it is time for the parents to resume using English. If the child reverts to baby talk after abandoning it, it may be a sign of regression due to some transient or permanent emotional strain. In such cases, baby talk is not something to be attacked directly. Indeed, nonorganic speech defects in general are cured not by direct attack but by providing the child with good speech models.

Probably the most frequent form of speech disorder in young children is **stuttering** (speech specialists today make no distinction between stuttering and stammering). Various theories to account for and various therapies to help stuttering have been advanced. Most theories, whether psychological (in terms of stuttering as a symptom of emotional disturbance) or physiological (in terms of short circuits in the brain), have not been able to withstand the facts, or else have been so abstract as to be untestable. One promising approach has placed stuttering partly under experimental control (Fillenbaum, 1963). It is possible that in "natural" stuttering, as well as in stuttering induced artificially in the laboratory, the critical factor is a disturbance of feedback. Studies indicate that a smooth flow of speech is dependent on the speaker's listening to and monitoring, without any particular awareness of the process, his own speech output. Normally, the lag between speaking and hearing oneself speak is infinitesimal. Stuttering can be induced experimentally in anyone simply by producing a time lag of about one quarter of a second between the time a person speaks and the time his voice comes back to him. This is accomplished by having the person speak into a tape recorder which after the predetermined interval plays his voice back to him through headphones. (One can also, using videotape recorders, produce delayed visual feedback, with similar results [Smith et al., 1960]).

Most therapies, it appears, at best can help the severe stutterer live more comfortably with his stuttering; few cures are claimed by responsible therapists. At worst, for reasons that will become clear in a moment, therapy—particularly if begun too early—may even exacerbate stuttering and make its removal more unlikely. For, along with Johnson (Johnson et al., 1942), the authors feel that the bulk of stuttering is created by adults who, reacting to normal speech hesitations and gropings, force the child to pay attention to his speech, generating a crippling self-consciousness about it, like that of the centipede who had gotten along perfectly well until an admiring ant asked him which leg he moved first, thereby rendering him unable to move.

All young children stumble and hesitate and make errors in speaking, but this only becomes a fixed pattern when parents hear the child's fumblings as stuttering and try to correct them. As with pronunciation, the child, left to himself, corrects his speech production and, with increasing practice, becomes more fluent. Once the child hears his own speech as stuttering, he becomes bound up in trying to control it, and then begins to stutter in earnest, exploding his words and writhing with the effort to keep his speech under control. Whatever other emotional or neurological factors may lie behind stuttering, there is ample evidence that it can be created; hence, it is a poor idea to tell a preschool child that he can talk better, that he should try to speak more slowly, or that he should repeat himself and "this time say it nicely"— which does not mean that parents should never correct those errors that have no special connection with stuttering.

Again in this section, let us emphasize that toddlerhood and the preschool years, too, have their normal "problems" calling for no special treatment whatever. Tantrums, negativism, destructiveness, toilet-training problems, thumb-sucking, masturbation, "selfishness," "cruelty," and so forth, are not at this age marks of derangement.

The Middle Years of Childhood

The most prominent difficulties of the middle years revolve around schooling and the child's ability to learn. **Learning difficulties** arise from many sources. First, there is **mental retardation**, intellectual disability not so severe as to incapacitate the child, but severe enough to interfere with school work. A number of retarded children have intellectual abilities equal to their daily childhood pursuits—and even, later on, to simple jobs and having a family—but insufficient to master all the sometimes artificial and arbitrary tasks demanded by school. The limitations of such a child's intelligence may not be evident until he goes to school and is asked to deal with abstract symbols.

Once his limitations have been detected and verified by careful individual testing and evaluation, two courses of management are possible. The child can be written off as a lost cause and left to suffer out the years he is legally required to spend in school—there is special help available for almost all severely handicapped children, but the merely dull child may not be eligible for it. When such a course is followed, as it all too often is, the child can easily develop a sense of failure and worthlessness. Even his classmates are likely to take over the school's opinion of him and treat him as an outcast—except, of course, when he has some special socially redeeming quality such as athletic ability. He can react to his sense of inadequacy passively, sharing the world's contempt, or he can deny it and rebel against it in truancy or delinquency. In any case, he is not likely to derive much benefit from his incarceration in school.

The second course is to make allowances for his limitations, to find out what things he can do well, to encourage him to pursue such talents as he may have, and, patiently and sympathetically, to give him as much formal education as possible. If this second course is followed, he can have the sense of worth that everybody is entitled to, he can accept his limitations realistically because he also knows his capabilities, and he stands a good chance of enjoying life and of making his own valuable, if modest, contribution to society.

Not all learning difficulties, however, are due to organic limitations. A large variety of factors, including malnutrition and low socioeconomic status, can interfere with learning. A number of children of apparently poor endowment, for instance, have turned out to be suffering from some degree of **hearing loss**, short of deafness, or **impaired vision**, short of blindness. With these disabilities brought to light and corrected as much as possible, children can be put into classes (if necessary, with special facilities) where they can go on to normal achievements—always provided that they have not already been damaged by the experience of failure. For another common source of learning difficulty, which sometimes appears as a secondary effect of physical handicaps, is emotional interference.

Emotional interferences with learning are generally referred to as **learning blocks**. They most often appear in a context of parental overambition and pressure, which turn the child away from the learning process and make of it something extrinsic to his own wishes. Some children try hard to measure up to their parents' expectations, but the very effort that goes into trying produces anxiety that interferes with learning; each failure becomes more frustrating, generating new anxiety and confusion and making the next failure all the more probable. For other children, nonachievement becomes a weapon in an unconscious revolt against parental pressures. The child goes through all the motions of studying hard, applying all the learning devices he has been urged to use, but still, somehow, nothing seems to stay with him. He is consciously blameless, but he can still manage a sort of secret satisfaction at the distress his parents feel at his failure. At the same time, he neutralizes his parents, since he is already apparently doing everything possible, so that they cannot blame him either. Sarason and collaborators (1964) have devoted a great deal of attention to the role of anxiety in school performance, to the relation between anxiety and intelligence-test performance, and to the special kind of "test anxiety" that afflicts some children in the course of being evaluated. There seems to be little doubt that anxiety or lack of it plays an important part in how well a child does in school, but the data so far do not permit any broad generalizations.

In addition to difficulty with school work in general, there are a number of special disabilities centered about particular kinds of skills or materials, such as reading, spelling, or arithmetic. Possibly the most important of these, because it involves the most basic and general academic skill, is **reading disability**. Theorists have had a field day explaining reading disability in terms of brain function, sinistrality, mixed cerebral dominance, emotional blocks, lack of perceptual maturation to the point of "reading readiness," in happy disregard of contrary evidence. It now seems likely that ease in learning to read hinges almost entirely on prior experience—with shape discrimination, with shape naming, with learning the alphabet, with being read to, with drawing, and with language in general—to the point where it seems safe to say that for most children learning to read happens before they reach school, and that reading instruction simply crystallizes and organizes the ways of perceiving that the child has already acquired. Reading disability, then, is probably most often the result of impoverished perceptual and linguistic experience in the years before school, which would account for its high incidence in deprived groups. Before we draw any sweeping conclusions, though, we should note that many people have a low opinion of the tests used to measure reading skills. **Arithmetic** or **number disability** used to be fairly common, but there is hope that the new approaches to teaching math starting in the early grades will help to eliminate this problem.

Lapouse (1966) has investigated the frequency of psychiatric symptoms in a representative sample of 482 school-age children. The incidence of single severe symptoms was surprisingly high (40 percent of the children had seven or more fears or worries and almost 20 percent wet the bed at least occasionally), but these were only somewhat correlated with chronic maladjustment. Younger children showed more symptoms than older ones, but there were no differences between boys and girls.

A study by Achenbach (1966) proposes a new classification for children's psychiatric conditions based on the clustering of symptoms. Achenbach's first classification is according to whether children show internalizing symptoms (those turned against the person himself), externalizing symptoms (directed against the outside world), or less clearly directed symptoms (unclassified). The boys in Achenbach's sample tend to be externalizers at all ages except, for reasons unknown, eleven, twelve, and fifteen. Girls tend to be internalizers from age six onward, except at age twelve. Boys and girls show somewhat different symptom groupings. Both male and female externalizers show aggressive and delinquent behavior, but only the boys have sexual problems. Many more male than female externalizers show hyper-reactive (emotionally explosive) behavior. Males from all three groups show schizoid thinking and behavior, but only internalizing and unclassified girls do so. Internalizing boys and girls had obsessions, compulsions, and phobias (one cluster) and somatic complaints, but internalizing girls also had trouble with obesity, depression, and anxiety. The female unclassified group included a few subjects who had trouble with bedwetting and other immaturities, which were not observed in the male subjects. Provocative though Achenbach's scheme is, it must be viewed as provisional until tested against an even larger sample of children.

Delinquency

Delinquency often has its beginnings in the school years, although its most serious manifestations usually occur in adolescence. It is simple enough to define delinquent acts—stealing, vandalism, physical aggression, and so forth—in social terms, defined by consequences, but all these acts may have quite different psychological sources in the individual. Therefore, we are forced to draw a number of distinctions among the psychological origins of delinquent acts. First, we can recognize **normal** or casual delinquent behavior. Individually, probably every six- or seven-year-old does a certain amount of experimental stealing from his mother's pocketbook. This is not serious and will usually be outgrown without any special measures. In the gang, especially the boy gang, there is usually a certain amount of prankishness which often has a superficially delinquent character. In addition, boys are expected to do a certain amount of street fighting to prove their mettle. These manifestations again are not serious, and most children develop their own inhibitions and controls without any action by the authorities.

Second, there is what we may term **subcultural** (sometimes called **socialized**) delinquency. This is the second most common

kind after normal delinquency. It is characteristic of the lower-class child who grows up into a ready-made delinquent culture within his own society, or turns to it when he finds himself blocked or rejected by the middle class. This is primarily gang delinquency, although it may be the breeding ground for later individual criminality. The important thing to recognize about subcultural delinquency is that, psychologically, it is not delinquency at all. It is only delinquency in terms of middle-class mores, which do not apply. The gang member is behaving in ways sanctioned by the culture he belongs to, and need feel absolutely no guilt. Indeed, to question the mores of the gang would be far more likely to make him feel guilty than almost any "delinquent" act he might perform. Subcultural delinquency, insofar as it is a gang enterprise, is more likely to be male than female. However, girl fighting gangs do exist. In addition, girls may be accepted into boy gangs, where they play the roll of queen bee or camp follower. Most female delinquency, though, including sexual delinquency, is likely to be of the neurotic or the acting-out type described below. A special form of subcultural delinquency is the "rat pack" gangs of middle-years and young adolescent boys that have sprung up in the city, robbing or beating victims of opportunity. They have a psychopathic indifference to the feelings of their victims, although closer questioning often reveals fierce hostility to the haves of society (Stevens, 1971).

Third, there is **neurotic** delinquency. This often takes the form of stealing from his parents (or sometimes a teacher) by a child who feels isolated. Such stealing is often symbolic. The child is not interested in the money as such (he may even throw it away or lose it, or simply forget what he

Ken Heyman

Crime and punishment. Large numbers of people are vocally concerned about what is perceived as a "breakdown of law and order," but few are willing to think through the issues involved.

did with it), but is, in effect, stealing the love he feels his parents will not give him. Or he may, unconsciously, steal as a way of punishing his parents for not loving him. He may steal in ways that seem to insure his being caught, as though seeking punishment to relieve some unconscious guilt. In some cases, children use the money they steal to buy favor with their peers, status they are otherwise denied. Obviously, neurotic delinquency does not call for punishment but for treatment. To avoid confusion, however, let us point out that neurotic delinquency is not a *neurosis*, a state of internal conflict which inhibits action and is expressed in particular symptoms such as diffuse anxiety, compulsive rituals, or somatic complaints. We call this delinquency neurotic because it is an *indirect* expression of an unformulated wish or need.

The fourth type of delinquency, **acting-out** delinquency, where the individual freely expresses his impulses, particularly hostile ones, has something in common with all the others. Acting out refers to the free, deliberate, and often malicious indulgence of impulse, particularly in the sphere of aggression but also in other areas of delinquency such as vandalism. It is essentially a form of revolt. Like subcultural delinquency, it may be more or less consciously directed against the middle-class morality. Unlike subcultural delinquency, it may be more an individual matter requiring less sanction from group mores. Furthermore, the acting-out delinquent may himself come from the middle or upper classes; he may be motivated by hostility either against the adult world in general or against his parents in particular, or by simple boredom. Like neurotic delinquency, acting out may express unformulated needs

520

that have nothing to do with the specific acts committed. In common with psychopathic behavior, to be described below, acting-out delinquency may betray a brutal disregard for other people's feelings. Unlike the psychopath, however, for whom other people's feelings simply do not count, the individual who acts out may quite consciously want to inflict pain, even though he may not know why, or he may simply move trancelike through an orgy of destruction. He may well be a relatively gifted and forceful individual, caught up in a pattern of resentments and unstructured cravings and impulses, who has not found constructive ways to use his gifts.

Fifth and finally, there is **psychopathic** delinquency. Psychopathy certainly begins very early in life. Indeed, some authors still speak of **constitutional** (that is, hereditary or "built-in") **psychopathic personality**. The consensus seems now to be that psychopathy represents a failure of the basic identification process in the first five years of life, so that the individual becomes incapable of true feelings for others. This failure can in some cases be traced to a disruption of normal family relationships. However, it is worth noting that the psychopath has an essentially intact personality, but lacks strong emotional ties to reality. The psychopath is remarkable for his emotional blandness, particularly in regard to actions that would profoundly shock the normal individual. He is virtually lacking in conscience or superego, although he professes a recognition of and can speak smoothly in terms of devotion to accepted values. He makes glib promises and resolutions, but meanwhile may be picking the pocket of the person he is talking to. He is profoundly egocentric and can never quite see his own responsibility for anything that goes wrong. The psychopath's measured intelligence is within the normal range but his thinking is essentially superficial and external. In spite of ability to learn things, he does not profit by the lessons of his own experience, so that his behavior is out of keeping with what he abstractly knows. In fact, he not only seems indifferent to the consequences for other people of what he does, he does not seem concerned about the almost certainly unfortunate consequences for himself—he is incurably, unrealistically optimistic.

The psychopath steals even when he is sure to be caught. He lies even when there is no earthly reason for lying. He may be assaultive or even murderous—although many psychopaths are not at all physically aggressive—but even his violence or sadism has a shallow, unfeeling quality quite unlike that of the child who has a chip on his shoulder. He does physical harm as casually and unthinkingly as he lies or steals. Because he can learn the formulas to which other people respond, he can manipulate people, at least until they come to detect the meaninglessness of what he says. It is not that he specifically wishes people ill, but only that their needs and feelings have no immediacy for him. His own needs and wishes are paramount and absolute. Because he is normally intelligent, he can undertake elaborate plans for getting what he wants, but his thinking, which does not take full account of other people's views, is likely to go awry, and his schemes to collapse. Childhood psychopaths used to supply the bulk of the adult criminal population, but not all of them end up as criminals. Some simply become unpleasant characters who exploit and betray their friends and families but stay within the law. Some become drifters or marginal personalities. Some settle down to shallow respectability on a low socioeconomic level. A few, turning their talents into socially acceptable channels, become financial successes, but it is doubtful that they are able to establish satisfactory personal relationships. The political rabble-rouser, the lynch-mob leader, is likely to be a psychopath. Because of the psychopath's lack of strong feeling, punishment does not change his ways, he is extremely hard to deal with in psychotherapy, and we cannot be hopeful about those who are already among us. In terms of prevention, considering the apparent origins of psychopathy in a disturbance of early emotional relationships, we can only point to all the things we have said so far about sound emotional relationships in infancy and early childhood.

Notice that we have left out of account in discussing delinquency a whole group of people who are in varying degrees branded as criminals: drug addicts, political extremists who use violent tactics, draft evaders, deserters, and those who simply feel alienated from present society. Some such people may indeed be psychopaths but this by no means explains the complex totality of motives in people who live outside society's customary framework.

Adolescence

The excesses of normal adolescent behavior, like those of normal preschool behavior, often reach emotional extremes that might lead some people to conclude that adolescence itself may be a form of insanity. We hope we have made clear that such is not the case. Nevertheless, adolescence is a vulnerable period, in terms of both the painful problems the adolescent has to face and the reawakening of past developmental issues that were only partially resolved. (Psychiatrists speak of the disturbances of adolescence as **hebetic** or **heboid**). It is during adolescence that a true **schizophrenic breakdown** may first occur; indeed, schizophrenia used to be known as **dementia praecox**, insanity of the young. Many normal adolescent traits in their extreme forms approximate schizophrenic behavior. Too persistent feelings of dislocation and estrangement, total docility or exaggerated rebelliousness, emotional volatility, feelings that everybody is against one, talk of suicide, and even idealism that seems to be a denial of reality may all have a schizophrenic flavor. Needless to say, most adolescents have developed a tough core of security and an anchorage in reality that permit them to withstand and thrive on the stresses of this period. Since, however, a few do break down, we should attempt to see the form that breakdowns are most likely to take.

Schizophrenia is actually a label that embraces several psychoses. All of these have in common a distortion of normal emotional responses and include ideas or feelings about reality which are incompatible with normal views. Ordinarily, the whole of reality is reshaped in keeping with a central conflict within the schizophrenic. This reshaping may take the form of **delusions**, unfounded but no less serious beliefs to the effect that people are trying to poison the individual, that they are accusing him of depraved practices or inviting him to engage in them, or that he has been endowed with special powers and dispensations. Schizophrenics may have delusions about their own bodies: that they are corrupted by strange diseases, that they are being controlled by malignant forces, that they are sensitive to radio waves, that their bodies contain various kinds of machines. Sometimes beliefs of this sort take the more concrete form of hallucinations, imaginary but nevertheless vivid experiences where the individual hears voices talking to him or about him, sees visions, or smells strange or foul odors. Notice that most sane people hallucinate occasionally, as when one hears his name called even though no one has spoken.

Schizophrenia does not always take such elaborate or explicit forms, however. Sometimes it is expressed in total apathy and inactivity, sometimes in grossly inappropriate emotional responses to standard reality. The individual may be quite unfeeling about something that is of vital importance to him, he may giggle foolishly in response to almost anything that happens, or he may fly into a rage over trifling setbacks. Some schizophrenics seem to be contented in their fantasy worlds, some seem to lack any emotion, some are at constant war with their surroundings, while others seem to seethe with bottled-up feelings. They may feel harried by their enemies, they may be verbally abusive, they may take pleasure in behaving outrageously, or they may be assaultive, self-destructive, or murderous. Two words of caution, however. At least some schizophrenic manifestations seem to be produced by the conditions of incarceration, so that what is taken for cause may actually be effect. Second, many people labeled as schizophrenic are diagnosed not so much on the content of their behavior as its manner. Thus, it is automatically assumed that a person must be "crazy" if he

harangues a bunch of perfect strangers on a street corner or a bus, even if the content of his harangue is nothing more than was said on the editorial page of the local paper.

Quite frequently, the central conflict of schizophrenia is a sexual (or homosexual) one, although often heavily disguised. Feelings of uncleanness, feelings of lack of control, a sense of being unwanted, a sense of vulnerability, all may enter into the schizophrenic pattern. We might add that males are more prone than females to schizophrenia (as to most forms of psychological disturbance), but some schizophrenic girls and women show the disorder in its most virulent forms. Most basically, the schizophrenic has a seriously disturbed self-image, and when he turns violent against the outside world it seems to be in an attempt to destroy the mirror in which he sees his own unbearably horrible reflection—or he may simply turn away from the world to deny the reality of his own feelings.

One hears schizophrenia spoken of as incurable. This is not necessarily the case. For one thing, the very notion of "curing" schizophrenia perpetuates the image of a "mental illness" rather than an orientation to the world. A number of schizophrenics recover, sometimes spontaneously, either temporarily or permanently. Some can live comfortably as long as they are in a sheltered environment, whether in a hospital or in a community that understands their vulnerabilities and needs. Some show improvement in response to a number of treatments used singly or in combination: tranquilizing drugs, energizing drugs, and individual or group psychotherapy, among others. Some respond well to arrangements that permit them to live in the hospital but work or go to school in the community, or to live at home and spend their days in therapeutic programs in the clinic or hospital.

There is continuing debate on the origins of schizophrenia (Rosenthal and Kety, 1968; reviewed by S. Kessler, 1969), with many authorities convinced that it is primarily genetic. Even among those of a genetic bent, however, there is considerable dispute about the mechanics involved. The evidence is conflicting, and suggestions that we dichotomize people not as normal and schizophrenic but as normal and schizoid seem hardly to help, since schizoid is too fluid a concept. The most promising research is of the kind pioneered by Sarnoff Mednick, in which children are followed from birth, and the children of schizophrenic mothers reared in nonschizophrenic families being compared with those reared by their own mothers and with adopted children without a schizophrenic background. In any event, whatever the genetic contribution, many schizophrenics do recover.

There is a great gulf between the legal and practical view of what constitutes **sexual delinquency** in boys. For girls, the discrepancy is not so great, particularly if a girl incurs the biological penalty of becoming pregnant. For this reason, and because the adolescent girl may use sexual promiscuity as a weapon of revolt, sex offenses make up a very sizable proportion of delinquent behavior in girls. Psychologically, as we might expect from what was said in Chapter 11 about female sexuality, sexually delinquent behavior in girls often seems to have nonsexual origins. We have just pointed out that it may be an expression of adolescent revolt. It is rather often associated with simple-mindedness and a passive inclination to do what other people say. It may express a need for affection, for emotional contact and support in girls who lack warm attachments. In some cases, and under certain kinds of pressures, it appears to stem from a need to conform to group mores, from the threat of ostracism if one does not do as the others do. In general, sex delinquency in girls is often symptomatic of a deeper emotional disturbance or of personal inadequacy. Punitive measures are of little help and may only force a girl into a life of prostitution. Sympathetic case work, however, which can help the girl make practical adjustments, often accomplishes a rapid change. The second major kind of female delinquency is shoplifting, sometimes for fun or profit but more often in response to neurotic needs.

Atypical sexual behavior may appear in adolescence. Let us stress that not all departures from the sexual norm connote disturbed psychological functioning. They do so only to the extent that they become monomaniac obsessions or are forced on other people. In girls, homosexuality as a fixed pattern, although less frequent than in boys, is probably the form which sexual deviation most often takes. There appear to be two main motivations behind female homosexuality. The first is deep-rooted hostility toward or fear of males. The second is psychological masculinity, a wish to assume the male role—this often extends beyond sexual practices to such matters as dress, mannerisms, speech, and so forth. In the latter case, men are viewed not as enemies but as competitors. The possibility has been raised, but not yet researched, that both male and female homosexuality may be related to early disturbances of hormonal functioning.

In boys, there are several forms of sexual

deviation which may become serious problems during adolescence. It should be noted, however, that all these deviations may play a part in normal adolescent fantasies, and that some of them may actually be practiced experimentally, without their having any abnormal significance. Forcible rape, which normal boys may fantasize but are extremely unlikely to execute, is ordinarily a part of subcultural delinquency, acting-out delinquency, or psychopathy, and does not require further discussion here. Closely allied to rape is sexual sadism. As we know, sex and violence do often become interwoven, and for certain unstable personalities may be interchangeable. Much of the pornographic literature addressed to late-school-age and adolescent boys (which they claim not to like but read avidly) is a compound of sex and sadism. For some normal children, such literature may serve a positive function by reassuring them that their fantasies are shared by other people. For a few near-psychotic or psychotic children, however, such literature may possibly be pernicious, supplying a prototype for acting-out behavior. For yet others, likewise unstable but less inclined to act out, it can serve further to confuse their own feelings and attitudes.

A more common form of deviation in adolescent males is homosexuality. As in the case of female homosexuality, male homosexuality as a permanent life style often reflects fear or hatred of the opposite sex, sometimes merged with an identification with it (ambivalence again). Negative feelings toward girls may be expressed as frank disgust or constant disparagement. Identification with the female role may lead to open adoption of feminine ways, and seems to be associated with a childhood in which there was no adequate adult male in the house. Some homosexuality, along with other atypical patterns, seems to go along with an alienation from experience, so that the individual needs some extraordinary stimulus, perhaps with elements of revulsion, to arouse him sexually.

In the past, homosexuals had to treat their sexual proclivities as a shameful secret, lest they be prosecuted, locked up in a mental hospital or coerced into psychiatric treatment, blackmailed, or fired from their jobs. Now, as we know, homosexuals (of all varieties) are "coming out of the closet" and asserting their right to freedom of choice. Only when legal and extralegal sanctions against homosexuality have been removed will we be in a position to know whether the psychological distress so often associated with homosexuality inheres in the role or is produced by social disapproval.

Yet another form of atypical sexual behavior is voyeurism, or Peeping Tom behavior. All youngsters, to satisfy their curiosity, do as much peeping and spying as they can get away with. However, when seeing nudity or near-nudity becomes an end in itself, rather than a source of knowledge or stimulation, it is apparent that the individual's sexual orientation has been dislocated. Both voyeurism and its reciprocal, exhibitionism, may be associated with feelings of sexual inadequacy, with sexual guilt that can be appeased as long as sex is enjoyed only at a distance, or with more serious and generalized disturbances of personality.

Although neurotic traits may appear earlier, it is ordinarily in adolescence or after, when the individual's ideal self has become differentiated from his other selves, that he is capable of full-blown neurosis, a state of conflict between antagonistic and often unformulated inner tendencies that drains his energies and hampers his functioning. As we mentioned previously, the neurotic individual's inner conflicts are seldom expressed directly. Basically, the neurotic person, unlike the psychotic or the psychopath, recognizes that he is blocked or ineffective by reason of characteristics within himself but beyond his voluntary control. The source of the neurosis is usually anxiety or guilt, against which the neurotic erects defenses which themselves impede his functioning. His tensions and defenses constitute the neurotic symptoms. Sometimes we find diffuse, "free-floating" anxiety ready to attach to any situation. However, the anxiety itself may be a defense against something else, such as pervasive but unacknowledged hostility. In some neurotics, the symptoms take more explicit, often symbolically meaningful forms, such as specific fears or phobias; ritualized, compulsive behavior; inability to make decisions (**abulia**); or a general sense of inadequacy, impotence, or worthlessness. These symptoms may affect only one sharply circumscribed area of functioning, or they may cripple the neurotic in all his activities.

One form of neurosis in adolescence is **hysteria**, inner conflict expressed usually through somatic symptoms. One form of hysterical behavior, now relatively rare (there are fashions in psychological disorders as in other things), is somatic dysfunction: hysterical blindness, deafness, paralysis, and so forth, where, although the affected organ is in good anatomical and physiological working order, the individual cannot use it. Such manifestations often seem to be a denial of the organ in an attempt to repudiate what it has experienced or done (a paralyzed hand, for instance, may serve to deny masturbation), to protect it from harm, to prevent its doing something in the future, or to justify the individual's helplessness—somatic dysfunctions are not uncommon among soldiers who would rather not fight, but they are wholly unconscious and thus different from deliberate shirking (Arluck, 1964). Hysteria may take the form of hypochondria, a constant inventory of the body to see what has gone wrong, and a tendency to interpret normal and usually unnoticed body sensations as warnings of some dread disease process. We can see how adolescents, with their heightened body awareness, might be prone to hypochondriacal symptoms; almost all adolescents have spells of hypochondria and almost all outgrow it. Yet another hysterical manifestation, and a more serious one, is the pseudo-suicide. This must be distinguished from the genuine suicide attempt, whether successful or not, which stems from a profound sense of despair or accompanies a psychotic breakdown. The hysterical gesture of suicide is usually an appeal for attention and affection and a means of reproaching an unsympathetic world. Even in cases where the danger of actual suicide is slight, suicidal gestures indicate emotional disturbance serious enough to call for professional help.

Hysteria often blends into **psychosomatic disorders**, where the body undergoes actual pathological changes as a result of corrosion by chronic conflicting emotions. As we said earlier, even dwarfism may have psychosomatic components. Persons who are very constricted emotionally are more prone to a host of rheumatoid diseases than normally expressive people. On the borderline between hysteria and psychosomatic disorders, there are manifestations such as fainting, where the physical changes that go with emotion interfere with the blood supply to the brain. Another borderline phenomenon, usually beginning in adolescence, is **anorexia nervosa**, a condition in which the individual finds food, or most foods, inedible or revolting. Anorexia nervosa seems to occur most often in girls, and, according to one interpretation, seems to be an unconscious expression of fear of sexuality, where anything taken into the body connotes, symbolically, sexual penetration. Although anorexia nervosa does not lead directly to physiological disorders, its victims may become badly emaciated and suffer tissue damage due to malnutrition. They generally survive on small quantities of a few selected foods, but they may have to be hospitalized and fed intravenously.

At the opposite pole from anorexia stands the far more common condition of **bulimia**, or compulsive overeating. Bulimia may begin long before adolescence, and appears to be an infantile oral character trait. It often is a symbolic expression of a hunger for love and support. It has psychosomatic consequences in obesity and metabolic changes. Other more directly psychosomatic disorders, such as gastric ulcers, migraine, and so forth, can also be observed. It is worth repeating that such somatic afflictions as eczema and asthma can be made worse or may even be triggered off by psychological upsets as early as infancy.

We might also say a word about individual differences in psychosomatic reactions. All strong emotions entail clearcut body changes. And, provided emotions are not so strong as to be disruptive, different emotions seem to entail different patterns of physiological change. But within this general framework, Lacey (1956), Wenger (1941), and others have demonstrated that individuals have their own characteristic ways of reacting to a variety of emotional stresses. It can easily be observed that some people react predominantly (although other systems are also involved in varying degrees) with their pharyngeal mucous membranes, becoming all stuffed up; some with their tear ducts; some react with their skin, flushing or paling; in some, blood pressure goes up, in others, down; some react with their muscles, tensing up; some with their digestive tracts, losing appetite or needing to eliminate. We are thus in a position to conjecture that the particular psychosomatic symptom that appears in individuals who live under prolonged emotional stress, and whose tissues break down before their personality organization, is a product of the particular chronic emotion which is at work within the person, of his idiosyncratic form of emotional response, and of tissue vulnerabilities such as a tendency to eczema or asthma.

As we can see, the adolescent has moved into a stage of individualized complexity where, like most adults, he is a mixture of normal and abnormal, of strengths and weaknesses, of virtues and faults. Even normal adolescents, when the strains get too great, may find it helpful to invoke psychotherapeutic assistance.

Help for Exceptional Children

Discussion of morbid conditions such as those described in this chapter may lead to certain anxieties, and we feel some obligation to try to put this discussion in its proper perspective. It is obvious that all the "abnormal" psychological symptoms we have described crop up in the most normal people. It is not necessarily the case that a child who shows some sign of psychological disturbance is ready for the psychiatrist. In the first place, his behavior may be a way of coping with essentially abnormal and stressful living conditions; in such cases, it is the environment that needs attention, and not the child. Furthermore, these symptoms by themselves do not indicate abnormal functioning. They express normal human potentialities shared by everybody. It is only when they begin to dominate the scene and interfere with effective living that they become abnormal and require special attention—which may occasionally consist of nothing more than the familiar prescription of a change of scene for a few weeks. At the other extreme, special attention may consist of prolonged psychotherapy. It should also be obvious that we are at a loss to explain in terms of situational influences many abnormalities thought to be psychological rather than organic, and we may need to give more consideration to constitutional sensitivities, strengths, weaknesses, capacities, and vulnerabilities. Some children survive objectively appalling childhoods without visible ill effects, while others seem to break down under apparently trifling stresses. Some break down or get off to a poor start and then recover with very little outside help, while others may spend a lifetime trying to find an identity they can call their own. Until the conditions of mental health and illness have been better defined, we can only offer the prescription that we have repeated throughout this book: love, emotional warmth, self-confidence and confidence in the child, solid but not overwhelming authority, enjoyment, op-

portunity for sound identifications, and encouragement—without coercion—to cognitive growth and to independence.

Meanwhile, some few children do have physical disabilities serious enough to affect their psychological functioning, and others do develop chronic psychological disorders. Fortunately, we live in an era when we can face such problems and try to deal with them realistically, instead of locking the child in a closet, castigating ourselves with guilt feelings, rattling family skeletons, and otherwise wasting valuable energies. It is hard for us to realize now that a generation ago people could not bring themselves to speak publicly of tuberculosis, cancer, or venereal disease, which, thanks largely to publicity by special interest groups, have been brought out into the open, where they can be dealt with. In the same way, we are now coming to acknowledge and attack such problems as emotional disturbance, schizophrenia, mental deficiency, epilepsy, cerebral palsy, and so forth. Possibly the most important effect of campaigns designed to focus public attention on these problems is that they have enabled parents to continue to be parents even when their children were severely disabled; they have made parents aware that children continue to be children in spite of disabilities, that they need the same basic emotional support that other children do.

Children with physical disabilities and severely disturbed children need outside professional help. Whether this kind of help is indicated for the child with emotional disturbances of slight or intermediate severity must be a matter for individual decision. Psychotherapy can help, but it cannot guarantee to do so. Furthermore it costs heavily, in terms both of money and psychic strain, and parents must weigh its possible benefits against its costs to them and to the child. And when they do elect psychotherapy—which often means psychotherapy for the entire family—they must be prepared to follow through wherever it leads. Sometimes, of course, less drastic measures than psychotherapy can be of therapeutic benefit. A good school or teacher, for instance, or participation in a recreation group, can often help a child immensely. Nevertheless, a professional opinion as to the most advisable measures is often helpful.

Unfortunately, there are not enough facilities to serve all those who need and want professional help. The rich, of course, can always look out for themselves, although they too can fall prey to frauds and charlatans. One of the more encouraging developments in antipoverty programs has been the trend to community mental health centers, sometimes in collaboration with hospitals and sometimes in storefront operations. One of the virtues of these centers is that they have helped break down some artificial distinctions among the professions and between professionals and nonprofessionals. There are, however, limits to what they can do. Too much of their energy is liable to go to treating drug abuse. Furthermore, it is very hard to solve people's psychological problems if one is unable to do anything about their economic circumstances. Meanwhile, an increasing number of graduate programs in clinical psychology are redirecting their programs toward community psychology. This means that they are training "paraprofessionals" such as child development specialists in addition to doctoral-level practitioners.

For those who can afford to pay for services, certain guidelines are in order. Various professional specialists are licensed or certified by a number of accrediting agencies, but the individual's best assurance of qualified help is to obtain information from a reliable source. To find out where reputable psychiatric or psychological services can be obtained, one might consult his pediatrician or family doctor, the nearest mental health clinic, his state psychological association, the American Psychological Association, or the psychology department or clinic of a college or university. For vocational guidance, a roster of qualified counselors is maintained by the National Vocational Guidance Association. In the case of particular disabilities, parent or citizen groups have been set up to provide services or maintain a directory of where services are available. Among these are the United Cerebral Palsy Association, the National Association for Retarded Children, the National Epilepsy League, the National Society for Crippled Children and Adults, the American Foundation for the Blind, the American Speech and Hearing Association, and the National Organization for Mentally Ill Children, plus, of course, many more. Many national foundation organizations have branch offices and clinics around the country, and application for help can be made directly to these. Otherwise, the national headquarters can direct applicants to the nearest facilities.

Pathology of the Environment

We have been talking thus far of problems which, regardless of their sources in the family or the social environment, are essentially problems of individual disturbance. These problems fall within the province of psychiatry and psychology. We should like to close our discussion of abnormalities of development with a discussion of the so-called sociopathies, pathologies of society, social organization, and family structure which may have deleterious effects on personality development. Obviously, we have taken some account of these throughout this book, and in the present chapter in references to mothering and to delinquency. We have implied earlier that intellectually sterile, unstimulating, and overrigid patterns of schooling may well stifle or deform personal creativity and development. The even more damaging effects of the usual sorts of institutionalization have also been alluded to. We have even suggested that some whole cultures seem to represent lunacy made the norm. Now we should like to give more attention to problems which are the province of social work, the field of child welfare, and, in terms of academic disciplines, of sociology.

*Family
pathology*

We should note that psychology and sociology are not exclusive disciplines. Their domains inevitably overlap a great deal. However, their emphases are quite different—so different at times that the same terms may have quite different meanings in the two disciplines. Sociologically, for instance, a "broken home" is one in which the parents are divorced or separated, or one or both parents dead, regardless of how successfully the remaining members live together as a family unit. Psychologically, on the other hand, a broken home is

one in which life is made difficult either by the loss or absence of a parent or by interpersonal strife, even though all the family members are present to participate in it. We shall feel free to use this and other terms in a way biased toward psychology, simply because psychology is our business.

The most immediately important **sociopathies**, from the standpoint of child development, are those having to do with the family structure, particularly those disruptions which are called broken homes. Until thirty or forty years ago, most such homes were broken up as a result of the death of one or both parents. The efforts of those who attempted to help the survivors of broken homes were largely aimed at placing the children, usually in orphanages. The orphanage is now a vanishing institution, for two reasons. First of all, parents live longer—especially mothers, for whom childbirth is now rarely a hazard. Second, there has been a general recognition that the usual form of group care provided in orphanages leaves much to be desired. However, a contrary trend is generated by a need to provide facilities for illegitimate babies who, for one reason or another, cannot be either kept or adopted. As substitutes for orphanages there have now been developed programs to place children without parents in private homes, and to enable a surviving parent to keep his or her family together. Instead of going to institutions, many homeless children are placed in foster homes (temporary placements, with the child's keep paid for by the public or private agency in whose legal custody he remains) or adoptive homes (permanent placements, with the child becoming a legal member of the family). The second substitute for orphanages is the provision through various state agencies and the federal Social Security system of subsidies for widows and their dependent children, enabling them to keep their families together.

Certain flaws have appeared in the foster care and adoptive placement programs. One is that it is hard to find enough foster homes. Another shortcoming is apparent in the case of children who have to move repeatedly from one foster home to another, because of incompatibility or changed circumstances; such children develop a sense of repeated loss and rejection, and often become victims of psychopathology. Yet another flaw lies in the implicit assumption that any foster home is better than any institution. Some people have moved to improve institutional care instead of scrapping it. By raising the quality, psychological warmth, understanding, and training of personnel, by providing continuity of attachment between child and a particular person responsible for his care, and by organizing children into *small* groups on a family plan, a number of institutions are improving to the point where they may yet provide the best solution for children with special kinds of emotional disturbance that prevent their forming attachments to a foster family, and for children past the early school years.

Illegitimacy no longer carries the moral and even criminal stigma that it once did, but it still poses serious problems. A few children are born out of wedlock to mothers who welcome them, but most illegitimate children are definitely unwanted. It is to be hoped that wide dissemination of birth control knowledge and materials, along with relaxed laws concerning abortion (and lowered costs), will help reduce the number of unwanted babies

and the problems they both bring and face. There is, of course, a demand for illegitimate babies by couples who want to adopt them. Adoption, of course, carries some risks. Some number of adoptive parents and children find that they were not made for each other. Every so often a biological mother changes her mind and decides she wants to take back her child from the family that adopted him, which can occasion great emotional turmoil and legal wrangling. By and large, however, the increasingly reasonable standards set by adoption agencies help insure a good match between adoptive parents and child. More than in the past, adoption agencies are willing to place flawed babies with families who want them, sometimes because the adoptive parents themselves are handicapped in some way. There is greater willingness to place babies with single women—it seems to be rare that single males seek to adopt a child. Interracial adoptions are more common than before, at least partly in reaction to the problem of children sired around the world by American servicemen. It has become accepted practice to let adopted children know early that they are adopted, that they are in fact *chosen*, as a safeguard against their learning the fact accidentally and being overwhelmed by the uncertainty and, perhaps, sense of rejection of not being with their own parents. On the other hand, too great an insistence on the child's adoptive status can raise a whole host of doubts and questions. A thorough study still needs to be made of how well adoption works, and of what factors help and hinder the process.

Nowadays, of course, although children less often have to face the problems of being orphaned or branded as illegitimate, they still are confronted with the problems of homes broken by marital discord. In the lowest stratum of society there are many families where intermittent or changing or absent fathers are the rule, where the children's only tie, if any, is to the mother. Such families are particularly likely to breed feelings of isolation and rejection, hostility against society, delinquency, and a gang orientation. A number of writers have commented on the special identification problems of males raised without fathers, a more common phenomenon than females raised without mothers. Nevertheless, a remarkably large number of fatherless families survive emotionally intact (Coles, 1967). Interestingly enough, a certain segment of upper-class society displays a similar pattern of multiple divorce (in the lowest-class families, of course, neither the marriage nor the divorce may be formalized), where there may be a tie with one parent but no clearcut, sustained family structure. For the children of such families, the boarding school may play the psychological role of orphanage and may be the only stable factor in the child's life.

In a sense even more disruptive is divorce in the middle-class family, founded as it is on a more definite assumption of permanence. Sometimes, of course, divorce seems to be the only answer. A family atmosphere of psychological divorce, permeated by coldness or open antagonism, may be even worse for the children. Divorce is simply an explicit acknowledgement that a marriage has failed, and, if anything, may have a stabilizing effect. Needless to say, even a badly spoiled marriage can sometimes be salvaged by putting it on a new footing where the parents' immaturities will not be in the forefront, and when this can be done—by family counseling, by psychotherapy, or otherwise —it is certainly preferable to divorce.

Divorce entails many secondary problems, of course, and these have to be met. Among the psychologically most important ones are those having to do with the children's divided loyalties and how their time is to be apportioned between the two parents. Some divorced parents work severe hardships on their children by trying to win exclusive affection, by using them as a weapon against the other parent, by trying to justify their own point of view, and even by treating children as substitute spouses. Traumatic as divorce can be, there is general agreement that it is better than trying to maintain a pretense "for the children's sake." The children can more easily understand and accept a real break than deceptions which do not deceive but only baffle and disturb. One of the subtle and neglected aspects of divorce is the disruption of countless accumulated habit patterns, leading to disorientation, aimlessness, and often a loneliness that sends the divorced person rushing into a new liaison.

Home conditions of poverty and economic privation or uncertainty can expose the child to ills ranging from malnutrition to extremes of psychopathology (Lustman, 1970; Mears, 1970; Pavenstedt, 1967). Although the acceptance of the principle of the welfare state has eliminated some of the conditions Dickens wrote about, we can still find nests of squalor on tenant farms, in migrant labor camps, and in the tenements of every city. Indeed, whole nations and, in the United States, whole regions, such as Appalachia, suffer from economic blight. Poverty may remove the child from the culture at large and deprive him of all the stimulation to growth that is the lot of more favored children. Some families, of course, maintain their group and individual integrity in the face of the most grinding hardships. Others, though, have been pounded into patterns of inadequacy and depravity that are beyond the reach of economic relief alone. Welfare regulations that force families apart contribute to pathology. Poor black people bear a special burden of prejudice. The social agencies in every community know certain families that can be counted on to produce more than their actuarial share of delinquency, psychopathic sexuality, drunkenness and disorderliness, disease, and crippled personalities who become the parents of yet other crippled personalities in a recurring sequence that led early theorists to talk of hereditary (rather than self-renewing) social incompetence.

While poverty is a monster, we should not forget that affluence has its dangers. Too many kids grow up muffled by money against the realities of the world. Ethnocentrism flourishes among those who do not have to wrestle a livelihood from a grudging world. We have already spoken of a loss of elementary skills among people who buy everything instead of making it. Most serious, many rich kids grow up without any sense of purpose, of having a future that will be both interesting and useful. Which is not to minimize the effects of poverty and the need to help poor families and their kids.

In giving such help, however, agencies and counselors must bear in mind the possibly devastating effects of conflicts in cultural values. This danger is brought sharply to our attention in a classic study by Hunt (1938) of the ecology of psychological disturbance. It came to Hunt's attention that a surprisingly large number of boys who had belonged to the same group

in a depressed section of Washington, D.C., developed one or another form of psychopathology. Investigating further, he found that the boys who broke down were those who had often taken part in the gang's atypical sexual activities *and* who had participated in neighborhood religious revivals. It was only when "deviant" sex was joined to religion in the same individual, implying a state of severe conflict, that psychological disturbance resulted. Programs that bring together would-be helpers from the middle class and people from the vastly different slum culture should be aware of the phenomenon of "culture shock" (which can work in both directions). It should be made explicit that programs for the poor are experiments in cultural engineering, which makes it necessary to consider and reconsider the cultural assumptions on which such programs operate.

We must insist that widespread prejudice against racial, ethnic, national, or religious groups is a form of social pathology. While the victims of prejudice may suffer immediate and obvious harm, the prejudiced are also the victims of culturally ordained unreason and suffer to the extent that their capacities for perceiving, feeling, and thinking are crippled by their misconceptions. It is obvious but often overlooked that prejudice generates reciprocal prejudice, so that minority groups may harbor irrational beliefs about and attitudes toward the prejudiced majority as well as crippling concepts of themselves.

Disaster and social disruption

Finally, we should point out that in recent years social scientists have begun to

Pathology of the environment

gather and organize information about what happens to children in times of major social crisis due to man-made or natural disasters: war, flood, earthquake, windstorm, panic. It has always been obvious that children suffer from such crises, but now we are beginning to see more precisely what they suffer and how, and what sort of psychological safety precautions can be incorporated in disaster preparations. The growth of our civilization has produced two parallel trends. First, we are able to create disasters on a gigantic scale, in the form of nuclear bombing, biological warfare, concentration camps, forced migrations, and genocide. Second, we have become able to stand apart from our acts of mass destruction, assess them, and plan against the day when we turn our destructive forces against ourselves. Needless to say, we shall reach real social maturity only when such assessments and planning are no longer necessary.

Studies of adult morale have shown that panic is most likely to occur when the individual feels cut loose from his moorings in the group and does not have clearcut tasks to perform. For the child, at least up to age ten and probably beyond, the essential moorings are in family ties. As we have said previously, it was found that, in general, children evacuated to safety from the threat of aerial bombardment, but removed from their parents, suffered far greater psychological strain than those who remained with their parents even in the face of actual danger. At one time, disaster rescue and relief workers had as their first intuitive impulse the need to collect children and take them to a safe place where they could be cared for in groups. In the Dutch flood disasters of the early 1950s, by contrast, a deliberate attempt was made to take account of World War II experience and keep children with their families, or at least with their mothers and siblings—fathers, for the most part, being required to take part in emergency operations (Querido and Mead, 1953).

American investigators, studying children's recovery from the psychological effects of such disasters as floods and tornadoes, have found that those children who had to step in and take over the functions and responsibilities of a dead or incapacitated parent or older sibling, and those who had the greatest opportunity to discuss and ventilate their experiences, were the first to recover. Ironically enough, "better-off" middle-class families, in which there was less likely to be a clearcut role for a child to assume, and which protectively tried to keep children from talking about the awful events they had witnessed, were likely to prevent children from discharging their accumulated feelings and thus helped perpetuate them. It should be noted, however, that adults are likely to misperceive the way children experience disaster; a superlative literary example of this is given in the novel *A High Wind in Jamaica*. Following a severe hurricane that demolished the family plantation, the mother observes:

"That awful night!" said Mrs. Thornton, once, when discussing their plan of sending [the children] home to school: "Oh, my dear, what the poor little things must have suffered! Think how much more acute Fear is to a child! And they were so brave, so English. . . . You know, I am terribly afraid what permanent, *inward* effect a shock like that may have on them. Have you noticed they never so much as mention it? . . ."

Meanwhile, the children, accepting the new life as a matter of course, were thoroughly enjoying it (Hughes, 1965, p. 41).

We might mention in passing the nomadic societies of children that sprang up in southern and eastern Europe following World Wars I and II. Children separated from their parents formed roving, predatory bands which developed their own cultures of a highly psychopathic turn. Again there is a literary depiction of such behavior in *Lord of the Flies* (Golding, 1954), which describes in harrowing detail the sociology of a group of castaway children (and which also teaches a Freud-like view of the intrinsic evil of human nature).

Studies on the effects of major social upheavals are, of course, only at the beginning, but their findings are important and dependable enough to make a vital difference in the thinking of those charged with planning for disaster relief. Meanwhile, we can see that we have our work cut out for us to provide a world fit for our children to grow up in.

references

Achenbach, T. M. The classification of children's psychiatric symptoms: A factor analytic study. *Psychological Monographs*, 1966, 80, no. 6.

Ader, R. F. Social factors affecting emotionality and resistance to disease in animals: III. Early weaning and susceptibility to gastric ulcers in the rat. A control for nutritional factors. *Journal of Comparative and Physiological Psychology*, 1962, 55, 600–602.

Ainsworth, M. D. S. *Infancy in Uganda*. Baltimore: Johns Hopkins University Press, 1967.

Ainsworth, M. D. S., Bell, S. M. V., & Stayton, D. J. Individual differences in strange-situation behavior of one-year-olds. In *The Origins of Human Social Relations*, edited by H. R. Schaffer. London: Academic Press, in press.

Alain-Fournier, H. *The Wanderer*. New York: New Directions, 1946 (originally 1913).

Albee, G. W. The uncertain future of clinical psychology. *American Psychologist*, 1970, 25, 1071–1080.

Allen, K. E., Hart, B., Buell, J. S., Harris, F. R., & Wolf, M. M. Effects of social reinforcement on isolate behavior of a nursery school child. *Child Development*, 1964, 35, 511–518.

Allport, G. W. *The Use of Personal Documents in Psychological Science*. New York: Social Science Research Council, 1942.

Allport, G. W. The fruits of eclecticism—bitter or sweet? *Psychologia*, 1964, 7, 1–14.

Altmann, S. A. Primate behavior in review. *Science*, 1965, 150, 1440–1442.

Altmann, S. A. (Ed.) *Social Communication among Primates*. Chicago: University of Chicago Press, 1966.

Altus, W. D. First born and last born children in a child development clinic. *Journal of Individual Psychology*, 1964, 20, 179–182.

Altus, W. D. Birth order and its sequelae. *Science*, 1966, 151, 44–49.

Ambrose, J. A. The development of the smiling response in early infancy. In *Determinants of Infant Behavior*, edited by B. M. Foss. New York: Wiley, 1961.

Ambrose, [J.] A. Remarks. In *Stimulation in Early Infancy*, edited by [J.] A. Ambrose. New York: Academic Press, 1969.

American Psychological Association. Education for research in psychology. *American Psychologist*, 1960, 15, 158–159.

Ames, L. B., & Learned, J. Imaginary companions

and related phenomena. *Journal of Genetic Psychology*, 1946, 69, 147–167.

Anastasi, A. Heredity, environment, and the question "How?" *Psychological Review*, 1958, 65, 197–208.

Anastasi, A. Psychology, psychologists, and psychological testing. *American Psychologist*, 1967, 22, 297–306.

Anonymous. Baby center adds ideas to its T.L.C., and Moscow is split on nursery issue. *New York Times*, March 22, 1971, 35.

Anonymous. New Hampshire girls may still marry at 13. *New York Times*, June 8, 1971, 19.

Apgar, V. Perinatal problems and the central nervous system. In *The Child with Central Nervous System Deficit*, U.S. Department of Health, Education, and Welfare, Welfare Administration, Children's Bureau. Washington, D.C.: U.S. Government Printing Office, 1965.

Apley, J., Davies, J., Davis, D. R., & Silk, B. Dwarfism without apparent physical cause. *Proceedings of the Royal Society of Medicine*, 1971, 64, 135–138.

Ardrey, R. *The Territorial Imperative*. New York: Atheneum, 1966.

Aries, P. *Centuries of Childhood*. New York: Knopf, 1962.

Arluck, E. W. *Hypnoanalysis: A Case Study*. New York: Random House, 1964.

Aronson, E., & Rosenbloom, S. Space perception in early infancy: Perception within a common auditory-visual space. *Science*, 1971, 172, 1161–1163.

Asch, S. E. Studies in the principles of judgments and attitudes: II. Determination of judgments by group and ego standards. *Journal of Social Psychology*, 1940, 12, 433–465.

Asch, S. E., & Nerlove, H. The development of double function terms in children. In *Perspectives in Psychological Theory*, edited by B. Kaplan & S. Wapner. New York: International Universities Press, 1960.

Ashton-Warner, S. *Teacher*. New York: Simon & Schuster, 1963.

Azrin, N. Pain and aggression. *Psychology Today*, May 1967, 27–33.

Babkin, P. S. The establishment of reflex behavior in early postnatal life. *Central Nervous System and Behavior*, 1956, 44, 10.

Ball, W., & Tronick, E. Infant responses to impending collision: Optical and real. *Science*, 1971, 171, 818–820.

Baltimore City Public Schools. *An Early School Admission Project: Progress Report 1963–1964*. Baltimore: Baltimore City Public Schools, 1964.

Bandura, A. (Ed.) *Psychological Modeling*. Chicago: Aldine-Atherton, 1971.

Bandura, A., Ross, D., Ross, S. A. A comparative test of the status envy, social power, and secondary reinforcement theories of identificatory learning. *Journal of Abnormal and Social Psychology*, 1963, 67, 527–534.

Barker, R. G., Dembo, T., & Lewin, K. Frustration and regression: An experiment with children. *University of Iowa Studies in Child Welfare*, 1941, 18, no. 1.

Bartoshuk, A. K. Human neonatal cardiac responses to sound: A power function. *Psychonomic Science*, 1964, 1, 151–152.

Bateson, G., Jackson, D., Haley, J., & Weakland, J. Toward a theory of schizophrenia. *Behavioral Science*, 1956, 1, 251–264.

Bateson, G., & Mead, M. *Balinese Character*. New York: New York Academy of Sciences, 1942.

Bayley, N. *Manual for the Bayley Scale of Infant Development*. New York: Psychological Corporation, 1969.

Beals, R. L., & Hoijer, H. *Introduction to Anthropology*. (3rd ed.) New York: Macmillan, 1965.

Beckwith, L. Relationships between infants' vocalizations and their mothers' behaviors. *Merrill-Palmer Quarterly*, 1971, 17, 211–226.

Bee, H. L., et al. Social class differences in maternal teaching strategies and speech patterns. *Developmental Psychology*, 1969, 1, 726–734.

Bell, R. Q. A reinterpretation of the direction of effects in studies of socialization. *Psychological Review*, 1968, 75, 81–95.

Bell, R. Q. Stimulus control of parent or caretaker behavior by offspring. *Developmental Psychology*, 1971, 4, 63–72.

Bell, R. Q., Weller, G. M., & Waldrop, M. F. Newborn and preschooler: Organization of behavior and relations between periods. *Monographs of the Society for Research in Child Development*, 1971, 36, nos. 1–2.

Bell, S. M. V. The effectiveness of various maternal responses as terminators of crying. Paper presented at meetings of the Society for Research in Child Development, 1971.

Bellugi, U. Simplification in children's language. In *Language Acquisition*, edited by R. Huxley and E. Ingram. London and New York: Academic Press, 1971.

Benedict, R. Continuities and discontinuities in cultural conditioning. *Psychiatry*, 1938, 1, 161–167.

Bennett, E. L., Diamond, M. C., Krech, D., & Rosenzweig, M. R. Chemical and anatomical plasticity of brain. *Science*, 1964, 146, 610–619.

Bennett, R., & Nahemov, L. Institutional totality and criteria of social adjustment in residences for the aged. *Journal of Social Issues*, 1965, 21, 44–78.

Bereiter, C., & Engelmann, S. *Teaching Disadvantaged Children in the Preschool*. Englewood Cliffs, N.J.: Prentice-Hall, 1966.

Berenda, R. W. *The Influence of the Group on the Judgments of Children*. New York: King's Crown Press, 1950.

Bernstein, B. Language and social class. *British Journal of Sociology*, 1960, 11, 271–276.

Bernstein, B. Elaborated and restricted codes: Their social origins and some consequences. *American Anthropologist*, 1964, 66, no. 6, part 2, 55–69.

Berzonsky, M. D. Interdependence of Inhelder and Piaget's model of logical thinking. *Developmental Psychology*, 1971, 4, 469–476.

Bettelheim, B. Joey: A "mechanical boy." *Scientific American*, March 1959.

Bettelheim, B. *The Empty Fortress*. New York: Free Press, 1967.

Bexton, W. H., Heron, W., & Scott, T. H. Effects of decreased variation in the sensory environment. *Canadian Journal of Psychology*, 1954, 8, 70–76.

Bialer, I. Conceptualizations of success and failure in mentally retarded and normal children. *Journal of Personality*, 1961, 29, 303–320.

Biber, B. Premature structuring as a deterrent to creativity. *American Journal of Orthopsychiatry*, 1959, 29, no. 2; *Bank Street College of Education Publications*, no. 67.

Billington, W. D. Trophoblast extensions from the placenta. *Proceedings of the Royal Society of Medicine*, 1970, 63, 57–59.

Birch, H. G., & Lefford, A. Intersensory development in children. *Monographs of the Society for Research in Child Development*, 1963, 28, no. 5.

Birns, B. Individual differences in human neonates' responses to stimulation. *Child Development*, 1965, 36, 249–256.

Bitterman, M. E., Wodinsky, J., & Candland, D. K. Some comparative psychology. *American Journal of Psychology*, 1958, 71, 94–110.

Blank, M., & Bridger, W. H. Cross-modal transfer in nursery-school children. *Journal of Comparative and Physiological Psychology*, 1964, 58, 277–282.

Blank, M., & Solomon, F. A tutorial language program to develop abstract thinking in socially disadvantaged preschool children. *Child Development*, 1968, 39, 379–389.

Blank, M., & Solomon F. How shall the disadvantaged child be taught? *Child Development*, 1969, 40, 47–61.

Blauvelt, H. Dynamics of the mother-newborn relationship in goats. In *Group Processes*, edited by B. Schaffner. New York: Macy Foundation, 1955.

Blauvelt, H., & McKenna, J. Capacity of the human newborn for orientation. In *Determinants of Infant Behavior*, edited by B. M. Foss. New York: Wiley, 1961.

Bousfield, W. A. The occurrence of clustering in the recall of randomly arranged associates. *Journal of General Psychology*, 1953, 49, 229–240.

Bower, T. G. R. Discrimination of depth in premotor infants. *Psychonomic Science*, 1964, 1, 368.

Bower, T. G. R. Stimulus variables determining space perception in infants. *Science*, 1965, 149, 88–89.

Bower, T. G. R. Perceptual functioning in early infancy. In *Brain and Early Behavior*, edited by R. J. Robinson. New York and London: Academic Press, 1969.

Bower, T. G. R., Broughton, J. M., & Moore, M. K. Demonstration of intention in the reaching behaviour of neonate humans. *Nature*, 1970a, 228, 679–681.

Bower, T. G. R., Broughton, J. M., & Moore, M. K. Infant responses to approaching objects. *Perception and Psychophysics*, 1970b, 9, 193–196.

Bower, T. G. R., Broughton, J. M., & Moore, M. K. Development of the object concept as manifested by changes in the tracking behavior of infants between 7 and 20 weeks of age. *Journal of Experimental Child Psychology*, 1971 (in press).

References

Bowes, W. A., Brackbill, Y., Conway, E., & Steinschneider, A. The effects of obstetrical medication on fetus and infant. *Monographs of the Society for Research in Child Development*, 1970, 35, no. 4.

Bowlby, J. *Attachment and Loss.* Vol. 1. *Attachment.* New York: Basic Books, 1969.

Brackbill, Y., & O'Hara, J. The relative effectiveness of reward and punishment for discrimination learning in children. *Journal of Comparative and Physiological Psychology*, 1958, 51, 747–751.

Brady, R. O., Uhlendorf, B. W., & Jacobson, C. B. Fabry's disease: Antenatal detection. *Science*, 1971, 172, 174–175.

Braine, M. D. S., Heimer, C. B., Wortis, H., & Freedman, A. M. Factors associated with impairment of the early development of prematures. *Monographs of the Society for Research in Child Development*, 1966, 31, no. 4.

Brazelton, T. B. Behavioral and neurological assessment scale. (Rev. ed.) Unpublished manuscript, 1970.

Brian, C. R., & Goodenough, F. L. Relative potency of color and form perception at various ages. *Journal of Experimental Psychology*, 1929, 12, 197–213.

Bridges, K. M. B. Emotional development in early infancy. *Child Development*, 1932, 3, 324–341.

Brody, J. E. Study of adolescents confirms some beliefs on marijuana use. *New York Times*, September 15, 1971, 40.

Bronfenbrenner, U. *Two Worlds of Childhood: U.S. and U.S.S.R.* New York: Russell Sage Foundation, 1970.

Bronowski, J., & Bellugi, U. Language, name, and concept. *Science*, 1970, 168, 669–673.

Bronson, G. Infants' reactions to an unfamiliar person. Paper presented at meetings of the Society for Research in Child Development, 1971.

Brophy, J. E. Mothers as teachers of their own preschool children. *Child Development*, 1970, 41, 79–94.

Brown, F. A. Living clocks. *Science*, 1959, 130, 1535–1544.

Bruce, H. M. A block to pregnancy in the mouse caused by the proximity of strange males. *Journal of Reproductive Fertility*, 1960, 1, 96.

Bruner, J. S. *The Process of Education.* Cambridge: Harvard University Press, 1960.

Bruner, J. S. After John Dewey, what? *Saturday Review*, June 17, 1961; *Bank Street College of Education Publications*, 1961, no. 54.

Bruner, J. S. *On Knowing.* Cambridge: Harvard University Press–Belknap Press, 1962.

Bruner, J. S. *Process of Cognitive Growth: Infancy.* Worcester, Mass.: Clark University Press, 1968.

Bunce, G. E. Milk and blindness in Brazil. *Natural History*, February 1969, 52–55.

Burghardt, G. M., & Hess, E. H. Food imprinting in the snapping turtle, Chelydra serpentina. *Science*, 1966, 151, 108–109.

Burton, R. V. Validity of retrospective reports assessed by the multi-trait-multimethod analysis. *Developmental Psychology Monographs*, 1970, 3, no. 3, part 2.

Cairns, N. U., & Steward, M. S. Young children's orientation of letters as a function of axis of symmetry and stimulus alignment. *Child Development*, 1970, 41, 993–1002.

Caldwell, B. M. Mother-infant interaction in monomatric and polymatric families. *American Journal of Orthopsychiatry*, 1963, 33, 653–664.

Caldwell, B. M. The effects of infant care. In *Review of Child Development Research*, vol. 1, edited by M. L. Hoffman and L. W. Hoffman. New York: Russell Sage Foundation, 1964.

Caldwell, B. M. Impact of interest in early cognitive stimulation. In *Perspectives in Child Psychopathology*, edited by H. E. Rie. Chicago: Aldine-Atherton, 1971.

Calhoun, J. G. Population density and social pathology. *Scientific American*, February 1962, 139–148.

Campbell, D. T. Social attitudes and other acquired behavioral dispositions. In *Psychology: A Study of a Science*, vol. 6, edited by S. Koch. New York: McGraw-Hill, 1963.

Campos, J. J., Langer, A., & Karowitz, A. Cardiac responses on the visual cliff in prelocomotor human infants. *Science*, 1970, 170, 196–197.

Cannon, W. B. *Wisdom of the Body.* New York: Norton, 1939.

Carlson, P., & Anisfeld, M. Some observations on the linguistic competence of a two-year-old child. *Child Development*, 1969, 40, 569–575.

Carne, S. The immigrant patient in general practice. *Proceedings of the Royal Society of Medicine*, 1970, 63, 629–631.

References

Carpenter, E., Varley, F., & Flaherty, R. *Eskimo.* Toronto: University of Toronto Press, 1959.

Carpenter, G. C., Tecce, J. J., Stechler, G., & Friedman, S. Differential behavior to human and humanoid faces in early infancy. *Merrill-Palmer Quarterly,* 1970, 16, 91–108.

Carr, H. S., & Watson, J. B. Orientation in the white rat. *Journal of Comparative Neurology,* 1908, 18, 27–44.

Carroll, J. B. (Ed.) *Language, Thought, and Reality: Selected Writings of Benjamin Whorf.* New York and Cambridge: Wiley; M.I.T. Press, 1956.

Cary, J. *A House of Children.* New York: Harper, 1955.

Cattell, P. *Infant Intelligence Scale.* New York: Psychological Corporation, 1940.

Caudill, W., & Weinstein, H. Maternal care and infant behavior in Japanese and American urban middle class families. In *Yearbook of the International Sociological Association,* edited by R. König and R. Hill, 1966.

Caviness, J. A., & Gibson, J. J. The equivalence of visual and tactual stimulation for the perception of solid forms. Paper presented at meetings of the Eastern Psychological Association, 1962.

Cazden, C. B. Some implications of research on language development for pre-school education. In *Early Education,* edited by R. D. Hess and R. M. Bear. Chicago: Aldine-Atherton, 1968a.

Cazden, C. B. The acquisition of noun and verb inflections. *Child Development,* 1968b, 39, 433–448.

Cazden, C. B. Language in early childhood and reading: A review for 1969. Washington, D.C.: ERIC Clearinghouse in Linguistics, mimeographed, no date.

Cazden, C. B. The situation: A neglected source of social class differences in language use. *Journal of Social Issues,* 1970, 26, 35–59.

Center for Cognitive Studies, Harvard University. *Annual Report,* 1968–1969. Cambridge: Harvard University, Center for Cognitive Studies.

Charlesworth, W. R. Cognition in infancy: Where do we stand in the mid-sixties? *Merrill-Palmer Quarterly,* 1968, 14, 25–46.

Chastaing, M. Premiers sourires enfantins. In *Rencontre/Encounter/Begegnung.* Utrecht and Antwerp: Spectrum, 1957.

Chesler, M. A. Ethnocentrism and attitudes toward the physically disabled. *Journal of Personality and Social Psychology,* 1965, 2, 877–882.

Chesler, P. Maternal influences in learning by observation in kittens. *Science,* 1969, 166, 901–903.

Child Study Association. *Parents' Guide to Facts of Life for Children.* New York: Maco, 1965.

Chodoff, P. A critique of Freud's theory of infantile sexuality. *American Journal of Psychiatry,* 1966, 123, 507–518.

Chomsky, N. Review of *Verbal Behavior,* by B. F. Skinner. *Language,* 1959, 35, 26–58.

Chomsky, N. *Language and Mind.* New York: Harcourt, Brace & World, 1968.

Chomsky, N. The case against B. F. Skinner. *New York Review of Books,* December 30, 1971, 18–24.

Chukovsky, K. *From Two to Five.* Berkeley and Los Angeles: University of California Press, 1963.

Church, J. Innovations, excellence, and children's learning. *School and Society,* 1962, 90, 401–404; *Bank Street College of Education Publications,* 1962, no. 65.

Church, J. *Language and the Discovery of Reality.* New York: Vintage, 1966 (originally 1961).

Church, J. (Ed.) *Three Babies: Biographies of Cognitive Development.* New York: Vintage, 1968 (originally 1966).

Church, J. Cognitive consequences of social disadvantage. Paper presented at meetings of the New York State Psychological Association, 1969.

Church, J. Techniques for the differential study of cognition in early childhood. In *Cognitive Studies,* vol. 1, edited by J. Hellmuth. New York: Brunner/Mazel, 1970.

Church, J. The ontogeny of language. In *Ontogeny of Vertebrate Behavior,* edited by H. Moltz. New York: Academic Press, 1971.

Church, J., & Insko, C. A. Ethnic and sex differences in sexual values. *Psychologia,* 1965, 8, 153–157.

Clock, R. O. *Our Baby.* New York and London: Appleton, 1912.

Cohen, W. Spatial and textural characteristics of the *Ganzfeld. American Journal of Psychology,* 1957, 70, 403–410.

Cole, M., & Bruner, J. S. Cultural differences and inferences about psychological processes. *American Psychologist,* 1971, 26, 867–876.

Cole, M., Gay, J., Glick, J. A., & Sharp, D. W. *The Cultural Context of Learning and Thinking.* New York: Basic Books, 1971.

References

Coles, R. *Children of Crisis: A Study of Courage and Fear*. Boston: Atlantic-Little, Brown, 1967.

Collard, R. R. Fear of strangers and play behavior in kittens with varied social experience. *Child Development*, 1968, 39, 877–891.

Comalli, P., Jr., Wapner, S., & Werner, H. Interference effects of Stroop color-word test in childhood, adulthood, and aging. *Journal of Genetic Psychology*, 1962, 100, 47–53.

Commager, H. S. (Ed.) *America in Perspective*. New York: New American Library, 1947.

Connolly, K. J. Perceptual processing in the neonate. Final report to the [British] Medical Research Council, 1970.

Crabtree, C. A. Effects of structuring on productiveness of children's thinking. In *Human Development*, edited by I. J. Gordon. Chicago: Scott, Foresman, 1965.

Cravioto, J. Nutritional deficiencies and mental performance in childhood. In *Environmental Influences*, edited by D. C. Glass. New York: Rockefeller University Press, 1968.

Crites, J. O. Measurement of vocational maturity in adolescence: I. Attitude test of the vocational development inventory. *Psychological Monographs*, 1965, 79, no. 2.

Crowell, D. H., Davis, C. M., Chun, B. J., & Spellacy, F. J. Galvanic skin reflex in newborn humans. *Science*, 1965, 148, 1108–1111.

Currie, G. A. The conceptus as an allograft: Immunological reactivity of the mother. *Proceedings of the Royal Society of Medicine*, 1970, 63, 61–64.

Curzen, P. The antigenicity of the human placenta. *Proceedings of the Royal Society of Medicine*, 1970, 63, 65–66.

Danielsson, B. *Love in the South Seas*. London: Allen & Unwin, 1956.

Darby, C. L., & Riopelle, A. J. Observational learning in the rhesus monkey. *Journal of Comparative and Physiological Psychology*, 1959, 52, 94–98.

Dart, F. E., & Pradhan, P. L. Cross-cultural teaching of science. *Science*, 1967, 155, 649–656.

Davis, A. E., & Bolin, T. D. Milk intolerance in southeast Asia. *Natural History*, February 1969, 54–55.

Davis, C. M. Results of the self-selection of diets by young children. *Canadian Medical Association Journal*, 1939, 41, 257–261.

Davis, H. V., Sears, R. R., Miller, N. C., & Brodbeck, A. J. Effects of cup, bottle, and breast feeding on oral activities of newborn infants. *Pediatrics*, 1948, 2, 549–558.

Davis, K. Final note on a case of extreme isolation. *American Journal of Sociology*, 1947, 52, 432–437.

Davis, R. C., Buchwald, A. M., & Frankman, R. W. Autonomic and muscular responses, and their relation to simple stimuli. *Psychological Monographs*, 1955, 69, no. 405.

Davis, R. C., Garafalo, L., & Kveim, K. Conditions associated with gastrointestinal activity. *Journal of Comparative and Physiological Psychology*, 1959, 52, 466–475.

Dawe, H. C. An analysis of two hundred quarrels of preschool children. *Child Development*, 1934, 5, 139–157.

Dayton, D. H. Early malnutrition and human development. *Children*, 1969, 16, 210–217.

Denenberg, V. H., Hudgens, G. A., & Zarrow, M. X. Mice reared with rats: Modification of behavior by early experience with another species. *Science*, 1963, 143, 380–381.

Denenberg, V. H., & Whimbey, A. E. Behavior of adult rats is modified by the experience their mothers had as infants. *Science*, 1963a, 142, 1192–1193.

Denenberg, V. H., & Whimbey, A. E. Infantile stimulation and animal husbandry: A methodological study. *Journal of Comparative and Physiological Psychology*, 1963b, 56, 877–878.

Dennis, W. Animistic thinking among college and university students. *Scientific Monthly*, 1953, 76, 247–250.

Dennis, W. Racial change in Negro drawings. *Journal of Psychology*, 1968, 69, 129–130.

Dennis, W., & Najarian, P. Infant development under environmental handicap. *Psychological Monographs*, 1957, 71, no. 7.

De Vries, R. Constancy of generic identity in the years three to six. *Monographs of the Society for Research in Child Development*, 1969, 34, no. 3.

Douvan, E., & Adelson, J. *The Adolescent Experience*. New York: Wiley, 1966.

Doxiades, S., Valaes, T., Karaklis, A., & Stavrakakis, D. Risk of severe jaundice in glucose-6-phosphate-dehydrogenase deficiency of the newborn. *Lancet*, December 5, 1964, 1210–1212.

Drillien, C. M. *The Growth and Development of the Prematurely Born Infant*. Baltimore: Williams & Wilkins, 1964.

References

542

Dubignon, J., & Campbell, D. Discrimination between nutriments by the human neonate. *Psychonomic Science*, 1969, 16, 186–187.

Dukes, W. F. N=1. *Psychological Bulletin*, 1965, 64, 74–79.

Dumas, G. *Traité de Psychologie*. Paris: Alcan, 1923.

Dyer, H. S. Is testing a menace to education? *New York State Education*, 1961, 49.

Edwards, R. G., & Fowler, R. E. Human embryos in the laboratory. *Scientific American*, December 1970, 44–54.

Ehrman, L. Mating success and genotype frequency in *Drosophila*. *Animal Behaviour*, 1966, 14, 332–339.

Eimas, P. D., Siqueland, E. R., Jusczyk, P., & Vigorito, J. Speech perception in infants. *Science*, 1971, 171, 303–306.

Eisenberg, L., & Kanner, L. Early infantile autism, 1943–55. *American Journal of Orthopsychiatry*, 1956, 27, 556–566.

Eisenberg, R. B. Auditory behavior in the human neonate: Functional properties of sound and their ontogenetic implications. *International Audiology*, 1969, 8, 34–45.

Eisenberg, R. B., Coursin, D. B., & Rupp, N. R. Habituation to an acoustic pattern as an index of differences among human neonates. *Journal of Auditory Research*, 1966, 6, 239–248.

Eleftheriou, B. E. Unpublished doctoral dissertation, Purdue University, 1961.

Eleftheriou, B., Bronson, F. H., & Zarrow, M. X. Interaction of olfactory and other environmental stimuli on implantation in the deer mouse. *Science*, 1962, 137, 764.

Elkind, D. *Children and Adolescence: Interpretative Essays on Jean Piaget*. New York: Oxford University Press, 1971.

Elkind, D., & Weiss, J. Studies in perceptual development, III: Perceptual exploration. *Child Development*, 1967, 38, 553–561.

Elmer, E. *Children in Jeopardy*. Pittsburgh: University of Pittsburgh Press, 1967.

Elmer, E., & Gregg, G. S. Developmental characteristics of abused children. *Pediatrics*, 1967, 40, 596–602.

Emde, R. N., & Koenig, K. L. Neonatal smiling, frowning, and rapid eye movement states: II. Sleep-cycle study. *Journal of the American Academy of Child Psychiatry*, 1969, 8, 637–656.

Emde, R. N., & Harmon, R. J. Endogenous and exogenous smiling systems in early infancy. *Journal of the American Academy of Child Psychiatry*, 1972, 11, 177–200.

Emde, R. N., Harmon, R. J., Metcalf, D., Koenig, K. L., & Wagonfeld, S. Stress and neonatal sleep. *Psychosomatic Medicine*, 1971, 33, 491–497.

Engen, T., Lipsitt, L. P., & Kaye, H. Olfactory responses and adaptation in the human neonate. *Journal of Comparative and Physiological Psychology*, 1963, 56, 73–77.

Erikson, E. H. *Childhood and Society*. (2nd ed.) New York: Norton, 1963.

Escalona, S., & Heider, G. M. *Prediction and Outcome*. New York: Basic Books, 1959.

Essex, M. F. L. Unpublished data.

Estes, W. K. *Learning Theory and Mental Development*. New York: Academic Press, 1970.

Evans, B. *The Natural History of Nonsense*. New York: Vintage, 1958 (originally 1946).

Fagot, B. I., & Patterson, G. R. An in vivo analysis of reinforcing contingencies for sex-role behaviors in the preschool child. *Developmental Psychology*, 1969, 1, 563–568.

Fantz, R. L. Visual perception from birth as shown by pattern sensitivity. *Annals of the New York Academy of Sciences*, 1963, 118, 793–814.

Faust, M. S. Developmental maturity as a determinant in prestige of adolescent girls. *Child Development*, 1960, 31, 173–184.

Featherstone, J. *Schools Where Children Learn*. New York: Liveright, 1971a.

Featherstone, J. Tempering a fad. *New Republic*, September 25, 1971b, 17–21.

Fillenbaum, S. Impairment in performance with delayed auditory feedback as related to task characteristics. *Journal of Verbal Learning and Verbal Behavior*, 1963, 2, 136–141.

Fisher, C., Gross, J., & Zuch, J. A cycle of penile erections synchronous with dreaming (REM) sleep. *Archives of General Psychiatry*, 1965, 12, 29–45.

Flavell, J. H. *Development Psychology of Jean Piaget*. New York: Van Nostrand-Reinhold, 1963.

Forgays, D. G., & Forgays, J. W. The nature of the effect of free environmental experience in the rat. *Journal of Comparative and Physiological Psychology*, 1952, 45, 322–328.

Fowler, W. Cognitive learning in infancy and early childhood. *Psychological Bulletin*, 1962, 59, 116–152.

References

543

Freda, V. J., Gorman, J. G., & Pollack, W. Rh factor: Prevention of isoimmunization and clinical trial on mothers. *Science*, 1966, 151, 828–829.

Freedman, D. G. Remarks. In *Stimulation in Early Infancy*, edited by [J.] A. Ambrose. New York: Academic Press, 1969.

Freedman, D. G., King, J. A., & Elliot, O. Critical period in the social development of dogs. *Science*, 1961, 133, 1016.

Freedman, M. B. As older sexual codes crumble on campus, a newer honesty takes their place. In *Young Americans*. New York: Time-Life Books, 1966.

Friedan, B. *The Feminine Mystique*. New York: Norton, 1963.

Friedenberg, E. Z. *The Vanishing Adolescent*. Boston: Beacon, 1959.

Friedman, S., Carpenter, G. C., & Nagy, A. N. Decrement and recovery of response to visual stimuli in the newborn human. *Proceedings of the 78th Annual Convention of the American Psychological Association*, 1970a, 5, 273–274.

Friedman, S., Nagy, A. N., & Carpenter, G. C. Newborn attention: Differential response decrement to visual stimuli. *Journal of Experimental Child Psychology*, 1970b, 10, 44–51.

Frisch, R. E., & Revelle, R. Height and weight at menarche and a hypothesis of critical body weights and adolescent events. *Science*, 1970, 169, 397–399.

Gaines, R. Children's selective attention to stimuli: Stage or set? *Child Development*, 1970, 41, 979–991.

Galambos, J. W. *A Guide to Discipline*. Washington, D.C.: National Association for the Education of Young Children, 1969.

Galambos, J. W. *Discipline and Self-Control*. Washington, D.C.: U.S. Government Printing Office, 1970.

Gallup, G. G. Chimpanzees: Self-recognition. *Science*, 1970, 167, 86–87.

Gardner, J., & Gardner, H. A note on selective imitation by a six-week-old infant. *Child Development*, 1970, 41, 1209–1213.

Gardner, R. A., & Gardner, B. T. Teaching sign language to a chimpanzee. *Science*, 1969, 165, 664–672.

Garraty, J. A. The interrelations of psychology and biography. *Psychological Bulletin*, 1954, 51, 569–582.

Geber, M., & Dean, R. F. A. The state of development of newborn African children. *Lancet*, 1957, 1, 1216–1219.

Gellert, E. Children's conceptions of the content and functions of the human body. *Genetic Psychology Monographs*, 1962, 65, 293–405.

German, J. Studying human chromosomes today. *American Scientist*, 1970, 58, 182–201.

Gesell, A. L. *The Mental Growth of the Preschool Child: A Psychological Outline of Normal Development from Birth to the Sixth Year, Including a System of Developmental Diagnosis*. New York: Macmillan, 1925.

Gesell, A., Thompson, H., & Amatruda, C. S. *The Psychology of Early Growth*. New York: Macmillan, 1938.

Ghent, L. Form and its orientation: A child's-eye view. *American Journal of Psychology*, 1961, 74, 177–190.

Gibson, E. J. The ontogeny of reading. *American Psychologist*, 1970, 25, 136–143.

Goethe, J. W. v. *Leiden des jungen Werthers (The Sorrows of Young Werther)*, 1774.

Goldberg, S., & Lewis, M. Play behavior in the year-old infant: Early sex differences. *Child Development*, 1969, 40, 21–31.

Goldfarb, W. Psychological privation in infancy and subsequent adjustment. *American Journal of Orthopsychiatry*, 1945, 15, 247–255.

Golding, W. *Lord of the Flies*. New York: Coward-McCann, 1954.

Goldstein, K. *The Organism*. New York: American Book, 1939.

Goodman, M. E. Child's-eye view of the world of people. *Wheelock Alumnae Quarterly*, Winter 1965, 7–10.

Goodman, P. *Compulsory Mis-education*. New York: Horizon Press, 1964.

Goodman, P. Moral youth in an immoral society. In *Young Americans*. New York: Time-Life Books, 1966.

Goodman, P. No processing whatever. In *Radical School Reform*, edited by R. Gross and B. Gross. New York: Simon & Schuster, 1969.

Goodnow, J. J. Effects of active handling, illustrated by uses for objects. *Child Development*, 1969, 40, 201–212.

Gordon, I. J. Early child stimulation through parent education. Mimeographed, 1969.

Gottlieb, G., & Kuo, Z.-Y. Development of behavior in the duck embryo. *Journal of Comparative and Physiological Psychology*, 1965, 59, 183–188.

Graham, F. K. Behavioral differences between normal and traumatized newborns: I. The test procedures. *Psychological Monographs*, 1956, 70. no. 20.

Graham, F. K., Ernhart, C. B., Thurston, D., & Craft, M. Development three years after perinatal anoxia and other potentially damaging newborn experiences. *Psychological Monographs*, 1962, 76, no. 3.

Gratch, G. A study of the relative dominance of vision and touch in six month old infants. *Child Development*, 1972, 143, 615–623.

Grier, J. B., Counter, S. A., & Shearer, W. M. Prenatal auditory imprinting in chickens. *Science*, 1967, 155, 1692–1693.

Griffiths, C. *Hear.* New York: Exposition, 1966.

Griffiths, R. *The Abilities of Babies.* New York: McGraw-Hill, 1954.

Grose, R. F., & Birney, R. C. (Eds.) *Transfer of Learning.* Princeton, N.J.: Van Nostrand, 1963.

Grossberg, J. M. Behavior therapy: A review. *Psychological Bulletin*, 1964, 62, 73–88.

Guilford, J. P. Intelligence: 1965 model. *American Psychologist*, 1966, 21, 20–26.

Guilford, J. P. *The Nature of Human Intelligence.* New York: McGraw-Hill, 1967.

Gyorgy, P., Dhanamitta, S., & Steers, E. Protective effects of human milk in experimental staphylococcus infection. *Science*, 1962, 137, 338–340.

Haber, R. N., & Haber, R. B. Eidetic imagery: I. Frequency. *Perceptual and Motor Skills*, 1964, 19, 131–138.

Haber, W. B. Reactions to loss of limb: Physiological and psychological aspects. *Annals of the New York Academy of Sciences*, 1958, 74, 14–24.

Haeusserman, E. *Developmental Potential of Preschool Children.* New York: Grune & Stratton, 1958.

Haggard, E. A., Brekstad, A., & Skard, A. G. On the reliability of the anamnestic interview. *Journal of Abnormal and Social Psychology*, 1960, 61, 311–318.

Hahn, E. A reporter at large: Washoese. *The New Yorker*, December 11, 1971, 54–98.

Haith, M. M. Visual scanning in infants. Paper presented at regional meetings of the Society for Research in Child Development, 1968.

Haith, M. M. Infrared television recording and measurement of ocular behavior in the human infant. *American Psychologist*, 1969, 24, 279–283.

Hall, E. T. *The Silent Language.* Garden City, N.Y.: Doubleday, 1959.

Hall, G. S. *Adolescence.* New York: Appleton, 1904. 2 vols.

Halpern, E. The effects of incompatibility between perception and logic in Piaget's stage of concrete operations. *Child Development*, 1965, 36, 491–497.

Hansley, C., & Busse, T. V. Perceptual exploration in Negro children. *Developmental Psychology*, 1969, 1, 446.

Harlow, H. F. The nature of love. *American Psychologist*, 1958, 13, 673–685.

Harlow, H. F. The heterosexual affectional system in monkeys. *American Psychologist*, 1962, 17, 1–9.

Harlow, H. F., & Kuenne, M. Learning to think. *Scientific American*, 1949, 181, 36–39.

Harlow, H. F., & Harlow, M. K. Social deprivation in monkeys. *Scientific American*, 1962, 207, 136–146.

Harper, L. V. The young as a source of stimuli controlling caretaker behavior. *Developmental Psychology*, 1971, 4, 73–88.

Hashmi, F. Immigrants and emotional stress. *Proceedings of the Royal Society of Medicine*, 1970, 63, 631–632.

Hatch, A., Balazs, T., Wiberg, G. S., & Grice, H. C. Long-term isolation stress in rats. *Science*, 1963, 56, 877–878.

Hayes, C. *The Ape in Our House.* New York: Harper, 1951.

Haynes, H., White, B. L., & Held, R. Visual accommodation in human infants. *Science*, 1965, 148, 528–530.

Hebb, D. O. Heredity and environment in mammalian behaviour. *British Journal of Animal Behaviour*, 1953, 1, 43–47.

Hebb, D. O., & Riesen, A. H. The genesis of irrational fears. *Bulletin of the Canadian Psychological Association*, 1943, 3, 49–50.

Heider, F., & Simmel, M. An experimental study of apparent behavior. *American Journal of Psychology*, 1944, 57, 243–259.

References

Hein, A., Held, R., & Gower, E. C. Development and segmentation of visually controlled movement by selective exposure during rearing. *Journal of Comparative and Physiological Psychology*, 1970, 73, 181–187.

Held, R., & Hein, A. Movement-produced stimulation in the development of visually-guided behavior. *Journal of Comparative and Physiological Psychology*, 1963, 56, 872–876.

Hellmuth, J. (Ed.) *The Disadvantaged Child*. Vol. 3. New York: Brunner/Mazel, 1970.

Hendry, C. E., Lippitt, R., & Zander, A. *Reality Practice as Educational Method*. New York: Beacon House, 1944.

Herrnstein, R. I.Q. *Atlantic*, September 1971, 43–64.

Hess, E. H. Imprinting in birds. *Science*, 1964, 146, 1128–1139.

Hess, R. D., & Shipman, V. C. Early experience and the socialization of cognitive modes in children. *Child Development*, 1965, 36, 869–886.

Hess, R. D., Shipman, V. C., Brophy, J. E., & Bear, R. M. *Cognitive Environments of Urban Preschool Children: Follow-up Phase*. Chicago: University of Chicago, Graduate School of Education, 1969.

Hewett, F. M. Teaching speech to an autistic child through operant conditioning. *American Journal of Orthopsychiatry*, 1965, 35, 927–936.

Hilgard, E. R., & Bower, G. H. *Theories of Learning*. New York: Appleton-Century-Crofts, 1966.

Hilton, I. Differences in the behavior of mothers toward first- and later-born children. *Journal of Personality and Social Psychology*, 1967, 7, 282–290.

Hindley, C. B., Filliozat, A. M., Klakenberg, G., Nicolet-Meister, D., & Sand, E. A. Differences in age of walking in five European longitudinal samples. *Human Biology*, 1966, 38, 364–379.

Hirsch, J. Behavior-genetic analysis and its biosocial consequences. *Seminars in Psychiatry*, 1970, 2, 89–105.

Hochberg, J., & Brooks, V. Pictorial recognition as an unlearned ability: A study of one child's performance. *American Journal of Psychology*, 1962, 75, 624–628.

Homans, G. C. Group factors in worker productivity. In National Research Council Committee on Work in Industry, *Fatigue of Workers*. New York: Reinhold, 1941.

Horowitz, F. D. Infant learning and development: Retrospect and prospect. *Merrill-Palmer Quarterly*, 1968, 14, 101–120.

House, B. J., & Zeaman, D. Reward and nonreward in the discrimination learning of imbeciles. *Journal of Comparative and Physiological Psychology*, 1958, 51, 614–618.

Hughes, R. *A High Wind in Jamaica* (also published as *The Innocent Voyage*). New York: New American Library, 1965 (originally 1929).

Hunt, J. McV. An instance of the social origin of conflict resulting in psychoses. *American Journal of Orthopsychiatry*, 1938, 8, 158–164.

Hunt, J. McV. *Intelligence and Experience*. New York: Ronald Press, 1961.

Hunter, W. S. The delayed reaction in animals and children. *Behavior Monographs*, 1913, 2, no. 1.

Hunton, V. C. The recognition of inverted pictures by children. *Journal of Genetic Psychology*, 1955, 86, 281–288.

Hymes, D. Competence and performance in linguistic theory. In *Language Acquisition*, edited by R. Huxley and E. Ingram. London and New York: Academic Press, 1971.

Igel, G. J., & Calvin, A. D. The development of affectional responses in infant dogs. *Journal of Comparative and Physiological Psychology*, 1960, 53, 302–305.

Illich, I. *Deschooling Society*. New York: Harper & Row, 1971.

Inhelder, B. Criteria of the stages of mental development. In *Discussions on Child Development*, vol. 1, edited by J. M. Tanner and B. Inhelder. New York: International Universities Press, 1953.

Inhelder, B., & Piaget, J. *The Early Growth of Logic in the Child*. New York: Harper & Row, 1964.

Jenkins, J. J., & Palermo, D. S. Further changes in word association norms. *Journal of Personality and Social Psychology*, 1965, 1, 303–309.

Jenkins, J. J., & Russell, W. A. Systematic changes in word association norms: 1910–1952. *Journal of Abnormal and Social Psychology*, 1960, 60, 293–304.

Jensen, A. R. Learning abilities of Mexican-American and Anglo children. *California Journal of Educational Research*, 1961, 12, 147–159.

References

Jensen, A. R. How much can we boost IQ and scholastic achievement? *Harvard Educational Review*, 1969, 39, 1–123.

Jirari, C. Form perception, innate form preferences, and visually-mediated head-turning in the human neonate. Unpublished doctoral dissertation, University of Chicago, 1970.

Johnson, E. W. *Love and Sex in Plain Language* (Rev. ed.) Philadelphia: Lippincott, 1965.

Johnson, R. Murderers, in study, called victims of child abuse. *New York Times*, December 9, 1971, 54.

Johnson, R. C. Similarity in IQ of separated identical twins as related to length of time spent in same environment. *Child Development*, 1963, 34, 745–749.

Johnson, W., et al. A study of the onset and development of stuttering. *Journal of Speech and Hearing Disorders*, 1942, 7, 251–257.

Johnston, F. E., Malina, R. M., & Galbraith, M. A. Height, weight, and age at menarche and the "critical weight" hypothesis. *Science*, 1971, 174, 1148.

Jones, M. C. Psychological correlates of somatic development. *Child Development*, 1965, 36, 899–911.

Joyce, J. *A Portrait of the Artist as a Young Man.* New York: Modern Library, 1928 (originally 1917).

Kagan, J. Attention and psychological change in the young child. *Science*, 1970, 170, 826–832.

Kagan, J., & Moss, H. A. *Birth to Maturity.* New York: Wiley, 1962.

Kalish, R. A. The aged and the dying process: The inevitable decisions. *Journal of Social Issues*, 1965, 21, 87–96.

Kanner, L. Early infantile autism. *Journal of Pediatrics*, 1944, 25, 211–217.

Karnes, M. B., Teska, J. A., Hodgins, A. S., & Badger, E. D. Educational intervention at home by mothers of disadvantaged infants. *Child Development*, 1970, 41, 925–935.

Kasdorf, C. A., III, & Schnall, M. Developmental differences in the integration of picture series: Effects of variations in object-attribute relationships. *Human Development*, 1970, 13, 188–200.

Kavanau, J. L. Behavior of captive white-footed mice. *Science*, 1967, 155, 1623–1639.

Kawi, A. A., & Pasamanick, B. Prenatal and paranatal factors in the development of childhood reading disorders. *Monographs of the Society for Research in Child Development*, 1959, 24, no. 4.

Kay, H., & Oldfield-Box, H. A study of learning-sets in rats using 3-dimensional shapes. *Animal Behaviour*, 1965, 13, 19–23.

Kaye, K. Learning by imitation in infants and young children. Paper presented at meetings of the Society for Research in Child Development, 1971.

Keister, M. E. *The "Good Life" for Infants and Toddlers: Group Care of Infants.* Washington, D.C.: National Association for the Education of Young Children, 1970.

Keller, L., Cole, M., Burke, C. J., & Estes, W. K. Reward and information values of trial outcomes in paired-associate learning. *Psychological Monographs*, 1965, 79, no. 12.

Kendler, T. S., & Kendler, H. H. Reversal and nonreversal shifts in kindergarten children. *Journal of Experimental Psychology*, 1959, 58, 56–60.

Keniston, K. *Young Radicals: Notes on Uncommitted Youth.* New York: Harcourt, Brace & World, 1968.

Kessler, J. W. *Psychopathology of Childhood.* Englewood Cliffs, N.J.: Prentice-Hall, 1966.

Kessler, S. The etiological question in mental illness. *Science*, 1969, 165, 1341–1342. (Review of Rosenthal and Kety, 1968.)

Kilbride, J. E., Robbins, M. C., & Kilbride, P. L. The comparative motor development of Baganda, American white, and American black infants. *American Anthropologist*, 1970, 72, 1422–1428.

Kinsey, A. C., et al. *Sexual Behavior in the Human Male.* Philadelphia: Saunders, 1948.

Kirby, D. R. S. The egg and immunology. *Proceedings of the Royal Society of Medicine*, 1970, 63, 59–61.

Kirk, S. A. *Early Education of the Mentally Retarded.* Urbana: University of Illinois Press, 1958.

Kirk, S. A. *Educating Exceptional Children.* Boston: Houghton Mifflin, 1962.

Kirkendall, L. A., & Libby, R. W. Interpersonal relationships—crux of the sexual renaissance. *Journal of Social Issues*, 1966, 22, 45–59.

Kirschner Associates. *A National Survey of the Impacts of Head Start Centers on Community Institutions.* Washington, D.C.: U.S. Department of Health, Education, and Welfare, Office of Child Development, Project Head Start, 1970.

Klatskin, E. H., Jackson, E. B., & Wilkin, L. C. The influence of degree of flexibility in maternal child care practices on early child behavior. *American Journal of Orthopsychiatry*, 1956, 26, 79–93.

Klüver, H. The study of personality and the method of equivalent and non-equivalent stimuli. *Character and Personality*, 1936, 5, 91–112.

Knox, W. E. Inherited enzyme defects. *Hospital Practice*, November 1969, 33–41.

Koff, R. H. Systematic changes in children's word-association norms 1916–63. *Child Development*, 1965, 36, 299–305.

Kohlberg, L. The development of children's orientations toward a moral order: I. Sequence in the development of moral thought. *Vita Humana*, 1963, 6, 11–33.

Kohlberg, L. The development of moral character and moral ideology. In *Review of Child Development Research*, vol. 1, edited by M. L. Hoffman and L. W. Hoffman. New York: Russell Sage Foundation, 1964.

Kohler, I. *On the Structuring and Transformation of the Perceptual World*. New York: International Universities Press, 1964.

Kohnstamm, G. A. Experiments on teaching Piagetian thought operations. In *Cognitive Studies*, vol. 1, edited by J. Hellmuth. New York: Brunner/Mazel, 1970.

Korner, A. F. Neonatal startles, smiles, erections, and reflex sucks as related to state, sex, and individuality. *Child Development*, 1969, 40, 1039–1053.

Korner, A. F. State as variable, as obstacle and as mediator of stimulation in infant research. Paper presented at Merrill-Palmer Institute conference on infancy, 1971.

Korner, A. F., & Thoman, E. B. Visual alertness in neonates as evoked by maternal care. *Journal of Experimental Child Psychology*, 1970, 10, 67–78.

Krasner, L. Studies of the conditioning of verbal behavior. *Psychological Bulletin*, 1958, 55, 148–170.

Krasner, L. Behavior therapy. *Annual Review of Psychology*, 1971, 22, 483–532.

Kreezer, G., & Dallenbach, K. M. Learning the relation of opposition. *American Journal of Psychology*, 1929, 41, 432–441.

Kreutter, M. The teacher in the brown paper bag. *Urban Review*, May 1966.

Kron, R. E., Ipsen, J., & Goddard, K. E. Consistent individual differences in the nutritive sucking behavior of the human newborn. *Psychosomatic Medicine*, 1968, 30, 151–161.

Kugelmass, S., & Lieblich, A. Perceptual exploration in Israeli children. *Child Development*, 1970, 41, 1125–1131.

Kuo, Z-Y. *The Dynamics of Behavior Development*. New York: Random House, 1967.

LaBarba, R. C., White, J. L., Lazar, J., & Klein, M. Early maternal separation and the response to Ehrlich carcinoma in BALB/c mice. *Developmental Psychology*, 1970, 3, 78–80.

Labov, W. *The Study of Non-standard English*. Washington, D.C.: Center for Applied Linguistics, 1969.

Lacey, J. I. The evaluation of autonomic responses: Toward a general solution. *Annals of the New York Academy of Sciences*, 1956, 67, 123–164.

LaCrosse, E. R. Primary influences on the development of competence: The development of a maternal behavior scale. Paper presented at meetings of the Society for Research in Child Development, 1969.

Langness, L. L. *The Life History in Anthropological Science*. New York: Holt, Rinehart and Winston, 1965.

Lapouse, R. The epidemiology of behavior disorders in children. *American Journal of Diseases of Children*, 1966, 111, 594–599.

Lavatelli, C. B. *Piaget's Theory Applied to an Early Childhood Curriculum*. Boston: American Science and Engineering, 1970.

Leacock, E. At play in African villages. *Natural History*, December 1971, 60–65.

Lehr, S., & Rossetto, L., Jr. The new right credo—libertarianism. *New York Times Magazine*, January 10, 1971, 24–25, 86–88, 93–94.

Lenneberg, E. H. *Biological Bases of Language*. New York: Wiley, 1968.

Leon, M. A., & Moltz, H. Discrimination of a maternal pheromone by preweaning albino rats. Paper presented at meetings of the Eastern Psychological Association, 1971.

Leonard, M. F., Rhymes, J. P., & Solnit, A. J. Failure to thrive in infants. *American Journal of Diseases of Children*, 1966, 111, 600–612.

References

Levine, J., Fishman, C., & Kagan, J. Social class and sex as determinants of maternal behavior. Paper presented at meetings of the American Orthopsychiatric Association, 1967.

Levine, S. Psychophysiological effects of infantile stimulation. In *Roots of Behavior*, edited by E. D. Bliss. New York: Harper, 1962.

Levine, S. Infantile stimulation: A perspective. In *Stimulation in Early Infancy*, edited by [J.] A. Ambrose. New York: Academic Press, 1969.

Levine, S., & Mullins, R. F. Hormonal influences on brain organization in infant rats. *Science*, 1966, 152, 1585–1592.

Lévi-Strauss, C. *The Savage Mind*. Chicago: University of Chicago Press, 1966.

Levy, D. M. Experiments on the sucking reflex and social behavior in dogs. *American Journal of Orthopsychiatry*, 1934, 4, 203–224.

Levy, D. M. On instinct-satiation: An experiment on the pecking behavior of chickens. *Journal of Genetic Psychology*, 1938, 18, 327–348.

Levy, D. M. Psychic trauma of operations in children. *American Journal of Diseases of Children*, 1945, 69, 7–25.

Levy, D. M. Advice and reassurance. *American Journal of Public Health*, 1954, 44, 1113–1118.

Levy, D. M. The infant's earliest memory of inoculation: A contribution to public health procedures. *Journal of Genetic Psychology*, 1960, 96, 2–46.

Lewin, K. Behavior and development as a function of the total situation. In *Manual of Child Psychology*, edited by L. Carmichael. New York: Wiley, 1954.

Lewin, K., Lippitt, R., & White, R. K. Patterns of aggressive behavior in experimentally created "social climates." *Journal of Social Psychology*, 1939, 10, 271–299.

Lewis, M. Infant attention: Response decrement as a measure of cognitive process, or what's new, Baby Jane? Paper presented at meetings of the Society for Research in Child Development, 1967.

Lewis, M. M. *How Children Learn to Speak*. New York: Basic Books, 1959.

Lipsitt, L. P., Engen, T., & Kaye, H. Developmental changes in the olfactory threshold of the neonate. *Child Development*, 1963, 34, 371–376.

Lipsitt, L. P., & Levy, N. Electrotactual thresholds in the neonate. *Child Development*, 1959, 30, 547–554.

Lipton, E. L., Steinschneider, A., & Richmond, J. B. Swaddling, a child care practice. *Pediatrics*, 1965, 35, 521–567.

Litman, F. Environmental influences on the development of abilities. Paper presented at meetings of the Society for Research in Child Development, 1969.

Lobb, H. Vision *versus* touch in form discrimination. *Canadian Journal of Psychology*, 1965, 19, 175–187.

Looft, W. R., & Charles, D. C. Modification of the life concept in children. *Developmental Psychology*, 1969, 1, 445.

Lorenz, K. *King Solomon's Ring*. New York: Crowell, 1952.

Lorenz, K. *On Aggression*. New York: Harcourt, Brace & World, 1966.

Lowie, R. H. Review of *Die Feuerlander Indianer*, by M. Gusinde. *American Anthropologist*, 1938, 40, 495–503.

Lubs, H. A., & Ruddle, F. H. Chromosomal abnormalities in the human population: Estimation of rates based on New Haven newborn study. *Science*, 1970, 169, 495–597.

Lustman, S. L. Cultural deprivation. *Psychoanalytic Study of the Child*, 1970, 25, 483–502.

Lynd, H. M. Some questions raised by experiences of shame. Paper presented at meetings of the American Psychological Association, 1966.

Lyon, M. F. X-chromosome inactivation in mammals. In *Advances in Teratology*, vol. 1, edited by D. H. M. Woollam. London and New York: Academic Press, 1966.

Maccoby, E. E., & Bee, H. L. Some speculations concerning the lag between perceiving and performing. *Child Development*, 1965, 36, 368–377.

Macfarlane, J., Allen, L., & Honzik, M. P. *A Developmental Study of the Behavior Problems of Normal Children between Twenty-one Months and Fourteen Years*. Berkeley and Los Angeles: University of California Press, 1954.

Machotka, P. The development of esthetic criteria in childhood: I. Justifications of preference. *Child Development*, 1966, 37, 877–885.

Maier, N. R. F. Reasoning in children. *Journal of Comparative Psychology*, 1936, 21, 357–366.

Maier, N. R. F. Maier's Law. *American Psychologist*, 1960, 15, 208–212.

Maltz, H. E. Ontogenetic changes in the meaning of concepts as measured by the semantic differential. *Child Development*, 1963, 34, 667–674.

Maretzki, T. W., & Maretzki, H. *Taira: An Okinawan Village*. New York: Wiley, 1966.

Marler, P., & Tamura, M. Culturally transmitted patterns of vocal behavior in sparrows. *Science*, 1964, 146, 1483–1486.

Maslow, A. H. Self-actualizing people: A study of psychological health. *Personality Symposia*, 1950, 1, 11–34.

Mason, M. K. Learning to speak after years of silence. *Journal of Speech and Hearing Disorders*, 1942, 7, 295–304.

Masters, W. H., & Johnson, V. E. *Human Sexual Response*. Boston: Little, Brown, 1966.

McCall, R. B., & Kagan, J. Stimulus-schema discrepancy and attention in the infant. *Journal of Experimental Child Psychology*, 1967, 5, 381–390.

McClelland, D. *The Achieving Society*. Princeton, N.J.: Van Nostrand, 1961.

McCreary-Juhasz, A. How accurate are student evaluations of the extent of their knowledge of human sexuality? *Journal of School Health*, 1967, 37, 409–412.

McGaugh, J. L., Jennings, R. D., & Thompson, C. W. Effect of distribution of practice on the maze learning of descendants of the Tryon maze bright and maze dull strains. *Psychological Reports*, 1962, 9, 147–150.

McGinley, P. *Times Three*. New York: Viking, 1952.

Mead, M. *And Keep Your Powder Dry*. New York: Morrow, 1942.

Mears, D. R. Contributions of a ghetto culture to symptom formation. *Psychoanalytic Study of the Child*, 1970, 25, 209–230.

Mecklenburger, J. A., & Wilson, J. A. Learning C.O.D. Can the schools buy success? *Saturday Review*, September 18, 1971, 62–64, 76–79.

Medawar, P. H. *The Future of Man*. New York: Basic Books, 1959.

Meichenbaum, D. H. Implications of cognitive training research for educational television: Ways of improving Sesame Street. *Proceedings of the 79th Annual Convention of the American Psychological Association*, 1971, 195–196.

Meier, G. W. Other data on the effects of social isolation during rearing upon adult reproductive behaviour in the rhesus monkey (Macaca-Mulattta). *Animal Behaviour*, 1965, 13, 228–231.

Melson, W. H., & McCall, R. B. Attentional responses of five-month girls to discrepant auditory stimuli. *Child Development*, 1970, 41, 1159–1171.

Melzack, R., Penick, E., & Beckett, A. The problem of "innate fear" of the hawk shape. *Journal of Comparative and Physiological Psychology*, 1959, 52, 694–698.

Meredith, H. V. Body size of contemporary groups of eight-year-old children studied in different parts of the world. *Monographs of the Society for Research in Child Development*, 1969a, 34, no. 1.

Meredith, H. V. Body size of contemporary youth in different parts of the world. *Monographs of the Society for Research in Child Development*, 1969b, 34, no. 7.

Merton, R. K. *On the Shoulders of Giants*. New York: Free Press, 1965.

Meyer, W. J., & Offenbach, S. I. Effectiveness of reward and punishment as a function of task complexity. *Journal of Comparative and Physiological Psychology*, 1962, 55, 532–534.

Michotte, A. *La Perception de la Causalité*. Louvain: Institut Supérieure de Philosophie, 1946.

Milgram, S. The experience of living in cities. *Science*, 1970, 167, 1461–1468.

Miller, G. A., Galanter, E., & Pribram, K. H. *Plans and the Structure of Behavior*. New York: Holt, Rinehart and Winston, 1960.

Miller, L. Children and money. *Redbook*, November 1959, 39–41, 66, 68.

Miller, N. Psychosomatic effects of specific types of training. *Annals of the New York Academy of Sciences*, 1969, 159, 1025–1040.

Miller, W., & Ervin, S. The development of grammar in child language. In *The Acquisition of Language*, edited by U. Bellugi and R. Brown. *Monographs of the Society for Research in Child Development*, 1964, 29, no. 1.

Mintz, B. (Ed.) *Environmental Influences on Prenatal Development*. Chicago: University of Chicago Press, 1958.

Minuchin, P., & Biber, B. A child development approach to language in the preschool disadvantaged child. Paper presented at meetings of the Society for Research in Child Development, 1967.

Mischel, W., & Metzner, R. Preference for delayed reward as a function of age, intelligence, and length of delay interval. *Journal of Abnormal and Social Psychology*, 1962, 64, 425–431.

References

Moltz, H., & Stettner, L. J. The influence of patterned-light deprivation on the critical period for imprinting. *Journal of Comparative and Physiological Psychology*, 1961, 54, 279–283.

Mönks, F. Future time perspective in adolescents. *Human Development*, 1968, 11, 107–123.

Montagu, M. F. A. *The Direction of Human Development*. New York: Harper, 1955.

Montagu, M. F. A. *Prenatal Influences*. Springfield, Ill.: Thomas, 1962.

Montagu, [M. F.] A. (Ed.) *Man and Aggression*. New York: Oxford, 1968.

Moore, A. U. Studies on the formation of the mother-neonate bond in sheep and goat. Paper presented at meetings of the American Psychological Association, 1960.

Moore, T., & Ucko, L. E. Night waking in early infancy. *Archives of Disease in Childhood*, 1957, 32, 333–342.

Moorehead, A. Our far-flung correspondents: It won't bite you. *The New Yorker*, November 19, 1966, 186–191.

Morgan, G. A., & Ricciuti, H. N. Infants' responses to strangers in the first year. In *Determinants of Infant Behaviour IV*, edited by B. M. Foss. London: Methuen, 1969.

Moriarty, A. E., & Toussieng, P. W. Renewal without rebellion: A Midwest spectrum. Mimeographed, 1970.

Moss, H. A. Sex, age, and state as determinants of mother-infant interaction. *Merrill-Palmer Quarterly*, 1967, 13, 19–36.

Mowrer, O. H. *Learning Theory and the Symbolic Processes*. New York: Wiley, 1960.

Mumford, L. *The Myth of the Machine: The Pentagon of Power*. New York: Harcourt Brace Jovanovich, 1970.

Murphy, G. *Human Potentialities*. New York: Basic Books, 1958.

Murphy, L. B. *Social Behavior and Child Personality*. New York: Columbia University Press, 1937.

Murphy, L. B., & associates. *Personality in Young Children*. New York: Basic Books, 1956.

Neff, W. S. Socioeconomic status and intelligence: A critical survey. *Psychological Bulletin*, 1938, 35, 727–757.

Nelson, T. H. The Hypertext. *International Federation for Documentation: Abstracts, 1965 Congress*, p. 80.

Nelson, T. H. No more teachers' dirty looks. *Computer Decisions*, September 1970, 16–23.

Newman, H. H., Freeman, F. N., & Holzinger, K. J. *Twins*. Chicago: University of Chicago Press, 1937.

Nixon, R. *The Art of Growing*. New York: Random House, 1962.

O'Brien, J. S., Okada, S., Fillerup, D. L., Veath, M. L., Adornato, B., Brenner, P. H., & Leroy, J. G. Tay-Sachs disease: Prenatal diagnosis. *Science*, 1971, 172, 61–64.

Ogburn, W. F., & Bose, N. K. On the trail of the wolf-children. *Genetic Psychology Monographs*, 1959, 60, 117–193.

Ogilvie, D. M. Distinguishing social behaviors of competent and incompetent three to six year old children. Paper presented at meetings of the Society for Research in Child Development, 1969.

Olton, R. M., & Crutchfield, R. S. Developing the skills of productive thinking. In *Trends and Issues in Developmental Psychology*, edited by P. H. Mussen, J. Langer, and M. Covington. New York: Holt, Rinehart and Winston, 1969.

Olum, V. Developmental differences in the perception of causality. *American Journal of Psychology*, 1956, 69, 417–423.

Opie, I., & Opie, P. *The Lore and Language of School Children*. Oxford: Clarendon, 1959.

O'Reilly, E., & Steger, J. A. Children's use of context in judgment of weight. *Child Development*, 1970, 41, 1095–1101.

Ortar, G. R. Classification of speech directed at children by mothers of different level of education and cultural background. Paper presented at meetings of the Eighteenth International Congress of Psychology, 1966.

Osgood, C. E. On understanding and creating sentences. *American Psychologist*, 1963, 18, 735–751.

Osgood, C. E., Suci, G. J., & Tannenbaum, P. H. *The Measurement of Meaning*. Urbana: University of Illinois Press, 1957.

Palermo, D. S., & Jenkins, J. J. Changes in word associations of fourth- and fifth-grade children from 1916 to 1961. *Journal of Verbal Learning and Verbal Behavior*, 1965, 4, 180–187.

References

551

Papoušek, H. Conditioning during early postnatal development. In *Behavior in Infancy and Early Childhood*, edited by Y. Brackbill and G. G. Thompson. New York: Free Press, 1967.

Parker, R. K., Ambron, S., Danielson, G. I., Halbrook, M. C., & Levine, J. A. *Overview of Cognitive and Language Programs for 3, 4, and 5 Year Old Children.* New York: Center for Advanced Study in Education, no date.

Parkin, J. M., & Warren, N. A comparative study of neonatal behaviour and development. Paper presented at the University of East Africa Social Science Conference, 1969.

Parloff, M. B. Group therapy and the small-group field: An encounter. *International Journal of Group Psychotherapy*, 1970, 20, 267–304.

Parry, W. H. Health and welfare of immigrants. *Proceedings of the Royal Society of Medicine*, 1970, 63, 633–636.

Pasamanick, B., & Knobloch, H. Early feeding and birth difficulties in childhood schizophrenia: An explanatory note. *Journal of Psychology*, 1963, 56, 73–77.

Pavenstedt, E. (Ed.) *The Drifters: Children of Disorganized Lower-Class Families.* Boston: Little, Brown, 1967.

Piaget, J. Das Umdrehen des Gegenstandes beim Kind unter einem Jahr. *Psychologische Rundschau*, 1932, 4, 110–115.

Piaget, J. *The Moral Judgment of the Child.* Glencoe, Ill.: Free Press, 1948 (originally 1932).

Piaget, J. *The Construction of Reality in the Child.* New York: Basic Books, 1954.

Platt, J. R. The step to man. *Science*, 1965, 149, 607–613.

Polanyi, M. *Personal Knowledge.* Chicago: University of Chicago Press, 1958.

Porter, I. H. *Heredity and Disease.* New York: McGraw-Hill–Blakiston, 1968.

Postman, N., & Weingartner, C. *Teaching as a Subversive Activity.* New York: Delta, 1969.

Pratt, K. C. The neonate. In *Manual of Child Psychology*, edited by L. Carmichael. New York: Wiley, 1954.

Prechtl, H. F. R. The directed head turning response and allied movements of the human baby. *Behaviour*, 1958, 13, 212–242.

Prechtl, H. F. R. Neurological findings in newborn infants after pre- and paranatal complications. In *Aspects of Praematurity and Dysmaturity*, edited by J. H. P. Jonxis et al. Leiden: Kroese, 1968.

Premack, D. Language in chimpanzees? *Science*, 1971, 172, 808–822.

Provence, S., & Lipton, R. *Children in Institutions.* New York: International Universities Press, 1962.

Pyles, M. K., Stolz, H. R., & Macfarlane, J. S. The accuracy of mothers' reports on birth and developmental data. *Child Development*, 1935, 6, 165–176.

Querido, A., & Mead, M. Mental health and the flood in Holland. *World Mental Health*, 1953, 5, 34–38.

Rainwater, L. Some aspects of lower class sexual behavior. *Journal of Social Issues*, 1966, 22, 96–108.

Reich, C. J. *The Greening of America.* New York: Random House, 1970.

Rheingold, H. L. The social and socializing infant. In *Handbook of Socialization Theory and Research*, edited by D. A. Goslin. New York: Rand McNally, 1969a.

Rheingold, H. L. The effect of a strange environment on the behavior of infants. In *Determinants of Infant Behaviour IV*, edited by B. M. Foss. London: Methuen, 1969b.

Rheingold, H. L., & Eckerman, C. O. The infant's free entry into a new environment. *Journal of Experimental Child Psychology*, 1969, 8, 271–283.

Rheingold, H. L., & Samuels, H. R. Maintaining the positive behavior of infants by increased stimulation. *Developmental Psychology*, 1969, 1, 520–527.

Ribble, M. A. *The Rights of Infants.* (Rev. ed.) New York: Columbia University Press, 1965.

Richards, M. P. M. Maternal behavior in the golden hamster: Responsiveness to young in virgin, pregnant, and lactating females. *Animal Behaviour*, 1966, 14, 310–313.

Richardson, C., & Church, J. A developmental analysis of proverb interpretations. *Journal of Genetic Psychology*, 1959, 194, 169–179.

Richter, C. P. Total self-regulatory functions in animals and human beings. *Harvey Lectures*, 1942–1943, 38, 63–103.

Rimland, B. *Infantile Autism.* New York: Appleton-Century-Crofts, 1964.

Ring, K., Lipinski, C. E., & Braginsky, D. The

relationship of birth order to self-evaluation, anxiety reduction, and susceptibility to emotional contagion. *Psychological Monographs*, 1965, 79, no. 10.

Riopelle, A. J. Observational learning of a position habit by monkeys. *Journal of Comparative and Physiological Psychology*, 1960, 53, 426–428.

Ripley, A. Birth defects in livestock linked to toxic weeds. *New York Times*, January 31, 1971, 29.

Roberts, E. Thumb and finger sucking in relation to feeding in early infancy. *American Journal of Disease in Children*, 1944, 68, 7–8.

Roberts, K. E., & Schoellkopf, J. A. Eating, sleeping, and elimination practices of a group of two-and-one-half-year-old children. *American Journal of Diseases of Children*, 1951, 92, 121–152.

Robertson, J. *Young Children in Hospital.* (2nd ed.) London: Tavistock, and New York: Barnes & Noble, 1970.

Robinowitz, R. Learning the relation of opposition as related to scores on the Wechsler Intelligence Scale for Children. *Journal of Genetic Psychology*, 1956, 88, 25–30.

Robinson, A., & Puck, T. T. Sex chromatin in newborns: Presumptive evidence for external factors in human nondisjunction. *Science*, 1965, 148, 83–85.

Robinson, H. B. An experimental examination of the size-weight illusion in young children. *Child Development*, 1964, 35, 91–107.

Robson, K. S., Pedersen, F. A., & Moss, H. A. Developmental observations of diadic gazing in relation to the fear of strangers and social approach behavior. *Child Development*, 1969, 40, 619–627.

Rock, I., & Victor, J. Vision and touch: An experimentally created conflict between the two senses. *Science*, 1964, 143, 594–596.

Roffwarg, H. P., Muzio, J. N., & Dement, W. C. Ontogenetic development of the human sleep-dream cycle. *Science*, 1966, 152, 604–619.

Rosenblatt, J. S., Turkevitz, G., & Schneirla, T. C. Early socialization in the domestic cat as based on feeding and other relationships between female and young. In *Determinants of Infant Behavior*, edited by B. M. Foss. New York: Wiley, 1961.

Rosenblith, J. F. The modified Graham behavior test for neonates: Test-retest reliability, normative data, and hypotheses for future work. *Biology of the Neonate*, 1961, 3, 174.

Rosenthal, D., & Kety, S. (Eds.) *The Transmission of Schizophrenia.* New York: Pergamon, 1968.

Rosenzweig, M. R. Environmental complexity, cerebral change, and behavior. *American Psychologist*, 1966, 21, 321–332.

Rosenzweig, S., & Kogan, K. L. *Psychodiagnostics.* New York: Grune & Stratton, 1949.

Ross, J. B., & McLaughlin, M. M. (Eds.) *A Portable Medieval Reader.* New York: Viking, 1949.

Rossi, E. L., & Rossi, S. I. Concept utilization, serial order and recall in nursery-school children. *Child Development*, 1965, 36, 771–778.

Roth, P. *Letting Go.* New York: Random House, 1962.

Rothbart, M. K., & Maccoby, E. E. Parents' differential reactions to sons and daughters. *Journal of Personality and Social Psychology*, 1966, 4, 237–243.

Rowan, C. T. Child development head refreshingly bold. *Washington Star*, July 5, 1970.

Rubenstein, J. Maternal attentiveness and subsequent exploratory behavior. *Child Development*, 1967, 38, 1089–1100.

Rubin, T. I. *Jordi.* New York: Macmillan, 1960.

Rudin, S. A. National motives predict psychogenic death rates 25 years later. *Science*, 1968, 160, 901–903.

Sackett, G. P. Effect of rearing conditions upon the behavior of rhesus monkeys. *Child Development*, 1965, 36, 855–868.

Salapatek, P., & Kessen, W. Visual scanning of triangles by the human newborn. *Journal of Experimental Child Psychology*, 1966, 3, 155–167.

Salinger, J. D. *The Catcher in the Rye.* Boston: Little, Brown, 1951.

Sampson, E. E. The study of ordinal position: Antecedents and outcomes. Mimeographed, 1964.

Sander, L. W. Regulation and organization in the early infant-caretaker system. In *Brain and Early Behavior*, edited by R. J. Robinson. New York: Academic Press, 1969.

Sanger, M. D. Language learning in infancy: A review of the autistic hypothesis and an observational study of infants. Unpublished Ed. D. dissertation, Harvard University, 1955.

Sarason, S. B., Hill, K. T., & Zimbardo, P. G. A longitudinal study of the relation of test anxiety to performance on intelligence and achievement tests. *Monographs of the Society for Research in Child Development*, 1964, 29, no. 7.

Sayegh, Y., & Dennis, W. The effect of supplementary experiences upon the behavioral development of infants in institutions. *Child Development*, 1965, 36, 81–90.

Scarr-Salapatek, S. Unknowns in the IQ equation. *Science*, 1971a, 174, 1223–1228. (Review of the Jensen controversy, the Herrnstein article, and a more recent book: Eysenck, H. J. *The IQ Argument*. New York: Library Press, 1971.)

Scarr-Salapatek, S. Race, social class, and IQ. *Science*, 1971b, 174, 1285–1295.

Schaefer, E. S. A configurational analysis of children's reports of parent behavior. *Journal of Consulting Psychology*, 1965, 29, 552–557.

Schaefer, E. S. A home tutoring program. *Children*, March-April, 1969, 59–61.

Schaffer, H. R., & Emerson, P. The development of social attachments in infancy. *Monographs of the Society for Research in Child Development*, 1964, 29, no. 3.

Schaffer, H. R., & Emerson, P. Patterns of response to physical contact in early human development. *Journal of Child Psychology and Psychiatry*, 1965, 5, 1–13.

Schein, M. W., & Hale, E. B. The effect of early social experience on male sexual behavior of androgen-injected turkeys. *Animal Behaviour*, 1959, 7, 189–200.

Schiff, W. The perception of impending collision. A study of visually directed avoidant behavior. *Psychological Monographs*, 1965, 79, no. 11.

Schmidt, W. H. O., & Nzimande, A. Cultural differences in color/form preference and in classificatory behavior. *Human Development*, 1970, 13, 140–148.

Schnall, M. Age differences in the integration of progressively changing visual patterns. *Human Development*, 1968, 11, 287–295.

Scott, J. P. *Animal Behavior*. Chicago: University of Chicago Press, 1958. .

Scott, J. P. Critical periods in behavioral development. *Science*, 1962, 138, 949–958.

Scott, J. P. Biology and human aggression. *American Journal of Orthopsychiatry*, 1970, 40, 568–576.

Scott, J. P., & Fuller, J. L. *Genetics and the Social Behavior of the Dog*. Chicago: University of Chicago Press, 1965.

Scrimshaw, N. S. Early malnutrition and central

nervous system function. *Merrill-Palmer Quarterly*, 1969, 15, 375–388.

Searle, L. V. The organization of hereditary maze-brightness and maze-dullness. *Genetic Psychology Monographs*, 1949, 39, 279–325.

Shantz, C. U., & Watson, J. S. Spatial abilities and spatial egocentrism in the young child. *Child Development*, 1971, 42, 171–181.

Sherif, M., Harvey, O. J., White, B. J., Hood, W. R., & Sherif, C. W. *Intergroup Conflict and Cooperation*. Norman, Okla.: University Book Exchange, 1961.

Sherman, M. The differentiation of emotional responses. *Journal of Comparative Psychology*, 1927, 7, 265–284.

Sherwin, R. V. The law and sexual relationships. *Journal of Social Issues*, 1966, 22, 109–122.

Shesh, D. B. Measurement of aesthetic sense of children. *Psychologia*, 1966, 9, 236–238.

Sichel, J. L., and Chandler, K. A. The color-word interference test: The effects of varied color-word combination upon verbal response latency. *Journal of Psychology*, 1969, 72, 219–231.

Sigel, I. E. How intelligence tests limit understanding of intelligence. *Merrill-Palmer Quarterly*, 1963, 9, 39–56.

Silberman, C. E. *Crisis in the Classroom*. New York: Random House, 1970.

Simmel, M. L. The absence of phantoms for congenitally missing limbs. *American Journal of Psychology*, 1961, 74, 467–470.

Simpson, G. G. The biological nature of man. *Science*, 1966, 152, 472–478.

Singer, J. L. *Daydreaming*. New York: Random House, 1966.

Siqueland, E. R. The development of instrumental exploratory behavior during the first year of human life. Paper presented at meetings of the Society for Research in Child Development, 1969.

Siqueland, E. R. Biological and experimental determinants of exploration in infancy. Paper presented at the First National Biological Conference, 1970.

Siqueland, E. R., & Lipsitt, L. P. Conditioned head-turning in human newborns. *Journal of Experimental Psychology*, 1966, 3, 356–376.

Skeels, H. M. Adult status of children with contrasting early life experiences. *Monographs of the Society for Research in Child Development*, 1966, 31, no. 3.

References

Skinner, B. F. *Walden Two.* New York: Macmillan, 1948.

Skinner, B. F. *Verbal Behavior.* New York: Appleton-Century-Crofts, 1957.

Skinner, B. F. Behaviorism at fifty. *Science,* 1963, 140, 951–958.

Skinner, B. F. *Beyond Freedom and Dignity.* New York: Knopf, 1971.

Smith, C. J. Mass action and early environment in the rat. *Journal of Comparative and Physiological Psychology,* 1959, 52, 154–156.

Smith, R. P. *"Where Did You Go?" "Out." "What Did You Do?" "Nothing."* New York: Norton, 1957.

Smith, R. P. *How to Do Nothing with Nobody, All Alone by Yourself.* New York: Norton, 1958.

Smith, S. M., Brown, H. O., Toman, J. E. P., & Goodman, L. S. The lack of cerebral effects of D-Tubocurarine. *Anesthesiology,* 1947, 8, 1–14.

Smith, W. M., McCrary, J. W., & Smith, K. U. Delayed visual feedback and behavior. *Science,* 1960, 132, 1013–1014.

Solomon, R. L. Punishment. *American Psychologist,* 1963, 18, 329–253.

Spears, W. C. Assessment of visual preference and discrimination in the four-month-old infant. *Journal of Comparative and Physiological Psychology,* 1964, 57, 381–386.

Spence, K. W. Cognitive factors in the extinction of the conditioned eyelid response in humans. *Science,* 1963, 140, 1224–1225.

Sperry, R. W. Summation. In *The Anatomy of Memory,* edited by D. P. Kimble. Palo Alto, Calif.: Science and Behavior Books, 1965.

Spiker, C. C., & McCandless, B. R. The concept of intelligence and the philosophy of science. *Psychological Review,* 1954, 61, 255–266.

Spiro, M. E. *Children of the Kibbutz.* Cambridge: Harvard University Press, 1958.

Spitz, R. A. The smiling response: A contribution to the ontogenesis of social relations. *Genetic Psychology Monographs,* 1946, 34, 57–125.

Spitz, R. A. The psychogenic diseases in infancy: An attempt at their etiologic classification. *Psychoanalytic Study of the Child,* 1951, 6, 255–275.

Spitz, R. A. Paper presented at meetings of the New York Psychoanalytic Society, March 1966.

Spock, B. *Baby and Child Care.* New York: Pocket Books, 1957.

Staats, A. W., & Butterfield, W. H. Treatment of nonreading in a culturally deprived juvenile delinquent: An application of reinforcement principles. *Child Development,* 1965, 36, 925–949.

Stanley, W. C., Bacon, W. E., & Fehr, C. Discriminated instrumental learning in neonatal dogs. *Journal of Comparative and Physiological Psychology,* 1970, 70, 335–443.

Staples, R. The responses of infants to color. *Journal of Experimental Psychology,* 1932, 15, 119–141.

Stechler, G. Newborn attention as affected by medication during labor. *Science,* 1964, 144, 315–317.

Sternglass, E. J. Cancer: Relation of prenatal radiation to development of the disease in childhood. *Science,* 1963, 140, 1102–1104.

Stevens, S. The "rat packs" of New York. *New York Times Magazine,* November 28, 1971, 29, 91–95.

Stevenson, H. W. The taxonomy of tasks. Paper presented at meetings of the International Society for the Study of Behavioral Development, 1971.

Stevenson, H. W., Hale, G. A., Klein, R. E., & Miller, L. K. Interrelations and correlates in children's learning and problem solving. *Monographs of the Society for Research in Child Development,* 1968, 33, no. 7.

Stevenson, H. W., & McBee, G. The learning of object and pattern discrimination by children. *Journal of Comparative and Physiological Psychology,* 1958, 51, 752–754.

Stevenson, H. W., Williams, A. M., & Coleman, E. Interrelations among learning and performance tasks in disadvantaged children. *Journal of Educational Psychology,* 1971, 62, 179–184.

Stoddard, G. D. *The Meaning of Intelligence.* New York: Macmillan, 1943.

Stoller, A. Virus-chromosome interaction as a possible cause of cases of Down's syndrome (mongolism) and other congenital anomalies. In *Advances in Teratology,* vol. 3, edited by D. H. M. Woollam. London and New York: Academic Press, 1968.

Stone, L. J. Unpublished data.

Stone, L. J. A critique of studies of infant isolation. *Child Development,* 1954, 25, 9–20.

Stone, L. J. Letter to the editor. *Science,* 1965, 148, 1173–1174.

Stone, L. J. A child's world. Mimeographed, 1966. (This 52-page compilation of Stuart's comments may be obtained from Professor Stone at Department of Psychology, Vassar College, Poughkeepsie, N.Y., 12601, for $2.)

Stone, L. J., Smith, H. T., & Murphy, L. B. (Eds.). *The Competent Infant: Readings and Commentary.* New York: Basic Books (in press).

Stone, L. J., & associates. *Incitement to Reading.* 16 mm., black and white, sound. 37 min. New York University Film Library.

Stone, L. J., & associates. *Learning Is Searching: A Third Grade Studies Man's Early Tools.* 16 mm., black and white, sound. 30 min. New York University Film Library.

Stotland, E., & Dunn, R. E. Identification, "oppositeness," authoritarianism, self-esteem, and birth order. *Psychological Monographs,* 1962, 76, no. 9.

Stott, L. H., & Ball, R. S. Infant and preschool mental tests. *Monographs of the Society for Research in Child Development,* 1965, 30, no. 3.

Sullivan, W. Boys and girls are now maturing earlier. *New York Times,* January 24, 1971, 1, 36. (This article is based on research by H. Bakwin, A. Damon, S. F. Daw, F. Falkner, Rose E. Frisch [see Frisch and Revelle, 1970], J. McClung, M. Schatzoff, H. C. Stuart, J. M. Tanner, A. E. Treloar, Isabelle Valadian, R. J. Wurtman, and Leonora Zacharias.)

Szasz, T. S. The uses of naming and the myth of mental illness. *American Psychologist,* 1961, 16, 59–65.

Tauber, E. S., & Koffler, S. Optomotor response in human infants to apparent motion: Evidence of innateness. *Science,* 1966, 152, 382–383.

Taussig, H. B. The thalidomide syndrome. *Scientific American,* August 1962, 29–35.

Teicher, J. D., & Jacobs, J. Adolescents who attempt suicide. *American Journal of Psychiatry,* 1966, 11, 122.

Telfer, M. A., Baker, D., Clark, G. R., & Richardson, C. E. Incidence of gross chromosomal errors among tall criminal American males. *Science,* 1967, 159, 1249–1250.

Thiessen, D. D., & Rodgers, D. A. Population density and endocrine function. *Psychological Bulletin,* 1961, 58, 441–451.

Thoman, E. B., & Korner, A. F. Effects of vestibular stimulation on the behavior and development of infant rats. *Developmental Psychology,* 1971, 5, 92–98.

Thoman, E. B., Turner, A. M., Leiderman, P. H., & Barnett, C. R. Neonate-mother interaction: Effects of parity on feeding behavior. *Child Development,* 1970, 41, 1103–1111.

Thomas, A., Chess, S., Birch, H. G., Hertzig, M., & Korn, S. *Behavioral Individuality in Early Childhood.* New York: New York University Press, 1963.

Thompson, W. R., & Schaefer, T. Early environmental stimulation. In *Functions of Varied Experience,* edited by D. W. Fiske and S. R. Maddi. Homewood, Ill.: Dorsey, 1961.

Thorpe, W. H. The development of song patterns by birds as evidence for sensitive periods in learning. *Acta Psychologica,* 1964, 23, 99–100.

Tiger, L. *Men in Groups.* New York: Random House, 1969.

Tiger, L., & Fox, R. *The Imperial Animal.* New York: Holt, Rinehart and Winston, 1971.

Tighe, T. J. Reversal and nonreversal shifts in monkeys. *Journal of Comparative and Physiological Psychology,* 1964, 58, 324–326.

Tinklepaugh, O. L. An experimental study of representative factors in monkeys. *Journal of Comparative Psychology,* 1928, 8, 197–236.

Torrance, E. P. *Guiding Creative Talent.* Englewood Cliffs, N.J.: Prentice-Hall, 1962.

Touwen, B. C. L., & Prechtl, H. F. R. The neurological examination of the child with minor nervous dysfunction. *Clinics in Developmental Medicine,* No. 38. London: Heinemann, and Philadelphia: Lippincott, 1970.

Tryon, R. C. Genetic differences in maze-learning ability in rats. *Thirty-ninth Yearbook of the National Society for the Study of Education,* 1940, 111–119.

Tuccille, J. *Radical Libertarianism.* Indianapolis: Bobbs-Merrill, 1970.

Tulkin, S. F. Mother-infant interaction in the first year of life. An inquiry into the influences of social class. Unpublished doctoral dissertation, Harvard University, 1970.

Turkewitz, G., Birch, H. G., Moreau, T., Levy, L., & Cornwell, A. C. Effect of intensity of auditory stimulation on directional eye movements in the human neonate. *Animal Behaviour,* 1966, 14, 93–101.

Tyler, L. E. *Tests and Measurements.* Englewood Cliffs, N.J.: Prentice-Hall, 1963.

References

Tyler, L. E. *The Psychology of Human Differences.* New York: Appleton-Century-Crofts, 1965.

U.S. Department of Commerce, Bureau of the Census. *Statistical Abstract of the United States.* Washington, D.C.: U.S. Government Printing Office, 1968.

U.S. Department of Health, Education, and Welfare, Children's Bureau. *Infant Care.* Washington, D.C.: U.S. Government Printing Office, periodically revised.

U.S. Department of Health, Education, and Welfare. *Minimal Brain Dysfunction in Children.* Washington, D.C.: U.S. Government Printing Office, National Institute of Neurological Diseases and Blindness Monograph no. 3, 1966.

U.S. Department of Health, Education, and Welfare, Public Health Service, Health Services and Mental Health Administration. Height and weight of children in the United States, India, and the United Arab Republic. *Vital and Health Statistics,* Series 3, no. 14, 1970.

Uzgiris, I. C. Patterns of vocal and gestural imitation. Paper presented at meetings of the International Society for the Study of Behavioral Development, 1971.

Valentine, C. W. The colour perception and colour preferences of an infant during its fourth and eighth months. *British Journal of Psychology,* 1913–1914, 6, 363–386.

Van den Berg, J. H. *The Changing Nature of Man.* New York: Dell, 1964.

Verplanck, W. S. A glossary of some terms used in the objective science of behavior. *Psychological Review,* 1957, 64, Supplement 8.

Walk, R. D., & Dodge, S. H. Visual depth perception of a 10-month-old monocular human infant. *Science,* 1962, 137, 529–530.

Walk, R. D., & Gibson, E. J. A comparative and analytical study of visual depth perception. *Psychological Monographs,* 1961, 75, no. 15.

Wardrop, J. L., Goodwin, W. L., Klausmeier, H. J., Olton, R. M., Covington, M. V., Crutchfield, R. S., & Ronda, T. The development of productive thinking skills in 5th-grade children. *Journal of Experimental Education,* 1969, 37, 67–77.

Warfield, F. *Cotton in My Ears.* New York: Viking, 1948.

Warren, N. African infant precocity. *Psychological Bulletin,* 1972 (in press).

Watson, J. B. *Psychology from the Standpoint of a Behaviorist.* Philadelphia: Lippincott, 1919.

Watson, J. B. *Psychological Care of Infant and Child.* New York: Norton, 1928.

Watson, J. S. Smiling, cooing, and "the game." Paper presented at meetings of the American Psychological Association, 1970.

Weatherly, D. Self-perceived rate of physical maturation and personality in late adolescence. *Child Development,* 1964, 35, 1197–1210.

Weber, L. *The English Infant School and Informal Education.* Englewood Cliffs, N.J.: Prentice-Hall, 1971.

Weikart, D. P., & Lambie, D. Z. Early enrichment in infants. Paper presented at meetings of the American Association for the Advancement of Science, 1969.

Weiner, B., Frieze, I., Kukla, A., Reed, L., Rest, S., & Rosenbaum R. M. Perceiving the causes of success and failure. In *Attribution: Perceiving the Causes of Behavior,* edited by E. E. Jones, D. Kanouse, H. H. Kelley, R. E. Nisbett, S. Valins, and B. Weiner. Los Angeles: McCaleb-Seiler, 1971. (Available as a separate from General Learning Press, 79 Madison Avenue, New York City, 10016.)

Weinreich, U. Travels through semantic space. *Word,* 1958, 14, 346–366. (Review of Osgood et al., 1957.)

Weinreich, U. On the semantic structure of language. In *Universals of Language,* edited by J. H. Greenberg, Cambridge: M.I.T. Press, 1963.

Weir, M. W. Developmental changes in problem-solving strategies. *Psychological Review,* 1964, 71, 473–490.

Weir, R. H. *Language in the Crib.* The Hague: Mouton, 1962.

Wenger, M. A. The measurement of individual differences in autonomic balance. *Psychosomatic Medicine,* 1941, 3, 427–434.

Werner, H., & Kaplan, E. The acquisition of word meanings. *Monographs of the Society for Research in Child Development,* 1950, 25, no. 1.

Wertheimer, M. Psychomotor coordination of auditory and visual space at birth. *Science,* 1961, 134, 1962.

Westinghouse Learning Corporation. *The Impact of Head Start.* Athens, Ohio: Ohio University Press, 1969.

References

White, B. L. The development of perception during the first six months of life. Paper presented at meetings of the American Association for the Advancement of Science, 1963.

White, B. L., & Held, R. Plasticity of sensori-motor development in the human infant. In *The Causes of Behavior*, edited by J. F. Rosenblith and W. Allinsmith. (2nd ed.) Boston: Allyn & Bacon, 1966.

White, R. W. Motivation reconsidered: The concept of competence. *Psychological Review*, 1959, 66, 297–333.

White, R. W. Ego and reality in psychoanalytic theory. *Psychological Issues*, 1963, Monograph No. 11.

White, R. W. *Lives in Progress.* (2nd ed.) New York: Holt, Rinehart and Winston, 1966.

Whiting, J. S. M., & Child, I. L. *Child Training and Personality.* New Haven, Conn.: Yale University Press, 1953.

Willerman, L., Naylor, A. F., & Myrianthopoulos, N. C. Intellectual development of children from interracial matings. *Science*, 1970, 170, 1329–1330.

Wilson, J. J., Wilson, B. C., & Swinyard, C. A. Two-point discrimination in congenital amputees. *Journal of Comparative and Physiological Psychology*, 1962, 55, 482–485.

Withers, C. *A Rocket in My Pocket.* New York: Holt, 1948.

Witkin, H. A., & associates. *Personality through Perception.* New York: Harper, 1954.

Wohlwill, J. F. The perception of size and distance relationships in perspective drawings. Paper presented at meetings of the Eastern Psychological Association, 1962.

Wohlwill, J. F., & Wiener, M. Discrimination of form orientation in young children. *Child Development*, 1964, 35, 1113–1125.

Wolf, M. M., Risley, T., & Mees, H. Application of operant conditioning procedures to the behavior problems of an autistic child. *Behavior Research and Therapy*, 1964, 1, 305–312.

Wolfenstein, M. The emergence of fun morality. *Journal of Social Issues*, 1951, 7, 15–25.

Wolff, P. H. Observations on newborn infants. *Psychosomatic Medicine*, 1959, 21, 110–118.

Wolff, P. H. Observations on the early development of smiling. In *Determinants of Infant Behavior II*, edited by B. M. Foss. London: Methuen, and New York: Wiley, 1963.

Wolff, W. *The Expression of Personality.* New York: Harper, 1943.

Woodcock, L. P. *Life and Ways of the Two-Year-Old.* New York: Dutton, 1941.

Yarrow, L. J., Goodwin, M. S., Manheimer, H., & Milowe, I. D. Infancy experiences and cognitive and personality development at ten years. Paper presented at meetings of the American Orthopsychiatric Association, 1971.

Yarrow, L. J., & Goodwin, M. S. The immediate impact of separation: Reactions of infants to a change in mother-figures. In *The Competent Infant*, edited by L. J. Stone, H. T. Smith, and L. B. Murphy. New York: Basic Books (in press).

Zamenhof, S., Mosley, J., & Schuller, E. Stimulation of the proliferation of cortical neurons by prenatal treatment with growth hormone. *Science*, 1966, 152, 1396–1397.

Zamenhof, S., van Marthens, E., & Grauel, L. DNA (cell number) in neonatal brain: Second generation (F_2) alteration by maternal (F_0) dietary protein restriction. *Science*, 1971, 172, 850–851.

Zazzo, R. Le problème de l'imitation chez le nouveau-né. *Enfance*, 1957, 2, 135–152.

Zeigler, H. P., & Leibowitz, H. W. Apparent visual size as a function of distance for children and adults. *American Journal of Psychology*, 1957, 70, 106–107.

References

subject index

Index

Conflict, generational, 483
Conformity, 355, 446, 448, 450
Congenital defects, 36, 42–43, 504–505
Conjugate reinforcement, 20
Consciousness I, II, and III, 137
Conservation, 77, 301–302, 388. *See also* Object permanence
Conservative reformers, adolescent, 457
Constancy, perceptual, 94–95
Contagion, behavioral, 264
Contingent learning, 132
Continuity, 201, 290–291. *See also* Discontinuity of growth rate; Discontinuity theory
Continuum of reproductive casualty, 506
Contraception, 470
Conventionalists, adolescent, 454–455, 475
Convergent thinking, 409
Conversations, of preschoolers, 238, 264–266, 281. *See also* Language
Cooking, 322
Cooperative play, 237–238
Counseling for adolescents, 487, 488. *See also* Psychotherapy
Crawling, 73. *See also* Creeping
Creativity, test of, 282
Creeping, 73, 74–77, 82
Criminal behavior, genetics and, 40
Critical periods, 32–33, 162–163
Cross-fostering, 170–171
Cross-implantation, 171
Cross-sectional method, 172
Crowding, 128
Crushes, 396
Crying, 12, 59–60, 117, 118, 119, 130, 141, 157
Cultural disadvantage: in adolescence, 450–451, 482; and cognition, 302–303; and education, 331, 404–405; and intelligence, 333–334; and learning, 295, 388; in middle years of childhood, 347; and preschool children, 257–258; and psychological abnormalities, 502, 532–533; and reaction to mirrors, 79; and self-awareness, 290–291; and space perception, 312
Cultural differences, 146–147; and adolescence, 418–419; and attitude toward time, 307–308; in continuity of sex roles, 375; and education, 138; and games, 236; in infant care, 70; in middle years of childhood, 347, 353–354; in preschool years, 302–303; and space perception, 311; and stranger anxiety, 67; and intelligence tests, 333. *See also* Culture; Individual differences
Cultural shaping, 147–152
Cultural transmission, 142–144, 357–363
Culture: and adolescence, 425–432, 486–489; American, 134–138; and canalization, 166–168; of childhood, 354–363; definition of, 133–134; and development, 493; and ethnocentrism, 68; and food habits, 127, 251; and pathology, 529–533; and perceptual differences, 86; and sexuality, 148, 466, 467–472; and sibling rivalry, 251, and social-affective play, 235; universals of, 138–144. *See also* Cultural differences; Peer culture; Subcultures; Youth culture
Curriculum, 324–330, 341–342

Dancing, 212, 444
Dating, 430
Day care centers, 112. *See also* Preschools
Deafness, 505, 507
Death, 135, 289. *See also* Bereavement
Death wish, 175
Deep structure of language, 230
Defense mechanisms, 177–178, 397
Deformities. *See* Congenital defects
Delayed-reaction experiment, 85
Delayed reinforcement, 117
Delinquency, 413–414, 475, 519–522
Delusions, 522–523
Demand feeding, 122
Demand qualities, 91
Dementia praecox, 522
Democratic style, 410
Denial, 397
Denomination, in language learning, 227–228
Dependency, sex differences in, 151
Depression, 473
Deprivation. *See* Cultural deprivation; Sensory deprivation
Depth perception, 75–77
Determinism, 201–202
Detour ability, 76–77
Developmental principles, 156–168
Developmental scales, 55–56, 244
Deviation IQ, 335
Diet, 61–62. *See also* Feeding; Feeding problems; Food preferences; Malnutrition; Self-feeding
Differentiation principle, 156–159
Digestion, neonatal, 9–10
Diploidy, 42
"Dirty" language. *See* Scatology
Disadvantaged children. *See* Cultural deprivation
Discipline: during first year, 121; in liberal school, 409–411; and setting limits, 252–253. *See also* Authoritarianism; Authority; Battered child syndrome
Discontinuity of growth rate, 158
Discontinuity theory, 201
Disobedience, 239
Discrepancy hypothesis, 69
Distributive traits, 41–42
Divergent thinking, 409
Divorce, 136, 532
Doctor, reaction to, 78

Index

Index

name index

Index

Index

581